Lecture Notes in Computer Science 12487

More information about this series at http://www.springer.com/series/7410

Xiaofeng Chen · Hongyang Yan ·
Qiben Yan · Xiangliang Zhang (Eds.)

Machine Learning
for Cyber Security

Third International Conference, ML4CS 2020
Guangzhou, China, October 8–10, 2020
Proceedings, Part II

 Springer

Editors
Xiaofeng Chen
Xidian University
Xi'an, China

Qiben Yan
Michigan State University
East Lansing, MI, USA

Hongyang Yan
Guangzhou University
Guangzhou, China

Xiangliang Zhang
Division of Computer, Electrical
and Mathematical Sciences and Engineering
King Abdullah University of Science
Thuwal, Saudi Arabia

ISSN 0302-9743 ISSN 1611-3349 (electronic)
Lecture Notes in Computer Science
ISBN 978-3-030-62459-0 ISBN 978-3-030-62460-6 (eBook)
https://doi.org/10.1007/978-3-030-62460-6

LNCS Sublibrary: SL4 – Security and Cryptology

This Springer imprint is published by the registered company Springer Nature Switzerland AG
The registered company address is: Gewerbestrasse 11, 6330 Cham, Switzerland

Preface

The Third International Conference on Machine Learning for Cyber Security (ML4CS 2020) was held in Guangzhou, China, during October 8–10, 2020. ML4CS is a well-recognized annual international forum for AI-driven security researchers to exchange ideas and present their works. This volume contains papers presented at ML4CS 2020.

The conference received 360 submissions. The committee accepted 118 regular papers and 40 short papers to be included in the conference program. The proceedings contain revised versions of the accepted papers. While revisions are expected to take the referees comments into account, this was not enforced and the authors bear full responsibility for the content of their papers.

ML4CS 2020 was organized by the Institute of Artificial Intelligence and Blockchain, Guangzhou University, China. Furthermore, ML4CS 2020 was supported by the Peng Cheng Laboratory, Shenzhen, China. The conference would not have been such a success without the support of these organizations, and we sincerely thank them for their continued assistance and support.

We would also like to thank the authors who submitted their papers to ML4CS 2020, and the conference attendees for their interest and support. We thank the Organizing Committee for their time and effort dedicated to arranging the conference. This allowed us to focus on the paper selection and deal with the scientific program. We thank the Program Committee members and the external reviewers for their hard work in reviewing the submissions; the conference would not have been possible without their expert reviews. Finally, we thank the EasyChair system and its operators, for making the entire process of managing the conference convenient.

September 2020

Fengwei Zhang
Jin Li

Organization

General Chairs

Fengwei Zhang   Southern University of Science and Technology, China
Jin Li   Guangzhou University, China

Program Chairs

Xiaofeng Chen   Xidian University, China
Qiben Yan   Michigan State University, USA
Xiangliang Zhang   King Abdullah University of Science and Technology,
                       Saudi Arabia

Track Chairs

Hao Wang   Shandong Normal University, China
Xianmin Wang   Guangzhou University, China
Yinghui Zhang   Xi'an University of Posts and Telecommunications,
                       China
Wei Zhou   Yunnan University, China

Workshop Chairs

Sheng Hong   Beihang University, China
Ting Hu   Queen's University, Canada
Nan Jiang   East China Jiaotong University, China
Liangqun Li   Shenzhen University, China
Jungang Lou   Hunan Normal University, China
Hui Tian   Huaqiao University, China
Feng Wang   Wuhan University, China
Zhi Wang   Nankai University, China
Tao Xiang   Chongqing University, China

Publication Chairs

Hongyang Yan   Guangzhou University, China
Yu Wang   Guangzhou University, China

Publicity Chair

Lianyong Qi   Qufu Normal University, China

Steering Committee

Xiaofeng Chen	Xidian University, China
Iqbal Gondal	Federation University Australia, Australia
Ryan Ko	University of Waikato, New Zealand
Jonathan Oliver	Trend Micro, USA
Islam Rafiqul	Charles Sturt University, Australia
Vijay Varadharajan	The University of Newcastle, Australia
Ian Welch	Victoria University of Wellington, New Zealand
Yang Xiang	Swinburne University of Technology, Australia
Jun Zhang	Swinburne University of Technology, Australia
Wanlei Zhou	Deakin University, Australia

Program Committee

Silvio Barra	University of Salerno, Italy
M. Z. Alam Bhuiyan	Guangzhou University, China
Carlo Blundo	University of Salerno, Italy
Yiqiao Cai	Huaqiao University, China
Luigi Catuogno	University of Salerno, Italy
Lorenzo Cavallaro	King's College London, UK
Liang Chang	Guilin University of Electronic Technology, China
Fei Chen	Shenzhen University, China
Xiaofeng Chen	Xidian University, China
Zhe Chen	Singapore Management University, Singapore
Xiaochun Cheng	Middlesex University, UK
Frédéric Cuppens	Télécom Bretagne, France
Changyu Dong	Newcastle University, UK
Guangjie Dong	East China Jiaotong University, China
Mohammed EI-Abd	American University of Kuwait, Kuwait
Wei Gao	Yunnan Normal University, China
Dieter Gollmann	Hamburg University of Technology, Germany
Zheng Gong	South China Normal University, China
Zhitao Guan	North China Electric Power University, China
Zhaolu Guo	Chinese Academy of Sciences, China
Jinguang Han	Queen's University Belfast, UK
Saeid Hosseini	Singapore University of Technology and Design Singapore
Chingfang Hsu	Huazhong University of Science and Technology, China
Haibo Hu	The Hong Kong Polytechnic University, Hong Kong
Teng Huang	Guangzhou University, China
Xinyi Huang	Fujian Normal University, China
Wenchao Jiang	Guangdong University of Technology, China
Lutful Karim	Seneca College of Applied Arts and Technology, Canada

Hadis Karimipour	University of Guelph, Canada
Sokratis Katsikas	Open University of Cyprus, Cyprus
Neeraj Kumar	Thapar Institute of Engineering and Technology, India
Ping Li	South China Normal University, China
Tong Li	Guangzhou University, China
Wei Li	Jiangxi University of Science and Technology, China
Xuejun Li	Anhui University, China
Kaitai Liang	University of Surrey, UK
Hui Liu	University of Calgary, Canada
Wei Lu	Sun Yat-sen University, China
Xiaobo Ma	Xi'an Jiaotong University, China
Fabio Martinelli	IIT-CNR, Italy
Ficco Massimo	Second University of Naples, Italy
Weizhi Meng	Technical University of Denmark, Denmark
Vincenzo Moscato	University of Naples, Italy
Francesco Palmieri	University of Salerno, Italy
Fei Peng	Hunan University, China
Hu Peng	Wuhan University, China
Lizhi Peng	Jinan University, China
Umberto Petrillo	Sapienza University of Rome, Italy
Lianyong Qi	Qufu Normal University, China
Shahryar Rahnamayan	Ontario Tech University, Canada
Khaled Riad	Guangzhou University, China
Yu Sun	Guangxi University, China
Yu-An Tan	Beijing Institute of Technology, China
Zhiyuan Tan	Edinburgh Napier University, UK
Ming Tao	Dongguan University of Technology, China
Donghai Tian	Beijing Institute of Technology, China
Chundong Wang	Tianjin University of Technology, China
Ding Wang	Peking University, China
Hui Wang	Nanchang Institute of Technology, China
Jianfeng Wang	Xidian University, China
Jin Wang	Soochow University, China
Licheng Wang	Beijing University of Posts and Telecommunications, China
Lingyu Wang	Concordia University, Canada
Tianyin Wang	Luoyang Normal University, China
Wei Wang	Beijing Jiaotong University, China
Sheng Wen	Swinburne University of Technology, Australia
Yang Xiang	Swinburne University of Technology, Australia
Run Xie	Yibin University, China
Xiaolong Xu	Nanjing University of Information Science and Technology, China
Li Yang	Xidian University, China
ShaoJun Yang	Fujian Normal University, China
Zhe Yang	Northwestern Polytechnical University, China

Yanqing Yao	Beihang University, China
Xu Yuan	University of Louisiana at Lafayette, USA
Qikun Zhang	Beijing Institute of Technology, China
Xiao Zhang	Beihang University, China
Xiaosong Zhang	Tangshan University, China
Xuyun Zhang	Macquarie University, Australia
Yuan Zhang	Nanjing University, China
Xianfeng Zhao	Chinese Academy of Sciences, China
Lei Zhu	Huazhong University of Science and Technology, China
Tianqing Zhu	China University of Geosciences, China

Track Committee

Jin Cao	Xidian University, China
Hui Cui	Murdoch University, Australia
Rui Guo	Xi'an University of Posts and Telecommunications, China
Qi Li	Nanjing University of Posts and Telecommunications, China
Muhammad Baqer Mollah	Nanyang Technological University, Singapore
Ben Niu	Chinese Academy of Sciences, China
Fatemeh Rezaeibagha	Murdoch University, Australia

Contents – Part II

Vulnerability Variants and Path Factors in Networks

Linli Zhu[1]([✉]) [iD], Haci Mehmet Baskonus[2] [iD], and Wei Gao[2] [iD]

[1] School of Computer Engineering, Jiangsu University of Technology,
Changzhou 213001, China
`zhulinli@jsut.edu.cn`
[2] Department of Mathematics and Science Education, Faculty of Education,
Harran University, Sanliurfa, Turkey
`hmbaskonus@gmail.com, gaowei@ynnu.edu.cn`

Abstract. The vulnerability of the network is one of the core contents of network security research, and there are several variables to test the network vulnerability from the perspective of network structure. For example, toughness, isolated toughness and their variants are defined from graph theory point of view, and these parameters works during the design phase to test the firmness of network. This paper studies the relationship between the existence of path factor and some variants which connect with vulnerability of networks. Moreover, we show that some of bounds of these variants are sharp.

Keywords: Network · Vulnerability · Toughness · Path factor

1 Introduction

When modelling the network structure, sites in the network are represented by vertices, the channels between which are denoted by edges between the vertices, so the entire network is represented by a graph model. In what follows, we use a graph G to express a specific network.

According to the limitation of data transmission direction, the network is divided into directed network and undirected network. In our article, we only deal with simple graph, i.e., finite and undirected graphs without loops or multiple edges. Assume $G = (V(G), E(G))$ as a graph with vertex set $V(G)$ and edge set $E(G)$. Set $G[S]$ as the subgraph deduced by $S \subseteq V(G)$, and set $G - S = G[V(G) \setminus S]$. For a detailed vertex x of G, assume $N_G(x)$ and $d_G(x) = |N_G(x)|$ as neighbourhood and the degree of x in G. For $E' \subseteq E(G)$, $G - E'$ is denoted as the subgraph by removing edges in E' from G. A path factor of a graph G is a spanning subgraph of G so every component is a path. We set P_n as the path

Supported by Modern Education Technology Research Project in Jiangsu Province (No. 2019-R-75637) and Design of equipment access system based on 3D printing cloud service platform (No. 2019530101000686).

© Springer Nature Switzerland AG 2020
X. Chen et al. (Eds.): ML4CS 2020, LNCS 12487, pp. 1–11, 2020.
https://doi.org/10.1007/978-3-030-62460-6_1

with n vertices. A P_n-factor is a spanning subgraph of G with every component isomorphic to P_n, and a $P_{\geq n}$-factor is a special path factor with every component at lowest n vertices.

If the resulting graph still has a $P_{\geq n}$-factor, after any k vertices from G removed, a graph G is called a $(P_{\geq n}, k)$-factor critical graph. If the resulting graph admits a $P_{\geq n}$-factor, after any m edges removed, a graph G is called a $(P_{\geq n}, m)$-factor deleted graph. When $m = 1$, a $(P_{\geq n}, m)$-factor deleted graph is a $P_{\geq n}$-factor deleted graph. If for any $e \in E(G)$, G possesses a $P_{\geq k}$-factor having e, a graph G is assured as a $P_{\geq k}$-factor covered graph.

If $R - \{x\}$ possesses a perfect matching for each vertex x in R, a graph R is a factor-critical graph. If $H = K_1$, $H = K_2$ or H is the corona of a factor-critical graph R with at lowest three vertices, a graph H is called a sun which contains at lowest six vertices. If it is isomorphic to a sun, and $sun(G)$ is used to represent the number of sun components of G, an element of G is called a sun component.

In the graph setting, the researchers use some variants to measure the vulnerability of networks, where toughness and isolated toughness are two classic parameters. Chvátal [1] first introduced the notation of toughness to test the vulnerable of networks: $t(G) = +\infty$ if G is a complete graph; otherwise

$$t(G) = \min\{\frac{|S|}{\omega(G - S)} : \omega(G - S) \geq 2\}$$

in which $\omega(G - S)$ is the number of connected elements of $G - S$. Yang et al. [2] borrowed the definition of isolated toughness which was stated below: if G is complete, then $I(G) = +\infty$; else wise,

$$I(G) = \min\{\frac{|S|}{i(G - S)} \,\bigg|\, S \subset V(G), i(G - S) \geq 2\},$$

where $i(G - S)$ is the number of isolated vertices of $G - S$.

Enomoto et al. [3] introduced a variant of toughness, remarked as $\tau(G)$. If G is completed, then $\tau(G) = +\infty$; else wise,

$$\tau(G) = \min\{\frac{|S|}{\omega(G - S) - 1} : \omega(G - S) \geq 2\}.$$

For this variant, Enomoto [4] showed that $\tau(G) \leq \kappa(G)$ if G is not completed, where $\kappa(G)$ is a connectivity of graph G. Combining with the well-know fact that $\kappa(G) \leq \lambda(G) \leq \delta(G)$ for every graph G, we get

$$\tau(G) \leq \kappa(G) \leq \lambda(G) \leq \delta(G)$$

for a non-completed graph G, where $\lambda(G)$ and $\delta(G)$ are edge-connectivity and minimum degree of G, respectively.

Zhang and Liu [5] introduced a variant of isolated toughness, denoted by $I'(G)$. If G is completed, then $I'(G) = +\infty$; else wise,

$$I'(G) = \min\{\frac{|S|}{i(G - S) - 1} \,\bigg|\, S \subset V(G), i(G - S) \geq 2\}.$$

In computer science, many problems on network design, file transfer, building blocks, coding design, scheduling problems are connected to the factors and factorizations of graphs [6]. Specifically, the problem of file transfer can be transformed as factorizations of graphs. Meanwhile, the problem of telephone network design can be transformed into path factors of graphs. In recent years, the researchers found that there is strong relationship between vulnerability variants and the existence of path factor (see Zhou et al. [7–11] for more details). More related results on factor and fractional factor can be referred to Gao et al. [12–16].

The paper proposes some sufficient conditions of the existence of $P_{\geq n}$-factor related to two variants $\tau(G)$ and $I'(G)$. The main results are listed as follows.

Theorem 1. *Let $m \geq 1$ be an integer, and set G as a graph with $\kappa(G) \geq \frac{3m+1}{2}$. If $\tau(G) > \frac{3m+1}{2(2m+1)}$, G is a $(P_{\geq 3}, m)$-factor deleted graph.*

Theorem 2. *Let k be a non-negative integer. Graph G with $\kappa(G) \geq k+2$ is a $(P_{\geq 3}, k)$-factor critical graph if $\tau(G) \geq k+1$.*

Theorem 3. *Assume G as a connected graph with at lowest three vertices. If $\tau(G) > 1$, then G is a $P_{\geq 3}$-factor covered graph.*

Theorem 4. *Assume G as a connected graph with at lowest three vertices. If $I'(G) > 3$, G is a $P_{\geq 3}$-factor covered graph.*

Theorem 5. *Let k be a positive integer. Graph G with $\kappa(G) \geq k+2$ is a $(P_{\geq 3}, k)$-factor critical graph if $I'(G) > \frac{k+7}{4}$.*

The lemmas below determines the proof process.

Lemma 1 (Kaneko [17]). *If and only if $sun(G - S) \leq 2|S|$ for each $S \subseteq V(G)$ a graph G possesses a $P_{\geq 3}$-factor.*

Lemma 2 (Zhang and Zhou [18]). *Assume G as a connected graph. If and only if $sun(G-S) \leq 2|S| - \varepsilon(S)$ for any subsetvS of $V(G)$, G is a $P_{\geq 3}$-factor covered graph, in which $\varepsilon(S)$ is assured by*

$$\varepsilon(S) = \begin{cases} 2, & \text{if } S \neq \emptyset \text{ and } S \text{ is not independent,} \\ 1, & \text{if } S \neq \emptyset, S \text{ is independent and a} \\ & \text{non-sun component of } G\text{-}S \text{ exists,} \\ 0, & \text{otherwise,} \end{cases}$$

2 Proof of Theorem 1

Under the condition that G is a complete graph, the result is clearly followed by the definition of $(P_{\geq 3}, m)$-factor deleted graph and $\lambda(G) \geq \kappa(G) \geq \frac{3m+1}{2}$. Therefore, it's supposed that G is a non-complete graph in the following discussion.

Set $G' = G - E'$ for arbitrary given $E' \subseteq E(G)$ having m edges. Apparently, we have $E(G') = E(G) - E'$ and $V(G') = V(G)$. In order to prove Theorem 1, we only need to prove that G' has a $P_{\geq 3}$-factor. On the contrary, assume G' has no $P_{\geq 3}$-factor. Hence, in terms of Lemma 1 that some subset S of $V(G')$ exists such that

$$2|S| < sun(G' - S). \tag{1}$$

In view of $\lambda(G) \geq \kappa(G) \geq \frac{3m+1}{2}$, we verify that $G' = G - E'$ is related, and then

$$1 = \omega(G') \geq sun(G'). \tag{2}$$

Claim. $|S| \geq 1$.

Proof. If $|S| = 0$, then according to (1) and (2) we get $sun(G') = \omega(G') = 1$. Using the fact that $m \geq 1$ is an integer, we yield $\lambda(G) \geq \kappa(G) \geq \frac{3m+1}{2} \geq 2$ and thus $|V(G')| = |V(G)| \geq 3$. Furthermore, we infer $\lambda(G') = \lambda(G - E') \geq \lambda(G) - |E'| \geq \frac{3m+1}{2} - m = \frac{m+1}{2}$.

If $m = 1$, then $G' = G - E'$ is a big sun follow from the above derivation. Assume R as the factor-critical graph in $G' = G - E'$. Clearly, a vertex x exists in R satisfy $\omega(G - \{x\}) = 2$. Therefore, we deduce $\frac{3m+1}{2(2m+1)} < \tau(G) \leq \frac{|\{x\}|}{G - \{x\}} = 1$, a contradiction.

If $m \geq 2$, then $\lambda(G') \geq 2$ by means of $\lambda(G') \geq \frac{m+1}{2} > 1$. Thus, $sun(G') = 0$, a contradiction.

In what follows, we consider two cases according to whether S is a vertex cut of G.

Case 1. $G - S$ is a connected subgraph.
Using the assumption $\kappa(G) \geq \frac{3m+1}{2}$, it's defined that G is a connected graph. Hence, $\omega(G - S) = \omega(G) = 1$ is got. Since the number of its components adds at most 1 after removing an edge from a graph, we get

$$m + 1 = \omega(G - S) + m \geq \omega(G - E' - S) \geq \omega(G' - S) \geq sun(G' - S). \tag{3}$$

In light of (1) and (3), we get $m + 1 \geq sun(G' - S) > 2|S|$, i.e., $|S| < \frac{m+1}{2}$. Combining it with $\lambda(G - S) \geq \kappa(G - S)$ and $\kappa(G) \geq \frac{3m+1}{2}$, we obtain

$$m = \frac{3m+1}{2} - \frac{m+1}{2} < \kappa(G) - |S| \leq \kappa(G - S) \leq \lambda(G - S).$$

Since $\lambda(G - S)$ is an integer, we infer $\lambda(G - S) \geq m + 1$, and thus

$$1 \leq \lambda(G - S) - m \leq \lambda(G' - S)$$

and

$$1 = \omega(G' - S) \geq sun(G' - S),$$

which contradicts (1) in light of Claim 2.

Case 2. $G - S$ is not a connected subgraph.

Since $\kappa(G) \geq \frac{3m+1}{2}$ and $G - S$ is not a connected subgraph, we get $\omega(G-S) \geq 2$ and

$$|S| \geq \frac{3m+1}{2}. \tag{4}$$

Combining (1) with the fact $\omega(G - S) + m \geq \omega(G' - S) \geq sun(G' - S)$, we get $\omega(G-S) + m \geq sun(G' - S) \geq 2|S| + 1$, which implies

$$2|S| - m + 1 \leq \omega(G-S). \tag{5}$$

By means of (5), the definition of $\tau(G)$ and $\tau(G) > \frac{3m+1}{2(2m+1)}$, we yield

$$\frac{3m+1}{2(2m+1)} < \tau(G) \leq \frac{|S|}{\omega(G-S)-1} \leq \frac{|S|}{2|S|-m}.$$

It means

$$|S| < \frac{3m+1}{2}$$

which contradicts (4).

In all, the proof of Theorem 1 is completed.

3   Proof of Theorem 2

If G is a complete graph, then the result follows from the condition $\kappa(G) \geq k+2$. Thus, it is supposed that G is not a complete graph below.

Set $G' = G - U$ where U is a vertex subset with k vertices. To prove the Theorem 2, the only need is to prove G' permits a $P_{\geq 3}$-factor. In contrast, it's assumed that G' without $P_{\geq 3}$-factor. Hence, in terms of Lemma 1 some subset $S \subseteq V(G')$ exists to meet

$$2|S| + 1 \leq sun(G' - S). \tag{6}$$

If $|S| = 0$, then we get $sun(G-U) = sun(G') = 0$ in view of $\kappa(G) \geq k+2$ and $|U| = k$, which conflicts (6). Therefore, we suppose that $|S| > 0$, and consider two cases on the basis of the value of $sun(G' - S)$.

Case 1. $sun(G' - S) \leq 1$.
In light of (6) and $|S| \geq 1$, we yield $sun(G' - S) \geq 2|S| + 1 \geq 3$, which conflicts $sun(G' - S) \leq 1$.

Case 2. $sun(G' - S) \geq 2$.
Using the fact $2 \leq sun(G' - S) \leq \omega(G' - S) = \omega(G - (S \cup U))$, $\tau(G) \geq k + 1$ and the definition of $\tau(G)$, we infer

$$k + 1 \leq \tau(G) \leq \frac{|S \cup U|}{\omega(G - (S \cup U)) - 1} \leq \frac{|S| + k}{sun(G' - S) - 1}$$

$$= \frac{|S|}{sun(G' - S) - 1} + \frac{k}{sun(G' - S) - 1} \leq \frac{|S|}{sun(G' - S) - 1} + k.$$

It reveals

$$sun(G' - S) \leq |S| + 1$$

which contradicts (6). Thus, we finish the proof of Theorem 2.

4   Proof of Theorem 3

The result is obtained by the definition of $P_{\geq 3}$-factor covered graph and the assumption $|V(G)| \geq 3$, if G is a complete graph. We suppose that G is not complete. Using contradiction, it's assumed that G meets the conditions of in Theorem 3, but it's not a $P_{\geq 3}$-factor covered graph. In terms of Theorem 3, a subset $S \subseteq V(G)$ exists to meet

$$2|S| - \varepsilon(S) < sun(G - S). \tag{7}$$

Three cases are discussed by the value of $|S|$ and a conflict in every case is got respectively.

Case 1. $S = \emptyset$.
Here, we infer $\varepsilon(S) = 0$. By means of (7), we have

$$sun(G) \geq 1. \tag{8}$$

We get $sun(G) \leq w(G) = 1$ since G is connected. Connecting it to (8), $sun(G) = w(G) = 1$ is got. On the basis of the definition of sun and $|V(G)| \geq 3$, we ensure that G is a big sun. Let R be the factor-critical subgraph of G, and set $X = \{u\}$ for arbitrary $u \in V(R)$. Easily, $w(G - X) \geq 2$. Thus, based on the definition of $\tau(G)$, we get $\tau(G) \leq \frac{|X|}{w(G-X)-1} \leq 1$, which contradicts $\tau(G) > 1$.

Case 2. S contains one vertex.
Here, we deduce $\varepsilon(S) \leq 1$. In terms of (7), we yield $sun(G - S) > 2|S| - \varepsilon(S) \geq 2 - 1 = 1$, which reveals $sun(G - S) \geq 2$ since $sun(G - S)$ is an integer.
In view of $w(G - S) \geq sun(G - S)$ and $\tau(G) > 1$, we obtain

$$1 < \tau(G) \leq \frac{|S|}{w(G - S) - 1} \leq \frac{|S|}{sun(G - S) - 1} \leq 1$$

which contradicts.

Case 3. $|S| \geq 2$.
Here, we get $\varepsilon(S) \leq 2$. According to (7), we have $2|S| - 1 \leq 2|S| - \varepsilon(S) + 1 \leq sun(G - S)$, which reveals $\frac{sun(G-S)+1}{2} \geq |S|$ and $sun(G - S) \geq 3$. Furthermore, using the definition of τ, we obtain

$$\tau(G) \leq \frac{|S|}{w(G - S) - 1} \leq \frac{|S|}{sun(G - S) - 1} \leq \frac{sun(G - S) + 1}{2(sun(G - S) - 1)}$$

$$= \frac{1}{2} + \frac{1}{sun(G - S) - 1} \leq 1,$$

which contradicts $\tau(G) > 1$.
Hence, the proof of Theorem 3 is completed.

5 Proof of Theorem 4

It is easy to check that G is a $P_{\geq 3}$-factor covered graph using $|V(G)| \geq 3$, if G is complete. It's focused that G is not complete. Assume G meet the hypothesis of Theorem 4, but it is not a $P_{\geq 3}$-factor covered graph. In terms of Lemma 2, a subset S of $V(G)$ exists to meet

$$sun(G - S) \geq 2|S| - \varepsilon(S) + 1. \tag{9}$$

By the value of $|S|$, three cases will be considered and the contradiction in each case is obtained.

Case 1. $S = \emptyset$.
According to the definition of $\varepsilon(S)$, we get $\varepsilon(S) = 0$. Using the similar discussion presented in last section, we obtain $sun(G) = \omega(G) = 1$.

By the definition of sun and $|V(G)| \geq 3$, it can be easily verify that G is a big sun. Assume R as the factor-critical subgraph of G. Set $U = V(R)$. Apparently, $i(G - U) = |U| \geq 3$. Considering the connection of definition of $I'(G)$ and $I'(G) > 3$, we get $3 < I'(G) \leq \frac{|U|}{i(G-U)-1} = 1 + \frac{1}{i(G-U)-1} \leq \frac{3}{2}$, which leads a contradiction.

Case 2. S contains only one vertex.
Apparently, $\varepsilon(S) \leq 1$. By means of (9), we infer

$$2 \leq 2|S| - \varepsilon(S) + 1 \leq sun(G - S). \tag{10}$$

It's supposed that a isolated vertices exists, b K_2's and c big sun components $H_1, H_2, \cdots, H_c$, where $|V(H_i)| \geq 6$, in $G - S$. Hence, in terms of (10), we get

$$sun(G - S) = a + b + c \geq 2. \tag{11}$$

We select a vertex from each K_2 component of $G - S$, and X is denoted as the set of these vertices. For every H_i, set R_i as the factor-critical subgraph of H_i. We select one vertex $y_i \in V(R_i)$ for $i \in \{1, \cdots, c\}$, and set $Y = \{y_1, y_2, \cdots, y_c\}$. Clearly, we infer $i(G - (S \cup X \cup Y)) = a + b + c \geq 2$.

According to (9), (11), $\varepsilon(S) \leq 1$, the definition of $I'(G)$ and $I'(G) > 3$, we verify

$$3 < I'(G) \leq \frac{|S \cup X \cup Y|}{i(G - (S \cup X \cup Y)) - 1} = \frac{|S| + b + c}{a + b + c - 1}$$

$$= \frac{|S| + sun(G - S) - a}{sun(G - S) - 1} \leq \frac{\frac{sun(G-S)+\varepsilon(S)-1}{2} + sun(G - S)}{sun(G - S) - 1} \leq 3,$$

which get a confliction.

Case 3. S has at least two vertices.
In this case, we have $\varepsilon(S) \leq 2$. Connecting this to (9), we deduce

$$sun(G - S) \geq 2|S| - \varepsilon(S) + 1 \geq 2|S| - 1 \geq 3. \tag{12}$$

It's assumed that there are a isolated vertices, b K_2s and c big sun components $H_1, H_2, \cdots, H_c$ with $|V(H_i)| \geq 6$ in $G - S$. In this way, we obtain $sun(G - S) = a + b + c$. We select one vertex from every K_2 of $G - S$, and note X as the set of these vertices. Set R_i as the factor-critical subgraph of H_i for every H_i, and set $Y_i = V(R_i)$. We yield $|X| = b$ and $i(H_i - Y_i) = |Y_i| = \frac{|V(H_i)|}{2}$. Set $Y = \cup_{i=1}^c Y_i$. Then in light of (12), we deduce

$$i(G - (X \cup Y \cup S)) = \sum_{i=1}^c |Y_i| + a + b = \sum_{i=1}^c \frac{|V(H_i)|}{2} + a + b$$

$$\geq a + b + c = sun(G - S) \geq 3.$$

Connecting this fact to the assumption $I'(G) > 3$ and using the definition of $I'(G)$, we obtain

$$3 < I'(G) \frac{|S \cup X \cup Y|}{i(G - (S \cup X \cup Y)) - 1} = \frac{|S| + b + \sum_{i=1}^c \frac{|V(H_i)|}{2}}{\sum_{i=1}^c \frac{|V(H_i)|}{2} + a + b - 1},$$

which implies

$$|S| > 3a + 2b + 2 \sum_{i=1}^c \frac{|V(H_i)|}{2} - 3. \tag{13}$$

By means of $|V(H_i)| \geq 6$, $sun(G - S) = a + b + c$, (12) and (13), we verify

$$|S| > 3a + 2b + 2 \sum_{i=1}^c \frac{|V(H_i)|}{2} - 3 \geq 3a + 2b + 6c - 3$$

$$\geq 2(a + b + c) - 3 = 2sun(G - S) - 3 \geq 2(2|S| - 1) - 3,$$

which means $|S| < \frac{5}{3}$. It is a contradiction to $|S| \geq 2$.

Hence, the proof of Theorem 4 is hold.

6   Proof of Theorem 5

The proof of Theorem 5 is similar to the proof of above theorems, and some duplicates will be omitted. The discussion on complete graph is obtained in the proof of Theorem 2, we only consider the non-complete graph in the following contents.

Let $G' = G - U$ for each $U \in V(G)$ with $|U| = k$. We assume that G' does't contain $P_{\geq 3}$-factor. Then it follows from Lemma 1 that

$$2|S| + 1 \leq sun(G' - S). \tag{14}$$

for some vertex subset S of G'.

By means of $|U| = k$, $\kappa(G) \geq k + 2$ and $G' = G - U$, we yield $\kappa(G') = \kappa(G - U) \geq \kappa(G) - |U| = \kappa(G) - k \geq (k + 2) - k = 2$, which implies $sun(G') = 0$. If $|S| = 0$, in terms of (14), we deduce $sun(G') > 0$, a contradiction. If $|S| = 1$, then $\lambda(G'-S) \geq \kappa(G'-S) = \kappa(G-U-S) \geq \kappa(G)-|U|-|S| = \kappa(G)-k-1 \geq 1$, which reveals $1 = \omega(G'-S) \geq sun(G'-S) \geq 2|S|+1 = 3$, a contradiction. In the following, we always assume that $|S| \geq 2$.

It's supposed that a isolated vertices exists, b K_2's and c big sun components $H_1, H_2, \cdots, H_c$, where $|V(H_i)| \geq 6$, in $G'-S$. Hence, we get

$$sun(G'-S) = a+b+c \geq 2|S|+1 \geq 5. \tag{15}$$

We select one vertex from every K_2 component in $G'-S$ and denote Y as the set of these vertices. Let R_i be the factor-critical subgraph of H_i, $Z_i = V(R_i)$ for $i \in \{1, \cdots, c\}$ and $Z = \cup_{i=1}^{c} Z_i$. Clearly, $|Y| = b$, $i(H_i - Z_i) = |Z_i| = \frac{|V(H_i)|}{2}$ for $i \in \{1, \cdots, c\}$, and

$$i(G - (U \cup Z \cup Y \cup S)) = i(G' - (Z \cup Y \cup S)) = \sum_{i=1}^{c} |Y_i| + a + b$$

$$= \sum_{i=1}^{c} \frac{|V(H_i)|}{2} + a + b \geq a + b + 3c \geq a + b + c \geq 5.$$

Combining this with the definition of $I'(G)$ and the assumption $I'(G) > \frac{k+7}{4}$, we yield

$$\frac{k+7}{4} < I'(G) \leq \frac{|U \cup S \cup Y \cup Z|}{i(G - (U \cup S \cup Y \cup Z)) - 1} = \frac{|S| + k + b + \sum_{i=1}^{c} \frac{|V(H_i)|}{2}}{\sum_{i=1}^{c} \frac{|V(H_i)|}{2} + a + b - 1},$$

which implies

$$4|S| > (k+7)a + (k+3)b + (k+3)\sum_{i=1}^{c} \frac{|V(H_i)|}{2} - (5k+7)$$

$$\geq (k+3)(a+b+c) - (5k+7)$$

$$\geq (k+3)(2|S|+1) - (5k+7)$$

$$= (2k+6)|S| - (4k+4).$$

Thus, we get $|S| < 2$ which leads a contradiction.

7   Sharpness

Its aim is to represent that our results are best in some sense.

To show the $\tau(G)$ bound in Theorem 1 is best in some sense, we build a graph $G = 2(m+1)K_2 \vee K_{\frac{3m+1}{2}}$, where $m \geq 1$ is an integer with $m \equiv 1(\text{mod}2)$. We can check that $\tau(G) = \frac{\frac{3m+1}{2}}{2(m+1)-1} = \frac{3m+1}{2(2m+1)}$. Set $E' \subseteq E(2(m+1)K_2)$ with m edges and $G' = G - E'$. In G', let $S = V(K_{\frac{3m+1}{2}})$, then $|S| = \frac{3m+1}{2}$ and

$$sun(G'-S) = 3m+2 > 3m+1 = 2|S|.$$

10   L. Zhu et al.

Based on Lemma 1, G' doesn't contain $P_{\geq 3}$-factor, and thus G is not a $(P_{\geq 3}, m)$-factor deleted graph.

Set k is a non-negative integer. We now explain that the bounds $\tau(G) \geq k+1$ and $\kappa(G) \geq k+2$ in Theorem 2 can't be alternated by $\tau(G) \geq \frac{k+1}{2}$ and $\kappa(G) \geq k+1$. We focus on the graph $G = 3K_2 \vee K_{k+1}$, and select $U \subseteq V(K_{k+1})$ such that $|U| = k$. Let $G' = G - U$. For $S = V(K_{k+1}) \setminus U$, we deduce

$$sun(G' - S) = 3 > 2 = 2|S|.$$

Based on Lemma 1, G' possesses no $P_{\geq 3}$-factor, and thus G is not $(P_{\geq 3}, k)$-factor critical.

To verify the τ bound in Theorem 3 is tight, we build $G = (H_1 \cup H_2 \cup H_3) \vee K_2$, where H_1, H_2, H_3 are sun. Set $S = V(K_2)$. We infer that $\omega(G-S) = sun(G - S) = 3$ and $\tau(G) = \frac{|S|}{\omega(G-S)-1} = 1$. Therefore, we yield $sun(G - S) = 3 > 2 = 2|S| - \varepsilon(S)$ in light of $\varepsilon(S) = 2$. Using Lemma 2, we confirm that G is not a $P_{\geq 3}$-factor covered graph.

Next, we show that in Theorem 4, $I'(G) > 3$ can't be alternated by $I'(G) \geq 3$. Let's consider a graph $G = K_1 \vee (2K_2 \cup K_t)$ where t is enough large and K_t is not a sun. It's easily seen that $I'(G) = 3$. Set $S = V(K_1)$, and thus $|S| = 1$. By the definition of $\varepsilon(S)$, $\varepsilon(S) = 1$ is got. Therefore, $sun(G - S) = 2 > 1 = 2|S| - \varepsilon(S)$ is yielded. In light of Lemma 2, G is not a $P_{\geq 3}$-factor covered graph.

Finally, let's present an example to show the condition $I'(G) > \frac{k+7}{4}$ in Theorem 5 can't be replaced by $I'(G) \geq \frac{k+7}{4}$. Let $G = 5K_2 \vee K_{k+2}$ where k is a positive number. Clearly, $\kappa(G) = k + 2$ and $I'(G) = \frac{k+7}{4}$. Take $U \subseteq V(K_{k+2})$ with $|U| = k$ and $G' = G - U$. Hence, we yield $sun(G' - S) = 5 > 4 = 2|S|$ by taking $S = V(K_{k+2}) - U$. Based on Lemma 1, G' possesses no $P_{\geq 3}$-factor, and thus G is not $(P_{\geq 3}, k)$-factor critical. Using the example with regard to Theorem 2, we know that the condition $\kappa(G) \geq k + 2$ in Theorem 5 can't be replaced by $\kappa(G) \geq k + 1$.

Acknowledgments. We thank the reviewers for their constructive comments in improving the quality of this paper.

References

1. Chvátal, V.: Tough graphs and Hamiltonian circuits. Disc. Math. **5**, 215–228 (1973)
2. Yang, J., Ma, Y., Liu, G.: Fractional (g, f)-factors in graphs. Appl. Math.- J. Chin. Univ. Seri. A **16**, 385–390 (2001)
3. Enomoto, H., Jackson, B., Katerinis, P., Saito, A.: Toughness and the existence of k-factors. J. Graph Theory **9**, 87–95 (1985)
4. Enomoto, H.: Toughness and the existence of k-factors II. Disc. Math. **189**, 277–282 (1998)
5. Zhang, L., Liu, G.: Fractional k-factor of graphs. J. Syst. Sci. Math. Sci. **21**(1), 88–92 (2001)
6. Alspach, B., Heinrich, K., Liu, G.: Orthogonal factorizations of graphs. In: Diuctz, J.H., Stinson, D.R. (eds.) Contemporary DesignTheory: A Collection of Surveys, pp. 13–37. Wiley, New York (1992)

7. Zhou, S.: Remarks on path factors in graphs. RAIRO-Oper. Res. **54**(6), 1827–1834 (2020). https://doi.org/10.1051/ro/2019111
8. Zhou, S.: Some results about component factors in graphs. RAIRO-Oper. Res. **53**(3), 723–730 (2019)
9. Zhou, S., Wu, J., Zhang, T.: The existence of $P_{\geq 3}$-factor covered graphs. Discussiones Math. Graph Theory **37**(4), 1055–1065 (2017)
10. Zhou, S., Yang, F., Xu, L.: Two sufficient conditions for the existence of path factors in graphs. Scientia Iranica (2019). https://doi.org/10.24200/SCI.2018.5151.1122
11. Zhou, S.Z., Sun, Z.R.: Some existence theorems on path factors with given properties in graphs. Acta Math. Sinica Engl. Ser. **36**(8), 917–928 (2020). https://doi.org/10.1007/s10114-020-9224-5
12. Gao, W., Wang, W., Dimitrov, D.: Toughness condition for a graph to be all fractional (g, f, n)-critical deleted. Filomat **33**(9), 2735–2746 (2019)
13. Gao, W., Guirao, J.L.G., Chen, Y.: A toughness condition for fractional (k, m)-deleted graphs revisited. Acta Math. Sinica Engl. Ser. **35**(7), 1227–1237 (2019)
14. Gao, W., Guirao, J.L.G.: Parameters and fractional factors in different settings. J. Inequalities Appl. **2019**(1), 1–16 (2019). https://doi.org/10.1186/s13660-019-2106-7
15. Gao, W., Guirao, J.L.G., Abdel-Aty, M., Xi, W.: An independent set degree condition for fractional critical deleted graphs. Disc. Continuous Dyn. Syst.-Ser. S **12**(4–5), 877–886 (2019)
16. Gao, W., Guirao, J.L.G., Wu, H.: Two tight independent set conditions for fractional (g, f, m)-deleted graphs systems. Qual. Theory Dyn. Syst. **17**(1), 231–243 (2018)
17. Kaneko, A.: A necessary and sufficient condition for the existence of a path factor every component of which is a path of length at least two. J. Comb. Theory Ser. B **88**, 195–218 (2003)
18. Zhang, H., Zhou, S.: Characterizations for $P_{\geq 2}$-factor and $P_{\geq 3}$-factor covered graphs. Disc. Math. **309**, 2067–2076 (2009)

A Variant of Sun Toughness and the Existence of Path Factors in Networks

Linli Zhu[1]([✉])[iD], Haci Mehmet Baskonus[2][iD], and Wei Gao[2][iD]

[1] School of Computer Engineering, Jiangsu University of Technology,
Changzhou 213001, China
zhulinli@jsut.edu.cn
[2] Department of Mathematics and Science Education, Faculty of Education,
Harran University, Sanliurfa, Turkey
hmbaskonus@gmail.com, gaowei@ynnu.edu.cn

Abstract. Among several parameters in computer networks to measure its vulnerability, toughness is the most important one which has raised widespread concern from mathematicians and computer scientists. Starting from the requirements of network security, other toughness related parameters are successively defined and applied to related engineering fields. Very recently, Zhou et al. [1] defined a new parameter called "sun toughness" and also show the essential connection with path factors. We first introduce a new variant related on sun toughness, and then we give the bounds of this variant to ensure a graph has path factor in different settings in this paper. Furthermore, we show that the sun toughness bounds are sharp in some sense.

Keywords: Network · Vulnerability · Toughness · Sun toughness · Path factor

1 Introduction

The modelling of network is often described by using a graph in which sites are denoted by vertices and channels are expressed by edges. The paper's consideration is limited only into simple graph, i.e., no directed or multiple edges, and no loops.

Assume G as a graph with vertex set $V(G)$ and edge set $E(G)$. We use $d_G(x)$ to denote the degree of any $x \in V(G)$ in G. For any subset S of $V(G)$ and E' of $E(G)$, we denote $G - S$ and $G - E'$ as the subgraphs by making the vertices of S and edges of E' from G deleted respectively. $\omega(G)$ is used to denote the amount of connected components of a graph G. The path which has n vertices is represented by P_n in which $n \geq 2$ is an integer. A path factor of a graph G is

Supported by Modern Education Technology Research Project in Jiangsu Province (No. 2019-R-75637) and horizontal foundation "Design of equipment access system based on 3D printing cloud service platform" (No. 2019530101000686).

X. Chen et al. (Eds.): ML4CS 2020, LNCS 12487, pp. 12–19, 2020.
https://doi.org/10.1007/978-3-030-62460-6_2

defined as a spanning subgraph whose components are paths. A $P_{\geq n}$-factor is a path factor such that every component contains at lowest n vertices.

Assume k and m as non-negative integers. A graph G is called a $(P_{\geq n}, k)$-factor critical graph if the resulting subgraph has a $P_{\geq n}$-factor, even after any k vertices from G deleted. A graph G is called a $(P_{\geq n}, m)$-factor deleted graph if the resulting subgraph has a $P_{\geq n}$-factor, even after any m edges from G deleted. Specially, when $m = 1$, then $(P_{\geq n}, m)$-factor deleted graph and $(P_{\geq n}, k)$-factor critical graph become $P_{\geq n}$-factor critical graph and $P_{\geq n}$-factor deleted graph, respectively. If for any $e \in E(G)$, G has a $P_{\geq n}$-factor e included, a graph G is defined as a $P_{\geq n}$-factor covered graph.

If for every vertex $x \in V(R)$, $R - x$ has a perfect matching, graph R is a factor-critical graph. If $H = K_1$, $H = K_2$ or H is the corona of a factor-critical graph R having at least 3 vertices, graph H is called a sun. A sun with at least six vertices is regarded as big. Then, the component refers to the component of G if it is isomorphic to a sun, and the amount of sun components of G can be denoted by $sun(G)$.

In the field of cyber security, there are several parameters as ways for the measurement of network vulnerability. Toughness is one of such parameters which introduced from the perspective of graph theory by Chvátal [2] in year 1973. If graph is completed, we thought it has the highest level of defense, which means $t(G) = \infty$. The toughness of non-completed graph is described by

$$t(G) = \min\{\frac{|S|}{\omega(G - S)} : \omega(G - S) \geq 2\}.$$

Yang et al. [3] introduced a transform version of toughness called isolated toughness: if G is a complete graph, $I(G) = \infty$; else wise,

$$I(G) = \min\{\frac{|S|}{i(G - S)} \Big| S \subset V(G), i(G - S) \geq 2\},$$

where $i(G - S)$ is the number of isolated vertices of $G - S$.

A variant of toughness is introduced by Enomoto et al. [4] denoted as $\tau(G)$. If G is a completed graph, then $\tau(G) = +\infty$; otherwise,

$$\tau(G) = \min\{\frac{|S|}{\omega(G - S) - 1} : \omega(G - S) \geq 2\}.$$

Enomoto [5] continue studied this variant and showed that $\tau(G) \leq \kappa(G)$ if G is not a completed graph, where $\kappa(G)$ is a connectivity of graph G. Combining with the well-know fact that $\kappa(G) \leq \lambda(G) \leq \delta(G)$ for any graph G, we get

$$\tau(G) \leq \kappa(G) \leq \lambda(G) \leq \delta(G)$$

for a non-completed graph G, where $\delta(G)$ and $\lambda(G)$ are minimum degree and edge-connectivity of G, respectively. Zhang and Liu [6] introduced a variant of isolated toughness, denoted by $I'(G)$. If G is a completed graph, and $I'(G) = +\infty$; otherwise,

$$I'(G) = \min\{\frac{|S|}{i(G-S)-1} \Big| S \subset V(G), i(G-S) \geq 2\}.$$

Recently, Zhou et al. [1] defined a new toughness parameter called sun toughness $s(G)$ which stated as follows

$$s(G) = \min\{\frac{|S|}{sun(G-S)} : sun(G-S) \geq 2\}$$

if G is not completed graph; else wise, $s(G) = +\infty$.

2   Main Results and Proofs

Some theoretical studies have pointed out that there is an inevitable connection between sun component and the existence of path factors. Kaneko [7] proofed the sufficient and necessary condition for a graph contain $P_{\geq 3}$-factor from view of sun component.

Lemma 1 (Kaneko [7]). *If and only if $sun(G - S) \leq 2|S|$ for every $S \subseteq V(G)$, a graph G permits a $P_{\geq 3}$-factor.*

Zhang and Zhou [8] provided the necessary and sufficient condition of $P_{\geq 3}$-factor covered graph from angle of sun component.

Lemma 2 (Zhang and Zhou [8]). *Assume G as a connected graph. Then G is a $P_{\geq 3}$-factor covered graph if and only if $sun(G - S) \leq 2|S| - \varepsilon(S)$ for any subset S of $V(G)$, in which $\varepsilon(S)$ is represented by*

$$\varepsilon(S) = \begin{cases} 2, \text{if } S \neq \emptyset \text{ and } S \text{ is not an independent set,} \\ 1, \text{if } S \neq \emptyset, \ S \text{ is independent and there exists a} \\ \quad \text{non-sun component of } G\text{-}S, \\ 0, \text{otherwise,} \end{cases}$$

More results on the existence of various factors can be referred to Gao et al. [9–12] and [13].

Inspired by $\tau(G)$ and $I'(G)$, we introduce the variant of sun toughness denoted by $s'(G)$ which is stated as follows:

$$s'(G) = \min\{\frac{|S|}{sun(G-S)-1} : sun(G-S) \geq 2\}$$

if G is not completed graph; otherwise, $s'(G) = +\infty$.

The paper aims to explore the connections between $s'(G)$ and the existence of path factor. Our fist main results is stated as follows.

Theorem 1. *Assume G as a 2-edge-connected graph. If $s'(G) > 1$, then G is a $P_{\geq 3}$-factor deleted graph.*

Proof. If G is a complete graph with $s'(G) = +\infty$, then it is not hard to directly confirm that G is a $P_{\geq 3}$-factor deleted graph. In what follows, it is supposed that G isn't a complete graph.

For any $e \in E(G)$, let $H = G - e$. In order to check the correctness of Theorem 1, It is waiting to prove that H permits a $P_{\geq 3}$-factor. On the contrary, H has no $P_{\geq 3}$-factor. Considering Lemma 1, subset $S \subseteq V(H) = V(G)$ meets

$$sun(H - S) > 2|S|. \tag{1}$$

If $|S| = 0$, then in view of (1) we yield

$$sun(H) > 0. \tag{2}$$

According to graph G is 2-edge-connected and $H = G - e$. Thus, we infer $sun(H) \leq \omega(H) = 1$. Together this fact with (2) and using the integrity of $sun(H)$, we deduce $sun(H) = \omega(H) = 1$.

Following from the condition G is a 2-edge-connected graph, we obtain $|V(G)| = |V(H)| \geq 3$. Hence, in light of the definitions of a sun and a big sun, we verify that $H = G - e$ is a big sun. Therefore, there exists a factor-critical graph R in $H = G - e$ with $d_H(x) = 1$ for every $x \in V(H) - V(R)$ and $|V(R)| = \frac{|V(H)|}{2} \geq 3$. Clearly, $G = H + e$ has at least one vertex with degree 1, which conflicts the supposition: G is 2-edge- connected.

If $|S| \geq 2$, in view of (1) we get

$$5 \leq 2|S| + 1 \leq sun(H - S). \tag{3}$$

Combining with $sun(G - S) + 2 \geq sun(G - S - e) = sun(H - S)$, we get

$$3 \leq sun(H - S) - 2 \leq sun(G - S). \tag{4}$$

According to (1), (3), (4), the definition of $s'(G)$ and $s'(G) > 1$, we have

$$1 < s'(G) \leq \frac{|S|}{sun(G - S) - 1} \leq \frac{|S|}{sun(H - S) - 3} \leq \frac{|S|}{2|S| + 1 - 3} = \frac{|S|}{2|S| - 2}.$$

It reveals that $|S| < 2$, which conflicts with $|S| \geq 2$.

At last, we only discuss the case of $|S| = 1$. By means of (1), we obtain

$$3 = 2|S| + 1 \leq sun(H - S). \tag{5}$$

Consider $sun(G - S) + 2 \geq sun(G - S - e) = sun(H - S)$. The two cases below is considered in light of the relationship between $sun(G - S)$ and $sun(H - S)$.

Case 1: $sun(H - S) - 1 \leq sun(G - S)$.
Using (5), we confirm $sun(G - S) \geq 2$. In light of (5), the definition of $s'(G)$ and $s'(G) > 1$, we infer

$$1 < s'(G) \leq \frac{|S|}{sun(G - S) - 1} \leq \frac{|S|}{sun(H - S) - 2} \leq \frac{|S|}{2|S| + 1 - 2} = \frac{|S|}{2|S| - 1} = 1,$$

which leads a contradiction.

Case 2: $sun(H - S) - 2 = sun(G - S)$.
If $sun(G - S) \geq 2$, then concerning the meaning of $s'(G)$ and $|S| = 1$, we confirm $s'(G) \leq \frac{|S|}{sun(G-S)-1} \leq 1$ which contradicts that $s'(G) > 1$. That is to say, $sun(G - S) = 1$, and thus $sun(H - S) = 3$. Denote C_1 as the unique sun component of $G - S$. In light of $sun(H - S) = 3$ and $H = G - e$, we ensure that C_1 is also a sun component of $H - S$, and thus the other two sun components of $H - S$ can be expressed by C_2 and C_3 respectively. Next, our discussion is divided according to the different case of sun components of $H - S$.

Subcase 1: $C_2 = C_3 = K_1$.
In this subcase, we obtain $K_2 = C_2 \cup C_3 + e$ is a sun component of $G - S$. It means $sun(G - S) = 2$, which conflicts $sun(G - S) = 1$.

Subcase 2: $C_2 \neq K_1$ or $C_3 \neq K_1$.
Without loss of generality, it is supposed that $C_3 \neq K_1$. After that, C_3 is a big sun or $C_3 = K_2$. Suppose $e = uv$ where $u \in V(C_3)$.
If $C_3 = K_2$, then we deduce $3 = sun(H - S \cup \{u\}) = sun(G - S \cup \{u\})$. Followed by the definition of $s'(G)$ and $|S| = 1$, we infer

$$s'(G) \leq \frac{|S \cup \{u\}|}{sun(G - S \cup \{u\}) - 1} = \frac{2}{3 - 1} = 1$$

which conflicts the assumption that $s'(G) > 1$.

Furthermore, C_3 is a big sun. Therefore, it contains a factor-critical graph R' in C_3 satisfies $d_{C_3}(x) = 1$ for each $x \in V(C_3) - V(R')$ and $|V(R')| = \frac{|V(C_3)|}{2} \geq 3$. If $u \in V(R')$, then we have $|V(R')| + 2 = sun(H - S \cup V(R')) = sun(G - S \cup V(R'))$. Thus, in light of the definition of $s'(G)$ and $|S| = 1$, we yield

$$s'(G) \leq \frac{|S \cup V(R')|}{sun(G - S \cup V(R')) - 1} \leq \frac{|V(R')| + 1}{|V(R')| + 2 - 1} = 1,$$

which conflicts $s'(G) > 1$. If $u \in V(C_3) - V(R')$, then there exists $u' \in V(R')$ such that $uu' \in E(C_3)$. Hence, we obtain

$$sun(G - S \cup (V(R') - \{u'\}) \cup \{u\})$$
$$= sun(H - S \cup (V(R') - \{u'\}) \cup \{u\})$$
$$= |V(R')| + 2.$$

Again, using the definition of $s'(G)$ and $|S| = 1$, we have

$$s'(G) \leq \frac{|S \cup (V(R') - \{u'\}) \cup \{u\}|}{sun(G - S \cup (V(R') - \{u'\}) \cup \{u\}) - 1} = \frac{|V(R')| + 1}{|V(R')| + 2 - 1} = 1$$

which conflicts the assumption $s'(G) > 1$.

Our next main outcome studies the relationship between $s'(G)$ and $P_{\geq 3}$-factor covered graphs stated as follows.

Theorem 2. *Assume G as a connected graph G with order at lowest three. If $s'(G) > 1$, then G is a $P_{\geq 3}$-factor covered graph.*

Proof. If G is a complete graph with $s'(G) = +\infty$, then it is not hard to directly confirm that G is a $P_{\geq 3}$-factor covered graph. In the below, it's always supposed that G is not a complete graph.

Let G meet the hypothesis of Theorem 2, but not a $P_{\geq 3}$- factor covered graph. Then in terms of Lemma 2, a vertex subset S of G existed to satisfy

$$2|S| - \varepsilon(S) < sun(G - S). \tag{6}$$

If $|S| = 0$, then according to (6) and the definition of $\varepsilon(S)$, we have $sun(G) > 0$. By means of the assumption that G is a connected graph, $sun(G) \leq \omega(G)$ and $sun(G)$ is an integer, we verify that $1 \leq sun(G) \leq \omega(G) = 1$, which implies $1 = \omega(G) = sun(G)$. Combining the fact that $|V(G)| \geq 3$, we confirm that G is a big sun with at least 6 vertices. Hence, there exists a factor- critical graph R in G such that $d_G(x) = 1$ for every $x \in V(G) \setminus V(R)$ and $|V(R)| = \frac{|V(G)|}{2} \geq 3$. Set $X = V(R) \setminus \{u\}$ for any $u \in V(R)$. Clearly, $sun(G - X) = |V(R)| \geq 3$. According to $s'(G)$, we yield

$$s'(G) \leq \frac{|X|}{sun(G - X) - 1} = \frac{|V(R)| - 1}{|V(R)| - 1} = 1,$$

which conflicts $s'(G) > 1$.

If $|S| = 1$, then it is easy to see that $\varepsilon(S) \leq 1$. Using (6), we have $sun(G - S) \geq 2|S| - \varepsilon(S) + 1 \geq 2|S| \geq 2$. Considering the definition of $s'(G)$, we infer $s'(G) \leq \frac{|S|}{sun(G-S)-1} \leq 1$, which conflicts $s'(G) > 1$.

From what we discussed above, we conclude $|S| \geq 2$. In view of the definition of $\varepsilon(S)$, we get $\varepsilon(S) \leq 2$. By means of $|S| \geq 2$ and (6), we deduce

$$sun(G - S) \geq 2|S| - \varepsilon(S) + 1 \geq 2|S| - 1 \geq |S| + 1 \geq 3. \tag{7}$$

On the other hand, followed by the definition of $s'(G)$ and $s'(G) > 1$, we get $1 < s'(G) \leq \frac{|S|}{sun(G-S)-1}$ which reveals $sun(G - S) < |S| + 1$. It conflicts (7).

In all, we get the desired conclusion.

3   Sharpness

First, it is shown that the condition $s'(G) > 1$ in Theorem 1 is sharp. Let H_1 be a big sun and R be the factor-critical graph of H_1 such that $d_{H_1}(x) = 1$ for arbitrary $x \in V(H_1) \setminus V(R)$ and $|V(R)| = \frac{|V(H_1)|}{2} \geq 3$. Set $v \in V(H_1) - V(R)$ and $u \neq V(H_1)$. A graph H' is constructed as follows:$V(H') = V(H_1) \cup \{u\}$ and $E(H') = E(H_1) \cup \{e\}$ with $e = uv$. Moreover, a graph G is constructed as $G = (K_2 \cup H') \vee K_1$. We select $X = \{v\} \cup (V(R) - \{w\}) \cup V(K_1)$, where $w \in V(R)$ and $vw \in E(R)$. Hence, we obtain $|V(R)| + 2 = sun(G - X - e) =$

18   L. Zhu et al.

$sun(G-X)$, $|V(R)|+1 = |X|$, and it is easy to verify that $s'(G) = \frac{|X|}{sun(G-X)-1} = \frac{|V(R)|+1}{|V(R)|+2-1} = 1$.

On the other hand, let $S = V(K_1)$. Then we get $sun(G-S-e) = 3 > 2|S| = 2$. According to Lemma 1, $G - e$ has no $P_{\geq 3}$-factor, i.e., G is not a $P_{\geq 3}$-factor deleted graph.

Second, we manifest that $s'(G) > 1$ in Theorem 2 is also in tight condition. Let G be a big sun. Hence, there exists a factor-critical graph R in G such that $d_G(x) = 1$ for any $x \in V(G)\backslash V(R)$ and $|V(R)| = \frac{|V(G)|}{2} \geq 3$. Set $X = V(R)\backslash\{u\}$ for arbitrary $u \in V(R)$. We can check easily that $sun(G - X) = |V(R)| \geq 3$. By means of definition of $s'(G)$, we have $s'(G) = \frac{|X|}{sun(G-X)-1} = \frac{(|V(R)|-1)}{(|V(R)|-1)} = 1$.

On the other hand, set $S = \emptyset$, and thus $\varepsilon(S) = 0$. Then we yield $sun(G-S) = 1 > 2|S| - \varepsilon(S) = 0$. In light of Lemma 2, G is not a $P_{\geq 3}$-factor covered graph.

4 Open Problems

We raise the following open problems as the end of our paper.

Problem 1. What are the tight bounds of $s(G)$ and $s'(G)$ for a graph G to be $(P_{\geq 3}, k)$-factor critical graph or $(P_{\geq 3}, m)$-factor deleted graph?

Problem 2. So far, there are lots of results on the toughness or isolated toughness condition for a graph admits factor or fractional factor. On the other hand, according to its definition, sun toughness is between toughness and isolated toughness. It is natural to ask what is the relation between sun toughness and a graph has fractional factor in various settings.

Acknowledgments. We thank the reviewers for their constructive comments in improving the quality of this paper.

References

1. Zhou, S., Sun, Z., Liu, H.: Sun toutheness and $P_{\geq 3}$-factors in graphs. Contrib. Disc. Math. **14**(1), 167–174 (2019)
2. Chvátal, V.: Tough graphs and Hamiltonian circuits. Disc. Math. **5**, 215–228 (1973)
3. Yang, J.B., Ma, Y.H., Liu, G.Z.: Fractional (g, f)-factors in graphs. Appl. Math.- J. Chin. Univ. Ser. A **16**, 385–390 (2001)
4. Enomoto, H., Jackson, B., Katerinis, P., Saito, A.: Toughness and the existence of k-factors. J. Graph Theory **9**, 87–95 (1985)
5. Enomoto, H.: Toughness and the existence of k-factors II. Disc. Math. **189**, 277–282 (1998)
6. Zhang, L., Liu, G.: Fractional k-factor of graphs. J. Syst. Sci. Math. Sci. **21**(1), 88–92 (2001)
7. Kaneko, A.: A necessary and sufficient condition for the existence of a path factor every component of which is a path of length at least two. J. Comb. Theory Ser. B **88**(2), 195–218 (2003)

8. Zhang, H., Zhou, S.: Characterizations for $P_{\geq 2}$-factor and $P_{\geq 3}$-factor covered graphs. Disc. Math. **309**, 2067–2076 (2009)
9. Gao, W., Wang, W., Dimitrov, D.: Toughness condition for a graph to be all fractional (g, f, n)-critical deleted. Filomat **33**(9), 2735–2746 (2019)
10. Gao, W., Guirao, J.L.G., Chen, Y.: A toughness condition for fractional (k, m)-deleted graphs revisited. Acta Math. Sinica Engl. Ser. **35**(7), 1227–1237 (2019)
11. Gao, W., Guirao, J.L.G.: Parameters and fractional factors in different settings. J. Inequalities Appl. **2019**(1), 1–16 (2019). https://doi.org/10.1186/s13660-019-2106-7
12. Gao, W., Guirao, J.L.G., Abdel-Aty, M., Xi, W.: An independent set degree condition for fractional critical deleted graphs. Disc. Continuous Dyn. Syst.-Ser. S **12**(4–5), 877–886 (2019)
13. Gao, W., Guirao, J.L.G., Wu, H.: Two tight independent set conditions for fractional (g, f, m)-deleted graphs systems. Qual. Theory Dyn. Syst. **17**(1), 231–243 (2018)

Network Adjacency Condition for Fractional (g, f, n', m)-Critical Covered Graphs

Yu Pan[1](✉), Haci Mehmet Baskonus[2]⑩, and Wei Gao[2]⑩

[1] School of Computer Engineering, Jiangsu University of Technology,
Changzhou 213001, China
ypan@jsut.edu.cn
[2] Department of Mathematics and Science Education, Faculty of Education,
Harran University, Sanliurfa, Turkey
hmbaskonus@gmail.com, gaowei@ynnu.edu.cn

Abstract. In resource scheduling network, the availability of resource scheduling can be converted into the existing the fractional factor of the related network graph. The study of the existence of fractional factors in specific graph structure is helpful for engineers design and the building of the network that possesses effective resources. If after any n' vertices from G removed, the remaining graph is still a fractional (g, f, m)-covered graph, a graph G is a fractional (g, f, n', m)-critical covered graph. The paper presents a network adjacency condition for a graph to be fractional (g, f, n', m)-critical covered.

Keywords: Network · Data transmission · Fractional factor · Fractional (g, f, n', m)-critical covered graph

1 Introduction

Introduced from the field of industry, Network functions virtualization (NFV) aims to solve the aforementioned inconveniences, and avoid the hardware constant proliferation in the engineering applications. This trick improves the revolution in the network in terms of leveraging virtualization technology to provide a new method in network designing. There was a piece of breaking news in 2012 that seven leading telecom network operators in the world choose the ETSI (European Telecom Standards Institute) as the home of the industry specification group of network functions virtualization. With the pattern of NFV, traditional middleboxes acted as a special VNF (Virtual Network Function) which works as single modules in software. It enables each function to be modularity

Supported by Modern Education Technology Research Project in Jiangsu Province (No. 2019-R-75637) and horizontal foundation "Design of equipment access system based on 3D printing cloud service platform" in Yunnan Normal University (No. 2019530101000686).

© Springer Nature Switzerland AG 2020
X. Chen et al. (Eds.): ML4CS 2020, LNCS 12487, pp. 20–30, 2020.
https://doi.org/10.1007/978-3-030-62460-6_3

and isolation, and thus can be dealt with independently. Furthermore, servers are easy to install and deploy the VNFs by means of related technologies, and thus it allows VNFs dynamic migration from one server to another.

As an envisioned framework, NFV can solve most of the current network problems in light of widely using the particular hardware appliances. Moreover, it offers chances in cost decline and network optimization, and helps to configure hybrid scenarios. The availability of resource scheduling in NFV network equals as the existence of the fractional factor in its related NFV network graph. It inspires us to consider the problem of resource scheduling from a theoretical point of view. In what follows, we transform it into the mathematical context and begin with the notations and settings.

Take $G = (V(G), E(G))$ as a graph (represent a special NFV network) having vertex set $V(G)$ (set of sites) and edge set $E(G)$ (set of channels). Assume $N_G(x)$ and $d_G(x)$ as the open neighbourhood and degree of $x \in V(G)$, respectively. Take $N_G[x] = N_G(x) \cup \{x\}$, and $G[S]$ denoted as the subgraph induced by $S \subset V(G)$. For any $S \subseteq V(G)$, denote $G - S = G[V(G) \setminus S]$. Set $e_G(S, T) = |\{e = xy | x \in S, y \in T\}|$ for any two subsets $S, T \subset V(G)$ with $S \cap T = \emptyset$. The smallest degree of G is denoted by $\delta(G) = \min\{d_G(x) : x \in V(G)\}$. In short, $d(x)$ is used to express $d_G(x)$ for any $x \in V(G)$. It can be referred to Bondy and Mutry [1] for more terminologies and notations used but undefined here.

Assume that for any vertex x, f and g are two integer-valued functions on $V(G)$ with $0 \le g(x) \le f(x)$. We can see fractional (g, f)-factor as a function h assigning every edge a real number in $[0, 1]$ and meets $g(x) \le \sum\limits_{e \in E(x)} h(e) \le f(x)$ for each $x \in V(G)$. When $g(x) = f(x)$ for any $x \in V(G)$, a fractional f-factor is a special case of fractional (g, f)-factor. A fractional (g, f)-factor is called a fractional $[a, b]$-factor if $g(x) = a$ and $f(x) = b$ for any vertex x. Moreover, a fractional (g, f)-factor is a fractional k-factor if for any vertex x, $g(x) = f(x) = k$. In what follows, we take the assumption $n = |V(G)|$.

Under the condition that a fractional (g, f)-factor with $h(e) = 1$ exists for any $e \in E(H)$ for every sub-graph H with m edges, a graph G is fractional (g, f, m)-covered. A fractional (g, f, m)-covered graph is a fractional (g, f)-covered graph once $m = 1$. If the resulting graph is still a fractional (g, f, m)-covered graph after any n' vertices from G removed, G is called a fractional (g, f, n', m)-critical covered graph. If $m = 1$, a fractional (g, f, n', m)-critical covered graph is a fractional (g, f, n')-critical covered graph. Previous results related to fractional covered graphs, fractional factor, fractional critical applications can be referred to Gao and Wang [2,3] and [4], Gao et al. [5,6] and [7].

The effective use of resources in NFV network can be reflected by the concept of fractional (g, f, n', m)-critical covered graph. The aim of this paper is to show a network adjacency condition condition for a graph to be fractional (g, f, n', m)-critical covered. The primary result in our paper is listed below.

Theorem 1. *Assume a, b, n', Δ and m non-negative integers with $2 \le a \le b - \Delta$, and set n as the order of graph G with $n \ge \frac{(a+b-2)(2a+b+\Delta-3)}{a+\Delta} + \frac{(a+\Delta)n'}{a+\Delta-1} + m$. Assume g, f as two integer-valued functions assured on $V(G)$ so $a \le g(x) \le$*

$f(x) - \Delta \leq b - \Delta$ for each $x \in V(G)$. If for every $X \subseteq V(G)$, we get

$$N_G(X) = V(G) \quad if \quad |X| \geq \lfloor \frac{((b-\Delta)(n-1) - (a+\Delta)n' - 2m)n}{(a+b-1)(n-1)} \rfloor; \quad or$$

$$|N_G(X)| \geq \frac{(a+b-1)(n-1)}{(b-\Delta)(n-1) - (a+\Delta)n' - 2m}|X|$$

$$if \quad |X| < \lfloor \frac{((b-\Delta)(n-1) - (a+\Delta)n' - 2m)n}{(a+b-1)(n-1)} \rfloor.$$

Here G is a fractional (g, f, n', m)-critical covered graph.

From the example presented in Gao et al. [9], we see that the bound on neighborhood $N_G(X) = V(G)$ or $|N_G(X)| \geq \frac{(a+b-1)(n-1)}{(b-\Delta)(n-1)-(a+\Delta)n'-2m}|X|$ for all $X \subseteq V(G)$ is sharp in Theorem 1 when m is small.

In Theorem 1, take $n' = 0$ and the result below on fractional (g, f, m)-covered graphs is obtained.

Corollary 1. *Assume a, b, Δ and m non-negative integers with $2 \leq a \leq b - \Delta$, and assume n as the order of graph G with $n \geq \frac{(a+b-2)(2a+b+\Delta-3)}{a+\Delta} + m$. Assume g, f as two integer-valued functions assured on $V(G)$ so for every $x \in V(G)$ $a \leq g(x) \leq f(x) - \Delta \leq b - \Delta$. If for every $X \subseteq V(G)$, we have*

$$N_G(X) = V(G) \quad if \quad |X| \geq \lfloor \frac{((b-\Delta)(n-1) - 2m)n}{(a+b-1)(n-1)} \rfloor; \quad or$$

$$|N_G(X)| \geq \frac{(a+b-1)(n-1)}{(b-\Delta)(n-1) - 2m}|X| \quad if \quad |X| < \lfloor \frac{((b-\Delta)(n-1) - 2m)n}{(a+b-1)(n-1)} \rfloor.$$

Here G is a fractional (g, f, m)-covered graph.

In Theorem 1, let $m = 0$ and the following result on fractional (g, f, n')-critical graphs is obtained.

Corollary 2. *Assume a, b, Δ, n' and m non-negative integers with $2 \leq a \leq b - \Delta$, and n as the order of graph G with $n \geq \frac{(a+b-2)(2a+b+\Delta-3)}{a+\Delta} + \frac{(a+\Delta)n'}{a+\Delta-1}$. Make g, f as two integer-valued functions assured on $V(G)$ then for every $x \in V(G)$ $a \leq g(x) \leq f(x) - \Delta \leq b - \Delta$. If for every $X \subseteq V(G)$, we have*

$$N_G(X) = V(G) \quad if \quad |X| \geq \lfloor \frac{((b-\Delta)(n-1) - (a+\Delta)n')n}{(a+b-1)(n-1)} \rfloor; \quad or$$

$$|N_G(X)| \geq \frac{(a+b-1)(n-1)}{(b-\Delta)(n-1) - (a+\Delta)n'}|X|$$

$$if \quad |X| < \lfloor \frac{((b-\Delta)(n-1) - (a+\Delta)n')n}{(a+b-1)(n-1)} \rfloor.$$

After which, G is a fractional (g, f, n')-critical graph.

From the proof which described in next section, we see that if set $\Delta = 0$, then the first equation becomes

$$d_{G-S}(T) - b|T| + a|S| \le d_{G-S}(T) - g(T) + f(S) \le f(U) + \sum_{x \in S} d_H(x) - e_H(T, S) - 1 \le bn' + 2m - 1.$$

Hence, we have the following conclusion in the setting $\Delta = 0$.

Corollary 3. *Assume a, b, n' and m non-negative integers with $2 \le a \le b$, and set n as the order of graph G with $n \ge \frac{(a+b-2)(a+2b-3)}{a} + \frac{bn'}{a-1} + m$. Let g, f be two integer-valued functions assured on $V(G)$ so that for each $x \in V(G)$, $a \le g(x) \le f(x) \le b$. If for every $X \subseteq V(G)$, we have*

$$N_G(X) = V(G) \quad if \quad |X| \ge \lfloor \frac{(a(n-1) - bn' - 2m)n}{(a+b-1)(n-1)} \rfloor; \quad or$$

$$|N_G(X)| \ge \frac{(a+b-1)(n-1)}{a(n-1) - bn' - 2m} |X| \quad if \quad |X| < \lfloor \frac{(a(n-1) - bn' - 2m)n}{(a+b-1)(n-1)} \rfloor.$$

After which G is a fractional (g, f, n', m)-critical covered graph.

In Theorem 3, set $n' = 0$ and when $\Delta = 0$, the following result on fractional (g, f, m)-covered graphs is obtained.

Corollary 4. *Assume m and a, b non-negative integers with $2 \le a \le b$, and set n as the order of graph G with $n \ge \frac{(a+b-2)(a+2b-3)}{a} + m$. Assume g, f as two integer-valued functions assured on $V(G)$ such that for every $x \in V(G)$, $a \le g(x) \le f(x) \le b$. If for every $X \subseteq V(G)$, we have*

$$N_G(X) = V(G) \quad if \quad |X| \ge \lfloor \frac{(a(n-1) - 2m)n}{(a+b-1)(n-1)} \rfloor; \quad or$$

$$|N_G(X)| \ge \frac{(a+b-1)(n-1)}{a(n-1) - 2m} |X| \quad if \quad |X| < \lfloor \frac{(a(n-1) - 2m)n}{(a+b-1)(n-1)} \rfloor.$$

After which G is a fractional (g, f, m)-covered graph.

In Theorem 3, set $m = 0$ and when $\Delta = 0$, the following result on fractional (g, f, n')-critical graphs is got.

Corollary 5. *Assume n' and a, b non-negative integers with $2 \le a \le b$, and let n be the order of graph G with $n \ge \frac{(a+b-2)(a+2b-3)}{a} + \frac{bn'}{a-1}$. Assume g, f be two integer-valued functions assured on $V(G)$ such that for each $x \in V(G)$, $a \le g(x) \le f(x) \le b$. If for every $X \subseteq V(G)$, we get*

$$N_G(X) = V(G) \quad if \quad |X| \ge \lfloor \frac{(a(n-1) - bn')n}{(a+b-1)(n-1)} \rfloor; \quad or$$

$$|N_G(X)| \ge \frac{(a+b-1)(n-1)}{a(n-1) - bn'} |X| \quad if \quad |X| < \lfloor \frac{(a(n-1) - bn')n}{(a+b-1)(n-1)} \rfloor.$$

After which G is a fractional (g, f, n')-critical graph.

On the basis of the lemma below which serves to be the necessary and sufficient condition of fractional (g, f, n', m)-critical covered graphs, the proof is completed.

Lemma 1 *(Gao and Wang [8]). Assume G as a graph, g, g be two non-negative integer-valued functions assured on $V(G)$ such that for every $x \in V(G)$, $g(x) \leq f(x)$. Assume n', m as non-negative integers. If and only if for any $S \subseteq V(G)$ with $|S| \geq n'$, G is a fractional (g, f, n', m)-critical covered graph.*

$$d_{G-S}(T) - g(T) + f(S)$$

$$\geq \max_{U \subseteq S, |U|=n', H \subseteq E(G-U), |H|=m} \{f(U) + \sum_{x \in S} d_H(x) - e_H(T, S)\}, \qquad (1)$$

where $T = \{x : x \in V(G) \setminus S, d_{G-S}(x) \leq g(x) - 1\}$.

2   Proof of Theorem 1

Here, the proof of Theorem 1 is stated in detail, and our main tricks follows from Gao et al. [9].

Suppose that G meets the assumption of Theorem 1, but isn't an all fractional (g, f, n', m)-critical covered graph. By Lemma 1 and the fact that for any $H \subseteq E(G)$ with m edges, $\sum_{x \in S} d_H(x) - e_H(T, S) \leq 2m$, subsets $S \subseteq V(G)$ exists to satisfy

$$f(S) + d_{G-S}(T) - g(T) \leq \max_{U \subseteq S, |U|=n'} f(U) + 2m - 1$$

or

$$(|S| - n')(\Delta + a) + \sum_{x \in T} d_{G-S}(x) - (b - \Delta)|T|$$

$$\leq f(S - U) - g(T) + d_{G-S}(T) \leq 2m - 1, \qquad (2)$$

where $|S| \geq n'$ and $T = \{x : x \in V(G) \setminus S, d_{G-S}(x) \leq g(x) - 1\}$.

Claim. $\delta(G) \geq \frac{(a+\Delta-1)n + (b-\Delta) + (a+\Delta)n' + 2m}{a+b-1}$.

Proof. Assume x as a vertex of G with degree $\delta(G)$. Set $X = V(G) - N_G(x)$. Obviously, $x \notin N_G(X)$ and $N_G(X) \neq V(G)$. Therefore, we get

$$n - 1 \geq |N_G(X)| \geq \frac{(a+b-1)(n-1)}{(b-\Delta)(n-1) - (a+\Delta)n' - 2m}|X|,$$

that is

$$(a+b-1)(n-1)|X| \leq ((b-\Delta)(n-1) - (a+\Delta)n' - 2m)(n-1). \qquad (3)$$

By means of (3) and $|X| = n - \delta(G)$, we have

$$(a+b-1)(n-1)(n - \delta(G)) \leq ((b-\Delta)(n-1) - (a+\Delta)n' - 2m)(n-1).$$

Hence,

$$\delta(G) \geq \frac{(a+\Delta-1)n + (b-\Delta) + (a+\Delta)n' + 2m}{a+b-1}.$$

Let $d = \min\{d_{G-S}(x) : x \in T\}$ and we get $0 \le d \le g(x) - 1 \le b - \Delta - 1$ and

$$(\Delta + a)n' + 2m - 1 \ge (\Delta + a)|S| - (b - \Delta - d)|T|. \tag{4}$$

$x_1 \in T$ is selected to satisfy $d_{G-S}(x_1) = d$. Then according to the value of d, the discussion can be divided into the two cases below. Concerning Claim 2 and the definition of d, we have

$$|S| + d \ge \delta(G) \ge \frac{(b - \Delta - 1)n + (b - \Delta) + (a + \Delta)n' + 2m}{a + b - 1}. \tag{5}$$

Case 1. $2 \le d \le b - \Delta - 1$.

According to (4), (5) and $|S| + |T| \le n$, we get

$$(\Delta + a)|S| + \sum_{x \in T} d_{G-S}(x) - (b - \Delta)|T| - (\Delta + a)n' - 2m$$

$$\ge (a + \Delta)|S| - (b - \Delta - d)|T| - (\Delta + a)n' - 2m$$

$$\ge (a + \Delta)|S| - (b - \Delta - d)(n - |S|) - (a + \Delta)n' - 2m$$

$$= (a + b - d)|S| - (b - \Delta - d)n - (a + \Delta)n' - 2m$$

$$\ge (a + b - d)(\frac{(b - \Delta - 1)n + (b - \Delta) + (a + \Delta)n' + 2m}{a + b - 1} - d)$$

$$-(b - \Delta - d)n - (a + \Delta)n' - 2m.$$

Set $h(d) = (a + b - d)(\frac{(b-\Delta-1)n+(b-\Delta)+(a+\Delta)n'+2m}{a+b-1} - d) - (b - \Delta - d)n - (a + \Delta)n' - 2m$. We have

$$(\Delta + a)|S| + \sum_{x \in T} d_{G-S}(x) - (b - \Delta)|T| - (\Delta + a)n' - 2m \ge h(d). \tag{6}$$

Taking $n \ge \frac{(a+b-2)(2a+b+\Delta-3)}{a+\Delta} + \frac{bn'}{a+\Delta-1} + m$ and $2 \le d \le b - \Delta - 1$, we infer

$$h'(d) = -(\frac{(b - \Delta - 1)n + (b - \Delta) + (a + \Delta)n' + 2m}{a + b - 1} - d) - (a + b - d) + n$$

$$= 2d + \frac{(b - \Delta - 1)n + (b - \Delta) + (a + \Delta)n' + 2m}{a + b - 1} - a - b$$

$$\ge 4 + \frac{(b - \Delta - 1)n + (b - \Delta) + (a + \Delta)n' + 2m}{a + b - 1} - a - b > 0.$$

After the combination of it and $2 \le d \le b - \Delta - 1$, we indicate

$$h(d) \ge h(2). \tag{7}$$

Taking (6) and (7), we have

$$-1 \ge (a + \Delta)|S| + \sum_{x \in T} d_{G-S}(x) - (b - \Delta)|T| - (a + \Delta)n' - 2m$$

$$\ge h(d) \ge h(2)$$

$$= (a + b - 2)(\frac{(b - \Delta - 1)n + (b - \Delta) + (a + \Delta)n' + 2m}{a + b - 1} - 2)$$

$$-(b - \Delta - 2)n - (a + \Delta)n' - 2m,$$

which implies

$$n \le \frac{(a+b-2)(2a+b+\Delta-3)-1}{a} + \frac{2m}{a+\Delta} + n'$$
$$< \frac{(a+b-2)(2a+b+\Delta-3)}{a} + \frac{bn'}{a-1} + m,$$

which conflicts with $n \ge \frac{(a+b-2)(2a+b+\Delta-3)}{a+\Delta} + \frac{bn'}{a+\Delta-1} + m$.

Case 2. $d = 1$.
In this case, we initially prove the two claims below.

Claim. $|T| \le \lfloor \frac{((b-\Delta)n-(b-\Delta)-(a+\Delta)n'-2m)n}{(a+b-1)(n-1)} \rfloor$.

Proof. If $|T| \ge \lfloor \frac{((b-\Delta)n-(b-\Delta)-(a+\Delta)n'-2m)n}{(a+b-1)(n-1)} \rfloor + 1$, then using $d_{G-S}(x_1) = d = 1$, we get

$$|T - N_G(x_1)| \ge |T| - 1 \ge \lfloor \frac{((b-\Delta)n-(b-\Delta)-(a+\Delta)n'-2m)n}{(a+b-1)(n-1)} \rfloor. \qquad (8)$$

Considering (8) and the assumption of Theorem 1, we get

$$N_G(T - N_G(x_1)) = V(G). \qquad (9)$$

Moreover, obviously $x_1 \notin N_G(T - N_G(x_1))$ which get contradictions to (9).

Claim. $|T| \le \frac{(a+\Delta)n-(b-\Delta)-(a+\Delta)n'-2m}{a+b-1}$.

Proof. Take $|T| > \frac{(a+\Delta)n-(b-\Delta)-(a+\Delta)n'-2m}{a+b-1}$. Considering (5) and $d = 1$, we have

$$n \ge |S| + |T|$$
$$> \frac{(b-\Delta-1)n+(b-\Delta)+(a+\Delta)n'+2m}{a+b-1} - 1$$
$$+ \frac{(a+\Delta)n-(b-\Delta)-(a+\Delta)n'-2m}{a+b-1}$$
$$= n - 1$$

which means

$$|S| + |T| = n. \qquad (10)$$

On the basis of (10) and Claim 2, we obtain

$$(a + \Delta)n' + 2m - 1$$
$$\geq (a + \Delta)|S| + \sum_{x \in T} d_{G-S}(x) - (b - \Delta)|T|$$
$$\geq (a + \Delta)|S| + |T| - (b - \Delta)|T|$$
$$= (a + \Delta)(n - |T|) - (b - \Delta - 1)|T|$$
$$= (a + \Delta)n - (a + b - 1)|T|$$
$$\geq (a + \Delta)n - (a + b - 1)\frac{(a + \Delta)n - (b - \Delta) - (a + \Delta)n' - 2m}{a + b - 1}$$
$$= (a + \Delta)n - ((a + \Delta)n - (b - \Delta) - (a + \Delta)n' - 2m)$$
$$\geq (a + \Delta)n' + 2m,$$

a conflict. Therefore, the Claim 2 is hold.

$t' = |\{x : x \in T, d_{G-S}(x) = 1\}|$ is set. Apparently, $t' \geq 1$ and $|T| \geq t'$. Considering (5), $d = 1$ and Claim 2, we get

$$(\Delta + a)|S| + \sum_{x \in T} d_{G-S}(x) - (b - \Delta)|T| - (\Delta + a)n' - 2m$$
$$\geq (\Delta + a)|S| + 2|T| - t' - (b - \Delta)|T| - (a + \Delta)n' - 2m$$
$$= (\Delta + a)|S| - (b - \Delta - 2)|T| - t' - (a + \Delta)n' - 2m$$
$$\geq (\Delta + a)(\frac{(b - \Delta - 1)n + (b - \Delta) + (\Delta + a)n' + 2m}{a + b - 1} - 1)$$
$$-(b - \Delta - 2)\frac{((b - \Delta)n - (b - \Delta) - (\Delta + a)n' - 2m)n}{(a + b - 1)(n - 1)} - t' - (\Delta + a)n' - 2m$$
$$= \frac{(b - \Delta)n - (b - \Delta) - (\Delta + a)n' - 2m}{a + b - 1} - t'$$
$$\geq |T| - t' \geq 0$$

which gets a contradiction.

Case 3. $d = 0$.
Take $r = |\{x : x \in T, d_{G?S}(x) = 0\}|$ and $Y = V(G) - S$. Apparently, $r \geq 1$ and $N_G(Y) \neq V(G)$. Connecting it to the assumption of Theorem 1, we deduce

$$n - r \geq |N_G(Y)| \geq \frac{(b + a - 1)(n - 1)}{(b - \Delta)(n - 1) - (a + \Delta)n' - 2m}|Y|$$
$$= \frac{(b + a - 1)(n - 1)}{(b - \Delta)(n - 1) - (a + \Delta)n' - 2m}(n - |S|),$$

which indicates

$$|S| \geq n - \frac{(n - r)((b - \Delta)(n - 1) - (a + \Delta)n' - 2m)}{(a + b - 1)(n - 1)}. \tag{11}$$

Considering $n \geq \frac{(a+b-2)(2a+b+\Delta-3)}{a+\Delta} + \frac{(a+\Delta)n'}{a+\Delta-1} + m$, we determine that

$$\frac{an - a - bn' - 2m}{n-1} > 1. \tag{12}$$

By means of (11), (12) and $|T| + |S| \leq n$, we indicate

$$(a + \Delta)n' + 2m - 1$$
$$\geq (\Delta + a)|S| + \sum_{x \in T} d_{G-S}(x) - (b - \Delta)|T|$$
$$\geq (\Delta + a)|S| - (b - \Delta - 1)|T| - r$$
$$\geq (\Delta + a)|S| - (b - \Delta - 1)(n - |S|) - r$$
$$= (b + a - 1)|S| - (b - \Delta - 1)n - r$$
$$\geq (b + a - 1)(n - \frac{(n-r)((b-\Delta)n - (b-\Delta) - (\Delta+a)n' - 2m)}{(b+a-1)(n-1)})$$
$$-(b - \Delta - 1)n - r$$
$$= (b - \Delta)n - \frac{(n-r)((b-\Delta)n - (b-\Delta) - (a+\Delta)n' - 2m)}{n-1} - r$$
$$\geq (b - \Delta)n - \frac{(n-1)((b-\Delta)n - (b-\Delta) - (\Delta+a)n' - 2m)}{n-1} - 1$$
$$= (b - \Delta)n - ((b-\Delta)n - (b-\Delta) - (\Delta+a)n' - 2m) - 1$$
$$= (\Delta + a)n' + 2m + (b - \Delta) - 1 > (\Delta + a)n' + 2m,$$

get conflicted.

To sum up, the proof of Theorem 1 is obtained.

3 Results on Fractional (g, f, n', m)-Critical Uniform Graphs

From the proofing procedure presented in above section and the necessary and sufficient condition of fractional (g, f, n', m)-critical deleted graphs similar to it is in critical covered graph setting, we get the following conclusion directly.

Theorem 2. *Assume b, a, Δ, n' and m non-negative integers with $2 \leq a \leq b - \Delta$, and let n be the order of graph G with $n \geq \frac{(a+b-2)(2a+b+\Delta-3)}{a+\Delta} + \frac{(a+\Delta)n'}{a+\Delta-1} + m$. Assume g, f as two integer-valued functions assured on $V(G)$ such that for every $x \in V(G)$ $a \leq g(x) \leq f(x) - \Delta \leq b - \Delta$. If for every $X \subseteq V(G)$, we have*

$$N_G(X) = V(G) \quad if \quad |X| \geq \lfloor \frac{((b-\Delta)(n-1) - (a+\Delta)n' - 2m)n}{(a+b-1)(n-1)} \rfloor; \quad or$$

$$|N_G(X)| \geq \frac{(a+b-1)(n-1)}{(b-\Delta)(n-1) - (a+\Delta)n' - 2m}|X|$$

$$if \quad |X| < \lfloor \frac{((b-\Delta)(n-1) - (a+\Delta)n' - 2m)n}{(a+b-1)(n-1)} \rfloor.$$

Then G is a fractional (g, f, n', m)-critical deleted graph.

If for any edge set E_1 and E_2 with $|E_1| = |E_2| = m$, a graph is a fractional (g, f, m)-uniform graph, it contains a fractional (g, f)-factor such that $h(e) = 1$ for any $e \in E_1$ and $h(e) = 0$ for any $e \in E_2$. So, fractional (g, f, m)-uniform graph is a combination of fractional (g, f, m)-deleted graph and fractional (g, f, m)-covered graph.

Recall that if after any n' removed, it still contains a fractional (g, f)-factor with any m edges $h(e) = 1$, a graph G is a fractional (g, f, n', m)-critical uniform graph. Any m edges satisfy $h(e) = 0$, i.e., it both a fractional (g, f, n', m)-critical deleted graph and a fractional (g, f, n', m)-critical covered graph. That is to say,if after any n' removed, the resulting graph is a fractional (g, f, m)-uniform graph, a graph G is a fractional (g, f, n', m)-critical uniform graph i. Combining Theorem 1 and Theorem 2, we deduce the results on fractional (g, f, n', m)-critical uniform graphs.

Theorem 3. *Assume b, a, Δ, n' and m non-negative integers with $2 \leq a \leq b - \Delta$, and assume n as the order of graph G with $n \geq \frac{(a+b-2)(2a+b+\Delta-3)}{a+\Delta} + \frac{(a+\Delta)n'}{a+\Delta-1} + m$. Assume g, f as two integer-valued functions assured on $V(G)$ such that for every $x \in V(G)$, $a \leq g(x) \leq f(x) - \Delta \leq b - \Delta$. If for every $X \subseteq V(G)$, we have*

$$N_G(X) = V(G) \quad if \quad |X| \geq \lfloor \frac{((b-\Delta)(n-1) - (a+\Delta)n' - 2m)n}{(a+b-1)(n-1)} \rfloor; \quad or$$

$$|N_G(X)| \geq \frac{(a+b-1)(n-1)}{(b-\Delta)(n-1) - (a+\Delta)n' - 2m} |X|$$

$$if \quad |X| < \lfloor \frac{((b-\Delta)(n-1) - (a+\Delta)n' - 2m)n}{(a+b-1)(n-1)} \rfloor.$$

After which G is a fractional (g, f, n', m)-critical uniform graph.

Also, using the example showed in above section, we ensure that the result presented in Theorem 3 on fractional (g, f, n', m)-critical uniform graphs is sharp when m is a small number. Set $n' = 0$ and $\Delta = 0$ in Theorem 3 respectively, we get the following corollaries.

Corollary 6. *Assume b, a, Δ and m non-negative integers with $2 \leq a \leq b - \Delta$, and assume n as the order of graph G with $n \geq \frac{(a+b-2)(2a+b+\Delta-3)}{a+\Delta} + m$. Set f, g as two integer-valued functions assured on $V(G)$ such that for every $x \in V(G)$, $a \leq g(x) \leq f(x) - \Delta \leq b - \Delta$. If for every $X \subseteq V(G)$, we get*

$$N_G(X) = V(G) \quad if \quad |X| \geq \lfloor \frac{((b-\Delta)(n-1) - 2m)n}{(a+b-1)(n-1)} \rfloor; \quad or$$

$$|N_G(X)| \geq \frac{(a+b-1)(n-1)}{(b-\Delta)(n-1) - 2m} |X| \quad if \quad |X| < \lfloor \frac{((b-\Delta)(n-1) - 2m)n}{(a+b-1)(n-1)} \rfloor.$$

After which, G is a fractional (g, f, m)-uniform graph.

Corollary 7. *Assume b, a, n' and m non-negative integers with $2 \leq a \leq b$, and take n as the order of graph G with $n \geq \frac{(b+a-2)(2b+a-3)}{a} + \frac{bn'}{a-1} + m$. Assume f, g as two integer-valued functions assured on $V(G)$ such that for every $x \in V(G)$ $a \leq g(x) \leq f(x) \leq b$. If for every $X \subseteq V(G)$, we get*

$$N_G(X) = V(G) \quad if \quad |X| \geq \lfloor \frac{(a(n-1) - bn' - 2m)n}{(a+b-1)(n-1)} \rfloor; \quad or$$

$$|N_G(X)| \geq \frac{(a+b-1)(n-1)}{a(n-1) - bn' - 2m}|X| \quad if \quad |X| < \lfloor \frac{(a(n-1) - bn' - 2m)n}{(a+b-1)(n-1)} \rfloor.$$

After which, G is a fractional (g, f, n', m)-critical uniform graph.

Using the same trick, we can get the corresponding results on fractional (a, b, n', m)-critical covered graph, fractional (a, b, n', m)-critical deleted graph and fractional (a, b, n', m)-critical uniform graph by setting $g(x) = a$ and $f(x) = b$ for all $x \in V(G)$. We don't list all these results here.

Acknowledgments. We thank the reviewers for their constructive comments in improving the quality of this paper.

References

1. Bondy, J.A., Mutry, U.S.R.: Graph Theory. Springer, Berlin (2008)
2. Gao, W., Wang, W.: New isolated toughness condition for fractional (g, f, n)-critical graphs. Colloquium Mathematicum **147**, 55–66 (2017)
3. Gao, W., Wang, W.: A tight neighborhood union condition on fractional (g, f, n, m)-critical deleted graphs. Colloquium Mathematicum **147**, 291–298 (2017)
4. Gao, W., Wang, W.: Toughness and fractional critical deleted graph. Utilitas Math. **98**, 295–310 (2015)
5. Gao, W., Guirao, J.L.G., Wu, H.: Two tight independent set conditions for fractional (g, f, m)-deleted graphs systems. Qual. Theory Dyn. Syst. **17**, 231–243 (2018)
6. Gao, W., Liang, L., Xu, T., Zhou, J.: Degree conditions for fractional (g, f, n', m)-critical deleted graphs and fractional ID-(g, f, m)-deleted graphs. Bull. Malays. Math. Sci. Soc. **39**, 315–330 (2016)
7. Gao, W., Liang, L., Xu, T., Zhou, J.: Tight toughness condition for fractional (g, f, n)-critical graphs. J. Korean Math. Soc. **51**, 55–65 (2014)
8. Gao, W., Wang, W.: On fractional (g, f, n', m)-critical covered graphs. Manuscript
9. Gao, W., Zhang, Y., Chen, Y.: Neighborhood condition for all fractional (g, f, n', m)-critical deleted graphs. Open Phys. **16**, 544–553 (2018)

An Effective Remote Data Disaster Recovery Plan for the Space TT&C System

Weijie Han[1,2(✉)], Jingfeng Xue[1], Fuquan Zhang[3], and Zhonghui Sun[4]

[1] School of Computer Science and Technology, Beijing Institute of Technology,
Beijing, China
bit_hwj2016@126.com
[2] School of Space Information, Space Engineering University, Beijing, China
[3] Fujian Provincial Key Laboratory of Information Processing and Intelligent
Control, Minjiang University, Fuzhou, China
[4] Baicheng Weapon Test Center of China, Baicheng 137001, China

Abstract. The critical asset data of the Space Tracking Telemetry and Command (TT&C) System plays an important role in fulfilling space missions. According to analyze the current storing methods and disaster recovery requirements of the data, the remote data disaster recovery techniques are studied based on the remote replication capability of the Oracle database, and the remote data disaster recovery plan is developed for the space TT&C system. Furthermore, the experiment is conducted to validate the plan by building a simulation environment. The experiment results demonstrate that the plan can reach the fifth degree of the disaster recovery level and satisfy the following three performance requirements including recoverability, reliability and real-time performance, and therefore realize remote disaster recovery of the critical asset data for the space TT&C system efficiently.

Keywords: The space TT&C system · Remote data disaster recovery · Database disaster recovery · Oracle DataGuard · Oracle GoldenGate

1 Introduction

Being the link of space communication, control, and command, the Space Tracking Telemetry and Command (TT&C) system plays an important role in fulfilling space missions. The safety and reliability of the system influences the success of the missions directly [1]. During the space missions, some critical data will be produced and takes effect on space missions. However, the Space TT&C System may encounter various kinds of unexpected problems during the missions. Subsequently, the system may break down and the operation data may be corrupted all of a sudden. Finally, the space missions may fail due to the data loss. In order to ensure its reliability, stability and security, we must deploy corresponding measures to guarantee the system's stable running even though the system is faced with great challenges.

Disaster recovery technique is one of the useful schemes that can make IT systems tolerant and recoverable from the damages due to disasters [2]. The disaster recovery goal is mainly realized by deploying a primary site infrastructure to respond in normal

X. Chen et al. (Eds.): ML4CS 2020, LNCS 12487, pp. 31–41, 2020.
https://doi.org/10.1007/978-3-030-62460-6_4

runtime, plus a backup secondary site in a remote geographical location. When the primary site fails in time of disaster, the secondary site can fulfill the role of the primary site efficiently [3].

According to the backup requirements of the space TT&C system, we propose a remote data disaster recovery plan so as to ensure its safety and reliability based on the remote replication capability of the Oracle database [4]. Our recovery scheme is implemented based on DataGuard and GoldenGate of the Oracle database mainly, which can fulfill the recovery goal in terms of efficiency and effectiveness.

In summary, this paper makes the following contributions:

(1) We make a detailed list of the mission data of the space TT&C system that needs to back up, and set the disaster recovery standards according to the mission requirement.
(2) We propose an effective remote disaster recovery play based on the data replication engine of the Oracle database. The data replication engine is embedded in the database of the production system.
(3) We conduct comprehensive evaluations about the plan and verify its performance.

2   Related Work

The disaster recovery technique has been employed widely in IT community. There have existed handful of ways to implement a disaster recovery plan [5]. The classical approach is to establish a backup and restore site for the production center [6]. This approach usually takes consistent snapshots of the data periodically produced by the production center, and writes the data into the storage devices away from the production site. Although this approach has the advantage of being low-cost, its disadvantage is also obvious because that it usually takes a long recovery time and restore the system to its outdated state. Compared with the above scheme, the remote mirroring approach continuously replicate its data to a remote online mirror site [6]. Based on continuous replication scheme, this approach guarantees the stability of the production site in case of a disaster. In spite of being more expensive than the above approach, this technique can substantially ensure the reliability and stability more than the aforementioned method.

During the disaster recovery process, the data replication operation is a key point [7, 8]. Usually, the data replication between these two sites can be performed in two ways: synchronously and asynchronously. In synchronously replication mode, the performance of the system may fail a bit as the primary site can only return successfully from a write operation after it has been acknowledged by the secondary site. In asynchronous replication mode, the primary site is allowed to proceed its execution without waiting for the synchronization between sites to complete. This type of replication overcomes the performance limitations of synchronous replication at the expense of allowing recent updates to be lost if a failure occurs.

In this paper, we employ the data replication functions provided by the Oracle database, design a data replication engine and embed it in the database of the production system, so as to ensure the recoverability, reliability and real-time performance.

3 The Current Backup Status and Disaster Recovery Requirements of the Critical Data

In the space TT&C system, the data related to the space missions including the technical plans, software documents, codes, software configurations, raw data of the missions and mission results are the essential objects, which need to be backed up. However, the data currently is stored and managed dispersedly that result in data loss easily. According to the disaster recovery requirements of the space TT&C system and the international general standards Share78 [9], the required disaster recovery levels for the data of the mission are shown as Table 1.

Table 1. The current storage status and disaster recovery requirements of the mission data

Name	Current storage status	Disaster recovery requirement
External input files/technical plans/mission processes/faults handling countermeasures	Paper documents/disk files	The fifth level RTO < 10 min RPO < 5 min
Software design and development documents	Configuration database	
Software codes	Configuration database	
Software configuration status	Configuration database/configuration file	
Raw data/real-time results/final analyzing results	Disk file/database	

4 Design of the Disaster Recovery Plan for the Space TT&C System

Currently, the critical asset data of the space TT&C system are stored in Oracle. Therefore, the disaster recovery plan can be designed and implemented based on the remote replication capability provided by Oracle.

4.1 Remote Data Disaster Recovery Based on Oracle

Oracle DataGuard. The Oracle DataGuard [10] ensures high availability, data protection, and disaster recovery for enterprise data. Oracle transfers data from the main database to a standby database, and in case of failures, Oracle will switch over to the standby database. A standby database can be one of two types: a physical standby database or a logical standby database. The physical standby database has to match the schema structure of the source database. And the archived redo logs are applied directly to the standby database. Logical standby is different from physical standby. Logical standby does not have to match the schema structure of the source database. Logical standby uses LogMiner techniques to transform the archived redo logs to native DML statements. This DML is transported and applied to the standby database. For physical disaster recovery, the archived and online log files are used, but for logical disaster recovery, only the SQL commands extracted from the archived and online log files are used. That is the greatest difference. The standby database can keep consistency with the primary not only in logical but also in physical by physical data disaster recovery. But the only logical structure of the standby database can be consistent by logical recovery. During the logical recovery, it is necessary for the logical standby database to be open, but LOB filed is not supported. The replication is implemented by the log writer process or the archive process.

Oracle GoldenGate. The Oracle GoldenGate [10] is software that replicates structured data based on log files. It captures primary database changes by reading redo records from a source database online redo log file, transforming those records into a platform-independent trail file format, and transmitting the trail file to a target database. Oracle GoldenGate maintains a logical replica by converting the trail file into SQL and applying SQL to a target database. It reads the log files from one database and updates another database by changes of data. So that data can be consistent between source and target. GoldenGate can be used for replicating the mass data between heterogeneous infrastructures under one second, so it is widely used in the emergency system, data synchronization, disaster recovery, database upgrade, double business centers and so on.

4.2 The Remote Data Disaster Recovery Plan for the Space TT&C System Based on Database

In the disaster recovery plan, the data replication engine is embedded in the database of the production system. By the means, the data updating is implemented by the database management system shown as Fig. 1. The update operations in the database can be divided into two kinds: metadata update and user data update. The former means to change the structure of the database, for example, extend tables in the database. The latter means to change the records of the user table. The structure of the database can be

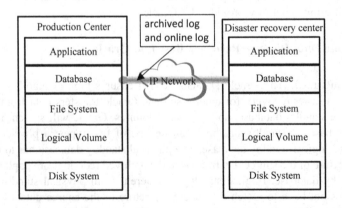

Fig. 1. Remote data disaster recovery plan for the space TT&C system

changed by metadata update for example by extending the database tablespace. The database table records can be changed by a user data update [11, 12].

As shown in Fig. 1, the database log files of the production center are transferred to the disaster recovery center in order to ensure the data synchronization between the two centers. In this way, because only the archived log files are replicated instead of the online log files, the impact on the production center due to the long-distance replication operation can be reduced effectively. Furthermore, the replication process is transparent to the disk system and OS, so the current system can be used directly without any significant modification. However, the disaster recovery process will put a little load on the system because of the database monitoring and replicating operations.

5 Evaluations

The simulated experimental environment is built so as to test and validate the disaster recovery plan based on both Oracle DataGuard and Oracle GoldenGate. The experiment aims to test the following important performance including recoverability, reliability and real-time performance, and evaluate the performance influence on the production system due to the disaster recovery system.

5.1 Testing Environment

Hardware Components. As shown in Fig. 2, the test environment consists of the following hardware components:

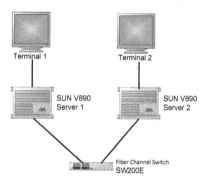

Fig. 2. The experimental environment

(1) 2 Sun Fire V890 servers (4 CPUs);
(2) 1 Brocade SW200E 4 GB fiber channel switch (16 ports);
(3) 2 computer terminals;
(4) The two servers are connected with each other through two Gigabit Ethernet ports.

Software Components. The test environment consists of the following software components:

(1) 2 Oracle 10 g databases (with DataGuard). The databases are configured as follows:

The source database: IP: 11.10.10.1; ORACLE_SID=db1
The destination database: IP: 11.10.10.2;
ORACLE_SID=db2

(2) 1 Oracle GoldenGate software.
The Solaris 10 OS and the Oracle 10 g database are installed on the servers so as to store, manage and back up the experiment data.

5.2   Configuration of the Environment

The two databases installed on the two servers keep consistent before testing, and the production database runs in the archive mode.

Configuring Oracle DataGuard

(1) Configuring the source database
    1) Modifying the initial parameters
        alter   system   set   log_charchiive_config='dg_config=(db1,standby)'
        scope=both;
        alter system set db_unique_name='db' scope=both;
    2) Producing the control file for the destination database
        alter database create standby controlfile as '/oracle/rmanback/ctontrl01.ctl';
    3) Configuring the tnsnames.ora file
        db1 = (DESCRIPTION =
        (ADDRESS_LIST = (ADDRESS = (PROTOCOL = TCP) (HOST = 11.10.1
        0.1)(PORT = 1521)))
        (CONNECT_DATA = (SERVICE_NAME = db1)))
        standby = (DESCRIPTION =
        (ADDRESS_LIST = (ADDRESS = (PROTOCOL = TCP)   (HOST = 11.10.
        10.2)(PORT = 1521)))
        (CONNECT_DATA = (SERVICE_NAME = db2)))

(2) Configuring the backup database
  1) Creating the parameter file and setting the parameters as follows:
     fal_server = 'db1' fal_client = 'db2'
     log_archive_dest_2 = 'SERVICE = db1 REOPEN=300'
     log_archive_dest_stat_2 = 'ENABLE'
  2) Copying the control file to the destination database
  3) Launching the destination database by the control file and setting the database into the mount mode
  4) Configuring the tnsnames.ora file as same as the source database.

Configuring Oracle GoldenGate.

(1) Configuring the source database
  1) Configuring the mgr process
     GGSCI>edit param mgr
     Input: PORT 7809
  2) Creating the capturing process
     GGSCI>add extract ext1, tranlog, begin now, threads 2
  3) Configuring the capturing process
     GGSCI>edit param ext1
     Input:

     > Extract ext1
     > userid ggtest, password ggtest
     > rmthost 11.10.10.2, mgrport 7809
     > rmttrail/ggs

5.3   Experiment Data

The experiment data include:

(1) The software and the tracking and telemetry data of space crafts that are stored in the database;
(2) The software codes;
(3) The space mission parameters;
(4) The technical plans;
(5) The raw data of the space missions;
(6) The processing results of the space missions.

5.4   Testing Process

(1) Recoverability testing

  The testing process and results of recoverability are shown in Table 2.

Table 2. Testing process and results of the recoverability

Testing content/Method/Step	Testing results	
	DataGuard	GoldenGate
According to the ascent stage plan of Shenzhou, starting the simulation, processing the telemetry data and loading the data. Ten minutes later, closing the production database and switching the redo log manually	The backup database has to be launched manually and some data are lost. The switching delay is less than 4 min	The production and backup databases can be switched real-time and no data are lost. The switching delay is less than 1 min
According to the ascent stage plan of Shenzhou, starting the simulation, processing the telemetry data and loading the data. Ten minutes later, closing the production database. Then switching operational stage, restarting the production database and stopping the data storage after one hour, and switching the redo log manually	The data can be fully recovered. The recovery time is less than 4 min	The data can be fully recovered. The recovery time is less than 1 min
Remarks	When switching between the production and backup database by DataGuard, the mode of the database has to be switched between mount and open. Some data may be lost due to the switching process and the amount of data loss depends on the switching time	

Both the production and backup databases can recover the data fully. The recovery time of DataGuard is longer because of switching the redo log manually.

(2) Reliability testing

The testing process and results of reliability are shown in Table 3.

Table 3. Testing process and results of reliability

Testing content/Method/Step	Testing results	
	DataGuard	GoldenGate
According to the operation stage plan of Tiangong, starting the simulation, processing the telemetry data and loading the data. Ten hours later, closing the production database. After succeeding ten hours, switching to the production database and stopping loading data and forcing log switch manually. Switching the redo log manually	Data-loading and database-switching are both normal	Data-loading and database-switching are both normal
Remarks	When switching between the production and backup database by DataGuard, the mode of the database has to be switched between mount and open. Some data may be lost due to the switching process and the amount of data loss depends on the switching time	

(3) Real-time performance testing

The testing process and results of real-time performance are shown in Table 4.

Table 4. Testing process and results of real-time performance

Testing content/Method/Step	Testing results	
	DataGuard	GoldenGate
Starting loading data and sending 100 commands of remote control. Switching redoes log manually	The results can be found in the backup database simultaneously	The results can be found in the backup database simultaneously
Starting loading data and sending 100 thousand telemetry data in 10 times averagely. Switching redoes log manually	The results can be found in the backup database after 2 min and 50 s	The results can be found in the backup database after 10 s
	The results can be found in the backup database after 2 min and 46 s	The results can be found in the backup database after 9 s
	The results can be found in the backup database after 2 min and 48 s	The results can be found in the backup database after 11 s
Starting loading data and sending 500 thousand telemetry data in 50 times averagely. Switching redoes log manually	The results can be found in the backup database after 3 min and 47 s	The results can be found in the backup database after 11 s
	The results can be found in the backup database after 3 min and 49 s	The results can be found in the backup database after 10 s
	The results can be found in the backup database after 3 min and 52 s	The results can be found in the backup database after 11 s
Remarks	The backup database is in the mounted state and needs to be turned to the open state. The switching process will take some time	

5.5 Evaluating the Performance Influence on the Production System Due to the Disaster Recovery System

The performance influence on the production system due to the disaster recovery system is validated including the network bandwidth, I/O throughput and CPU usage so on. The testing process and results are shown in Table 5.

Table 5. Testing process and results of the performance influence on the production system

Testing content	Pre-deployment (peak value)	Testing results	
		DataGuard (peak value)	GoldenGate (peak value)
Network bandwidth	1000 M	1004 M	1002 M
I/O throughput: Creating tables in both the production and backup databases which include 1 timestamp field and 999 float fields. Writing 100 thousand records and repeating 5 times	2' 45" 63 2' 48" 02 2' 47" 12 2' 46" 56 2' 47" 33	2' 46" 52 2' 47" 10 2' 48" 23 2' 45" 76 2' 46" 23	2' 47" 21 2' 45" 34 2' 46" 23 2' 48" 12 2' 47" 63
CPU usage: Starting simulation, processing telemetry data, and loading data. Repeating 5 times	35.8% 34.2% 37.5% 36.8% 34.9%	36.1% 37.3% 34.3% 35.7% 35.2%	38.8% 39.2% 39.9% 40.2% 38.9%

Because GoldenGate runs as a system process and DataGuard runs as an Oracle process, GoldenGate consumes 5%–7% more CPU resources than DataGuard. Additionally, DataGuard consumes more bandwidth than GoldenGate because of the difference in the replication mechanism.

5.6 Analysis of the Experiment Results

The results show that both DataGuard and GoldenGate can meet the data disaster recovery requirements of the system (RTO < 10 min, RPO < 5 min) which can reach the fifth level of the disaster recovery standards. DataGuard is a free tool provided by Oracle but GoldenGate is an expensive component need to pay. GoldenGate is better than DataGuard in terms of bandwidth consumption, data synchronization performance and the backup database status except for the higher cost.

6 Conclusions

The remote data disaster recovery technologies are introduced and a data disaster recovery plan is designed based on Oracle for the space TT&C system so as to protect the critical space data. In order to validate the effectiveness and performance of the plan, an experimental environment is built. The experiment aims to test the recoverability, reliability and real-time performance, and evaluate the performance influence on the production system due to the disaster recovery system. The experiment results show that the plan can reach the fifth level of the disaster recovery standards and meet the disaster recovery requirements for the space TT&C system.

Acknowledgments. This work was supported by the National Key Research and Development Program of China under Grant 2016QY06X1205.

References

1. Wu, W., Li, H., Li, Z., Wang, G., Kang, Y.: Status and prospect of China's deep space TT&C network. SCIENTIA SINICA Inform. **50**(1), 87–108 (2020). http://engine.scichina.com/doi/10.1360/SSI-2019-0242
2. Alcântara, J., Oliveira, T., Bessani, A.: GINJA: one-dollar cloud-based disaster recovery for databases. In: Proceedings of Middleware 2017, Las Vegas, NV, USA, 11–15 December 2017, 13 pages (2017). https://doi.org/10.1145/3135974.3135985
3. Ping, Y., Bo, K., Jinping, L., Mengxia, L.: Remote disaster recovery system architecture based on database replication technology. In: Proceedings of 2010 International Conference on Computer and Communication Technologies in Agriculture Engineering, Chengdu, China, 12–13 June 2010. https://doi.org/10.1109/CCTAE.2010.5544352
4. Jain, A., Mahajan, N.: Disaster Recovery Options. The Cloud DBA-Oracle. Apress, Berkeley (2017). https://doi.org/10.1007/978-1-4842-2635-3_5
5. Kokkinos, P., Kalogeras, D., Levin, A., Varvarigos, E.: Survey: live migration and disaster recovery over long-distance networks. ACM Comput. Surv. **49**(2), 26 (2016). https://doi.org/10.1145/2940295
6. Faisal, F.: The backup recovery strategy selection to maintain the business continuity plan. J. Appl. Sci. Adv. Technol. **1**(1), 23–30 (2018). https://doi.org/10.24853/jasat.1.1.23-30
7. Choy, M., Leong, H.V., Wong, M.H.: Disaster recovery techniques for database systems. Commun. ACM **43**(11), 6-es (2000). https://doi.org/10.1145/352515.352521
8. Zheng, L., Shen, C., Tang, L., et al.: Data mining meets the needs of disaster information management. IEEE Trans. Hum.-Mach. Syst. **43**(5), 451–464 (2013). https://doi.org/10.1109/THMS.2013.2281762
9. Dhanujati, N., Girsang, A.S.: Data center-disaster recovery center (DC-DRC) for high availability IT service. In: Proceedings of 2018 International Conference on Information Management and Technology, Jakarta, Indonesia, 3–5 September (2018). https://doi.org/10.1109/ICIMTech.2018.8528170
10. Alawanthan, D., et al.: Information technology disaster recovery process improvement in organization. In: Proceedings of 2017 International Conference on Research and Innovation in Information Systems, Langkawi, Malaysia, 16–17 July 2017. https://doi.org/10.1109/ICRIIS.2017.8002530
11. Mukherjee, N., et al.: Fault-tolerant real-time analytics with distributed oracle database in-memory. In: Proceedings of 2016 IEEE 32nd International Conference on Data Engineering, Helsinki, Finland, 16–20 May 2016. https://doi.org/10.1109/ICDE.2016.7498333
12. Han, W., Xue, J., Yan, H.: Detecting anomalous traffic in the controlled network based on cross entropy and support vector machine. IET Inf. Secur. **13**(2), 109–116 (2019). https://doi.org/10.1049/iet-ifs.2018.5186

Research on Progress and Inspiration of Entity Relation Extraction in English Open Domain

Xu Jian[1,2], Yao Xianming[2(✉)], Gan Jianhou[1], and Sun Yu[3]

[1] Key Laboratory of Educational Informatization for Nationalities (YNNU),
Kunming 650500, China
qjncxj@126.com
[2] School of Information Engineering, QuJing Normal University,
Qujing 655011, China
yxm176@qq.com
[3] School of Information Science and Technology, Yunnan Normal University,
Kunming 650500, China
sunyu_km@hotmail.com

Abstract. In the era of big data, how to extract unrestricted type of entity relations from open domain text is a challenging topic. In order to further understand related deep issues, this paper summarized the latest progress in the field of English entity relation extraction, ranging from binary to n-ary entity relation extraction; furthermore, some milestone systems are introduced in detail. This paper makes a preliminary exploration on the extraction of entity relations in the Chinese open domain. In particular, the inspiration of English to Chinese has also promoted the development of Chinese entity relation extraction.

Keywords: English open domain · Binary entity relation · N-ary entity relation · Entity relation extraction

1 Preface

With the advent of the era of big data, traditional entity relation extraction algorithms are faced with a series of problems such as weak domain expansion capabilities, restricted entity types, and heavy manual labor. Therefore, the extraction of open domain entity relations has become a hot spot.

The research of English open domain entity relation extraction has started earlier, and gone through the process from binary to n-ary entity relation extraction. Lots of milestone systems such as Reverb [1], OLLIE [2], Kraken [3], ClausIE [4] and so on emerged. The relation extraction in the open domain of English is becoming more and more mature. Nevertheless, relevant research in the field of Chinese has just begun, and there is still much room for exploration.

In order to promote the development of related research in the field of Chinese, this paper makes a review of English open domain entity relation extraction, ranging from binary relation to n-ary entity relation. Several milestone systems are presented in detail as typical cases. Furthermore, this paper also makes a preliminary exploration of entity

X. Chen et al. (Eds.): ML4CS 2020, LNCS 12487, pp. 42–55, 2020.
https://doi.org/10.1007/978-3-030-62460-6_5

relation extraction in Chinese open domain, and analyzes the Inspiration of English to Chinese. Considering the lack of relevant research in the field of Chinese, we hope this paper can contribute to the current work.

2 Summaries

In order to have a comprehensive understanding of open domain entity relation extraction, we would like to introduce its definition, tasks and applications in this section.

2.1 Definition

Entity relation extraction refers to extract semantic relations between entities and expressions from text. This kind of semantic relations could reflect interactions between them [5]. Currently, there is no authoritative definition to open domain entity relation extraction. Definition defined in paper [6] is generally accepted: Open information extraction is a novel extraction paradigm that tackles an unbounded number of relations. It usually refers to extending the traditional entity relation extraction from specific domain to general domain. For example, in the sentence of "Einstein was born in Ulm, Germany", there exists a relation of (Einstein, be born in, Ulm Germany).

Let E be a set of entities in text, e_i and e_j ($0 < i, j < |E|$) are elements in E, and let R be a relation set in the same text, $r_k (0 < k < |R|)$ is an element of R, so that I is a set of random combination of e_i, e_j, r_k in the form of (e_i, r_k, e_j), and the task of entity relation extraction is to extract $\delta = \; < E, R, I >$.

In the triple of (e_i, r_k, e_j), r_k is usually called as relation or relation phrase consisting of one or more words. In the task of extracting relations delivered by predicate, r_k is a predicate or P for short. e_i and e_j are often called entities, appropriately, the relation between them is expressed as r_k. In some studies, e_i and e_j are named as arguments of r_k. Also, in the task of extracting relation delivered by predicate, e_i and e_j act as subject and object respectively; and this kind of relation could be expressed as (Subject, Predicate, Object), or (S, P, O) for short.

2.2 Tasks

The task of entity relation extraction is to extract the semantic relation between entities represented by a continuous word. Based on the analysis of previous studies, this paper divides these relations into three categories.

- **Relations delivered by verbs.** Since verbs between subject and object could clearly reflect their interaction in sentence, verbs are a good choice for relation extraction. For example, in sentence of "*Bin Laden masterminded the 9/11 attacks*", the verb of "*masterminded*" could reflect interaction of "*Bin Laden*" and "*9/11 attacks*", so that it could be selected as the relation of them. In systems such as Reverb [1], WOE [6] and TextRunner [7], verb phrases are the main target for extracting target in the domain of English, as is the domain of Chinese.

- **Relations delivered by common nouns.** In natural language, there is a structure in the form of "*proper noun + common noun + proper noun*", in which *proper noun* is noun or adjective of location, people, organization, etc. *Common noun* is general concept which can be considered as attribute. In this kind of structure, triples of (Entity, Attribute, Value) could be mined as entity relation. For example, in the sentence of "*American President Obama is going to cooperate with their western allies*", there is a fragment of "*American President Obama*" which satisfies this kind of structure, and we could find an entity relation of (*America, President, Obama*). However, due to inversed order, long distance dependency, and instable structure, extraction of this kind of entity relation is rarely mentioned except for OLLIE in paper [2].
- **Relations established contextually.** With the passage of time, people's understanding of objective laws will also change, which means that certain triples extracted from previous rules will be invalid, so a certain dependence should be given. Therefore, extracting relations established contextually is particularly important for open domain entity relation extraction. For example, we could extract relation of (*the earth; be the center of; the universe*) from the sentence of "*Early astronomers believed that the earth is the center of the universe.*" However, we know that this relation is invalid, and the valid relation should be ((*the earth; be the center of; the universe*) *AttributedTo believe; Early astronomers*). The OLLIE system extends the representation of open information extraction and allows it to accept other contextual information, such as attributes and clause modifiers, thereby solving this type of problem. Systems such as TIE [9] and Yago2 [10] extended temporal constraints and achieved certain success in given types of entity relation extraction. Yao uses relation nested in subjects and objects to extract compound entity relations, thus resolving this problem. For example, they could extract the relation of (*Early astronomers, believed, (the earth, is the center of, the universe)*) from above example.

Of course, not only the above relations exist, but with the development of research, more types of entity relations will be discovered in the future. In addition, there are other types of relations in other studies, but this paper has not been found. Yang Bo [12] proposed implicit entity relation extraction, which is different from the method of extracting explicit entity relations in this paper, so it is not taken into account.

2.3   Application

Because the open domain entity relation extraction can expand the types of entities and relations, and also has the domain extension function, it has been applied in many applications and played an important role.

- **Knowledge base construction** [13, 14]. Generally speaking, knowledge base consists of domain ontology and knowledge graph. It is composed of vertexes and edges. Vertexes refer to concepts and entities, and edges refer to relations between concepts and entities in knowledge base. This kind of structure is similar to triple discussed in this paper, so entity relation extraction is especially important to the construction of knowledge base. Prior studies on the construction of knowledge base mainly focus on a given domain, thereby limiting the types of entities and relations. By the introduction of open domain entity relation extraction, these problems could be resolved perfectly. Nowadays, lots of knowledge graphs have appeared, such as Google Knowledge Graph, Satori of Microsoft, etc. There are also some general knowledge graphs in the Chinese field, such as Baidu ZhiXin, Sogou ZhiLiFang, and CN-DBpedia developed by Knowledge Works Research Laboratory in Fudan University. The emergence of these knowledge graphs has greatly promoted the development of in-depth question answering, intelligent information retrieval and knowledge reasoning.

- **Semantic Search** [15]. Traditional search engine works in a workflow of analyzing question raised by user, extracting key words as well as computing similarity between key words and web pages, relevant pages with higher similarity will be provided to user. This kind of information retrieval can only match at the word level, and cannot understand users' purpose, so relevant pages cannot meet users' needs. If the task of entity relation extraction is introduced into traditional information retrieval to capture the relation between entities and perform semantic level information retrieval, it will increase the probability of information retrieval to find more closely related pages and even give direct answers to improve user-friendliness.

- **Question Answering System** [16, 17]. This is nearly the same problem with information retrieval, for entity relation extraction could catch semantic relation between entities, these information could be provided to question answering system for modeling user's attention, deep analysis to sentences will help positioning answer. In addition, for the uncertainty of answer types, any kind of entity relation could be treated as candidate answer, extracting relation from answer nested sentences will be helpful to the generation of answer.

Generally, as one of the most important tasks in information extraction, entity relation extraction not only plays an important role in the above three applications, but also has a wide range of applications in natural language processing, machine translation and machine reading. Due to space limitations, these applications will not be discussed here.

3 Summaries on English Open Doman Entity Relation Extraction

Since the relevant research in the field of English is earlier than Chinese and has accumulated a lot of experience, these studies have good reference value for other languages. Here we will introduce some excellent research. According to the summary of some domestic scholars, the open domain entity relation extraction in English can be divided into two stages: binary entity relation extraction stage and n-ary entity relation extraction attachment. Next, we will introduce some milestone systems based on this summary. The presentation includes tasks, techniques, experiments and deficiencies.

3.1   Binary Entity Relation Extractions

Binary entity relation extraction is the earliest research work, and has the most fruitful work and the most mature technical solutions in the open English domain. Extensive research has been conducted on the extraction of relation phrases, relation arguments, conditional dependence, juxtaposition and other issues. Data size and speed as well as the precision and recall rate have been improved greatly. In the meantime, it also provides technical premise to n-ary entity relation extraction. The research results at this stage mainly have six systems, namely, KnowItAll [18], TextRunner [7], WOE [6], Reverb [1], R2A2 [19] and OLLIE [2].

KnowItAll

KnowItAll system is an advantageous attempt to extract information from restricted domain to open domain. Its main purpose is to solve the problem of obtaining concept examples in an open domain environment. You can give concept name to be queried, the system can use a search engine to retrieve the text in the Web and return its instance.

KnowItAll first constructs a baseline system based on Hearst patterns [20], and instances of these patterns will be provided to search engine to retrieve more instances which will be added to knowledge base. KnowItAll also proposes the tasks of Pattern Learning, Subclass Extraction and List Extraction. Task of Pattern Learning is to learn and evaluate domain specific patterns automatically according to Hearst which belong to open domain. Task of Subclass Extraction can learn subclass of a given concept so as to construct concept tree. Task of List Extraction is the population of concept with instances according to structural similarity of web pages.

TextRunner

TextRunner can be regarded as the first generation open domain entity relation extraction system [21]. This is the first work to incorporate remote supervision into the research of entity relation extraction. TextRunner transforms the relation extraction problem into a classification problem, aiming to identify relation phrases to achieve its goal.

Rule-based patterns are adopted to automatically tag training instances. Tagged entities mainly include noun phrases, and relation phrases are composed of continuous words in syntactic structure between entities. Classification features include universal features such as POS, length of relation phrase as well as the number of stop words in relation etc. Deep syntactic features are not in consideration so as to speed up system performance. Finally, naïve Bayes was borrowed to train classification model.

WOE

Alike to TextRunner, WOE (Wikipedia-based Open Extractor) adopted distant super-vision to automatically tagging training instances. After extracting effective features, instances will be sent to train classification model. Unlike TextRunner which performs the task of tagging based on hand crafted rules, Wikipedia inforbox information was selected as tagging data source. For the high quality of tagging data, classification model can outperform TextRunner.

WOE trained two kinds of systems: WOE^{pos} and WOE^{parse}. Both of them realized the same purpose of extracting entity relation, but WOE^{pos} uses shallow syntactic features which is same to TextRunner, while WOE^{parse} uses deep syntactic features both in training and recognizing. Probability model and conditional random field model were chosen as training model respectively.

The performance of two systems is as expected. The performance of WOE^{pos} is almost the same as TextRunner, but lower than WOE^{parse}. In consideration of speed, WOE^{pos} is also the same as TextRunner, and far faster than WOE^{parse} which is attributed to deep syntactic analysis. The comparison of two systems shows that deep syntactic features are not fit for open domain entity relation extraction, since they are time-consumed, but the speed is especially important to open domain.

Reverb

Previous studies like TextRunner generically take continuous words between entities as relation phrase which may take incoherent and uninformative extractions. The greatest contribution of Reverb is to find the boundary of relation phrase. Reverb introduced LVCs (light verb constructions) theory, furthermore, lexical and syntactic constraints were defined to extract relation phrase.

Syntactic constraint could reduce incoherent and uninformative extractions errors. Lexical constraint could reduce wrong relation phrases with lowest occurrence which cannot be filtered by syntactic constraint. At the stage of implementation, syntactic constraints were encoded as regular expressions to match corresponding relation phrase in sentence; entities were extracted from left and right side of relation phrase to form a triple. In the following, over-specified relation phrases will be filtered by threshold, defined by lexical constraints. Finally, linear regression classifier was adopted to assign a confidence score to each triple, aiming to find a balance between precision and recall rate.

R2A2

Entity relation extraction should focus on three kinds of extraction tasks as triple listed: first entity, relation phrase and second entity. As far as the relation phrase extraction task is concerned, Reverb has provided technical solution. Previous studies had no deep studies in entity extraction. R2A2 (REVERB relation phrases with ARGLEARNER's arguments) is just this kind of system, which focuses on extracting entity that makes open domain entity relation more perfect.

The analysis of R2A2 to real text shows that the left and right position for first entity and second entity could be divided into several categories which enable supervised method to be borrowed for recognizing the boundary of each entity. R2A2 designed 3 classifiers. The first classifier is the left boundary recognizer for first argument (R2A2 names entity as argument, which means argument for relation). The second classifier is right boundary recognizer for first argument. The third classifier is right boundary recognizer for second argument. Note that there is no left boundary recognizer for second argument, and statistics show that almost all the left boundary of second argument is just at the end of relation phrase. Contextual features, length of sentence, POS, case and punctuation were selected as features. Training instances come from sematic role labeling. Relation phrases come from the result of Reverb. CRF, REPTree and CRF were chosen as training models for each classifier respectively.

Evaluation shows that the precision of first argument increased by 10%, and 20% for second argument which is better than previous systems. It also outperforms previous systems in other respects.

OLLIE

OLLIE (Open Language Learning for Information Extraction) is a more perfect system in the field of open domain entity relation extraction. As introduced above, systems such as Reverb and R2A2 had made great contributions to the recognition of relation phrase and entity (argument). However, there are still two problems. The first is that relation phrases delivered by noun were hardly mentioned, while the second problem is that contextually established relations were rarely mentioned. Aimed at resolving these problems, OLLIE promoted two methods: (1) expanding the syntactic scope of relation phrases to cover a much larger number of relation expressions, and (2) expanding the Open IE representation to allow additional context information such as attribution and clausal modifiers.

In the implementation stage, OLLIE involves three steps. First, seeds of entity relation with high quality provided by Reverb will be created to bootstrap a very large training set which encapsulates the multitudes of ways in which information is expressed as text. Second, open pattern templates will be learned by identifying dependency path between relation phrase and corresponding arguments. Finally, extracting new entity relations using learned pattern templates.

Experiments show that the correct extraction rate of OLLIE is 4.4 times higher than REVERB, 4.8 times higher than WOE^{parse}, and the accuracy is about 75%.

3.2   N-ary Entity Relation Extractions

After a series of studies, there may be a lot of research space in binary entity relation extraction. It has made great progress, making it difficult to improve accuracy and recall rate. Therefore, a lot of work has turned to n-ary entity relation extraction. Statistics in paper [22] show that n-ary entity relations occupy about 40% in all entity relations, and n-ary entity relation could make the extracted result easier to be understood. So the n-ary entity relation is a novel and fruitful direction.

TIE

Although n-ary entity relation extraction is pretty important, and relevant studies started at a later time, resulting in fewer achievements. TIE (Temporal Information Extractor) is one of such system which extracts n-ary entity relations. TIE believes that most entity relations have temporal constraint with start and end time, and temporal constraint will make relation meaningful. Temporal information was extracted from the text as an argument of entity relation. Temporal entropy was adopted to assess the performance of TIE. Experiments and its wide application had proved its usefulness. TIE is one of these systems that raised n-ary entity relation task, and certain progress has opened up a new direction for entity relation extraction.

Yago2

Yago2 is a relatively ripe knowledge base whose data comes from Wikipedia. It owns declarative rules including factual rules, implication rules, replacement rules and extraction rules, so the number of entities in its base increased greatly. Temporal information, space information and contextual information are also extracted as arguments of entities. Temporal information contains begin and end time of an entity. Space information includes longitude and latitude. Contextual information refers to textual context that entity occurred in Wikipedia pages. In this way, an entity relation with six parameters including predicate (relational phrase) is constructed, namely subject, predicate, object, temporal, space and context, which is called as SPOTLX for short. So Yago2 can trace the process of all entities and events in knowledge base from birth to death, including its specific geographic location information. Finally, Yago2 integrates information such as entities and events into the map, allowing users to query corresponding information in the form of visualization; therefore, the data is more intuitive.

The limitation of Yago2 is that it only considers time, space and environment information. The domain it focuses on has certain limitations, and it is difficult to expand to more constraints of entity relation arguments.

Kraken

In contrast, Kraken (N-ary OIE fact extraction system for facts of arbitrary arity) system [3] is a relatively more mature system in n-ary entity relation extraction. Based on dependency analysis, it can extract n-ary entity relation by locating the relation phrases and obtaining their corresponding arguments. The specific algorithm steps are as follows:

1. The detection of fact phrase. Detecting event relation phrase composed by verbs, modifiers and prepositions, such as "has been known", "claims to be". If there is only one predicate, it can be also considered as fact phrase.
2. To find argument heads. Finding subject heads for each fact phrase according to dependency path like "nsubj-↓", "nsubjpass-↓, rcmod-↑", "appos-↑" etc. Finding object heads according to dependency path like "dobj-↓", "prep-↓, pobj-↓" etc.
3. Detection of full arguments. Follow all downward links recursively from the argument head in order to get the full argument, excluding any links that were part of the type-path to the argument head.

Experiment shows that the precision of Kraken is 68% and the completeness is 79%, while the highest precision of Reverb is only 64% and the completeness is only 44%, which reflects the excellent performance of Kraken system. But in terms of extraction speed, Kraken consumes 319 ms for 500 sentences; Reverb only spends 13 ms, with a speed difference of nearly 20 times, which fully proves that deep syntactic analysis will have a greater impact on extraction speed.

ClausIE

ClausIE (Clause-based open Information Extraction) [4] is a relatively more mature and powerful open information extraction system, which can consider unary, binary, ternary and n-ary entity relation.

ClausIE uses linguistic knowledge of English grammar to detect clauses, and then recognizes the types of clauses according to grammatical functions of each clause component. It listed seven types of clauses: ① SVi; ② SVeA; ③ SVcC; ④ SVmtO; ⑤ SVdtOiO; ⑥ SVctOA; ⑦ SVctOC. For any given clause, ClausIE can determine the type of the clause by its predicate, and obtain the information of the clause from the dependency analysis results as well as the type of predicate in domain independent dictionary.

In the phase of system evaluation, they compared ClausIE to TextRunner, Reverb, WOE, OLLIE and Kraken. Experimental datasets include Reverb dataset, Wikipedia and New York Times. Statistics shows that ClausIE could extract more entity relation instances than other systems with equal or even higher recall and precision rate. Although OLLIE is better than other previous systems, the correct instance extracted by ClausIE is 2.5–3.5 times that of OLLIE. Errors of ClausIE are caused by the result of the wrongly analyzed dependency.

3.3   Reflections and Prospect of English Open Domain Entity Relation Extraction

Although the entity relation extraction in English open domain has begun very early, and has achieved many achievements and mature technical solutions, there are still some problems, which will have a certain impact on other research.

- **Lack of standard evaluation dataset and criterion** which would makes it difficult to evaluate the performance of each system horizontally. To evaluate datasets, KnowItAll adopted Tipster Gazetteer and Internet Movie Database, while TextRunner adopted their own data collected from 9 M web pages. WOE adopted Penn Treebank, Wikipedia and the general Web. Reverb used a test set of 500 sentences sampled from the Web, using Yahoo's random link service. OLLIE created a dataset of 300 random sentences from three sources: News, Wikipedia and Biology textbook. These evaluation datasets come from different sources with different quality. The performance of each system may vary greatly, so it cannot reflect the actual performance.

  To evaluate criterion, most of these systems adopted precision and recall rate, while Reverb and OLLIE partly or fully used AUC. As a result, the horizontal comparison between different systems is not very intuitive, and may hinder the development of open domain entity relation extraction indirectly. If we can carry out corresponding academic conferences and competitions, release standard evaluation corpus, and establish a unified evaluation standard, just like what traditional information extraction do, it will undoubtedly promote the development of open domain entity relation extraction.

- **Lack of standard definition of relevant concepts.** Different studies define these concepts from different perspectives. In the definition of binary entity relation extraction, most systems adopted the definition in Sect. 2 of this paper to extract entity relations in the form of (e_i, r_k, e_j) and name it as binary entity relation extraction. However, KnowItAll defines concept instance extraction as unary entity relation extraction, and others as n-ary. In the definition of n-ary entity relation extraction, Kraken aims to extract multiple triples of (e_i, r_k, e_j) from sentence, and this kind of extraction is considered as n-ary entity relation extraction by default which shares the same form with binary entity relation extraction defined in Sect. 2. Nevertheless, this kind of definition neglected their close relation between different triples extracted from the same sentence. ClausIE aimed at solving this problem and extract more entity relations from sentence. Unlike other studies, entities extracted from sentence are regarded as arguments of relation phrase, so their triples could be unified as an organic whole. But this kind of extraction is obviously different to other works.

- **Introduction of dependency parsing is controversial, but it is a trend.** Due to the long-distance dependence between entities and their relations in text, it can only be solved by dependency parsing. However, dependency parsing may be tedious and time-consuming, which makes it not suitable for processing large-scale data in open domain. In TextRunner and WOE^{parse} systems, they try to obtain syntactic features to improve system performance. Experiment shows that syntactic features do play an important role, but it is time-consuming. In the system of OLLIE, the dependency path is used as template directly, and achieved great success. Later, Kraken also used dependency parsing to extract n-ary entity relation. Although dependency parsing could be time-consuming, scientists are still willing to use it to improve the precision and recall rate, which proves the effectiveness of this technology indirectly. It is believed that with the improvement of computer speed and the development of natural language processing, dependency parsing should be one of the most promising directions in future, or at least achieve a certain balance between speed and performance.
- **Fewer researches reported on entity relation extraction in other languages.** At present, studies are mainly focus on the domain of English, and had achieved a large amount of research results. There are in-depth analysis and technical solutions to problems involved in English. But for other languages, due to various reasons, related studies were rarely mentioned. For example, in the domain of Chinese, although there have been some researches in open domain, it is mainly based on binary, and the research results are relatively fewer, while n-ary is rarely reported.

4 Chinese Open Domain Entity Relation Extraction and Its Inspiration

Compared with English, study of open domain entity relations in other languages is relatively lagging behind, and related results are relatively lacking too, which may be attributed to many factors. As one of the six official languages of the United Nations, Chinese has the most users in the world, which makes Chinese information work of great value. Similarly, it is equally important to do relevant studies in open domain of Chinese. If we can learn from the beneficial experience of English and carry out relevant research work in combination with the characteristics of Chinese, it will bring great impetus to relevant research.

4.1 Introduction of Chinese Open Domain Entity Relation Extraction

Chinese open domain entity relation extraction started at around 2014, and certain achievements have been reached at present, but representative systems have not yet appeared. This paper divides relevant researches into two categories: one is based on statistics, and the other is based on natural language processing.

Statistics-based methods design corresponding constraint rules according to objective statistical results of entity relations in text, aiming to extract entity relation instances. Qin bing [23] exploited using word distance and entity distance constraints to generate candidate relation triples from the corpus, and then adopted global ranking and domain ranking methods to discover relation words from candidate relation triples, and finally filtered candidate triples by using the extracted relation words and some sentence rules. Result shows that the precision is higher than 80% when extracting large scale relation triples. Yu li [24] adopted approximate method, by making statistics on part of speech, position, distance and other features of the relation words in geographical entity relation, Yu li also constructed an evaluation function to extract relation words, and obtained the accuracy rate of 80% and the recall rate of 87.79%.

Natural language processing based methods makes full use of dependency syntax analysis and utilizes dependency paths as templates or features to extract entity relations. These approaches benefit from the beneficial attempts of OLLIE, Kraken and other systems in English domain and have achieved success in Chinese [13]. Song qing [8] adopted method used by OLLIE system, and select relation with high confidence to extract seed set, matching it in open text, and then save the dependency path of entity relation as templates, and then templates used frequently are selected as seeds to extract new entity relation, so as to realize the automatic extraction of entity relation. Yao xianming [11] uses the idea of the Kraken system as reference, based on the characteristics of the Chinese language; take the verb as the relation indicator to extract its subject and object, and use the nested relation between entity relations to extract contextually dependent entity relations. Liu shen [25] takes dependency relation as the feature of entity relation, and deep learning is utilized to study the entity relation extraction problem. In addition, this paper also studied argument boundary identification problem similar to the R2A2 system in English domain.

In addition, there are other related studies. For example, literature [26–30] presents some different ideas and technical routes, which will not be introduced in-depth here.

4.2   Inspiration of English to Chinese

Through comparative analysis of Chinese and English, we can find that Chinese open domain entity relation extraction is relatively small, scattered, and lacks continuity. These problems make it difficult to formulate a complete technical solution. Once we can learn successful experiences from abroad and apply them to the Chinese field, technology development will be more rapid and beneficial.

- English open domain entity relation extraction experienced a process of relation phrase extraction, entity extraction, attribute extraction and contextual dependence extraction. Different systems have completed part of the tasks and brought them together to form a unified technical solution. Although accomplished by different researchers, these studies are continuous. But for Chinese, relevant studies are isolated, and have no special research to specific problem; therefore, these studies could not be bound together easily. If we can refer to the research ideas in English and break down tasks of entity relation extraction, we may be able to open a new situation for entity relation extraction in Chinese open domain.

- Extraction techniques in English went through the stages of distant supervision, lexical pattern, dependency syntactic pattern, dependency syntactic path analysis, and sentence clause analysis etc. These techniques could be implemented in Chinese directly or indirectly. Although Chinese is different from English, for example, Chinese has no space. Many of these languages are the same as each other. For example, part of speech is almost the same. Open domain named entity recognition includes time expression, location, person and organization recognition; sentences are also composed of subject, predicate, object, definition complement, etc. Therefore, transplanting these technologies into Chinese should work well, not to mention Chinese Has made great strides in natural language processing. At present, many Chinese studies have proved its feasibility in [8, 26, 31].
- Disadvantages of English could also be avoided, such as lack of evaluation dataset and criterion. Institutional advantages of our country could mobilize lots of talents to create such kinds of data, so as to provide to lots of researchers as reference.
- Accelerate the development of natural language processing, especially the ability to improve accuracy, speed and domain expansion. From the experience of English open domain entity relation extraction, we can find that relying on syntactic analysis is particularly important for relation extraction, but the premise of this technique is a series of natural language processing techniques. Therefore, natural language processing is particularly important. Considering that relation extraction is mainly applied in the open domain, and speed is particularly important, so speeding up the process of relying on syntactic analysis will help open subject relation extraction.

5 Conclusions

The development of Chinese open domain entity relation extraction research is bound to learn the successful experience of other languages. At the same time, it is necessary to combine the characteristics of this field to develop an effective extraction strategy, and even need a complete set of extraction technology solutions. Entity and relation research will the promote research progress in this area. This paper summarizes and analyzes the extraction of binary and n-ary entity relations in the field of English, and introduces the work related to Chinese, and puts forward some suggestions, hoping to provide reference for domestic research.

Acknowledgement. This research was partly supported by Yunnan Normal University Graduate Research and innovation fund in 2020.

References

1. Anthony F., Stephen S., Oren E.: Identifying relations for open information extraction. In: Proceedings of the 2011 Conference on Empirical Methods in Natural Language Processing, pp. 1535–1545. John McIntyre Conference Centre, Edinburgh (2011)

2. Michael, S., Robert, B., Stephen, S., Oren E.: Open language learning for information extraction. In: Proceedings of the 2012 Joint Conference on Empirical Methods in Natural Language Processing and Computational Natural Language Learning, vol. 4590, Eight Street, Stroudsburgm, United States, pp. 523–534 (2012)

3. Alan A., Alexander, L.: N-ary facts in open information extraction. In: Joint Workshop on Automatic Knowledge Base Construction and Web-Scale Knowledge Extraction, Montreal, Canada, pp. 52–56 (2012)

4. Luciano, D.C., Rainer, G.: ClausIE: clause-based open information extraction. In: International Conference on World Wide Web, Brazil, pp. 355–366 (2013)

5. Nancy, C., Elaine, M.: MUC-7 information extraction task definition. In: A Seventh Message Understanding Conference, Virginia, pp. 1–53 (1998)

6. Fei, W., Daniel, S.W.: Open information extraction using wikipedia. In: Meeting of the Association for Computational Linguistics, Sweden, pp. 118–127 (2010)

7. Alexander, Y., Michele, B., Matthew, B., Michael, C., Oren, E., Stephen, S.: TextRunner: open information extraction on the web. In: Human Language Technology Conference of the North American Chapter of the Association of Computational Linguistics, New York, pp. 25–26 (2007)

8. Song, Q., Qi, C.L., Yang, Y.: New Event Relation Extraction Approaches Based on Bootstrapping. J. Commun. Univ. China (Sci. Technol.) **4**, 46–50 (2017)

9. Xiao, L., Daniel, S.W.: Temporal information extraction. In: Twenty-Fourth AAAI Conference on Artificial Intelligence, UK, pp. 1385–1390 (2010)

10. Johannes, H., Fabian, M.S., Klaus, B.: YAGO2: exploring and querying world knowledge in time, space, context, and many languages. In: International Conference Companion on World Wide Web, India, pp. 229–232 (2011)

11. Yao, X.M., Gan, J.H., Xu, J.: Chinese open domain oriented N-ary entity relation extraction. CAAI Trans. Intell. Syst. **14**, 597–604 (2019)

12. Yang, B., Cai, D.F., Yang, H.: Progress in Open Information Extraction. J. Chin. Inf. Process. **28**, 1–11 (2014)

13. Sheng, J.B., Shijia, E., Li, M., Xiang, Y.: Chinese open relation extraction and knowledge base establishment. ACM Trans. Asian Low-Resour. Lang. Inf. Process. **17**, 1–22 (2018)

14. Ndapandula, N., Gerhard, W., Fabian, S.: Discovering and exploring relations on the Web. Proc. VLDB Endow. **5**, 1982–1985 (2012)

15. Sérgio, M., Arrais, J.P., Maia-Rodrigues, J., Oliveira, J.L.: Concept-based query expansion for retrieving gene related publications from MEDLINE. BMC Bioinform. **11**, 212–220 (2010). https://doi.org/10.1186/1471-2105-11-212

16. Roma, Y., Tandan, S.R.: N-ary relation approach for open domain question answering system based on information extraction through world wide web. Int. J. Eng. Appl. Sci. (IJEAS) **2**, 141–144 (2015)

17. Gosse, B., Ismail, F., Jori, M.: Relation extraction for open and closed domain question answering. In: van den Bosch, A., Bouma, G. (eds.) Interactive Multi-modal Question-Answering. Theory and Applications of Natural Language Processing, pp. 171–197. Springer, Heidelberg (2011). https://doi.org/10.1007/978-3-642-17525-1_8

18. Oren, E., Michael, C., Doug, D.: Unsupervised named-entity extraction from the web: an experimental study. Artif. Intell. **165**, 91–134 (2005)

19. Christensen, J., Mausam, Soderland, S., Etzioni, O.: Learning arguments for open information extraction. In: Proceedings of the Sixth International Conference on Knowledge Capture, USA, pp. 1–8 (2011)

20. Hearst, M.A.: Automatic acquisition of hyponyms from large text corpora. In: Proceedings of the 14th Conference on Computational Linguistics, France, pp. 539–545 (1992)

21. Oren, E., Anthony, F., Janara, C., Stephen, S.: Open information extraction: the second generation. In: International Joint Conference on IJCAI, Spain, pp. 3–10 (2011)
22. Janara, C., Mausam, Stephen, S., Oren, E.: An analysis of open information extraction based on semantic role labeling. In: K-CAP, Ganada, pp. 113–120 (2011)
23. Qin, B., Liu, A.A., Liu, T.: Unsupervised Chinese open entity relation extraction. J. Comput. Res. Dev. **52**, 1029–1035 (2015)
24. Yu, L., Lu, F., Liu, X.L.: A bootstrapping based approach for open geo-entity relation extraction. Acta Geodaetica Cartogr. Sin. **45**, 616–622 (2016)
25. Liu, S.: Chinese entity relation discovery for BigCilin. Harbin Institute of Technology (2016)
26. Li, M.Y., Yang, J.: Open Chinese entity relation extraction method based on dependency parsing. Comput. Eng. **42**, 201–207 (2016)
27. Yang, M.: Research and implementation of Chinese open relation extraction. Nanjing Normal University (2017)
28. Li, Y.: Research and implementation of Chinese open relation extraction. University of Electronic Science and Technology of China (2017)
29. Guo, X.Y.: Entity relation extraction for open domain text. Central China Normal University (2017)
30. Wang, Y., Zhou, G., Nan, Y., Zhen, Z.S., Tian, F.: Open entity relation extraction based on library of relation word. J. Inf. Eng. Univ. **18**, 242–247 (2017)
31. Li, Y.: N-ary Chinese open entity relation extraction. Taiyuan University of Technology (2017)

A SEU Immune Flip-Flop with Low Overhead

Zhengfeng Huang[1] , Xiandong Li[1] , Shangjie Pan[1] ,
Min Wang[1] , and Tianming Ni[2(✉)]

[1] Hefei University of Technology, Hefei 230009, China
[2] Anhui Polytechnic University, Wuhu 241000, China
timmyni126@126.com

Abstract. In nano-scale CMOS technologies, storage cells such as flip-flops are becoming increasingly sensitive to soft errors caused by harsh radiation effects. This paper proposes a radiation-hardened flip-flop with single event upset (SEU) immunity and low overhead. The flip-flop consists of a transfer unit, a storage unit and an output stage. The input signal propagates through transfer unit to the storage unit on the rising edge of the clock signal. The transfer unit uses the true single-phase clock (TSPC) scheme to simplify the clock distribution and reduce power consumption. The storage unit is composed of a radiation hardened memory (RHM) cell. Due to stacked PMOS structure and interlocked interconnect mechanism, SEU can be entirely tolerated. The C-element at output stage can filter any SEU occurred at storage unit. Compared with the existing radiation hardened flip-flops, the proposed flip-flop achieves 41.4% reduction in terms of delay on average, 82.6% reduction in terms of active power on average, 83.8% reduction in terms of power delay product on average and 39.7% reduction in terms of area on average.

Keywords: Single event upset · True single-phase clock · C-element

1 Introduction

As the feature size of the CMOS process is decreasing, the operating frequency of the circuit is continuously increasing, the supply voltage is continuously reducing, the capacitance of internal node is continuously reducing, the critical charge of the internal nodes is reducing continuously, the soft error rate in the circuit is rapidly increasing [1–3].

Soft errors can be caused by radioactive particles such as neutrons or alpha particles in terrestrial areas or protons, electrons, and heavy ions in space environments. When a particle with enough linear-energy-transfer hits the diffusion region of a reverse bias transistor, a voltage change in a node connected to the affected transistor will occur since the particle can allow current to flow through an off-state transistor temporarily. As for previous device processes, the issue of striking-particle-induced soft errors was mainly considered by researchers for on-board aerospace applications [4]. However, due to the aggressive shrinking of transistor feature sizes, soft errors at the earth level have also become a matter of concern. Soft errors mainly include single event upset (SEU) in flip-flops/latches and single event transient (SET) in combinatorial logic. Dual sampling and temporal redundancy can effectively handle the SET [5, 6]. SEU

X. Chen et al. (Eds.): ML4CS 2020, LNCS 12487, pp. 56–65, 2020.
https://doi.org/10.1007/978-3-030-62460-6_6

tolerance is the research focus. In general, the current soft error hardening of flip-flop includes radiation hardened by design (RHBD) and radiation hardened by process (RHBP) [7–9]. RHBD is more prevalent because it is scalable for different technology nodes. In aerospace applications, because the reliability requirements are very urgent, the most popular scheme of RHBD is triple modular redundancy (TMR). However, TMR does not always work in all situations because of high area overhead, high power consumption and speed penalty [10]. A lot of hardened scheme have been proposed to handle SEU in latches [11–17], memory cells [18–24] and flip-flops [23, 25–31].

This paper proposes a TSPC-RHM flip-flop which can achieve SEU immunity at the internal state nodes. Different from the previous hardened flip-flops, the proposed TSPC-RHM flip-flop utilizes the RHM cell to entirely tolerate SEU. Extensive SPICE simulations show that compared with other radiation hardened flip-flops mentioned in the paper, the proposed TSPC-RHM flip-flop makes great reduction in power consumption, delay and area.

The contribution of this paper can be summarized as follows. 1) a TSPC-RHM flip-flop which can achieve SEU immunity at the internal state nodes is proposed, 2) The power consumption of the clock tree is reduced by using the TSPC design in transfer unit, and 3) the area-powerperformance comparison and process, voltage and temperature (PVT) fluctuation analyse of the proposed TSPC-RHM and conventional flip-flops.

The following arrangements are as follows, Sect. 2 introduces the proposed flip-flop structure and its working principle. Section 3 discusses and compares the simulation results and overhead. Section 4 summarizes this paper.

2   Proposed TSPC-RHM Flip-Flop Design

2.1   Radiation Hardened Memory (RHM) Cell

The proposed flip-flop utilizes the RHM cell as the storage unit, because the RHM cell can effectively tolerate single event upset occurred at any internal state nodes. As shown in Fig. 1, the RHM cell structure consists of 10 transistors [22]. It is completely symmetric to get the optimal static noise margin. There are 4 internal state nodes (S0, S1, S2, S3). State nodes can be connected to the gate of transistors and reach full swings. The point is to using SEU physics mechanism to tolerate SEU. The RHM cell has following advantages:

1) Stacked PMOS structure to reduce sensitive state nodes. For example, when S0 = 0, S1 = 1, S2 = 1 and S3 = 0, only S0, S1, S3 are sensitive to SEU, S2 is not sensitive to SEU because S2 is only connected to PMOS transistors. When the node S2 is struck by high-energy particles, only positive pulses can be generated, which does not affect the logical value of the node S2. Since the RHM cell has a symmetric structure, when S0 = 1, S1 = 0, S2 = 0 and S3 = 1, only S0, S1, S2 are sensitive nodes, S3 is not sensitive to SEU.

2) Redundant state nodes and interlocked interconnect scheme to recover from SEU. There are four internal state nodes (S0, S1, S2, S3) to store the correct logic value.

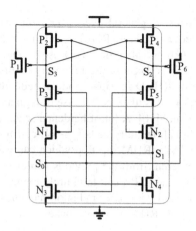

Fig. 1. RHM cell

In normal situation, S1 and S2 has the same logic value, S0 and S3 has the same logic value. When one state node is upset, the other three state nodes can recover the upset node quickly.

3) Cross coupled stable structure to keep the correct logic value. The first cross coupled stable structure consists of transistors P2, P3, P4 and P5. The second cross coupled stable structure consists of transistors N1, N2, N3 and N4. The interlocked scheme of two stable structure can effectively increase the ability to tolerate SEU.

2.2   TSPC-RHM Structure and Work Principle

Figure 2 shows that the proposed TSPC-RHM flip-flop is composed of transfer unit, storage unit and output stage. The transfer unit is a true single-phase clock transfer unit, which can effectively simplify the clock distribution and reduce the power consumption. The storage unit uses the RHM cell, which can tolerate all the SEU occurred at any internal state nodes. The output stage is based on C-element with two inputs. C-element works as an inverter when the two inputs have the same logic value. C-element can keep the output unchanged when the two inputs have different logic values. And the C-element at the output stage can filter SEU at either of the two inputs.

When CLK is low, the transfer unit is in the precharge phase. When CLK is high, the transfer unit is in the evaluation phase. At the rising edge of the clock, the transistor M10 turns on, the input data propagates from the transfer unit to the storage unit. For example, when CLK is low, if Data = 1, then the transistors M3 and M4 turn on, A = 0, B = 1. On the rising edge of CLK, transistors M8 and M9 turn on and S1 = 0. Transistor M10 turns on and S2 = 0. Transistor M12 turns on and S3 = 1, transistor M20 turns on and S0 = 1. Because there are 4 internal state nodes (S0, S1, S2, S3). S1 and S2 have the same logic value in normal situation. S0 and S3 have the same logic value in normal situation. The new value is written to RHM cell: S0 = 1, S1 = 0, S2 = 0, and S3 = 1. The node pairs (S1, S2) drive the output stage, and the output Q is high. Because the RHM cell is symmetric. If D = 0, the output Q is low.

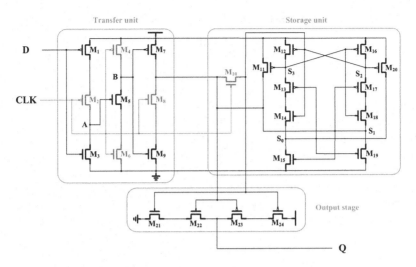

Fig. 2. The proposed TSPC-RHM flip-flop

In order to pull down the state nodes S1 and S2 of RHM cell, the pull-down strength of transistors M8 and M9 must be stronger than the pull-up strength of transistors M11 and M16. In order to pull up the state nodes S1 and S2 of the RHM cell, the pull-up strength of transistor M7 must be stronger than the pull-down strength of M19. The point is to increase the aspect ratio of transistors M7, M8 and M9.

3 Simulation and Discussion

3.1 Cost Comparison

We have simulated and compared the proposed TSPC-RHM flip-flop with CPQ, C2-DICE and TSPCER flip-flops [27], TMR-DICE flip-flop [28], the conventional Master Slave DICE (MSDICE) flip-flop without preset and clear [29], a PGDICE1 [30], a MSQuatro [23] and TSPC-DICE flip-flops [31] using the PTM 65 nm CMOS technology model. As we can see in Table 1, column 1 shows the name of the flip-flops, column 2 shows the reference, column 3 shows the setup time, column 4 shows the hold time, column 5 shows the D-Q delay, column 6 shows the power consumption (active and stand-by), column 7 shows the power delay product (PDP), PDP equals the product of active power and D-Q delay (t_{DQ}),column 8 shows the area in equivalent unit size transistors (UST) [32], column 9 shows the SEU tolerate rate. The performance of the flip-flops is evaluated using extensive SPICE simulations at a clock frequency of 500 MHz and a supply voltage of 1.1 V [33]. The delay of D-Q is the minimum D-Q delay (t_{DQ}). The active power consumption is measured when D-Q delay reaches the minimum value.

Table 1 shows the cost comparison among the proposed TSPC-RHM and other 8 hardened flip-flops. As we can see, the proposed TSPC-RHM flip-flop features the

Table 1. Performance and overhead comparison with other hardened flip-flops

	t_{setup} (DC)	t_{hold}	Delay (t_{DQ})	Power (µw)		PDP (aJ)	Area	SEU tolerate rate
	(ps)	(ps)	(ps)	Active	Stand-by		(UST)	
CPQ	17.49	−34.17	74.51	25.87	0.90	1927.71	116	75%
C^2-DICE	56.10	−20.58	121.28	25.35	0.45	3074.45	86	100%
TSPCER	20.94	−982.76	57.55	98.54	27.14	5671.10	79	75%
TMR-DICE	20.20	−3.47	87.58	19.71	0.38	1726.20	125	100%
MSDICE	42.85	7.56	106.41	13.64	1.10	1451.17	123	100%
PGDICE1	−42.05	−129.50	31.61	240.80	208.29	7611.54	192	100%
MSQuatro	136.39	79.76	182.43	28.41	0.64	5183.69	103	87.5%
TSPC-DICE	30.40	−5.04	66.22	9.02	0.17	597.30	67	100%
TSPC-RHM	15.52	−4.65	53.33	8.35	0.93	445.31	69	100%

smallest active power consumption and power delay product. Its setup time is only slightly longer than PGDICE1. Its delay overhead is only slightly higher than TSPCER flip-flop. Its area overhead is only slightly bigger than TSPC-DICE flip-flop.

Table 2. Relative cost comparison with other hardened flip-flops

	Ref.	ΔDelay	Δpower	ΔPDP	ΔArea
			Active		
CPQ	[27]	−28.43%	−67.73%	−77%	−40.52%
C^2-DICE	[27]	−56.03%	−67.06%	−86%	−19.77%
TSPCER	[27]	−7.33%	−91.53%	−92%	−12.66%
TMR-DICE	[28]	−39.11%	−57.64%	−74%	−44.80%
MSDICE	[29]	−49.88%	−38.77%	−69%	−43.90%
PGDICE1	[30]	−68.71%	−96.53%	−94%	−64.06%
MSQuatro	[23]	−70.77%	−70.61%	−91%	−33.01%
TSPC-DICE	[31]	−19.47%	−7.43%	−25%	2.99%
AVERAGE		−38.54%	−84.00%	−90%	−35.31%

Table 2 shows the relative cost comparison in terms of delay (Δdelay), power (Δpower), power delay product (ΔPDP) and area (Δarea). The relative results are calculated as following: Δ = (the TSPC-RHM − the compared flip-flop)/the compared flip-flop. If the result is negative, the proposed TSPC-RHM is better than the compared flip-flop. If the result is positive, the proposed TSPC-RHM is worse than the compared flip-flop. As we can see, the proposed TSPC-RHM flip-flop is only a little higher than PGDICE1 in terms of delay overhead and a little bigger than TSPC-DICE in terms of area. Compared with the other eight radiation hardened flip-flops, the proposed flip-flop achieves 38.54% reduction in terms of delay on average, 84% reduction in terms of active power on average, 90% reduction in terms of power delay product on average and 35.31% reduction in terms of area on average.

3.2 SEU Immunity

To verify the SEU immunity of the proposed TSPC-RHM flip-flop, fault injections are performed at each of the internal state nodes such as S0, S1, S2, and S3. A double exponential current pulse is generated to simulate a SEU induced by particle striking [34]. Figure 3 shows that fault injections are performed in turn at internal nodes S0, S1, S2 and S3 at different time windows. Results show that all nodes can fully immunize SEU. It is obvious that the logic value of internal state nodes can recover from SEU quickly, and output signal Q is completely undisturbed. The proposed TSPC-RHM flip-flop will not generate a short pulse at the output when SEU occurs at internal state nodes. C-element at the output stage can effectively filter the short pulse. It is important to note that S2 is not a sensitive node when S2 = 1, SEU at S2 only generates a positive pulse which will not upset the logic value. Because of the RHM is symmetric, S3 is not a sensitive node when S3 = 1.

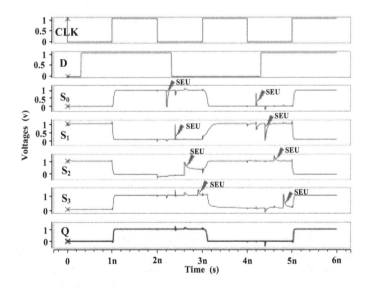

Fig. 3. Fault injection Waveform of TSPC-RHM flip flop

As you can see in Table 1, the proposed TSPC-RHM flip-flop is immune to SEU. In a word, the proposed TSPC-RHM flip-flop can tolerate SEU with a rate of 100%, while the CPQ and TSPCER flip-flops can only tolerate SEU with a rate of 75%, and the MSQuatro flip-flop can only tolerate SEU with a rate of 87.5%.

3.3   PVT Analysis

With the rapid development of CMOS technology and integrated circuit design, the size of integrated circuit technology is shrinking, and the influence of PVT fluctuation on the performance, stability and power consumption of integrated circuits is also increasing. Therefore, this paper evaluates the PVT variation sensitivity of the proposed flip-flop by extensive PVT analysis. The CPQ, C²-DICE, TSPCER, TMR-DICE, MSDICE, PGDICE1, MSQuatro, TSPC-DICE flip-flop and the flip-flop of the paper (TSPC-RHM) were simulated and analyzed under fluctuation to evaluate the delay and power consumption.

Figure 4 shows the delays and power consumption of various flip-flops under different process corner. That are including fast NMOS/fast PMOS process (NFF, PFF), fast NMOS/slow PMOS process (NFF, PSS), typical process (N, F), slow NMOS/fast PMOS process (NSS, PFF), and fast NMOS/slow PMOS process (NFF, PSS). Figure 5 shows he delays and power consumption of various flip-flops under different voltages. The normal supply voltage was set to 1 V and the supply voltage variation was varied from 0.8 V to 1.6 V. Figure 6 shows he delays and power consumption of various flip-flops under different temperatures. Note that the normal temperature was set to 25 °C and the temperature was varied from −20 °C to 50 °C.

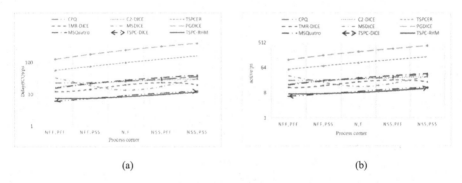

(a)   (b)

Fig. 4. Delay and power consumption under different process

It can be seen from Fig. 4a and Fig. 6a that compared with other flip-flops, the delay of TSPC-RHM flip-flop is less sensitive to the process and temperature variation, and the trend of the TSPC-DICE flip-flop curve is similar to the TSPC-RHM flip-flop, indicating that the TSPC-DICE is not sensitive to the process and temperature variation in term of the delay. It can be seen from Fig. 5a that the TSPC-RHM flip-flop delay is greatly affected by the power supply voltage. As can be seen from Fig. 4b to 6b, the power consumption of TSPC-RHM flip-flop is the least affected by PVT. In general, the stability of the design flip-flop of this paper has certain advantages when considering the PVT changes.

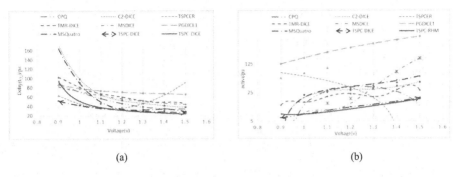

Fig. 5. Delay and power consumption under different voltages

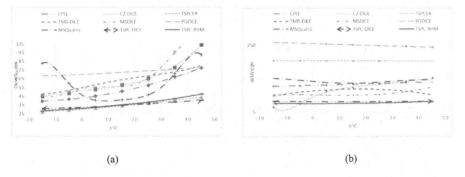

Fig. 6. Delay and power consumption under different temperatures

4 Conclusion

We have presented a SEU immune TSPC-RHM flip-flop with low overhead. The TSPC of transfer unit can simplify clock network and reduce power consumption. Storage unit of RHM cell can achieve SEU immunity. Output stage utilizes C-element to filter any short pulse induced by SEU occurred at internal state nodes. The proposed TSPC-RHM flip-flop features high performance, low power overhead and area overhead, at the same time, the TSPC-RHM flip-flop designed in this paper is not sensitive to PVT fluctuations. Compared with the other eight radiation hardened flip-flops, the proposed flip-flop achieves 38.54% reduction in terms of delay on average, 84% reduction in terms of active power on average, 90% reduction in terms of power delay product on average and 35.31% reduction in terms of area on average.

References

1. Baumann, R.C.: Radiation-induced soft errors in advanced semiconductor technologies. IEEE Trans. Device Mater. Rel. **5**, 305 (2005)

2. Akkerman, A., et al.: Role of elastic scattering of protons, muons, and electrons in inducing single-event upsets. IEEE Trans. Nucl. Sci. **64**, 2648 (2017)
3. Caron, P., et al.: Physical mechanisms inducing electron single-event upset. IEEE Trans. Nucl. Sci. **65**, 1759 (2018)
4. Aibin, Y., et al.: Quadruple cross-coupled dual-interlocked-storage-cells-based multiple-node-upset-tolerant latch designs. IEEE Trans. Circuits Syst. I: Regul. Papers **67**(3), 879–890 (2020)
5. Mongkolkachit, P., Bhuva, B.: Design technique for mitigation of alpha-particle-induced single-event transients in combinational logic. IEEE Trans. Device Mater. Rel. **3**, 89 (2003)
6. Huang, C., et al.: Robust circuit design for flexible electronics. IEEE Des. Test Comput. **28**, 8 (2011)
7. Fu, W., et al.: Alpha-particle-induced charge collection measurements and the effectiveness of a novel p-well protection barrier on VLSI memories. IEEE Trans. Device Mater. Rel. **32**, 49 (1985)
8. Chen, J., et al.: Characterization of the effect of pulse quenching on single-event transients in 65-nm twin-well and triple-well CMOS technologies. IEEE Trans. Device Mater. Rel. **18**, 12 (2018)
9. Rodbell, P., et al.: Low energy proton SEUs in 32-nm SOI SRAMs at Low Vdd. IEEE Trans. Nucl. Sci. **64**, 999 (2017)
10. Nicolaidis, M.: Design for soft error mitigation. IEEE Trans. Device. Mater. Rel. **64**, 405 (2017)
11. Hui, X.: Circuit and layout combination technique to enhance multiple nodes upset tolerance in latches. IEICE Electron. Exp. **12**, 20150286 (2015)
12. Huaguo, L., et al.: Highly robust double node upset resilient hardened latch design. IEICE Trans. Electron **E100-C**, 496 (2017)
13. Aibin, Y., et al.: A transient pulse dually filterable and online self-recoverable latch. IEICE Electron. Express **14**, 1 (2017)
14. Aibin, Y., et al.: A self-recoverable, frequency-aware and cost-effective robust latch design for nanoscale CMOS technology. IEICE Trans. Electron **E98-C**, 1171 (2015)
15. Huang, Z., Liang, H., Hellebrand, S.: A high performance SEU tolerant latch. J. Electron. Test. **31**(4), 349–359 (2015). https://doi.org/10.1007/s10836-015-5533-5
16. Aibin, Y., et al.: Double-node-upset-resilient latch design for nanoscale CMOS technology. IEEE Trans. VLSI Syst. **25**, 1978 (2017). https://doi.org/10.1007/s10836-015-5533-5
17. Aibin, Y., et al.: Single event double-upset fully immune and transient pulse filterable latch design for nanoscale CMOS. Microelectron. J. **61**, 43 (2017)
18. Calin, T., et al.: Upset hardened memory design for submicron CMOS technology. IEEE Trans. Nucl. Sci. **43**, 2874 (1996)
19. Jahinuzzaman, S., et al.: A soft error tolerant 10T SRAM bit-cell with differential read capability. IEEE Trans. Nucl. Sci. **56**, 3768 (2009)
20. Jung, S., et al.: A novel sort error hardened 10T SRAM cells for low voltage operation. In: IEEE MWSCAS Papers, p. 714 (2012)
21. Jing, G., et al.: Novel low-power and highly reliable radiation hardened memory cell for 65 nm CMOS technology. IEEE Trans. Circuits Syst. I **61**, 1994 (2014)
22. Jing, G., et al.: Soft error hardened memory design for nanoscale complementary metal oxide semiconductor technology. IEEE Trans. Rel. **64**, 596 (2015)
23. Li, Y., et al.: A quatro-based 65-nm flip-flop circuit for soft-error resilience. IEEE Trans. Nucl. Sci. **64**, 1554 (2017)
24. Shah, S., et al.: A 32 kb macro with 8T soft error robust, SRAM cell in 65-nm CMOS. IEEE Trans. Nucl. Sci. **62**, 1367 (2015)

25. Furuta, J., et al.: An area/delay efficient dual-modular flip-flop with higher SEU/SET immunity. IEEE Trans. Nucl. Sci. **93**, 340 (2010)
26. Wey, C., et al.: Robust C-element design for soft-error mitigation. IEEE Electron. Exp. **12**, 20150268 (2015)
27. Islam, R.: Low-power resonant clocking using soft error robust energy recovery flip-flops. J. Electron. Test. **34**(4), 471–485 (2018). https://doi.org/10.1007/s10836-018-5737-6
28. Knudsen, E., Clark, T.: An area and power efficient radiation hardened by design flip-flop. IEEE Trans. Nucl. Sci. **53**, 3392 (2006)
29. Wang, W., Gong, H.: Edge flip-floped pulse latch design with delayed latching edge for radiation hardened application. IEEE Trans. Nucl. Sci. **51**, 3626 (2004)
30. Singh, S., Manoj, S.: Radiation hardened pulsed-latches in 65-nm CMOS. In: Proceedings CCECE Papers, p. 1 (2016)
31. Jahinuzzaman, M., Islam, R.: TSPC-DICE: a single phase clock high performance SEU hardened flip-flop. In: Proceedings of MWSCAS, Papers, p. 73 (2010)
32. Katsarou, K., Tsiatouhas, Y.: Soft error interception latch: double node charge sharing SEU tolerant design. In: Proceedings of IET Paper, p. 330 (2015)
33. PTM: 65 nm Predictive Technology Model. http://ptm.asu.edu
34. Messenger, G.: Collection of charge on junction nodes from ion tracks. IEEE Trans. Nucl. Sci. **29**, 2024 (1982)

An Information and Power Simultaneous Transfer Strategy in UAV and Wireless Rechargeable Sensor Networks

Zhi Li[1,2], Jifeng Feng[1], Jian Li[1(✉)], and Xu Gou[1]

[1] College of Electronics and Information Engineering, Sichuan University,
Chengdu 610065, China
lijiandz@scu.edu.cn
[2] Key Laboratory of Wireless Power Transmission of Ministry of Education,
Sichuan University, Chengdu 610065, China

Abstract. Using UAV to Simultaneous Wireless Information and Power Transfer (SWIPT) can effectively solve sensor energy problems in Wireless Rechargeable Sensor Networks (WRSN). Among current charging techniques, radio frequency (RF) remote charging with a small transmit antenna is gaining interest when non-contact type charging is required for sensor nodes. In this article, we study how to obtain higher charging efficiency by RF charging on the basis of ensuring data collection efficiency. Considering the actual environmental parameters, by establishing the mathematical relationship between data transmission power and power transfer power, we realized the creation of UAV-WRSN SWIPT model. We propose the path planning strategy based on joint priority of node residual energy and position, and design the node optimal power transfer strategy based on data collection maximization. The simulation results show that the proposed path planning algorithm can improve the efficiency of the UAV for SWIPT on the premise of ensuring that the nodes do not die. On the other hand, using the charging strategy based on data collection maximization proposed by us, the residual energy of the node charging is significantly higher than that non-charging, and the working life of the sensor is prolonged.

Keywords: SWIPT · UAV pathing planning · RF energy harvesting · WRSN

1 Introduction

Currently, energy efficiency is an important objective in the analysis and design of wireless sensor networks [1]. In previous studies, the network life was extended mainly by reducing the energy consumption of nodes themselves, but the energy of nodes is limited after all. In order to address these issues, wireless power transfer (WPT) is a promising approach to harvest RF energy from wireless received signal and prolong the lifework time of wireless sensor networks. For wireless power transfer mode, distance is one of the key factors to limit its transmission efficiency. At first, researchers mainly sent RF energy to sensor nodes through fixed RF sources. In [2] the RF energy received by the receiving equipment from different RF energy sources and different distances is

© Springer Nature Switzerland AG 2020
X. Chen et al. (Eds.): ML4CS 2020, LNCS 12487, pp. 66–78, 2020.
https://doi.org/10.1007/978-3-030-62460-6_7

studied. However, because this way is limited by distance, it is only suitable for small networks. Therefore, the strategy of charging sensor nodes with mobile devices is proposed to solve the distance problem. The mobile charging car can realize the wireless power supply of short distance and non-contact, and its charging strategy and charging model have been widely studied. Compared with mobile charging car, UAV has better mobility and controllability. Using UAV charging can deal with emergencies in time and improve charging efficiency.

On the other hand, data perception and collection are the main task of sensor network, how to improve the efficiency of data collection for sensor has always been the focus of research. However, time variation of recharging rates in wireless rechargeable sensor networks imposes a great challenge in obtaining an optimal data gathering strategy [3]. Since radio signals carry both information and RF energy at the same time, simultaneous wireless information and power transfer (SWIPT) has recently been proposed and attracted much attention from academia and industry. As shown in Fig. 1, wireless charging and data collection are carried out simultaneously by UAV. In [4], the joint design problem of charging and mobile data collection in WRSN is studied to maximize the amount of data collection and to establish a network utility maximization model to optimize the amount of charging and node routing. In [5], the author proposes a method of separating data collection and mobile charging. At the same time, data collection car and mobile charging car are used to design adaptive algorithm to obtain the optimal scheduling strategy of data collection and energy supply. In [6], the network is divided into grids to enable mobile charging devices to move along the edge of the grid to charge the nodes, and the routing strategy based on this is studied. In [7] establishes a WRSN dynamic topology model to optimize the network dynamic routing and the working strategy of mobile charging devices with the goal of maximizing station-to-station ratio when mobile charging devices simultaneously have data collection capabilities.

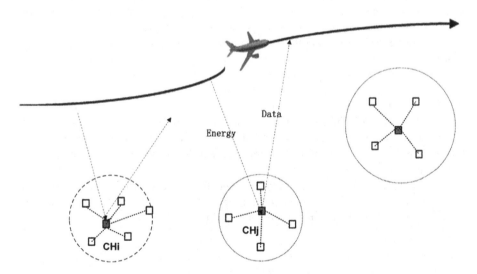

Fig. 1. The architecture of UAV-WRSN SWIPT.

In this paper, combined with the current research status of radio frequency wireless energy transmission technology, the collaborative design of UAV-WRSN data collection and charging strategy is carried out:

(1) Establishing UAV-WRSN SWIPT service model, the sensor node is charged by moving the RF energy source through UAV.
(2) We propose UAV path planning strategy of joint priority cluster head node residual energy (residual survival time) and location, achieve fast and accurate SWIPT.
(3) Under the premise of time constraint and energy constraint, the mathematical relationship between data collection and energy recharge is established by jointly optimizing the data transmission rate of cluster head node and the energy transmission power of UAV, and the optimal energy recharge is realized on the basis of maximizing data collection.

The rest of this paper is organized as follows. In Sect. 2, we establish and introduce UAV-WRSN SWIPT service model. Then, we design an UAV flight path for UAV-WRSN SWIPT in Sect. 3. Section 4 is the result of energy analyses. Finally, we conclude this paper in Sect. 5.

2 System Model

In WRSN, We Nonuniform arrange N sensors in the $L * L$ square area, $\{V_1, V_2, V_3, \ldots, V_i, \ldots V_n\}$ is the set of the Sensor node, the initial energy of each node is E_o. The base station is located at point $(0, 0)$, and the base station knows the location of each node. The flying speed of the UAV is expressed in terms of constant value V_c (uniform speed flight). In particular, during a cycle of mission execution, the UAV has enough energy to charge the joint and complete the traversal. Let the maximum effective distance of charging for UAV be fixed and less than the maximum effective distance of charging for cluster head and UAV. In particular, in a round of periodic mission execution, the UAV has enough energy to complete the mission. Let the distance between the node and the UAV be fixed and less than the charging effective distance.

In one task execution, the UAV traverses all nodes from the base station. when one node position is reached, data collection begins. if the energy of the node is lower than the charging threshold, it is charged at the same time as the data collection. If the energy of the node is higher than the charging threshold, the UAV only needs to receive data. When the UAV passes through all the nodes in the monitoring area, it finally returns to the base station for energy replenishment and transfers the collected data to the base station.

We set the node charging threshold E_c, when the node energy is below the charging threshold, UAV will charge it while collecting its data. The UAV carries out the mission according to the planned flight path, and the time to reach a certain node is as follows:

$$t_w^i = t_w^{i-1} + t_d^{i-1} + \frac{dist\{V_i, V_{i-1}\}}{V_c} \tag{1}$$

Where V_c is the flying speed of the UAV, t_w^{i-1} is the time to reach the previous node, t_d^{i-1} is the time to stay at the previous node. The residual survival time t_r^i of node i is determined by node energy and node self-digestion rate:

$$t_r^i = \frac{E_i}{p_i} \tag{2}$$

Where E_i denotes the remaining energy of node i, p_i is the node energy consumption rate (When collecting data). As long as the remaining survival time t_r^i is greater than the UAV arrival time t_w^i, the node can be charged in time to avoid death.

3   Research on the Strategy of SWIPT

3.1   The Path Planning Strategy

In UAV-WRSN SWIPT model, it is unreasonable to consider only the shortest UAV path in node position, in order to avoid the node dying before the UAV arrives, the residual energy of the node in the UAV path planning should also be considered. on the other hand, if only the residual energy of the node is considered, UAV traversing all nodes according to the remaining survival time of the node will increase the complexity of the path and reduce the efficiency of data collection. Therefore, this paper proposes a path planning strategy based on node location and energy.

We define the Node Energy Priority as the ratio of the residual survival time to the initial survival time of the node [8]:

$$p_t(i) = \frac{t_r^i}{\frac{E_o}{p_i}} \tag{3}$$

Where E_o is the initial energy of node, and $p_t(i) < 1$, As the residual survival time of the node is lower, the value $p_t(i)$ is smaller and the priority is higher, the UAV will priority access.

The shortest path problem of UAV with Node Position Priority is similar to the well-known Travelling Salesmen Problem (TSP) [9]. Therefore, the Ant Colony algorithm is used to solve the problem. The shortest path of the UAV is planned, mark the nodes according to the sequence of UAV arrival $\{P_1, P_2, P_3, \ldots, P_k, \ldots P_n\}$. P_1 is the first node to be arrived by UAV, P_n is the last node to be arrived by UAV. Therefore, the value of Node Position Priority of P_1 above the value of Node Position Priority of P_n. The value of Node Position Priority of the node i:

$$p_d(i) = \frac{k}{n} \quad (1 < k < n) \tag{4}$$

And $p_d(i) < 1$, the value $p_d(i)$ is higher, the UAV will priority access.

Finally, we consider the node location and residual energy, joint optimization of priority $p_t(i)$ and $p_d(i)$:

$$p(i) = \frac{1}{\delta * p_t(i) + (1 - \delta) * p_d(i)} \tag{5}$$

The greater the joint priority $p(i)$ of the node, it will be preferentially accessed by the UAV. And $0 < \delta < 1$, when $\delta = 1$, the joint priority strategy is equivalent to the energy priority strategy; when $\delta = 0$, the joint priority strategy is equivalent to the position priority strategy.

3.2   The Energy Strategy of SWIPT

The most important task of sensor nodes is to perceive and monitor environmental data. In periodic data collection, the data are real-time [10, 11]. Therefore, the SWIPT studied in this paper is based on the maximization of data collection, that is to say, the UAV should ensure that all the data are collected in the task execution of each cycle, so as to do a better study of the monitoring environment.

The residence time of the UAV at a certain node is determined by the data collection time and the charging time, but the two are not the same. Because of the high efficiency of data collection and the charging efficiency is low, the full charge time of node is longer than the data collection time. In order to improve the efficiency of data collection, we use continuous charging instead of one-time full charging. In a SWIPT task, we specify that the UAV residence time at each node is the data collection time of that node. After the data collection end, the charging will also end.

The UAV residence time (the data collection time) t_d^i is depending on the node data volume and the data transmission rate:

$$t_d^i = \frac{Q_{C_i}}{\omega} \tag{6}$$

Where Q_{C_i} is node data volume, ω is the data transmission rate.

In RF energy harvesting, the amount of energy that can be harvested depends on the transmit power, wavelength of the RF signals and the distance between an RF energy source and the harvesting node. The harvested RF power from a transmitter in free space can be calculated based on the Friis equation as follow [12]:

$$\varepsilon_i = \frac{\eta_i P_T G_i G_U \lambda^2}{(4\pi d_i)^2 L} \tag{7}$$

Where ε_i is the node i received power, η_i is the efficiency of converting RF energy into electrical energy, P_T is the transmit power, L is the path loss factor, G_U is the transmit antenna gain, G_i is the receive antenna gain, λ is the wavelength emitted, and d is the distance between UAV and node. Since all sensors are of the same structure and performance, the above parameters are determined except the distance:

$$\varepsilon_i = \frac{Z}{d_i^2} \tag{8}$$

And

$$Z = \frac{\eta_i P_T G_i G_U \lambda^2}{(4\pi)^2 L} \tag{9}$$

Finally, according to formulas (6) and (7), we can calculate the energy that node i obtains in a round of SWIPT:

$$e_i = \varepsilon_i * t_d^i \tag{10}$$

Where e_i is the energy that node i obtains in a round of SWIPT.

4 Simulation Results

4.1 Simulation Environment and Energy Model

In order to observe the energy consumption of WRSN, the energy model of the wireless channel must be studied. In this paper, we propose a simplified wireless channel energy consumption model [13].

The paper assumed that node energy consumption is mainly caused by sending and receiving data, and node consumes very little energy when not receiving or sending any data. The energy consumption of sending data can be divided into two parts: the transmitter consumes energy from the processing circuit and the sensor power amplifier to generate the required data transmission power. The receiver dissipates energy to run the receiving circuit.

The energy consumed of the sensor circuit to receive or send 1bit data is E_{elec} and the energy consumption of sending amplifier to send 1bit data is E_{mp} (when $d \geq d_0$) or E_{fs} (when $d < d_0$). The first-order RF model of energy consumption is shown in Fig. 2. Since the energy consumption of signal modulation and amplification is in

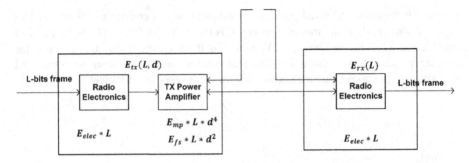

Fig. 2. The first-order RF model of energy consumption.

inverse proportion to the square of transmission distance, the energy consumed to send l bits packet is:

$$E_{tx}(l,d) = \begin{cases} E_{elec} * l + E_{fs} * l * d^2 & d < d_0 \\ E_{elec} * l + E_{mp} * l * d^4 & d \geq d_0 \end{cases} \tag{11}$$

The energy consumed to receive l bits packet is:

$$E_{rx}(l) = E_{elec} * l \tag{12}$$

And

$$d_0 = \sqrt{E_{fs}/E_{mp}} \tag{13}$$

In a WRSN environment, according to actual demand, we deploy nodes in the field of interest. The simulation was configured with a network size of 500×500 meters and with 15 nodes fixed deployed, and the base station was located at the position (0,0), it is represented with a X, as shown in Fig. 3. Use a hovering UAV to carry sufficient energy for the SWIPT mission. The simulation parameters are shown in Table 1. In particular, in the simulation, we need UAV to provide a stable link for data collection and energy supply, so the hover wing UAV is a better choice. Compared with the fixed wing UAV, the hover wing UAV can supply more stable energy to the sensor.

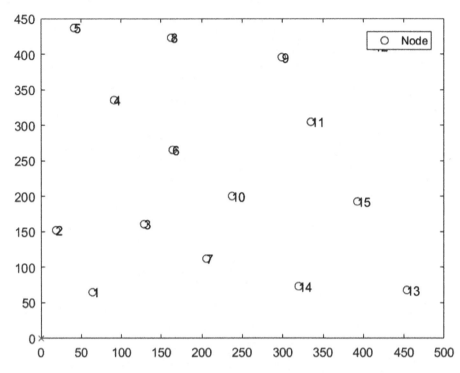

Fig. 3. The network size of 500 × 500 meters and with 15 nodes.

Table 1. Simulation parameter.

Parameter	Value	Parameter	Value
N	15	Z	5 mwm^2
E_{elec}	50 nJ/bit	d	5 m
E_0	4 J	ω	250 kbps
L	10 KB	δ	0.4
V_c	5 m/s	E_{mp}	0.0013 pJ/bit/m^4
E_c	3.5 J	rounds	4000
E_{fs}	10 pJ/bit/m^2	d_0	87.7 m

4.2 The Path Planning Simulation

In the same environment, we compare the joint priority strategy with position priority strategy and energy priority strategy. At this time, the remaining energy of each node is as shown in Fig. 4.

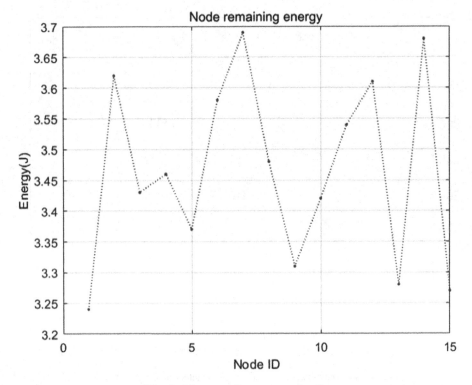

Fig. 4. The remaining energy of node.

Path Planning Strategy of Position Priority. Using ant colony algorithm, we plan the shortest flight path of UAV in the distance, as shown in the Fig. 5. The label on the node in the figure indicates the order of UAV access.

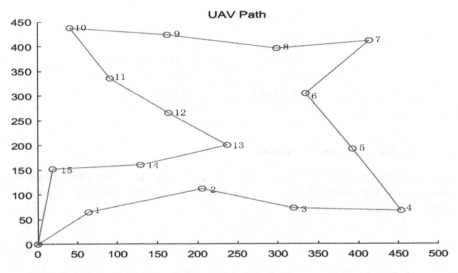

Fig. 5. UAV path planning based on Path Planning Strategy of Position Priority.

Path Planning Strategy of Energy Priority. According to the residual energy of nodes, the nodes with lower energy will be accessed first. The flight path of UAV is shown in Fig. 6.

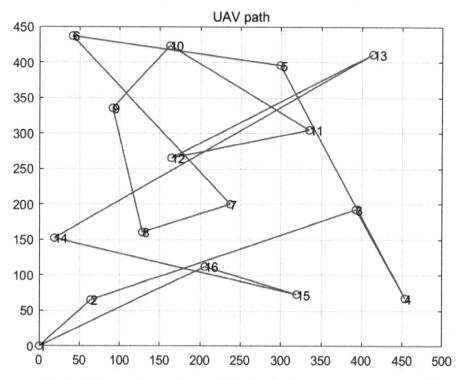

Fig. 6. UAV path planning based on Path Planning Strategy of Energy Priority.

Path Planning Strategy of Joint Priority of node energy and position. According to the node location and energy, using the node priority value calculated by formula (5), we plan the UAV path as shown in Fig. 7.

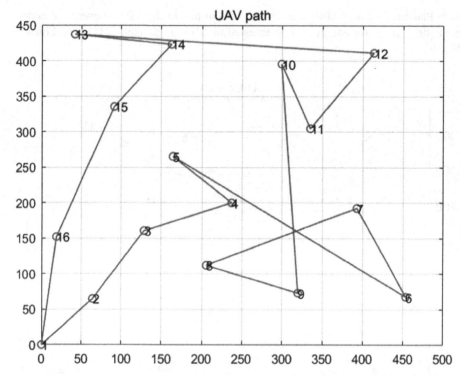

Fig. 7. UAV path planning based on Path Planning Strategy of Joint Priority of node energy and position.

Comparing the three UAV flight paths above, we can draw the following conclusions:

(1) The Path Planning Strategy of Position Priority has the shortest path, but it is only suitable for individual data collection task. In the SWIPT task, it is easy to cause the nodes accessed after UAV to die due to failing to charge in time.

(2) Although the Path Planning Strategy of Energy Priority can ensure that nodes get timely charging and avoid death, it can only be used for individual energy supply tasks. In the SWIPT task, due to considering data collection, and the low efficiency of this path, the real-time performance of data collection will be reduced.

(3) Compared with the other two strategies, the joint priority strategy proposed by us takes into account both data collection and energy supply, which is more suitable for UAV path planning in SWIPT tasks. Using our proposed strategy, UAV-WRSN can realize the simultaneous wireless information and power transfer quickly and accurately.

4.3 Energy Efficiency Analysis

Due to the fixed flight altitude of the UAV, the power received by each node from the UAV is the same, and the power charged by the node is only determined by the charging time (data collection time). On the other hand, the data transmission power of nodes is fixed and the same, so the data collection time is only related to the amount of data of nodes.

In order to analyze the energy change of node charging and non-charging, we compared the energy of a node charging and non-charging in 4000 SWIPT tasks. As shown in Fig. 8. We can see from the picture, the residual energy of the node charging is significantly higher than that non-charging. At 4000 rounds, the remaining energy of the node when charging is 16 times of that when not charging.

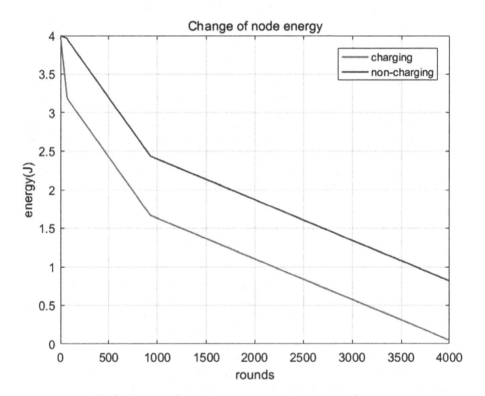

Fig. 8. Change of charging and non-charging energy of a node.

5 Conclusion

In this paper, we establish the UAV-WRSN SWIPT Model. Based on this model, an algorithm for path planning of UAV with joint priority of node residual energy (residual survival time) and position is proposed. Aiming at the charging efficiency based on data acquisition, the optimal charging strategy based on data acquisition maximization is proposed, and the optimal energy charging based on charging time is realized. Finally, according to the WRSN environmental characteristics, we simulated UAV-WRSN SWIPT energy analysis, which proves that our proposed strategy can achieve better data collection and energy recharge.

Acknowledgments. The work is supported by the Research Project of China Railway Eryuan Engineering Group CO. LTD (No. KYY2019033(19-20)) and the Support Project of Science and Technology Department of Sichuan Province, China (No. 2019YFG0205).

References

1. Xie, L., Shi, Y., Hou, Y.T.: Bundling mobile base station and wireless energy transfer: modeling and optimization. In: INFOCOM, 2013 Proceedings IEEE (2013)
2. Hongyan, Y., Yongqiang, Z., Songtao, G., et al.: Energy efficiency maximization for WRSN with simultaneous wireless information and power transfer. Sensors **17**(8), 1906 (2017)
3. Guo, S., Wang, C., Yang, Y.: Mobile data gathering with Wireless energy replenishment in rechargeable sensor networks. In: Infocom. IEEE (2013)
4. Guo, S., Wang, C., Yang, Y.: Joint mobile data gathering and energy provisioning in wireless rechargeable sensor networks. IEEE Trans. Mob. Comput. **13**(12), 2836–2852 (2014)
5. Wang, C., Li, J., Ye, F., et al.: A mobile data gathering framework for wireless rechargeable sensor networks with vehicle movement costs and capacity constraints. IEEE Trans. Comput. **2015**, 1 (2015)
6. Han, G., Qian, A., Jiang, J.: A grid-based joint routing and charging algorithm for industrial wireless rechargeable sensor networks. Comput. Netw.
7. Amaldi, E., Capone, A., Cesana, M., et al.: Design of wireless sensor networks for mobile target detection (2012)
8. Spuri, M., Buttazzo, G.C.: Efficient aperiodic service under earliest deadline scheduling. In: Real-Time Systems Symposium. IEEE Computer Society (1995)
9. Zhongrui, Y., Houyu, Y., Miaohua, H.: Improved ant colony optimization algorithm for intelligent vehicle path planning (2017)
10. Hu, C., Wang, Y.: Optimization of charging and data collection in wireless rechargeable sensor networks. In: Zu, Q., Hu, B. (eds.) HCC 2016. LNCS, vol. 9567, pp. 138–149. Springer, Cham (2016). https://doi.org/10.1007/978-3-319-31854-7_13
11. Liu, B.H., Nguyen, T.N., Pham, V.T., et al.: Novel methods for energy charging and data collection in wireless rechargeable sensor networks. Int. J. Commun. Syst. **30**(5), e3050.1–e3050.14 (2015)
12. Lu, X., Wang, P., Niyato, D., et al.: Wireless networks with RF energy harvesting: a contemporary survey. IEEE Commun. Surv. Tutor. **17**(2), 757–789 (2015)
13. Wang, Q., Hempstead, M., Yang, W.: A realistic power consumption model for wireless sensor network devices (2007)

Research on Adaptive Beacon Transmitting Power Based on Vehicle Forecast Error

Meng Wang[1], Guanxiang Yin[1,2], Fei Du[1], Juan Wang[1],
and Yuejin Zhang[1(✉)]

[1] School of Information Engineering, East China Jiaotong University,
Nanchang 330013, China
zyjecjtu@foxmail.com
[2] College of Computer and Control Engineering, Nankai University,
Tianjin 300071, China

Abstract. In view of the problem that the channel resources cannot be allocated optimally in Vehicular Ad Hoc NETwork (VANET) with nodes sending information at fixed power, we propose an adaptive VANET power control algorithm. The algorithm calculates the vehicle's position prediction error, dynamically adjusts the transmission power according to different error sizes, and then optimizes channel resource allocation and node routing performance. The experimental results show that our algorithm can adaptively adjust the transmission power, reduce the channel occupancy rate and increase the data packet delivery rate, so that the information transmission between vehicles becomes more effective.

Keywords: VANET · Forecast error · Adaptive transmitting power · SUMO · NS-2

1 Introduction

As an important part of ITS (Intelligent Transport System), the VANET aims to strengthen vehicle-to-vehicle connections and enhance road traffic safety, which has attracted wide attention from all walks of life [1–3]. Broadcasting beacon messages between vehicles to realize information exchange and perception of the surrounding environment is the basic condition for the realization of VANET and security applications [4, 5]. Messages of communication between vehicles are mainly divided into two categories: one is periodic beacon messages, which mainly contain core state information such as vehicle speed and position; and the other is event-driven safety messages, such as warning messages of emergency events such as car accidents [6, 7].

In Internet of Vehicles security applications, a high rate of beacon packet generation is required to update information such as vehicle location, but a higher message collision rate will occur. Therefore, Liu Mingjian et al. [8] adaptively control the transmission power according to the channel congestion status; Mo Yuanfu et al. [9] adaptively adjust the beacon transmission power within the communication range by presetting the channel load threshold; Xu Zhexin et al. [10] adjusted the transmission power of VANET according to the density change of traffic flow.

© Springer Nature Switzerland AG 2020
X. Chen et al. (Eds.): ML4CS 2020, LNCS 12487, pp. 79–86, 2020.
https://doi.org/10.1007/978-3-030-62460-6_8

However, the above-mentioned documents all adjust the overall power within the range, and do not consider the mobility of each node. Therefore, based on the vehicle's prediction error, this paper considers all vehicle nodes in the range, and designs a reasonable and effective power control function to avoid channel congestion, thereby ensuring low delay and high reliable transmission of messages.

2 Adaptive Beacon Transmission Power Transmission Control Algorithm Based on Prediction Error

2.1 Error Calculation

In the Internet of vehicle applications, in addition to errors in the positioning system itself, data transmission delay and packet loss rate are also factors that affect the accuracy of position prediction errors [11, 12]. Generally, vehicles reduce the error of other vehicles' perception of their position by reducing the broadcast period or increasing the transmission power, but it is impossible to make all vehicles broadcast with a smaller period or with higher power. Therefore, this paper proposes an adaptive beacon message transmission power algorithm, which adjusts the transmission power of the beacon message according to the position prediction error between vehicles, and the larger the prediction error increases the transmission power of the beacon message, the smaller the error Reduce transmission power. However, the traditional linear prediction algorithm is only suitable for linear motion, and the position prediction error when the vehicle turns is very large, so the use of the traditional linear prediction algorithm will make the prediction error very large. Taking an ordinary 90° turn as an example, Fig. 1 shows the movement trajectory of an ordinary vehicle turning. The drawing interval is 1 s, each point represents the position of the car at a certain moment, and the interval between successive points is 1 s.

As can be seen from Fig. 2, if the prediction of the traditional linear tracking algorithm occurs in the fourth or several seconds after the turn, the prediction error at this time will be very large. Therefore, predicting the turning of the vehicle in advance is the key to reducing the prediction error. As we all know, the turning of the vehicle is a relatively continuous process, and the turning speed of the vehicle is lower than the straight driving speed. Therefore, we use a linear combination model to reduce vehicle turning errors. The specific derivation process can be seen in the article [13]. We only discuss the prediction error after applying the model here:

$$\varepsilon = L_T - L_P \tag{1}$$

Where ε is the prediction error, L_T is the true distance, and L_P is the predicted distance.

2.2 Adaptive Transmission Power Control Algorithm

After the linear combination model, the obtained vehicle prediction error is more accurate. The safe braking distance of a general vehicle is 20 m, but for safety reasons,

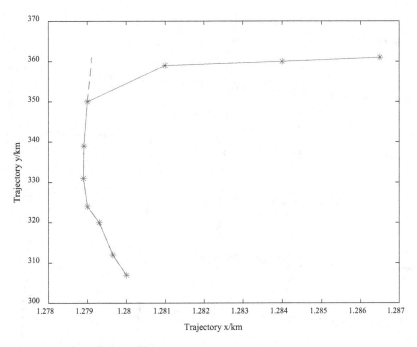

Fig. 1. Schematic diagram of vehicle turning

the safety distance is set to 15 m in this paper. If the prediction error is greater than 15 m, the transmission power of the beacon message needs to be increased, and vice versa. The adaptive beacon transmission power algorithm based on prediction error is as follows:

$$P_v = \left[P_\omega * e^{\frac{\theta}{15}-1} \right] + \theta \tag{2}$$

Among them, P_v is the adaptive beacon transmission power, P_ω is the fixed beacon transmission power, and θ is the balance parameter. In this paper, $\theta = 0.01$.

3 Experimental Simulation and Analysis

3.1 Experimental Parameter Settings

In order to ensure that the vehicle trajectory in the simulation scenario is as close as possible to the real vehicle trajectory, this paper uses SUMO (Simulation of Urban Mobility) traffic simulation to build a city two-way two-lane road model with a range of 1000 m × 1000 m and the number of vehicles is 20–120 Vehicles with a speed range of 15–20 m/s. The vehicles are randomly distributed on the street, and they will travel through the roads within 0 to 100 s. The vehicle will wait for traffic lights and make turns according to the situation of the road, so as to simulate the real driving environment as much as possible.

Fig. 2. City road topology

Subsequently, the power control algorithm was simulated and verified in NS-2, and the VANET protocol architecture was constructed as follows: At the application layer, The packet type uses the constant bitrate (CBR) data stream, the communication packet size is 800 bits, and the data transmission rate is 3 Mb/s. At the transport layer, the transport protocol used is UDP. At the network layer, routing algorithms are not the focus of this paper, so DSDV is selected as the network layer protocol for analysis. At the MAC layer, choose the IEEE 802.11p protocol that is mainly used for in-vehicle electronic communications. At the physical layer, various parameters of the vehicle-mounted equipment are set, and the Nakagami-m model is selected as the propagation model. The beacon message generation period is set to 100 ms; the power control period is set to 1 s, because the relative position change between vehicles within 1 s is small in the conventional case. According to the document (), the fixed transmission power is set to 18 dBm, which can ensure that all vehicles communicate normally within the communication range. The specific experimental parameters are shown in Table 1:

Table 1. Simulation parameter settings

Parameter	Value
Number of nodes	20–120
Vehicle speed	15–20 m/s
Scene size/m^2	1000 * 1000
Transmission range/m	1000
Data rate	3 Mb/s
Fixed transmit power	18 dBm
Packet size	800 bits
Mac layer protocol	IEEE 802.11p
Transport layer protocol	UDP
Routing protocol	DSDV
Antenna gain	4 dB
Antenna height	1.5 m
Type of data	CBR

3.2 Simulation Experiment Results Analysis

The simulation in this paper mainly analyzes the number of different vehicles, and the number of vehicles varies from 20 to 120. The simulated network performance parameters mainly include: 1) average transmit power, that is, the average transmit power of vehicle nodes in the network; 2) channel occupancy rate, which is the percentage of channel occupied time per unit time; 3) data packet delivery rate, that is The ratio of the number of status information packets received per unit time to the total number of packets sent by the source node.

Since the position of the vehicle is constantly changing during driving, its transmit power also changes dynamically. Figure 3 shows the variation curve of the vehicle node transmit power during the simulation. It can be seen from the figure that under the fixed transmission power, the transmission power is fixed; while under the adaptive power control algorithm proposed in this paper, the average power of the vehicle node fluctuates above and below the fixed power. This is because although the adaptive power is time-varying, it uses a uniform distribution, so the mean value does not change.

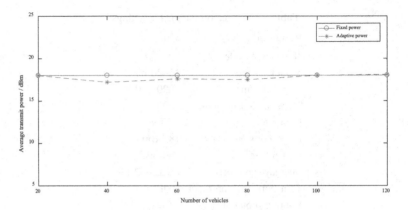

Fig. 3. Average transmit power under different numbers of vehicles

Figure 4 describes the channel occupancy under fixed transmission power and adaptive power control for different numbers of vehicles. In both cases, the channel occupancy rate increases with the number of vehicles, but the increase in fixed transmit power is significantly greater than adaptive power control. This is because the fixed transmission power always sends information at a fixed power. When the number of vehicle nodes increases, the competition between the nodes will increase. The adaptive power control will automatically adjust the transmission power according to the error, so the impact is not as large as the fixed transmission power.

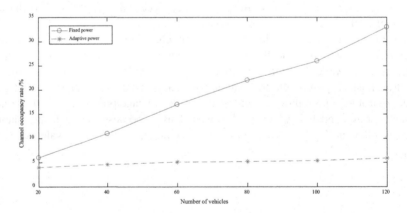

Fig. 4. Channel occupancy rate under different vehicle numbers

Figure 5 describes the fixed transmission power and adaptive power control packet delivery rate under different numbers of vehicles. As can be seen from the figure, as the number of vehicle nodes increases, the delivery rate decreases, but adaptive power control delivery rate Higher than the fixed transmit power, this is because the fixed power node competition is more intense.

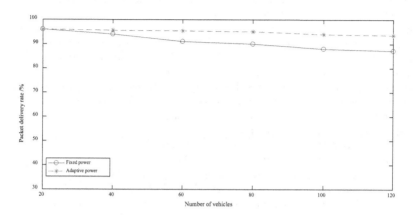

Fig. 5. Packet delivery rate under different vehicle numbers

It can be seen from Figs. 3, 4 and 5 that the performance of the adaptive beacon transmission power algorithm in this paper is better than that of the fixed beacon transmission power algorithm in all aspects. The channel occupancy rate is increased by 30% and the packet delivery rate is increased by about 10%. And we can get that with the increase of the number of vehicles, the advantages of our algorithm will be more and more obvious, and the performance is better than the fixed beacon transmission power algorithm. This shows that our algorithm has a strong ability to avoid channel congestion in the case of dense vehicles, so that the information transmission between vehicles becomes more effective.

4   Conclusion

In vehicle safety applications, due to limited channel resources, the safety warning information cannot accept continuous delay and packet loss. This paper proposes an adaptive beacon transmit power algorithm based on vehicle position prediction error. Vehicles with large prediction errors are very dangerous, so the transmission power can be increased appropriately. On the contrary, for vehicles with small errors, the transmission power can be reduced. Through the simulation of SUMO and NS-2 software, the results show that, compared with the fixed transmit power, the adaptive power in this paper can reduce the channel occupancy rate and increase the packet delivery rate, ensuring the effective transmission of security information. However, the number of experimental vehicles in this paper is small, so the research on adaptive power algorithm of vehicle beacon message under high density is our next direction.

References

1. Torrent-Moreno, M., Santi, P., Hartenstein, H.: Distributed fair transmit power adjustment for vehicular ad hoc networks. In: 2006 IEEE Communications Society on Sensor & Ad Hoc Communications & [2] Networks, Secon IEEE (2006)
2. Egea-Lopez, E.: Fair distributed congestion control with transmit power for vehicular networks. In: IEEE International Symposium on a World of Wireless. IEEE (2016)
3. Fallah, Y.P., Nasiriani, N., Krishnan, H.: Stable and fair power control in vehicle safety networks. IEEE Trans. Veh. Technol. 65(3), 1662–1675 (2016)
4. Mittag, J., Schmidt-Eisenlohr, F., Killat, M., Härri, J., Hartenstein, H.: Analysis and design of effective and low-overhead transmission power control for VANETs. In: Proceedings of the Fifth ACM International Workshop on VehiculAr Inter-NETworking - VANET 2008 (2008). https://doi.org/10.1145/1410043.1410051
5. Hu, R.N., Guo, A.H.: Transmission reliability algorithm based on power control in Internet of vehicles. Comput. Appl. 35(6), 1523–1526 (2015)
6. Zuo, Y.X., Guo, A.H., Huang, B., Wang, L.: Power control algorithm based on network utility maximization in Internet of vehicles, 37(12), 3345–3350 + 3380 (2017)
7. A safety collision avoidance algorithm based on comprehensive characteristics. Complexity 2020, Article ID 1616420, 13 p. (2020). https://doi.org/10.1155/2020/1616420
8. Liu, M.J., Tan, G.Z., Li, S.B., et al.: Adaptive message sending rate control method based on channel congestion cost calculation in VANET. J. Commun. 037(10), 108–116
9. Mo, Y.F., Yu, D.X., Bao, S.N., et al.: Beacon transmission power control algorithm based on the preset threshold in VANETs. J. Northeast. Univ.: Nat. Sci. Ed. 38, 334 (2017)
10. Xu, Z.X., Li, S.J., Lin, X., Wu, Y.: Power control mechanism for vehicle status message in VANET. Comput. Appl. 36(08), 2175–2180 (2016)
11. Killat, M., Hartenstein, H.: An empirical model for probability of packet reception in vehicular ad hoc networks. Eurasip J. Wirel. Commun. Netw. 2009(1), 1–12 (2009). https://doi.org/10.1155/2009/721301
12. Kloiber, B., Härri, J., Strang, T.: Dice the TX power - improving awareness quality in VANETs by random transmit power selection. In: IEEE Vehicular Networking Conference. IEEE (2012)
13. Zhang, Y., Wang, M., et al.: Research on adaptive beacon message broadcasting cycle based on vehicle driving stability. Int. J. Netw. Manag. (2020). https://doi.org/10.1002/nem.2091

Analysis of the Effective Scatters for Hyperloop Wireless Communications Using the Geometry-Based Model

Jiachi Zhang[1,2], Liu Liu[2(✉)], Kai Wang[2], Botao Han[2], Zheyan Piao[1], and Dong Wang[1]

[1] School of Rail Transportation, Shandong Jiaotong University, Jinan 250357, China
[2] School of Electronic and Information Engineering, Beijing Jiaotong University, Beijing 100044, China
bill0715@163.com

Abstract. A novel 3-dimensional (3D) non-stationary geometry-based deterministic model (GBDM) is proposed in this paper to analyze the effective scatters for the Hyperloop train-to-ground wireless communication. Different from the stochastic models, the channel gain of each propagation path is derived based on the Lambertian scattering pattern from the aspect of physical scattering mechanism. Besides, the channel gain can be obtained by superposing the line-of-sight (LOS) and single-bounced components. Then, we aim at capturing small-scale fading channel characteristics, mainly involving the effective scattering areas together with the arrival angular distribution. The simulation results show that the channel modeling computational complexity can be reduced greatly by using the effective scatters. Besides, the Von Mises distribution and Gaussian distribution are proved to characterize azimuth and elevation angular distribution with good fitting results, respectively. Our works provide some insights into the research on the Hyperloop train-to-ground wireless channel modeling and characterization.

Keywords: Hyperloop · Wireless communication · Geometry-based deterministic model · Effective scatters · Angular distribution

1 Introduction

Hyperloop, proposed by Robert Goddard in 1904 [1], is a maglev line (vactrain) using evacuated tubes that could be competitive to high-speed railways and airplanes in terms of travel time, velocity, and in-journey comfort for long distance. The low atmosphere or vacuum inside the tube enables the Hyperloop to travel at an ultra-high-speed (hypersonic) speed (over 1,000 km/h) with relatively little power consumption regardless of all weather conditions. Moreover, the noise generated from mechanical friction can be alleviated or avoided significantly due to the maglev technology. This means of transportation could improve the quality of journey services, yield greater customer satisfaction, and help to create socio-economically balanced societies. Rekindled by a white paper entitled "Hyperloop Alpha" published by Elon Musk in

© Springer Nature Switzerland AG 2020
X. Chen et al. (Eds.): ML4CS 2020, LNCS 12487, pp. 87–97, 2020.
https://doi.org/10.1007/978-3-030-62460-6_9

2013 [2], the Hyperloop began to draw worldwide attention due to its fascinating future envisions. A good review of the dynamics of vehicles and infrastructure can be found in [3] and references therein.

A reliable wireless train-to-ground connection link is pivotal not only to the vac-train safe operation but also to the passengers' in-journey communication quality of experience (QoE). The ultra-high-velocity of the Hyperloop brings some unprecedented challenges to the wireless communication system, e.g., the frequent handover, severe Doppler effect [4]. However, few works on the train-to-ground wireless communication have been performed except for the previous works we conducted in [4–9], to our best knowledge. These works lay a good foundation for the wireless communication system. Yet, some detailed channel characterization issues such as the angle analysis still need to be investigated.

Given the aforementioned background, the contributions of this paper are listed as follows:

1. A novel 3D non-stationary geometry-based deterministic wireless channel model is proposed. By using the Lambertian scattering pattern, the channel gain of each possible propagation path is derived.
2. The effective scatters of the Hyperloop propagation environment are investigated by using the proposed model. Based on the results, the channel modeling computational complexity can be reduced greatly by abandoning those scatters with less contributions.
3. We investigate the angular distribution of the azimuth and elevation angle of arrival (AOA) of the effective scatters, respectively. Besides, we present the fitting results of two prevailing angular distribution for those effective scatters.

The rest of this paper is organized as follows. We introduce the related works in Sect. 2 briefly. The system model of the 3D non-stationary channel model is formulated with details in Sect. 3. Section 4 presents the simulation results of the Hyperloop train-to-ground propagation environment and studies the effective scatters. Moreover, the angular distribution of azimuth and elevation AOA are investigated. Finally, conclusions are drawn in Sect. 5.

2 Related Works

The exact and detailed broadband wireless channel characterization is a prerequisite for the performance analysis as well as the deployment of the Hyperloop wireless communication system. Moreover, it provides an effective evaluation of further advanced transmission technologies such as multi-input and multi-output (MIMO) and resource management. In [8], Wei proposed a novel leak waveguide system dedicated to the Hyperloop to alleviate or avoid the Doppler effect in the physical layer. In [9], we analyzed some small-scale channel parameters of the train-to-ground channel. The simulation result reveals that the ultra-high-velocity leads to a drastic time-varying Doppler shift, especially near the roadside antenna. However, some detailed channel characterizations such as the angular distribution still need to be investigated.

Currently, numerous wireless channel models aiming to achieve a high accuracy and low computational complexity have been proposed. Generally, these models can be roughly classified as two types, i.e., the deterministic channel models and the stochastic channel models [10, 11]. Deterministic channel models aim to model the propagation channel based on the detailed description of the specific propagation environment along with antenna configuration. These models use intensive simulation calculations incorporating reflection, scattering, and refraction to obtain the detailed amplitudes, phases, and delays of every possible propagation path. Typical models include the ray tracing and propagation-graph methods [12, 13], which estimate the channel gain by thorough searching all possible paths connecting transmitter (Tx) and receiver (Rx). Hence, the deterministic models are physically meaningful and able to acquire accurate simulation results.

Despite the high accuracy, deterministic channel models require detailed descriptions of the propagation environments and extensive computational resources. To avoid the high complexity and maintain a desirable simulation accuracy, the geometry-based stochastic models (GBSM) are proposed. In GBSMs, the channel impulse response (CIR) can be obtained by the law of wave propagation considering the specific Tx, Rx, and scatters [14]. Besides, these theoretical models assume an infinite number of effective scatters that are predefined in a stochastic fashion according to some certain stochastic probability distributions such as the Von Mises distribution. Different types of GBSMs differ mainly in the scatters distributions. Obviously, such a simplification can accelerate the simulation speed evidently. Some works have been performed in the circle-shape tunnels by using the GBSM, e.g., [15]. However, the steel-made tube makes the near-field radiation different from the tunnel. Moreover, the angular distribution in the Hyperloop scenario has never been investigated, indicating that the current angular distributions fails to characterize this situation.

To fill the aforementioned research gaps, it is highly desirable to design an accurate channel model that consider the non-stationarity of Hyperloop scenarios by taking into account time-varying small-scale fading parameters, especially the angular information. Furthermore, it is essential to establish a cluster-based theoretical framework, which not only alleviates the computational burden of modeling but also characterizes the angular distribution for the vacuum tube scenarios.

3 System Model

3.1 Wireless Access Method

As the roadside antenna emits a signal to the on-board passengers, the electromagnetic wave will go through two severe penetration attenuations derived from the metal tube and train body. As such, we adopt the mobile relay station (MRS) method to cope with such a situation [16]. The MRS method is an explicit way with the merits of easy to deploy and low cost of equipment. As shown in Fig. 1, the Hyperloop is equipped with multi-input and multi-output (MIMO) antenna array for wireless connection to the ground active antenna units (AAUs). The on-board terminals connect with the inside-train antennas via WiFi technology, these antennas converge all terminals signal and forward them to the outside MIMO antennas via cable or vice versa. This two-hop relay structure avoids a radio wave penetration attenuation of the train body, guaranteeing a relatively stable received amplitude. Consequently, the wireless channel characterization between ground antennas and train antennas is crucial to the communication system performance.

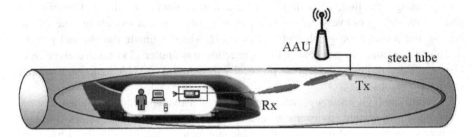

Fig. 1. The diagram of the wireless access method

3.2   Theoretical Model

To characterize the wireless channel accurately, we utilize the deterministic channel model theory since the shape and the size is provided in [2]. To better illustrate the simulation scenario, a 3D Cartesian coordinate system is established as shown in Fig. 1. The x-axis is parallel to the Hyperloop movement direction and plane x-O-y is parallel to the ground, the origin of the coordinate system lies in the lower-left end of the tube. The Tx linear antenna array embedded at the inside of the tube emits signals to the Rx linear antenna array located at the central axis of the tube. Besides, both two linear arrays are perpendicular to the movement direction to maximize the MIMO channel capacity (Fig. 2).

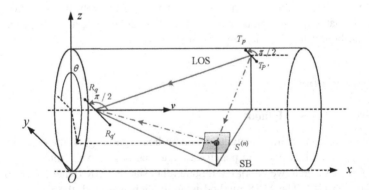

Fig. 2. Propagation environment inside the vacuum tube

Based on [10], the complex channel impulse response (CIR), $h_{pq}(t)$ from the p-th $(p = 1, 2, \ldots, N_T)$ Tx to the q-th $(q = 1, 2, \ldots, N_R)$ Rx is the superposition of line-of-sight (LOS) and single-bounced (SB) components, which can be expressed as

$$h_{pq}(t) = h_{pq}^{LOS}(t) + h_{pq}^{SB}(t). \tag{1}$$

In GBSM, the amplitude of these two components can be expressed as

$$\left\| h_{pq}^{LOS}(t) \right\| = \sqrt{\frac{K\Omega_{pq}}{K+1}}, \tag{2}$$

$$\left\| h_{pq}^{SB}(t) \right\| = \sqrt{\frac{\Omega_{pq}}{K+1}}, \tag{3}$$

where K denotes the Ricean K factor and Ω_{pq} means the total power of the p-th Tx to the q-th Rx link. These two key parameters depend heavily on the actual measured data, which constrains the application of the GBSM. Besides, the GBSMs are derived based on a certain predefined angular distribution. However, no actual channel measurement has been performed to our best knowledge, and the actual K factor along with the angular distribution remains to be investigated, indicating that the GBSMs cannot be applied for the Hyperloop scenario directly. To handle the above challenge, we aim to derive the closed-form expression of the channel gain based on the physical scattering mechanism in the following text.

As for the LOS component, it can be regarded as a free-space propagation model and its corresponding channel gain can be expressed as

$$h_{pq}^{LOS}(t) = \frac{\lambda}{4\pi \left\| \mathbf{D}_{pq}(t) \right\|} e^{-j\frac{2\pi \left\| \mathbf{D}_{pq}(t) \right\|}{\lambda}} \times e^{j2\pi f_{pq}^{LOS}(t)}, \tag{4}$$

where λ is the wavelength, $\mathbf{D}_{pq}(t)$ denotes the distance vector from the p-th Tx to the q-th Rx, $\| \cdot \|$ calculates the Frobenius norm, $f_{pq}^{LOS}(t)$ stands for the Doppler frequency shift and it can be obtained by

$$f_{pq}^{LOS}(t) = f_{T\max} \frac{\langle \mathbf{D}_{pq}(t), \mathbf{v}_0 \rangle}{\left\| \mathbf{D}_{pq}(t) \right\| \cdot \left\| \mathbf{v}_0 \right\|}, \tag{5}$$

where $\mathbf{v}_0$ represents the speed vector and its Frobenius norm denotes the velocity value, $\langle \cdot, \cdot \rangle$ is the inner product operator, $f_{T\max} = \| \mathbf{v}_0 \| / \lambda$ means the maximum Doppler shift. As for the SB component, we can obtain it from

$$h_{pq}^{SB}(t) = \sum_{n=1}^{N_1} \left(g_{pq}^{SB} e^{j(\psi_n - \frac{2\pi \left\| \mathbf{D}_{pq,n} \right\|}{\lambda})} \right) \times e^{j2\pi f_{pq,n}^{SB} t}, \tag{6}$$

where ψ_n means the additional phase caused by the reflection. $\|\mathbf{D}_{pq,n}(t)\|$ represents the distance from the p-th Tx via the n-th scatter to the q-th Rx, which can be expressed as

$$\|\mathbf{D}_{pq,n}(t)\| = \|\mathbf{D}_{pn}(t)\| + \|\mathbf{D}_{nq}(t)\|, \tag{7}$$

and

$$f_{pq,n}^{SB} = f_{T\max}\frac{\langle \mathbf{D}_{pn}(t), \mathbf{v}_0\rangle}{\|\mathbf{D}_{pn}(t)\| \cdot \|\mathbf{v}_0\|}. \tag{8}$$

To obtain the channel gain g_{pq}^{SB} of the SB component, we adopt the Lambertian scattering model mentioned in [13]. The diagram of the Lambertian model is presented in Fig. 3.

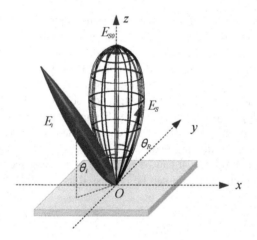

Fig. 3. The diagram of the Lambertian scattering pattern

As a signal with an amplitude of E_i impinges on a tile, it will be transformed into a beam with a certain width. Explicitly, the amplitude of the scattered signal in a certain direction can be expressed as

$$E_s = E_{s0}\sqrt{\cos(\theta_s)}, \tag{9}$$

where θ_s is the angle between the scattered wave and the normal direction of the tile, E_{s0} means the maximal amplitude of the scattering wave along the normal direction after scattering. It can be deduced that the maximum amplitude lies in the normal direction of the surface. Based on the derivations in [13], we can derive the channel gain of the SB component, which is expressed as

$$g_{pq}^{SB} = \frac{\lambda S\sqrt{dS}\cos(\theta_i)\cos(\theta_s)}{4\pi^{\frac{3}{2}}\|\mathbf{D}_{pn}(t)\| \cdot \|\mathbf{D}_{nq}(t)\|}, \tag{10}$$

where θ_i denotes the angle of incident, dS is the scattering area of the tile and S is a scattering loss parameter of which the square means the ratio of all scattered wave power and the incident wave power. Let $\mathbf{v}_n$ denote the norm vector of the n-th tile pointing to the inside of the tube, θ_i and θ_s can be expressed as

$$\cos(\theta_i) = \frac{\langle -\mathbf{D}_{pn_i}(t), \mathbf{v}_n \rangle}{\left\| \mathbf{D}_{pn_i}(t) \right\| \cdot \left\| \mathbf{v}_n \right\|}, \tag{11}$$

$$\cos(\theta_s) = \frac{\langle \mathbf{D}_{n_iq}(t), \mathbf{v}_n \rangle}{\left\| \mathbf{D}_{pn_i}(t) \right\| \cdot \left\| \mathbf{v}_n \right\|}. \tag{12}$$

It is worth mentioning that, in Eq. (4) and (6), we have time-varying parameters $\mathbf{D}_{pq}(t)$ and $\mathbf{D}_{pq,n}(t)$, which makes the proposed GBDM a nonstationary one.

4 Simulation and Results

In this section, we will emulate the propagation scenario as depicted in Fig. 1. The total length of the vacuum tube is 40 meters and the vactrain-embedded Rx is set in the middle of the tube. In [9], we have already conducted a series of research on the small-scale channel parameters including the time delay spread, K factor, MIMO system capacity during the whole process. Herein, the effective scatters will be investigated. Specifically, we focus on a scenario where the Hyperloop travels at position (5, 0, 0) m. First, a digital simulation map is established including Tx, Rx, and all tube scatters. The frequency carrier is set to 5 GHz and the scattering loss factor is 0.6 according to [13]. Then, the vacuum tube wall is divided into 130×36 tiles, i.e., 130 equal parts in the central axis direction and 36 equal parts along the perimeter of the cylindrical cross-section. Each tile is assigned with a scatter located at the center. Finally, the Lambertian scattering model is implemented to each tile and the received signal of Rx is the sum of all scattered signals and the LOS component.

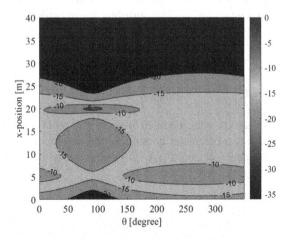

Fig. 4. The normalized channel gain of different scatters

Figure 4 depicts the normalized channel gain of different scatters considering the single bounce. Obviously, those scatters between Tx and Rx located from 5 m to 20 m pose some major influences on the received power and those scatters outside this range, with an average value lower than −15 dB, can be neglected. Moreover, the received amplitude contour curves are drawn and we mainly focus on those scatters with a contribution over −10 dB.

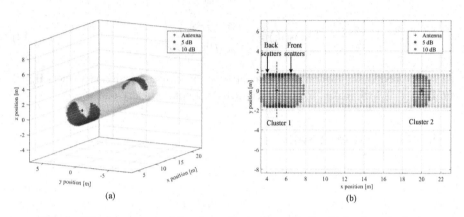

(a)   (b)

Fig. 5. Effective scatters with a channel gain over −10 dB. (Color figure online)

Figure 5 presents those scatters with a relatively large channel gain contribution, among which the red scatters denotes the propagation paths with a channel gain over −5 dB, the blues ones over −10 dB, and the yellow ones stand for the rest scatters with low contributions. Clearly, the blue scatters can be categorized into two clusters, of which each cluster is located near an antenna array. The first cluster near the Rx involves a larger effective scattering area, whereas the second cluster located near the Tx refers to a small effective area with a large scattering contribution, i.e., the red area.

Without loss of generality and to demonstrate a better statistical result, we choose the first cluster to investigate the angular distribution. According to [10], the distribution of the azimuth angle is usually characterized by the Von Mises distribution, which can be expressed as

$$f(\alpha) = \frac{e^{k\,\cos(\alpha-\mu)}}{2\pi I_0(k)}, -\pi < \alpha \leq \pi, \tag{13}$$

where $I_0(\cdot)$ means the zeroth-order modified Bessel function of the first kind, μ is the mean value of α, and k is a parameter controlling the angular spread of α. Then, we gather all the azimuth angle of arrival (AAOA) information of the first cluster and demonstrate them in Fig. 6.

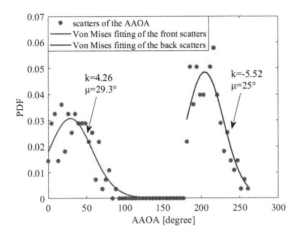

Fig. 6. The distribution of the AAOA and fitting results.

From Fig. 6, it can be learned that the first cluster yields two different distributions. The first one ranges from 0° to 180°, which is derived from the front scatters, the other one varies from 180° to 360° stemmed from the back scatters as marked in Fig. 5(b). Then, the Von Mises function is used to fit these two angular distributions. The fitting results are marked as two curves with different colors, among which the red one denotes an angular spread of 29.3° and the blue curve refers to an angular spread of 25°.

In terms of the elevation angle of arrival (EAOA), some literatures stated that the EAOA follows the Gaussian distribution [10] or the cosine distribution [17], which can be expressed as

$$f_{cosine}(\beta) = \frac{\pi}{4\beta_m} \cos\left(\frac{\pi}{2} \frac{\beta - \beta_\mu}{\beta_m}\right) \tag{14}$$

where β_μ is the mean angle and β_m refers to the absolute value of the maximum elevation angle. Herein, we use both of them and compare their fitting performances.

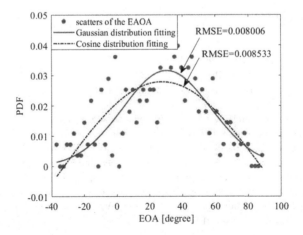

Fig. 7. The distribution of the EAOA and the fitting results.

Figure 7 shows the EAOA information of the first scattering cluster and the fitting results of above two mentioned distributions. The EAOA varies from −40° to 90° and a majority of them is larger than 0°, which corresponds to the geometrical results mentioned in Fig. 5(a). Two different distribution functions are used to fit the EAOA values and the results are presented in two curves with different colors. Obviously, the Gaussian distribution can yield a better fitting result with a root mean squared error (RMSE) smaller than that of the cosine distribution function.

5   Conclusions

In this paper, we propose a novel 3D geometry-based deterministic channel modeling method by using the Lambertian scattering pattern. Based on this, we analyze the effective scatters for the Hyperloop propagation scenarios considering the LOS and SB components. Simulation results show that those scatters around the Tx and Rx make a large contribution to the received signal. Moreover, the feasibility of the Von Mises distribution for the AAOA is verified based on the emulated results. Besides, the Gaussian distribution is a better fitting function option for the EAOA. The work we conducted provides some meaningful insights into further channel analysis especially in terms of the GBSMs that require the pre-defined angular distribution.

Acknowledgements. The research was supported by the Beijing Municipal Natural Science Foundation-Haidian Original Innovation Foundation (No. L172030), Research Fund of Shandong Jiaotong University under grant Z201924, Fundamental Research Funds for the Central Universities under grant 2018JBZ102 and Beijing Nova Program Interdisciplinary Cooperation Project (Z191100001119016).

References

1. Aksenov, N.A.: Maglev: as a new stage of high-speed transport development. Transp. Syst. Technol. **3**(1), 24–34 (2017)
2. Hyperloop Alpha (2013). https://www.spacex.com/sites/spacex/files/hyperloop_alpha-2013 0812.pdf
3. Janzen, R.: TransPod ultra-high-speed tube transportation: dynamics of vehicles and infrastructure. Procedia Eng. **199**, 8–17 (2017)
4. Qiu, C.C., Liu, L., Han, B.T., Zhang, J.C., Li, Z., Zhou, T.: Broadband wireless communication systems for vacuum tube high-speed flying train. Appl. Sci. **10**(4), 1379–1399 (2020)
5. Han, B.T., et al.: Research on resource migration based on novel RRH-BBU mapping in cloud radio access network for HSR scenarios. IEEE Access **7**, 108542–108550 (2019)
6. Qiu, C.C., Liu, L., Liu, Y., Li, Z., Zhang, J.C., Zhou, T.: Key technologies of broadband wireless communication for vacuum tube high-speed flying train. In: 2019 IEEE 89th Vehicular Technology Conference (VTC2019-Spring), pp. 1–5. IEEE (2019)
7. Zhang, J.C., et al.: Two novel structures of broadband wireless communication for high-speed flying train in vacuum tube. In: 2019 28th Wireless and Optical Communications Conference (WOCC), pp. 1–5. IEEE (2019)

8. Wei, B., Li, Z., Liu, L., Wang, J.H.: Field distribution characteristics of leaky-wave system in the vacuum tube for high-speed rail. In: 2018 12th International Symposium on Antennas, Propagation and EM Theory (ISAPE), pp. 1–3. CIE (2018)
9. Han, B.T., Zhang, J.C., Liu, L., Tao, C.: Position-based wireless channel characterization for the high-speed vactrains in vacuum tube scenarios using propagation-graph modeling theory. Radio Sci. 55(4) (2020)
10. Wang, C.X., Ghazal, A., Ai, B., Liu, Y., Fan, P.Z.: Channel measurements and models for high-speed train communication systems: a survey. IEEE Commun. Surv. Tutor. 18(2), 974–987 (2016)
11. Wang, C.X., Bian, J., Sun, J., Zhang, W.S., Zhang, M.G.: A survey of 5G channel measurements and models. IEEE Commun. Surv. Tutor. 20(4), 3142–3168 (2018)
12. Hussain, S., Brennan, C.: Efficient preprocessed ray tracing for 5G mobile transmitter scenarios in urban microcellular environments. IEEE Trans. Antennas Propag. 67(5), 3323–3333 (2019)
13. Tian, L., Degli-Esposti, V., Vitucci, E.M., Yin, X.F.: Semi-deterministic radio channel modeling based on graph theory and ray-tracing. IEEE Trans. Antennas Propag. 64(6), 2475–2486 (2016)
14. Wu, S.B., Wang, C.X., Aggoune, E.M., Alwakeel, M.M., You, X.H.: A general 3-D non-stationary 5G wireless channel model. IEEE Trans. Commun. 66(7), 3065–3078 (2018)
15. Liu, Y., Wang, C.X., Lopez, C.F., Goussetis, G., Yang, Y., Karagiannidis, G.K.: 3D non-stationary wideband tunnel channel models for 5G high-speed train wireless communications. IEEE Trans. Intell. Transp. Syst. 21(1), 259–272 (2020)
16. Liu, L., et al.: Position-based modeling for wireless channel on high-speed railway under a viaduct at 2.35 GHz. IEEE J. Sel. Areas Commun. 30(4), 834–845 (2012)
17. Ma, Z.F., Ai, B., He, R.S., Wang, G.P., Niu, Y., Zhong, Z.D.: A wideband non-stationary air-to-air channel model for UAV communications. IEEE Trans. Veh. Technol. 64(2), 1214–1226 (2020)

Finite-Time Consensus of Second-Order Multi-agent Systems with External Disturbances and Without Velocity Measurements

Yuling Li[1,2], Hongyong Yang[1,2(✉)], Yize Yang[2,3],
and Yuanshan Liu[1,2]

[1] School of Information and Electrical Engineering, Ludong University,
Yantai 264025, China
hyyang@yeah.net
[2] School of Electrical and Electronic Engineering, University of Adelaide,
Adelaide, Australia
[3] Key Laboratory of Cyber-Physical System and Intelligent Control in
Universities of Shandong, Ludong University, Yantai 264025, China

Abstract. In order to solve the problem of flocking for multi-agent systems with external disturbances, this paper studies the finite-time consensus of second-order multi-agent systems with external disturbances. Based on the disturbance estimations of external disturbances, a control protocol is proposed without velocity information, to deal with the leader-following consensus tracking problem of multi-agent systems. With the aid of algebraic graph theory and modern control theory, the finite-time consensus of second-order multi-agent systems with external disturbances is studied. The simulation results are provided to verify that the finite-time consensus algorithm of systems can make the states of followers converge to the states of one leader, and the state consistency of the second-order multi-agent systems with external disturbances is achieved.

Keywords: Multi-agent systems · Finite-time consensus · External disturbances

1 Introduction

In recent years, increasing attention has been paid to multi-agent systems due to their broad application in mobile robots cooperation control [1], military reconnaissance [2, 3], formation control of drones [4] and so on. Distributed cooperative control of multi-agent systems which is motivated by biology promotes the rapid development of multi-agent systems research. The consensus problem of multi-agent systems, as an important research direction of distributed cooperative control problem, is to design a distributed algorithm to make all agents reach an agreement through information exchange between neighbors. Distinguished by the number of leaders, consensus of multi-agent systems includes leaderless consensus [5, 6], leader-following consensus [7–9], and containment control [10, 11].

© Springer Nature Switzerland AG 2020
X. Chen et al. (Eds.): ML4CS 2020, LNCS 12487, pp. 98–111, 2020.
https://doi.org/10.1007/978-3-030-62460-6_10

The leader-following consensus means that the leader is followed by all other agents. Xie et al. [12] have investigated the global leader-following consensus problem for discrete-time neutrally stable linear systems subject to actuator saturation. The consensus problem for the multi-agent systems with a smart leader was studied in [13], and a sufficient condition was provided to ensure the boundedness of the position-tracking error and velocity-tracking error. Note that, most of the aforementioned consensus algorithms were asymptotically convergent in infinite time and the tracking errors of the systems can't be guaranteed to decrease to zero in finite time. However, in some practical control systems, such as brake control systems, the faster the convergence speed of the system is, the higher the control precision will be. In these situations, compared with general consensus protocols, finite-time consensus protocols are more desirable. Moreover, besides faster convergence, other advantages of the finite-time consensus are that it has better disturbance rejection and robustness against uncertainties. A finite-time exponential consensus problem was addressed for multi-agent systems in [14]. Zhao et al. [15] studied a finite-time control algorithm for the stochastic multi-agent systems to guarantee all agents converge to consensus in finite time. Sakthivel et al. [16] proposed a non-fragile control protocol that guaranteed the finite-time stability of the closed-loop system even in the presence of time-varying delay. A distributed consensus protocol was presented to make multi-agent systems reach consensus in finite time in [17]. He et al. [18] investigated the leaderless finite-time consensus for second-order Lipschitz nonlinear multi-agent systems with partial-state coupling.

It should be pointed out that, in practical applications, external disturbances are inevitable in multi-agent systems under uncertain environments, which may degrade the consensus performance or even destroy the consensus. Thus, how to solve the consensus problem for multi-agent systems with external disturbances turns out to be an important and interesting issue. Wang et al. [19] studied the consensus disturbance rejection problem for multi-agent systems with directed fixed as well as switching communication topologies in the presence of deterministic disturbances. The consensus problem of linear multi-agent systems subject to external disturbances via distributed event-triggered adaptive control was studied in [20]. A distributed self-triggered adaptive output feedback control strategy was designed to solve the consensus problem. Wang et al. [21] investigated distributed dynamic average consensus for a class of nonlinear multi-agent systems in the presence of local disturbances, and a consensus algorithm was proposed to guarantee that positions and velocities of the system converge exponentially to the average of multiple time-varying inputs. Yu et al. [22] investigated the distributed finite-time consensus of second-order multi-agent systems in the presence of bounded disturbances. Franceschelli et al. [23] investigated a consensus algorithm for a network of continuous-time integrators subject to time-varying disturbances, and it has been proven that the agents achieve an approximated consensus condition by attenuating the destabilizing effect of the disturbances. Distributed leader-following consensus for multi-agent systems with unknown bounded external disturbances in [24–26], then they proven that the multi-agent systems can achieve global asymptotic consensus even in the presence of external disturbances. The problem of robust consensus for fractional multi-agent systems with external disturbances was investigated in [27, 28].

It has come to our notice that a lot of finite-time consensus algorithms for multi-agent systems mainly depend on the availability of full states of the systems, very few works have been done when velocity information is not available. Actually, such situation is often happened when vehicles are not equipped with velocity sensors, or velocity might be more difficult to be accurately measured compared with the position. Hence, it's of great significance to design finite-time consensus algorithms without velocity information to stabilize the systems. Gui et al. [29] investigated global finite-time attitude consensus of multiple spacecraft without velocity measurements, where distributed finite-time attitude consensus laws were proposed for leader-following and leaderless multi-agent systems. Zheng et al. [30] have investigated the finite-time consensus of the heterogeneous multi-agent systems, where two kinds of consensus protocols with and without velocity measurements were proposed. Liu et al. [31] investigated finite-time consensus protocols for second-order multi-agent systems without velocity measurements, then obtained that the goal of finite-time consensus can be achieved when the velocity information is unavailable. The consensus problem of second-order multi-agent systems without measuring the velocity states of the agents was investigated in [32], and some necessary and sufficient conditions were derived for reaching second-order consensus in the systems. Abdessameud et al. [33] have proposed a consensus algorithm lack of velocity measurement to achieve consensus for the multi-agent systems.

In comparison to the existing above literatures, the innovations of this paper are that we investigate the leader-following finite-time consensus problem for second-order multi-agent systems with external disturbances. And we propose a control protocol, which is independent of velocity information, to deal with the finite-time consensus tracking problem. On account of the external disturbances, a disturbance observer is established to estimate them. The control algorithm studied in this paper has very important practical significance. When the velocities can't be obtained or there are no velocity sensors in the systems, the control systems can avoid the influence of the disturbances to achieve consensus. The rest of this paper is organized as follows. In Sect. 2, some preliminaries about algebraic graph theory are shown, and we recall some useful definitions and supporting lemmas. Finite-time consensus of multi-agent systems with external disturbances without velocity measurements is studied in Sect. 3. In Sect. 4, numerical simulations are used to verify the theoretical analysis. Finally, conclusions are drawn in Sect. 5.

2   Preliminaries

Assume that n agents constitute a network topology graph $G = (V, E, A)$, in which $V = \{v_1, v_2, \ldots, v_n\}$ represents a set of n nodes, and its edges set is $E \subseteq V \times V$. $A = [a_{ij}] \in R^{n \times n}$ is an adjacency matrix with elements $a_{ij} \geq 0$. An edge of the graph G is denoted by $e_{ij} = (v_i, v_j) \in E$. If $e_{ij} \in E$, the adjacency element $a_{ij} > 0$, otherwise $a_{ij} = 0$. The neighbors' set of node i is denoted by $N_i = \{v_j \in V | (v_i, v_j) \in E\}$.

Let graph G be a weighted graph without self-loops, i.e. $a_{ii} = 0$, and let matrix $D = \mathrm{diag}\{d_1, d_2, \ldots, d_n\} \in R^{n \times n}$ be the diagonal matrix with the diagonal elements

$d_i = \sum_{j=1}^{n} a_{ij}$. $L = D - A \in R^{n \times n}$ is the Laplacian matrix of the weighted graph G. For two nodes v_i and v_j, if there is an information transmission linked path between node v_i and v_j, we say node v_i can transfer the information to node v_j. If node v_i can find a path to reach any node of the graph, then node v_i is globally reachable from every other node in the digraph.

Assumption 1. For each follower, there exists at least one leader that has a directed path to that follower.

Assumption 2. There exists some scalars $p_i > 0$ and $p_j > 0$, such that $p_j a_{ij} = p_i a_{ji}$, for all $i, j = \{1, \ldots, n\}$, where a_{ij} is the $(i,j) - th$ entry of the weighted adjacency matrix A.

Definition 1. Consider the following nonlinear continuous system

$$\dot{x} = f(x), \, x(0) = x_0 \in R^n \tag{1}$$

where a continuous vector function $f(x) = (f_1(x), f_2(x), \ldots, f_n(x))^T$ is said to be homogeneous of degree $\kappa \in R$ with respect to $r = (r_1, r_2, \ldots, r_n)$, $r_i > 0$, if for any given $\varepsilon > 0$, $x \in R^n$,

$$f_i(\varepsilon^{r_1} x_1, \varepsilon^{r_2} x_2, \ldots, \varepsilon^{r_n} x_n) = \varepsilon^{\kappa + r_i} f_i(x), i = 1, 2, \ldots, n$$

Lemma 1. Consider the following system

$$\dot{x} = f(x) + \tilde{f}(x), f(0) = 0 \tag{2}$$

where $f(x)$ is a continuous homogeneous vector function of degree $\kappa < 0$ with respect to $r = (r_1, r_2, \ldots, r_n)$, and $\tilde{f}$ satisfies $\tilde{f}(0) = 0$. Assume $x = 0$ is an asymptotically stable equilibrium point of the system $\dot{x} = f(x)$. Then the system (2) is a locally finite-time stable if

$$\lim_{\varepsilon \to 0} \frac{\tilde{f}_i(\varepsilon^{r_1} x_1, \ldots, \varepsilon^{r_n} x_n)}{\varepsilon^{\kappa + r_i}} = 0, i = 1, 2, \ldots, n$$

Lemma 2. Suppose $f(x, u, t)$ is continuously differentiable and globally Lipschitz in (x, u), uniformly in t. If the unforced system $\dot{x} = f(x, 0, t)$ is globally uniformly exponentially stable at the origin, when $\lim_{t \to \infty} u(t) = 0$, then system $\dot{x} = f(x, u, t)$ is asymptotically converged to zero, i.e., $\lim_{t \to \infty} x(t) = 0$.

3 Finite-Time Consensus of Multi-agent Systems with External Disturbances Without Velocity Measurements

Suppose that the multi-agent systems with external disturbances are consisted of n followers and one leader. The dynamics of n followers are defined as

$$\begin{cases} \dot{q}_i(t) = p_i(t) \\ \dot{p}_i(t) = u_i(t) + d_i(t) \end{cases} \quad i = 1,\ldots,n \tag{3a}$$

where $q_i(t)$ and $p_i(t)$ are respectively the position and velocity of the i-th agent, $u_i(t)$ is the control input and $d_i(t)$ is external disturbance.

The dynamics of the leader is defined as

$$\begin{cases} \dot{q}_{n+1}(t) = p_{n+1}(t) \\ \dot{p}_{n+1}(t) = 0 \end{cases} \tag{3b}$$

where $q_{n+1}(t)$ and $p_{n+1}(t)$ are the position and velocity of the leader, respectively.

Assumption 3. The disturbance $d_i(t)$ is bounded in the system (3a).

Define the following auxiliary variables

$$\begin{cases} r_i(t) = \displaystyle\sum_{j=1}^{n+1} a_{ij}(q_i(t) - q_j(t)) \\ s_i(t) = \displaystyle\sum_{j=1}^{n+1} a_{ij}(p_i(t) - p_j(t)) \end{cases} \tag{4}$$

A control protocol is designed for agent i as follows

$$\begin{cases} u_i(t) = -l_1 \tanh(sig(\theta_i(t))^{\alpha_1}) - l_2 \tanh(sig(\eta_i(t))^{\alpha_2}) - \hat{d}_i(t) \\ \dot{\theta}_i(t) = \eta_i(t) - l_3 sig(\theta_i(t) - r_i(t))^{\sigma_1} \\ \dot{\eta}_i(t) = \displaystyle\sum_{j=1}^{n} a_{ij}(u_i(t) - u_j(t)) + a_{i,n+1}u_i(t) - l_4 sig(\theta_i(t) - r_i(t))^{\sigma_2} \end{cases} \tag{5}$$

where $\alpha_1, \alpha_2, \sigma_1, \sigma_2$ are undetermined parameters, l_1, l_2, l_3, l_4 are feedback gains, $\theta_i(t)$ and $\eta_i(t)$ are the states of the control protocol to estimate the auxiliary variables $r_i(t)$ and $s_i(t)$.

Suppose the external disturbance $d_i(t)$ of the systems can be described as

$$\begin{cases} \dot{\xi}_i(t) = W\xi_i(t) \\ d_i(t) = V\xi_i(t) \end{cases} \quad i = 1,\ldots,n \tag{6}$$

where W and V are the matrices of the system with (W, V) observable.

A disturbance observer is designed for the system (6)

$$\begin{cases} \dot{z}_i(t) = (W - KV)z_i(t) + WKp_i(t) - K(u_i(t) + VKp_i(t)) \\ \hat{\xi}_i(t) = z_i(t) + Kp_i(t) \\ \hat{d}_i(t) = V\hat{\xi}_i(t) \end{cases} \tag{7}$$

where $z_i(t)$ is the internal state variable of the observer, $\hat{\xi}_i(t)$ and $\hat{d}_i(t)$ are the estimations of $\xi_i(t)$ and $d_i(t)$ respectively, and K is a control gain to be designed.

Remark 1. The disturbances in this paper are generated by external disturbance system (6). We propose the disturbance observer (7) to estimate the unknown disturbances in the system (3a), so that the control protocol (5) can enhance the disturbance attenuation ability and avoid the disturbances to the stability of system (3a, 3b).

Let $q(t) = [q_1(t), q_2(t), \ldots, q_n(t)]^T$, $p(t) = [p_1(t), p_2(t), \ldots, p_n(t)]^T$, $u(t) = [u_1(t),$ $u_2(t), \ldots, u_n(t)]^T$, $\theta(t) = [\theta_1(t), \theta_2(t), \ldots, \theta_n(t)]^T$, $\eta(t) = [\eta_1(t), \eta_2(t), \ldots, \eta_n(t)]^T$, $r(t) = [r_1(t), r_2(t), \ldots, r_n(t)]^T$, $s(t) = [s_1(t), s_2(t), \ldots, s_n(t)]^T$, $\xi(t) = [\xi_1(t), \xi_2(t),$ $\ldots, \xi_n(t)]^T$, $d(t) = [d_1(t), d_2(t), \ldots, d_n(t)]^T$, $z(t) = [z_1(t), z_2(t), \ldots, z_n(t)]^T$, and then according to the systems (3a, 3b) and (5), the system (3a, 3b) can be rewritten in the vector form

$$
\begin{cases}
\dot{q}(t) = p(t) \\
\dot{p}(t) = -l_1 \tanh(sig(\theta(t))^{\alpha_1}) - l_2 \tanh(sig(\eta(t))^{\alpha_2}) + d(t) - \hat{d}(t)
\end{cases}
\tag{8}
$$

where
$$
\begin{cases}
\dot{\theta}(t) = \eta(t) - l_3 sig(\theta(t) - r(t))^{\sigma_1} \\
\dot{\eta}(t) = -l_1(L_1 \otimes I_n) \tanh(sig(\theta(t))^{\alpha_1}) - l_2(L_1 \otimes I_n) \tanh(sig(\eta(t))^{\alpha_2}) - l_4 sig(\theta(t) - r(t))^{\sigma_2}
\end{cases}.
$$
The external disturbance system (6) can be rewritten as

$$
\begin{cases}
\dot{\xi}(t) = (W \otimes I_n)\xi(t) \\
d(t) = (V \otimes I_n)\xi(t)
\end{cases}
\tag{9}
$$

The disturbance observer (7) can be rewritten as

$$
\begin{cases}
\dot{z}(t) = ((W - KV) \otimes I_n)z(t) + ((WK) \otimes I_n)p(t) - (K \otimes I_n)(u(t) + ((VK) \otimes I_n)p(t)) \\
\hat{\xi}(t) = z(t) + (K \otimes I_n)p(t) \\
\hat{d}(t) = (V \otimes I_n)\hat{\xi}(t)
\end{cases}
\tag{10}
$$

Taking the derivatives of the auxiliary variables gives

$$
\begin{cases}
\dot{r}(t) = s(t) \\
\dot{s}(t) = -l_1(L_1 \otimes I_n) \tanh(sig(\theta(t))^{\alpha_1}) - l_2(L_1 \otimes I_n) \tanh(sig(\eta(t))^{\alpha_2}) + (L_1 \otimes I_n)(d(t) - \hat{d}(t))
\end{cases}
\tag{11}
$$

In order to show the followers can track the leader in finite time, define the observation errors as $\bar{q}(t) = q(t) - 1_n \otimes q_{n+1}(t)$, $\bar{p}(t) = p(t) - 1_n \otimes p_{n+1}(t)$. Then according to the system (3a, 3b), taking the derivatives of the observation errors gives

$$\begin{cases} \dot{\bar{q}}(t) = \bar{p}(t) \\ \dot{\bar{p}}(t) = -l_1 \tanh(sig(\theta(t))^{\alpha_1}) - l_2 \tanh(sig(\eta(t))^{\alpha_2}) + d(t) - \hat{d}(t) \end{cases} \tag{12}$$

Thus, it can be seen that the leader-following consensus of the systems (3a, 3b) can be achieved in finite time if and only if the system (12) is globally finite-time stable.

Theorem 1. For the multi-agent systems (3a, 3b), suppose that both Assumption 1 and Assumption 2 hold, then

1) If control gains l_1, l_2 satisfy $l_1 + l_2 \leq M$, then for any $M > \|\hat{d}(t)\|$, there is $\|u\|_\infty \leq M$.
2) If $0 < \alpha_1, \sigma_2 < 1$, $\alpha_2 = \frac{2\alpha_1}{1+\alpha_1}$, $\sigma_1 = \frac{1+\sigma_2}{2}$ and the matrix $W - KV$ is negative definite, then the systems (3a, 3b) can achieve finite-time consensus with external disturbances.

Proof:
As the fact that for any $x \in R^n$, there is $\|\tanh(x)\|_\infty \leq 1$. Therefore, according to control protocol (5), there is $\|u_i\|_\infty \leq l_1 + l_2 + \|\hat{d}(t)\|$. Define the observation error as $e_\xi(t) = \xi(t) - \hat{\xi}(t)$, taking the derivative of it gives

$$\begin{aligned} \dot{e}_\xi(t) &= \dot{\xi}(t) - \dot{\hat{\xi}}(t) \\ &= W\xi_i(t) - \dot{z}_i(t) - K\dot{p}_i(t) \\ &= ((W - KV) \otimes I_n)e_\xi(t) \end{aligned} \tag{13}$$

We can find a matrix K to make the matrix $W - KV$ negative definite because (W, V) is observable. Therefore, it is easy to prove that the system (13) is asymptotically stable.

Then define the observation error of disturbances as $e_d(t) = d(t) - \hat{d}(t)$. It can be obtained from the system (6) and the observer (7) that

$$e_d(t) = (V \otimes I_n)e_\xi(t) \tag{14}$$

According to the Eq. (14), $e_d(t)$ is asymptotically stable because the system (13) is asymptotically stable, i.e. $\lim_{t\to\infty} e_d(t) = 0$. It can be known from the Assumption 3 that $d(t)$ is bounded, so it's easy to obtain that $\hat{d}(t)$ is also bounded. Therefore, the control input satisfies $\|u_i\|_\infty \leq l_1 + l_2 + \|\hat{d}(t)\|$. Because the control gains l_1, l_2 satisfy $l_1 + l_2 \leq M - \|\hat{d}(t)\|$, for any $M > \|\hat{d}(t)\|$, there is $\|u\|_\infty \leq M$.

Next, we will prove the system (12) is globally finite-time stable. Let $\bar{r}(t) = \theta(t) - r(t)$, $\bar{s}(t) = \eta(t) - s(t)$, and then according to (8) and (11), taking the derivatives of $\bar{r}(t)$ and $\bar{s}(t)$ gives

$$\begin{cases} \dot{\bar{r}}(t) = \bar{s}(t) - l_3 sig(\bar{r}(t))^{\sigma_1} \\ \dot{\bar{s}}(t) = -l_4 sig(\bar{r}(t))^{\sigma_2} - (L_1 \otimes I_n)e_d(t) \end{cases} \tag{15}$$

Then choose Lyapunov function as $V(t) = l_4|\bar{r}(t)|^{\sigma_2+1} + \frac{1+\sigma_2}{2}\bar{s}^2(t)$ and taking the derivative of it gives

$$
\begin{aligned}
\dot{V}(t) &= l_4(\sigma_2+1)|\bar{r}(t)|^{\sigma_2} \cdot |\dot{\bar{r}}(t)| + (1+\sigma_2)\bar{s}(t) \cdot \dot{\bar{s}}(t) \\
&= l_4(\sigma_2+1)|\bar{r}(t)|^{\sigma_2} \cdot \mathrm{sgn}(\bar{r}(t)) \cdot \dot{\bar{r}}(t) + (1+\sigma_2)\bar{s}(t) \cdot \dot{\bar{s}}(t) \\
&= l_4(\sigma_2+1) \cdot sig(\bar{r}(t))^{\sigma_2}(\bar{s}(t) - l_3 sig(\bar{r}(t))^{\sigma_1}) \\
&\quad + (1+\sigma_2)\bar{s}(t) \cdot (-l_4 sig(\bar{r}(t))^{\sigma_2} - (L_1 \otimes I_n)e_d(t)) \\
&= -l_3 l_4(\sigma_2+1)|\bar{r}(t)|^{\sigma_1+\sigma_2} - (1+\sigma_2)\bar{s}(t)e_d(t)
\end{aligned}
\tag{16}
$$

By applying the Lemma 2, $e_d(t)$ is regarded as the input of the system (16). On the basis of above analysis, it can be obtained that $\lim\limits_{t\to\infty} e_d(t) = 0$. When $e_d(t) = 0$, the Eq. (16) can be rewritten as

$$
\begin{aligned}
\dot{V}(t) &= -l_3 l_4(\sigma_2+1)|\bar{r}(t)|^{\sigma_1+\sigma_2} \\
&\leq 0
\end{aligned}
\tag{17}
$$

When $\dot{V}(t) \equiv 0$, there is $\bar{r}(t) = 0$, and then that is $\bar{s}(t) = 0$. Based on ISS theorem, it can be obtained that the system (16) is also asymptotically convergent.

It follows from the above analysis that $\bar{r}(t)$ and $\bar{s}(t)$ can globally asymptotically converges to 0. That is, there exists $T > 0$, when $t > T$, such that $\theta(t) = r(t)$, $\eta(t) = s(t)$. Then the system (12) can be changed to

$$
\begin{cases}
\dot{\bar{q}}(t) = \bar{p}(t) \\
\dot{\bar{p}}(t) = -l_1 \tanh(sig(r(t))^{\alpha_1}) - l_2 \tanh(sig(s(t))^{\alpha_2}) + e_d(t)
\end{cases}
\tag{18}
$$

Multiplying both sides of (18) by $(L_1 \otimes I_n)$ gives

$$
\begin{cases}
(L_1 \otimes I_n)\dot{\bar{q}}(t) = (L_1 \otimes I_n)\bar{p}(t) \\
(L_1 \otimes I_n)\dot{\bar{p}}(t) = -l_1(L_1 \otimes I_n)\tanh(sig(r(t))^{\alpha_1}) - l_2(L_1 \otimes I_n)\tanh(sig(s(t))^{\alpha_2}) + (L_1 \otimes I_n)e_d(t)
\end{cases}
\tag{19}
$$

It can be obtained from the auxiliary variables (4) that

$$
\begin{cases}
r(t) = (L_1 \otimes I_n)\bar{q}(t) \\
s(t) = (L_1 \otimes I_n)\bar{p}(t)
\end{cases}
\tag{20}
$$

Denote $\begin{cases} X = (L_1 \otimes I_n)\bar{q}(t) \\ Y = (L_1 \otimes I_n)\bar{p}(t) \end{cases}$, and then the Eq. (19) can be transformed to

$$\begin{cases} \dot{X} = Y \\ \dot{Y} = -l_1(L_1 \otimes I_n)\tanh(sig(X)^{\alpha_1}) - l_2(L_1 \otimes I_n)\tanh(sig(Y)^{\alpha_2}) + (L_1 \otimes I_n)e_d(t) \end{cases}$$

$$(21)$$

With the fact that $\tanh(sig(x)^{\alpha}) = sig(x)^{\alpha} + o(sig(x)^{\alpha})$, the system (21) can be rewritten as

$$\begin{cases} \dot{X} = Y \\ \dot{Y} = -l_1(L_1 \otimes I_n)sig(X)^{\alpha_1} - l_2(L_1 \otimes I_n)sig(Y)^{\alpha_2} + \hat{f}(X,Y) + (L_1 \otimes I_n)e_d(t) \end{cases} \quad (22)$$

where $\hat{f}(X,Y) = o((L_1 \otimes I_n)sig(X)^{\alpha_1}) + o((L_1 \otimes I_n)sig(Y)^{\alpha_2})$.

The Lyapunov function candidate is chosen as

$$V_1 = \frac{1}{2}Y^T((L_1 p(t))^{-1} \otimes I_n)Y + l_1(p^{-1}(t) \otimes I_n)\int_0^X \tanh(sig(\rho)^{\alpha_1})d\rho \quad (23)$$

Taking the derivative of V_1 gives

$$\begin{aligned} \dot{V}_1 &= Y^T(p^{-1}(t) \otimes I_n)\dot{Y} + l_1\dot{X}^T(p^{-1}(t) \otimes I_n)\tanh(sig(X)^{\alpha_1}) \\ &= Y^T(p^{-1}(t) \otimes I_n)(-l_1(L_1 \otimes I_n)\tanh(sig(X)^{\alpha_1}) - l_2(L_1 \otimes I_n)\tanh(sig(Y)^{\alpha_2}) \\ &\quad + (L_1 \otimes I_n)e_d(t)) + l_1 Y^T(p^{-1}(t) \otimes I_n)\tanh(sig(X)^{\alpha_1}) \\ &= -l_2 Y^T(p^{-1}(t) \otimes I_n)\tanh(sig(Y)^{\alpha_2}) + Y^T(p^{-1}(t) \otimes I_n)e_d(t) \end{aligned}$$

$$(24)$$

Using the same analytical method as (16), we can know that $Y = 0$, and then $\dot{Y} = 0$. It follows from (21) that $X = 0$. The system (21) is globally asymptotically stable by LaSalle's invariant principle and ISS theorem.

The system (22) can be transformed to the following reduced system

$$\begin{cases} \dot{X} = Y \\ \dot{Y} = -l_1(L_1 \otimes I_n)sig(X)^{\alpha_1} - l_2(L_1 \otimes I_n)sig(Y)^{\alpha_2} + (L_1 \otimes I_n)e_d(t) \end{cases} \quad (25)$$

Next, we will prove the system (25) is also asymptotically stable and homogeneous. Then choosing Lyapunov function as

$$V_2 = \frac{1}{2}Y^T((L_1 p(t))^{-1} \otimes I_n)Y + \frac{l_1}{1+\alpha_1}(p(t)^{-1} \otimes I_n)|X|^{1+\alpha_1} \quad (26)$$

And taking the derivative of V_2 gives

$$\dot{V}_2 = Y^T((L_1p(t))^{-1} \otimes I_n)\dot{Y} + l_1(p(t)^{-1} \otimes I_n)|X|^{\alpha_1}|\dot{X}|$$
$$= Y^T(p(t)^{-1} \otimes I_n)(-l_1 sig(X)^{\alpha_1} - l_2 sig(Y)^{\alpha_2} + e_d(t)) + l_1 Y^T(p(t)^{-1} \otimes I_n)sig(X)^{\alpha_1}$$
$$= -l_2 Y^T(p(t)^{-1} \otimes I_n)sig(Y)^{\alpha_2} + Y^T(p(t)^{-1} \otimes I_n)e_d(t)$$

$$(27)$$

By applying the same analytical method as V_1, based on LaSalle's invariant principle and ISS theorem, the system (25) is also asymptotically stable.

Moreover, the system (25) is homogeneous of degree $\kappa = \alpha_1 - 1 < 0$ with respect

to dilation $(\underbrace{2, 2, \ldots, 2}_{n}, \underbrace{\alpha_1 + 1, \alpha_1 + 1, \ldots, \alpha_1 + 1}_{n})$, and $\lim_{\varepsilon \to 0} \dfrac{\hat{f}(\varepsilon^{r_1}X, \varepsilon^{r_2}Y)}{\varepsilon^{k+r_2}} =$

$$\lim_{\varepsilon \to 0} \frac{o((L_1 \otimes I_n)sig(\varepsilon^2 X)^{\alpha_1}) + o((L_1 \otimes I_n)sig(\varepsilon^{1+\alpha_1} Y)^{\frac{2\alpha_1}{1+\alpha_1}})}{\varepsilon^{2\alpha_1}} = 0.$$

Above all, it follows from the Lemma 1 that the system (21) is globally finite-time stable. That is, based on the control protocol (5) and the disturbance observer (7), the multi-agent system (3a, 3b) can achieve leader-following consensus in finite time. $\square$

4 Numerical Simulations

In order to verify the effectiveness of the control protocols (5), consider the communication topology with four followers (illustrated as 1, 2, 3, 4) and one leader shown in Fig. 1.

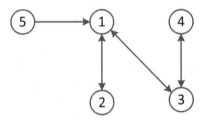

Fig. 1. The communication topology of multi-agent systems

Assume the connection weights of each edge are 1, the adjacent matrix of communication topology is $A = \begin{bmatrix} 0 & 1 & 1 & 0 & 1 \\ 1 & 0 & 0 & 0 & 0 \\ 1 & 0 & 0 & 1 & 0 \\ 0 & 0 & 1 & 0 & 0 \\ 0 & 0 & 0 & 0 & 0 \end{bmatrix}$, and then the Laplacian matrix of

systems (3a, 3b) is as follows $L = \begin{bmatrix} 3 & -1 & -1 & 0 & -1 \\ -1 & 1 & 0 & 0 & 0 \\ -1 & 0 & 2 & -1 & 0 \\ 0 & 0 & -1 & 1 & 0 \\ 0 & 0 & 0 & 0 & 0 \end{bmatrix}$.

Assume that the initial positions and velocities of four followers are respectively taken as $q(0) = [3, 2, 0, -2]^T$ and $p(0) = [6, 5, 0, -1]^T$. The initial position and velocity of the leader are respectively taken as $q_5(0) = 1$ and $p_5(0) = 2$. The parameters of the control protocols (5) are taken as $l_1 = 15$, $l_2 = 10$, $l_3 = 20$, $l_4 = 15$, $\alpha_1 = 0.25$, $\alpha_2 = 0.4$, $\sigma_1 = 0.6$, $\sigma_2 = 0.2$. The parameters of the external disturbance system (6) are taken as $W = \begin{bmatrix} 0 & 2 \\ -2 & 0 \end{bmatrix}$ and $V = [0 \ \ 1]$, with initialized values $\xi_1(0) = [1, 1]^T$, $\xi_2(0) = [1, 2]^T$, $\xi_3(0) = [1, 3]^T$ and $\xi_4(0) = [1, 4]^T$. The parameters of the disturbance observer (7) are taken as $K = [1, 2]^T$, with initialized value $z_i(0) = [1, 1]^T$.

Figure 2 shows the actual values of the positions of five agents. It can be seen that the position states of four followers can gradually approach to the position of the leader in finite time around 3 s. Figure 3 shows the actual values of the velocities of five agents. It can be seen that the velocity states of four followers can gradually approach to the velocity of the leader in finite time around 6 s. Hence, it can be obtained that the states of followers can be traced to the leader states in finite time under the control protocol (5) and the multi-agent systems (3a, 3b) can achieve consensus.

Figure 4 shows the actual values of external disturbances in the systems (3a, 3b). The external disturbances of the four followers are respectively taken $d_1 = \cos t$, $d_2 = 2\cos t$, $d_3 = 3\cos t$ and $d_4 = 4\cos t$. Figure 5 shows the estimated values of external disturbances which can be obtained by the disturbance observer (7). Figure 6 shows the observation errors of the disturbances. It can be obtained that the observer (7) observes the accurate estimations of the disturbances in the systems, and the estimation errors approach to 0 in finite time about 6 s. The observer (7) has a good observation effect.

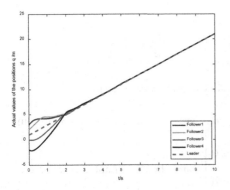

Fig. 2. Actual values of the positions

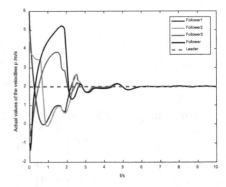

Fig. 3. Actual values of the velocities

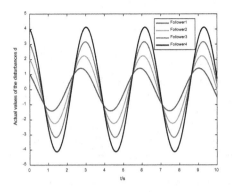

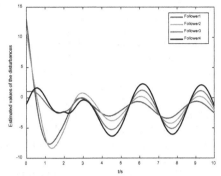

Fig. 4. Actual values of the disturbances   **Fig. 5.** Estimated values of the disturbance

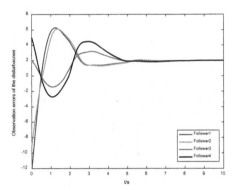

Fig. 6. Observation errors of the disturbances

5 Conclusions

1) In this paper, the finite-time consensus of second-order multi-agent systems with external disturbances has been investigated. The disturbance observer is designed to estimate the unknown external disturbances. Simulation results show that the control protocol without velocity information based on disturbance observer can make the multi-agent systems achieve finite-time consensus.

2) Because of the external disturbances in the systems, a lot of data traffic is sometimes generated and the multi-agent systems take a long time to achieve consensus. Therefore, the next step is to research the optimal control algorithm for the multi-agent systems to make the systems achieve stable faster.

Acknowledgements. The research is supported by the National Natural Science Foundation of China (61673200, 61771231), the Major Basic Research Project of Natural Science Foundation of Shandong Province of China (ZR2018ZC0438) and the Key Research and Development Program of Yantai City of China (2019XDHZ085).

References

1. Mazdin, P., Arbanas, B., Haus, T., et al.: Trust consensus protocol for heterogeneous underwater robotic systems. IFAC-PapersOnLine **49**(23), 341–346 (2016)
2. Jiang, Z., Wei, D., Shuchun, Z., et al.: Hyper-network multi agent model for military system and its use case. In: IEEE 7th Joint International Information Technology & Artificial Intelligence Conference, vol. 20–21, pp. 358–362 (2014)
3. Ekanayake, S., Pathirana, P.: Smart cluster bombs-control of multi-agent systems for military applications. In: Proceedings of 2007 IEEE International Conference on Networking, Sensing and Control, Institute of Electrical and Electronics Engineers, Piscataway, N.J., pp. 471–476 (2007)
4. Kim, M., Matson, E.T.: A cost-optimization model in multi-agent system routing for drone delivery. In: Bajo, J., et al. (eds.) PAAMS 2017. CCIS, vol. 722, pp. 40–51. Springer, Cham (2017). https://doi.org/10.1007/978-3-319-60285-1_4
5. Sakthivel, R., Sakthivel, R., Kaviarasan, B., et al.: Finite-time leaderless consensus of uncertain multi-agent systems against time-varying actuator faults. Neurocomputing **325**, 159–171 (2019)
6. Liu, W., Zhou, S., Qi, Y., et al.: Leaderless consensus of multi-agent systems with Lipschitz nonlinear dynamics and switching topologies. Neurocomputing **173**, 1322–1329 (2016)
7. Zou, W., Ahn, C.K., Xiang, Z.: Leader-following consensus of second-order nonlinear multi-agent systems with unmodeled dynamics. Neurocomputing **322**, 120–129 (2018)
8. Cai, Y., Zhang, H., Zhang, K., et al.: Distributed leader-following consensus of heterogeneous second-order time-varying nonlinear multi-agent systems under directed switching topology. Neurocomputing **325**, 31–47 (2019)
9. Deng, C., Yang, G.H.: Leaderless and leader-following consensus of linear multi-agent systems with distributed event-triggered estimators. J. Franklin Inst. **356**, 309–333 (2019)
10. Wang, Q., Fu, J., Wang, J.: Fully distributed containment control of high-order multi-agent systems with nonlinear dynamics. Syst. Control Lett. **99**, 33–39 (2017)
11. Fu, J., Wang, J.: Robust finite-time containment control of general linear multi-agent systems under directed communication graphs. J. Franklin Inst. **353**, 2670–2689 (2016)
12. Xie, Y., Lin, Z.: Global leader-following consensus of a group of discrete-time neutrally stable linear systems by event-triggered bounded controls. Inf. Sci. **459**, 302–316 (2018)
13. Ma, Z., Liu, Z., Chen, Z.: Leader-following consensus of multi-agent system with a smart leader. Neurocomputing **214**, 401–408 (2016)
14. Jin, X.Z., Zhao, X.F., Qin, J.H., et al.: Adaptive finite-time consensus of a class of disturbed multi-agent systems. J. Franklin Inst. **355**, 4644–4664 (2018)
15. Zhao, L., Jia, Y.: Finite-time consensus for second-order stochastic multi-agent systems with nonlinear dynamics. Appl. Math. Comput. **270**, 278–290 (2015)
16. Sakthivel, R., Kanakalakshmi, S., Kaviarasan, B., et al.: Finite-time consensus of input delayed multi-agent systems via non-fragile controller subject to switching topology. Neurocomputing **325**, 225–233 (2019)
17. Tong, P., Chen, S., Wang, L.: Finite-time consensus of multi-agent systems with continuous time-varying interaction topology. Neurocomputing **284**, 187–193 (2018)
18. He, X., Hao, Y., Wang, Q.: Leaderless finite-time consensus for second-order Lipschitz nonlinear multi-agent systems with settling time estimation. Physica A **514**, 280–289 (2019)
19. Wang, P., Wen, G., Yu, X., et al.: Consensus disturbance rejection for linear multiagent systems with directed switching communication topologies. IEEE Trans. Control Netw. Syst. **7**(1), 254–265 (2020)

20. Qian, Y.Y., Liu, L., Feng, G.: Distributed event-triggered adaptive control for consensus of linear multi-agent systems with external disturbances. IEEE Trans. Cybern. **50**(5), 2197–2208 (2020)
21. Wang, Z., Wang, D., Wang, W.: Distributed dynamic average consensus for nonlinear multi-agent systems in the presence of external disturbances over a directed graph. Inf. Sci. **479**, 40–54 (2019)
22. Yu, S., Long, X.: Finite-time consensus for second-order multi-agent systems with disturbances by integral sliding mode. Automatica **54**, 158–165 (2015)
23. Franceschelli, M., Giua, A., Pisano, A., et al.: Finite-time consensus for switching network topologies with disturbances. Nonlinear Anal. Hybrid Syst. **10**(1), 83–93 (2013)
24. Yang, Y., Yang, H., Liu, F.: Group motion of autonomous vehicles with anti-disturbance protection. J. Netw. Comput. Appl. **162**, 102661 (2020)
25. Yang, H., Zhang, Z., Zhang, S.: Consensus of second-order multi-agent systems with exogenous disturbances. Int. J. Robust Nonlinear Control **21**(9), 945–956 (2010)
26. Yang, H., Zhu, X., Zhang, S.: Consensus of second-order delayed multi-agent systems with leader-following. Eur. J. Control **16**(2), 188–199 (2010)
27. Yang, H., Wang, F., Han, F.: Containment control of fractional order multi-agent systems with time delays. IEEE/CAA J. Automatica Sinica **5**(3), 727–732 (2018)
28. Yang, H., Yang, Y., Han, F., Zhao, M., Guo, L.: Containment control of heterogeneous fractional-order multi-agent systems. J. Franklin Inst. **356**(2), 752–765 (2019)
29. Gui, H., Vukovich, G.: Distributed almost global finite-time attitude consensus of multiple spacecraft without velocity measurements. Aerosp. Sci. Technol. **75**, 284–296 (2018)
30. Zheng, Y.S., Wang, L.: Finite-time consensus of heterogeneous multi-agent systems with and without velocity measurements. Syst. Control Lett. **61**, 871–878 (2012)
31. Liu, X., Cao, J., Hao, G.: Finite-time consensus of second-order multi-agent systems via auxiliary system approach. J. Franklin Inst. **353**(7), 1479–1493 (2016)
32. Wen, C.L., Liu, F., Feng, X., et al.: Observer-based consensus of second-order multi-agent systems without velocity measurements. Neurocomputing **179**, 298–306 (2016)
33. Abdessameud, A., Tayebi, A.: On consensus algorithms for double-integrator dynamics without velocity measurement and with input constraints. Syst. Control Lett. **59**(12), 812–821 (2010)

A Comparative Study on Key Technologies of Ultra-Reliable Low Latency Communication

Mingju Yuan$^{(\boxtimes)}$ ⓘ, Dongxiang Song ⓘ, and Bing Li ⓘ

School of Information, Dehong Teachers' College, Mangshi 678400, China
yuanmingju@qq.com

Abstract. The three typical business scenarios of 5G are Enhanced Mobile Broadband, Massive Machine Type Communication, and Ultra-Reliable Low Latency Communication. Among them, Ultra-Reliable Low Latency Communication is one of the key application scenarios of 5G. Different from the traditional communication system which should pay more attention to the throughput, it requires the wireless and the carrier to have the ability of ultra-low delay and ultra-high reliability processing, and has high requirements on the network design. Therefore, based on the analysis of ITU and 3GPP's demand for URLLC's performance indicators, this paper discusses the key technologies of reducing URLLC's delay and increasing its reliability, and proposes the design objectives of URLLC, as well as the key technologies of solving the delay and increasing URLLC's reliability at design time, which provides a reference for designers and peers.

Keywords: URLLC · Highly reliable · Low latency · Mobile communication

1 Introduction

In June 2019, The Ministry of Industry and Information Technology granted China Telecom a "fifth-generation digital cellular mobile communications business" business license, marking China has entered the 5G era. At present, LTE technology is widely used in various industries, it provides enough wireless access latency for most mobile broadband applications, but for delays in critical applications such as traffic safety, healthcare or emerging industrial Internet applications, far from meeting the requirements.

High reliability and low latency are one of the key directions of 5G technology research, as early as in 2017 3GPP R15 [1] report discusses delay reduction techniques such as subcarrier, key frame structure and short slot scheduling, in 2018 3GPP R16 [2] report focus on the reliability and low delay of URLLC put forward a higher standard, low latency, high reliability and the reuse of URLLC and EMMB technologies are studied. 5G communication is not yet universal, EMMB technology is used a lot, there are few applications and researches on URLLC, most of which are mainly based on LTE technology, And MMTC technology similar to 4G technology. At present, there is less research on 5G at home and abroad, and there is not much analysis and research on URLLC. Among them Zhang [3] studied the standardization process of URLLC in the update of 3GPP version and summarized the key technologies of physical layer in

© Springer Nature Switzerland AG 2020
X. Chen et al. (Eds.): ML4CS 2020, LNCS 12487, pp. 112–124, 2020.
https://doi.org/10.1007/978-3-030-62460-6_11

URLLC, it lists URLLC use cases and requirements, and introduces the research progress of each stage. Zhu [4] analyzes 5G URLLC standard, summarize of URLLC's network architecture, key technologies and network architecture. Liang [5] according to 3GPP's analysis of the requirements of different service network indicators, combined with ITU's requirements for URLLC scenario delay and reliability indicators, the potential applications in URLLC scenarios are analyzed, and the deployment plan of 5G URLLC wireless network is discussed. AN Krasilov [6] research on 5G network capacity under URLLC, and analyze the dependency relationship between URLLC and the main parameters of 5G network. Murtaza Ahmed Siddiqi [7] analyzes the operational problems in the implementation of 5G ultra-reliable low-delay communication IOT devices. The above-mentioned domestic and foreign studies have introduced the basic technology of 5G. With regard to the future prospects of 5G development, there is little analysis of the key points in URLLC, especially how to improve the widespread use of URLLC in 5G. This paper discusses the key technology of ultra-reliable Low Latency Communication, and takes the requirements of ITU and 3GPP on URLLC performance indexes as the starting point, Compare URLLC delay and reliability with LTE, Based on the analysis of user plane latency, control plane latency and reliability, the key technologies of URLLC with high reliability and low latency were proposed by effectively scheduling the transmission data structure, resource allocation and multiple access schemes, So as to get an effective solution.

2 The ITU Defines Three Application Scenarios for 5G

5G technology is committed to dealing with the explosive growth of mobile data traffic, massive device connections, emerging new businesses and application scenarios in the future, at the same time, deep integration with the industry, to meet the diverse needs of vertical industry terminal interconnection, and to create a new world of "Internet of everything". International Telecommunication Union-Radiocommunication (ITU-R) defined three typical business scenarios of 5G: Enhanced Mobile Broadband (EMBB), Massive Machine Type Communication (MMTC), Ultra-Reliable Low Latency Communication (URLLC) [8]. The definition of three typical 5G services makes the communication system no longer only focus on human-centric communication, machine-type communication has become an important communication method. The following Table 1 shows us differences and characteristics of the three types of scenarios.

Table 1. Differences and characteristics of EMBB, MMTC and URLLC scenarios

Classification	EMBB	MMTC	URLLC
Main target	Improving spectral efficiency and peak throughput	Increase the number of support devices to support low cost devices	Reduce end-to-end delay and improve the robustness of data transmission
Key demand	20× peak Throughput 100× zone throughput 5× spectral efficiency	10^6 equipment/km^2 100× energy efficiency	End-to-end delay: 10 ms Physical layer delay: 0.5 ms BLER $< 10^{-5}$ within 1 ms
Package size	≫100 bytes	Several hundreds bytes	Dozens to hundreds bytes
Physical layer	Large-scale antenna, millimeter wave, bandwidth aggregation, new waveform	Non-Orthogonal Access Technology, overloaded data transfer and active user detection	Real time access, error free transmission
Application and features	For large-traffic mobile broadband applications such as Ultra-HD video, VR/AR, high-speed mobile Internet access, 5G enhances the 4G mobile broadband scene	Application scenarios such as the Internet of things with sensor and data collection as targets have the characteristics of small data packets, massive connections, and more cooperation between base stations	For the special applications of vertical industries such as Internet of vehicles, industrial control, perception network, etc., 5 g wireless and bearer are required to have ultra-low delay, high reliability and other processing capabilities

3 URLLC Performance Evaluation Index

As one of the typical 5G business scenarios, URLLC has high technical requirements for URLLC. This paper gives the URLLC performance assessment definitions and recommendations as defined by ITU and 3GPP.

3.1 The ITU Defines the Performance Indicator of URLLC

The ITU research performance index report is:Minimum requirements related to technical performance for IMT-2020 radio interface. Including three performance indicators of URLLC, user plane latency, control plane latency, reliability. User plane latency is the contribution of the radio network to the time from when the source sends a packet to when the destination receives it (in ms). It is defined as the one-way time it takes to successfully deliver an application layer packet/message from the radio pro-tocol layer 2/3 SDU (Service Data Unit) ingress point to the radio protocol layer 2/3 SDU egress point of the radio [9]. Interface in either uplink or downlink in the network for a given service in unloaded conditions, assuming the mobile station is in the active state. ITU recommends that the URLLC user plane delay is: 1 ms.

Control plane latency refers to the transition time from a most "battery efficient" state (e.g. Idle state) to the start of continuous data transfer (e.g. Active state). The ITU recommends that URLLC control plane delay: 20 ms, encouraged up to 10 ms.

Reliability relates to the capability of transmitting a given amount of traffic within a predetermined time duration with high success probability. Reliability is the success probability of transmitting a layer 2/3 packet within a required maximum time, which is the time it takes to deliver a small data packet from the radio protocol layer 2/3 SDU ingress point to the radio protocol layer 2/3 SDU egress point of the radio interface at a certain channel quality. The minimum requirement for the reliability is $1-10^{-5}$ success probability of transmitting a layer 2 PDU (Protocol Data Unit) of 32 bytes within 1 ms in channel quality of coverage edge for the Urban Macro-URLLC test environment, assuming small application data (e.g. 20 bytes application data + protocol overhead).

3.2   URLLC Performance Index Defined by 3GPP

The 3GPP research performance index requirements report is: Study on scenarios and requirements for next generation access technologies. The URLLC performance index defined by 3GPP is different from ITU, the time it takes to successfully deliver an application layer packet/message from the radio protocol layer 2/3 SDU ingress point to the radio protocol layer 2/3 SDU egress point via the radio interface in both uplink and downlink directions, where neither device nor Base Station reception is restricted by DRX (Discontinuous Reception) [10]. 3GPP recommends that the URLLC user plane Upper chain: 0.5 ms, Lower chain: 0.5 ms: EMBB, Upper chain: 4 ms, Lower chain: 4 ms.

Control plane latency refers to the time to move from a battery efficient state (e.g., IDLE) to start of continuous data transfer (e.g., ACTIVE). 3GPP recommends that the URLLC control plane delay is: 10 ms. For infrequent application layer small packet/message transfer, the time it takes to successfully deliver an application layer packet/message from the radio protocol layer 2/3 SDU ingress point at the mobile device to the radio protocol layer 2/3 SDU egress point in the RAN, when the mobile device starts from its most "battery efficient" state. For the definition above, the latency shall be no worse than 10 s on the uplink for a 20 byte application packet (with uncompressed IP header corresponding to 105 bytes physical layer) measured at the maximum coupling loss (MaxCL) of 164 dB.

In 3GPP reliability can be evaluated by the success probability of transmitting X bytes within a certain delay, which is the time it takes to deliver a small data packet from the radio protocol layer 2/3 SDU ingress point to the radio protocol layer 2/3 SDU egress point of the radio interface, at a certain channel quality (e.g., coverage-edge). A general URLLC reliability requirement for one transmission of a packet is $1-10^{-5}$ for 32 bytes with a user plane latency of 1 ms [11].

Foe V2X, Transfer a 300 bytes packet, its reliability: $1-10^{-5}$, control plane latency: 3–10 ms, Direct communication through sidelink, with a range of several meters. Another transmission mode is transmitted through the base station, and the reliability and user interface delay remain the same.

Availability is the probability that the network can support Mu to meet the target QoS requirements under delay and reliability, it is also a key indicator of URLLC [12].

3.3   LTE Delay

3GPP 36.913 R15 the report shows the user side delay and control side delay of LTE system. Compare urllc delay with LTE delay evaluation index, the C-Plane latency takes into account RAN and CN latencies (excluding the transfer latency on the S1 interface) in unloaded conditions. The target for transition time from Idle mode (with IP address allocated) to Connected mode is less than 50 ms including the establishment of the user plane (excluding the S1 transfer delay) [13]. The target for the transition from a "dormant state" in Connected Mode (i.e. DRX substate in Connected Mode in E UTRAN) is less than 10 ms (excluding the DRX delay). According to 3GPP 36.881 R15 report, the end-to-end delay of LTE system connecting ues is contributed by multiple components, including the receiving distance, wireless technology, mobility, network architecture and the number of active network users.

3.4   URLLC Design Objectives

For URLLC, ITU and 3GPP are more concerned with their delay and reliability. In the design of URLLC system, the most direct goal is to achieve the highest reliability with the lowest delay. But this is ideal, and a real URLLC system requires additional considerations such as throughput, connection density, spectrum efficiency, energy efficiency, cost efficiency, and compatibility with other existing services. Figure 1 [14] theoretically shows that low latency, high reliability and high throughput are difficult to achieve at the same time. Figure 1 [15] defines reliability as the probability that the delay does not exceed a predetermined time, using the convention that discarded packets have infinite delay, among, the asymptote of Cumulative Distribution Function is $1 - Pe$, Pe Is the probability of packet loss or mistake.

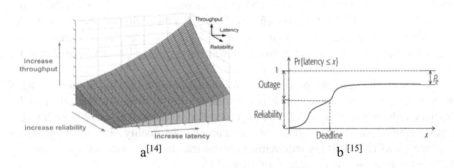

Fig. 1. Outage, Reliability, Deadline and Latency

4   URLLC Implementation Method/Technology

Firstly, the delay should be reduced in terms of transmission data structure and transmission time interval; Second, minimize overhead, for example, remove or merge user scheduling, resource allocation; Then, the packet error rate of the first transmission is significantly improved because the packet retransmission mechanism fails to meet the delay requirement. In addition, the URLLC package should be transferred as soon as it is generated; In addition, URLLC packages should be transferred immediately after they are generated. Therefore, methods such as frame structure, multiple access scheme, multiplexing scheme and efficient resource scheduling are expected to improve transmission delay and ensure the reliability of URLLC.

4.1   Ways to Reduce Latency

When designing URLLC networks, optimizing the frame structure and time-slot structure is considered one of the most common methods. Figure 2 shows the relationship between LTE's Frame, Subframe, Slot, and Symbol.

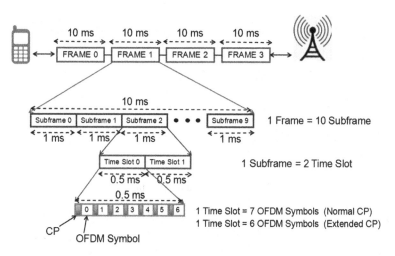

Fig. 2. Relationships among Frames, Subframes, Slots, and Symbols

Delay Calculation Method. Calculate physical layer delay with formula (1) [16], expressed as T_L:

$$T_L = T_{ttt} + T_{prop} + T_{proc} + T_{reTx} \tag{1}$$

where T_{ttt} represents the time required to transmit a packet, T_{prop} represents the propagation delay, which is the delay from the transmitter to the receiver, T_{proc} is the channel estimation process time, which is the first transmission codec-decode time, and T_{reTx} represents the retransmit time. According to the requirement of 3GPP, physical layer delay T_L cannot exceed 0.5 ms, so T_{ttt} should be in hundreds of us. The end-to-end latency calculation method is the sum of physical layer latency and network layer latency.

Optimize Package Structure. The primary goal of URLLC package design is to minimize T_{proc} in formula (1), this includes receiving data symbols, acquiring channel information, extracting control information, unpacking, and checking for errors. In order to further reduce the delay, the three parts of the packet, namely pilot frequency, control and data, are grouped. It then transmits in sequence, which makes it possible to manage channel estimation, control channel decoding, and monitor data. In the control part, we need a simple and fast decoding scheme, rather than relying on time-consuming processes such as channel decoding, blind search, and CRC testing [17].

Optimize Frame Structure. In LTE, the transfer subframe interval is 1 ms, The LTE frame consists of 10 TTI [4]. Obviously, the delay cannot meet the needs of URLLC. In order to reduce the transmission delay, the short frame structure is used [18], ts frame duration is one TTI, with the exception of the UL and DL data transfer phases, each frame contains a control signaling phase (see Fig. 3). Short frame structure for channel encoding of short length blocks, encoding delay does not exceed transmission time, so queue blocking delay is not considered.

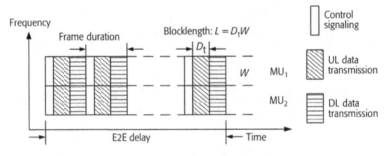

Fig. 3. Short Frame Structure

Optimize Time Slot Structure. To reduce the T_{ttt} delay of formula (1), the symbol period can be shortened by controlling the subcarrier interval with the carrier of a higher frequency band. For example, when the 15 kHz subcarrier interval is increased to 30 kHz, the symbol length decreases from 72 μs to 36 μs, it can send 28 OFDM symbols within 1 ms cycle. In 4G, if a packet consists of 14 OFDM symbols, T_{ttt} can be reduced by 0.5 ms. Another way to control the T_{ttt} delay in formula (1) is by reducing the number of symbols in the frame, this is also the idea of Mini Frames. The latest NR standard achieves low latency by increasing the carrier frequency and reducing the number of symbols (Mini time slots) [19]. Both LTE and NR use OFDM-based waveforms. Intersymbol interference will only be introduced if the delay extension of the signal exceeds the length of the CPs (so in complex propagation scenarios where the delay extension is longer, the short CPs with low latency need to be considered carefully). NR also encourages the use of different subcarriers to transmit data, and windowing is used to reduce intersymbol interference, thereby improving

Table 2. NR and LTE OFDM numerologies

	Sub-carrier spacing	Symbol duration	Cyclic prefix	Slot (14 symbols)	Mini-slot (7 symbols)	(4 symbols)	(2 symbols)
NR and LTE	15 kHz	66.67 μs	4.76 μs	1000 μs	500 μs	286 μs	143 μs
NR	30 kHz	33.33 μs	2.38 μs	500 μs	250 μs	143 μs	71 μs
NR	60 kHz	16.67 μs	1.19 μs	250 μs	125 μs	71 μs	36 μs
NR	120 kHz	8.33 μs	0.59 μs	125 μs	63 μs	36 μs	18 μs

spectral efficiency and reducing latency. The upstream chains are processed by DFT to reduce the peak average power ratio. Table 2 clearly describes the OFDM parameter sets (numerologies) for NR and LTE.

Multiplexing/Preemption Policy. Multiplexing is a technique for simultaneous transmission of multiple signals over a single channel. A scheduling solution for resource and latency efficiency is to use different TTI lengths (in resource-constrained cases), making high-priority data use resources from low-priority data, this type of multiplexing, also known as preemption, includes instant access, semi-static reservation, and dynamic reservation.

Multiple Access Policy. Multiplexing different multiple access techniques do not require information from various quarters together, instead, each is modulated to a channel, and the required information obtained by removing the modulation from each channel. The current LTE system establishes wireless access through OMA (Orthogonal Multiple Access) technology, which requires base stations to identify users first through competitive random access. As the number of user's increases, this strategy can cause severe congestion and high latency. Non-orthogonal multiple-access (NOMA) is a candidate access scheme, which mainly includes power domain and code domain. Different from different power levels assigned to different users in the power domain, the code domain distinguishes users by assigning unique channel codes, unauthorized management is now available [20]. A large number of papers have proved that NOMA can be more conducive to resource management, reduce delay and improve reliability, the paper also points out that NOMA has an advantage in URLLC scenarios where a large number of users frequently join and leave the network.

Optimize Resource/Wireless Management. Network availability is closely related to coverage or downtime probability. Some studies use SINR values to characterize availability [21]. They used multiple connections to reduce the probability of SINR below the threshold (disruption probability). But this is not perfect, because whether data packets can be successfully transmitted with short delay and high reliability depends not only on the SINR, but also on the allocated time/frequency resources. Therefore, a mathematical tool is needed to describe the relationship between achievable rate, transmission error probability, and resources. Further, a mathematical analysis tool is needed to transform the queuing delay requirement into a resource optimization constraint problem. The resources to be optimized include: antenna, maximum transmission power, bandwidth, transmission period, multiple MUs, etc.

a. Ensure transmission error requirements

The accessibility rate of SISO, SIMO and MISO under finite block length is accurately estimated [22], such as formula (2).

$$R(\varepsilon_t) \approx \frac{W}{\ln 2} \left[\ln\left(1 + \frac{\alpha P_t g}{N_0 W}\right) - \sqrt{\frac{V}{D_t W}} f_Q^{-1}(\varepsilon_t) \right] (b/s), \quad V = 1 + \left(1/\left(1 + \frac{\alpha P_t g}{N_0 W}\right)^2\right)$$

$$(2)$$

where ε_t is the transmission error probability, W is bandwidth, P_t is the transmission power, α is the average channel gain of path loss and shadow fading, g is the normalized instantaneous channel gain, N_0 is the single side noise spectral density, D_t is the transmission cycle, $f_Q^{-1}(x)$ is the reciprocal of Gaussian Q function. For MIMO Systems, g need to replace with $HH^\dagger$, H is the channel matrix. It is worth noting that when the block length is relatively large, formula (2) satisfies Shannon capacity. But the formula is difficult to achieve the global optimal (power, bandwidth, time).

b. Ensure queuing delay requirements

The method of network calculus [23] is used to analyze the queuing delay conflict, use SINR to optimize formula (2). The idea is to convert the accumulated data and the arriving data from the bit domain to the signal-to-noise ratio domain to obtain an upper bound on the probability of delay collision.

c. Ensure network availability

The average channel gain in formula (2) is determined by shadow fading, the distance between transceivers, and the instantaneous channel gain, therefore, the transmission error rates of UL and DL are random. At present, there is a lack of an appropriate and rigorous framework to describe the availability as a constraint of resource allocation.

Coding and Modulation. Unlike many communication systems that use Turbo codes and LDPC codes as data for FEC, URLLC uses convolutional codes and block codes to reduce decoding delay. If M diversity channels are deployed, the code rate must be low enough so that the free distance (convolutional code) or minimum Hamming distance (block code) is sufficiently larger than M. The selection of code rate should match the modulation, and the modulation with 256-qam order at most should be selected [23], simulation found that higher-order modulation can improve the spectral efficiency.

Improve CSI Acquisition Efficiency. CSI acquisition is a very important concern in URLLC. Wei [3] proposed and implemented an improved channel estimation method to reduce the delay of channel estimation, The basic idea is to use least squares estimation to extract the CSI related to the reference symbol, Then an advanced low-complexity two-dimensional dual harmonic interpolation method is used to obtain the CSI of the entire resource block. The simulation results show that the proposed channel estimation method can reduce the computation time by about 60% at B = 5 MHz compared with MMSE method. In the case of MIMO, a parallel interference cancellation algorithm based on DSC (decision statistical combining) is proposed [24], compared with serial interference cancellation method, pic has shorter delay.

Massive MIMO designed for URLLC requires the following features: (1) Very high signal-to-noise ratio link; (2) Accurately qualitative link, not affected by fading; (3) Extreme spatial reuse capability. Massive MIMO reduces the need for strong coding schemes, maintains high reliability for shorter packages, and significantly reduces the occurrence of retransmissions. But these advantages are built on the premise that Masive BS can get CSI instantly. This requires a lot of reliability/delay depending on the auxiliary process. In a mobile environment that is required by channel coherence time and extreme delay, the acquisition of instantaneous CSI becomes one of the most serious limitations of URLLC.

4.2 Ways to Improve Reliability

Diversity Thought. Diversity is a method to achieve highly robust communication using the spatial, frequency, and time-dependent characteristics of fading channels, it may include spatial diversity using multiple transmit and receive antennas, frequency diversity using multiple independent fading coefficient resource blocks, and time diversity using independent fading coefficient time slots.

a. Spatial diversity

In the case of multiple transmit antennas, an open-loop transmit diversity technique, such as precoder cycling, which circulates over the transmission bandwidth through a set of precoding matrices, can provide spatial diversity. Relative to multiple receive antennas, different versions of the same signal will be available on the receiver. It is unlikely that these signal versions will all be in deep fading, thereby increasing SINR. Transmit diversity can be achieved using space-frequency codes combined with forward error correction codes.

b. Frequency diversity

The physical boundaries of channels and available bandwidth can be developed by using distributed resource mapping and frequency modulation techniques.

c. Time diversity

The channel fading can be overcome by repeated or feedback-based retransmission methods, but it is necessary to consider whether the URLLC delay needs to be less than the channel coherence time, and if so, time diversity cannot be used. Of course, in a typical URLLC scenario, the delay requirement will be less than the coherence time of the channel (it will cause queuing decoding problems, and it will be uncontrollable depending on the channel status), in order to meet the requirements of queuing delay for limited transmission power, when the channel is in deep fading, some packets that cannot be transmitted even if the transmission power is maximum can be actively dropped [25].

Double Link/Multiple Connection. In multi-connection, UE is connected to the wireless network through multi-carrier. In recent years, 3GPP has defined several different multi-connection modes. Multi-connection has evolved from the initial CA (Carrier aggregation) technology by aggregating different used carrier resources to improve throughput. In CA, the aggregation point is a media access control (MAC) entity that allows a centralized scheduler to distribute packages and allocate resources. Subsequently, Release-12 proposed the concept of dual-link DC (Dual Connectivity), moving the aggregation point to the packet data aggregation layer. In Release-15, both CA and DC are used in LTE and NR, which can improve the reliable transmission of a higher layer. Multiple connections using packet replication on PDCP have the advantage of effectively using the underlying retransmission scheme (HARQ and RLC retransmission), thereby reducing latency and ensuring certain reliability. In addition, multi-connection based on dual connection is possible to achieve reliable switching without interrupting user plane data switching: One carrier moves from the source node to the target node at a time, so the UE always maintains at least one connection. During this process, packet replication makes the packet available for uninterrupted transmission to the UE at both nodes.

Short Error Control Code. In traditional communication systems, long low-density parity-check codes LDPC and Turbo codes are used to achieve low-error transmission. When the data rate is lower than the Shannon channel capacity, even error-free transmission can be achieved. But low latency requires a lower TTI, which requires a shorter code, but Shannon's theoretical model is not suitable for short codes. PPV (polyansky-poor-verdu) [26] analyzed the balance of delay, throughput and reliability on a limited block length by introducing a new basic parameter called "channel dispersion". The paper [27] shows that LDPC and Polar codes are constrained by 95% PPV, the BER is as low as 10^{-7}, and the block length is only a few hundred symbols, but the main disadvantage of PPV is the large decoding delay. As the complexity of the codec algorithm increases, the delay problem is almost inevitable, in addition, CSI estimation at the receiver, CSI feedback to the transmitter, code rate and modulation selection, and block length are all considerations.

Adaptive coding may also be used for URLLC. Adaptive coding is also called rateless code. The code rate can be adjusted to adapt to channel changes by sending the exact amount of encoded symbols required for successful decoding. This adaptation does not require any CSI at the transmitter, thereby eliminating channel estimation overhead and delay. The simulated fountain [24] code proposed by some studies is a code with a capacity close to the rateless code.

5   Conclusion

URLLC is one of the most critical application scenarios of 5G. Based on the requirements of 3GPP and ITU for URLLC, this paper analyzes the application requirements of URLLC. The performance evaluation index of URLLC by 3GPP and ITU is presented. The user surface delay requirement is about 0.5^{-1} ms, and the reliability requirement of BLER is about 10^{-7}–10^{-5}. URLLC requires higher technical requirements than LTE.

In this paper, URLLC's delay and reliability are compared with the corresponding parameters of LTE, and the key technologies of URLLC are analyzed from the aspects of reducing delay and increasing reliability. In terms of reducing latency, the use of new frame parameter sets (packet structure, frame structure, time slot structure) and shortened transmission time (TTI) are the most direct methods, improved multiplexing/preemption strategies, multiple access strategies, channel estimation methods, wireless management/resource optimization and other technologies can also reduce latency. In terms of improving reliability, methods such as diversity (spatial diversity, frequency diversity, time diversity), multiple connections, and short error control codes can improve the reliability of transmission.

When designing the URLLC system, factors such as data throughput, connection density, spectrum efficiency, energy efficiency, cost efficiency, and compatibility with other existing services are also considered, combining the above key technical points can make the URLLC system more complete and scientific during deployment, and finally achieve the optimal solution for 5G communication.

Acknowledgements. This study was supported by the research project of Dehong Teachers' College (XJ201812), Dr. Gan Jianhou workstation, Funded by the Science Research Fund of Yunnan Provincial Department of Education (2020J0835), Computer Science and Technology discipline innovation team building for intelligent education in ethnic areas (2020xhxtd07).

References

1. GPP.3GPP TR 38.913: Study on Scenarios and Requirements for Next Generation Access Technologies (Release 15) (2018)
2. GPP. 3GPP TR 38.824: Study on physical layer enhancements for NR ultra-reliable and low latency case (URLLC) (Release 16) (2019)
3. Yi, Z., Xia, L., et al.: The URLLC standardization progresses in 3GPP. Mob. Commun. **44** (2), 2–7 (2020)
4. Zhu, H., Lin, Y., et al.: Research on URLLC standard key technique and network architecture for 5G. Mob. Commun. **41**(17), 28–33 (2017)
5. Liang, H., Han, X., Li, F.: Analysis on 5G URLLC wireless network deployment scheme. Des. Technol. Post Telecommun. (3), 15–18 (2020)
6. Krasilov, A.N., Khorov, E.M., Tsaritsyn, M.V.: On the capacity of a 5G network for URLLC. J. Commun. Technol. Electron. **64**(12), 1513–1516 (2019)
7. Siddiqi, M.A., Yu, H., Joung, J.: 5G ultra-reliable low-latency communication. Implementation Challenges Oper. Issues IoT Devices **8**(9) (2019)
8. IMT-2020(5G) Propulsion group, 5g vision and requirements white paper V1.0[Z] (2014)
9. Zhang, P., Pang, S., et al.: Research advance and development trend of wireless channel measurement technology in 5G high frequency band. Mob. Commun. **41**(18), 67–72 (2017)
10. Wei, S., Wu, C.: Traffic latency charcterization and fingerprinting in mobile cellular networks. J. Comput. Res. Dev. **56**(2), 363–374 (2019)
11. Xie, R., Lian, X.: Survey on computation offloading in mobile edge computing. J. Commun. (11), 138–155 (2018)

12. She, C., Yang, C., Quek, T.Q.: Radio resource management for ultra-reliable and low-latency communications. IEEE Commun. Mag. **55**, 72–78 (2017)
13. Gao, Y., Li, L.: Analysis and research on URLLC Service Probability Delay Constraint And Resource Reservation. J. Beijing Univ. Posts Telecommun. **41**(5), 98–102 (2018)
14. Chen, H., et al.: Ultra-reliable low latency cellular networks: use cases, challenges and approaches. IEEE Commun. Mag. **56**, 119–125 (2018)
15. Öhmann, D., Awada, A., Viering, I., Simsek, M., Fettweis, G.P.: Achieving high availability in wireless networks by inter-frequency multi-connectivity. In: 2016 IEEE International Conference on Communications (ICC), pp. 1–7 (2016)
16. Wang, Y., Qiu, G., Lu, Z., et al.: The design of multi-TRP based URLLC transmission scheme in 5G. Appl. Electron. Tech. **45**(8), 10–13 (2019)
17. Lu, W., Fang, Y.: The solutions and key technologies for URLLC ultra-low latency. Mob. Commun. **44**(2), 8–14 (2020)
18. Li, X., Liu, J.: From LTE to 5G mobile communication system-technical principles and LabVIEW implementation. Tsinghua University Press (2019)
19. Ding, C.: Application scenarios and key technologies of 5G communication technology. Telecom World **26**(5), 98–99 (2019)
20. Shirvanimoghaddam, M., Dohler, M., Johnson, S.J.: Massive non-orthogonal multiple access for cellular IoT: potentials and limitations. IEEE Commun. Mag. **55**, 55–61 (2017)
21. Chen, H., Li, F.: Intelligent computer and applications. Res. Fifth Gener. Mob. Commun. Method Based eMBB mMTC uRLLC Scenarios **6**(9), 13–21 (2019)
22. Popovski, P., et al.: Ultra-reliable low-latency communication (URLLC): principles and building blocks. IEEE Netw. **32**, 16–23 (2018)
23. Chen, J.: Key technical specifications and development of 5G mobile communication. Telecom Eng. Technol. Stand. **31**(6), 36–41 (2018)
24. Panigrahi, S.R., Bjorsell, N., Bengtsson, M.: Feasibility of large antenna arrays towards low latency ultra reliable communication. In: IEEE International Conference on Industrial Technology (2017)
25. Jing, L., Carvalho, E.D., Popovski, P., Martinez, A.O.: Design and performance analysis of non-coherent detection systems with massive receiver arrays. In: IEEE Transactions on Signal Processing, vol. 64, pp. 5000–5010 (2016)
26. Polyanskiy, Y., Poor, H.V., Verdú, S.: Channel coding rate in the finite blocklength regime. IEEE Trans. Inf. Theory **56**, 2307 (2010)
27. Li, S.: 5G key technology introduction of NOMA. Electron. Prod. (4), 139–140 (2015)

Research on the Construction of College Campus Sports Culture and the Participation of College Students in Sports Activities

Guan Li[✉] and Xin Xin Huang

Guangdong University of Science and Technology, Dongguan 523083, China
675288845@qq.com

Abstract. This article selects male and female college students from 5 colleges and universities in Dongguan, Guangdong Province as the research object, using the theoretical background of college students' participation in sports activities and the construction of campus sports culture, employing literature data method, expert interview method, questionnaire survey method, logic analysis method, mathematical statistics method, carrying in-depth investigation and research on the current status of college students' participation in sports activities and the construction of campus sports culture, aims to explore the interrelated characteristics of college campus sports culture and college students' participation in sports activities, to strengthen the construction of college campus sports culture and put forward reasonable and effective measures and suggestions for promoting college students' sports activities participation, and to provide the necessary basis for the future development of college physical education.

Keywords: College campus culture · College students' participation in sports activities · Campus sports culture construction

1 Introduction

The stage of college education is the best period for the cultivation of physical fitness of young people. The awareness of college students' participation in sports activities and the behavior of participation in sports activities will directly affect their sports concepts and participation in sports after they enter the society. During college, college students contact the school sports environment and campus sports culture most frequently. Campus sports culture has become the main factor affecting students' participation in sports activities and awareness of sports activities. To encourage the strengthening of college campus sports culture will promote the formation of lifelong exercise awareness for college students and help them develop good physical exercise habits, which play a vital role in further improving physical fitness.

X. Chen et al. (Eds.): ML4CS 2020, LNCS 12487, pp. 125–136, 2020.
https://doi.org/10.1007/978-3-030-62460-6_12

2   Research Objects, Methods and Steps

2.1   Research Object

The male and female college students of 5 universities in Dongguan City, Guangdong Province were selected as the research objects, namely Guangdong University of Science and Technology, Dongguan University of Technology, Guangdong Medical University, Xinhua College of Sun Yat-sen University, and Dongguan City University of Technology. Each university selected 200 male and 200 female students, totaling 400 people, including 50 male and female students from each grade. Thus a total of 2,000 samples were taken, a total of 2000 questionnaires were distributed, 1741 valid questionnaires were retrieved, from 880 boys and 861 girls. The efficiency is 87.05%, and the related problems are analyzed.

2.2   Research Methods

Adopt literature information method, interview method, questionnaire survey method, mathematical statistics method, logic analysis method.

3   Results and Analysis

By consulting relevant literatures and materials, the relevant connotation of campus sports culture can be summarized, that is, campus sports culture is a concentrated expression of the sports values, will quality, and spiritual outlook regarding sports, of specific groups in schools. College campus sports culture is an important part of college campus culture and an important reflection of the purpose, significance and value of college sports education. It has direct or indirect influence on college students' sports awareness, sports motivation, sports attitude and sports value, thereby increasing the interest of college students in participating in sports activities, to meet the college students' own sports needs.

3.1   Analysis of the General Situation of College Students Participating in Sports Activities

Analysis of the Frequency and Time of College Students Participating in Physical Exercise
As can be seen from Fig. 1, the overall number of college students participating in physical exercise less than once, once, twice, three times or more per week is 336, 475, 446, and 484, which shows, 1405 people, accounting for 80.7% of the total number of college students, participate in physical exercise every week, but there are still 336 people, accounting for 19.3% of the total number of college students, participate in physical exercise at a frequency of less than once. This is not an ideal proportion of college students participating in physical exercise, as many college students' weekly participation in physical exercise is relatively infrequent, not attaching enough

importance to sports activities. This is also a problem that schools and society need to take seriously.

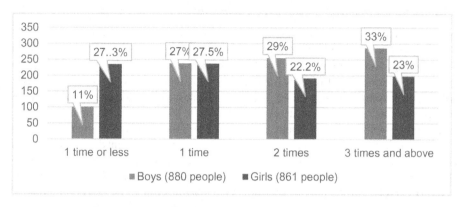

Fig. 1. Statistics on the frequency of college students participating in physical exercise (weekly)

The General Administration of Sport of China points out in the criteria for judging the sports population: the average time for physical exercise is required to be over 30 min or more. The China General Public Sports Status research team has manifested that a physical load and frequency of 3 times a week, over 20 min each time of active physical activity, has a significant effect on the maintenance and improvement of the respiratory and circulatory systems.

It can be seen from Table 1 that the total number of college students who participated in physical exercise for more than 20 min each time was 1478, accounting for 84.89%. Among them, the total number of college students who participated in physical exercise for 31–60 min each time is 551, accounting for 31.65%, which is a relatively high proportion, which shows that most college students can still guarantee an appropriate length of time to participate in physical exercise.

Table 1. Statistics of college students' participation in physical exercise time (each time)

Per exercise time	Within 20 min	21–30 min	31–60 min	60 min or more
Boys (880 people)	106	185	290	299
Girls (861 people)	157	353	261	90
Overall (1741 people)	263	538	551	389

There is a significant difference in the time of participation in physical exercise between college students of different genders. The number of college girls participating in physical exercise for 21–30 min each time is 353, accounting for 41%. The proportion of short-term physical exercise for girls is significantly higher than that for boys, while the number of male college students who participated in physical exercise for more than 30 min each time was 589, accounting for 67%, while the number of girls was only 351, accounting for 40.76%. The number of boys who participated in physical exercise for a long time was much higher than that of girls, which shows that boys comparatively exercises for more scientific and reasonable time lengths, and can benefit from a more effective physical exercise effect.

Analysis on the Choice of Sports Activities Among College Students

Statistics on the choice of sports activities among college students, has been obtained by surveying. It can be seen from Fig. 2 that boys mainly play ball games with a large amount of exercise and strong confrontation, while girls choose light and flexible items with less confrontation for exercise. It can also be seen from Fig. 2 that among all the college students' sports items surveyed, table tennis, badminton and running are three items most popular among female students. The fitness effect of running is very obvious, which can make up for the impact on college students' participation in physical exercise by the lack of sports facilities in colleges and universities. The figure also reflects that most college students like to choose sports activities of moderate-intensity exercise, strong interaction, and less demanding venues and sports equipment, on the other hand, it may also reflect that sports facilities in colleges needs to be improved to meet the needs of college students.

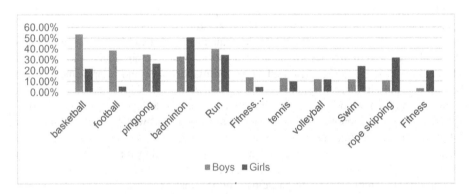

Fig. 2. Statistics on the selection of college students participating in sports

The Analysis of the Venues and Forms of Participation of College Students in Physical Exercise

As can be seen from Fig. 3, when college students participate in physical exercise, the proportion of boys and girls who choose outdoor stadiums is higher, the overall proportion is 78.8%. The proportion of male and female students who choose gyms is relatively low, and girls are more willing to choose gyms for physical exercise than boys. This also shows that most college students still prefer to choose outdoor sports venues for physical exercise, on one hand, because of the insufficient number of gymnasium venues and their own limited economic conditions, on the other hand, because there are more outdoor stadium sports activities to choose from, suitable for the participation of most college students. In the survey data on the form of participation, it can be seen that male and female college students who choose to participate in physical exercise mainly work with their classmates, accounting for 58.2% of the total number of people. This also illustrates the "conformity psychology" of college students when participating in physical exercise, compared with boys, girls are more willing to participate in physical exercise in classes and organizations, which shows that boys take a more active form of physical exercise, and girls are relatively dependent and blind.

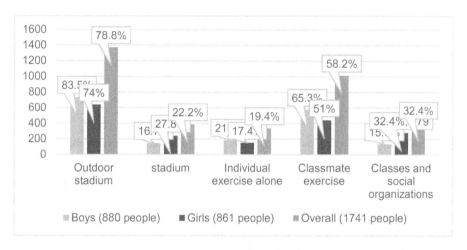

Fig. 3. Statistics on the venues and forms of college students participating in physical exercise

Analysis of Learning Channels of Sports Skills and Sports Methods for College Students

As can be seen from Fig. 4, the overall situation shows that the proportion of classroom sports learning is the highest, accounting for 51.8%. It can be seen that the learning of sports skills and sports methods for college students is still mainly from sports classrooms, and sports classroom teaching is the most direct and effective way for college students. to master sports skills and sports methods, which reflects the importance of college physical education. The second way to learn is to exchange and study with classmates, accounting for 49.7%, which reflects that most college students are more likely to be affected by the external sports atmosphere when they participate in physical exercise.

3.2   Analysis of the Influencing Factors of College Campus Sports Culture on College Students' Participation in Sports Activities

Evaluation and Analysis of the Use of Sports Venues and Equipment

College sports venues and equipment facilities is part of the material and cultural structure of campus sports culture, which is the basis and guarantee for the development of campus sports and cultural activities. With the increase in the number of college students, the existing sports venues and equipment facilities of colleges and universities have been unable to satisfy college students' need to participate in sports

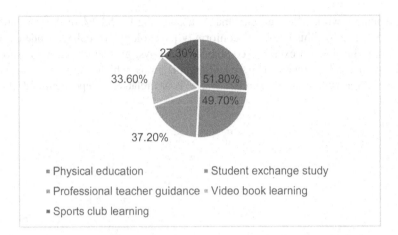

Fig. 4. Statistics on learning channels of sports skills and sports methods of college students

activities. It can be seen from Fig. 5 that the satisfaction of college students with sports venues and facilities and equipment is not high. Overall, 47.8% of college students believe that sports venues and facilities and equipment are average, so it can be seen that the current college sports venues, facilities and equipment are relatively lagging, and they can not meet the needs of college students to participate in sports activities, which is also the main problem of the construction of sports materials and culture on college campuses.

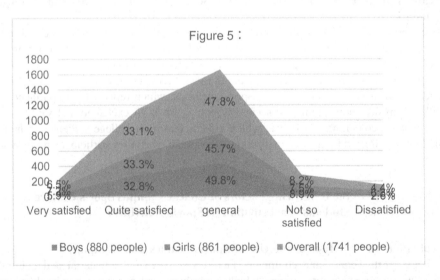

Fig. 5. Statistics on the evaluation of college students on the status quo of the use of sports venues and facilities

Evaluation and Analysis of the Current Status of Physical Education Teaching
As can be seen from Fig. 6, the total number of university students who are very satisfied and satisfied with the evaluation of physical education in colleges and universities is 1449, accounting for 83.2% of the total. This shows that the majority of university students have a higher evaluation of physical education, and physical education in colleges and universities pays more attention to stay student-oriented, curriculum and teaching process more in line with college students' sports psychology and physical activity participation needs. It can also be seen from Fig. 6 that 35.9% of male students are very satisfied with the teaching of physical education courses and 26.7% of female students. The ratio of male students is significantly higher than that of female students. In comparison, male students are more likely to accept physical education.

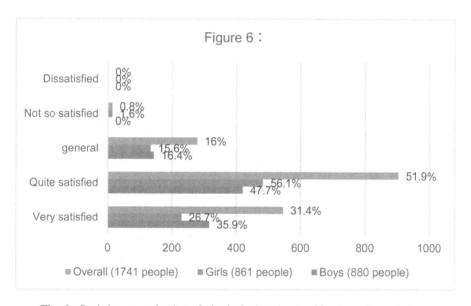

Fig. 6. Statistics on evaluation of physical education teaching by college students

Evaluation and Analysis of Extracurricular Sports Activities and the Development of Sports Clubs
The development of extracurricular sports activities and sports clubs is an effective supplement to the teaching of physical education in colleges and universities. Extracurricular sports activities can give full play to the fitness and entertainment characteristics of sports. As a "second classroom", sports clubs can effectively mobilize the enthusiasm of college students to participate sports activities on their initiative, which can become an effective way for college students to adjust their nervous learning state and increase their interest in participating in sports activities. It can be seen from Fig. 7 that they are very satisfied, relatively satisfied and generally account for 15.3%, 34% and 43.2% of the overall extracurricular sports activities, which shows that college students do not have high recognition of extracurricular sports activities. How to play extracurricular activities' positive role in sports activities is also a problem to be solved

in campus sports culture. Very satisfied, relatively satisfied and general accounted for 13.7%, 22.3% and 52.4% of the total for sports clubs, which shows that with its current organizational form, content of activities and development methods, the existing sports clubs have not mobilized college students' interest of participating in activities. Most college students will not choose to participate in the activities of sports clubs. College sports clubs are the "second classroom" for college students' sports learning and communication. How to effectively manage and cultivate college sports clubs is also a problem that needs attention.

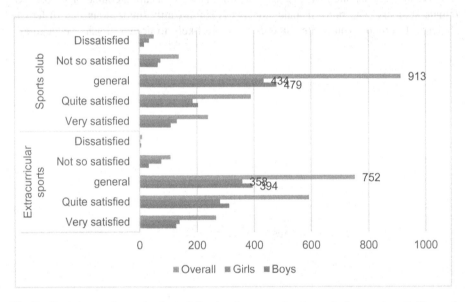

Fig. 7. Statistics on the evaluation of the development of extracurricular sports activities and sports associations by college students.

Evaluation and Analysis of the Current Situation of College Campus Sports Spirit Culture

The campus sports spirit culture in colleges and universities is the core of campus sports culture, with rich extension and profound connotation. Establishing a good sports spirit and cultural atmosphere has a positive effect on shaping college students' good character and will quality.

As can be seen from the survey data on college students' sports concepts in Fig. 8, the overall sports concepts of college students are correct, but most of them recognize that sports are of health and entertainment functions, which are the apparent functions, but they failed to recognize the deep-seated connotation of sports, such as personality training, interpersonal communication and the development of intelligence.

As can be seen from the survey data on the sports behaviors of college students in Fig. 9, 28.6% often participate in physical exercise, and 52.8% of college students only occasionally participate in physical exercise. Of these three aspects of often paying attention to sports news, watching sports events and reading sports books and

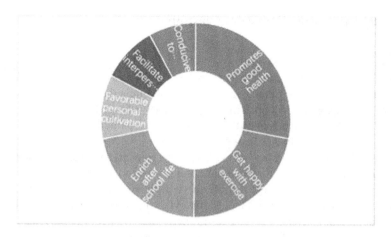

Fig. 8. Statistics of college students' sports concepts (overall proportion).

periodicals, 37.6% students often pay attention to sports news, which is significantly higher than the other two aspects. In general, most college students have not formed good habits of consciously participating in physical exercise, and have not yet formed a relatively stable fashion of sports behavior.

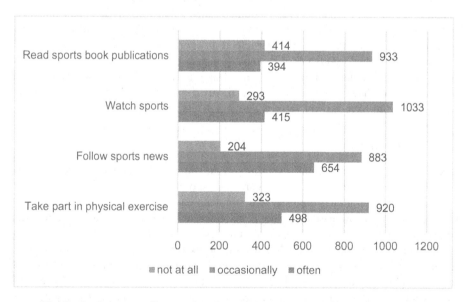

Fig. 9. Statistics on college students' sports behavior trends (overall proportion).

4 Conclusions and Recommendations

4.1 Conclusion

The proportion of college students participating in physical exercise is not ideal. The gender of college students differs significantly in the time they participate in physical exercise. The proportion of short-term physical exercise for girls is significantly higher than that of boys, and the number of male students who participate in physical exercise for a long time is much higher than girls.

In the selection of sports activities for college students, male students are mainly engaged in ball sports with a large amount of exercise and strong confrontation, while female students choose light and flexible sports with weak confrontation for exercise. Among all the female college students surveyed, the three sports options are table tennis, badminton, and running. This also reflects that most college students prefer to choose sports activities of moderate exercise intensity, strong interaction, and less requirements for venues and sports equipment.

College students are not very satisfied with the sports grounds and facilities, and most college students still prefer to choose outdoor sports venues for physical exercise. In the form of physical exercise participation, they mainly work with their classmates. Girls are more willing to participate in physical exercises in classes or organizations than boys.

The recognition of extracurricular sports activities by college students is not high. Existing sports clubs have not fully mobilized their interest in participating in sports activities in terms of organization form, content and development methods. Most college students will not choose to participate in sports club activities.

College students' sports concepts mostly focus on superficial cognition of sports health and entertainment, while ignoring the deeper meaning of sports. In general, most college students have not formed a good habit of participating in physical exercise consciously, and have not yet formed a relatively stable fashion of sports behavior.

4.2 Recommendation

Stadiums and facilities are the material carriers for college physical education and college students to participate in extracurricular sports activities. Differences in sports materials and cultural environments will stimulate the interest and enthusiasm of college students in participating in sports activities and meet the needs of individual college students. Therefore, colleges and universities should increase their investment in stadiums and facilities, make full use of the existing campus space and material resources, rationally arrange and allocate sports venues and facilities, increase and improve sports venues and facilities, improve the utilization rate of stadiums and gymnasiums, create a good sports environment, and provide material guarantee for improving the quality of physical education courses in colleges and universities and promoting the construction and inheritance of campus sports culture.

The teaching of college physical education courses is the core work of college physical education and the basic path of the construction and spread of college campus sports culture. Improving the teaching quality of college physical education courses is also the foundation of college campus sports culture construction. Therefore, it is necessary to focus on deepening the reform of physical education in colleges and universities, and strengthen the teaching of college students' basic knowledge, principles and methods of sports, sports hygiene and health care, human sports anatomy and sports injuries, and sports appreciation, so that college students in the systematic and standardized physical education process, can integrate the learned sports-related knowledge and the basic skills of physical education, and combine physical and mental pleasure in the individual participation of college students physical activities, so as to continuously increase the active participation in physical activities, gradually develop good habits of physical exercise to achieve the purpose of lifelong sports.

Extracurricular sports activities and sports clubs are part of the campus sports culture of colleges and universities, which not only enables students to exercise in sports practice and social adaptability, but also improves students' physical fitness and health. In view of the current situation of extracurricular sports activities, a variety of extracurricular sports activities including national sports, leisure sports, competitive sports, health care sports, etc. should be set up, and stadiums and equipment facilities and tutors should be regularly arranged to guide college students to participate in different extracurricular sports activities. Sports clubs, as a student sports organization participated voluntarily by college students, with the main purpose of fitness and entertainment, their learning and activities are more attractive to the student community. Therefore, the interest and hobbies of college students in sports should be fully considered, and the scientific guide and standardized management of sports clubs should be strengthened, to create a good sports space for college students, to promote the exchange between sports clubs inside and outside the school, and to enable college students to carry out sports activities independently in sports clubs, and gradually form a healthy lifestyle.

The cultivation of campus sports spirit culture in colleges and universities is an important content of campus culture construction in colleges and universities, and is also one of the important goals. The participation of college students in physical activities can enhance physical fitness and build the quality of will, and more importantly, it can cultivate the character of students and spread the spirit of sports. Therefore, we should focus on guiding college students to establish correct sports concepts and sports awareness, from simple physical enhancement to coordinated physical and mental development, from the transfer of skills to training physical fitness ability. At the same time, we must be good at using the new media environment, creating a more active sports culture atmosphere, and exerting the role of the campus network, campus broadcasting and other media, so that college students can obtain sports humanities knowledge, sports news and event information. Regularly carry out sports knowledge lectures, enrich the content of campus sports events, strengthen the exchange of sports events inside and outside the school, improve the sports cultural literacy of college students, and then translate into interest and motivation for sports activities participation, which has a positive significance for promoting the construction of college campus sports culture.

References

1. Yang, L., Chen, H., Wang, W., Song, J.: The guarantee mechanism of college sports culture education. J. Phys. Educ. (03) (2016)
2. Cai, S.: The construction of college campus sports culture under the new normal. J. Suzhou Univ. (03) (2016)
3. Mao, X.: A survey of the current status of college campus sports culture. Educ. Theory Pract. (33) (2012)
4. Wang, T.: Analysis of the function and development of college campus sports culture. Soc. Sci. (S1) (2012)
5. Liu, S.: Research on the construction of college campus sports culture. Soc. Sci. Forum (08) (2012)
6. Yan, Y.: The construction of the evaluation index system for the construction of sports culture in colleges and universities in China. Bull. Sports Sci. Technol. (07) (2012)
7. Wang, W.: Research on the construction of college sports culture. J. Beijing Printing Univ. (05) (2010)
8. Gu, C., He, W., Hu, B.: The status quo and countermeasures of the construction of campus sports culture in colleges and universities in China. J. Chengdu Sport Univ. (08) (2010)
9. Gu, C., Wu, H., Xiao, B., He, W.: Study on the campus sports culture index system of colleges and universities in China. Sports Sci. (08) (2010)

Group Movement of Multi-agent Systems with Diverse Delays

Yize Yang[1,2] (ID), Hongyong Yang[1(✉)] (ID), Fei Liu[1] (ID), and Li Liu[1] (ID)

[1] School of Information and Electrical Engineering, Ludong University,
Yantai 264025, People's Republic of China
yangyz1994@126.com, hyyang@yeah.net
[2] School of Electrical and Electronic Engineering, University of Adelaide,
Adelaide, Australia

Abstract. Wireless sensor network, which is an important part of Cyber-physical systems, has been widely applied in the fields of artificial intelligence. However, there exist communication delays between nodes in wireless communication network, which may reduce the performance and stability of the network. In this paper, we study cooperative control of multi-agent dynamical systems with communication delays. With the hypothesis of multiple agents groups, we propose group cooperative algorithm of multi-agent systems with diverse delays. By applying generalized Nyquist criterion, we analyze the group consensus of multi-agent systems with fixed coupling weights and obtain convergence condition of group movement, which is an upper value of the communication delays, to ensue the group consensus of dynamical systems. Finally, a simulation example illustrates the effectiveness of the results.

Keywords: Multi-agent systems · Group consensus · Diverse delays · Convergence condition

1 Introduction

Motivated by the distributed mobile autonomous agents, the cooperative control problem for multi-agent systems has attracted more and more research recently ([1–6], and their references). Consensus of multi-agent systems means multiple agents reach an agreement behavior by means of adjusting their moving states. The cooperation technologies of multi-agent systems have been applied in many areas including formation control of mobile robots, flocking movement of unmanned air vehicles, cooperative working of autonomous underwater vehicles, and so on.

The work is supported by the National Natural Science Foundation of China (61673200, 61771231), the Major Basic Research Project of Natural Science Foundation of Shandong Province of China (ZR2018ZC0438) and the Key Research and Development Program of YantaiCityof China (2019XDHZ085).

X. Chen et al. (Eds.): ML4CS 2020, LNCS 12487, pp. 137–146, 2020.
https://doi.org/10.1007/978-3-030-62460-6_13

Since the complexity of actual network puts forward high requirements for distributed systems, many researches focus on the group movement of multi-agent systems. The group consensus of multi-agent systems is a control strategy based on the cooperation and competition mechanism. Supposing the multiple agents are cut apart many groups, the convergence of the agents in the same group is achieved by designing the communication protocol, while the agents in different group converge to different states. In [7], group consensus algorithms of multi-agent systems are studied on preference relations. In [8], the heterogeneous agents with parametric uncertainties are investigated by the Euler-Lagrange model. By discussing the effect of coupling strength among agents in two group, group consensus of multi-agent systems is analyzed in [9]. Group consensus problem of multi-agent systems with discontinuous information transmissions and switching topologies is studied in [10,11], respectively.

When the information is transmitted in network, there are usually communication delays between the nodes in reality. Since communication delays may reduce the performance and stability of the network, the cooperation of multi-agent systems will be effected by the communication delays [12–14]. In [15,16], group consensus for second-order multi-agent systems with time delays is studied. Group consensus in multi-agent systems with switching topologies and communication delays are investigated in [17–19] respectively. Although delay problems of control systems have been extensively studied in classic control theory [20–22], there are a few reports on the delays group consensus problems up to now, to our knowledge.

However, most studies of the delayed consensus algorithms are on the hypothesis of same delays in network, and rarely a few results of the consensus problems with diverse delays are reported. In this paper, we present a consensus algorithms with multiple group agents. Based on the frequency-domain analysis, the group consensus algorithm with diverse communication delays is studied, and decentralized consensus condition is obtained for the multi-agent systems with coupling weights.

The rest of this paper is organized as follows. Some preliminaries are introduced in Sect. 2. In Sect. 3, we propose a group consensus algorithm with different communication delays. The main result for the group consensus of the delayed multi-agent systems is obtained in Sect. 4. In Sect. 5, an example is applied to illustrate the design scheme of the communication delays on the theoretical results. Finally, conclusions are drawn in Sect. 6.

2 Preliminaries

Assuming the agents communicate with each other through the sensor, a network topology can be made with bidirectional communication. Three tuple $\mathcal{G} = \{V, E, A\}$ is use to describe a weighted directed graph with a set of vertices $V = \{v_1, v_2, ..., v_n\}$, a set of edges $E \subseteq V \times V$ and an adjacency matrix $A = [a_{ij}] \in R^{n \times n}$. An edge of the weighted diagraph $\mathcal{G}$ is denoted by $e_{ij} = (v_i, v_j) \in E$. The adjacency element satisfies $a_{ij} \neq 0$ when $e_{ij} \in E$; otherwise, $a_{ij} = 0$. The set of neighbors of node i is denoted by $N_i = \{j : a_{ij} \neq 0\}$.

Let $\mathcal{G}$ be a weighted directed graph without self-loops, i.e., $a_{ii} = 0$, matrix D be the diagonal matrix with the elements d_i along the diagonal, where $d_i = \sum_{j=1}^{n} a_{ij}$ is the out-degree of the node i. The Laplacian matrix of the graph is defined as $L = D - A$.

For any node i and j, if there are a set of nodes $\{k_1, k_2, ...k_l\}$ satisfying $a_{ik_1} > 0$, $a_{k_1 k_2} > 0$, ..., $a_{k_l j} > 0$, node j is said to be reachable from i. If node i is reachable from every other node in the digraph, it is said to be globally reachable.

3   Group Consensus Algorithm of Delayed Multi-agent Systems

In this section, we discuss the group movement of multi-agent dynamical systems with diverse delays. Assume the dynamic equation of the system, for $i = 1, 2, ..., n$

$$\dot{x}_i(t) = u_i(t), \tag{1}$$

where $x_i \in R$ and $u_i \in R$ are the position and velocity, respectively, of agent i. Suppose multiple agents are composed of two group with vertices sets V_1 and V_2 in graph $\mathcal{G}$, where $V_1 \cup V_2 = V$ and $V_1 \cap V_2 = \Phi$. If the node $v_i, v_j \in V_k, k = 1, 2$, it is defined as $\hat{i} = \hat{j}$; otherwise, $\hat{i} \neq \hat{j}$. If for any initial condition $x(0) = [x_1(0), ..., x_n(0)]$ of the system (1), there are $\lim_{t \to \infty} |x_i(t) - x_j(t)| = 0$ for $\hat{i} = \hat{j}$ and $\lim_{t \to \infty} |x_i(t) - x_j(t)| > 0$ for $\hat{i} \neq \hat{j}$, it is said the multi-agent systems (1) will be reach group consensus asymptotically.

In order to achieve the group consensus, the group movement protocol for multi-agent systems will be proposed as following:

$$u_i(t) = \kappa_i \left(\sum_{j=1}^{n} a_{ij}(x_j(t) - x_i(t)) \right), \tag{2}$$

where control gains $\kappa_i \in R$ are positive constants.

Assumption 1. There are a balance of effect between the subgraph V_1 and V_2, i.e., $\sum_{j \in V_2} a_{ij} = 0$ for $i \in V_1$ and $\sum_{j \in V_1} a_{ij} = 0$ for $i \in V_2$.

Based on the Assumption 1, the control protocol can be rewritten as

$$u_i(t) = \begin{cases} \kappa_i \left(\sum_{j \in V_1} a_{ij}(x_j(t) - x_i(t)) \right) + \kappa_i \sum_{j \in V_2} a_{ij} x_j(t), \forall i \in V_1, \\ \kappa_i \left(\sum_{j \in V_2} a_{ij}(x_j(t) - x_i(t)) \right) + \kappa_i \sum_{j \in V_1} a_{ij} x_j(t), \forall i \in V_2 \end{cases} \tag{3}$$

Suppose there are communication delays in multi-agent systems, where T_i is used to denote the delay at agent i which is different with other agent. When each agent is subject to a communication delay T_i, the system (1) can be described as

$$\dot{x}_i(t) = u_i(t - T_i), i = 1, ..., n. \tag{4}$$

then, the group movement protocol for multi-agent systems with diverse communication delays becomes

$$u_i(t - T_i) = \begin{cases} \kappa_i \left(\sum_{j \in V_1} a_{ij}(x_j(t - T_i) - x_i(t - T_i)) \right) \\ \quad + \kappa_i \sum_{j \in V_2} a_{ij} x_j(t - T_i), \forall i \in V_1, \\ \kappa_i \left(\sum_{j \in V_2} a_{ij}(x_j(t - T_i) - x_i(t - T_i)) \right) \\ \quad + \kappa_i \sum_{j \in V_1} a_{ij} x_j(t - T_i), \forall i \in V_2 \end{cases} \tag{5}$$

In this paper, we study the group consensus algorithm of the multi-agent systems (4) with diverse delays in the weighted network.

Lemma 1 [23]. Assume the interconnection topology graph of n agents in system (4) has a globally reachable node. Then, the matrix L has one zero eigenvalue and $1_n = [1, ..., 1]^T$ is the corresponding right eigenvector, where L is the Laplacian matrix of the interconnection topology of n agents.

Corollary 1. Assume the interconnection topology graph of n agents in system (4) is composed of two group, there is a globally reachable node in each group. With the help of Assumption 1, the matrix L has two zero eigenvalue, $1_n = a[1, ..., 1, 0, ..., 0]^T + b[0, ..., 0, -1, ..., -1]^T$ is the corresponding right eigenvector, where L is the Laplacian matrix, a and b is any real number.

4   Group Consensus of Multi-agent Systems with Heterogenous Delays

In this section, we will discuss the group consensus of the delayed multi-agent systems. Now, we analyze the consensus condition of the multi-agent systems (4) with heterogenous delays. The system (4) can be rewritten as

$$x_i(t) = \begin{cases} \kappa_i \left(\sum_{j \in V_1} a_{ij}(x_j(t - T_i) - x_i(t - T_i)) \right) \\ \quad + \kappa_i \sum_{j \in V_2} a_{ij} x_j(t - T_i), \forall i \in V_1, \\ \kappa_i \left(\sum_{j \in V_2} a_{ij}(x_j(t - T_i) - x_i(t - T_i)) \right) \\ \quad + \kappa_i \sum_{j \in V_1} a_{ij} x_j(t - T_i), \forall i \in V_2 \end{cases} \tag{6}$$

Assumption 2. Suppose the nodes of the graph $\mathcal{G}$ are composed of two group V_1 and V_2, the subgraph $\mathcal{G}_1$ constituted by V_1 and the subgraph $\mathcal{G}_2$ constituted by V_2 have a globally reachable node, respectively.

Theorem 1. Based on Assumption 1 and Assumption 2, the multi-agent systems (6) with heterogenous delays can reach the group consensus asymptotically, if the following equation is satisfied

$$2\kappa_i T_i < \pi/\lambda_{max}, \tag{7}$$

where λ_{max} is the maximum eigenvalue of the matrix L.

Proof. Applying the Laplace transform, we get

$$sX_i(s) - X_i(0) = \begin{cases} \kappa_i \left(\sum_{j \in V_1} a_{ij}(e^{-sT_i}X_j(s) - e^{-sT_i}X_i(s)) \right) \\ + \kappa_i \sum_{j \in V_2} a_{ij}e^{-sT_i}X_j(s), \forall i \in V_1, \\ \kappa_i \left(\sum_{j \in V_2} a_{ij}(e^{-sT_i}X_j(s) - e^{-sT_i}X_i(s)) \right) \\ + \kappa_i \sum_{j \in V_1} a_{ij}e^{-sT_i}X_j(s), \forall i \in V_2 \end{cases} \tag{8}$$

where $X_i(s)$ is the Laplace transform of $x_i(t)$. Let $K = diag\{\kappa_i, i = 1, ..., n\}$, $X(s) = [X_1(s), ..., X_n(s)]^T$, we have

$$sX(s) - X(0) = -KL(s))X(s), \tag{9}$$

where $L(s) = [l_{ij}(s)]$, the elements of matrix $L(s)$ satisfy

$$l_{ij}(s) = \begin{cases} -a_{ij}e^{-sT_i}, & j \in N_i \\ \sum_{j=1}^n a_{ij}e^{-sT_i}, & j = i \\ 0, & otherwise \end{cases} \tag{10}$$

Thus, we get the characteristic equation of the system (8)

$$det(sI + KE(s)L) = 0. \tag{11}$$

where $E(s) = diag\{e^{-sT_1}, ..., e^{-sT_n}\}$.

Defining $D(s) = det(sI + KE(s)L)$, we can get $D(0) = det(KL))$ when $s = 0$. Based on Assumption 1 and Assumption 2, the bipartite graph $\mathcal{G}_1$ and $\mathcal{G}_2$ have a globally reachable node, respectively, then we obtain $D(0) = 0$ and matrix L has exactly two simple zero eigenvalues in Corollary 1.

When $s \neq 0$, let $F(s) = det(I + \frac{KE(s)L}{s})$. If we prove the zeros of $F(s)$ are on the open left complex plane, the consensus of multi-agent delayed system will be obtained. Let $C(s) = \frac{KE(s)L}{s}$, $s = j\omega$, we get

$$C(j\omega) = \frac{KE(j\omega)L}{j\omega}, \tag{12}$$

Based on the general Nyquist stability criterion [24], if the trajectory path of the eigenvalue $\lambda(C(j\omega))$ does not enclose the point $(-1, j0)$ for all $\omega \in R$, the zeros of matrix $F(s)$ lie on the open left half complex plane. Let $s = j\omega$, it has

$$C(j\omega) = H(j\omega)L, \tag{13}$$

where

$$H(j\omega) = diag\{\frac{\kappa_i}{\omega}e^{-j(\omega T_i + \pi/2)}, i = 1, ..., n\} \tag{14}$$

Let $M = diag\{\pi/(2k_iT_i), , i = 1, ..., n\}$, the matrix $MH(i\omega)$ is a diagonal matrix with the Nyquist graph line of its element passing over the point $(-1, j0)$. We have

$$\lambda(C(j\omega)) = \lambda(MH(j\omega)M^{-1}L) \in \rho(M^{-1}L) \times Co(0 \cup MH(j\omega)), \tag{15}$$

where $\rho(M^{-1}L)$ is used to express the spectral radius of matrix $M^{-1}L$, and $Co(\zeta)$ is the convex hull of ζ. Since

$$\rho(M^{-1}L) = max\{2\kappa_i T_i \lambda_i / \pi, i = 1, ..., n\}, \tag{16}$$

where λ_i is the eigenvalue of the matrix L, we can obtain from the hypothesis $2\kappa_i T_i < \pi\lambda_{max}$ that

$$\rho(M^{-1}L) < 1. \tag{17}$$

Thus $\lambda(C(j\omega))$ does not enclose the point $(-1, j0)$ for $\omega \in R$. Then the system is stable asymptotically. Based on Corollary 1, we can obtain vector $a[1, ..., 1, 0, ..., 0]^T + b[0, ..., 0, -1, ..., -1]^T$ is the eigenvector with the zero eigenvalue of matrix L. It is proved the group consensus is achieved. The proof of Theorem 1 is finished.

Remark 1. The result of Theorem 1 presents a range of time delays for the convergence of multi-agent systems with diverse delays, which can be used to design the parameter values of the system.

Corollary 2. Assume two subgraphs of multi-agent systems have a globally reachable node respectively and the communication delays is indistinctive with each agent, The multi-agent systems can reach group consensus asymptotically if

$$\kappa_i T < \frac{\pi}{2\lambda_i}. \tag{18}$$

where T is the indistinctive delay of multi-agent systems.

Proof. The process is similar to the proof of Theorem 1, we can obtain the group consensus condition in Corollary 2.

Remark 2. If the control gain $\kappa_i = 1$ and the no-subgroup, the consensus result in Corollary 2 for multi-agent systems is identical with the results in reference [4].

5   Simulation Examples

Consider multi-agent systems of 7 agents with the connected topology in Fig. 1. There are two group with group one (composed of agent 1, agent 2 and agent 3) and group two (composed of agent 4, agent 5, agent 6 and agent 7). The weights of the edges are shown in graph. Based on the config of the system, we design the control gains so that the agents converge to the leader's state asymptotically.

According to the consensus condition in Theorem 1, we can obtain the different critical values of communication delays for the different parameter κ_i (Fig. 2). From Fig. 2, when $\kappa_i = 1$ we have

$$T_i \in (0, 1.5708), \tag{19}$$

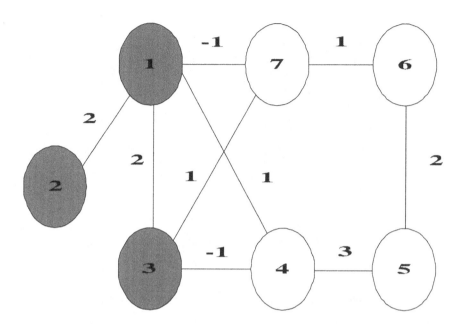

Fig. 1. Topology graph of multi-agent systems

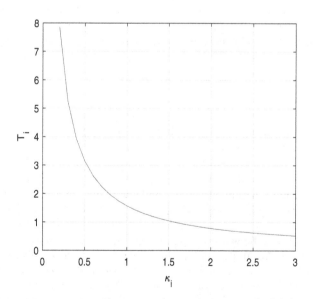

Fig. 2. Critical value of time delays for different parameter κ_i

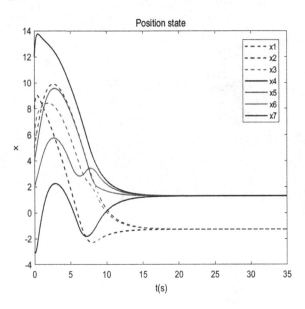

Fig. 3. Group consensus of multi-agent systems with diverse delays.

Then, we validate the group consensus condition obtained in this paper. Suppose the parameters $\kappa_i = 1$, $i = 1, ..., 7$, we select the time delays $T_1 = 0.9\,\text{s}$, $T_2 = 1.5\,\text{s}$, $T_3 = 1.2\,\text{s}$, $T_4 = 1.1\,\text{s}$, $T_5 = 1.0\,\text{s}$, $T_6 = 1.0\,\text{s}$, $T_7 = 0.8\,\text{s}$ based on the illustration in Fig. 2. Suppose the initial states generated randomly, the movement trajectory of the agents asymptotically converge to two stable states (Fig. 3). The group consensus of multi-agent systems is reached with condition of Theorem 1.

6   Conclusion

In this paper, we study group consensus of multi-agents systems with hetero-geneous communication delays. Suppose there are two group agents in the dis-tributed systems and there is a globally reachable node in every group, we ana-lyze group movement of delayed multi-agent systems and obtain a convergence consensus condition. In the future, we will focus on the optimization of group movement for heterogenous multi-agent systems time delays.

Acknowledgement. The work is supported by the National Natural Science Foun-dation of China (61673200, 61771231), the Major Basic Research Project of Natural Science Foundation of Shandong Province of China (ZR2018ZC0438) and the Key Research and Development Program of Yantai City of China(2019XDHZ085). The authors thank the anonymous reviewers for theirs valuable comments to significantly improve the quality of this paper.

References

1. Olfati-Saber, R., Fax, J.A., Murray, R.M.: Consensus and cooperation in networked multi-agent systems. Proc. IEEE **95**(1), 215–233 (2007)
2. Ren, W., Beard, R.W., Atlkins, E.: Information consensus in multivehicle cooperative control: collective group behavior through local interaction. IEEE Control Syst. Mag. **27**(2), 71–82 (2007)
3. Jadbabaie, A., Lin, J., Morse, A.S.: Coordination of groups of mobile agents using nearest neighbor rules. IEEE Trans. Autom. Control **48**(6), 988–1001 (2003)
4. Olfati-Saber, R., Murray, R.M.: Consensus problems in networks of agents with switching topology and time-delays. IEEE Trans. Autom. Control **49**(9), 1520–1533 (2004)
5. Yang, H.-Y., Zhu, X.-L., Zhang, S.-Y.: Consensus of second-order delayed multi-agent systems with leader-following. Eur. J. Control **16**(2), 188–199 (2010)
6. Yang, H.-Y., Yang, Y., Han, F., et al.: Containment control of heterogeneous fractional-order multi-agent systems. J. Franklin Inst. **356**, 752–765 (2019)
7. Xu, Z., Cai, X.: Group consensus algorithms based on preference relations. Inf. Sci. **181**(1), 150–162 (2011)
8. Hu, H.X., Yu, W., Xuan, Q., et al.: Group consensus for heterogeneous multi-agent systems with parametric uncertainties. Neurocomputing **142**(1), 383–392 (2014)
9. Gao, Y., Yu, J., Shao, J., et al.: Group consensus for multi-agent systems under the effect of coupling strength among groups. IFAC-PapersOnLine **48**(28), 449–454 (2015)
10. Hu, H.X., Yu, L., Zhang, W.A., et al.: Group consensus in multi-agent systems with hybrid protocol. J. Franklin Inst. **350**(3), 575–597 (2013)
11. Yu, J., Wang, L.: Group consensus in multi-agent systems with switching topologies. Syst. Control Lett. **59**(6), 340–348 (2010)
12. Hu, J., Hong, Y.: Leader-following coordination of multi-agent systems with coupling time delays. Phys. A **374**, 853–863 (2007)
13. Xiao, F., Wang, L.: State consensus for multi-agent systems with switching topologies and time-varying delays. Int. J. Control **52**(8), 1469–1475 (2007)
14. Yang, H., Guo, L., Zou, H.: Robust consensus of multi-agent systems with time-delays and exogenous disturbances. Int. J. Control Autom. Syst. **10**(10), 797–805 (2012)
15. Xie, D., Liang, T.: Second-order group consensus for multi-agent systems with time delays. Neurocomputing **153**, 133–139 (2015)
16. Gao, Y.L., Yu, J.Y., Shao, J.L., et al.: Group consensus for second-order discrete-time multi-agent systems with time-varying delays under switching topologies. Neurocomputing **207**, 805–812 (2016)
17. Yu, J., Wang, L.: Group consensus in multi-agent systems with switching topologies and communication delays. Syst. Control Lett. **59**, 340–348 (2010)
18. Wen, G., Yu, Y., Peng, Z., et al.: Dynamical group consensus of heterogenous multi-agent systems with input time delays. Neurocomputing **175**, 278–286 (2016)
19. Xia, H., Huang, T.Z., Shao, J.-L., et al.: Group consensus of multi-agent systems with communication delays. Neurocomputing **171**, 1666–1673 (2016)
20. Wang, F., Yang, H., Yang, Y.: Swarming movement of dynamical multi-agent systems with sampling control and time delays. Soft Comput. **23**, 707–714 (2019)
21. Tian, Y., Liu, C.: Consensus of multi-agent systems with diverse input and communication delays. IEEE Trans. Autom. Control **53**(9), 2122–2128 (2008)

22. Yang, H., Zhang, Z., Zhang, S.: Consensus of second-order multi-agent systems with exogenous disturbances. Int. J. Robust Nonlinear Control **21**(9), 945–956 (2011)
23. Ren, W., Beard, R.W.: Distributed Consensus in Multi-Vehicle Cooperative Control: Theory and Applications. Springer, Heidelberg (2008). https://doi.org/10.1007/978-1-84800-015-5
24. Desoer, C.A., Wang, Y.T.: On the generalized Nyquist stability criterion. IEEE Trans. Autom. Control **25**(1), 187–196 (1980)

Online Task Allocation in Mobile Crowdsensing with Sweep Coverage and Stability Control

Jiaang Duan[1,3], Shasha Yang[2,3(✉)], Jianfeng Lu[1,3], Wenchao Jiang[2,3], Haibo Liu[1,3], and Shuo Zhang[1,3]

[1] Department of Computer Science and Engineering,
Zhejiang Normal University, Jinhua 321004, China
duanqz21@zjnu.edu.cn, lujianfeng@zjnu.cn,
lhbzjnu@163.com, zssdut@163.com
[2] Xingzhi College, Zhejiang Normal University, Jinhua 321004, China
yssl3910109@126.com, jiangwenchao@gdut.edu.cn
[3] School of Computer, Guangzhou University of Technology,
Guangzhou 510006, China

Abstract. Mobile crowdsensing (MCS) harnesses the sensing capabilities of sensors built into a large number of smart devices to collect and analyze data, which can be used by a large number of mobile participants to perform numerous sensing tasks. Stability control and quality coverage are two key issues in mobile crowdsensing as the platform aims to ensure the maximum benefits of the system. However, with the participant's autonomy and mobility, it is difficult to achieve the quality of coverage in a specific area for task assignment. Furthermore, the stochasticity of tasks causes the stability control being another challenge. To address these issues, in this paper, we design a sweep coverage framework in mobile crowdsensing consisting of a reward rule and a task assignment rule. We first formalize the task queue and participant coverage in the current time slot and introduce disturbance parameters to prevent tasks underflow and waste participant resources. Then, we design a Lyapunov optimization algorithm to solve the stability control and the sweep coverage, which can maintain system stability and achieve a time average social welfare within $O(1/V)$ of the optimum for a tunable parameter $V > 0$. Finally, compared to the random control algorithm and the greedy control algorithm, our algorithm is 40%–50% higher than the greedy control algorithm, and 60%–70% higher than the random control algorithm in terms of social welfare.

Keywords: Lyapunov optimization · Mobile crowdsensing · Stability control · Sweep coverage · Task allocation

This work was supported in part by the National Natural Science Foundation of China (No. 62072411, 61872323, 61751303), in part by the Social Development Project of Zhejiang Provincial Public Technology Research (No. 2017C33054), in part by the Natural Science Foundation of Guangdong Province (No. 2018A030313061), and in part by the Guangdong Science and Technology Plan (no. 2017B010124001, 201902020016, 2019B010139001).

X. Chen et al. (Eds.): ML4CS 2020, LNCS 12487, pp. 147–163, 2020.
https://doi.org/10.1007/978-3-030-62460-6_14

1 Introduction

The emergence of 4G communication has led to the growth of a new type of sensing technology based on portable mobile devices and digital signals, namely mobile crowdsensing (MCS) [1, 2]. Compared with traditional static sensor-aware networks, MCS utilizes powerful processors and sensors in a large number of mobile devices to enable the collection and processing of large-scale data without spending a lot of cost and time [3, 4]. Such a technology has become a new paradigm for pervasive sensory data collection, analysis, and exploration beyond the scale of which was previously possible, which significantly improves citizens' everyday life and provides new perspectives to smart city. Currently, a large variety of applications have been stimulated for crowdsensing, which cover many aspects of our life, such as public safety [5], intelligent traffic [6], environmental monitoring [7], etc.

To obtain high-quality sensory data, MCS requires the active participation of a large number of participants. However, for specific tasks, the quality of their sensory data in the same area at different time may be different. Hence, it is a critical issue in mobile computing to study the task allocation rules which is a coverage method that enables participants to maximize the regional needs of coverage tasks [3, 4, 8]. Compared with other coverage problems such as barrier coverage, area coverage, sweep coverage is long-term, heterogeneous, and dynamic, and it is an economical and effective choice for solving task allocation rules. Although the sweep coverage problem has always been applied in the field of wireless networks, it is mainly used to study the approximation algorithm for reducing the number of static sensors or the coverage problem [9, 10], and these methods are not suitable for the field of MCS. Consequently, sweep coverage is invaluable to study the dynamic task assignment rules in MCS.

When studying coverage problems with time-varying features in mobile crowdsensing, the system stability caused by incomplete information also needs to be considered. Due to the dynamic nature of tasks and participants, we do not know the future information about tasks and participants, where we are not sure about the tasks and participants when they will come in the next time slot. Therefore, we need to control the number of tasks that enter the system, control how tasks are allocated to participants, and control the coverage status to ensure system stability.

In this paper, we are motivated to address an online task allocation problem with sweep coverage and stability control. First, on account of the dynamic nature of tasks and participants, we introduce an indicator to represent the quality of the sweep coverage of the area. Second, we construct a location-based mobile crowdsensing model with sweep coverage quality requirements. Third, we control the stability of the system to prevent waste of resources caused by underflow of tasks without knowing the future information by using Lyapunov optimization theory. Finally, we realize the optimization of social benefits under stability control. Simulation experiments verify the stability and effectiveness of the mobile crowdsensing system. The main contributions of this article are summarized as follows.

- We design a sweep coverage framework in mobile crowdsensing consisting of a reward rule and a task assignment rule, where the reward rule for participant is designed to maintain the sustainability of the platform, and the task assignment rule that takes into account coverage quality to motivate participants to provide a high level of coverage quality.

- We construct task queues and virtual queues based on sweep coverage quality and participant budgets to solve the problem of stability control in MCS, and propose an algorithm based on Lyapunov optimization theory to control tasks entry into the system and task assignment process to control the quality of sweep coverage.
- Compared to the random control algorithm and the greedy control algorithm, experimental results show that our proposed algorithm is 60%–70% higher than the other two algorithms in terms of social welfare. Meanwhile, in terms of stability, task queue backlog is also much lower than the other two algorithms.

The rest of this article is organized as follows. Section 2 reviews previous studies related to this article. Section 3 presents a system model that includes the sweep coverage quality model and the reward rule. In Sect. 4, we formulate our queue model and propose task assignment algorithm based on Lyapunov optimization. We evaluate the performance of our algorithms in Sect. 5 and conclude this article in Sect. 6.

2 Related Work

The rise of the mobile crowdsensing paradigm has brought many mobile applications, and their research focuses on task allocation and quality requirements. Task allocation is an important research content in MCS, and researchers have paid a lot of attention in recent years.

Most literatures on multi-task allocation in MCS focus on incentive mechanisms to maximize social welfare or the security of mobile crowdsensing systems. Yucel et al. [5] proposed a task allocation method based on user satisfaction and social welfare, and proposed two heuristic algorithms. Jin et al. [6] proposed a multi-requester integration framework for a novel MCS system consisting of an incentive mechanism and data aggregation. Lin et al. [7] design an online incentive mechanism to prevent the Sybil attack for crowdsensing.

All of the above documents have designed different multi-task allocation mechanisms for different goals, but these documents have not considered the actual factor of spatio-temporal attributes. For example, considering the traffic congestion in a city, of course, it only makes sense to target the traffic conditions in a particular urban area. Wang et al. [11] proposes position perception and position diversity based on crowdsensing system to maximize task value. Yucel et al. [12] based on opportunity sensing, proposes two task allocation protocols, which can accurately measure the effectiveness of users to solve network resources when they perform tasks in specific areas. An innovative geo-social model is proposed by Cardone et al. [13] to analyze users based on different variables such as time, location, social interaction, and human activities.

Data coverage quality is a very important measure based on the spatiotemporal attribute literature, and stability control is a significant means to make the system run normally. However, these research contents are only based on spatiotemporal properties, and do not consider the quality of data coverage and system stability. Participants may 'free-riding', that is, participants choose to submit low-quality data in order to maximize personal earning. So how to assign tasks to participants to get the maximum data coverage quality is a question worth studying. However, due to the dynamic nature of participants and tasks, the quality of coverage varies with area and time. Therefore, sweep coverage is introduced into mobile crowdsensing as a coverage method, while the existing research directions on sweep coverage cannot be applied to the field of mobile crowdsensing. Liang et al. [9] studied the approximate algorithm of barrier sweep coverage and the base station distance constrained sweep coverage algorithm. Gorain et al. [10] aims to minimize the number of sensors required to solve the energy consumption problem in sweep coverage. Wang et al. [14] considered the diversity of participant types, cooperated with various participants to complete the task, and met the user's quality.

While we aim to consider the allocation between participants and tasks to meet the sweep coverage quality and maintain system stability. In summary, our work differs from them mainly in the following two aspects: First, we consider the quality of sweep coverage based on the spatiotemporal properties. Second, we consider the stability of the entire system to prevent congestion. Only when the system is running steadily can participants complete tasks in the area and provide persistent sweep coverage data.

3 System Model and Preliminary Work

3.1 System Overview

In a mobile crowdsensing platform, there is a set of tasks and several participants $W = \{1, 2, \ldots, N\}$ to complete the tasks. Participants are randomly distributed in a specified grid area, who have the sensing range centered on their respective positions that changes as the participants move in a slotted time $t \in \{0, 1, 2, \ldots, \tau, \ldots\}$. In addition, each participant i can complete at most k_i tasks within each time slot due to time and area constraints. For grid regions, we assume that these grids can be divided into k sub-regions $L = \{l_1, l_2, \ldots, l_k\}$, with different coverage quality requirements, and participants need to complete tasks to meet the coverage quality of the sub-region. The running process of the system is shown in Fig. 1. First, within a time slot τ, for a newly arrived task in the sub-region l_j, the platform needs to make a decision whether the system allows the task to enter the platform. Next, the platform needs to perform task allocation control and task coverage quality control on tasks and participants in the system. Third, participants submit task awareness data and records and the platform pays a certain amount of compensation to the participants.

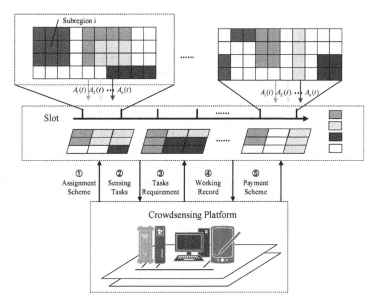

Fig. 1. Task allocation framework with participant incentive process and control process.

As a result, we can obtain a task assignment scheme for each task based on a specific optimization strategy in each slot. For ease of the following presentation, we list the notations used frequently in this article in Table 1.

Table 1. Notations of the article

Notations	Meanings
$W = \{1, 2, \ldots, n\}$	The set of participants
$L = \{l_1, l_2, \ldots, l_k\}$	The set of sub-regions
$t \in \{0, 1, 2, \ldots, \tau, \ldots\}$	The time slot
$E_i(t)$, $e_{iM}(t)$	The professional ability vector
ω, Ω_j	The reference contribution value
$a_j(t), A_j$	The number of tasks in the newly arrived sub-region, the number of tasks allowed to enter the system
$b_j(t)$	The total number of tasks assigned
Q	The sweep coverage quality of the entire target area
$R(l_k)$	The coverage of the task in the sub-area j
$c_i(t)$, B_i	The participant's cost, The participant's budget

3.2   Sweep Coverage Threshold and Quality

In this section, on account of the dynamic nature of participants and tasks, the coverage requirements of each sub-region in each time slice are also different. Consequently, we consider the sweep coverage quality of the region and give a model of the reference contribution value and sweep coverage quality details as follows:

Definition 1 (Reference Contribution Value).   The reference contribution value required for sweep coverage the sub-region can be calculated by:

$$\Omega_j = \omega_j \cdot n \tag{1}$$

where ω_j is denoted as the sweep coverage quality, and n is the number of grids.

The entire target area is divided into several **subregions** by aggregating the grids that have the same sweep coverage quality weights and are similar in spatial distances. As shown in Fig. 1, the dashed box in slot τ shows the three subregions, which are composed of three, two and four girds, respectively, whose reference contribution value required for sweep coverage in subregion are and $3\omega_1$, $2\omega_2$ and $4\omega_3$. Also, we assume that each participant has his own professional ability $E_i(t) = [e_{i1}(t), e_{i2}(t), \ldots e_{iM}(t)]$ for each regional task. For each sub-region, there is sweep coverage quality that requires participants to provide the reference contribution value to meet the requirements.

$$\overline{e_j} = \lim_{T \to \infty} \frac{1}{T} \Sigma_{t=0}^{T-1} E[\Sigma_{i \in N}(e_{ij}(t))] \geq \Omega_j$$

where $n(l_j)$ is the number of cells in the j-th task sub-region.

Definition 2 (Sweep Coverage Quality).   The sweep coverage quality of the entire target area in a time slot can be denoted as:

$$Q = \Sigma_{j=1}^{m} n(l_j) R(l_j) = \Sigma_{j=1}^{m} \frac{n(l_j) \Sigma_{i=1}^{N} e_{ij}(t)}{\Omega_j} \tag{2}$$

where $\Sigma_{j=1}^{m} n(l_j)$ is the number of grids in the entire area, and $R(l_j) = \frac{\Sigma_{i=1}^{N} e_{ij}}{\Omega_j}$ indicates the coverage ratio of the task in the sub-area j.

3.3   Social Welfare and Objective Function

As participating in the allocation, the participant inevitably incurs a cost. To motivate participants to actively participate in the task, the platform must reward the participants. In addition, each participant has a budget because it is impossible for participants to complete all the tasks. Therefore, the cost of each participant cannot exceed the budget.

Based on the above, the participant's cost to complete the task is c_{ij}, and we can derive the cost of a participant in a time slot t as:

$$c_i(t) = b_{ij}(t) c_{ij} \tag{3}$$

with the time average expected cost $\overline{c_i} = \lim_{T \to \infty} \frac{1}{T} \Sigma_{t=0}^{T-1} E[c_i(t)] \leq B_i$. Therefore, the total cost of all participants is

$$C = \Sigma_{i=1}^{n} c_i(t) = \Sigma_{i=1}^{n} b_{ij}(t) c_{ij} \tag{4}$$

Furthermore, in order to maintain the sustainability of the system and motivate participants to sense tasks in the system, the platform needs to give participants a certain reward, denoted as p_i. Therefore, the utility for all participants is

$$u^w = \Sigma_{i=1}^{N} p_i - C \tag{5}$$

In addition, the utility of the platform is:

$$u^p = Q - \sum_{i=1}^{N} p_i \tag{6}$$

Above all, we formulate Task Allocation with Sweep Coverage and Stability Control (TA-SC) problem as the following programming:

Definition 3 (The TA-SC Problem). The system wishes to maximize the social welfare under the constraints of participant's budget and ability:

$$\begin{cases} & \max \quad U \\ \text{s.t.} & \begin{cases} \overline{e_j} \geq \Omega_j, \forall j \in M \\ \overline{c_i} \leq B_i, \forall i \in N \\ b_{ij}(t) \in \{0, 1, \ldots k_i\}, \forall i \in N, j \in M \\ Q_j(t) \ is \ stable, \forall j \in M \end{cases} \end{cases} \tag{7}$$

4   Sweep Coverage-Guaranteed Online Control Framework

In this section, we will propose an algorithm based on Lyapunov optimization theory to solve the task assignment problem of mobile crowdsensing. The advantage of Lyapunov theory is that there is no need to know the future information, only the current information is used for task allocation. At the same time, the stability of the system is guaranteed.

4.1   Queue Dynamics and Lyapunov Function

Let $A_j(t)$ denote the number of tasks in the newly arrived sub-region l_j and bounded by A_j^{max}, $a_j(t)$ denote the number of tasks allowed to enter the system in the new arrival position l_j. Meanwhile, the task queue of sub-region l_j is represented by $Q_j(t)$ in time slot t. $b_{ij}(t) \in \{0, 1, \ldots, k_i\}$ indicates whether the worker i is assigned to the task t_j in the time slot t, then the total number of tasks processed can be expressed as $b_j(t) = \Sigma_{i=1}^{n} b_{ij}(t)$. Then in a time slot, the dynamic queue is:

$$Q_j(t+1) = max[Q_j(t) - b_j(t), 0] + a_j(t) \tag{8}$$

with $\{Q_j(0) = 0, \forall j \in M\}$. In this paper, we introduce the concept of stable for all queues are stable, that is, $Q_j(t)$ is stable if

$$lim_{t\to\infty} sup \frac{1}{t} \Sigma_{\tau=0}^{t-1} E\left[Q_j(t)\right] < \infty, \forall j \in M \tag{9}$$

In addition, the set of participants who choose the sensing task needs to meet the sweep coverage requirements of the sub-regions. Each sub-region has a sweep coverage requirement Ω_j. The sum of the contribution value of the participants to complete the task needs to meet the sweep coverage requirements of each sub-region, hence we maintain a virtual sweep coverage request queue $Y_j(t)$ for sub-region l_j. The queue dynamics of $Y_j(t)$ is:

$$Y_j(t+1) = max\left[Y_j(t) + e_j(t) - \Omega_j, 0\right] \tag{10}$$

Each participant i has a cost budget B_i with $\overline{c_i} \le B_i$. Hence, we need to maintain a (virtual) cost queue $Z_i(t)$ for participant. The queue dynamics of $Z_i(t)$ is:

$$Z_i(t+1) = max[Z_i(t) + c_i(t) - B_i, 0] \tag{11}$$

In each time slot, we are supposed to make the decision based on the current available information. Lyapunov optimization dispenses us with the unreliable prediction of future system state. Denote $Y(t) = \{Y_j(t) : j \in M\}, Z(t) = \{Z_i(t) : i \in N\}$, and $\Theta(t) = (Q(t); Y(t); Z(t))$.

Definition 4. Lyapunov function in terms of $\Theta(t)$.

$$L(\Theta(t)) = \frac{1}{2}||Q(t) - \theta|| + \frac{1}{2}||Y(t)|| + \frac{1}{2}||Z(t)|| = \frac{1}{2}\Sigma_{j\in M}(Q_j(t) - \theta_j)^2 + \frac{1}{2}\Sigma_{j\in M}Y_j^2(t) + \frac{1}{2}\Sigma_{i\in N}Z_i^2(t) \tag{12}$$

The smaller $L(\Theta(t))$ becomes, the more stable all actual and virtual queue are. Therefore, we define one slot (conditional) *Lyapunov drift*:

$$\Delta(\Theta(t)) = E[L(\Theta(t+1)) - L(\Theta(t))|\Theta(t)] \tag{13}$$

Then, *drift-minus-utility* is considered:

$$\Delta(\Theta(t)) - VE[U|\Theta(t)] \tag{14}$$

where $V > 0$ is an adjustable control parameter that balance the social welfare and the network stability.

Lemma 1. Drift-minus-utility $\Delta(\Theta(t)) - VE[U|\Theta(t)]$ satisfies:

$$\Delta(\Theta(t)) - VE[U|\Theta(t)] \leq D - \Sigma_{i=1}^{N}E[Z_i(t)B_i|\Theta(t)] + \Sigma_{j=1}^{M}E[Y_j(t)\Omega_j|\Theta(t)] +$$
$$\Sigma_{j=1}^{M}E[a_j(t)(Q_j(t) - \theta_j)|\Theta(t)] - \Sigma_{i=1}^{N}\Sigma_{j=1}^{M}E\{b_{ij}(t)[(Q_j(t) - \theta_j) - Z_i(t)c_{ij} -$$
$$Vc_{ij}]|\Theta(t)\} - \Sigma_{i=1}^{N}\Sigma_{j=1}^{M}E\{e_{ij}(t)[Y_j(t) + V\frac{n(l_j)}{\Omega_j}]|\Theta(t)\} \tag{15}$$

where

$$D = \tfrac{1}{2}\Sigma_{j=1}^{M}\left(max[(\Sigma_{i=1}^{N}k_i)^2, A_j^2(t)] + max\left[\Omega_j^2, 1\right]\right) + \tfrac{1}{2}\Sigma_{i=1}^{N}(max[B_i^2, (k_i \underset{j}{max}\, c_{ij})^2]).$$

Proof: First, we all know the facts that $(max[A, 0])^2 \leq A^2$ and $x \in [a, b]$, $x^2 \leq max$ $[a^2, b^2]$. According to the dynamic queue of $Q_j(t)$, we have $Q_j(t+1) = max$ $[Q_j(t) - b_j(t), 0] + a_j(t)$. Therefore,

$$\tfrac{1}{2}[(Q_j(t+1) - \theta_j)^2 - (Q_j(t) - \theta_j)^2] \leq \tfrac{1}{2}(a_j(t) - b_j(t))^2 + (Q_j(t) - \theta_j)(a_j(t) - b_j(t)) \tag{16}$$

Due to $a_j(t) \leq A_j(t)$ and $b_{jk}(t) \leq \Sigma_{i=1}^{n}k_i$, then we can get $-\Sigma_{i=1}^{n}k_i \leq a_j(t)$ $-b_j(t) \leq A_j(t)$, and square the above inequality. We have

$$max(a_j(t) - b_j(t))^2 \leq max\left[(\Sigma_{i=1}^{n}k_i)^2, A_j^2(t)\right]$$

Apart from $Q_j(t)$, we also need to calculate cost queue $Z_i(t)$ and coverage queue $Y_j(t)$. The proof process is the same as the above.

Consequently, the lemma is proved. $\square$

4.2   Design of Coverage-Guaranteed Control Algorithm

We design a Coverage-Guaranteed Control Algorithm (CGCA) for drift-minus-utility bound minimization problem based on Lyapunov optimization with the current information, that can achieve $O(\frac{1}{V})$ of the maximum social welfare. From Eq. (15), we can see that minimizing the upper bound needs to be control three modules as follows, namely task admission control, participant-task allocation control, and coverage-guaranteed control.

Task Admission Control: To refrain over-saturation in each task queue $Q_j(t)$, $a_j(t)$, with $0 \leq a_j(t) \leq A_j(t)$, is the number of tasks admitted into $Q_{jk}(t)$. Hence, minimizing the inequality in Eq. (15) is equivalent to minimize $a_{jk}(t)$:

$$min\, a_j(t)[Q_j(t) - \theta_j]$$
$$s.t.\ 0 \leq a_j(t) \leq A_j(t) \tag{17}$$

Note that the value of $a_j(t)$ depends on the current queue backlog $Q_j(t)$. Consequently, the optimal solution of $a_j(t)$ can be determined in the following way:

$$a_j(t) = \begin{cases} 0 & if \ Q_j(t) \geq \theta_j \\ A_j(t) & if \ Q_j(t) < \theta_j \end{cases} \tag{18}$$

Participant-Task Assignment Control: Due to the participants' mobility and the limitation of sensing range, each participant cannot be assigned more than k_i tasks, i.e., $\sum_{j=1}^{M} b_{ij}(t) \leq k_i$. Similar as the admission control above, maximizing the inequality in Eq. (15) is equivalent to maximize $b_{ijk}(t)$ as the following:

$$\begin{aligned} &max\{b_{ij}(t)[(Q_j - \theta_j) - Z_j(t)c_{ij} - Vc_{ij}]\} \\ &s.t. \sum_{j=1}^{M} b_{ij}(t) \leq k_i, \forall i \in N \\ &b_{ij}(t) \in \{0, 1, \ldots, k_i\}, \forall i \in N, \forall j \in M \end{aligned} \tag{19}$$

Note that Eq. (19) depends on the value of $b_{ij}(t)$, while $\sum_{j=1}^{M} b_{ij}(t) \leq k_i$, where $(Q_j - \theta_j) - Z_j(t)c_{ij} - Vc_{ij}$ can be viewed as the weight of the $b_{ij}(t)$. Therefore, CGCA uses to select the participant with the largest weight to find the optimal solution of $b_{ij}(t)$, which can be determined in the following way:

$$b_{ij}(t) = \begin{cases} k_i & if \ (Q_j - \theta_j) - Z_j(t)c_{ij} - Vc_{ij} \geq 0 \\ 0 & if \ (Q_j - \theta_j) - Z_j(t)c_{ij} - Vc_{ij} < 0 \end{cases} \tag{20}$$

Coverage-Guaranteed Control: Participants need to meet the coverage quality required by the sub-region in the coverage problem.

$$max\{e_{ij}(t)[V\frac{n(A_j)}{\Omega_j} + Y_j(t)]\} \tag{21}$$

$$s.t. \ b_{ij} \in \{0, 1, \ldots, k_i\}, i \in N, j \in M$$

As for this intuition, the participant takes a greedy strategy that ranks $e_{ij}(t)$ according to their weight as large as possible.

Queue Update: After CGCA, update $Q_j(t)$, $Y_j(t)$ and $Z_i(t)$ according to Eq. (8), Eq. (10), Eq. (11).

4.3   Performance Analysis

For CGCA, we theoretically analyzed the optimal solution of the algorithm and the boundedness of the queue, details as follows in this part:

Theorem 1 (Boundary of Queue). The backlog of task queue $Q_j(t)$ in CGCA is bounded by

$$0 \le Q_j(t) \le \theta_j + A_j^{max} \tag{22}$$

Proof: We use mathematical induction to prove the inequality. For $t = 0$, the above inequality is true:

$$0 \le Q_j(0) = 0 \le \theta_j + A_j^{max} \tag{23}$$

Note that we assume that Eq. (22) is true while $t = \tau$, which is

---
Algorithm 1 CGCA: Coverage-Guaranteed Control Algorithm.

1: **Input**: Worker $i \in W$, Subregion $j \in M$ costs c_{ij}, budgets B_i, expertise E_{ij},
   $Q_j(0) = 0, Z_i(0) = 0, Y_j(0) = 0$, A_j^{max}, k_i, Ω_j
2: **Output:** $a_j(t)$, $b_{ij}(t)$, $e_{ij}(t)$
3: **For $\tau \in t$, the platform:**
4: Admission control:
5: **If $Q_j(t) \ge \theta_j$:**
$$a_j(t) = 0$$
6: **else:**
$$a_j(t) = A_j(t)$$
7: Selection control:
8: **If $(Q_j - \theta_j) - Z_j(t)c_{ij} - Vc_{ij} \ge 0$:**
$$b_{ij}(t) = k_i$$
9: **else:**
$$b_{ij}(t) = 0$$
10 Quality control:
11: Maximizes
$$e_{ij}(t)[V \frac{n(A_j)}{\Omega_j} + Y_j(t)]$$
12: **Updates $Q_j(t)$, $Y_j(t)$ and $Z_i(t)$ according to Eq.(8), Eq.(10), Eq.(11)**

$$0 \le Q_j(\tau) \le \theta_j + A_j^{max} \tag{24}$$

Next, we will verify that Eq. (22) is true for $t = \tau + 1$. We analyze from the following two perspectives. First, with $0 \le Q_j(t)(\tau) \le \theta_j$, according to Eq. (18), we have $A_j(t)$. By substituting it into Eq. (9) yields

$$0 \le Q_j(\tau+1) \le Q_j(\tau) + A_i(\tau) \le \theta_j + A_j^{max} \tag{25}$$

Second, while $VQ \le Q_j(t) \le VQ + A_j^{max}$, according to Eq. (18), we acquire $a_j(\tau) = 0$ and $Q_i(\tau+1) \le Q_i(\tau)$. Thus,

$$0 \leq Q_j(\tau+1) \leq Q_j(\tau) \leq \theta_j + A_j^{max} \tag{26}$$

Therefore, we can conclude that Eq. (22) holds for any $\tau \in t$ and any $j \in M$.

Corollary 1. All queues are stable, that is, $Q_j(t)$ is stable with

$$\lim_{t \to \infty} \sup \frac{1}{t} \Sigma_{\tau=0}^{t-1} E[Q_j(t)] < \infty, \forall j \in M$$

Proof: Based on Eq. (22), by taking expectations of the above, summing every $\tau \in t$, dividing t, and taking $t \to \infty$, we can get:

$$0 \leq \lim_{t \to \infty} \sup \frac{1}{t} \Sigma_{\tau=0}^{t-1} E[Q_j(t)] \leq \theta_j + A_j^{max} < \infty \tag{27}$$

We can prove that all queues in the system are stable. Therefore, the entire system is also stable.

Theorem 2. The gap between the time average fair social welfare achieved by CGCA and the optimal social welfare u^* satisfies:

$$\lim_{T \to \infty} \frac{1}{T} E[U] \geq u^* - \frac{D}{V} \tag{28}$$

Proof: if we want to prove (28), we need to require the following lemma:

Lemma 2: For any arbitrarily small $\delta > 0$, there exists a stationary and randomized policies of control algorithm σ for arbitrary task queue yields:

$$E[U^\sigma(t)] \geq U^{opt} - \delta \tag{29}$$

$$E\left[a_j^\sigma(t)\right] \leq E\left[b_j^\sigma(t)\right] + \delta \tag{30}$$

This lemma derives from [15].

For every time slot t, on account of CGCA minimizing the upper bound of Eq. (15), i.e., $\Delta(\Theta(t)) - VE[U|\Theta(t)]$, $\Delta(\Theta(t)) - VE[U|\Theta(t)]$ in CGCA is smaller than that under policy σ. We acquire:

$$\Delta(\Theta(t)) - VE[U|\Theta(t)]$$
$$\leq B + E[\Sigma_{j \in M} Q_j(t)(a_j(t) - b_j(t))|\Theta(t)] + E[\Sigma_{i \in N} Z_i(t)(c_i(t)$$
$$- B_i)|\Theta(t)] + E[\Sigma_{j \in M} Y_j(t)(e_j(t) - \Omega_j)|\Theta(t)] + - VE[U(t)|\Theta(t)]$$

Now we turn to consider the Lyapunov drift at any time slot τ, and take expectations of the above to yield

$$E[L(\tau+1)] - E[L(\tau)] - VE[U(\tau)] \leq D - VU^{opt}$$

By summing up the inequality over $t = 0, 1, ..., T-1$, we can find that the intermediate terms from $t = 1, 2, ...t - 2$ are all eliminated, which yields:

$$E[L(t)] - E[L(0)] - V\sum_{t=0}^{T-1} E[P(t)] \leq T(D - VU^{opt}) \qquad (31)$$

According to $L(0) = 0$ and dividing by Vt on both sides of the Eq. (34), the following perform:

$$\frac{1}{t}\sum_{\tau=0}^{t-1} E[U(t)] \geq U^{opt} - \frac{D}{V} + \frac{E\{L(t)\}}{Vt} \geq U^{opt} - \frac{D}{V} \qquad (32)$$

Let $T \to \infty$ then $\lim_{T\to\infty} \frac{E[Y_k(T)]}{T} \to 0$, we can prove Eq. (28).

5   Performance Evaluation

In this section, we evaluate the performance of the crowdsensing system, as well as comparing the results of the proposed methods to baseline methods.

5.1   Data Set and Parameter Settings

We conduct simulation experiments in the following scenarios. The platform serves medium-sized virtual cities with a size of 1000 m × 1000 m and each grid size 50 m × 50 m. This means that the entire detection area is split into 400 grids. A total of 50 participants participate in the system. We simply define the detection area of each participant j as the circle O_j, with the center the location of j and the radius randomly picked from [40 m, 80 m]. If grid j fully covered with O_j, then $b_{ij} = 1$. Qualified expertise E_i takes values in (0.5, 1). c_i is uniformly sampled in. Budget is randomly valued in (1.0, 1.5), while constraint of limited time slot length is a random integer in [4, 6]. The reference contribution value for each sub-region area in each time slot is a random integer [500,1000]. In addition, we compare the experimental results with the following two control algorithms.

Random Algorithm (RA): In this algorithm, each participant randomly assigns tasks under restricted conditions.

Greedy Algorithm (GA): The algorithm completes the greedy strategy as much as possible in each time slot, that is, as many tasks as possible are allowed to enter the system. At the same time, each task is assigned to participants with high professional level as much as possible.

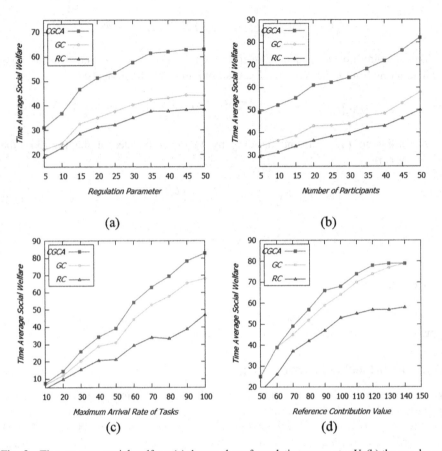

Fig. 2. Time average social welfare: (a) the number of regulation parameter V; (b) the number of participants N; (c) the maximum arrival rate of tasks; (d) the reference contribution value.

5.2 Time Average Social Welfare

We conducted four sets of experiments to verify the effect of the regulation parameter, the number of participants N, the arrival rate of tasks A^{max}, and the reference contribution value on social welfare Ω.

As shown in Fig. 2(a), we fix the number of participants $N = 50$, the maximum arrival rate of tasks $A^{max} = 100$, the reference contribution value $\Omega = 200$ and compare the time averaged social profit achieved by three algorithms as the number of V varies from 5 to 50. We can see that the time average social welfare of the CGCA algorithm and the GA and RA algorithms, from which we can find that the performance presented by the three algorithms is CGCA > GA > RA, where the CGCA algorithm is 40%–50% average higher than the greedy control algorithm and 60%–70% average higher than the random control algorithm in terms of social welfare.

In the case of Fig. 2(b), we draw the time average social welfare with the number of participants changing. We fix $V = 50, A^{max} = 100, \Omega = 200$, and compare the time averaged social welfare achieved by three algorithms as the number of participants varies from 5 to 50. We find that the time average social welfare achieved by three algorithms increases as the number of participants becomes larger on account of more participants can finish more works. While compared to the random control algorithm and the greedy control algorithm, our algorithm is 43%–46% higher than the greedy control algorithm, and 58%–62% higher than the random control algorithm in terms of social welfare.

We consider the impact of the arrival rate of tasks reached on social welfare by fixing $N = 50$, $V = 50$, and $\Omega = 100$. Vary A^{max} from 10 to 100, the time average social welfare are drawn in Fig. 2(c). We can find that when the initial task arrival rate is low, the social welfare of the three algorithms are almost the same. With the increase of the task arrival rate, the social welfare of our algorithm and the two comparison algorithms are ranked as CGCA > GA > RA.

Finally, we provide how the reference contribute value influences the social welfare. By fixing $V = 50$, $N = 50$, $A^{max} = 100$, we can see that the time average social welfare achieved by three algorithms increases as the reference contribute value becomes larger. However, when a certain value is reached, the social benefits start to grow slowly, and finally tend to be flat, because the participant resources and task resources are already insufficient.

5.3 Queue Stability

We have conducted experiments on the backlogs of task queue, cost queue, and sweep quality queue in Fig. 3. We can find that all queues are limited and maintained at a low state, that is, the entire system is stable. At the beginning of the experiment, the backlog of cost queue and sweep quality queue continue to increase, but as queue backlog continues to increase, the final queue backlog would not exceed the threshold, but tended to stabilize.

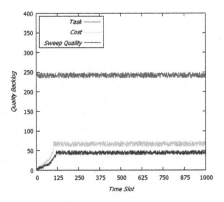

Fig. 3. Queue stability

6 Conclusion and Future Work

In this paper, we propose the sweep coverage based the mobile crowdsensing systems. We mainly consider the quality and stability control of sweep coverage in MCS, whose participants and tasks are dynamic. We use current information to solve random feature problems based on Lyapunov optimization theory, and design an algorithm for task allocation. We prove that the algorithm has strong theoretical guarantees. Performance evaluation of the simulation data sets have proved the efficiency of the system. In the future, we will consider the 'free-riding' of participants during the completion of tasks. Therefore, we need to add a certain incentive mechanism to prevent participants from 'free-riding', so that participants tend to provide high-quality services.

References

1. Wang, J., et al.: Multi-task allocation in mobile crowd sensing with individual task quality assurance. IEEE Trans. Mob. Comput. **17**(9), 2101–2113 (2018)
2. Zhang, D., Wang, L., Xiong, H., et al.: 4W1H in mobile crowdsensing. IEEE Commun. Mag. **52**(8), 42–48 (2014)
3. Gong, W., Zhang, B., Li, C.: Location-based online task assignment and path planning for mobile crowdsensing. IEEE Trans. Veh. Technol. **68**(2), 1772–1783 (2019)
4. Wu, L., Xiong, Y., Wu, M., He, Y., She, J.: A task assignment method for sweep coverage optimization based on crowdsensing. IEEE Internet Things J. **6**(6), 10686–10699 (2019)
5. Yucel, F., Bulut, E.: User satisfaction aware maximum utility task assignment in mobile crowdsensing. Comput. Netw. **172**, 107156 (2020)
6. Jin, H., Su, L., Nahrstedt, K.: CENTURION: incentivizing multi-requester mobile crowd sensing. In: Proceedings of the IEEE INFORCOM (2017)
7. Lin, J., Li, M., Yang, D., Xue, G.: Sybil-proof online incentive mechanisms for crowdsensing. In: IEEE INFOCOM 2018 - IEEE Conference on Computer Communications, Honolulu, HI, pp. 2438–2446 (2018)
8. Wang, L., Yu, Z., Zhang, D., Guo, B., Liu, C.H.: Heterogeneous multi-task assignment in mobile crowdsensing using spatiotemporal correlation. IEEE Trans. Mob. Comput. **18**(1), 84–97 (2019)
9. Liang, J., Huang, X., Zhang, Z.: Approximation algorithms for distance constraint sweep coverage with base stations. J. Comb. Optim. **37**(4), 1111–1125 (2018). https://doi.org/10.1007/s10878-018-0341-3
10. Gorain, B., Mandal, P.: Approximation algorithms for barrier sweep coverage. Int. J. Found. Comput. Sci. **30**(03), 425–448 (2019)
11. Wang, X., Jia, R., Tian, X., Gan, X.: Dynamic task assignment in crowdsensing with location awareness and location diversity. In: IEEE INFOCOM 2018 - IEEE Conference on Computer Communications, Honolulu, HI, pp. 2420–2428 (2018)
12. Yucel, F., Bulut, E.: Location-dependent task assignment for opportunistic mobile crowdsensing. In: 2020 IEEE 17th Annual Consumer Communications & Networking Conference (CCNC), pp. 1–6 (2020)
13. Cardone, G., et al.: Fostering participaction in smart cities: a geo-social crowdsensing platform. IEEE Commun. Mag. **51**(6), 112–119 (2013)

14. Wang, A., Zhang, L., Guo, L., Ren, M., Li, P., Yan, B.: A task assignment approach with maximizing user type diversity in mobile crowdsensing. In: Li, Y., Cardei, M., Huang, Y. (eds.) COCOA 2019. LNCS, vol. 11949, pp. 496–506. Springer, Cham (2019). https://doi.org/10.1007/978-3-030-36412-0_40
15. Neely, J.: Stochastic Network Optimization with Application to Communication and Queueing Systems. Morgan and Claypool Publishers, San Rafael (2010)

Max-Min Fairness Multi-task Allocation in Mobile Crowdsensing

Shasha Yang[1], Wenchao Jiang[2(✉)], Jiaang Duan[3], Zhengjie Huang[3], and Jianfeng Lu[3]

[1] Xingzhi College, Zhejiang Normal University, Jinhua 321004, China
yss13910109@126.com
[2] School of Computer, Guangdong University of Technology,
Guangzhou 510006, China
jiangwenchao@gdut.edu.cn
[3] Department of Computer Science and Engineering,
Zhejiang Normal University, Jinhua 321004, China
{duanqz21, lujianfeng}@zjnu.edu.cn,
hzj2118124379@163.com

Abstract. Mobile Crowdsensing (MCS) has become a new paradigm of collecting and merging a large number of sensory data by using rich sensor-equipped mobile terminals. Existing studies focusing on multi-task allocation with the objective of maximizing the social utility may result in the problem of unbalanced allocation due to the limited resources of workers, which may damage the social fairness, and requesters who suffer unfairness will choose to leave the system, thereby destroying the long-term stability of the system. To address this issue, we introduce max-min fairness into the design of a novel fairness-aware incentive mechanism for MCS. We first formalize the max-min fairness-aware multi-task allocation problem by using the sensing time threshold of tasks as a constraint. By modeling the max-min fairness-aware multi-task allocation problem as a Stackelberg game consisting of multi-leader and multi-follower, we next compute the unique Stackelberg equilibrium at which the utilities of both requesters and workers are maximized. Then, we design a greedy algorithm to achieve max-min fairness while meeting the sensing time threshold required by the task. Finally, simulation results further demonstrate the impact of intrinsic parameters on social utility and price of fairness, as well as the feasibility and effectiveness of our proposed max-min fairness-aware incentive mechanism.

Keywords: Mobile crowdsensing · Incentive mechanism · Multi-task allocation · Max-Min fairness · Stackelberg game

This work was supported in part by the National Natural Science Foundation of China (No. 62072411, 61872323, 61751303), in part by the Social Development Project of Zhejiang Provincial Public Technology Research (No. 2017C33054), in part by the Natural Science Foundation of Guangdong Province (No. 2018A030313061), and in part by the Guangdong Science and Technology Plan (no. 2017B010124001, 201902020016, 2019B010139001).

© Springer Nature Switzerland AG 2020
X. Chen et al. (Eds.): ML4CS 2020, LNCS 12487, pp. 164–179, 2020.
https://doi.org/10.1007/978-3-030-62460-6_15

1   Introduction

With the rapid development of sensor technology, wireless communication, and the market of handheld mobile terminal, mobile terminals have integrated rich built-in sensors including accelerometers, gyroscopes, contact image sensors, cameras, microphones, and global positioning systems (GPS), have become an interface for mobile users to obtain important information such as the surrounding environment, which has catalyzed and evolved mobile crowdsensing (MCS) [1]. MCS uses handheld mobile terminals carried by ubiquitous mobile users to collect and merge sensory data [2, 3], a series of research results have been achieved in the fields of communication (WiFi-Scout [4]), environmental monitoring (Third-Eye [5],Creekwatch [6]), traffic conditions (Vtrack [7], ContriSense: Bus [8]), and health caring (HealthAware [9]).

The success of MCS often depends on the active participation of a large number of workers and high quality of sensory data contributed by them. However, collecting sensory data often consumes a high cost in terms of resource consumption and even exposes workers to potential privacy risks, which greatly inhibits the enthusiasm of workers [10]. Meanwhile, with the development of MCS, tasks continue to emerge, and worker resources are relatively limited and it is difficult to grow simultaneously. In the multi-task allocation for the purpose of maximizing social utility, strategic workers will give priority to tasks with high rewards in the worker-centric model, while the platform will give priority to assigning highly capable and reliable workers to tasks with high value in the requester-centric model. The unbalanced allocation of heterogeneous worker resources will widen the gap in utility between requesters, and thus leading to unfair resource allocation. Requesters who suffer unfairness will choose to leave the system, thereby destroying the long-term stability of the system. Therefore, considering social fairness from the perspective of requesters' utility distribution is an important issue to be solved urgently for multi-task allocation in MCS.

In the literature, many efforts with social fairness have been devoted to incentivizing users in MCS. Huang et al. [11] focused on the crowdsensing task assignment problem with multiple data consumers, and proposed an auction mechanism which can achieve max-min fairness and the essential economic properties, such as truthfulness, individual rationality and budget balance. Li et al. [12] designed the framework for publishing tasks based on decoy effect mechanism on the platform side, and the payoff allocation based on fairness preference mechanism for the user side, respectively, which can increase the utility of the platform and the users. However, in addition to classic fairness concepts, most of the existing literatures combine the system model to define the special fairness concept. By considering the effects of malicious competition behavior and the "free-riding" phenomenon, Zhu et al. [13] proposed incentive mechanism based on an auction combining the concepts of reverse auctions and Vickrey auctions, which can effectively improve fairness of the bidding and the quality of the sensory data. Tao et al. [14] used Jain's fairness index to evaluate the fairness of tasks, which measures whether tasks receive a fair share of system resources. And the maximum value **1** of Jain's fairness index is achieved when all tasks receive the same number of data samples. Sooksatra et al. [15] considered multi-dimensional fairness while selecting winning providers, and designed a fairness-aware auction mechanism to incentive users to stay in the system in a long run. Unfortunately, the above literature lacks indicators such as price of fairness to measure social fairness and social utility are usually based on empirical models without accurate mathematical models to formulate and quantify the fairness, and some fairness concepts are difficult to apply directly to the general MCS system. In contrast, we initiate the study of strategy-proof and fairness-aware incentive mechanism for multi-task allocation in MCS for the first time, and show that our mechanism maintains max-min fairness at a low cost.

Our main contributions are summarized as follows:

- We introduce the concept of max-min fairness, and formalize the max-min fairness-aware multi-task allocation problem by taking into account the sensing time threshold of tasks.
- We model the multi-task allocation as a Stackelberg game consisting of multi-requester and multi-worker, and then transform the max-min fairness-aware multi-task allocation problem into the max-min fairness-aware incentive mechanism design problem.
- We show how to compute the unique Stackelberg equilibrium, consisting of a unique Nash equilibrium for the sensing plan game and a unique Nash equilibrium for the reward declaration game, at which the utilities of both requesters and workers are maximized.
- We design a greedy algorithm to achieve max-min fairness while meeting the sensing time threshold required by the task. Simulation results further demonstrate how intrinsic parameters impact on the social utility, and the price of fairness.

In the rest of this article, we first introduce the preliminaries and formulate the problem in Sect. 2, and develop a max-min fairness-aware incentive mechanism as well as the design details of our mechanism in Sect. 3. Section 4 evaluates the performance, and conclusions are drawn in Sect. 5.

2 Preliminaries and Problem Formulation

2.1 System Model

Multi-task allocation is a MCS framework consisting of a platform, a set $W = \{w_1, \ldots, w_i, \ldots, w_n\}$ of workers, and a set $\mathcal{R} = \{r_1, \ldots, r_j, \ldots, r_m\}$ of requesters. Taking into account the practical factors (e.g., time, location, effort, etc.), without loss of generality, a worker (or requester) is usually assumed to be able to participate in (or publicize) only one task. It is easy to find that this paper is not limited to this assumption, when a worker (or requester) chooses to participate in (or publicize) multiple tasks, we simply treat her as multiple workers (or requesters). As illustrated in Fig. 1, a typical transaction of multi-task allocation in MCS can be described as follows: First, each requester r_j posts a task τ_j with its budget B_j, unit value κ_j, and sensing time threshold V_j, which are sent to the platform (step 1). The platform collects and publishes the set $T = \{\tau_1, \ldots, \tau_j, \ldots, \tau_m\}$, $B = \{B_1, \ldots, B_j, \ldots, B_m\}$ as well as $K = \{\kappa_1, \ldots, \kappa_j, \ldots, \kappa_m\}$ of tasks (step 2). After reading the description of tasks, each worker w_i submits a set Γ_i of tasks that she is interested and her unit cost c_i to the platform (step 3). After collecting the workers' unit cost set $C = \{c_1, \ldots, c_i, \ldots, c_n\}$, the tasks' unit value set K and sensing time threshold set V, the platform will decide each task is allocated to which users, and the winning workers set for each task τ_j is denoted as S_j (step 4). Then each worker $w_i \in S_j$ determines her sensing time t_{ij}, uploads the sensory data to the platform and gets the payment from the platform as her reward (step 6). Conveniently, Table 1 lists frequently used notions in this paper.

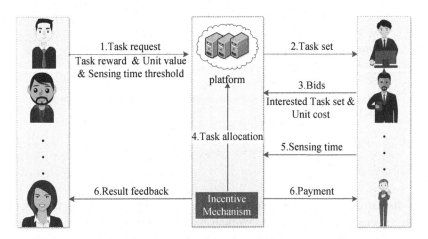

Fig. 1. Framework of multi-task allocation in mobile crowdsensing

Each rational and selfish worker will not participate in a task unless there exists a sufficient payment to compensate for her cost. Given the budget B_j and the winning workers set S_j for task τ_j, as well as the unit cost c_i, the worker w_i is only interested in maximizing her own utility by making her optimal sensing time t_{ij}.

Definition 1 (Worker's Utility). *A worker $w_i's$ utility u_i^w is defined as*

$$u_i^w = \begin{cases} p_{ij}(B_j, T_j) - c_i t_{ij}, & \text{if } w_i \in S_j \text{ and } t_{ij} \neq 0 \\ 0, & \text{otherwise} \end{cases} \tag{1}$$

Where $c_i t_{ij}$ is the total cost of w_i performing the task τ_j, t_{-ij} is the sensing time strategy profile for a set S_j excluding w_i, and thus the set of sensing time strategy profile of all workers in S_j can be written as $T_j = (t_{ij}, t_{-ij})$. The reward received by worker w_i is proportional to her sensing time t_{ij}, $p_{ij}(B_j, T_j)$ based on the task $\tau_j's$ budget B_j and the sensing time strategy profile T_j is defined as

$$p_{ij}(B_j, T_j) = B_j \times \frac{t_{ij}}{\sum_{x:w_x \in S_j} t_{xj}} \tag{2}$$

Substituting (2) into (1), a worker $w_i's$ utility u_i^w can be rewritten as

Table 1. Summary of notations in this paper.

Variable	Description
$r_j, \mathcal{R}$	j_{th} requesters, $\mathcal{R} = \{r_1, \ldots, r_j, \ldots, r_m\}$
$\tau_j, \mathcal{T}$	j_{th} task, $\mathcal{T} = \{\tau_1, \ldots, \tau_j, \ldots, \tau_m\}$
κ_j, K	Unit value of τ_j, $\mathrm{K} = \{\kappa_1, \ldots, \kappa_j, \ldots, \kappa_m\}$
B_j, B	Budget of τ_j, $B = \{B_1, \ldots, B_j, \ldots, B_m\}$
V_j, V	Sensing time threshold of τ_j, $V = \{V_1, \ldots, V_j, \ldots, V_m\}$
$w_i, \mathcal{W}$	i_{th} worker, $\mathcal{W} = \{w_1, \ldots, w_i, \ldots, w_n\}$
Γ_i, Γ	Interested task set of w_i, $\Gamma = \{\Gamma_1, \ldots, \Gamma_i, \ldots, \Gamma_n\}$
$c_i, \mathcal{C}$	Cost of w_i, $\mathcal{C} = \{c_1, \ldots, c_i, \ldots, c_n\}$
$\mathcal{S}_j$	Winning worker set of τ_j
t_{ij}, t_{-ij}	Sensing time of w_i when she participated in τ_j, sensing time profile for τ_j excluding w_i

$$u_i^w = \begin{cases} B_j \times \dfrac{t_{ij}}{\sum_{x:w_x \in \mathcal{S}_j} t_{xj}} - c_i t_{ij}, & \text{if } w_i \in \mathcal{S}_j \text{ and } t_{ij} \neq 0 \\ 0, & \text{otherwise} \end{cases} \tag{3}$$

At the requester side, a requester r_j will receive a service benefit as long as there exists a non-empty set $\mathcal{S}_j$ of workers participating in her publicized task τ_j, and the total sensing time is not lower than the threshold V_j. The service benefit $b_j(\kappa_j, T_j)$ based on the task τ_j's unit value κ_j and the sensing time strategy profile T_j is defined as

$$b_j(\kappa_j, T_j) = \begin{cases} \left(\kappa_j \sum_{x:w_x \in \mathcal{S}_j} t_{xj} \right)^\theta, & \text{if } \mathcal{S}_j \neq \varnothing \text{ and } \sum_{x:w_x \in \mathcal{S}_j} t_{xj} \geq V_j \\ 0, & \text{otherwise} \end{cases} \tag{4}$$

Definition 2 (Requester's Utility). *A requester r_j's utility u_j^r is defined as*

$$u_j^r = \begin{cases} \left(\kappa_j \sum_{x:w_x \in \mathcal{S}_j} t_{xj} \right)^\theta - B_j, & \text{if } \mathcal{S}_j \neq \varnothing \text{ and } \sum_{x:w_x \in \mathcal{S}_j} t_{xj} \geq V_j \\ -B_j, & \text{otherwise} \end{cases} \tag{5}$$

where the range of $\theta \in (0, 1)$ makes u_j^r a strictly concave function in $\sum_{x:w_x \in \mathcal{S}_j} t_{xj}$, which reflects the common phenomenon of diminishing marginal utility in economics.

2.2 Max-Min Fairness-Aware Multi-task Allocation Problem

We consider the multi-task allocation in MCS as a general resource allocation problem assigning different quantities of the given workers to different tasks. Formally, such a problem is given for a set of m tasks $\mathcal{T} = \{\tau_1, \ldots, \tau_j, \ldots, \tau_m\}$, and defined by the set of all feasible solution X, i.e., allocations and m utility functions $u_j : X \to R^+$ for each requester r_j. Note that, χ_1 and χ_2 will be regarded as equivalent if $u_j(\chi_1) = u_j(\chi_2), \forall j : r_j \in \mathcal{R}$.

Definition 3 *(Max-Min Fairness). A solution χ_{MM} is max-min fairness if the requester obtaining the lowest utility, still receives the highest possible utility.*

$$\chi_{MM} = arg \max_{\chi \in X} \min_{j=1,\ldots,m} u_j(\chi) \qquad (6)$$

Given the definition of max-min fairness, we now study the multi-task allocation problem, that is, the platform, as a decision maker, allocates which workers to which task in a balanced way under the constraint of sensing time threshold to balance the utilities of requesters, such a problem can formulated as follows:

Definition 4 *(MMFMTA). The max-min fairness-aware multi-task allocation problem can be formulated as follows:*

$$\begin{cases} \chi_{MM} = arg \max_{\chi \in X} \min_{j=1,\ldots,m} u_j(\chi) \\ s.t. \sum_{x:w_x \in \mathcal{S}_j} t_{xj} \geq V_j, \forall j : r_j \in \mathcal{R} \end{cases} \qquad (7)$$

3 Max-Min Fairness-Aware Incentive Mechanism

We model the interaction between requesters and workers as a two-stage Stackelberg game consisting of multi-requester and multi-worker. In the first stage, a requester r_j's strategy is her budget B_j. After the platform allocates the winning worker set $\mathcal{S}_j$ to the task τ_j, in the second stage, a worker w_i choose her optimal strategy, i.e., sensing time t_{ij}.

Given Eq. (5), the utility maximization problem for each requester r_j can be formulated as:

$$\begin{cases} u_j^r \triangleq \max_{B_j} \left(\kappa_j \sum_{x:w_x \in \mathcal{S}_j} t_{xj} \right)^\theta - B_j \\ s.t. B_j \geq 0, \forall j : r_j \in \mathcal{R} \end{cases} \qquad (8)$$

Given Eq. (3), the utility maximization problem for each worker w_i can be formulated as:

$$\begin{cases} u_i^w \triangleq \max_{t_{ij}} B_j \times \dfrac{t_{ij}}{\sum_{x:w_x \in \mathcal{S}_j} t_{xj}} - c_i t_{ij} \\ s.t. t_{ij} \geq 0, \forall i, j : w_i \in \mathcal{S}_j \end{cases} \qquad (9)$$

Aiming at the max-min fairness-aware multi-task allocation problem (7), we design a fair incentive mechanism based on Stackelberg game, which includes the sensing time game, the reward declaration game, and the max-min fairness-aware multi-task allocation algorithm. The Nash equilibria in the sensing time game and the reward declaration game are defined as follows.

Definition 5. *A set of strategies* $T^* = \{t_1^*, \ldots, t_n^*\}$ *is a NE of the sensing time game, if the following condition is satisfied*

$$u_i^w\left(t_i^*, t_{-i}^*\right) \geq u_i^w\left(t_i, t_{-i}^*\right), \forall i : w_i \in \mathcal{W} \tag{10}$$

Definition 6. *A set of strategies* $B^* = \{B_1^*, \ldots, B_m^*\}$ *is a NE of the reward declaration game, if the following condition is satisfied*

$$u_j^r\left(B_j^*\right) \geq u_j^r(B_j), \forall j : r_j \in \mathcal{R} \tag{11}$$

For the proposed multi-requester multi-worker Stackelberg game, Eq. (10) and Eq. (11) together form a Stackelberg equilibrium, which is defined as follows.

Definition 7. *Let* $T^* = \{t_1^*, \ldots, t_n^*\}$ *be a NE of the sensing time game, and* $B^* = \{B_1^*, \ldots, B_m^*\}$ *be a NE of the reward declaration game, the point* (T^*, B^*) *is an equilibrium for the Stackelberg game if for any* (T, B) *that* $T \neq T^*$ *and* $B \neq B^*$, *the following conditions are satisfied:*

$$\begin{cases} u_i^w\left(B^*, t_{ij}^*, t_{-ij}^*\right) \geq u_i^w\left(B^*, t_{ij}, t_{-ij}^*\right), & \forall i : w_i \in \mathcal{W} \\ u_j^r\left(B_j^*, T^*\right) \geq u_j^r(B_j, T^*), & \forall j : r_j \in \mathcal{R} \end{cases} \tag{12}$$

At the Stackelberg equilibrium, neither the requesters nor the workers have incentive to deviate, and thus the fairness-aware multi-task allocation problem can be transformed to the fairness-aware incentive mechanism design problem:

Definition 8 (MMFIM). *The max-min fairness-aware incentive mechanism design problem can be formulated as follows*

$$\begin{cases} \chi_{MM} = \arg\max\limits_{\chi \in X} \min\limits_{j=1,\ldots,m} u_j(\chi) \\ \\ s.t. \begin{cases} \sum\limits_{x:w_x \in \mathcal{S}_j} t_{xj} \geq V_j, \forall j : r_j \in \mathcal{R} \\ u_i^w = \max\limits_{t_{ij} \geq 0} u_i^w, \forall i : w_i \in \mathcal{W} \\ u_j^r = \max\limits_{B_j \geq 0} u_j^r, \forall j : r_j \in \mathcal{R} \end{cases} \end{cases} \tag{13}$$

3.1   NE in the Sensing Time Game

Given the set of winning workers $\mathcal{S}_j$ for task τ_j allocated by the platform, we focus on determining whether there exists a NE in the sensing time game, and whether the NE is unique. If the answers to the above two questions are affirmative, then how to calculate the unique NE is very necessary. In order to address these issues, we first introduce the concept of optimal sensing time strategy for the workers.

Definition 9 (Optimal Sensing Time Strategy). *Given* B_j, $\mathcal{S}_j$ *and* t_{-ij}, *a worker* $w_i's$ *optimal sensing time strategy* $\bar{t}_{ij}$ *maximizes* $u_i^w\left(\bar{t}_{ij}, t_{-ij}\right)$ *over all* $\bar{t}_{ij} \geq 0$.

According to Definition 5, each worker will choose her optimal sensing time strategy in a NE, and hence we can obtain the value of $\bar{t}_{ij}$, as shown in Lemma 1.

Lemma 1. *Given a task τ_j with the corresponding budget B_j and the set of winning workers S_j, the optimal sensing time strategy for worker $w_i \in \mathcal{W}$ is*

$$\bar{t}_{ij} = \begin{cases} \epsilon, & \text{if } l = 1 \\ 0, & \text{if } i \geq z \\ \dfrac{B_j\left(|S_j|-1\right)\left[\sum_{x:w_x\in S_j} c_x - c_i\left(|S_j|-1\right)\right]}{\left(\sum_{x:w_x\in S_j} c_x\right)^2}, & \text{otherwise} \end{cases} \quad (14)$$

where the workers in S_j are sorted by the unit cost such that $c_1 \leq c_2 \leq \cdots \leq c_l$, $z = \max\left\{x : 2 \leq x \leq l, c_x \leq \dfrac{\sum_{y=1}^{x} c_y}{x-1}\right\}$ and ϵ is a sufficiently small positive number, which is approximately 0 here.

Proof: For the special case of $|S_j| = 1$, the single worker w_i can enjoy the total reward B_j by contributing a small sensing time, denoted as $\bar{t}_{ij} = \epsilon$.

For the other cases, we know that $t_{ij} \in \left[0, \frac{B_j}{c_i}\right]$ as $u_i^w \geq 0$ according to Eq. (3). The first-order and second-order derivatives of u_i^w with respect to t_{ij} are shown as follows

$$\begin{cases} \dfrac{\partial u_i^w}{\partial t_{ij}} = \dfrac{B_j\left(\sum_{x:w_x\in S_j} t_{xj} - t_{ij}\right)}{\left(\sum_{x:w_x\in S_j} t_{xj}\right)^2} - c_i \\ \dfrac{\partial^2 u_i^w}{\partial^2 t_{ij}} = \dfrac{-2B_j \sum_{x:w_x\in S_j\setminus\{w_i\}} t_{xj}}{\left(\sum_{x:w_x\in S_j} t_{xj}\right)^3} \end{cases} \quad (15)$$

Algorithm 1: Computation of the NE for the sensing time game

Input: $B = \{B_1, \dots B_j, \dots, B_m\}, C = \{c_1, \dots c_i, \dots, c_n\}, S = \{S_1, \dots S_j, \dots, S_m\}$

Output: $T^* = \{t_1^*, \dots, t_i^*, \dots t_n^*\}, \forall i : w_i \in S$

1   for $j = 1; j \leq m; j + +$ do
2   if $S_j \neq \emptyset$ and $\sum_{x:w_x\in S_j} t_{xj} \geq V_j$ then
3   for $i = 1; i \leq |S_j|; j + +$ do
4   compute $\bar{t}_{ij}, \forall w_i \in S_j$ according to Eq. (18) ;
5   else
6   break;
7   foreach $i \in \mathcal{W}$ do
8   if $w_i \in S_j$ and $S_j \neq \emptyset$ and $\sum_{x:w_x\in S_j} t_{xj} \geq V_j$ then
9           $t_i^* = \bar{t}_{ij}$;
10   else
11          $t_i^* = 0$;
12   return $T^* = \{t_1^*, \dots, t_i^*, \dots t_n^*\}$

Given any $B_j > 0$, we know that $\frac{\partial^2 u_i^w}{\partial^2 t_{ij}} < 0$, which implies that u_i^w is a strictly concave function in t_{ij}, and thus the optimal sensing time $\bar{t}_{ij}$ is unique if it exists. Let $\frac{\partial u_i^w}{\partial t_{ij}} = 0$, we obtain

$$B_j \left(\sum_{x:w_x \in \mathcal{S}_j} t_{xj} - t_{ij} \right) = c_i \left(\sum_{x:w_x \in \mathcal{S}_j} t_{xj} \right)^2 \tag{16}$$

Denote $\mathcal{S}_j^+ = \{ w_i \in \mathcal{S}_j : t_{ij} > 0 \}$. By summing up Eq. (16) over all workers in $\mathcal{S}_j^+$, we have

$$\sum_{x:w_x \in \mathcal{S}_j^+} t_{xj} = \frac{B_j \left(\left| \mathcal{S}_j^+ \right| - 1 \right)}{\sum_{x:w_x \in \mathcal{S}_j^+} c_x} \tag{17}$$

Since $t_{ij} = 0$ for $w_x \in \mathcal{S}_j \backslash \mathcal{S}_j^+$, we know that $\sum_{x:w_x \in \mathcal{S}_j^+} t_{xj} = \sum_{y:w_y \in \mathcal{S}_j} t_{yj}$. By substituting Eq. (17) into Eq. (16), we have

$$t_{ij} = \frac{B_j \left(\left| \mathcal{S}_j^+ \right| - 1 \right) \left[\sum_{x:w_x \in \mathcal{S}_j^+} c_x - c_i \left(\left| \mathcal{S}_j^+ \right| - 1 \right) \right]}{\left(\sum_{x:w_x \in \mathcal{S}_j^+} c_x \right)^2} \tag{18}$$

Algorithm 2: Computation of the NE for the reward declaration game

Input: $\kappa = \{ \kappa_1, \dots \kappa_j, \dots, \kappa_m \}, \mathcal{S} = \{ \mathcal{S}_1, \dots \mathcal{S}_j, \dots, \mathcal{S}_m \}, T^* = \{ t_1^*, \dots, t_i^*, \dots t_n^* \}$

Output: $B^* = \{ B_1^*, \dots, B_j^*, \dots B_m^* \}, u = \{ u_1^r, \dots, u_j^r, \dots, u_m^r \}, \sum_{j:r_j \in \mathcal{R}} u_j^r$

1	initialize $B_j = 0, \forall j \in [1, m]$ and $t = 1$;
2	for $j = 1; j \leq m; j + +$ do
3	if $\mathcal{S}_j \neq \emptyset$ and $\sum_{x:w_x \in \mathcal{S}_j} t_{xj} \geq V_j$ then
4	update B_j^t by solving Eq.(21)with given $B_k^t, \forall j \in (j, m]$ and $B_k^{t-1}, \forall j \in [1, j)$;
5	compute $u_j^{r^t}$ by solving Eq. (8);
6	if $\left| u_j^{r^{t-1}} - u_j^{r^t} / u_j^{r^t} \right| < \epsilon$
7	$B_j^* = B_j^t$;
8	$u_j^r = u_j^{r^t}$;
9	$t = t + 1$;
10	break;
11	else
12	$B_j^* = 0$;
13	$u_j^r = 0$;
14	return $B^* = \{ B_1^*, \dots, B_j^*, \dots B_m^* \}, u = \{ u_1^r, \dots, u_j^r, \dots, u_m^r \}, \sum_{j:r_j \in \mathcal{R}} u_j^r$

Next, we determine the set $\mathcal{S}_j^+$. Any worker $w_i \in \mathcal{S}_j$ with $c_i < \frac{\sum_{x:w_x \in \mathcal{S}_j^+} c_x}{|\mathcal{S}_j^+|-1}$ has $t_{ij} > 0$, such a worker belongs to $\mathcal{S}_j^+$. Furthermore, it can be seen that t_{ij} is a monotonically decreasing function on variable c_i. Therefore, a worker with smaller cost has more incentive to devote more time. And hence $\mathcal{S}_j^+$ consists of a consecutive set of workers, namely $\mathcal{S}_j^+ = \{w_1, \ldots, w_s\}$ for some $s \in [2, l]$. Notice that if $c_x \geq \frac{\sum_{y=1}^{x} c_y}{x-1}$ then $c_{x+1} \geq \frac{\sum_{y=1}^{x+1} c_y}{x}$. Thus s must be the last index x satisfying

$$c_x \leq \frac{\sum_{y=1}^{x} c_y}{x - 1} \tag{19}$$

Then the lemma follows.

By substituting Eq. (14) into Eq. (9), the maximum utility u_i^w of a worker w_i is

$$u_i^w = \begin{cases} B_j, & \text{if } l = 1 \\ 0, & \text{if } i \geq z \\ B_j \times \left[1 - \frac{c_i(z-1)}{\sum_{x:w_x \in \mathcal{S}_j} c_x}\right]^2, & \text{otherwise} \end{cases} \tag{20}$$

As a result, the output of Algorithm 1 is the unique NE of the sensing time game.

3.2 NE in the Reward Declaration Game

Given the set of winning workers $\mathcal{S}_j$ for task τ_j and the NE T^* in the sensing time game, rational and self-interested requesters will strategically declare the budget B_j to maximize her own utility. We now introduce the concept of optimal reward declaration strategy for the requesters.

Definition 10 (*Optimal Reward Declaration Strategy*). *Given $\mathcal{S}_j$ and T_j^*, a requester r_j's optimal reward declaration strategy $\bar{B}_j$ maximizes u_j^r over all $\bar{B}_j \geq 0$.*

According to Definition 6, each strategic requester will choose her optimal reward declaration strategy in a NE, and hence we can obtain the value of $\bar{B}_j, \forall j : r_j \in \mathcal{R}$.

Lemma 3. *Given T_j^*, the optimal reward declaration strategy $\bar{B}_j$ of requester $r_j \in \mathcal{R}$ is*

$$\bar{B}_j = \max_{B_j \geq 0} \left(\kappa_j \sum_{x:w_x \in \mathcal{S}_j} t_{xj} \right)^{\theta} - B_j \tag{21}$$

Algorithm 3: Greedy max-min fairness-aware multi-task allocation algorithm

Input: $V = \{V_1, ..., V_j, ..., V_m\}, C = \{c_1, ..., c_i, ..., c_n\}$,

$\quad\quad K = \{\kappa_1, ..., \kappa_j, ..., \kappa_m\}, \{\Gamma_i | \forall i : w_i \in \mathcal{W}\}$

Output: $S = \{S_1, ..., S_j, ..., S_m\}$

1   Reorder elements in $\mathcal{W}$ so that $c_1 \leq c_2 \leq \cdots \leq c_n$.

2   Initialize $f_j = 0; S_j = \emptyset$.

3   **for** $i = 1; i \leq n; i + + $ **do**

4   reorder elements in Γ_i so that $\kappa_1 \geq \kappa_2 ... \geq \kappa_z$.

5   **for** $j = 1; j \leq z; j + + $ **do**

6   **if** $f_j = 0$ **then**

7   **if** $S_j = \emptyset$ **then**

8      $S_j = S_j \cup \{w_i\}$.

9      $u_j^r = -B_j$.

10   **else**

11   **if** $c_i < \sum_{y:y \in S_j \cup \{w_i\}} c_y / |S_j|$ **then**

12      $S_j = S_j \cup \{w_i\}$.

13   compute $\sum_{x=1}^{z} t_{xj}$ according to Eq(17).

14   **if** $\sum_{x=1}^{z} t_{xj} \geq V_j$ **then**

15   Update $f_j = 1$;

16   Update u_j^r according to Eq.(5).

17   **else**

18      $S_j = \emptyset, u_j^r = 0$.

19      $\mathcal{T} = \mathcal{T} \backslash \{\tau_j\}$.

20   **else**

21   **if** $f_j = 1, \forall j : \tau_j \in \Gamma_i$ **then**

22   find the requester with minimum utility u_{min}^r.

23   repeat line 11 to 19.

24   **else**

25   break;

26   **Return** $S = \{S_1, ... S_j, ..., S_m\}$

Proof: This proof can be directly obtained by substituting T_j^* into Eq. (8), and is omitted here.

As a result, the output of Algorithm 2 is the unique NE of the reward declaration game.

3.3 Max-Min Fairness-Aware Multi-task Allocation Algorithm

In this section, we design a greedy max-min fairness-aware multi-task allocation two-stage algorithm, i.e., allocate a set of winning workers S_j for each task τ_j that satisfies the sensing time threshold V_j, as shown in Algorithm 3. In the first stage, the platform allocates workers to tasks in sequence to meet the sensing time threshold. In the second stage, the platform gives priority to allocating workers to the requester with the lowest utility to maintain the max-min fairness.

Firstly, the platform reorders elements in $\mathcal{C}$ so that $c_1 \leq c_2 \leq \ldots \leq c_n$, and initializes $S_j = \varnothing, \forall j : r_j \in \mathcal{R}$. Similarly, reorder elements in K so that $\kappa_1 \geq \kappa_2 \ldots \geq \kappa_z$. In the first stage (lines 6–20), the platform judges whether the sensing time threshold V_j of task τ_j is satisfied according to the order of K, and then judges the next task. Otherwise, it is judged whether the unit cost c_i of the worker w_i meets the condition for joining the set of winning workers S_j, and update the set S_j, the sum of sensing time $\sum\limits_{x:w_x \in S_j} t_{xj}$ and the requester $r'_j s$ utility u^r_j. Otherwise, delete τ_j from the task set $\mathcal{T}$, update $S_j = \varnothing$ and $u^r_j = 0$. When the sensing time threshold of all tasks are satisfied, the algorithm runs in the second stage (lines 21–25). The platform will find the requester with minimum utility value r_{jmin} and allocate the following workers to the task τ_{jmin} until the set $\mathcal{W}$ is empty.

4   Performance Evaluation

4.1   Simulation Setup

In this section, we provide numerical results to evaluate the performance of the max-min fairness-aware incentive mechanism, and verify the impact of intrinsic parameters on social utility and price of fairness (PoF). Throughout our experiments, we assume that the value of $\kappa_j, \forall j \in [1, m]$ is subject to a Gaussian distribution $\kappa_j \sim N(\mu_1, \sigma_1^2)$ (here, we fix $\mu_1 = 100$). Similarly, we assume that the value of $V_j, \forall j \in [1, m]$ and the value of $C_i, \forall i \in [1, n]$ are subject to a Gaussian distribution $V_j \sim N(\mu_2, \sigma_2^2)$ and $C_i \sim N(\mu_3, \sigma_3^2)$ respectively (here, we fix $\mu_2 = 3$ and $\mu_3 = 5$).

4.2   Social Utility

Figure 2 illustrates how the social utility $U \triangleq \sum_{j:r_j \in \mathcal{R}} u^r_j$ is impacted by intrinsic parameters: (a) m; (b) n; (c) σ_1^2; (d) σ_2^2; (e) σ_3^2. The social utility under the proposed max-min fairness-aware incentive mechanism is denoted as U_F, and the social optimum without considering fairness is denoted as U.

First, the max-min fairness-aware multi-task allocation algorithm sacrifices some utilities of requesters, which leads to no matter how the intrinsic parameters change, U_F is lower than U.

In Fig. 2(a), we fixed $n = 150$ and $\sigma_1^2 = \sigma_2^2 = \sigma_3^2 = 5$, as the number of requesters increases, workers have more freedom of choice and avoid fierce competition, thus increasing the social optimum U. Similarly, in Fig. 2(b) we fixed $m = 10$ and $\sigma_1^2 = \sigma_2^2 = \sigma_3^2 = 5$, as the number of workers increases, more workers can contribute more sensing time and bring greater service benefit, which increases the social optimum U. While in Fig. 2(a) and Fig. 2(b), as the number of requesters or workers increases, the social utility U_F has fluctuated. This is because the interested task set Γ_i

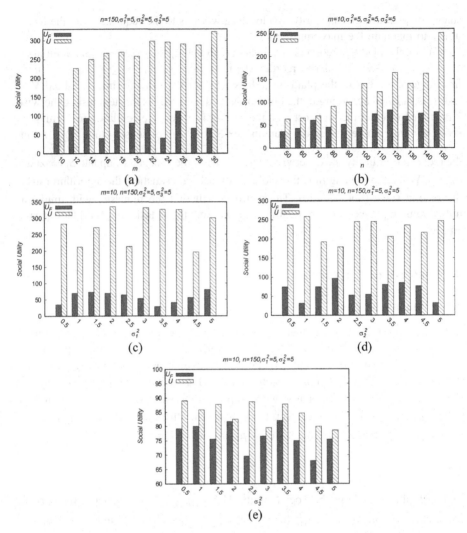

Fig. 2. The impact of intrinsic parameters against social utility: (a) m; (b) n; (c) σ_1^2; (d) σ_2^2; (e) σ_3^2.

of w_i is randomly generated based on the task set $\mathcal{T}$, which leads to the difference and randomness of the winning workers set $\mathcal{S}_j$ allocated to the task.

In Fig. 2(c), we fixed $m = 10$, $n = 150$ and $\sigma_2^2 = \sigma_3^2 = 5$, it can be found that as σ_1^2 increases, that is, as the unit value of tasks become more diverse, the social utility U_F and social optimum U all have fluctuated and the gap between U_F and U is obvious. This is because workers will be assigned to high-value tasks preferentially without considering fairness, while some workers may be assigned to tasks with low value, which increases the gap between U and U_F.

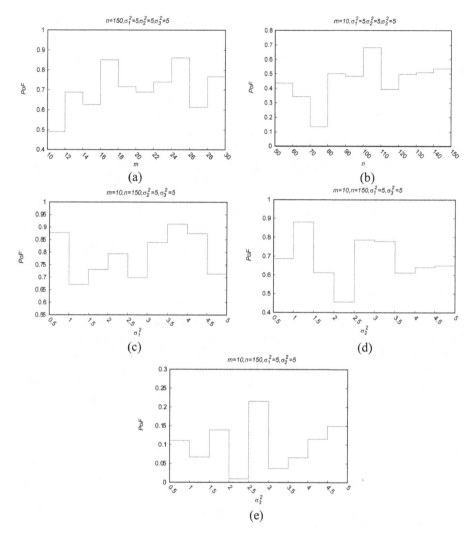

Fig. 3. The impact of intrinsic parameters against PoF: (a) m; (b) n; (c) σ_1^2; (d) σ_2^2; (e) σ_3^2.

A similar phenomenon can be found in Fig. 2(d) and Fig. 2(e), as σ_2^2 and σ_3^2 increase respectively, U_F and U all have fluctuated, and it is easy to find that the gap between U_F and U in Fig. 2(d) is more significant than Fig. 2(e). In Fig. 2(d), as σ_2^2 increases, i.e., the sensing time threshold of tasks become more diverse, some tasks with higher value cannot meet the sensing time threshold, which will cause a relatively large loss of service benefit, and thus U_F is far less than U. Whereas, in Fig. 2(e), as σ_3^2 increases, thus as the cost of workers become more diverse, workers with high cost have more opportunities to be assigned to tasks with lower value, which avoids bidding failures caused by too many workers competing for the same task and increases the number of winning workers, and thus U_F is close to U.

4.3 Price of Fairness

In order to measure the loss of social utility U_F compared to the social optimum U, we study the price of fairness in this section. Price of fairness is defined as $PoF = \frac{U-U_F}{U}$, it is easy to find that the range of PoF is $[0, 1]$. Similarly, from Fig. 2, we demonstrate how intrinsic parameters (a) m; (b) n; (c) σ_1^2; (d) σ_2^2; (e) σ_3^2 impact on PoF. When the gap between U_F and U is small, the value of PoF will be small, otherwise, the value of PoF will be large. As shown in Fig. 3(a), when the number of requesters m ranges from 16 to 20, the gap between U_F and U is small, and thus the value of PoF is small. However, when m ranges from 26 to 30, the gap between U_F and U becomes more significant and thus the value of PoF becomes larger. Figure 3(b), Fig. 3(c), Fig. 3(d) and Fig. 3(e) are consistent with the situation in Fig. 3(a), and the reasons are similar.

5   Conclusion

In this paper, we modeled the interaction between requesters and workers as a Stackelberg game consisting of multi-requester and multi-worker and developed a max-min fairness-aware incentive mechanism to address the dilemma that tasks are constantly emerging and worker resources are relatively limited in MCS. Under the proposed multi-task allocation algorithm, the distribution of requesters' utility satisfies max-min fairness, which incentives users to keep sustainability in MCS effectively.

References

1. Zhang, X.: Incentives for mobile crowd sensing: a survey. IEEE Commun. Surv. Tutor. **18**(1), 1 (2015)
2. Liu, Y.: Data-oriented mobile crowdsensing: a comprehensive survey. IEEE Commun. Surv. Tutor. **21**(3), 2849–2885 (2019)
3. Guo, B., Yu, Z., Zhou, X., et al.: From participatory sensing to mobile crowd sensing. In: International Conference on Pervasive Computing, pp. 593–598 (2014)
4. Wu, F., Luo, T.: WiFiScout: a crowdsensing WiFi advisory system with gamification-based incentive. In: Mobile Ad Hoc and Sensor Systems, pp. 533–534 (2014)
5. Liu, L., Liu, W., Zheng, Y., et al.: Third-eye: a mobilephone-enabled crowdsensing system for air quality monitoring. Mobile Wearable Ubiquit. Technol. **2**(1), 1–26 (2018)
6. Kim, S., Robson, C., Zimmerman, T., et al.: Creek watch: pairing usefulness and usability for successful citizen science. In: Human Factors Computing Systems, pp. 2125–2134 (2011)
7. Thiagarajan, A., Ravindranath, L., Lacurts, K., et al.: VTrack: accurate, energy-aware road traffic delay estimation using mobile phones. In: International Conference on Embedded Networked Sensor Systems, pp. 85–98 (2009)
8. Lau, J.K., Tham, C., Luo, T., et al.: Participatory cyber physical system in public transport application. In: Utility and Cloud Computing, pp. 355–360 (2011)

9. Gao, C., Kong, F., Tan, J., et al.: HealthAware: tackling obesity with health aware smart phone systems. In: Robotics and Biomimetics, pp. 1549–1554 (2009)
10. Capponi, A., Fiandrino, C., Kantarci, B., et al.: A survey on mobile crowdsensing systems: challenges, solutions, and opportunities. IEEE Commun. Surv. Tutor. **21**(3), 2419–2465 (2019)
11. Huang, H., Xin, Y., Sun, Y., et al.: A truthful double auction mechanism for crowdsensing systems with max-min fairness. In: Wireless Communications and Networking Conference, pp. 1–6 (2017)
12. Li, D., Yang, L., Liu, J., et al.: Considering decoy effect and fairness preference: an incentive mechanism for crowdsensing. IEEE Internet Things J. **6**(5), 8835–8852 (2019)
13. Zhu, X., An, J., Yang, M., et al.: A fair incentive mechanism for crowdsourcing in crowd sensing. IEEE Internet Things J. **3**(6), 1364–1372 (2016)
14. Tao, X., Song, W.: Location-dependent task allocation for mobile crowdsensing with clustering effect. IEEE Internet Things J. **6**(1), 1029–1045 (2019)
15. Sooksatra, K., Li, R., Li, Y., Guan, X., Li, W.: Fairness-aware auction mechanism for sustainable mobile crowdsensing. In: Biagioni, E.S., Zheng, Y., Cheng, S. (eds.) WASA 2019. LNCS, vol. 11604, pp. 310–321. Springer, Cham (2019). https://doi.org/10.1007/978-3-030-23597-0_25

Research on High Reliable Wireless Channel Data Cleaning Method

Lingfan Zhuang, Liu Liu$^{(\boxtimes)}$, Shuoshuo Dong, Yuanyuan Fan,
and Jiachi Zhang

School of Electronic and Information Engineering, Beijing Jiaotong University,
Beijing 100044, China
bill0715@163.com

Abstract. Recent developments in the 5th generation wireless communication system have heightened the need for the propagation characteristics and modeling of wireless channels. As the propagation characteristics and variation rules of radio waves in different scenes, frequency points and bandwidth are all hidden in the channel test massive data that have the big data features, it is necessary to carry out effective data cleaning methods to make better use of test data. This paper analyzes and compares a variety of data cleaning methods first, then designs a data cleaning strategy according to the characteristics of wireless channel test data. Finally, the effectiveness of the data cleaning strategy is verified through simulation. This paper provided significant theoretical and technical support for the wireless environment reconstruction and model construction in the big data era.

Keywords: Data cleaning · Big data mining · Channel modeling · 5G · High reliable

1 Introduction

Millimeter-wave (MMW) has become an important technic of the 5th generation wireless systems (5G) due to its characteristics of large bandwidth, low diffraction capability, and the concentrated beam [1]. Thus, the propagation characteristics and modeling of MMW wireless channel become a major area of interest within the field of wireless communication. However, the wireless channel measurement and experiments under the ITU-R MMW candidate frequency band and typical application scenarios [2] at home and abroad are not sufficient at present. The difficulty lies in the fact that the measured MMW channel data includes the fading information of the channel in the time domain, frequency domain, airspace, scene, and other dimensions which is quite different from that of a traditional channel. Traditional channel modeling method using simple statistics, geometrical optics of time and space of locally finite data (such as specific scenarios and the measured data of a specific frequency) to carry on the analysis and modeling, and using the least-squares to build the model which makes the conclusion one-sided. On the other hand, the traditional model lacks universality and portability issues, greatly limits the accuracy and depth of channel data parameter

X. Chen et al. (Eds.): ML4CS 2020, LNCS 12487, pp. 180–189, 2020.
https://doi.org/10.1007/978-3-030-62460-6_16

extraction, loss of channel fading characteristics extraction of information, so it is not appropriate to conduct channel modeling traditionally in big data era.

Data mining [3] is a process of searching hidden rules or information in huge amount of data through algorithms. It realizes the mining of deep-rooted rules of data through statistics, online analysis and processing, machine learning, expert system, and pattern recognition. If data mining methods are used to process the fading character-istics of mass data and analyze the measured channel characteristics by data cleaning, data dimension reduction, and compression [4], we can obtain the internal relation between channel parameters in different typical scenes under the candidate frequency band of 5G more effectively.

Due to the "garbage in, garbage out" principle [5], analyzing the MMW wireless channel measured data directly will get inaccurate or even wrong conclusions because raw data is characterized by complexity, high dimension, and sparsity, thus the validity of data preprocessing directly determines whether valuable information can be mined from massive data. In this paper, we use data cleaning methods which are high reli-ability, high efficiency, and high precision for measured MMW wireless channel data to provide effective theoretical and technical support for the wireless environment reconstruction and model construction in the MMW wireless channel big data environment.

The structure of this paper is organized as follows. In Sect. 2, we introduce data cleaning methods. In Sect. 3, we introduced the simulation steps of data cleaning and results, and compare the channel impulse response before and after data cleaning. In Sect. 4 we conclude the paper.

2   Methods of Data Cleaning

Foreign research on data cleaning technology first appeared in the United States, starting from the correction of the social security number errors in the United States [6]. Abnormal detection of the data set refers to the cleaning of the record properties of the data set. There are the following types [7]: missing value, outlier (outlier), duplicate data, and noise. In this section, we describe how to clean different types of data through different methods.

2.1   Duplicate Records

The problem of cleaning duplicate records is often called *the merge/purge problem*, we list and compare several methods below.

Proximity Ordering Method
Article [8] put out the sorted neighborhood method (SNM) to reduce the complexity of the merge/purge problem. SNM includes three steps: First, sorts data according to the *key*, then compares records in pairs by sliding a fixed-size window over a sorted database, finally delete duplicate data according to rules (in general, duplicate records is always in the adjacent position after preliminary sorting). The three steps of SNM respectively cost $O(N)$, $O(N * \log N)$ and $O(N * \log N)$, N represent the number of

records. Its effectiveness depends largely on the ability of the *key* to tie together imprecise duplicates.

Based on SNM, the multi-pass SNM method (MPN) is also proposed, which assumes that no *key* is good enough to put all imprecise duplicates together, which employ SNM loops several times. each loop uses different index to sort the database to reduce the chance of missing duplicates.

Article [9] proposes a knowledge-based cleaning framework based on SNM, Java Expert System Shell and other methods was proposed for data Cleaning. The experimental results showed that the Framework could better identify repetition and anomaly, and had high recall and precision. Article [10] proposes an efficient Variegated Data Swabbing algorithm to removing duplicity from the structured data.

Cluster

Article [11] proposes a new clustering technique for processing large databases, *canopy*. The main idea of it is to perform clustering in two stages: the first stage is to roughly and quickly divide the data into overlapping subsets which is called *canopy*; in the second phase, more precise measurements are used to cluster the points in the canopy, then we get the duplicate records. The key to using *canopy* clustering technology is to roughly divide the data into possibly overlapping classes using approximate distance calculation which cost little, then cluster those classes again using precise distance calculation. This method greatly reduces the computing complexity, and if the accuracy of the first stage can be guaranteed, the result is accurate.

2.2   Outlier Detection

The detection of outliers is always divided into three steps: define and determine the type of outliers; search and identify the case of outliers; correct the outliers found. There are mainly several methods to detect outliers in the data set.

Statistical Method

According to Chebyshev's theorem [12], the mean value, standard deviation, and confidence interval of each field are used to identify abnormal fields and records.

Cluster

Article [13, 14] summarizes several clustering methods. Cluster is to group data into multiple classes or clusters. The data objects in the same cluster have a high degree of similarity while the objects in different clusters are quite different. Scattered data that cannot be merged into any clusters is called an "outlier" or a "singularity." Cluster usually represents the degree of similarity between objects by distance, includes Euclidean distance, absolute distance (Manhattan distance), Murkowski distance, etc. The methods used to measure the distance between clusters are minimum distance, maximum distance, and so on.

The advantages of the cluster include: First, clustering techniques based on linear and near-linear complexity (like K-means) may be highly effective; Second, the definition of cluster is usually the complement of outliers, so it is possible to find clusters and outliers at the same time. However, the set of outliers generated and their scores may be very dependent on the number of clusters and the existence of outliers in the data.

Pattern-Based Approach

Pattern recognition [15] allows us to find fields and records that do not conform to existing patterns in data. A pattern is defined as a set of records in a dataset with P % (P is a user-specified value, usually above 90%) fields having similar characteristics. If the algorithm is applied to a subset of the records generated based on domain knowledge, rather than the entire dataset, the chance of discovering a pattern increases. However, it is difficult to apply to most of the recorded patterns because real-world data sets are highly irrelevant.

Association Rule Method

Association rules [16] with a high degree of confidence and support define another outlier detection patterns, and records that do not conform to these patterns or rules are considered abnormal records. In Article [17], ordinal association rules are defined to discover rules that give more information.

Model-Based Detection

Model-based detection builds a data model first. Outliers are those objects that can't fit the model perfectly. If the model is a collection of clusters, the exception is an object that does not significantly belong to any cluster. When using a regression model, exceptions are objects that are relatively far from the predicted value.

Density-Based Approach

A point is classified as an outlier when its local density is significantly lower than that of most of its nearest neighbors. This approach is suited for non-uniformly distributed data. However, it is hard to choose parameter selection, although the algorithm deals with this problem by observing different K values and obtaining the maximum outlier score, the upper and lower bounds of these values still need to be selected.

2.3   Noise

Noise includes error values or deviations from expected outliers, but it does not mean that noise contains outliers, although most data mining methods discard outliers as noise or anomalies. However, in some applications (e.g., fraud detection), analysis or exception mining is performed for outliers. Moreover, some points are local outliers, but they are normal from a global perspective. The noise is mainly treated by the binning and regression method.

Binning

The binning soothes the ordered data values by examining the "nearest neighbor" of the data. These ordered values are distributed into "buckets" or boxes. Because the partition method looks at the value of the nearest neighbor, it performs local smoothing. Generally, the wider the width, the smoother the data is.

Regression

Using regression to find mathematical equations that fit the data can help eliminate noise. Linear regression involves finding the "best" line fitting two properties (or variables) so that one property can predict the other. Multilinear regression is an extension of linear regression that involves more than two properties and data fitting into a multidimensional surface.

2.4 Missing Value

Missing value is usually treated differently depending on its importance and the missing rate, as Fig. 1 shows.

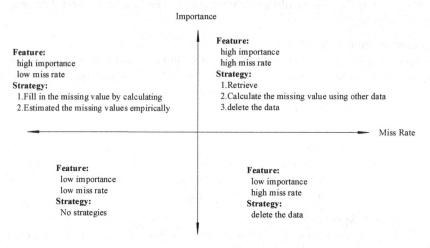

Fig. 1. Principle of treating the missing value.

Padding Method

The data can be filled simply according to the data distribution when the missing rate and importance of attributes are low and the attributes are numeric. For example, if the data is evenly distributed, the mean value can be used to fill the data. If the data distribution is skewed, fill it with the median is an efficient way. If the property is a category property, you can populate it with a global constant, 'Unknow,' but it is rarely used because it often gets bad result, after all the algorithm might recognize it as a completely new category.

Delete

When the miss rate is high (>95%) and the attribute is of low importance, or the miss rate is high and the attribute is of low importance, the data can be deleted directly. However, when the missing value is high and the degree of attribute is high, deleting the attribute directly will have a bad effect on the result of the algorithm.

Interpolation Method

The interpolation methods include random interpolation, multiple interpolations, and hot platform interpolation [18], often used in image processing. Different methods should be chosen according to the characteristics of the data. Random interpolation selects samples randomly from the population to replace the missing samples. The multiple interpolation methods predict the missing data through the relationship between variables, then generate multiple complete data sets by the Monte Carlo method, analyze these data sets, and finally summarizes the analysis results.

The advantage of the interpolation method is its simplicity and high accuracy while its disadvantage is obvious: when the number of variables is large, it is usually difficult to find the sample that is the same as the sample that needs to be interpolated. There is no unified process for the processing of data missing values, and the method must be selected according to the distribution of actual data, the degree of skew, and the proportion of missing values. In addition to the simple filling method and deletion method, the modeling method is more often used for filling. The main reason is that the modeling method can predict the unknown value based on the existing value, with high accuracy. However, the modeling method may also cause a correlation between attributes to become larger, which may affect the training of the final model.

3 Simulation

MMW wireless channel measured data has big data features: volume, variety, value and velocity, which is called 4 V. Channel test data that does not meet the requirements will be introduced in the process of acquisition and import, including abnormal data, inconsistent data, repetitive data, missing data, etc. They mainly come from the abnormal changes in the channel, the sudden abnormal of the channel test equipment, the abnormal physical jitter of the antenna and so on. Therefore, it is necessary to clean the data before channel modeling. This section describes the data cleaning process in the simulation. First, duplicate values in the test data are deleted, then abnormal data are cleared, and finally, missing values are filled in and noise is removed. The data cleaning process is shown in Fig. 2.

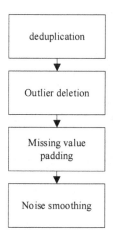

Fig. 2. The process of data cleaning is presented.

Measurement of the channel impulse response (CIR) is the most important part of the channel modeling, the accuracy of CIR directly determines the accuracy and reliability of the channel characteristic parameters, Therefore, this paper generates channel test data through channel simulator, and uses big data mining to clean the channel test data, and compares the CIR before and after data cleaning.

Step 1: SNM method is utilized to clear the two norms of the selection signal as the sorting keyword, and then uses a sliding window to sort similar data twice (according to the Euclidean distance between signals) after sorting, and finally removes duplicate data.

Step 2: Clustering Using Representatives (CURE) algorithm choose fixed number in the data space, some representative together to represent the corresponding class, it can identify with complex shape and different sizes of clustering, and good isolation outliers, so this article chooses CURE algorithm clear channel test outliers in the data, as shown in Fig. 3, good CURE algorithm identify the isolated point.

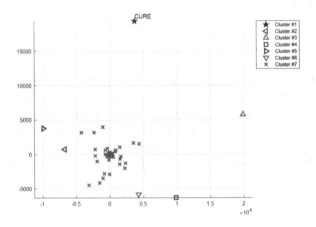

Fig. 3. Outliers are resolved by CURE algorithm.

Figure 4 compares the CIR obtained from the original test data with the one after removing the outliers. The channel impulse response after removing the outliers with the CURE algorithm is cleaner and more reliable than the channel impulse response obtained from the original test data, which is more conducive to extracting accurate channel parameters.

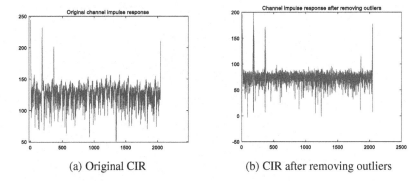

(a) Original CIR   (b) CIR after removing outliers

Fig. 4. comparison of CIR

Step 3: The binning method is utilized to supplement the missing value by the average and smooth the noise to further enhance the robustness of the channel test data, which is conducive to the extraction of accurate parameters and the establishment of the channel model. Figure 5 shows the CIR after using the binning method. Compared with the original data, it is found that multipath clusters are easier to be distinguished and channel parameters can be easier extracted due to the obvious reduction of noise.

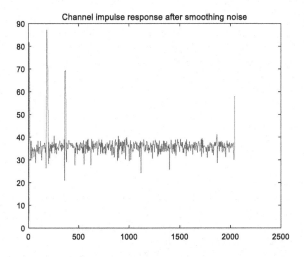

Fig. 5. CIR after all data cleaning steps.

The reason why we did not choose regression to smooth the noise is that the overfitting or underfitting problems often occur if the parameters are not appropriate. Figure 6 shows the CIR after least-square regression analysis under different parameters.

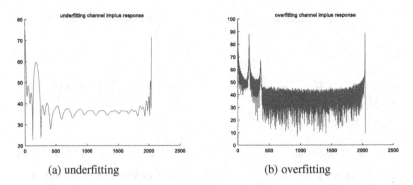

(a) underfitting   (b) overfitting

Fig. 6. Different parameter selection results in CIR overfitting or underfitting.

4   Conclusions

In this paper, the performance of channel data cleaning is investigated by comparing the CIR before and after data cleaning. The results show that the data cleaning can effectively clean the duplicate data, outlier data and noise in the original channel measurement data, so as to obtain the clean and effective channel measurement data, improve the accuracy and reliability of channel feature parameter extraction, which provides effective theoretical and technical support for wireless environment reconstruction and model construction in the big data environment of MMW channel.

Acknowledgment. The research was supported by the Beijing Municipal Natural Science Foundation-Haidian Original Innovation Foundation (No. L172030), Fundamental Research Funds for the Central Universities under grant 2018JBZ102 and Beijing Nova Program Interdisciplinary Cooperation Project (Z191100001119016).

References

1. Molisch, A.F.: Wireless Communications. Wiley, Hoboken (2011)
2. Manyika, J., Chui, M., Brown, B., et al.: Big data: the next frontier for innovation, competition, and productivity (2011)
3. Wu, X., Zhu, X., Wu, G., Ding, W.: Data mining with big data. IEEE Trans. Knowl. Data Eng. **26**(1), 97–107 (2014)
4. Zhang, J., Zhang, P., Tian, L., et al.: A wireless channel modeling method based on big data mining. CN 106126807A, 16 November 2016
5. Ganti, V., Sarma, A.D.: Data cleaning: a practical perspective. In: Data Cleaning: A Practical Perspective. Morgan & Claypool (2013)
6. Galhardas, H., Florescu, D.: An extensible framework for data cleaning. Technical report, Institute National de Recherche en Informatique et en Automatique (1999)
7. Maletic, J.I., Marcus, A.: Data cleansing: beyond integrity analysis. In: IQ 2000. Division of Computer, Science, 23 June 2000

8. Hernandez, M., Stolfo, S.: The merge/purge problem for large databases. In: Proceedings of the ACM SIGMOD International Conference on Management of Data, pp. 127–138, May 1995

9. Lee, M.L., Ling, T.W., Low, W.L., et al.: IntelliClean: a knowledge—based intelligent data cleaner. In: Proceedings of the 6th ACM SIGKDD International Conference on Knowledge Discovery and Data Mining, pp. 290–294 (2000)

10. Virmani, D., Arora, P., Sethi, E., Sharma, N.: Variegated data swabbing: an improved purge approach for data cleaning. In: 2017 7th International Conference on Cloud Computing, Data Science & Engineering - Confluence, Noida, pp. 226–230 (2017)

11. McCallum, A., Nigam, K., Ungar, L.: Efficient clustering of high-dimensional data sets with application to reference matching. In: Proceedings of the Sixth International Conference on Knowledge Discovery and Data Mining, pp. 169–178 (2000)

12. Fayyad, U., Piatetsky-shapiro, G., Smyth, P., et al.: A statistical perspective on knowledge discovery in databases. In: Advances in Knowledge Discovery and Data Mining. AAAI/MIT Press, Cambridge (1996)

13. He, L., Wu, L., Cai, Y.: Summary of clustering algorithm in data mining. Comput. Appl. Res. (01), 10–13 (2007)

14. Tang, Y., Zhong, D., Yan, X.: Data cleaning technology based on clustering model. Comput. Appl. (05), 118–121 (2004)

15. Duda, R.O., Hart, P.E., Stork, D.H.: Pattern Classification, 2nd edn. Wiley, Hoboken (2000)

16. Hernandez, M.A., Stolfo, J.S.: Real—world data is dirty: data cleaning and the merge/purge problem. J. Data Min. Knowl. Discov. 2(1), 9–37 (1998)

17. Marcus, A., Maletic, J.I.: Utilizing association rules for the identification of errors in data. Technical report C& 00-04

18. Kokaram, A.C., Morris, R.D., Fitzgerald, W.J., Rayner, P.J.W.: Interpolation of missing data in image sequences. IEEE Trans. Image Process. 4(11), 1509–1519 (1995)

A New Health Assessment Approach of Lithium-Ion Batteries Under Variable Operation Conditions

Sheng Hong[1(✉)] and Yining Zeng[2]

[1] Beihang University, Beijing, China
shenghong@buaa.edu.cn
[2] Nanchang University, Nanchang, Jiangxi, China

Abstract. The monitoring information of the Lithium-ion batteries is influenced by variable operation conditions. Many health assessment approaches acquire the battery monitoring information to assess the battery health status. However, these approaches have poor adaptability under variable operation conditions. This paper presents a new health assessment approach of the Lithium-ion batteries under variable operation conditions. Specifically, it extracts the geometrical characteristics of charging and discharging curves of the lithium-ion batteries. Furthermore, it adapts a multiple dimensionality reduction approach based on the locally linear embedding and Isomap. Moreover, the synthetical correlation coefficient is proposed to evaluate the ability of the method to be immune to variable operation conditions. Finally, the example illustrates the effectiveness of the proposed method.

Keywords: Health assessment · Locally linear embedding · Isomap · Lithium-ion battery

1 Introduction

As a popular energy storage device, lithium-ion batteries are widely utilized in electric vehicle, three-dimensional printing, and other industries [1–3]. The researches of health assessment of lithium-ion batteries are attracting increasing attention [4]. Considering the situation of cascading failure, the cascading failure analysis and restoration strategy have a significant contribution to health assessment of lithium-ion batteries [5–7]. Many efficient approaches are developed for health assessment of lithium-ion batteries in the past years. A self-adaptive health evaluation method is proposed [8], which based on the online measurable parameters. An effective health indicator is presented in literature [9], and moving-window-based method is utilized to evaluate the battery remaining useful time. A health assessment approach based on the least square method is introduced in the literature [10]. The decreasing battery V_{0+} model and the increasing constant voltage charge capacity model is proposed to estimate the state of health (SOH) of lithium-ion batteries [11]. Considering the requirement in engineering applications, the impedance and the available capacity of the battery are considered in

© Springer Nature Switzerland AG 2020
X. Chen et al. (Eds.): ML4CS 2020, LNCS 12487, pp. 190–200, 2020.
https://doi.org/10.1007/978-3-030-62460-6_17

the new evaluation method of SOH [12]. Meanwhile, the methods based on network models are suitable for the health assessment of lithium-ion batteries [13, 14].

However, variable operation conditions of lithium-ion batteries have serious impacts on the evaluation process, which is unable solved by the methods mentioned above. This paper proposed a health assessment method of the lithium-ion batteries under variable operation conditions. Aiming at the inefficiency of a single algorithm, a multiple dimensionality reduction method is introduced.

The remainder of this paper is presented as follows. The procedures and backgrounds of proposed method are provided in Sect. 2. An illustrative example is given in Sect. 3. Section 4 shows the conclusion of this paper.

2 Procedures of Proposed Method

2.1 Feature Extraction

The Extraction of Geometrical Characteristics. Feature extraction is a necessary part of health assessment and health trend prediction [15, 16]. It is difficult to obtain the internal electrochemical information of lithium-ion batteries for health assessment [17]. However, the SOH of lithium-ion batteries will change with charging and discharging behavior. Meanwhile, the data of the charge-discharge cycles can be easily obtained by sensors. Figure 1(a) shows the charging current curve of the 60th, 110th, and 160th charge-discharge cycle [18]. The charging current curve moving left with the increasing number of charge-discharge cycles. As shown in Fig. 1(b), the discharging voltage curve moving left with the increasing number of charge-discharge cycles [18]. These specific trends contain information about battery performance recession.

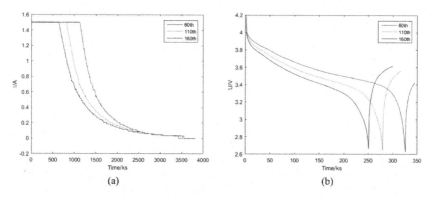

(a)   (b)

Fig. 1. The charging and discharging curves of lithium-ion batteries ((a) charging, (b) discharging).

Four geometrical characteristics are utilized to assess the SOH of lithium-ion batteries. The details of these geometrical characteristics are shown in Table 1.

Table 1. The details of four geometrical characteristics

Behavior	Geometrical characteristic	Symbol	Describe
Charge	Duration of the constant current mode	T_c	T_c decreased with increasing cycle number
	The area between the current curve and the x-axis	S_c	S_c decreased with increasing cycle number
Discharge	The area between the voltage curve and the x-axis	S_d	S_d decreased with increasing cycle number
	Average offset coefficient of voltage	K_d	K_d increased with increasing cycle number

The average offset coefficient of voltage is calculated by the degree of the curve deviates from the standard value before increasing. It is assumed that the standard value is 4 V in this paper. The battery B0036 is chosen as an example for showing the trends of four geometrical characteristics as shown in Fig. 2.

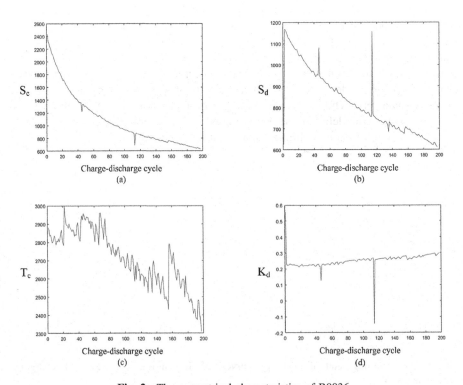

Fig. 2. The geometrical characteristics of B0036

Normalization Processing. For the normalization processing, it is assumed that there are m cycles and n geometrical characteristics. The decision matrix A is constructed as:

$$A = \begin{pmatrix} a_{11} & \cdots & a_{1n} \\ \vdots & \ddots & \vdots \\ a_{m1} & \cdots & a_{mn} \end{pmatrix} \tag{1}$$

where a_{ij} represents the geometrical characteristic value of attribute j in cycle i.

The values and dimensions among attributes are different before we normalize the decision matrix. Comparing these attributes directly would cause a considerable deviation of the result. Therefore, the Min-Max normalization method is utilized to normalize the decision matrix [19].

The decision matrix $A = (a_{ij})_{m*n}$ is converted into the normalizing decision matrix $X = (x_{ij})_{m*n}$ by Eq. 2.

$$x_{ij} = \frac{a_{ij} - \min_j(a_{ij})}{\max_j(a_{ij}) - \min_j(a_{ij})} \tag{2}$$

where $i = 1, 2, \cdots, m, j = 1, 2, \cdots, n$.

2.2 Health Assessment of Lithium-Ion Battery

Locally Linear Embedding. Locally linear embedding (LLE) is a novel dimensionality reduction method for nonlinear data [20]. The main idea of LLE is that the data point is defined as a linear combination of its local neighbors, and a lower dimensional embedding that contains local linear relationships is utilized to reduce the dimensionality of data [21].

LLE can deal with non-linear manifold geometries. This method fits locally along the manifold and analyzes the relationships of the original structure of the data. The procedures of LLE is shown as follows:

1. Find nearest neighbors
   The parameter k must be defined before the application of LLE algorithm, and different values of k seriously influence the result. The k-nearest neighbor (KNN) algorithm is utilized to find k nearest neighbors of each data point:

$$\begin{cases} N_i = KNN(x_i, k) \\ N_i = [x_{1i}, \ldots, x_{ki}] \\ i = 1, \ldots, n, j = 1, \ldots k \end{cases} \tag{3}$$

   where x_i represents the data point, and x_{ij} represents the nearest neighbor of x_i
2. Calculate optimal weights
   The optimal weights are calculated by solving optimization problem:

$$\begin{cases} J(W) = \min\left(\sum_{i=1}^{n}\left\|x_i - \sum_{j=1}^{k} w_{ij}x_j\right\|^2\right) \\ s.t. \sum_{j=1}^{k} w_{ij} = 1 \end{cases} \qquad (4)$$

where $W = [w_{ij}]_{n*n}$ is the weight matrix.

3. Map to lower dimensional space

Map original data to lower dimensional space through solving the optimization problem:

$$\begin{cases} J(Y) = \min\left(\sum_{i=1}^{n}\left\|y_i - \sum_{j=1}^{k} w_{ij}y_j\right\|^2\right) \\ s.t. \sum_{j=1}^{k} y_j = 0, \frac{1}{m}\sum_{i=1}^{n} y_i y_i^T = I \end{cases} \qquad (5)$$

where $Y = (y_1, y_2, \ldots, y_n)^T$ is output matrix which in lower dimensional space.

Isomap. Isomap is an improved MDS (multidimensional scaling) and inherits the advantages of MDS [22, 23]. The procedures of Isomap is shown as follows:

1. Construct the graph G

Connect all pairs of points to construct the neighborhood graph G. Let edge lengths equal to the Euclidean distance $d_X(x_i, x_j)$ if the following conditions are satisfied.

- A nearest neighbor of x_j is x_i.
- x_i and x_j are linked by the same edge.

2. Compute the matrix D_G

The shortest paths matrix $D_G = (d_G(x_i, x_j))_{n*n} = (d_{ij})_{n*n}$ is calculated as follows:

$$d_{ij} = \min\{d_X(x_i, x_j), d_G(x_i, x_k) + d_G(x_k, x_j)\} \qquad (6)$$

The shortest paths matrix D_G contains the shortest path distances among all points in graph G.

3. MDS algorithm

Let D_G be the inputs of the MDS algorithm. The main idea of MDS algorithm is keeping the distance between data points which from high-dimensional to low-dimensional space [24–26]. Set $Y = (y_1, y_2, \ldots, y_n)^T$ be the outputs which calculated by following equations:

$$\begin{cases} d_{ij}^2 = \|y_i\|^2 + \|y_i\|^2 - 2y_i^T y_j \\ \quad = b_{ii} + b_{jj} - 2b_{ij} \\ d_{i\cdot}^2 = \frac{1}{n}[tr(B)] + nb_{ii} \\ d_{\cdot i}^2 = \frac{1}{n}[tr(B)] + nb_{jj} \\ d_{\cdot\cdot}^2 = \frac{2}{n}tr(B) \\ b_{ij} = -\frac{1}{2}\left(d_{ij}^2 - d_{i\cdot}^2 - d_{\cdot i}^2 + d_{\cdot\cdot}^2\right) \end{cases} \tag{7}$$

where $B = Y^T Y$, $tr(B)$ is the trace of matrix B.

A Multiple Dimensionality Reduction Method. LLE and Isomap are unsupervised learning algorithms, and each has its own advantages and disadvantages. Isomap can produce a globally optimal low dimensional Euclidean representation. LLE recovers global nonlinear structure from locally linear fits.

However, using a single algorithm to reduce the dimension of the data will cause the loss and distortion of the intrinsic features of the data, and the single algorithm have poor adaptability under variable operation conditions. This paper presents a new multiple dimensionality reduction method that combined LLE and Isomap. Specifically, it adopts Isomap algorithm map the inputs from high dimensional space to a lower dimensional space, and the LLE algorithm is utilized to map the data from low-dimensional space to one dimension. Finally, the health assessment of lithium-ion batteries is processed based on the outputs. The illustrated example shows the effectiveness of the proposed method.

3 Case Study

Figure 3 shows the procedures of proposed health assessment approach. In this paper, the monitoring data of lithium-ion batteries provided by NASA PCoE research center are utilized to prove the effectiveness of the proposed approach. The operating conditions of different lithium-ion batteries are shown in Table 2. The temperature, output current, and output voltage(ending) are chosen as three operating conditions in this paper.

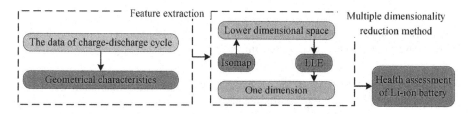

Fig. 3. The procedures of proposed health assessment approach

The Fig. 4(a) and Fig. 4(b) show the results of LLE and Isomap respectively. It can be seen from the result that the single algorithm has poor adaptability under different

Table 2. Operating conditions of different lithium-ion batteries

Number	Temperature	Output current	Output voltage(ending)
B0029	43	4 A	2 V
B0033	24	4 A	2 V
B0042	4	Variable (4 A and 1 A)	2.2 V
B0045	3	2 A	2 V
B0048	3	1 A	2.7 V

operating conditions. However, the proposed method has relatively good adaptability under variable operation conditions as shown in Fig. 4(c) which at the next page.

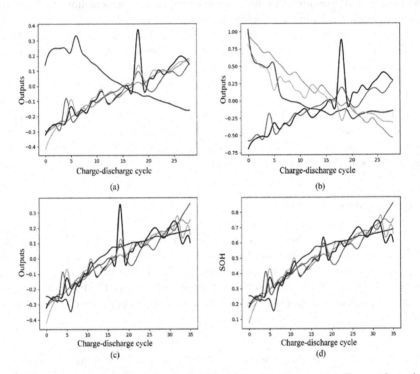

Fig. 4. The outputs of different methods ((a) LLE, (b) Isomap, (c) Proposed method, (d) Performance of assessed values of lithium-ion batteries).

Aiming at some significant fluctuations in Fig. 4(c), the explanation of NASA PCoE research center is given as follows [18]:

"Note that there are several discharges runs where the capacity as well as voltage levels were very low. Reasons for this have not been fully analyzed."

The average curve and a threshold k are established to deal with the large fluctuations in outputs. The average curve is calculated by Eq. 8, and the threshold k is equal to 0.2 in this paper. If the significant deviations have occurred between the output data point the average data point, the output data point will be replaced by the average data point. Meanwhile, the curves are shifted upwards to assess the health status of the battery easily the Fig. 4(d) shows the processed curves.

$$a = (s_d + s_c + t_c + k_d) \times \frac{1}{4} \qquad (8)$$

It needs to be explained that the SOH value does not starts from 0 since the health assessment starts from the first cycle instead of 0.

The synthetical correlation coefficient (SCC) evaluation method based on the Pearson correlation coefficient (PCC) is proposed to quantify the differences between the various methods. The PCC is universally acknowledged as an approach of measuring the correlation between the curves and has a range of +1 (perfect correlation) to −1 (perfect but negative correlation) with 0 denoting the absence of a relationship [27–29].

Different from the Euclidean distance similarity score, PCC evaluates how highly correlated are two curves. Technically, the PCC quantifies how well two data objects fit a line. PCC has several advantages, and one of them is that the PCC adjusts for any scaling within an attribute. Therefore, PCC is utilized to quantify the objects that describe the same data but use different values.

SCC is an improved PCC. For an intuitive result, the SCC has range +1 (perfect correlation) to 0 (absence of a relationship). The procedures of SCC evaluation method are given as follows:

1. Calculate the PCC of each pair of curves
   The PCC of each pair of curves is given as follows:

$$PCC_{ij} = \frac{\text{cov}(i,j)}{\sigma_i \sigma_j} \qquad (9)$$

where the $\text{cov}(i, j)$ represents the covariance of curves i and j, and the σ represents standard deviation. There are four equivalent formulas for calculating PCC:

$$PCC_{ij} = \frac{E(ij) - E(i)E(j)}{\sqrt{E(i^2) - E^2(i)}\sqrt{E(j^2) - E^2(j)}} \qquad (10)$$

$$PCC_{ij} = \frac{N\sum ij - \sum i \sum j}{\sqrt{N\sum i^2 - (\sum i)^2}\sqrt{N\sum j^2 - (\sum j)^2}} \qquad (11)$$

$$PCC_{ij} = \frac{\sum (i - \bar{i})(j - \bar{j})}{\sqrt{\sum (i - \bar{i})^2 \sum (j - \bar{j})^2}} \qquad (12)$$

$$PCC_{ij} = \frac{\sum ij - \frac{\sum i \sum j}{N}}{\sqrt{\left(\sum i^2 - \frac{(\sum i)^2}{N}\right)\left(\sum j^2 - \frac{(\sum j)^2}{N}\right)}} \tag{13}$$

where N represents the number of charge-discharge cycles.

2. Pairwise comparison matrix P

$$P = \begin{pmatrix} PCC_{11} & \cdots & PCC_{1n} \\ \vdots & \ddots & \vdots \\ PCC_{n1} & \cdots & PCC_{nn} \end{pmatrix} = \begin{pmatrix} 1 & \cdots & PCC_{1n} \\ \vdots & \ddots & \vdots \\ PCC_{n1} & \cdots & 1 \end{pmatrix} \tag{14}$$

The pairwise comparison matrix P is constructed by PCC_{ij}. Each curve completely coincides with itself. Therefore, PCC_{ii} is equal to 1. The pairwise comparison matrix of Isomap and the proposed method are shown in Table 3 as an example.

Table 3. The pairwise comparison matrix of Isomap and proposed method

Method	P				
Isomap	1	0.9213	0.0575	0.0364	0.9771
	0.9213	1	0.1309	0.0926	0.9231
	0.0575	0.1309	1	0.9434	0.0338
	0.0364	0.0926	0.9434	1	0.043
	0.9771	0.9231	0.0338	0.043	1
Proposed method	1	0.9695	0.9738	0.9749	0.976
	0.9695	1	0.9606	0.9477	0.9542
	0.9738	0.9606	1	0.9366	0.9879
	0.9749	0.9477	0.9366	1	0.9461
	0.976	0.9542	0.9879	0.9461	1

3. Compute the SCC.

$$\begin{cases} S = P \times 0.5 + 0.5 \\ SCC = \frac{1}{n \times m} \sum_{i=1}^{m} \sum_{j=1}^{n} S_{ij} \end{cases} \tag{15}$$

where $i = 1, 2, \ldots, m$, $j = 1, 2, \ldots, n$.

The elements of the matrix S have a reasonable range through processing the matrix P. Moreover, SCC is obtained by averaging all the elements of the matrix S.

Table 4 shows the SCC of different methods. Compared with other methods, the SCC of the proposed method is remarkably close to 1, which means the SOH curves under variable operation conditions are highly correlated. More specifically, the proposed method is less affected by variable operation conditions.

Table 4. The SCC of different methods

Method	LLE	Isomap	Proposed method
SCC	0.6799	0.5327	0.9702

4 Conclusion

In this paper, a new health assessment approach of the lithium-ion batteries under variable operation conditions is proposed. Additionally, four typical geometrical characteristics of charging and discharging curves are utilized to assess the SOH of the lithium-ion batteries. Aiming at the disadvantages of single dimensionality reduction algorithm, a multiple dimensionality reduction method is introduced. The illustrated example shows that the proposed method has relatively good adaptability under variable operation conditions, and the SCC is proposed for evaluating the ability of the method to be immune to variable operation conditions.

Acknowledgments. The authors are highly thankful for National Key Research Program (2019YFB1706001), National Natural Science Foundation of China (61773001), Industrial Internet Innovation Development Project (TC190H46B).

References

1. Yang, Y., Yuan, W., Zhang, X., et al.: Overview on the applications of three-dimensional printing for rechargeable lithium-ion batteries. Appl. Energy **257**(1), 114002 (2020)
2. Gong, X., Xiong, R., Mi, C.C.: Study of the characteristics of battery packs in electric vehicles with parallel-connected lithium-ion battery cells. IEEE Trans. Ind. Appl. **51**(2), 1872–1879 (2015)
3. Hannan, M.A., Hoque, M.M., Peng, S.E., et al.: Lithium-ion battery charge equalization algorithm for electric vehicle applications. IEEE Trans. Ind. Appl. **53**(3), 2541–2549 (2017)
4. Giordano, G., Klass, V., Behm, M., et al.: Model-based lithium-ion battery resistance estimation from electric vehicle operating data. IEEE Trans. Veh. Technol. **67**(5), 3720–3728 (2018)
5. Hong, S., Lv, C., Zhao, T., et al.: Cascading failure analysis and restoration strategy in an interdependent network. J. Phys. A: Math. Theor. **19**(49), 195101 (2016)
6. Hong, S., Wang, B., Ma, X., et al.: Failure cascade in interdependent network with traffic loads. J. Phys. A: Math. Theor. **48**(48), 485101 (2015)
7. Hong, S., Zhu, J., Braunstein, L.A., et al.: Cascading failure and recovery of spatially interdependent networks. J. Stat. Mech.-Theory Exp. **10**, 103208 (2017)
8. Liu, D., Song, Y., Li, L., et al.: On-line life cycle health assessment for lithium-ion battery in electric vehicles. J. Clean. Prod. **199**(20), 1050–1065 (2018)
9. Xiong, R., Zhang, Y., Wang, J., et al.: Lithium-ion battery health prognosis based on a real battery management system used in electric vehicles. IEEE Trans. Veh. Technol. **68**(5), 4110–4121 (2019)
10. Yang, Q., Xu, J., Cao, B., et al.: State-of-health Estimation of Lithium-ion Battery Based on Interval Capacity. Energy Procedia **105**, 2342–2347 (2017)

11. Kong, X.R., Bonakdarpour, A., Wetton, B., et al.: State of health estimation for lithium-ion batteries. IFAC-PapersOnline **51**, 667–671 (2018)
12. Jiang, J., Lin, Z., Ju, Q., et al.: Electrochemical impedance spectra for lithium-ion battery ageing considering the rate of discharge ability. Energy Procedia **105**, 844–849 (2017)
13. Hong, S., Yang, H., Zhao, T., et al.: Epidemic spreading model of complex dynamical network with the heterogeneity of nodes. Int. J. Syst. Sci. **11**(47), 2745–2752 (2016)
14. Hong, S., Zhang, X., Zhu, J., et al.: Suppressing failure cascades in interconnected networks: considering capacity allocation pattern and load redistribution. Modern Phys. Lett. B **5**(30), 1650049 (2016)
15. Hong, S., Zhou, Z., Zio, E., et al.: Condition assessment for the performance degradation of bearing based on a combinatorial feature extraction method. Digit. Sig. Process. **27**, 159–166 (2014)
16. Hong, S., Zhou, Z., Zio, E., et al.: An adaptive method for health trend prediction of rotating bearings. Digit. Sig. Process. **35**, 117–123 (2014)
17. Bao, T., Ma, J., Gan, Z.: Performance assessment of lithium-ion battery based on geometric features and manifold distance. J. Shandong Univ. (Eng. Sci.) **47**(5), 157–165 (2017)
18. Saha, B., Goebel, K.: Battery data set. NASA ames prognostics data repository. NASA Ames Research Center, Moffett Field (2007). http://ti.arc.nasa.gov/project/prognostic-data-repository
19. Li, W., Liu, Z.: A method of SVM with normalization in intrusion detection. Procedia Environ. Sci. **11**(Part A), 256–262 (2011)
20. Ward, J.L., Lumsden, S.L.: Locally linear embedding: dimension reduction of massive protostellar spectra. Mon. Not. Roy. Astron. Soc. **461**(2), 2250–2256 (2016)
21. Roweis, S., Saul, L.: Nonlinear dimensionality reduction by locally linear embedding. Science **290**(5500), 2323–2326 (2000)
22. Xu, K., Li, H., Liu, Z.: ISOMAP-based spatiotemporal modeling for lithium-ion battery thermal process. IEEE Trans. Ind. Inform. **14**(2), 569–577 (2018)
23. Tenenbaum, J.B., De Silva, V., Langford, J.C.: A global geometric framework for nonlinear dimensionality reduction. Science **290**(5500), 2319–2323 (2000)
24. Amar, A., Wang, Y., Leus, G.: Extending the classical multidimensional scaling algorithm given partial pairwise distance measurements. IEEE Sig. Process. Lett. **17**(5), 473–476 (2010)
25. Pohlheim, H.: Multidimensional scaling for evolutionary algorithms—visualization of the path through search space and solution space using sammon mapping. Artif. Life **12**(2), 203–209 (2006)
26. Chen, Z., Wei, H., Wan, Q., Ye, S., et al.: A supplement to multidimensional scaling framework for mobile location: a unified view. IEEE Trans. Sig. Process. **57**(5), 2030–2034 (2009)
27. Gillham, E.M.: A Life of Sir Francis Galton. Oxford University Press, Oxford (2001)
28. Ren, L., Zhao, L., Hong, S., et al.: Remaining useful life prediction for lithium-ion battery: a deep learning approach. IEEE Access **6**, 50587–50598 (2018)
29. Adler, J., Parmryd, I.: Quantifying colocalization by correlation: the Pearson correlation coefficient is superior to the Mander's overlap coefficient. Cytometry Part A **77**, 733–742 (2010)

Health Evaluation of Lithium Ion Battery Based on Weighted Kalman Filter Algorithm

Sheng Hong$^{(\boxtimes)}$ and Tianyu Yue

School of Cyber Science and Technology, Beihang University,
No. 37, Xue Yuan Road, Beijing 100191, China
shenghong@buaa.edu.cn

Abstract. With the wide application of lithium ion batteries in various fields, the safety and reliability of lithium ion batteries have been put forward higher requirements, and the health evaluation of lithium ion batteries is very important. In this paper, a new health evaluation method for lithium ion batteries based on weighted kalman filter algorithm is proposed by investigating and analyzing the existing health evaluation methods for lithium ion batteries. Based on the general kalman filter, the weighted kalman filter algorithm was proposed to evaluate the health of lithium ion batteries by constructing the battery SOH double-exponential recession model and the gaussian-type feature correlation mapping model for the health characteristics of lithium ion batteries. Four lithium ion battery data sets provided by NASA were used to simulate and verify the proposed health evaluation method. The verification results show that the health evaluation method of lithium ion battery based on weighted kalman filter proposed in this paper has better evaluation accuracy than the ordinary kalman filter method, with an average percentage error of 0.61%. Moreover, the average absolute percentage error of the health evaluation method for different types of batteries was less than 0.9%, and the method was applicable to all types of lithium ion batteries.

Keywords: Lithium ion battery · Health evaluation · Weighted kalman filtering

1 Introduction

The performance of lithium ion battery will decrease with the continuous cycle of battery use. When the performance of lithium ion battery is reduced to a certain extent, failure will occur, which may even lead to serious or even catastrophic consequences. Therefore, it is important to conduct health evaluation research on lithium ion battery and develop battery health management technology [1–4].

The health evaluation of lithium ion batteries can be divided into SOC evaluation and SOH evaluation, and the existing methods can be roughly divided into direct measurement, model-based method and data-driven method [5, 6]. Direct measurement method is to directly measure the battery resistance or capacity to achieve the battery health evaluation. Yuan et al. used a rapid and effective three-point impedance extraction method to estimate the health status of lithium ion batteries [7]. Guo et al. monitored the charging curves of different battery life, and evaluated SOH using transformation function and nonlinear least square method [8]. The direct measurement

© Springer Nature Switzerland AG 2020
X. Chen et al. (Eds.): ML4CS 2020, LNCS 12487, pp. 201–213, 2020.
https://doi.org/10.1007/978-3-030-62460-6_18

method is simple to calculate and easy to realize, but the stability and robustness of this method are weak, the estimation accuracy is easily affected by noise, and the actual operation is difficult.

The model-based method constructs the battery decay model and establishes the empirical formula based on the characteristic parameters to realize the battery health evaluation. Wang et al. used the first-order equivalent circuit model to describe the aging phenomenon of batteries, reflecting the characteristics of battery SOH [9]. Lysander et al. performed a comprehensive parameter evaluation of the fractional differential model, which proved that the model was more accurate than the traditional equivalent circuit model [10]. Li et al. proposed a capacitance-voltage model based on the charging process curve, and estimated the SOH of lithium ion batteries [11]. Liu et al. established a double-exponential degradation model of battery, which has good accuracy robustness and the ability of uncertainty characterization [12]. Yang et al. proposed a semi-empirical model based on the relationship between coulomb efficiency and battery degradation, and used particle filter to update the model parameters regularly [13]. The model-based method has good robustness and stability, but it relies too much on the accuracy of the specific model for specific target objects and is complicated in calculation, which limits its application in practice.

The data-driven method extracts available battery features as input and evaluates predicted values as output [14]. Various algorithms such as self-organizing mapping [15], gaussian process regression [16] and empirical modal decomposition [17, 18] are used flexibly to study the correlation between input and output, so as to achieve the purpose of evaluating battery health. Song et al. used the sparsity training nonlinear mapping model of the correlation vector machine model to obtain the health evaluation results with uncertainty representation [19]. Ding et al. proposed a health evaluation method for lithium ion batteries based on multi-layer feature integration and deep learning [20]. Verena et al. proposed a SOH estimation method based on support vector machine model and virtual standard performance test to detect battery degradation online [21]. Wang et al. proposed a training method for multiple capacity prediction of lithium ion battery based on recursive neural network, which has a significant improvement in reliability compared with the single-sample training method [22]. Deng et al. proposed a new least squares support vector machine training set design idea, and established a SOH estimation model for lithium ion batteries under multiple working conditions [23]. The data-driven method can further improve the reliability and accuracy of battery health state estimation, but it requires a large amount of computation and takes a long time to run.

Therefore, this paper proposes a lithium ion battery health evaluation method based on weighted kalman filter algorithm. The gaussian-type feature correlation mapping model was constructed based on the health characteristics, combined with the SOH double-exponential recession model, on the basis of the kalman filter, a weighted kalman filter algorithm was proposed to evaluate the health of lithium ion batteries.

The structure of the rest of this paper is as follows. Section 2 introduces the principle and steps of the traditional kalman filtering algorithm, and the improvement of the weighted kalman filtering algorithm proposed in this paper. Section 3 establishes the health evaluation model based on the feature correlation mapping model and the SOH double-exponential recession model. In Sect. 4, the accuracy and applicability of the proposed health evaluation method for lithium ion batteries are verified by simulation and comparative analysis. Section 5 summarizes the whole paper.

2 Evaluation Method

2.1 Kalman Filtering Algorithm

Kalman filter algorithm is a recursive estimation algorithm that adopts minimum mean square error as the optimal criterion for estimating results, and it can estimate and predict the real-time running state of dynamic signals [24, 25]. The steps are as follows:

Construct the state equation of the estimated signal

$$X(k) = A \cdot X(k-1) + B \cdot F(k) + W(k) \tag{1}$$

where $X(k)$, $X(k-1)$ are the quantity of system state at time k, $k-1$, the covariance of $X(k)$ is denoted as P, $F(k)$ is the control quantity of system state at time k, $W(k)$ is the noise of system state at time k, and the covariance of $W(k)$ is denoted as Q, A and B are the parameters of system state equation.

Establish the system measurement equation based on the actual measured value

$$Z(k) = C \cdot M(k) + V(k) \tag{2}$$

where $Z(k)$, $M(k)$ are the system measurement variable and actual measurement value at time k, $V(k)$ is the noise in the measurement at time k, the covariance of $V(k)$ is R, and C is the system parameter.

Estimate the current system state

$$X(k|k-1) = A \cdot X(k-1|k-1) + B \cdot F(k) + W(k) \tag{3}$$

where $X(k|k-1)$ is the system state estimated by the state quantity at $k-1$, $X(k-1|k-1)$ is the optimal estimation of system state at $k-1$.

Update the covariance of the current system state quantity

$$P(k|k-1) = A \cdot P(k-1|k-1) + Q \tag{4}$$

where $P(k|k-1)$ is the covariance of $X(k|k-1)$, $P(k-1|k-1)$ is the covariance of $X(k-1|k-1)$ at time $k-1$.

Calculate the optimal estimate of the current state

$$X(k|k) = X(k|k-1) + Kg(k)(Z(k) - C \cdot X(k|k-1)) \tag{5}$$

where $Kg(k)$ is the kalman gain

$$Kg(k) = \frac{P(k|k-1) \cdot H}{P(k|k-1) \cdot H + R} \tag{6}$$

Update the covariance of the optimal estimate under the current state

$$P(k|k) = (I - Kg(k) \cdot C) \cdot P(k|k - 1) \tag{7}$$

where I is all 1 matrix.

Repeat the above steps until the optimal estimation of the whole system is made.

Kalman filter is an effective data prediction and evaluation method, but ordinary kalman filter has poor processing effect on nonlinear system, so some scholars further proposed extended kalman filter [26], unscented kalman filter [27] and multi-scale kalman filter [28].

2.2 Weighted Kalman Filtering Algorithm

The essence of the ordinary kalman filter is to modify the system state estimation according to the measured value, but in many practical cases, there is a large noise in the measurement of the signal, resulting in a large error in the measured value, which is even much larger than the error in the estimated value of the system state. At this time, if the ordinary kalman filtering method is still used for estimation and prediction, it will not improve the estimation result, or even make the estimation result worse.

Based on this problem, this paper proposes a weighted kalman filter algorithm based on the kalman filter algorithm. The weighted kalman filter algorithm does not simply adopt the measured value to modify the estimation of system state variables, but introduces the trend estimation, compares the error of measured value and the error of the trend estimation, and sets the weight of the two. The weight ratio of large error is small, and the weight ratio of small error is large. The weighted value is used as the input of kalman filter measurement equation, so as to improve the effect of kalman filter and reduce the estimation error caused by excessive measurement noise. According to this idea, rewrite Eq. 2 as

$$Z(k) = C \cdot (w_m \cdot M(k) + w_T \cdot T(k)) + V(k) \tag{8}$$

Where $T(k)$ is the current trend estimate at time k, w_m is the weight coefficient of the actual measured value and w_T is the weight coefficient of the trend estimate, and they add up to 100%. If the error of the measured value $M(k)$ is small, a large weight coefficient will be assigned to $M(k)$, otherwise, a large weight coefficient will be assigned to $T(k)$. The influence of measurement error on the evaluation results is improved by the distribution of weight coefficient, and the accuracy and superiority of the algorithm for estimation and prediction are improved.

3 Construction of Health Evaluation Model

3.1 Battery SOH Double Exponential Recession Model

With the continuous charging and discharging of the lithium ion battery, the battery's capacity decreases, the internal resistance increases, and the battery's healthy SOH also declines. By analyzing the decline curve of battery SOH along with the number of battery cycles, it was found that with the increase of battery cycles, battery health SOH showed an overall decline and a partial rise. The recession model of lithium ion battery SOH was constructed to reflect the decay of battery SOH. Through previous literature review, it is found that the overall decline trend of battery SOH follows the form of exponential function, and the decline model generally adopts the exponential model. Therefore, this paper adopts the double-exponential recession model of lithium ion battery SOH constructed by Liu et al. [12] to characterize the decline trend of battery SOH. The specific formula of the double-exponential recession model of battery SOH is as follows

$$SOH = a \times e^{bk} + c \times e^{dk} \tag{9}$$

where k is the number of battery cycles, and a, b, c and d are all parameters of the model.

The least square method was used to identify the parameters of the double-exponential recession model of battery health state, and the results of parameter identification were $a = 0.788$, $b = -0.005483$, $c = 0.2238$, $d = 0.001126$. The identification parameters were substituted into the formula to construct the SOH double-exponential recession model of the healthy state of the lithium ion battery.

The double-exponential recession model well reflects the decline of lithium ion battery's continuous cycle use over time, that is, the state of battery SOH under the current cycle use times. Therefore, the battery SOH double-exponential recession model can be applied to the trend estimation variable $T(k)$ in the measurement equation to build the measurement equation model of the weighted kalman filter algorithm.

3.2 Gaussian Type Feature Correlation Mapping Model

The charge and discharge curve data of lithium ion battery were analyzed to extract the characteristic index HI for health evaluation. In order to apply the extracted characteristic index HI to the evaluation of battery SOH, it is necessary to build a feature correlation mapping model of lithium ion battery, explore the correlation characteristics between health characteristic index HI and battery SOH, and map the health characteristic index HI to battery SOH for the next step of battery health evaluation.

Through research and analysis, it was found that the extracted health characteristic indexes HI and battery SOH were approximately linearly correlated. Based on this finding, Liu [12] et al. constructed a linear correlation mapping model between health characteristic indexes and battery SOH. This paper continued to explore and analyze and found that although the linear feature correlation mapping model can reflect the overall correspondence between battery SOH and the feature index HI, there are still some deviations in some details, and the corresponding relationship between battery SOH and the feature index is not accurately reflected.

In this paper, after many studies and comparisons, it is found that the gaussian function is used to construct the feature correlation mapping model, especially the feature correlation mapping model based on the second order gaussian function is more effective. Therefore, this paper constructs a second-order gaussian model of feature correlation mapping, whose formula is as follows

$$SOH = a1 \times e^{-\left(\frac{HI-b1}{c1}\right)^2} + a2 \times e^{-\left(\frac{HI-b2}{c2}\right)^2}$$

(10)

where HI is the health characteristic index, and $a1$, $b1$, $c1$, $a2$, $b2$ and $c2$ are all parameters of the model.

The least square method is used to identify the model parameters, and the gaussian model of feature correlation mapping is obtained, as shown in Fig. 1. The health feature index is extracted from the measured data of the charging and discharging process of the lithium ion battery. Therefore, the feature correlation mapping model can be applied to the measured value $M(k)$ in the measured equation in the weighted kalman filter algorithm to construct the measured equation model of the weighted kalman filter algorithm.

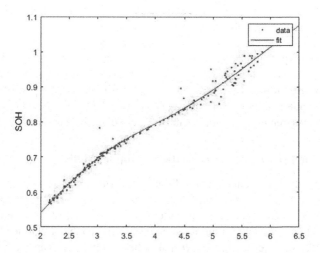

Fig. 1. Gaussian type feature correlation mapping model

4   Simulation Verification and Analysis

4.1   Evaluation Index of Simulation Verification

In order to have a clearer understanding of the health evaluation results of the battery, it is necessary to set up quantitative evaluation indexes for the health evaluation of the lithium ion battery, and compare and analyze the results and errors of the battery health evaluation. Quantitative evaluation indexes include: root mean square error RMSE, average absolute error MAE and average absolute percentage error MAPE. The specific calculation formulas of each quantitative evaluation index are as follows.

Root mean square error RMSE

$$\text{RMSE} = \frac{1}{N}\sqrt{\sum_{k=1}^{N}(SOH^k - SOH^k_{estimated})^2} \tag{11}$$

where SOH^k represents the true value of battery health state SOH under the k-th cycle, $SOH^k_{estimated}$ represents the estimated value of battery health state SOH under the k-th cycle, and N represents the total number of battery cycle life in the data.

Average absolute error MAE

$$\text{MAE} = \frac{1}{N}\sum_{k=1}^{N}\left|SOH^k - SOH^k_{estimated}\right| \tag{12}$$

where SOH^k represents the true value of battery health state SOH under the k-th cycle, $SOH^k_{estimated}$ represents the estimated value of battery health state SOH under the k-th cycle, and N represents the total number of battery cycle life in the data.

Average absolute percentage error MAPE

$$\text{MAPE} = \frac{1}{N}\sum_{k=1}^{N}\left|\frac{SOH^k - SOH^k_{estimated}}{SOH^k}\right| \tag{13}$$

where SOH^k represents the true value of battery health state SOH under the k-th cycle, $SOH^k_{estimated}$ represents the estimated value of battery health state SOH under the k-th cycle, and N represents the total number of battery cycle life in the data.

4.2 Comparison of Evaluation Accuracy

Kalman filter algorithm has a good effect on data estimation and prediction, so it has been used by many researchers to evaluate battery health SOH.

However, kalman filter algorithm is mostly used for the adaptive prediction and identification of battery SOH evaluation model parameters, so that the evaluation model can be adaptive optimization, so as to achieve the accurate evaluation of battery SOH.

Through research, it is found that kalman filter itself is a recursive estimation algorithm for data, so this paper directly uses kalman filter to evaluate battery SOH. The battery SOH double-exponential recession model [12] and the feature correlation mapping model is applied to kalman filter's measurement equation (Eq. 2). Based on the general kalman filter algorithm and the weighted kalman filter algorithm, the battery health was evaluated and compared. The evaluation results and errors based on the general kalman filter algorithm are shown in Fig. 2, and the evaluation results and errors based on the weighted kalman filter algorithm are shown in Fig. 3. The comparison of the evaluation error indexes between the kalman filter and the weighted kalman filter is shown in Table 1.

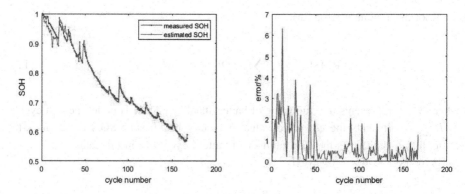

Fig. 2. SOH evaluation results and errors of ordinary kalman filtering

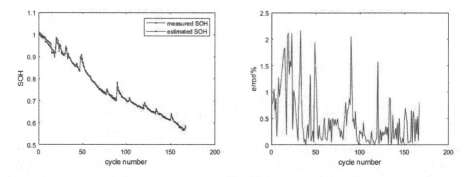

Fig. 3. SOH evaluation results and errors of weighted kalman filter

Table 1. SOH evaluation comparison

	KF	Weighted KF
RMSE	0.0117	0.0071
MAE	0.0074	0.0049
MAPE	0.91%	0.61%

It can be seen from Table 1 that both the evaluation of battery SOH based on kalman filter algorithm and weighted kalman filter algorithm have good estimation effects, with root mean square error less than 0.02, average absolute error less than 0.01, and average absolute percentage error less than 1%. It proves that the kalman filter algorithm and the weighted kalman filter algorithm are effective and accurate in battery health evaluation.

According to Table 1, the evaluation error based on weighted kalman filter algorithm is smaller than that based on kalman filter algorithm. According to the comparison between Figs. 3 and 4, it can be found that the maximum percentage error of SOH evaluation of the kalman filter algorithm is 6.5%, and the maximum percentage error of SOH evaluation of the weighted kalman filter algorithm is 2.5%. The above chart shows the effective improvement of weighted kalman filter algorithm to further reduce errors and improve the accuracy of data estimation and prediction.

4.3   Validation of the Evaluation Method's Applicability

In order to further verify the effectiveness and applicability of the method proposed in this paper, the evaluation method was applied to four batteries in the NASA battery data set.

Health features were extracted from four battery data of B0005, B0006, B0007, B0018, and an evaluation model of feature correlation mapping was constructed. The feature correlation mapping evaluation model and the battery SOH recession evaluation model were substituted into the weighted kalman filter algorithm for battery health evaluation. The results and errors of health evaluation are shown in Figs. 4, 5, 6 and 7. The root mean square error, average absolute error and average absolute percentage error of four batteries were calculated and recorded in Table 2.

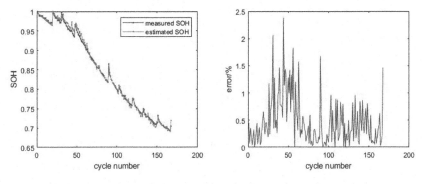

Fig. 4. Health evaluation results and errors of B0005 battery

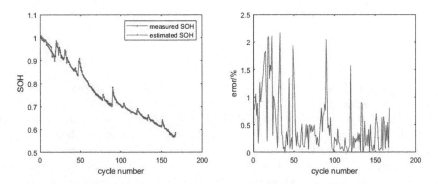

Fig. 5. Health evaluation results and errors of B0006 battery

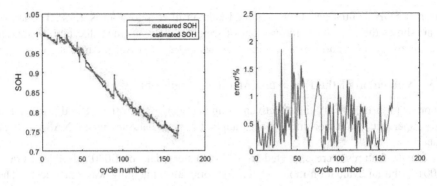

Fig. 6. Health evaluation results and errors of B0007 battery

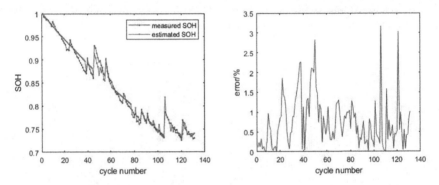

Fig. 7. Health evaluation results and errors of B0018 battery

Table 2. The weighted kalman health evaluation error of four batteries

	B0005	B0006	B0007	B0018
RMSE	0.0064	0.0071	0.0066	0.0099
MAE	0.0047	0.0049	0.0053	0.0075
MAPE	0.54%	0.61%	0.61%	0.89%

As shown in Figs. 4, 5, 6 and 7, the health evaluation method based on weighted kalman filter algorithm has a high coincidence degree between the estimated SOH value of four batteries and the measured SOH value, and the estimated error percentage is less than 2.5%, 2.5% and 3.5%, respectively, indicating that this method has a good accuracy of evaluation. The evaluation error indexes calculated in Table 2 also reflect the accuracy of this method. For the four verification test batteries, the root mean square error of the evaluation results was less than 0.01, the average absolute error was less than 0.008, and the average absolute percentage error was less than 0.9%.

Four battery data provided by NASA are used to verify the health evaluation method of lithium ion battery proposed in this paper, and the applicability of this method is proved.

5 Conclusion

In this paper, a new health evaluation method for lithium ion batteries based on weighted kalman filter algorithm is proposed by investigating and analyzing the existing health evaluation methods for lithium ion batteries. The gauss feature correlation mapping model between battery health characteristics and SOH was constructed, and the gauss feature correlation mapping model was combined with the double-exponential decay model of battery SOH to establish a health evaluation model. A weighted kalman filter algorithm was proposed on the basis of the ordinary kalman filter to carry out the battery health evaluation. Four battery data sets from the NASA battery database were used to verify the proposed health evaluation method for lithium ion batteries. The verification results show that the health evaluation method of lithium ion battery based on weighted kalman filter proposed in this paper has good evaluation accuracy. The evaluation errors are lower than that of ordinary kalman filter. The root mean square error is 0.0071, the average absolute error is 0.0049, and the average absolute percentage error is 0.61%. Moreover, for different types of batteries, the root mean square error of the evaluation results is less than 0.01, the average absolute error is less than 0.008, and the average absolute percentage error is less than 0.9%, which has better applicability. The health assessment method can effectively realize health assessment of lithium ion power battery, but with the continuous development of Internet technology, the power battery power system security defense is not only to need assessment to the health of lithium ion power battery, you also need to further explore the interdependencies and cascading relationships between the network [29, 30], put forward the method to suppress fault cascade no cost defense [31], build a recovery failure node boundary recovery strategy [32], effective defense against hackers for power battery power system security attacks.

Acknowledgements. The authors thank NASA for providing the battery data set for this study. The authors are highly thankful for National Key Research Program (2019YFB1706001), National Natural Science Foundation of China (61773001), Industrial Internet Innovation Development Project (TC190H46B).

References

1. Etacheri, V., et al.: Challenges in the development of advanced Li-ion batteries: a review. Energy Environ. Sci. **4**, 3243–3262 (2011)
2. Palacin, M.R., de Guibert, A.: Why do batteries fail. Science **351**, 1253292 (2016)
3. Feng, X., et al.: Thermal runaway mechanism of lithium ion battery for electric vehicles: a review. Energy Storage Mater. **10**, 246–267 (2018)
4. Waag, W., Fleischer, C., Sauer, D.U.: Critical review of the methods for monitoring of lithium-ion batteries in electric and hybrid vehicles. J. Power Sources **258**, 321–339 (2014)

5. Hossain, L.M.S., et al.: A review of state of health and remaining useful life estimation methods for lithium-ion battery in electric vehicles: challenges and recommendations. J. Clean. Prod. **205**, 115–133 (2018)
6. Yang, A., et al.: Lithium-ion battery SOH estimation and fault diagnosis with missing data. In: IEEE International Instrumentation and Measurement Technology Conference, pp. 1–6. IEEE Instrumentation and Measurement Society, Auckland, New Zealand (2019)
7. Yuan, H.F., Dung, L.: Off-line state-of-health estimation for high power lithium-ion batteries using three-point impedance extraction method. IEEE Trans. Veh. Technol. **66**, 2019–2032 (2017)
8. Guo, Z., et al.: State of health estimation for lithium ion batteries based on charging curves. Power Sources **249**, 457–462 (2014)
9. Wang, Z., et al.: State of health estimation of lithium-ion batteries based on the constant voltage charging curve. Energy **167**, 661–669 (2019)
10. Lysander, D.S., et al.: Battery aging assessment and parametric study of lithium-ion batteries by means of a fractional differential model. Electrochim. Acta **305**, 24–36 (2019)
11. Li, X., et al.: A capacity model based on charging process for state of health estimation of lithium ion batteries. Appl. Energy **177**, 537–543 (2016)
12. Liu, D., et al.: An on-line state of health estimation of lithium-ion battery using unscented particle filter. IEEE Access **6**, 40990–41001 (2018)
13. Yang, F., et al.: A coulombic efficiency-based model for prognostics and health estimation of lithium-ion batteries. Energy **171**, 1173–1182 (2019)
14. Ren, L., Zhao, L., Hong, S.: Remaining useful life prediction for lithium-ion battery: a deep learning approach. IEEE Access **6**, 50587–50598 (2018)
15. Hong, S., Zhou, Z., Zio, E., Wang, W.: An adaptive method for health trend prediction of rotating bearings. Digit. Signal Proc. **35**, 117–123 (2014)
16. Hong, S., Zhou, Z., Lu, C., Wang, B., Zhao, T.: Bearing remaining life prediction using Gaussian process regression with composite kernel functions. J. VibroEng. **17**, 695–704 (2015)
17. Hong, S., Wang, B., Li, G., Hong, Q.: Performance degradation assessment for bearing based on ensemble empirical mode decomposition and Gaussian mixture model. J. Vib. Acoust. **136**, 1–8 (2014)
18. Hong, S., Zhou, Z., Zio, E., Hong, K.: Condition assessment for the performance degradation of bearing based on a combinatorial feature extraction method. Digit. Signal Proc. **27**, 159–166 (2014)
19. Song, Y., Liu, D., Peng, Y.: Data-driven on-line health assessment for lithium-ion battery with uncertainty presentation. In: 2018 IEEE International Conference on Prognostics and Health Management, pp. 1–7. IEEE Instrumentation and Measurement Society, Seattle, WA, USA (2018)
20. Ding, Y., Lu, C., Ma, J.: Li-ion battery health estimation based on multi-layer characteristic fusion and deep learning. In: 2017 IEEE Vehicle Power and Propulsion Conference, pp. 1–5. Institute of Electrical and Electronics Engineers Inc, Belfort, France (2017)
21. Verena, K., et al.: A support vector machine-based state-of-health estimation method for lithium-ion batteries under electric vehicle operation. J. Power Sources **270**, 262–272 (2014)
22. Wang, J.X., et al.: Improved long-term capacity prognosis using Recurrent Softplus Neural Network modeling with initial states trained for individual lithium-ion batteries. IEEE Trans. Veh. Technol. 1–10 (2019)
23. Deng, Y., et al.: Feature parameter extraction and intelligent estimation of the State-of-Health of lithium-ion batteries. Energy **176**, 91–102 (2019)

24. Andre, D., et al.: Comparative study of a structured neural network and an extended Kalman filter for state of health determination of lithium-ion batteries in hybrid electric vehicles. Eng. Appl. Artif. Intell. **26**, 951–961 (2013)
25. Andre, D., et al.: Advanced mathematical methods of SOC and SOH estimation for lithium-ion batteries. J. Power Sources **224**, 20–27 (2013)
26. Gregory, L.P.: Extended Kalman filtering for battery management systems of LiPB-based HEV battery packs Part 3. State and parameter estimation. J. Power Sources **134**, 277–292 (2004)
27. Zheng, X.J., Fang, H.J.: An integrated unscented kalman filter and relevance vector regression approach for lithium-ion battery remaining useful life and short-term capacity prediction. Reliabil. Eng. Syst. Saf. **144**, 74–82 (2015)
28. Xiong, R., et al.: A data-driven multi-scale extended Kalman filtering based parameter and state estimation approach of lithium-ion polymer battery in electric vehicles. Appl. Energy **113**, 463–476 (2014)
29. Hong, S., Lv, C., Zhao, T.D., et al.: Cascading failure analysis and restoration strategy in an interdependent network. J. Phys. A: Math. Theor. **49**, 195101 (2016)
30. Hong, S., Zhang, X.J., Zhu, J.X., et al.: Suppressing failure cascades in interconnected networks: considering capacity allocation pattern and load redistribution. Mod. Phys. Lett. B **30**, 1650049 (2016)
31. Hong, S., Wang, B.Q., Ma, X.M., et al.: Failure cascade in interdependent network with traffic loads. J. Phys. A: Math. Theor. **48**, 485101 (2015)
32. Hong, S., Zhu, J.X., Braunstein, L.A., et al.: Cascading failure and recovery of spatially interdependent networks. J. Stat. Mech: Theory Exp. **10**, 103208 (2017)

Location Planning of UAVs for WSNs Data Collection Based on Adaptive Search Algorithm

Xueqiang Li$^{(\boxtimes)}$ and Ming Tao

School of Computer Science and Technology,
Dongguan University of Technology,
Dongguan 523808, People's Republic of China
lxqchn@163.com, ming.tao@mail.scut.edu.cn

Abstract. Unmanned Aerial Vehicles (UAVs) have been widely used in data collection, tracking and monitoring in wireless sensor networks (WSNs). By considering the three factors of sensor coverage, energy consumption and Quality of Service (QoS), the WSNs data collection problem is transformed into a location planning model for optimizing K-location of UAVs. Besides, an adaptive search algorithm contains two crucial methods are proposed to address this issue, form which one is the optimal matching method between sensors and UAVs, and the other is automatic location generation strategy of UAVs. Finally, analytical and simulation-based results show that the proposed algorithm has obvious advantages over the KMeans algorithm in location planning option of UAVs.

Keywords: WSNs data collection · Location planning · Adaptive search

1 Introduction

With the era of big data, the applications of the Internet of Things (IoT), associated with the federally deployed wireless sensor networks, is widely used in data collection, location tracking, environmental, industrial and traffic monitoring, etc., and has been regarded as a challenging research topic for many years [1–3], and the WSNs data collection has become one of the most critical in the IoT [4].

In the process of data collection in wireless sensor networks, the monitored data may be routed to the sink after multiple hop counts, and finally reach the management node through the internet or satellites [5, 6]. In which the three unacceptable defects mainly encountered: First, the problem of unbalanced energy consumption during information transmission shortens the lifetime of the network [7]. Second, the QoS imbalance of the sensor is not conducive to the timeliness and reliability of data transmission [8]. Third, the data collected by uncovered or isolated sensors will not be transmitted to sinks, and eventually the collected data will be discarded [9].

In recent years, due to the characteristics of high maneuverability, flexibility, reachable line-of-sight points, and low cost of UAVs, the use of UAVs as sinks to assist WSNs in data collection has gradually been proposed. Direct access to all or part of the

© Springer Nature Switzerland AG 2020
X. Chen et al. (Eds.): ML4CS 2020, LNCS 12487, pp. 214–223, 2020.
https://doi.org/10.1007/978-3-030-62460-6_19

sensors through UAVs can effectively reduce the data forwarding hop counts of WSNs, reduce the energy consumption of the network and improve the reliability of data transmission, etc. [10]. Therefore, how to deploy the UAVs as sinks plays a decisive role in the overall performance of WSNs.

In recent years, many scholars have conducted a lot of research on minimizing the energy consumption of WSNs and the delay of mobile data collection, and have achieved certain results. Miao et al. attempted to achieve both time efficient and energy efficient for data collection by combining the amount of concurrent uploaded data, the number of neighbors and the moving tour length of sink in one metric [11]. Zhou et al. proposed a three-phase energy-balanced heuristic algorithm to schedule mobile sinks and prolong the network lifetime, in which the uniformly divided grid cells is assigned to clusters through an algorithm inspired by the k-dimensional tree algorithm to keep the energy consumption of each cluster is similar [12]. Chang et al. proposed a novel tree-based power saving scheme to reduce the data transmission distances of the sensor nodes [13].

Although the proposed algorithms are very effective in collecting data in specific monitoring regions, each still has some limitations for further discussion. Inspired by the previous achievements and employing UAVs to act as mobile sinks, the location planning of UAVs for WSNs data collection based on adaptive search algorithm (LPUAV-ASA) is proposed. The main contributions of this study can be summarized as follows.

(1) Convert the WSNs data collection problem into location planning of UAVs. This model simplifies the problem of WSNs data collection and increases the scope of its application.
(2) Discuss the location planning of UAVs under different sensor distribution conditions is, and the disadvantages of the KMeans algorithm [14] in the deployment of drones are analyzed. Also an experiment is conducted on larger-scale WSNs data collection problems to reasonably compare the effectiveness of the proposed algorithm with the KMeans algorithm.

The remainder of this paper is organized as follows. The mathematical model of location planning of UAVs for WSNs data collection and some definitions are introduced in Sect. 2. The optimal matching method between sensors and UAVs and automatic location generation strategy of UAVs, also the detailed steps of LPUAV-ASA is described in Sect. 3. The experimental studies have been conducted to show the performance of LPUAV-ASA on larger-scale WSNs data collection in Sect. 4. Finally, Sect. 5 concludes this paper.

2   The Mathematical Model of Location Planning of UAVs

2.1   The Network Model of WSNs Data Collection

Without loss of generality, the WSNs data collection network is defined in an undirected weighted graph $G(V, E)$, where V and E stand for a set of vertices and a set of edges respectively. The set $V = \{W, U\}$ is composed of two kinds of nodes: (1) a subset of N sensors $W = \{w_1, \cdots, w_N\}$, (2) a subset of K UAVs $U = \{u_1, u_2, \cdots, u_K\}$. These nodes are distributed in a size of L^2. $E = \{(v_i, v_j) | v_i, v_j \in V, (v_i, v_j) \notin U \times U\}$ represents edges connecting UAVs with sensors, and the interconnecting sensors.

Some basic definitions are given for introducing the following algorithms and models:

Definition 1 (Adjacent). For any two nodes $v_i(x_i, y_i)$ and $v_j(x_j, y_j)$, v_i and v_j are adjacent if and only if one of the following conditions hold:

(1) For $v_i, v_j \in W$, $d(v_i, v_j) \leq r$, where $d(v_i, v_j) = \sqrt{(x_i - x_j)^2 + (y_i - y_j)^2}$ and r is the communication radius of sensor.
(2) For $v_i \in U, v_j \in W$, $d(v_i, v_j) \leq R$, where R is the communication radius of UAV.

Definition 2 (Chain). The alternating sequence $\Gamma = v_0 e_1 v_1 e_2 \cdots e_l v_l$ of nodes and edges in graph G is called a chain if and only if one of the following conditions hold:

(1) For $\forall v_i \in W$, $|e_i| \leq r$, $(i = 1, \cdots, l)$.
(2) For $v_0 \in U$ and $\forall v_i \in W$, $(i = 1, \cdots, l)$, $|e_1| \leq R$, $|e_i| \leq r$, $(i = 2, \cdots, l)$.

where v_{i-1} and v_i are the two endpoints of edge e_i, $|e_i|$ is the length of edge e_i, $v_i \neq v_j$, $e_i \neq e_j$ for $\forall i, j \in \{1, \cdots, l\}$.

Definition 3 (Connected). For any two nodes v_i and v_j, if there is a chain between v_i and v_j, then v_i and v_j are connected.

Definition 4 (Hop count). For any two nodes v_i and v_j, if v_i and v_j are connected, and the total number of connected edge is l, then the hop count between v_i and v_j is defined $T(v_i, v_j) = l$, if v_i and v_j are not connected, then the hop count between v_i and v_j is $T(v_i, v_j) = T_{\max}$, where $T_{\max}$ is an artificially defined large value.

Definition 5 (Transmission distance). Given a chain $\Gamma = v_0 e_1 v_1 e_2 \cdots e_l v_l$, then the transmission distance from v_0 to v_l is $D(v_0, v_l) = \sum_{i=1}^{l} |e_i|$; if v_0 and v_l are not connected, then the transmission distance from v_0 to v_l is $D(v_0, v_l) = D_{\max} + d(v_0, v_l)$, where $D_{\max}$ is also an artificially defined large value.

2.2   The Mathematical Model of WSNs Data Collection

In the IoT application with federally deployed WSNs, first of all, a sensor must be served by an UAV, which requires the coverage of sensors should be as large as possible. Second, to ensure rapid and efficient data collection, the energy consumption among the sensors should be as small as possible. Finally, unbalanced energy consumption and unbalanced QoS can adversely affect network performance. In order to address these three issues, the dual optimization problem of coverage and energy consumption is converted into a single optimization problem by Definition 4 firstly. It is clearly that the more uncovered sensors in WSNs, the more energy consumption will be required. In addition, the transmission distance is introduced to balance the energy consumption. Obviously, a longer transmission distance will inevitably lead to more energy consumption of the sensors, and the worse of QoS. Therefore, Minimizing the transmission distance can effectively balance energy consumption and improve the QoS of sensors.

The WSNs data collection problem is transformed into a goal programming model, in which the priority of energy consumption is much higher than the energy consumption balance, and the mathematical model is defined as follows.

$$\min F = \sum_{k=1}^{K} \sum_{i=1}^{N} p_1 \cdot e \cdot T(u_k, w_i) + p_2 \cdot D(u_k, w_i) \tag{1}$$

$$\text{Subject to } \sum_{k=1}^{K} z_{ki} = 1, \ \forall \, i = 1, \cdots, N \tag{2}$$

$$\sum_{k=1}^{K} \max \left\{ \sum_{i=1}^{N} z_{ki}, 1 \right\} \leq K \tag{3}$$

$$u_k, w_i, \in L^2, \forall \, k = 1, \cdots, K. \ \forall \, i = 1, \cdots, N. \tag{4}$$

Where p_1 and p_2 are the priority coefficients of the target, and $p_1 \gg p_2$. $e \cdot T(u_k, w_i)$ is the energy consumption for one data delivery between the sensor w_i and its UAV u_k, e is a constant. $T(u_k, w_i)$ is the hop count between u_k and w_i defined in Definition 4. $D(u_k, w_i)$ is the transmission distance from w_i to u_k defined in Definition 5. $z_{ki} = 1$ represents the sensor w_i is served by UAV u_k, otherwise $z_{ki} = 0$.

In the above mathematical model, the objective function (1) represents minimize the transmission distance on the basis of minimizing the transmission energy. Constraints (2) indicates each sensor must be served by one and only one UAV. Constraints (3) represents the total number of UAVs cannot exceed K. Constraints (4) represents the location of all sensors and UAVs fall within the specified area. The key to solving this problem is to reasonably plan the location of UAVs to minimize the total target value.

3 Adaptive Search Algorithm for Location Planning of UAVs

3.1 Optimal Matching Method Between Sensors with UAVs

The next inference is to illustrate the optimal matching method between sensors with UAVs. Assume the sensor w_i has the smallest cost for data transmission when it through the UAV u_k, and the transmission chain is $w_i e_i w_{i1} e_{i2} \cdots w_{il} e_{il} u_k$. It is easy to prove that for any sensor in this chain, the smallest cost must be served by the UAV u_k, and the transmission chain is the sub-chain of $w_i e_i w_{i1} e_{i2} \cdots w_{il} e_{il} u_k$.

According to the above analysis, each UAV u_k can find the service sensors according to cost from small to large, and then add the found service sensors to its own set S_k. It is easy to verify that the proposed matching method is a global optimal match, and the specific process of the matching method is as follows:

Algorithm1: Optimal matching method between sensors with UAVs

---

Input: the coordinates of sensors and UAVs.

Output: the set $\{S_1,\cdots,S_K\}$ of UAVs.

    Step1: Initial K sets $S_1, S_2, \cdots, S_K$, $S_k \leftarrow \varnothing, k = 1, \cdots, K$.

    Step2: Calculate the minimum hop count matrix $A_{N\times N}$ and shortest transmission distance matrix $B_{N\times N}$ between sensors by Floyd algorithm.

    Step3: Search the smallest neighbor sensors set $\{S_1, S_2, \cdots, S_K\}$, where $S_k = \{w_{k1}, w_{k2}, \cdots, w_{kN_k}\}$ represent the sensor in set S_k have small value F when served by the UAV u_k, also $\sum_{k=1}^{K} N_k \leq N$. The specific process is as follows.

    for each node $w_i \in W$ do

        set $p \leftarrow \underset{k=1,\cdots,K}{\arg\min}\, d(w_i, u_k)$;

        if $d(w_i, u_p) \leq R$ then

            $S_p \leftarrow \langle w_i, S_p \rangle$;

        end if

    end for

    Step4: Divide each sensor into a set of UAV. The detail is as follows.

    for each node $w_i \in W$ do

        for $k = 1$ to K do

            set $d_k \leftarrow \min\{p_1 \cdot A_{i,k1} + p_2 \cdot B_{i,k1}, \cdots, p_1 \cdot A_{i,kN_k} + p_2 \cdot B_{i,kN_k}\}$;

        end for

        $q \leftarrow \underset{k=1,\cdots,K}{\arg\min}\, d_k$;

        $S_q \leftarrow \langle w_i, S_q \rangle$;

    end for

3.2   The Location Planning of UAVs

The problem in this paper can be regarded as a clustering problem of dividing N sensors into K categories. The center of the clusters are UAVs. Since the sensors are relatively evenly distributed in the square area, the KMeans algorithm has been proven to effectively deal with this problem. However, the problem is not quite the same as the traditional clustering problem. The clustering method is not based on the Euclidean distance, but the hop count to distinguish the attribution of sensor. To put it simply, one is that the transmission hop count is not necessarily small when the sensor near to a UAV. As shown in the Fig. 1, the Euclidean distance of node 5 is smaller than node 2, but the hop count of node 5 is larger than node 2. The second is that the sensor may not be assigned to the UAV with the Euclidean distance. As shown in the Fig. 1, node 5 is near to the right UAV, but it is divided into the left UAV at last.

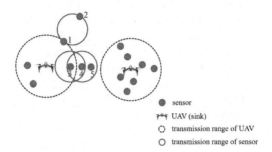

●   sensor
ᵗᵗᵗ   UAV (sink)
◌   transmission range of UAV
○   transmission range of sensor

Fig. 1. An example of UAVs serving sensors in WSNs data collection by UAVs

Based on above analysis, the optimal solution will not be obtained theoretically by the KMeans algorithm. Here are some examples to illustrate this case, where the locations of UAV on the left in Fig. 2 are created by the KMeans algorithm.

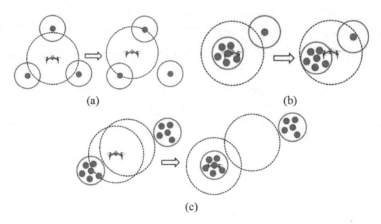

(a)   (b)

(c)

Fig. 2. The better location planning of UAVs on the right than the one on the left generated by the KMeans for WSNs data collection in three cases.

In the left of Fig. 2(a), the data of all sensors cannot be collected when the location of UAV generated by the Kmeans algorithm. In the left of Fig. 2(b), the location planning of the UAV will result in a low sensor coverage by the KMeans algorithm. In the left of Fig. 2(c), no matter how the location of UAV is set, all sensors cannot be completely covered. But the location planning of UAV on the right can significantly reduce the hop counts and transmission distances of the covered sensors.

Combined with the above analysis, two cases are discussed to generate the location of UAVs: (1) While sensors are adjacent to each other and the data of one sensor can be collected by a UAV, then the data of other sensors can also be transferred to the UAV. Obviously, the coverage does not need to be considered, only need to reduce the hop count and transmission distance in this case. So as with the KMeans algorithm, the location of the UAV can be set to the center of gravity of all sensors. (2) While sensors are not adjacent to each other, according to the analysis in Fig. 2. The first consideration is the issue of coverage, and the second is to reduce sensors hop counts and transmission distances. The detailed location generation steps of UAVs are as follows.

Algorithm 2: Automatic location generation strategy of UAVs

Input: the coordinates of Sensors.

Output: the coordinates of UAVs.

Step1: Extract adjacent sensors and group them, then set the center of gravity of sensors in each group as the location of UAV.

Step2: Extract sensor pairs that are not adjacent and have a spacing less than a $2R$.

Step3: For each sensor pair, generate three UAV locations, as shown in Fig.3.

Step4: Select the optimal location of UAVs from all generated locations according to equation (1).

Step5: Disturb the horizontal and vertical coordinates of the optimal location of UAVs in the range of $(-R, R)$, and randomly generate P new locations of UAVs.

Step6: Select the optimal location of UAVs from the P newly generated locations and the current optimal location of UAVs.

In Algorithm 2. Step1 handle the case that an UAV can only cover one adjacent area. Step2 to Step4 extract the sensor pairs to generate the location of UAVs to achieve a largest coverage. The extracted sensor pairs are not adjacent and the distance between each other is less than $2R$. Step5 to Step6 is the local search for the optimal location of UAVs.

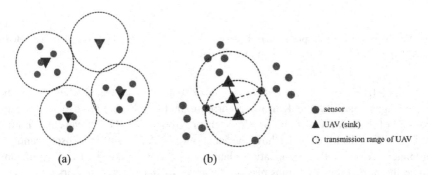

(a)   (b)

Fig. 3. Set the center of gravity of sensors in each group as the location of UAVs in (a). Generate three coordinates of UAVs on a two-point vertical bisector in (b).

3.3   The Flow of Adaptive Search Algorithm of UAVs

The adaptive search algorithm of UAVs draws on the basic idea of the KMeans algorithm, but it is significantly different from the KMeans algorithm in two steps. One is the matching method of the sensor and UAVs, and the other is the generation method of the optimal location of UAVs. The flow of the proposed algorithm is given below.

Algorithm 3: Adaptive Search Algorithm of UAVs

Input: the coordinates of Sensors.

Output: the coordinates of UAVs.

Step1: Randomly generate K locations of UAVs in the given area.

Step2: Assign sensors to different sets by Algorithm 1.

Step3: Regenerate new locations of UAVs for each set by Algorithm 2.

Step4: If the termination condition is reached, output the location of UAVs, otherwise go to Step2.

---

4   Experimental Results and Analysis

4.1   Test Problem and Related Parameter

The number of sensor $N = 2000$. The abscissa and ordinate of sensors for the test problem are randomly generated in the size of $(0, \sqrt{N})$. The transmission range R of UAV is 5, and the transmission range r of sensor is 1. $P = 100$ in local research. The termination condition of each algorithm is that the coverage is 100% for 3 consecutive iterations with the number of UAVs increases.

4.2   Experimental Results and Analysis

The figure of WSNs data collection served by 10 and 50 UAVs got by the proposed algorithm LPUAV-ASA are shown in Fig. 4, many sensors evidently are not covered as the number of UAVs are not enough. For different values of K, the coverage, energy consumption and transmission distance found by the proposed algorithm LPUAV-ASA and the KMeans algorithm are shown in the Fig. 5.

In Fig. 5(a), the coverage of the LPUAV-ASA algorithm has significant advantages over the KMeans algorithm. In Fig. 5(b), when the value of k is small, the total energy consumption of WSNs solved by LPUAV-ASA is higher than the KMeans algorithm. The reason is the amount of data collection by LPUAV-ASA is higher than the KMeans algorithm. At last the energy consumption gradually decreases and tends to be stable with the number of UAVs increases. Obviously, the increase of the number of UAVs bring about a reduction in energy consumption. In Fig. 5(c), As the coverage increases, the more sensors are covered, so the total transmission path are gradually increase and stabilize, and the two algorithms have similar performance.

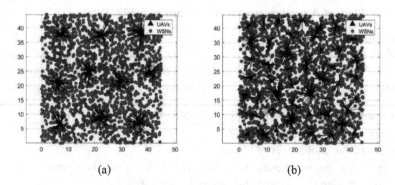

(a)   (b)

Fig. 4. The sensors are served by 10 UAVs for WSNs data collection in (a), and the sensors are served by 50 UAVs for WSNs data collection in (b).

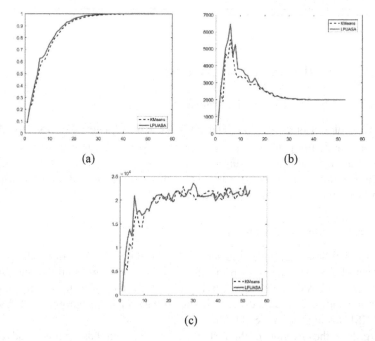

(a)   (b)

(c)

Fig. 5. The coverage (a), energy consumption (b) and transmission distance (c) found by the proposed algorithm LPUAV-ASA and the KMeans algorithm.

5   Conclusion

By considering the sensor coverage, energy consumption and QoS for WSNs sensor data collection, a general goal planning model is established, and an algorithm named LPUAV-ASA is proposed to address this issue. Finally, a large-scale data collection problem is experimented. By comparing with the KMeans algorithm, the experimental results show that this proposed algorithm has significant advantages of coverage, but there is no obvious increase in the two indicators of energy consumption and transmission distance. It indicates the effectiveness of the proposed algorithm.

Acknowledgments. This work is supported by the PhD Start-Up Fund of Dongguan University of Technology (GC300502-3),the Higher Education Innovation Strong School Project of Guangdong Province of China (2017KQNCX190), the Natural Science Foundation of Guangdong Province (Grant No. 2018A030313014), the research team project of Dongguan University of Technology (Grant No. TDY-B2019009), and the Guangdong University Key Project (2019KZDXM012).

References

1. Tao, M., Ota, K., Dong, M.: Locating compromised data sources in IoT-enabled smart cities: a great-alternative-region-based approach. IEEE Trans. Ind. Inform. **14**(6), 2579–2587 (2018)
2. Tao, M., Li, X., Yuan, H., Wei, W.: UAV-aided trustworthy data collection in federated-WSN-enabled IoT applications. Inf. Sci. **532**, 155–169 (2020)
3. Bera, S., Misra, S., Roy, S.K., et al.: Soft-WSN: software-defined WSN management system for IoT applications. IEEE Syst. J. **12**(3), 2074–2081 (2018)
4. Vijay, G., Bdira, E.B.A., Ibnkahla, M.: Cognition in wireless sensor networks: a perspective. IEEE Sens. J. **11**(3), 582–592 (2011)
5. Zhao, M., Yang, Y., Wang, C.: Mobile data gathering with load balanced clustering and dual data uploading in wireless sensor networks. IEEE Trans. Mob. Comput. **14**(4), 770–785 (2018)
6. Xie, K., Ning, X., Wang, X.: An efficient privacy-preserving compressive data gathering scheme in WSNs. Inf. Sci. **390**, 82–94 (2017)
7. Rani, S., Ahmed, S.H., Talwar, R., et al.: Can sensors collect big data? An energy-efficient big data gathering algorithm for a WSN. IEEE Trans. Ind. Inform. **13**(4), 1961–1968 (2017)
8. Farzana, A.H.F., Neduncheliyan, S.: Ant-based routing and QoS-effective data collection for mobile wireless sensor network. Wirel. Netw. **23**(6), 1697–1707 (2016). https://doi.org/10.1007/s11276-016-1239-6
9. Joshi, Y.K., Younis, M.: Restoring connectivity in a resource constrained WSN. J. Netw. Comput. Appl. **66**, 151–165 (2016)
10. Wu, Q., Liu, L., Zhang, R.: Fundamental tradeoffs in communication and trajectory design for UAV enabled wireless network. IEEE Wirel. Commun. **26**(1), 36–44 (2019)
11. Miao, Y., Sun, Z., Wang, N., et al.: Time efficient data collection with mobile sink and vMIMO technique in wireless sensor networks. IEEE Syst. J. **12**(1), 639–647 (2018)
12. Zhou, Z., Du, C., Shu, L.: An energy-balanced heuristic for mobile sink scheduling in hybrid WSNs. IEEE Trans. Ind. Inform. **12**(1), 28–40 (2016)
13. Chang, J.Y., Shen, T.H.: An efficient tree-based power saving scheme for wireless sensor networks with mobile sink. IEEE Sens. J. **16**(20), 7545–7557 (2016)
14. Ekanayake, J., Pallickara, S.: Map Reduce for data intensive scientific analysis. In: IEEE eScience, Piscataway, pp. 277–284 (2008)

Covid-19 Public Opinion Analysis Based on LDA Topic Modeling and Data Visualization

Li Chen[1], Xin Huang[1,2], Hao Zhang[2(✉)], and Ben Niu[1,2]

[1] College of Management, Shenzhen University, Shenzhen, China
[2] Greater Bay Area International Institute for Innovation, Shenzhen University, Shenzhen, China
zhanghaord@163.com

Abstract. The Coronavirus Disease 2019 has a huge impact on countries all over the world. The analysis of public opinions during this period is conducive to the government timely understanding and solving the difficulties faced by the people. In this paper, we crawled text data from different periods of "Wuhan lockdown" and "Wuhan lift lockdown" from Sina Weibo for analysis. Then we use LDA topic modeling and LDAvis visualization methods to compare the topics that people pay attention to in different periods. We find that people's concerns are indeed different in different periods. Therefore, public opinion analysis can enable decision-makers to understand a large amount of information in a short time, and the government can establish a good relationship with the public by solving hot and difficult issues of public concern. By analyzing the public opinions during the epidemic in China, we can also know the corresponding measures taken by the Chinese government. At present, many countries in the world are deeply affected by the epidemic, and this paper also provides reference for the reconstruction of these countries.

Keywords: Public opinion analysis · LDA topic modeling · LDAvis · Weibo

1 Introduction

In December 2019, an acute respiratory infection (Coronavirus Disease 2019, COVID-19) caused by a novel coronavirus infection in Wuhan, China became a major public health emergency with the fastest spread, the most widespread infection, and the most difficult prevention and control in China. With the outbreak of COVID-19 in China, COVID-19 cases have also appeared in many countries in the world. On January 31, 2020, the World Health Organization (WHO) listed the novel coronavirus outbreak as a public health emergency of international concern. In order to minimize the risk of infection, Wuhan was locked down the entire city immediately after the outbreak. After the epidemic was effectively controlled in China, the Chinese government announced on March 24, 2020 that Wuhan would be lift lockdown on April 8. After the outbreak of the epidemic, the majority of people stayed at home during the holidays to learn about the development of the epidemic through various channels. The masses generated their own opinions and comments on various events, and the analysis of online public opinions is conducive to understanding the psychological state, attitude and other information of the masses. The occurrence of public health events often affects many aspects of the society. In addition to the loss of life, it also causes public anxiety and panic, and even leads to riots and looting. For the government, if it does not pay attention to online public opinions and allows the dissemination of negative information arbitrarily, the credibility and authority of the government will be affected [1]. The measures taken by the Chinese government during the epidemic helped China effectively control the epidemic in a short period of time. Therefore, the analysis of domestic public opinion can also provide reference for the reconstruction of other countries.

Therefore, this paper intends to analyze the public opinion before and after the Wuhan lift lockdown. According to the release time of the lift lockdown message, we select two keywords (respectively "Wuhan lockdown" and "Wuhan lift lockdown"), and three time periods in 2020 (respectively 3.9–3.23, 3.24–4.7, 4.8–4.22) to crawls text data from Sina Weibo. Then use the method of LDA topic modeling to extract the topics discussed by people in each time period, and use LDAvis to visualize it. And then compare the differences of the topics discussed by people in different time periods.

2 Literature Review

Social media is rapidly becoming ubiquitous and has become one of the main channels for sharing information. Extracting and analyzing real-time information from social media data is a research hotspot in many fields [2]. According to a report on China's Internet development in 2019, the number of Internet users in China had reached 829 million by the end of 2018. China's online discussion platform is an important source for understanding the public opinion dynamics of specific issues and policies [3]. Sina Weibo as the Chinese largest microblog platform (the Chinese equivalent of Twitter), and many studies relied on data from Weibo to conduct public opinion analysis. For example, the user's emotions and opinions can be analyzed through Sina Weibo's text data "Take-away Food Safety" and natural language processing [4]. In view of some issues related to the vital interests of the people, the government can understand the situation through public opinion analysis. For example, text data on Weibo can be used to raise public awareness of haze management and provide references for the government to formulate environmental policies [5]. For the policy evaluation after the implementation of the second child policy (second stage) and the comprehensive second child policy, we can use text data on Weibo to study the online attitudes and reactions of the public [6].

Since the outbreak, scholars in different fields have conducted their own studies on COVID-19, but most of the researches are about prediction. Based on the population flow data of Wuhan city from January 1 to January 24, 2020, researcher established the risk source model, used the existing data for rapid and accurate risk assessment, and planned the allocation of limited resources before the outbreak [7]. Or collected text data on Weibo in Wuhan at the beginning of the COVID-19 outbreak, and judge whether text data on the Weibo can predict the number of reported cases based on the total number of COVID-19 cases per day in Wuhan [8]. And collected the social media search index (SMSI) of dry cough, fever, chest tightness, coronavirus and pneumonia from December 31, 2019 to February 9, 2020 and COVID-19 from January 20, 2020 to February 9, 2020 for the data of suspected cases, the lag sequence of SMSI is used to predict the number of new suspected COVID-19 cases in this period [9]. In addition, there are many COVID-19 researches related to medicine, but few researches related to public opinion analysis.

Latent Dirichlet Allocation (LDA) model is a generative theme model proposed by Blei et al., which can mine the potential themes in the data set and then analyze the focus of the data set and its related features [10]. Since then, LDA model has been widely used in various fields to help researchers extract effective information from a large number of texts. Based on newspaper articles published in each city, researcher used LDA to extract a number of perceptions that describe urban life, which are aspects of the urban identity file [11]. The technical themes generated by the LDA model can also be used to construct the evaluation model of the enterprise's technical competitiveness, which can provide rich information about the competitive situation in a certain field [12]. In this paper, LDA model was also used to extract information from Weibo during the epidemic period and to explore hot topics of public concern.

3   Methodology

3.1   Data Preparation

Since the Chinese government announced on March 24 that Wuhan would be lift lockdown on April 8, we chose three time periods: (1) From March 9 to March 23, 2020, 15 days before the Chinese government announced the lift lockdown of Wuhan; (2) From March 24 to April 7, 2020, the 15 day after the Chinese government announced that Wuhan will lift lockdown on April 8; (3) From April 8 to April 22, 2020, 15 days after Wuhan officially lift lockdown. After determining the time period, considering the specific situation, we determined two topic words and obtained the text data by crawling the data from the Weibo. What are the topics discussed by the people in different periods? First is during the lockdown of the city, second is after the announcement of the lift lockdown but before the official lift lockdown, and finally after the official lift lockdown. The crawled topics and data volume are shown in Table 1 below:

Table 1. The crawled topics and data volume.

Time periods	Topic words	Data volume
March 9 to March 23	#Wuhan lockdown#	1539
March 24 to April 7	#Wuhan lift lockdown#	1254
April 8 to April 22	#Wuhan lift lockdown#	3793

3.2   Latent Dirichlet Allocation

LDA believes that each word of each document selects a certain topic with a certain probability, and selects a certain word from this topic with a certain probability [13]. LDA can effectively model text, and compared with the traditional space vector model, it increases the probability of information [13]. As for how to find the optimal number of topics, we choose an adaptive optimal LDA model selection method based on similarity to determine the number of topics and conduct topic analysis. This method can find the optimal topic structure with relatively little iteration without manual debugging of the number of topics [13]. The cosine similarity between topics is used to measure the similarity between topics. Starting from word frequency, the similarity is calculated. The more similar the words are, the closer the content is and the least similarity is the most appropriate. In addition, we use another open source tool LDAvis [14] on LDA results to visualize the frequency and clustering of words in the text, and then judge what people discuss in different time periods.

3.3   Text Processing Flow

Before analyzing the data, it is necessary to preprocess the crawled data. First, remove invalid characters from the text, such as letters, numbers, symbols, and so on. Then, using the jieba word segmentation package to segment the text data, and at the same time create a user dictionary according to the text data, such as "Goodnight SMS Hubei Project", "COVID-19" etc. Next, we chose to summarize the stopword vocabulary of "Harbin Institute of Technology Stopword Thesaurus", "Sichuan University Machine Learning Intelligence Lab Stopword Thesaurus", "Baidu Stopword List" and so on to remove duplicates and extract stopwords.

After text preprocessing is completed, LDA topic modeling is carried out. We use an adaptive optimal LDA model selection method based on similarity to determine the K. Then LDA visualization is performed and the values of α, β, and λ are adjusted to determine the top 10 terms in each topic, representing the content expressed in each topic. Figure 1 is the flow chart for this article.

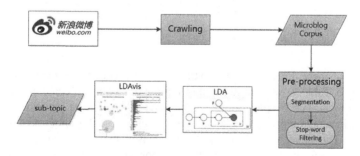

Fig. 1. Flow chart of this article

4 Experiment and Empirical Result

4.1 First Time Period: 3.9–3.23

The K value determined by the adaptive optimal LDA model selection method based on similarity is shown in Fig. 2 below. In this part we choose K = 3. And the final experimental results are shown in Fig. 3 below, where $\alpha = 0.5$, $\beta = 0.01$, $\lambda = 0.3$.

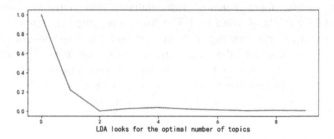

Fig. 2. Average cosine similarity graph between topics (3.9–3.23)

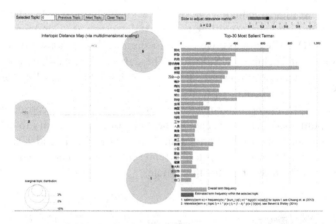

Fig. 3. Visualized results of LDAvis (3.9–3.23)

In each of these three topics, we extracted 10 words as representatives (Table 2). According to Table 2, we can know that topic 1 is about the epidemic situation in Hubei Province. The people are concerned about the epidemic situation, cheer for Hubei province, and fight against novel coronavirus. Topic 2 is about the home life of the people. The novel coronavirus not only caused the lockdown of city for two months, but also made the people only have to cook food at home, people look forward to lift lockdown and want to go out. Topic 3 is about fighting the novel coronavirus. The government, enterprises and residents work together to fight against the epidemic. Volunteers and medical staff have made great contributions to protecting people's health.

Table 2. 10 terms for each topics (3.9–3.23)

	Topic 1	Topic 2	Topic 3
Terms	Pneumonia	Life	Work
	Come on	Mother	People
	Fight	Food	Doctor
	Novel Coronavirus	Two months	Health
	All of one heart	Go out	Government
	Diagnose	Lift lockdown	Enterprise
	Prevention and control	At home	Condition
	Case	Go downstairs	Resident
	China	Eat	Medical workers
	Hubei province	Express delivery	Volunteer

4.2 Second Time Period:3.24–4.7

The K value determined by the adaptive optimal LDA model selection method based on similarity is shown in Fig. 4 below. In this part we choose K = 3. And the final experimental results are shown in Fig. 5 below, where $\alpha = 0.05$, $\beta = 0.01$, $\lambda = 0.3$.

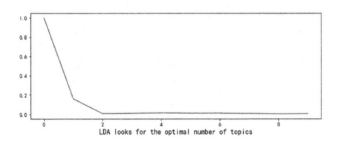

Fig. 4. Average cosine similarity graph between topics (3.24–4.7)

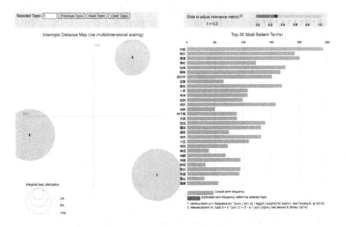

Fig. 5. Visualized results of LDAvis (3.24–4.7)

In each of these three topics, we extracted 10 words as representatives (Table 3). According to Table 3, we can know that topic 1 is about virus detection. After the lift lockdown of Wuhan, the population movement has increased. In order to further prevent viruses and reduce the potential risk of asymptomatic infections, it is necessary to perform nucleic acid testing on personnel and leave Wuhan with the health code green code. Topic 2 is about the mood of lift lockdown. After more than two months, Wuhan is finally going to lift lockdown, and the rare super moon appeared the night before the lift lockdown. People are full of anticipation for lift lockdown, and say "long time no see" to Wuhan residents. Topic 3 is about prepared before lift lockdown. Wuhan is going to lift lockdown, which means that all traffic will also be restored. All means of transportation and passenger transportation should be disinfected, including subways, buses, flights, airports, etc.

Table 3. 10 terms for each topics (3.24–4.7)

	Topic 1	Topic 2	Topic 3
Terms	People	Come on	Recover
	Orderly	Hot-and-dry Noodles	Operation
	Detect	Supermoon	Subway
	Prevention and control	Hero	Passenger transport
	Residence community	China	Flight
	Green code	City	Zero hour
	Nucleic acid	Eventually	Do business
	Health	Lift lockdown	Sterilize
	Asymptomatic carrier	Look forward to	Bus
	Mobility	Long time no see	Airport

4.3 Third Time Period: 4.8–4.22

The K value determined by the adaptive optimal LDA model selection method based on similarity is shown in Fig. 6 below. In this part we choose K = 6. And the final experimental results are shown in Fig. 7 below, where $\alpha = 0.8$, $\beta = 0.01$, $\lambda = 0.2$.

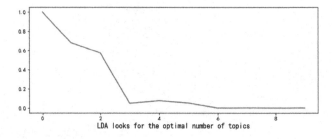

Fig. 6. Average cosine similarity graph between topics (4.8–4.22)

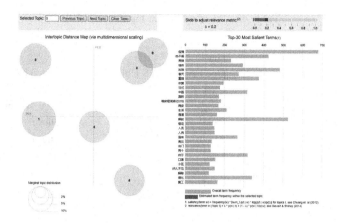

Fig. 7. Visualized results of LDAvis (4.8–4.22)

This part is also extracted 10 words for each topic (Table 4). According to Table 4, we can know that topic 1 is about international epidemic situation. The lift lockdown of Wuhan shows that China has achieved a staged victory in process of fighting against the epidemic. The next focus is about the asymptomatic infected people. At this time, the global epidemic situation is getting worse and worse, and the people's attention to the international epidemic has increased. Theme 2 involves saluting heroes. The public is grateful for the efforts made by Wuhan City during the lockdown and for the medical teams sent by other provinces and cities to stick to their posts. We pay tribute to all heroes, and also send sincere greetings to the people of Hubei through the Good Night SMS Hubei Project (Send a good night message to a stranger in Hubei). Topic 3 is about nucleic acid testing of floating population. After the lift lockdown of Wuhan, traffic recovery, so it is necessary to perform nucleic acid detection on the floating population to prevent the outbreak. Topic 4 is about City recovery. After lift lockdown, people can wear masks to go out, most people also start to work, there are more people on the street, and traffic jams also occur. Topic 5 is about people's mental state after lift lockdown. After the epidemic ended, many people were able to reunite with their families, and they were more confident in life and full of hope for tomorrow. Thanks for living and recording their daily life, students are also looking forward to the start of school. Topic 6 is about the activity after lift lockdown. Spring is coming and the cherry blossoms in Wuhan are in full bloom. The public celebrate the lift lockdown and can go out to eat hot-and-dry noodles and cray, they also miss the outdoor scenery that they haven't seen for a long time and plan a trip.

Table 4. 10 terms for each topics (4.8–4.22)

	Topic 1	Topic 2	Topic 3
Terms	Epidemic situation	Hero	Recover
	America	Good Night SMS Hubei Project	Traffic aisle
	Case	City	People
	Diagnose	People	Leave Wuhan
	Global	Gratitude	Relieve
	Virus	Salute	Control
	China	Life	Nucleic acid testing
	Asymptomatic carrier	Medical corps	Passenger
	Attention	Blessing	Flight
	Risk	Stick to a post	Leave
	Topic 4	Topic 5	Topic 6
Terms	Go out	Diary	Hot-and-dry Noodles
	Two months	Tomorrow	Sakura
	Residence community	Life	Spring blossoms
	First time	Beginning of term	Long time no see
	Mask	Daily	Live
	Working	Happy	Travel
	Take-away food	Sunshine	Celebrate
	Work resumption	Record	Cray
	Bus	Hope	Miss
	Traffic jam	Family	Happiness

5 Conclusion

After the above analysis, we can find that the focus of people in different time periods is not the same. In short, during the lockdown of the city, the focus was mainly about epidemic situation in Hubei Province. After the government released the news, people shared their feelings and looked forward to the lift lockdown. After the official lift lockdown, attention has shifted to asymptomatic infections in our country and to the international epidemic situation.

This paper has the following limitations: firstly, the main purpose of this paper is to analyze the changes of people's concerns during the Wuhan lockdown and the Wuhan lift lockdown in different periods, so this paper just used the most classic LDA topic modeling method for analysis. In the future we will attempt to use the multi-grain topic model for analysis. Secondly, this paper did not classify the text emotionally in the data preprocessing. In the future, we will further analyze people's emotional tendencies and explore people's concerns under different emotional tendencies.

The realistic contribution of this paper mainly has the following points. Firstly, through the public opinion analysis of Wuhan lockdown event, it can provide decision-makers with a large amount of objective and accurate public opinion information in a short time, which is conducive to improving decision-making efficiency and helping them make correct decisions. For example, in the process of public opinion analysis, the government can find hot issues and difficult problems that the public are concerned about, scientifically predict the future development, and issue statements or take measures to solve the plight of the public, so as to obtain the support and understanding of the public and maintain a good relationship between the public and the government. Secondly, through the analysis of public opinions during the epidemic period in China, we can also learn some measures taken by the Chinese government to prevent and control the epidemic. At present, there are still many countries in the world where the epidemic situation is severe. This paper provides certain reference for the reconstruction of these countries.

Acknowledgements. This study is supported by Guangdong Province Soft Science Project (2019A101002075), Guangdong Province Educational Science Plan 2019 (2019JKCY010), Guangdong Province Bachelor and Postgraduate Education Innovation Research Project (2019SFKC46).

References

1. Wang, G.F., Li, M.: Review and prospect of research on network public opinion in China. Mod. Intell. **36**(05), 172–176 (2016)
2. Chen, Y., Lv, Y., Wang, X., et al.: Detecting traffic information from social media texts with deep learning approaches. IEEE Trans. Intell. Transp. Syst. **99**, 1–10 (2018)
3. Medaglia, R., Yang, Y.: Online public deliberation in China: evolution of interaction patterns and network homophily in the Tianya discussion forum. Inf. Commun. Soc. **20**(5), 733–753 (2017)
4. Song, C., Guo, C., Hunt, K., et al.: An Analysis of Public Opinions Regarding Take-Away Food Safety: A 2015–2018 Case Study on Sina Weibo. Foods (Basel, Switzerland) (2020). https://doi.org/10.3390/foods9040511
5. Zhang, Q., Chen, J., Liu, X.: Public perception of haze weather based on Weibo comments. Int. J. Environ. Res. Publ. Health **16**, 4767 (2019). https://doi.org/10.3390/ijerph16234767
6. Wang, S., Song, Y.: Chinese online public opinions on the two-child policy. Online Inf. Rev. **43**(3), 387–403 (2019)
7. Jia, J., Lu, X., Yuan, Y., et al.: Population flow drives spatio-temporal distribution of COVID-19 in China. Nature, 1–11 (2020)
8. Li, J., Xu, Q., Cuomo, R., et al.: Data mining and content analysis of the Chinese social media platform Weibo during the early COVID-19 outbreak: retrospective observational infoveillance study. JMIR Publ. Health Surveill. **6**(2), e18700 (2020). https://doi.org/10.2196/18700
9. Qin, L., Sun, Q., Wang, Y., et al.: Prediction of number of cases of 2019 novel coronavirus (COVID-19) using social media search index. Int. J. Environ. Res. Publ. Health **17**(7) (2020). https://doi.org/10.3390/ijerph17072365
10. Blei, D., Ng, A., Jordan, M.: Latent Dirichlet allocation. J. Mach. Learn. Res. **3**(4–5), 993–1022 (2003)
11. Capela, F., Ramirez-Marquez, J.: Detecting urban identity perception via newspaper topic modeling. Cities **93**, 72–83 (2019)

234   L. Chen et al.

12. Wang, X., Yang, X., Wang, X., et al.: Evaluating the competitiveness of enterprise's technology based on LDA topic model. Technol. Anal. Strateg. Manag. 32(2), 208–222 (2020)
13. Zhang, L., Tan, L., Liu, M., et al.: Hands-on Data Analysis and Data Mining with Python, 2nd edn. China Machine Press, Beijing (2019)
14. Carson, S., Kenneth, S.: LDAvis: a method for visualizing and interpreting topics. In: Proceedings of the Workshop on Interactive Language Learning, Visualization, and Interfaces, pp. 63–70. Association for Computational Linguistics, Maryland (2014)

A Capacitated Vehicle Routing Problem with Order Release Time Based on a Hybrid Harmony Search

Ling Liu[1] , Sen Liu[1(✉)] , Ben Niu[2,3(✉)] , and Hui Tan[1]

[1] School of Logistics, Yunnan University of Finance and Economics,
Kunming 650221, China
liusencool@163.com
[2] College of Management, Shenzhen University, Shenzhen 518060, China
drniuben@gmail.com
[3] Institute of Big Data Intelligent Management and Decision,
Shenzhen University, Shenzhen, China

Abstract. With the popularity of Internet technology, e-commerce enterprises have rapidly developed. Orders need to be collected before delivery, and vehicles are waiting in the warehouse for most enterprises. This paper considers a capacitated vehicle routing problem with order release time, with the aim of minimizing the maximum order delivery time. A mathematical model is first built, and then, a hybrid harmony search algorithm is proposed to address the nearest optimal solutions, with three methods to generate initial harmony memory, an optimization algorithm to evaluate each harmony and a tabu search to improve initial solutions and neighbourhood solutions. The linear programming software CPLEX is applied to verify the rationality of the mathematical model. Computational results indicate that the average solution quality of all generated instances obtained by the hybrid harmony search is better than the current operational strategy of the enterprise, a tabu search algorithm and a genetic algorithm in the related articles.

Keywords: Vehicle routing problem · Order release time · Hybrid harmony search

1 Introduction

E-commerce enterprises have entered a stage of rapid development under advanced Internet technology; however, high logistics costs and other factors lead to lower profitability. Increasing numbers of e-commerce enterprises regard the optimization of logistics distribution as one of the means for improving enterprise efficiency. In particular, with the increasing demand for fully integrated omni-channel retail, an increasing number of researchers have begun to study "last-mile" logistics. "Last-mile" logistics refers to the journey of goods from the final distribution centre, collection site or local storehouse to the final destination (such as the address of the customer). In the B2C e-commerce mode, in the whole logistics chain, last-mile distribution is one of the most complicated and expensive segments. For the particularity of e-commerce

© Springer Nature Switzerland AG 2020
X. Chen et al. (Eds.): ML4CS 2020, LNCS 12487, pp. 235–249, 2020.
https://doi.org/10.1007/978-3-030-62460-6_21

logistics, such as a large number of small packages, high delivery frequency and the wide dispersion of customers, the probability of delivery in time will decrease. Owing to the inefficiency of the final delivery, the cost of last-mile delivery is high. Additionally, "last-mile" logistics play a crucial role in satisfaction with the online shopping experience. Therefore, the importance of the final distribution of e-commerce was realized when online shopping became popular. Many e-retail giants (e.g., Amazon, TMALL.com and JD.com) believe that the "last-mile" logistics capability is their core competitiveness in all competitions [1].

This research comes from a large-scale e-commerce retail enterprise, which mainly sells household appliances and electronic products. The enterprise is also responsible for "last-mile" logistics services in the city. The enterprise implements a multi-channel sales strategy that combines e-commerce and traditional retail. When an advance order is placed online, the warehouse receives a delivery notification. However, not all products are in stock in the warehouse, so these products must be supplied to the warehouse before they are ready for the final delivery. The preparation time of products for delivery is called the "order release time". First, the order is delivered in batches according to the principle of first come, first served; then the vehicle performs nearby deliveries first, and finally the far deliveries. When the enterprise arranges the orders in vehicles, vehicle routing is not considered, which results in many orders for different customers that are far away from each other being transported by the same vehicle, leading to a long completion time. Thus, considering the order collection activities and vehicle routing synergistically is necessary.

This paper considers the capacitated vehicle routing problem with order release time (CVRPORT). At the beginning of transportation, multiple vehicles with identical capacities are based at a single depot; each vehicle can leave the depot only after all orders have been loaded. Each order placed by the corresponding customer has an order release time (the collection time of all products of an order), which can be predicted during a powerful information system. Obviously, each vehicle's departure time is actually the latest order release time among the loading orders, which is defined as the vehicle waiting time. After a vehicle leaves, the transportation time between all customers is called the vehicle travelling time. Each vehicle's completion time is equal to the sum of vehicle waiting time and vehicle travelling time. The objective is to minimize the maximum vehicle completion time, that is, the maximum order delivery time, which is often used in vehicle routing problems [2, 3].

The main contributions of this paper are as follows. First, the order release time is considered, which is considered less in the common capacitated vehicle routing problem. Second, a hybrid harmony search (HHS) is proposed to solve CVRPORT, with three methods to generate initial harmony memory, an optimization algorithm to evaluate each harmony, a tabu search to improve initial solutions and neighbourhood solutions, and a simulated annealing principle to determine whether the inferior solution is acceptable. Finally, by comparing the result with CPLEX, the validity of the proposed HHS is verified. The computational results show that the HHS can obtain the optimal solution or approximate optimal solution, which is better than the existing operational method, a tabu search algorithm and a genetic algorithm in the existing literature.

Section 2 reviews the relevant literature of CVRPORT. Section 3 formulates the CVRPORT. Section 4 introduces a hybrid harmony search to solve this problem, and the performances are analysed in Sect. 5. Section 6 describes the main conclusions.

2 Literature Review

In fact, the capacitated vehicle routing problem with order release time (CVRPORT) belongs to the capacitated vehicle routing problem (CVRP). CVRP was first proposed by [4], which considers that each vehicle has identical limited capacity and assumes that all the goods to be delivered are available at the depot when the distribution starts. Since then, increasing attention has been paid to CVRP, which has become a front subject in logistics, operational research, and computer applications [5, 6]. Because the CVRP pertains to the kind of NP-complete problems, many intelligent optimization algorithms have been designed to solve it. For example, large-neighbourhood search algorithms [7], branch-and-cut algorithms [8, 9], artificial bee colony algorithms [5, 10], simulated annealing algorithms [11], and hybrid algorithms [12, 13]. In addition, as an increasing number of enterprises focus on logistics costs, the extended forms of CVRP have received increasing concern. The CVRP with time windows was studied by [14, 15]. The CVRP with simultaneous pickup and delivery was researched by [16–18]. The CVRP with stochastic demand was considered by [19–21]. The CVRP with multiple depots was studied by [22, 23]. The CVRP with heterogeneous vehicles was considered by [24–26].

In the past few years, CVRP with order release time has attracted increasing attention, which considers the depot's storage capacity and the order release times at the depot. Few studies have focused on the characteristics of order release times. It was assumed that the goods are not all available at the depot and vehicles are uncapacitated in [27]. They demonstrated that the problem can be solved in polynomial time if the underlying graph has a special structure, i.e., star and line. Based on the work in [27], the routing problems that have the constraints of release dates and deadlines were studied in [28], which proved that the problem can be solved in polynomial time if the underlying graph has a special structure. A travelling salesman problem that has the constraints of release dates was studied in [29], and only one vehicle was involved. An iterated local search algorithm was developed to solve the problem, which means minimizing the vehicle completion time. This paper studies the general graph and considers the limited fleet of capacitated vehicles. The context of e-commerce deliveries was studied in [30, 31], which handled the CVRP with order available time, regarding the minimization of the sum of the vehicle completion times as the objective. This paper considers the minimization of the maximum vehicle completion time as the objective. The vehicle routing problem with time windows and release dates was considered in [32, 33]. The objectives were to minimize the total travelling time and total distance. To solve the VRP with release and due dates, a path-relinking algorithm was proposed in [34]. The objective of the problem was to minimize the convex combination of the total distance and total weighted tardiness of delivery. A heterogeneous fleet vehicle routing problem was introduced by [35], which had the constraints of release and due dates. They proposed a mixed-integer programming model that minimizes the sum of inventory holding, transportation, tardiness, and backorder costs. This paper ignores the time windows or due dates for e-commerce distribution. In most cases, because customers are busy with work throughout the day, delivered goods are usually received by collection points, and then customers can pick them up according to their own time.

3   Problem Formulation

The CVRPORT is formulated in this section. A depot has a set of vehicles with limited capacity waiting for transportation. Multiple customers are in different geographical locations. let $V = \{0, 1, 2, ..., n\}$ represent a set of all points, with 0 representing the depot and other numbers representing customers. Each customer places a corresponding order, with a predictable order release time and order demand. When a vehicle completes loading a series of orders, the earliest time that the vehicle can leave is equal to the maximum order release time, which is called the vehicle waiting time. The objective is to minimizing the maximum order delivery time. Let the vehicle completion time be the sum of the vehicle waiting time and vehicle travelling time; then, the minimization of the maximum vehicle completion time is the objective function in this problem.

The problem is formulated based on the following assumptions: 1) each order can only be arranged in one vehicle and cannot be transported in batches, 2) each vehicle must start from and return to the depot after visiting at least one customer, 3) the total quantity of products loaded on each vehicle shall not exceed its volume, and 4) vehicle speed is constant, and the travel time between two points can be equal to the travel distance. All symbols used in the model are described as follows:

1)   Parameters;

i, j index of the customer, which belongs to the set of customers $C = \{1, 2, ..., n\}$;

k index of the vehicle, which belongs to the set of vehicles $V = \{1, 2, ..., K\}$;

q_i the goods demand of the order belonging to customer i;

r_i the order release time of customer i;

t_{ij} travel time between customer i and customer j;

Q capacity of each vehicle.

2)   Decision variables and variables

x_{ijk} is 1 if vehicle k travels from point i to point j and equal to 0 otherwise.

y_{jk} is 1 if vehicle K is loaded with the order that belongs to customer i and equal to 0 otherwise.

A_i^k the time when vehicle K arrives at customer i.

The mathematical model is presented below:

$$Min(\max_{k \in H}(\sum_{i=0}^{n}\sum_{j=0}^{n} t_{ij}x_{ijk} + \max_{j \in N}(r_j y_{jk}))) \tag{1}$$

$$\sum_{k=1}^{K}\sum_{j=0}^{n} x_{ijk} = 1, \qquad i = 1,\ldots,n \tag{2}$$

$$\sum_{i=0}^{n} x_{ihk} - \sum_{j=0}^{n} x_{hjk} = 0, \qquad h = 1,2,\ldots,n, \quad k = 1,\ldots,K \tag{3}$$

$$\sum_{i=1}^{n} q_i \sum_{j=0}^{n} x_{ijk} \le Q, \qquad k = 1,\ldots,K \tag{4}$$

$$A_i^k + t_{ij} - A_j^k \le (1 - x_{ijk})M, \; i = 0,\ldots,n, \; j = 0,\ldots,n, \; k = 1,\ldots,K \tag{5}$$

$$A_0^k \ge \max_{j \in N}(r_j y_{jk}), \; k = 1,\ldots,K \tag{6}$$

$$y_{jk} = \sum_{i=0}^{n} x_{ijk}, \; j = 1,\ldots,n, \; k = 1,\ldots,K \tag{7}$$

$$x_{ijk} \in \{0,1\}, \quad i = 0,\ldots,n, \quad j = 0,\ldots,n, \quad k = 1,\ldots,K \tag{8}$$

$$y_{jk} \in \{0,1\}, \quad j = 1,\ldots,n \; k = 1,\ldots,K \tag{9}$$

The goal is to minimize the maximum vehicle completion time. Formula (2) means that each order must be delivered by one vehicle. Equation (3) represents the flow conservation constraint. Constraint (4) indicates that the volume of each vehicle cannot be violated. In constraint (5), M is a large number, and constraint (5) eliminates the subcycle constraint. Constraint (6) indicates that each vehicle can leave the depot only after the order with the maximum release time is loaded. Constraint (7) means that if a customer is visited by a vehicle, the customer's order must be loaded. Constraints (8) and (9) are 0–1 variable constraints.

This problem is an NP-hard problem, including a classical NP-hard problem named CVRP. Therefore, the exact algorithm has difficulty solving large-scale examples; thus, to solve this problem, a heuristic algorithm is proposed.

4 Hybrid Harmony Search

As a kind of heuristic algorithm, harmony search (HS) was first proposed by [36] and is intended to imitate the process of musicians constantly adjusting their tone to produce beautiful music. HS first generates multiple initial harmonies in the harmony memory (HM), then generates new harmony according to certain rules, and then judges whether

240   L. Liu et al.

the new harmony is better than the worst harmony in HM. If so, it is replaced; otherwise, the memory remains unchanged. This process is repeated until the best solution is obtained. In this section, a hybrid harmony search (HHS) is designed, which embeds a local search algorithm based on the original HS. The detailed procedure of HHS is shown in Fig. 1.

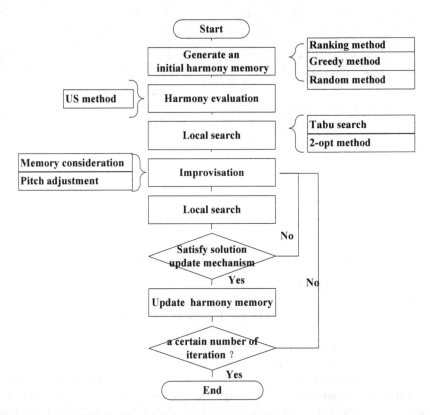

Fig. 1. The detailed procedure of hybrid harmony search.

Step 1: Harmony memory initialization. The ranking method, greedy method and random method are used to generate the initial harmony memory.

Step 2: Harmony evaluation. Each harmony is transformed into vehicle routings, and then each routing is optimized by a "US" method to calculate the objective value.

Step 3: Local search. The tabu search algorithm is used as a local optimization algorithm to optimize every harmony in memory.

Step 4: Improvisation. A new harmony is generated by memory consideration and pitch adjustment based on all harmonies in the current harmony memory. Then, the new harmony is optimized by the above local search algorithm.

Step 5: Update the harmony memory. It needs to judge which is better between the new harmony generated by improvisation and the worst harmony in the current memory. If the new harmony is better, the worst harmony is replaced. In contrast, the simulated annealing principle is used to judge whether to accept the bad harmony or not. Each updating can be regarded as a generation. If the generation reaches the specified number $I_{iteration}$, the HHS algorithm is stopped, or if the harmony memory has not been updated for I_{cons} consecutive times.

4.1   Harmony Memory Initialization

The initial harmony memory (HM) consists of a series of harmonies, the size of which is HMS. Each harmony consists of several different notes. Each note corresponds to an order, and then N orders correspond to N notes. Thus, a harmony is a sequence of orders. There are three methods to generate initial harmonies.

Ranking method: The notes of the first harmony are sequenced in ascending order of order release time.

Greedy method: starting from the depot, find the nearest customer, make its order as the first note, then find the customer closest to the nearest customer and add its order to the harmony as the second note, and so on, to build all the notes of the second harmony.

Random method: The remaining harmonies are generated by a random method, i.e., one order is randomly selected each time as a note to be added to the harmony.

4.2   Harmony Evaluation

The value of the objective function (1) of each harmony in HM is calculated according to the harmony evaluation. Given a harmony, i.e., order sequence, it is necessary to assign orders to different vehicles for transportation and decide routes.

First, starting from the first order in the sequence, add the orders to the first vehicle successively until the volume of the vehicle is exceeded; then, start the second vehicle. Add the subsequent orders to the second vehicle in turn, and so on, until all orders are added to the corresponding vehicle. Then, check whether all orders are added to the existing vehicle. If vehicles have been used up and an order remains, the remaining order is forced to join the last vehicle, and the value of the harmony will be a large number. Third, it is assumed that the routing of each vehicle is consistent with the order loading sequence. The waiting time of each vehicle is actually the same as the maximum order release time among the loaded orders. Fourth, the routing of each vehicle can be taken as a travelling salesman problem (TSP); a "US" method is applied to improve each routing to minimize the travel time. The "US" method in [30] is used to obtain a better solution by applying predesigned rules to change the order of customers in a TSP route. Finally, the value of the harmony is calculated, which is equal to the vehicle waiting time plus the vehicle travelling time.

4.3   Local Search

The tabu search (TS) is used to improve the current harmony (the harmony in the initial memory or the new harmonies generated in improvisation) as a local optimization algorithm. For the current harmony, the 2-opt method (i.e., swap two notes in the harmony) is used to generate multiple neighbourhood solutions (harmonies). Each neighbourhood solution is calculated by harmony evaluation, and then the best neighbourhood solution is recorded. If the best neighbourhood solution is tabu and worse than the current optimal solution, the best neighbourhood solution is not accepted, and the suboptimal neighbourhood solution is determined. However, if the best neighbourhood solution is non-tabu or superior to the current optimal solution, a new neighbourhood solution is generated by regarding the neighbourhood solution as the current optimal solution. The algorithm will not stop until the search time is reached.

4.4   Improvisation

Based on all harmonies in the HM, through the improvisation procedure, a new harmony is formed. Memory consideration and pitch adjustment are two main procedures in improvisation.

Memory consideration: the ith note (n_i) of the new harmony is selected from the ith note of the best harmony in the current memory according to the probability HMCR (harmony memory considering rate) or selected from the ith note of a random harmony in the current memory according to the probability (1-HMCR).

Pitch adjustment: when the note n_i is generated by memory consideration, pitch adjustment is executed. The note n_i is unchanged with probability (1-PAR) or adjusted with probability PAR (pitch adjusting rate).

When the note n_i needs to be changed, two notes (not in the new harmony) that are nearest and the second nearest to n_i are selected to replace n_i with 50% probability. If n_i is the last note of the new harmony, then n_i is unchanged. Then, the new harmony is improved by the local search introduced in Sect. 4.3.

4.5   Update Harmony Memory

If the improved new harmony h_{new} is better than the worst harmony h_{worst} in the current harmony memory, h_{worst} is replaced by h_{new}; otherwise, the simulated annealing principle is used to decide whether to accept h_{new}. The acceptance probability exp $v(h_{new}) - v(h_{worst})/T$ is calculated, where $v(h_{new})$ and $v(h_{worst})$ represent the objective values of the new harmony and the worst harmony, respectively; T is the current temperature, which is a large number and can be set as the objective value of the worst solution. If the acceptance probability is greater than the random number between [0, 1], the worst harmony is replaced with the new harmony. Otherwise, the current harmony memory is unchanged.

5   Numerical Experiments

To evaluate the performance of the proposed HHS, a series of numerical experiments are conducted based on two sets of data, and the CPLEX software, the enterprise method, and the tabu search algorithm introduced in Liu et al. [30] are compared with the proposed HHS.

5.1   Experimental Data and Settings

The performance of the proposed HHS is valued in the following sections. The experiments are run on a computer with an Intel Core i5 processor and 8 GB RAM. HHS the tabu search algorithm, and the genetic algorithm are coded in C++. A preliminary numerical test is executed, and the values of different parameters are selected. The harmony memory size HMS, harmony memory considering rate HMCR, pitch adjusting rate PAR, the number of iterations $I_{iteration}$, and I_{cons} are set as 10, 0.8, 0.4, 1000, and 100. Two sets of instances are generated according to [30]. The first set of small-sized instances includes 5–10 customers and two vehicles. The second set of larger-sized instances includes 72 instances, each with 18–100 customers and 2–15 vehicles, which were generated based on the well-known CVRP benchmark (A, B and P Series). The features of the customer coordinates of groups A, B and P are different and are reflected in Group A's customer coordinates being produced randomly, group B's customer coordinates being clustered, and group C's customer coordinates being almost the same distance. The distance between two points (customers or the plant) is set as the travel time for convenient calculation.

5.2   Comparing HHS with CPLEX for Small-Sized Instances

CPLEX is applied to verify the validity of the mathematical model for small instances. It is worth noting that Constraint (6) of the mathematical model in Sect. 3 is actually nonlinear; thus, a new variable P_{jk}, with $P_{jk} = r_j y_{jk}$, is defined to solve the problem. Then, Constraint (6) is replaced by the following linear Constraints (10)–(12), where M is a large number.

$$r_j \leq P_{jk} + M(1 - y_{jk}) \tag{10}$$

$$0 \leq P_{jk} + M y_{jk} \tag{11}$$

$$A_0^k \geq \max_{j \in N} P_{jk} \tag{12}$$

Table 1 shows the CPLEX and HHS solutions for small instances. The "case" list shows the name of the instance, "n" and "k" represent the number of customers and vehicles individually. The solutions obtained by the CPLEX algorithm and HHS are equal and optimal for small instances, while the completion time of HHS is less than that of CPLEX.

5.3   Comparing HHS with the Enterprise Method for Larger-Sized Instances

To verify whether the actual problem can be solved, the HHS is compared with the enterprise method for the larger-sized instances. As introduced in Sect. 1, in the actual operation of the e-commerce retail enterprise, the order shall be delivered in batches according to the principle of first come, first served, when one vehicle completes the loading task, start the loading task of the next vehicle. The routing of each vehicle

Table 1. Computational results of CPLEX and HHS.

Case	CPLEX		HHS		
	Objective	Time(s)	Objective	Time(s)	Optimal?
n5-k2	75	3	75	3	Yes
n6-k2	105	4	105	3	Yes
n7-k2	119	5	119	3	Yes
n8-k2	139	7	139	3	Yes
n9-k2	150	11	150	3	Yes
n10-k2	146	23	146	3	Yes

follows the principle of "close first and then far later", that is, the delivery shall be for the customers who are close first.

Table 2 gives the solutions of HHS and the enterprise method for larger-sized instances of groups A, B, and C. The column "Case" shows the name of the instance, "n" and "k" represent the number of customers and vehicles individually. Columns "Z2" and "Z1" show the solutions obtained by the enterprise method and HHS algorithm, respectively. The gap percentage between the enterprise method and the HHS algorithm is listed in "Gap1", with the calculation formula being $(Z2 - Z1)/Z1 *$ 100%. For the average solution of all instances, the gap percentage between the enterprise method and HHS is approximately 18%. Obviously, HHS is better than the enterprise method; that is, the joint decision of vehicle routing and order release time is better than the separate decision.

5.4 Comparing HHS with the Tabu Search Algorithm for Larger-Sized Instances

To further verify the effectiveness of HHS, a tabu search (TS) algorithm [30] and a genetic algorithm (GA) [2] are applied to solve the same larger-sized instances. The same problem (CVRPORT) is considered in [30] except for the objective is to minimize the sum of the vehicle completion times. The problem addressed in [2] considered an integrated machine scheduling and vehicle routing problem, in which orders have been processed by a distribution centre and then delivered to retailers within time windows. The objective is to minimize the maximum order delivery time, which is as same as this paper.

Table 3 gives the solutions of HHS, the TS, and the GA for larger-sized instances. Columns"Z3", "Z2" and "Z1" show the solutions obtained by the GA, the TS and HHS algorithms, respectively. The gap percentage between the GA and HHS algorithms is listed in "Gap2" and the gap percentage between the TS and HHS algorithms is listed in "Gap1", with the calculation formula being $(Z3 - Z1)/Z1 * 100\%$ and $(Z2 - Z1)/Z1 * 100\%$. HHS is inferior to TS, GA in only three instances and eight instances, respectively. For the average solution of all instances, the gap percentage between TS and HHS, GA and HHS are approximately 2.24%, 1.90%, respectively. Thus, HHS is slightly better than TS and GA. For TS, only one initial solution is constructed, and the

Table 2. Computational results of HHS and enterprise method.

Case	Z1	Z2	GAP1	Case	Z1	Z2	GAP1
A-n32-k5	364	419	0.55%	B-n45-k6	291	310	6.53%
A-n33-k5	273	362	32.60%	B-n50-k7	363	403	11.02%
A-n33-k6	287	340	18.47%	B-n50-k8	342	374	9.36%
A-n34-k5	299	381	27.42%	B-n51-k7	342	481	40.64%
A-n36-k5	362	386	6.63%	B-n52-k7	329	416	26.44%
A-n37-k5	290	398	37.24%	B-n56-k7	317	427	34.70%
A-n37-k6	316	404	27.85%	B-n57-k7	426	620	45.54%
A-n38-k5	365	443	21.37%	B-n57-k9	321	398	23.99%
A-n39-k5	381	419	9.97%	B-n63-k10	349	385	10.32%
A-n39-k6	334	366	9.58%	B-n64-k9	317	377	18.93%
A-n44-k6	356	459	28.93%	B-n66-k9	333	386	15.92%
A-n45-k6	402	514	27.86%	B-n67-k10	305	375	22.95%
A-n45-k7	305	355	16.39%	B-n68-k9	359	410	14.21%
A-n46-k7	331	369	11.48%	B-n78-k10	356	448	25.84%
A-n48-k7	364	383	5.22%	P-n16-k8	107	112	4.67%
A-n53-k7	359	407	13.37%	P-n19-k2	188	208	10.64%
A-n54-k7	397	489	23.17%	P-n20-k2	176	192	9.09%
A-n55-k9	327	366	11.93%	P-n21-k2	185	199	7.57%
A-n60-k9	350	412	17.71%	P-n22-k2	194	201	3.61%
A-n61-k9	328	363	10.67%	P-n22-k8	127	170	33.86%
A-n62-k8	387	444	14.73%	P-n23-k8	138	139	0.72%
A-n63-k9	384	407	5.99%	P-n40-k5	182	228	25.27%
A-n63-k10	302	409	35.43%	P-n45-k5	199	285	43.22%
A-n64-k9	358	402	12.29%	P-n50-k7	207	230	11.11%
A-n65-k9	401	470	17.21%	P-n50-k8	218	219	0.46%
A-n69-k9	419	455	8.59%	P-n50-k10	159	201	26.42%
A-n80-k10	444	479	7.88%	P-n51-k10	167	227	35.93%
B-n31-k5	271	300	10.70%	P-n55-k7	187	230	22.99%
B-n34-k5	298	336	12.75%	P-n55-k10	149	193	29.53%
B-n35-k5	369	430	16.53%	P-n60-k10	202	215	6.44%
B-n38-k6	290	343	18.28%	P-n60-k15	154	205	33.12%
B-n39-k5	279	339	21.51%	P-n65-k10	194	233	20.10%
B-n41-k6	328	352	7.32%	P-n70-k10	231	272	17.75%
B-n43-k6	249	291	16.87%	P-n76-k4	398	429	7.79%
B-n44-k7	275	325	18.18%	P-n76-k5	329	393	19.45%
B-n45-k5	365	462	26.58%	P-n101-k4	461	489	6.07%

neighborhood solution generated later depends on the initial solution. HHS constructs a set of initial solutions for generating neighborhood solutions. For GA, the genes of the best individuals are not specially preserved. HHS preserves the genes of the best individuals with a certain probability in the procedure of memory consideration.

Table 3. Computational results of HHS and enterprise method.

Case	Z1	Z2	Z3	GAP1	GAP2	Case	Z1	Z2	Z3	GAP1	GAP2
A-n32-k5	364	366	368	0.55%	1.02%	B-n45-k6	291	298	294	2.41%	0.97%
A-n33-k5	273	283	277	3.66%	1.34%	B-n50-k7	363	366	372	0.83%	2.57%
A-n33-k6	287	289	292	0.70%	1.87%	B-n50-k8	342	354	351	3.51%	2.73%
A-n34-k5	299	308	307	3.01%	2.54%	B-n51-k7	342	345	339	0.88%	0.88%
A-n36-k5	362	366	364	1.10%	0.66%	B-n52-k7	329	336	331	2.13%	0.75%
A-n37-k5	290	285	292	−1.72%	0.53%	B-n56-k7	317	328	321	3.47%	1.21%
A-n37-k6	316	332	317	5.06%	0.26%	B-n57-k7	426	432	430	1.41%	1.02%
A-n38-k5	365	376	368	3.01%	0.77%	B-n57-k9	321	331	326	3.12%	1.41%
A-n39-k5	381	393	384	3.15%	0.79%	B-n63-k10	349	355	352	1.72%	0.84%
A-n39-k6	334	336	332	0.60%	−0.60%	B-n64-k9	317	321	320	1.26%	0.79%
A-n44-k6	356	364	363	2.25%	1.92%	B-n66-k9	333	345	343	3.60%	2.99%
A-n45-k6	402	412	410	2.49%	2.07%	B-n67-k10	305	309	309	1.31%	1.22%
A-n45-k7	305	334	309	9.51%	1.26%	B-n68-k9	359	369	361	2.79%	0.53%
A-n46-k7	331	338	328	2.11%	-0.91%	B-n78-k10	356	368	359	3.37%	0.87%
A-n48-k7	364	373	367	2.47%	0.83%	P-n16-k8	107	109	117	1.87%	9.18%
A-n53-k7	359	365	367	1.67%	2.13%	P-n19-k2	188	191	195	1.60%	3.68%
A-n54-k7	397	406	402	2.27%	1.24%	P-n20-k2	176	177	181	0.57%	2.75%
A-n55-k9	327	332	334	1.53%	2.23%	P-n21-k2	185	187	192	1.08%	3.81%
A-n60-k9	350	358	352	2.29%	0.49%	P-n22-k2	194	199	199	2.58%	2.51%
A-n61-k9	328	331	325	0.91%	−0.91%	P-n22-k8	127	129	136	1.57%	7.15%
A-n62-k8	387	389	392	0.52%	1.27%	P-n23-k8	138	139	139	0.72%	0.72%
A-n63-k9	384	398	388	3.65%	0.93%	P-n40-k5	182	189	187	3.85%	2.56%
A-n63-k10	302	309	303	2.32%	0.44%	P-n45-k5	199	211	201	6.03%	0.96%
A-n64-k9	358	365	359	1.96%	0.40%	P-n50-k7	207	215	205	3.86%	−0.97%
A-n65-k9	401	413	409	2.99%	2.11%	P-n50-k8	218	221	221	1.38%	1.38%
A-n69-k9	419	425	416	1.43%	−0.72%	P-n50-k10	159	165	162	3.77%	1.75%
A-n80-k10	444	449	449	1.13%	1.15%	P-n51-k10	167	175	167	4.79%	0.23%
B-n31-k5	271	277	277	2.21%	2.12%	P-n55-k7	187	189	185	1.07%	−1.07%
B-n34-k5	298	287	308	−3.69%	3.29%	P-n55-k10	149	157	154	5.37%	3.25%
B-n35-k5	369	373	375	1.08%	1.53%	P-n60-k10	202	205	212	1.49%	4.81%
B-n38-k6	290	295	292	1.72%	0.82%	P-n60-k15	154	159	156	3.25%	1.23%
B-n39-k5	279	281	283	0.72%	1.53%	P-n65-k10	194	198	203	2.06%	4.46%
B-n41-k6	328	326	334	−0.61%	1.76%	P-n70-k10	231	241	236	4.33%	2.23%
B-n43-k6	249	251	251	0.80%	0.85%	P-n76-k4	398	401	391	0.75%	−1.76%
B-n44-k7	275	280	278	1.82%	0.92%	P-n76-k5	329	336	336	2.13%	2.23%
B-n45-k5	365	376	370	3.01%	1.40%	P-n101-k4	461	478	465	3.69%	0.87%

6 Conclusion

This paper addresses a capacitated vehicle routing problem with order release time in an e-commerce enterprise, regarding the minimization of the maximum order delivery time (maximum vehicle completion time) as the objective. The mathematical model is established, and the vehicle routing and the order release time are considered coordinated. The hybrid harmonic search is designed, and the local optimization algorithm is embedded. In the experimental part, the hybrid harmony search is compared with the actual operational methods of the enterprise, an existing tabu search algorithm and a genetic algorithm in the literature. The results show that the hybrid harmonic search is more effective.

This research will be helpful for improving the customer service level and intelligent logistics level for enterprises. Further research will focus on more real-world features, such as the constraints of heterogeneous vehicles and multiple depots.

Acknowledgments. This work was supported by the National Natural Science Foundation of China (No. 71862034 and 71862035); The Scientific Research Funding of Yunnan Department of Education (No. 2017ZZX004); The Scientific Research Funding of Yunnan University of Finance and Economics (No. 2019D04); The Yunnan Fundamental Research Project under grant NO. 2019FB085.

Conflicts of Interest. The authors declare no conflicts of interest.

References

1. Gevaers, R., Van de Voorde, E., Vanelslander, T.: Cost modelling and simulation of last-mile characteristics in an innovative B2C supply chain environment with implications on urban areas and cities. Proc. Soc. Behav. Sci. **125**, 398–411 (2014). https://doi.org/10.1016/j.sbspro.2014.01.1483
2. Low, C.Y., Li, R.K., Chang, C.M.: Integrated scheduling of production and delivery with time windows. Int. J. Logist. Res. Appl. **51**, 897–909 (2013). https://doi.org/10.1080/00207543.2012.677071
3. Li, K., Chen, B., Sivakumar, A.I., Wu, Y.: An inventory–routing problem with the objective of travel time minimization. Eur. J. Oper. Res. **236**, 936–945 (2014). https://doi.org/10.1016/j.ejor.2013.07.034
4. Dantzig, G.B., Ramser, J.H.: The truck dispatching problem. Manag. Sci. **6**, 80–91 (1959). https://doi.org/10.1287/mnsc.6.1.80
5. Szeto, W.Y., Wu, Y., Ho, S.C.: An artificial bee colony algorithm for the capacitated vehicle routing problem. Int. J. Prod. Res. **215**, 126–135 (2011). https://doi.org/10.1016/j.ejor.2011.06.006
6. Akpinar, S.: Hybrid large neighbourhood search algorithm for capacitated vehicle routing problem. Exp. Syst. Appl. **61**, 28–38 (2016). https://doi.org/10.1016/j.eswa.2016.05.023
7. Liu, R., Jiang, Z.: A hybrid large-neighborhood search algorithm for the cumulative capacitated vehicle routing problem with time-window constraints. Appl. Soft Comput. **80**, 18–30 (2019). https://doi.org/10.1016/j.asoc.2019.03.008

8. Liu, T., Luo, Z., Qin, H., Lim, A.: A branch-and-cut algorithm for the two-echelon capacitated vehicle routing problem with grouping constraints. Eur. J. Oper. Res. **266**, 487–497 (2018). https://doi.org/10.1016/j.ejor.2017.10.017

9. Marques, G., Sadykov, R., Deschamps, J.-C., Dupas, R.: An improved branch-cut-and-price algorithm for the two-echelon capacitated vehicle routing problem. Comput. Oper. Res. **114**, 104833 (2020). https://doi.org/10.1016/j.cor.2019.104833

10. Ng, K.K.H., Lee, C.K.M., Zhang, S.Z., Wu, K., Ho, W.: A multiple colonies artificial bee colony algorithm for a capacitated vehicle routing problem and re-routing strategies under time-dependent traffic congestion. Comput. Ind. Eng. **109**, 151–168 (2017). https://doi.org/10.1016/j.cie.2017.05.004

11. Wei, L., Zhang, Z., Zhang, D., Leung, S.C.H.: A simulated annealing algorithm for the capacitated vehicle routing problem with two-dimensional loading constraints. Eur. J. Oper. Res. **265**, 843–859 (2018). https://doi.org/10.1016/j.ejor.2017.08.035

12. Bortfeldt, A.: A hybrid algorithm for the capacitated vehicle routing problem with three-dimensional loading constraints. Comput. Oper. Res. **39**, 2248–2257 (2012). https://doi.org/10.1016/j.cor.2011.11.008

13. Allahyari, S., Salari, M., Vigo, D.: A hybrid metaheuristic algorithm for the multi-depot covering tour vehicle routing problem. Eur. J. Oper. Res. **242**, 756–768 (2015). https://doi.org/10.1016/j.ejor.2014.10.048

14. Xu, Z., Elomri, A., Pokharel, S., Mutlu, F.: A model for capacitated green vehicle routing problem with the time-varying vehicle speed and soft time windows. Comput. Ind. Eng. **137**, 106011 (2019). https://doi.org/10.1016/j.cie.2019.106011

15. Ciancio, C., Laganá, D., Vocaturo, F.: Branch-price-and-cut for the mixed capacitated general routing problem with time windows. Eur. J. Oper. Res. **267**, 187–199 (2018). https://doi.org/10.1016/j.ejor.2017.11.039

16. Madankumar, S., Rajendran, C.: Mathematical models for green vehicle routing problems with pickup and delivery: a case of semiconductor supply chain. Comput. Oper. Res. **89**, 183–192 (2018). https://doi.org/10.1016/j.cor.2016.03.013

17. Lu, E.H.-C., Yang, Y.-W.: A hybrid route planning approach for logistics with pickup and delivery. Exp. Syst. Appl. **118**, 482–492 (2019). https://doi.org/10.1016/j.eswa.2018.10.031

18. Hornstra, R.P., Silva, A., Roodbergen, K.J., Coelho, L.C.: The vehicle routing problem with simultaneous pickup and delivery and handling costs. Comput. Oper. Res. **115**, 104858 (2020). https://doi.org/10.1016/j.cor.2019.104858

19. Shi, Y., Boudouh, T., Grunder, O.: A hybrid genetic algorithm for a home health care routing problem with time window and fuzzy demand. Exp. Syst. Appl. **72**, 160–176 (2017). https://doi.org/10.1016/j.eswa.2016.12.013

20. Gutierrez, A., Dieulle, L., Labadie, N., Velasco, N.: A hybrid metaheuristic algorithm for the vehicle routing problem with stochastic demands. Comput. Oper. Res. **99**, 135–147 (2018). https://doi.org/10.1016/j.cor.2018.06.012

21. Bertazzi, L., Secomandi, N.: Faster rollout search for the vehicle routing problem with stochastic demands and restocking. Eur. J. Oper. Res. **270**, 487–497 (2018). https://doi.org/10.1016/j.ejor.2018.03.034

22. Contardo, C., Martinelli, R.: A new exact algorithm for the multi-depot vehicle routing problem under capacity and route length constraints. Discrete Optim. **12**, 129–146 (2014). https://doi.org/10.1016/j.disopt.2014.03.001

23. Li, Y., Soleimani, H., Zohal, M.: An improved ant colony optimization algorithm for the multi-depot green vehicle routing problem with multiple objectives. J. Clean. Prod. **227**, 1161–1172 (2019). https://doi.org/10.1016/j.jclepro.2019.03.185

24. Leggieri, V., Haouari, M.: Lifted polynomial size formulations for the homogeneous and heterogeneous vehicle routing problems. Eur. J. Oper. Res. **263**, 755–767 (2017). https://doi.org/10.1016/j.ejor.2017.05.039
25. Bevilaqua, A., Bevilaqua, D., Yamanaka, K.: Parallel island based memetic algorithm with Lin-Kernighan local search for a real-life two-echelon heterogeneous vehicle routing problem based on Brazilian wholesale companies. Appl. Soft Comput. **76**, 697–711 (2019). https://doi.org/10.1016/j.asoc.2018.12.036
26. Eskandarpour, M., Ouelhadj, D., Hatami, S., Juan, A.A., Khosravi, B.: Enhanced multi-directional local search for the bi-objective heterogeneous vehicle routing problem with multiple driving ranges. Eur. J. Oper. Res. **277**, 479–491 (2019). https://doi.org/10.1016/j.ejor.2019.02.048
27. Archetti, C., Feillet, D., Speranza, M.G.: Complexity of routing problems with release dates. Eur. J. Oper. Res. **247**, 797–803 (2015). https://doi.org/10.1016/j.ejor.2015.06.057
28. Reyes, D., Erera, A.L., Savelsbergh, M.W.P.: Complexity of routing problems with release dates and deadlines. Eur. J. Oper. Res. **266**, 29–34 (2018). https://doi.org/10.1016/j.ejor.2017.09.020
29. Archetti, C., Feillet, D., Mor, A., Speranza, M.G.: An iterated local search for the Traveling Salesman Problem with release dates and completion time minimization. Comput. Oper. Res. **98**, 24–37 (2018). https://doi.org/10.1016/j.cor.2018.05.001
30. Liu, L., Li, K., Liu, Z.: A capacitated vehicle routing problem with order available time in e-commerce industry. Eng. Optim. **49**, 449–465 (2017). https://doi.org/10.1080/0305215x.2016.1188092
31. Li, W., Wu, Y., Kumar, P.N.R., Li, K.: Multi-trip vehicle routing problem with order release time. Eng. Optim. **52**, 1279–1294 (2019). https://doi.org/10.1080/0305215x.2019.1642880
32. Cattaruzza, D., Absi, N., Feillet, D.: The multi-trip vehicle routing problem with time windows and release dates. Transp. Sci. **50**, 676–693 (2016). https://doi.org/10.1287/trsc.2015.0608
33. Zhen, L., Ma, C., Wang, K., Xiao, L., Zhang, W.: Multi-depot multi-trip vehicle routing problem with time windows and release dates. Transp. Res. E Logist. Transp. Rev. **135**, 101866 (2020). https://doi.org/10.1016/j.tre.2020.101866
34. Shelbourne, B.C., Battarra, M., Potts, C.N.: The vehicle routing problem with release and due dates. INFORMS J. Comput. **29**, 705–723 (2018). https://doi.org/10.1287/ijoc.2017.0756
35. Soman, J.T., Patil, R.J.: A scatter search method for heterogeneous fleet vehicle routing problem with release dates under lateness dependent tardiness costs. Expert Syst. Appl. **150**, 113302 (2020). https://doi.org/10.1016/j.eswa.2020.113302
36. Geem, Z.W., Kim, J.H., Loganathan, G.V.: A new heuristic optimization algorithm: harmony search. Simulation **76**, 60–68 (2001). https://doi.org/10.1177/003754970107600201

An Adaptive Data Protection Scheme for Optimizing Storage Space

Meng Ming[1,2], Gang Zhao[3], Xiaohui Kuang[3], Lu Liu[1],
and Ruyun Zhang[4(✉)]

[1] School of Computer Science and Technology, Beijing Institute of Technology,
Beijing 100081, China
2530715002@qq.com, liulu@bit.edu.cn
[2] Institute of Artificial Intelligence and Blockchain, Guangzhou University,
Guangzhou, China
[3] National Key Laboratory of Science and Technology on Information System
Security, Beijing, China
zhao-gang20@126.com, xiaohui_kuang@163.com
[4] Zhejiang Lab, Hangzhou, Zhejiang Province, China
zhangry@zhejianglab.com

Abstract. Data is the main driving factor of artificial intelligence represented by machine learning, and how to ensure data security is one of the severe challenges. In many traditional methods, a single snapshot strategy is used to protect data. In order to meet the flexibility of data protection and optimize storage space, this paper presents a new architecture and an implementation in the Linux kernel. The idea is to hook system calls and analyze the relationship between applications and files. By tracking system calls, the system can perceive the file modification and automatically adjust the time interval for generating snapshots. Time granularity changes with the application load to achieve on-demand protection. Extensive experiments have been carried out to show that the scheme can monitor the process of operating files, reduce storage costs and hardly affect the performance of system.

Keywords: Adaptive protection · Snapshot · Storage optimization

1 Introduction

In the era of artificial intelligence, machine learning as its representative technology has been applied to various fields including smart cities, smart medical care, human cognitive communication, privacy protection, etc. [1–3]. Data is the core driving element of machine learning [4, 5]. How to ensure its security in a complex network environment is a serious challenge [6]. A survey from IDC (Internet Data Center) shows that up to 60% of users often store important data in desktop or laptop computers outside the data center. Some dangerous situations often lead to data corruption or loss, such as user misuse, virus intrusion, hacker attack, etc.

In response to this concern, snapshot technology is widely used in data backup with its advantages of online backup and saving storage space [7, 8]. Many products

X. Chen et al. (Eds.): ML4CS 2020, LNCS 12487, pp. 250–260, 2020.
https://doi.org/10.1007/978-3-030-62460-6_22

including Sheepdog, NetApp NAS, IBM Total Storage SAN Volume Controller, Linux LVM, NetApp filers, Veritas File System, etc., all support the snapshot function [9, 10]. But these products still remain several drawbacks that they are mostly implemented at the operating system level and snapshots are performed with an inflexible way by users.

To solve above problems, Gsnapshot—a fine-grained universal snapshot across file systems, is implemented by Zhao [11] and others. This method is more flexible and less expensive than previous device-level snapshots, but it ignores the impact of the access status on data protection. Zhou [12] et al. proposed a logical volume snapshot protection system based on out-of-band storage virtualization. In this system, the interval between snapshot generations can be changed. But there also are some disadvantages, including complicated implementation process and lack of connection between applications and data blocks.

Previous studies have further addressed remaining issues. This paper proposes an adaptive data protection scheme to reduce storage costs by adopting flexible strategies for different data. We have hooked [13] system calls of VFS to intercept file operations, analyzed the relationship between applications and files and implemented a simple and efficient adaptive data protection strategy in Linux kernel.

The contribution of this article is as follows:

- We intercept file operations to monitor file access status.
- We adjust the protection granularity according to application load to ensure the security of data and save space.
- We do some related experiments and confirm that this method can optimize the use of storage space and hardly affect the performance of system.

The rest of this paper is organized as follows: Sect. 2 gives a brief introduction to the related work and background. Section 3 discusses the design process of this method and issues to be addressed. Section 4 describes implementation details in a specific environment. Section 5 evaluates the performance of the prototype. Section 6 gathers the conclusion and future work.

2 Related Work and Background

2.1 Snapshot Technology

With the increase of storage requirements, users need to protect data online. Snapshot is one of the effective methods to prevent data loss of online storage devices. It is usually implemented in data block layer or file system. The snapshot technology in the file system can ensure the consistency of the state, but the portability and flexibility are poor. Some FS support "fine-grained" snapshots, including Ext3Cow [14], Elephant [15], ZFS from Sun Solaris, BTRFS, NILFS, NILFS2 [16] and WAFL [17] (Write Anywhere File Layout).

BTRFS is a file system in Linux. It is based on Copy-on-Write (COW) technology, and it can achieve efficient snapshots and clones [18]. The literature [19] compares the I/O performance, flexibility, ease of use and so on. Results show that the performance of BTRFS is outstanding in terms of write and re-write. The snapshot of BTRFS is achieved by copying "subvolumes". Only metadata is copied during the snapshot process. When new data is written or existing data is updated, the COW-based system will generate a new snapshot. It can quickly recover data in the event of a hard disk write error, file corruption, or program failure[20]. The process is shown in Fig. 1.

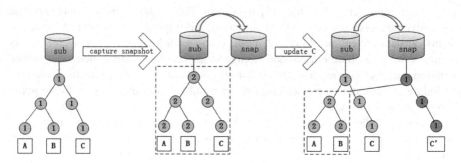

Fig. 1. Snapshot structure of BTRFS.

2.2 The/Proc

Proc is a virtual file system, and it only exists in memory. It is a communication bridge between kernel and user space [21, 22]. In Linux, each running process generates a directory named process number and produces some files in it to describe the running status [22]. In this article, we use/proc to transfer data between the monitoring module in kernel and the backup program in user space.

3   Design

In this section, we will introduce design ideas based on main problems to be solved during the implementation process, including intercepting file operations, and updating protection granularity.

3.1   Intercepting File Operations

Each file system in Linux has an independent organization and operation. In order to facilitate the unified operation of users, VFS provides a set of system calls so that users can transparently process files. When an application accesses a file, the process calls open (), read (), write (), etc., then maps them to sys_read (), sys_write () of the VFS, next transfers to call functions of the specific file system. In this article, we achieve the purpose of intercepting file operations by hooking system calls of the VFS.

When a process opens a file, a structure named file is created. This structure has a pointer named f_op, whose content is a function pointer that points to specific file manipulation functions. By modifying this pointer to point to a custom function, we can intercept file operations. However, we need to consider a problem. Due to the different implementation in each file system, not every function pointed to by the f_op is meaningful. At this time, the function pointer is NULL. Therefore, before replacing the file manipulation function, we should first make sure that the function has been defined. The process of hooking file operation functions is shown in Fig. 2.

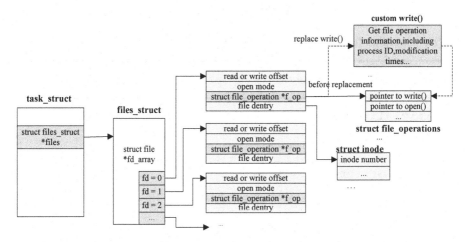

Fig. 2. The process of hooking file operations.

3.2   Updating Protection Granularity

This article adopts an adaptive snapshot generation mechanism to automatically create snapshots at dynamic intervals. It has the following characteristics:

Adaptive load change: When the frequency of data modification increases, the time interval for generating snapshots is shortened; On the contrary, the interval for generating snapshots is extended to save storage resources.

Simple counting structure: The structure that records the number of file modifications is stored in the cache, and it hardly affects the system performance.

High flexibility: This method provides an automatic snapshot generation policy based on the average number of modifications.

We propose two related concepts here: Granularity indicates the frequency of creating snapshots within a certain period of time; Threshold represents the interval between two snapshots. The relationship between two values in a certain period is shown as formula (1). Among them, T represents the interval from the last update time to the next update time.

$$threshold_T = \frac{1}{granularity_T} \tag{1}$$

We have designed an update strategy for protection granularity. The average modification strategy: Since the last update time, within the set multiple periods, the average value of modifications in these periods is used as the protection granularity.

The formula (2) is as follows. Among them, N is the number of periods set by the user, T is each period, and count is the frequency of file modification in each period.

$$file_{granularity} = \frac{\sum_{n=1}^{N} count_{T_n}}{N} \qquad (2)$$

The algorithm for updating the granularity is as follows:

Algorithm 1 Algorithm for updating granularity

```
1  initialize the current value.
2  granularity_last ← file_granularity
3  T represents a time interval.
4  F is the modification within a time interval.
5  set time intervals Time [T₁, T₂, ..., Tₙ].
6  Timer thread is started.
7  While the number of intervals does not reach the set
value
8        if T arrives then
9             Fᵢ ← file_frequency
10            restart Timer
11 if adopt the average modification strategy then
12       granularity_now ← [F₁, F₂, ... Fₙ]/N
13 else if use the maximum modification strategy then
14       granularity_now ← max[F₁, F₂, ... Fₙ]
```

---

4 Implementation

This section discusses the implementation of this scheme. It mainly describes the problems we need to solve. The process is divided into the following modules:

- Modifying file operation functions.
- Backup process in user layer.

4.1 Modifying File Operation Functions

We use struct file * filp_open (const char * filename, int open_mode, int mode) to open the protected file and obtain the file structure, and then determine whether the function pointer is defined under the f_op. If the file function is defined, the pointer will be set to point to the corresponding custom function. For example, we first define mywrite () with the same type and parameters as the original write (), and then define the temporary variable orig_write. When file-> f_op-> write is not null, the original value of file-> f_op-> write is assigned to orig_write. And then f_op-> write is transferred to point to mywrite (). There is a problem that the f_op is read-only and cannot be directly modified. It requires us to define the struct file_operations * fop ourselves, and then assign it to file-> f_op after pointing to a custom function.

In order to conveniently handle parameters, we define a structure to represent the relevant file operation information. As shown in Fig. 3. Among them, file_name is full path of protected file, app_path stores the application list in the host whitelist corresponding to the file, the third parameter is the threshold for current period, and write_count represents the frequency of modification.

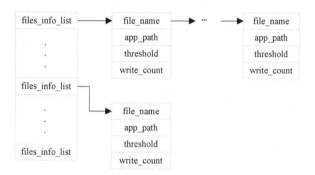

Fig. 3. Structure of protected objects.

4.2 Backup Process in User Layer

After intercepting system calls, we obtain the relevant information from mywrite (). Then we get the name of the application that is currently modifying the file based on the process ID. Next we determine whether the current application is on the whitelist or whether the number of modifications reaches the threshold. If not, the program jumps back to the original point to continue. Otherwise, it calls int call_usermodehelper (char * path, char ** argv, char ** envp, enum umh_wait wait) to run the backup program in the user space. The fourth parameter controls whether the current process waits for the result of application execution to return. The prototype is shown as Table 1. We hope to protect files before abnormal operations are performed, so we choose UMH_WAIT_PROC.

Table 1. Parametric prototypes.

Parameter type	Value	Effect
UMH_NO_WAIT	−1	Don't wait at all
UMH_WAIT_EXEC	0	Wait for the exec, but not the process
UMH_WAIT_PROC	1	Wait for the process to complete

The overall process is shown in Fig. 4.

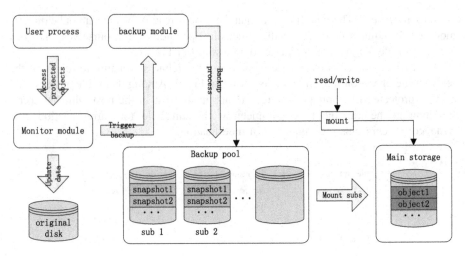

Fig. 4. The implementation process.

5   Test Evaluation

In this section, we evaluate the effectiveness and performance overhead of the proto-type. The test environment is shown in Table 2:

Table 2. Test environment.

VMware version	VMware Workstation 12.5.2
Operation system	Ubuntu-16.04.5
kernel version	Linux-kernel-5.6.0
Memory	4 GB
CPU	3.6 GHz

5.1   Effect on Reading and Writing Rate

We have set up several experiments to test the read and write rate before and after modification. We used IOzone to test and perform it 5 times to get a better average. We used the following command to initialize the experiment:

./iozone -a -n 64K -g 8M -r 4K -o -i 0 -i 1 -p -f file_path -Rb result_file

From the test results in Fig. 5, we can see that files with size is below 1 MB, our modification caused a certain degree of decline in read and write rate, and for files with size is above 1 MB, the read and write performance are basically consistent. This is due to the performance overhead we switch between the original function and the custom function. For large files, compared to the time consumption of reading data blocks multiple times, the switching overhead between functions is negligible.

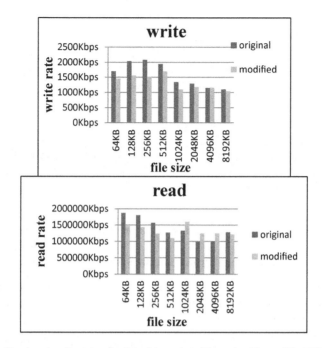

Fig. 5. Read and write rate of original kernel and kernel with modified VFS layer.

5.2 Comparative Experiment of Fixed Interval Snapshot and Adaptive Interval Snapshot

We have conducted a comparative test of generating snapshots at fixed intervals and adaptive intervals. We observed the frequency of modification of each file in the first three hours of normal use, and selected three files with different frequency of modification. We used the average number strategy to update protection granularity. We implemented six sets of comparative experiments and observed the space occupied by the corresponding snapshot volume. Each set of experiments lasted 180 min. In the six groups of experiments, the first five groups were tested with fixed time intervals (5 min, 10 min, 15 min, 20 min, 60 min), and the last group was tested using adaptive time interval. The experimental results are shown in Fig. 6.

From the experimental results, it can be seen that no matter how frequently the files are modified, the adaptive method can save storage space to a certain extent, and the saved capacity accounts for 22.6% ～ 29.2%. Compared with the fifth group of experiments with a large fixed time interval, this method will take up more space. However, because the protection granularity of reference group experiment is too large, the risk of data loss is higher, and the amount of lost data is up to 37%. Compared with the maximum percentage of data lost in the adaptive method within 10%, the difference of two sets of experimental storage space is only 5.8% ～ 6.15%, so it is meaningful to sacrifice a small amount of storage space in exchange for a lower risk of data loss.

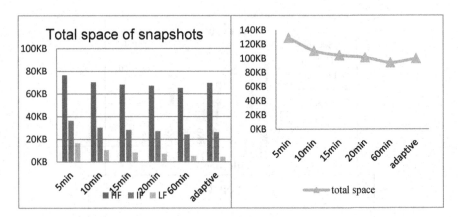

Fig. 6. The storage capacity of fixed interval snapshot and adaptive interval snapshot.

5.3   Impact of Adaptive Data Protection on System Performance

We choose an office software to simulate the normal environment to operate the file, and test the impact on system performance under normal conditions and adaptive data protection. The test results are shown in Figs. 7 and 8.

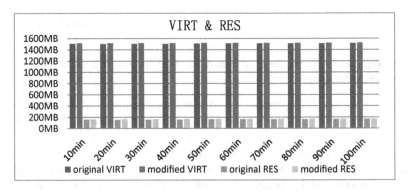

Fig. 7. Usage of VIRT and RES in fixed interval mode and adaptive interval mode.

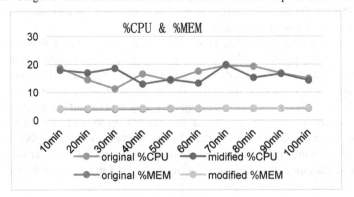

Fig. 8. Occupation of CPU and MEM by fixed interval and adaptive interval.

As can be seen in Fig. 7, the VIRT and RES of the adaptive method increase slightly, with the growth percentages within about 1% and 8%, respectively. % CPU is related to the data volume of each file. It can be obtained from the test results in Fig. 8, there is no significant difference in the change trend of the usage, both between 10% and 20%. Modified usage of CPU does not increase compared to normal conditions. Usage of memory after modification is basically the same as before. For SHR, it is 103388 Kb and 103772 Kb under two modes. From the above test results, it can be seen that the adaptive data protection method proposed in this paper does not bring significant overhead to the system performance, and the use of resources belongs to a reasonable range.

6 Conclusion and Future Work

To protect data, snapshot technology is applied to many devices and systems to reduce the risk of data corruption. However, in many existing snapshot protection systems, a unified protection granularity is generally used to protect data at different risk levels. Too fine granularity will waste space resources, and too coarse granularity will lose more data. In this paper, we proposed an adaptive data protection method to meet the protection of files with different security levels. We intercepted system calls to obtain the process of modifying the file and operational information. By tracking changes to protected objects, the protection granularity was dynamically adjusted with the change of the application load. The results show that this method proposed in this paper can sense the modification of files and save storage resources under the premise of protecting data. And the performance overhead is reasonable.

However, there are still some limitations. First, we can obtain the process information when the file is modified, but it does not deeply consider the semantic relationship between protected data and applications. Second, redirected file functions will reduce the read and write performance of small files. In the future work, we will study the semantic relationship between data and applications to improve specific protection, and optimize the read and write performance of small files.

Acknowledgements. This work was supported in part by the National Key Research and Development Program of China under Grant 2018YFB1004402, National Natural Science Foundation of China (No. U1936218, No. 61876019), and Zhejiang Lab (No. 2020LE0AB02).

References

1. Jacob, S., Menon, V.G., Al-Turjman, F., et al.: Artificial muscle intelligence system with deep learning for post-stroke assistance and rehabilitation. IEEE Access 7, 133463–133473 (2019)
2. Sangaiah, A.K., Lu, H., Hu, Q.: Cognitive science and artificial intelligence for human cognition and communication. IEEE Consum. Electron. Mag. 9(1), 72–73 (2019)
3. Zafar, S., Jangsher, S., Aloqaily, M., et al.: Resource allocation in moving small cell network using deep learning based interference determination. In: 2019 IEEE 30th Annual International Symposium on Personal, Indoor and Mobile Radio Communications (PIMRC). IEEE, pp. 1–6 (2019)

4. Sharma, G., Srivastava, G., Mago, V.: A framework for automatic categorization of social data into medical domains. IEEE Trans. Comput. Soc. Syst. **7**, 129–140 (2019)
5. Edwards, L.: data protection and e-privacy: from spam and cookies to big data, machine learning and profiling. Soc. Sci. Electron. Publ. (2018)
6. Ullah, F., Naeem, H., Jabbar, S., et al.: Cyber security threats detection in internet of things using deep learning approach. IEEE Access **7**, 124379–124389 (2019)
7. Elnozahy, E.N., Alvisi, L., Wang, Y.M., et al.: A survey of rollback-recovery protocols in message-passing systems. ACM Comput. Surv. (CSUR) **34**(3), 375–408 (2002)
8. Netzer, R.H.B., Xu, J.: Necessary and sufficient conditions for consistent global snapshots. IEEE Trans. Parallel Distrib. Syst. **6**(2), 165–169 (1995)
9. Johann, T.: Reward for return of sheepdog and pups. Farmers Weekly **169**(7), 1 (2018)
10. Chen, L., Kang, H., Jia, W.: Design and implementation of snapshot system in cloud storage log-structured file-system. Comput. Appl. Softw. **7** (2013)
11. Zhao, Z., Luo, Y.: Design and implementation of a remote disaster recovery system based on fine-grained snapshot. Comput. Eng. Sci. **7** (2008)
12. Zhou, W., Tan, H., Yi, L., et al.: High-performance snapshot of logical volumes based on out-of-band storage virtualization. J. Comput. Res. Dev. **49**(3), 636–645 (2012)
13. Li, C., Zhang, Q., Tan, J., Yan, Z.: Linux file system encryption design. Internet Things Technol. **8**(2): 77–79, 82 (2018)
14. Peterson, Z., Burns, R.: Ext3cow: a time-shifting file system for regulatory compliance. ACM Trans. Storage (TOS) **1**(2), 190–212 (2005)
15. Hitz, D., Lau, J., Malcolm, M.A.: File system design for an NFS file server appliance. USENIX Winter **94** (1994)
16. Duzy, G.: Match snaps to apps. Storage, Special Issue on Managing the Information that Drives the Enterprise, 46–52 (2005)
17. Xu, G., Gang, W., Jing, L.: Multi-point incremental snapshot design based on the same snapshot volume. Comput. Eng. Appl. **3**, 113–115 (2005)
18. Bhat, W.A., Wani, M.A.: Forensic analysis of B-tree file system (Btrfs). Digit. Investig. **27**, 57–70 (2018)
19. Wei, Y., Shin, D.: NAND flash storage device performance in Linux file system. In: 2011 6th International Conference on Computer Sciences and Convergence Information Technology (ICCIT). IEEE (2011)
20. Li, S., et al.: COW-IMM: a novel integrity measurement method based on copy-on-write for file in virtual machine. IEEE Access **6**, 51776–51790 (2018)
21. Guo, S., Xie, W.: Analysis in depth on Linux proc file system programming. J. Huaqiao Univ. (Nat. Sci.) **5** (2010)
22. Peng, G.-J., et al.: Abnormal file management activities identification system based on association analysis of behaviors. Comput. Eng. Des. (2015)

The Thinned Rectangular Array Based on Modified Interger Genetic Algorithm

Qingling Liu[1], Ding Yuan[1(✉)], and Shubin Wang[2]

[1] Department of Information and Communication Engineering,
Harbin Engineering University, Harbin 150001, China
{liuqingling,diandian}@hrbeu.edu.cn
[2] China Telecom Co. Ltd. Harbin Branch, Harbin 150001, China
125338156@qq.com

Abstract. Aiming at the optimization of peak sidelobe levels (PSLL) of rectangular thinned arrays with fixed thinned rate and array aperture constraints. This paper proposes a new coding mapping model and an improved integer genetic algorithm (MIGA). Applying this algorithm to a symmetric rectangular array of 108 elements, the PSLL and the directivity coefficient was also improved. MIGA uses a simple and direct integer coding strategy for thinned arrays, and abandons conventional binary coding and real coding. Under the premise of ensuring the thinned rate, the possibility of infeasible solutions in the optimization process of the algorithm is reduced, and the number of optimization variables is effectively reduced.

Keywords: Rectangular thinned arrays · Peak sidelobe levels (PSLL) · Coding mapping model · Improved integer genetic algorithm (MIGA)

1 Introduction

Since humans entered the radio age, radio systems such as radar, communications, navigation, and mapping have always played an important role [1]. The thinned array thinnedly arranges the array elements within the antenna aperture range, that is, the antenna elements are removed from the regular grid, which can reach the specified beam width with fewer elements, improve the radar resolution, and reduce the cost of radar system equipment [2–4]. Therefore, thinned arrays are widely used in array scenarios that do not require much gain, and require narrower scanning beams and lower side lobes [5–7].

From a mathematical point of view, the thinned array optimization problem is equivalent to obtaining an optimal solution to a non-linear function under conditions of multiple constraints and multiple variables. In mathematics, some optimization algorithms have been applied to thinned arrays one by one. The most effective optimization algorithm is the swarm intelligence optimization algorithm. With the rapid improvement of computer computing capabilities, genetic algorithms (GA) [8, 9], differential evolution algorithms (DE) [10, 11], particle swarm algorithms (PSO) [12, 13], ant colony algorithms (AC) [15], etc., have been used in thinned array optimization. Although these algorithms have been proved to have good results in array optimization, they are easily trapped in local optimal solutions, which will affect the algorithm's

© Springer Nature Switzerland AG 2020
X. Chen et al. (Eds.): ML4CS 2020, LNCS 12487, pp. 261–269, 2020.
https://doi.org/10.1007/978-3-030-62460-6_23

efficiency and convergence speed. Therefore, how to choose an appropriate algorithm, and how to improve the algorithm and the array model, so as to improve the algorithm's convergence speed and the degree of approaching the optimal value have become the hotspots of sparse array optimization algorithms.

In 1994, Randy [16] used GA to thinned a uniform linear array of 200 elements, and obtained an optimization result with a maximum sidelobe level of only −22.09 dB when the omnidirectional radiation element was used and the thinned rate was 77%; In 2007, Peng et al. [17] optimized the array model so that the GA can be applied to planar arrays with arbitrary thinned rates; In 2006, Chen et al. [18] proposed an improved real-coded genetic algorithm (Modified Genetic Algorithm, MGA) to optimize uniformly weighted linear arrays of thinned cloth, and simultaneously constrained the minimum spacing of array elements and the array aperture; In 2011, Zeng [19] introduced a planar thinned array optimization method based on an iterative FFT algorithm, and obtained good sidelobe level values. In 2012, Ling et al. [20] proposed a floating method that can improve search efficiency point genetic algorithm (Improved Genetic Algorithm, IGA), and integrated uniformly weighted and non-uniformly weighted thinned linear arrays; Heng [21] uses a differential evolution algorithm to sparse the rectangular array to obtain a peak side lobe level of −19.88 dB. In 2016, Jiang [22] applied an improved integer genetic algorithm (IIGA) to the concentric circle array and achieved good results.

The structure of this paper is as follows: The second part introduces the thinned rectangular array model and the improved integer genetic algorithm model, the third part introduces the simulation experimental results, and finally gives the experimental conclusions.

2   Symmetric Thinned Rectanglular Array Model

The symmetrical rectangular array has $2M \times 2N$ array elements, the array aperture is $2L \times 2H$, array element spacing is d_x in the x-axis direction, and d_y is in the y-axis direction. Since it is a symmetrical rectangular array, taking the geometric center of the array as the origin to establish a coordinate system, as shown in Fig. 1. The coordinates of each array element are (x_m, y_n), $1 \le m \le M$, $1 \le n \le N$ and the position coordinates of the thinned array element be $(0,0)$. It is assumed that all array elements are omnidirectional antenna arrays, and the current excitation of each array element is equal. $(I_{mn} = 1)$. To meet the antenna aperture constraints, the corner elements need to be fixed. According to the assumptions of the appeal, only the position of the first quadrant element is needed when calculating the antenna array factor, and the symmetrical rectangular array factor can be expressed as

$$AF(\theta, \varphi) = \begin{cases} \sum_{m=1}^{M} \sum_{n=1}^{N} \left(\begin{array}{l} e^{jk(x_m u + y_n v)} + e^{jk(-x_m u + y_n v)} \\ + e^{jk(x_m u - y_n v)} + e^{jk(-x_m u - y_n v)} \end{array} \right), & others \\ 0, & x_m = 0 \,\&\, y_n = 0 \end{cases} \quad (1)$$

where $k = 2\pi/\lambda$, λ is the wavelength; $u = \sin\theta\cos\varphi$, $v = \sin\theta\sin\varphi$, θ, φ are the pitch and azimuth angles in the spherical coordinate system.

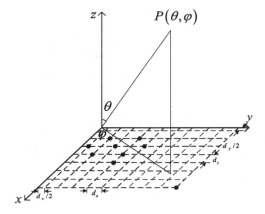

Fig. 1. Rectangular thinned array model

3 Algorithm Model

Traditional optimization algorithms often use binary or real number encoding, and binary encoding only has 0 and 1. Obviously, many infeasible solutions will appear during the optimization process. Then, because the array elements of the thinned rectangular array are evenly distributed on the rectangular grid, the integers are used to encode the positions of the grid points in order, which not only reduces the number of optimization variables, but also accurately controls the number of array elements to ensure the thinned rate. It is assumed that the number of elements in a rectangular thinned array is 2M × 2N, the number of elements in a quadrant is M × N and the thinned rate is $f(f > 50\%)$. The algorithm steps are as follows

1) Initial Population
When the thinned rate is greater than 50%, the reserved element number is taken as the optimization object. Set the number of population to NP and the number of array elements T to be optimized as

$$T = M \times N \times (1 - f) \tag{2}$$

So the initial population matrix generated is

$$POP_{init} = \begin{bmatrix} \alpha_{1,1} & \alpha_{1,2} & \alpha_{1,3} & \cdots & \alpha_{1,T} \\ \alpha_{2,1} & \alpha_{2,2} & \alpha_{2,3} & \cdots & \alpha_{2,T} \\ \alpha_{3,1} & \alpha_{3,2} & \alpha_{3,3} & \cdots & \alpha_{3,T} \\ \vdots & \vdots & \vdots & \ddots & \vdots \\ \alpha_{NP,1} & \alpha_{NP,2} & \alpha_{NP,3} & \cdots & \alpha_{NP,T} \end{bmatrix} \tag{3}$$

where $\alpha_{i,j} \in \{1, 2, \cdots, T\}$, $(1 \leq i \leq NP,\ 1 \leq j \leq T)$, each row is a non-repeating positive integer less than or equal to T.

At the same time, POP_{init} is sorted from row to row, from left to right, which is convenient for subsequent operations. The correspondence between the array element position number and the actual position is not unique, and calculation complexity needs to be given priority when given. The position coordinates of the array elements can be a complex matrix with x as the real part and y as the imaginary part, that is, $P = x + yi$.

2) Fitness Function
The number in the population is converted into the actual array element position that needs to be retained, and the fitness value of each individual in the population is calculated. In order to obtain a lower PSLL, the fitness function is defined here as follows

$$\text{fitness} = \max_{(u,v)\in S}\left(20\lg\left|\frac{AF(u,v)}{AF_{max}}\right|\right) \tag{4}$$

where, S is the side lobe region of the attenna pattern.

3) Crossover
The individuals are sorted according to the fitness value from large to small, and half of the individuals with better fitness are retained. The parent population can be expressed as

$$POP_{parent} = \begin{bmatrix} \beta_{1,1} & \beta_{1,2} & \cdots & \beta_{1,T} \\ \beta_{2,1} & \beta_{2,2} & \cdots & \beta_{2,T} \\ \vdots & \vdots & \ddots & \vdots \\ \beta_{NP/2,1} & \beta_{NP/2,2} & \cdots & \beta_{NP/2,T} \end{bmatrix} \tag{5}$$

After sorting all the elements in the parent population from small to large, a row vector $g = [\gamma_1, \gamma_2, \cdots, \gamma_{NP\times T/2}]$ is obtained, and then sliding extraction is performed at $NP/2$ intervals to form new offspring individuals, thereby generating a new offspring population.

$$POP_{new} = \begin{bmatrix} \gamma_{1,1} & \gamma_{1,2} & \cdots & \gamma_{1,T} \\ \gamma_{2,1} & \gamma_{2,2} & \cdots & \gamma_{2,T} \\ \vdots & \vdots & \ddots & \vdots \\ \gamma_{NP/2,1} & \gamma_{NP/2,2} & \cdots & \gamma_{NP/2,T} \end{bmatrix} \tag{6}$$

4) Multi-point Mutation
Define the similarity of individuals s as

$$\begin{cases} s = \sum_{j=1}^{T}\sum_{i=1}^{NP/2}|\gamma_{ij} - k\eta_j| \\ \eta_j = 2\sum_{i=1}^{NP/2}\gamma_{ij}/NP \end{cases} \tag{7}$$

where, k is a constant that can adjust the degree of similarity. In this article, $k = 2$. Set the number of iterations of the algorithm to Iter, and obtain an adaptive mutation probability through similarity. The expression is as follows

$$P_i = \begin{cases} 1 - \frac{i}{\text{Iter}} \cdot \frac{s_i}{s_1} & s_i < s_1 \\ \frac{i}{\text{Iter}} \cdot \frac{s_1}{s_i} & s_i \geq s_1 \end{cases} \tag{8}$$

where, s_1 is the similarity value of the initial children, and s_i is the similarity value of the i-th iteration.

Determine whether to mutate by comparing whether the mutation probability of each child is greater than the random number in [0,1]. A new mutation method is adopted here. Considering the uncertainty of genetic mutation in nature, the method of single point mutation is too single, so multi-point mutation is used to enhance the randomness of mutation. Because the number of mutated genes is generally small, the number of mutated genes is limited to 2% of the entire genome. Because the traditional mutation method can not guarantee that the coding position is not duplicated after mutation, this article adopts the mutation method exchanged with complementary space, which can not only guarantee the individual non-repetition after mutation but also speed up the calculation speed. The specific way is as follows

Defining the complete set $H = \{\gamma | 1 \leq \gamma \leq T, \gamma \in Z^+\}$. The complement of the individual $B = [\gamma_1, \gamma_2, \cdots, \gamma_T]$ in POP_{new} is $B_{mut} = \{\gamma | \gamma \in H, \gamma \neq B\}$. The number of mutated genes and the position of the mutated genes are randomly generated, and then exchanged with the elements of the random positions in the complement space, the mutated genes are obtained, that is, the final offspring population $POP_{offspring}$.

5) Genetic Recombination:
Combine POP_{parent} and $POP_{offspring}$ into a population of NP $\times$ T, the new initial population, and repeat the above steps.

In summary, MIGA mainly includes five parts: population initialization, selection of parent genes, generation (crossover) of offspring genes, calculation of mutation probability, and gene recombination. The specific flowchart of the algorithm is shown in Fig. 2.

4 Simulation Results

The algorithm of this paper is used to optimize the 108 elements in the rectangular grid of 20×10. Obviously the thinned rate is 54%. It is assumed that the elements are ideal point sources and the element spacing is $d_x = d_y = 0.5\lambda$. To facilitate comparison, the number of iterations here is Iter = 1000, the population size NP = 60, and the number of sampling points is 256. In order to reduce the uncertainty of the results, 10 Monte-Carlo experiments were performed.

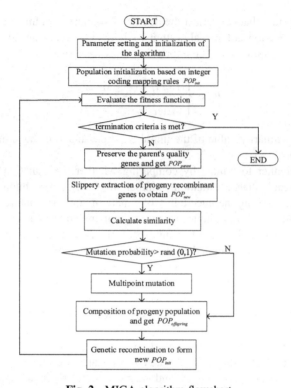

Fig. 2. MIGA algorithm flowchart

Symmetric rectangular array only optimizes the position of the element in one quadrant, and finally obtains PSLL = −20.5 dB, which is 1.82 dB lower than the reference [19], and the sidelobe level value is significantly reduced. It can be seen from Table 1 that compared with the existing methods, the PSLL method has been greatly improved, and the gain has been improved under the same 3-dB beam width of the main lobe.

Table 1. Symmetric optimization result comparison

Method	PSLL/dB	$\Theta_{3dBE}/(°)$	$\Theta_{3dBH}/(°)$	D/dB
GA [16]	−16.10	6.05	11.88	24.51
MGA [18]	−17.38	5.64	11.24	–
IFT [19]	−18.68	6.72	12.78	24.74
DE [20]	−19.88	6.94	12.11	25.32
MIGA	−20.50	6.30	12.08	25.34

The best thinned rectangular array element distribution are shown in Fig. 3.

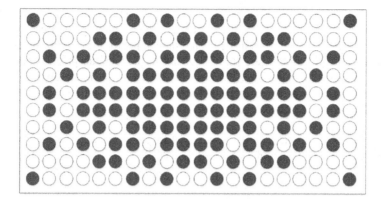

Fig. 3. Element distribution of symmetric rectangular thinned array

Where, the solid points represent the reserved array elements, and the hollow dots represent the removed array element positions. It can be seen that the array elements near the center of the array are densely arranged, and the array elements far from the center of the array are thinnedly arranged, which conforms to the general rule of thinned array optimization.

The 3D far-field pattern corresponding to the best element position of the thinned rectangular array, as shown in the Fig. 4.

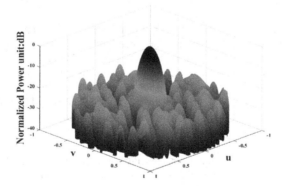

Fig. 4. Symmetric rectangular thinned array pattern

5   Conclusion

When the random evolution algorithm optimizes the thinned array, the individual thinned rate is easily destroyed, which results in a large number of infeasible solutions that do not satisfy the thinned rate, which seriously affects the search performance of the algorithm. Because of the characteristics of thinned arrays, integer coding is preferred over binary and real coding. Based on this, this paper proposes a MIGA algorithm based on traditional genetic algorithms and applies it to sparse rectangular arrays. The simulation results show that the rectangular array pattern can effectively reduce the PSLL in the entire airspace. At the same time, for the optimization of small-scale planar arrays, adopting the strategy of integer coding can greatly speed up the operation speed of the algorithm. But how to adopt a better mutation and crossover strategy to make the convergence value of the algorithm closer to the optimal solution is a question worthy of further study.

Funding. This paper is funded by the International Exchange Program of Harbin Engineering University for Innovation-oriented Talents Cultivation.

References

1. Balanis, C.A.: Antenna Theory: Analysis and Design, pp. 283–293. Wiley-Interscience, Hoboken (2005)
2. Fabrizio, G.A.: High Frequency Over-The-Horizon Radar: Fundamental Principles, Signal Processing, and Practical Applications, pp. 28–39. McGraw-Hill Education, New York (2013)
3. Kumar, B.P., Branner, G.: Generalized analytical technique for the synthesis of unequally spaced arrays with linear, planar, cylindrical or spherical geometry. IEEE Trans. Antennas Propag. 53(2), 621–634 (2005)
4. Kumar, B.P., Branner, G.: Design of unequally spaced arrays for performance improvement. IEEE Trans. Antennas Propag. 47(3), 511–523 (1999)
5. Wang, X., Aboutanios, E., Amin, M.G.: Thinned array beampattern synthesis by iterative soft-thresholding-based optimization algorithms. IEEE Trans. Antennas Propag. 62(12), 6102–6113 (2014)
6. Rubio, J., Corcoles, J., Izquierdo, J.F., et al.: Array thinning of coupled antennas based on the orthogonal matching pursuit method and a spherical-wave expansion for far-field synthesis. IEEE Trans. Antennas Propag. 63(12), 5425–5432 (2015)
7. Plessis, W.P.D., Bin, Ghannam A.: Improved seeding schemes for interleaved thinned array synthesis. IEEE Trans. Antennas Propag. 62(11), 5906–5910 (2014)
8. Schlosser, E.R., Heckler, M.V.T., Machado, R., et al.: Synthesis and implementation aspects of linear antenna arrays with shaped radiation pattern for mobile communications. IET Microwaves Antennas Propag. 10(4), 442–452 (2016)
9. Clauzier, S., Mikki, S.M., Antar, Y.M.M.: Design of near-field synthesis arrays through global optimization. IEEE Trans. Antennas Propag. 63(1), 151–165 (2015)
10. Das, S., Suganthan, P.N.: Differential evolution: a survey of the state-of-the-art. IEEE Trans. Evol. Comput. 15(1), 4–31 (2011)
11. Oliveri, G., Rocca, P., Massa, A.: Differential evolution as applied to electromagnetics: advances, comparisons, and applications. In: Proceedings of the European Conference on Antennas and Propagation, pp. 3058–3059 (2012)
12. Basu, B., Mahanti, G.K.: A comparative study of Modified Particle Swarm Optimization, Differential Evolution and Artificial Bees Colony optimization in synthesis of circular array. In: Proceedings of the 2010 International Conference on Power, Control and Embedded Systems (ICPCES), pp. 1–5 (2010)
13. Jang, C.H., Hu, F., He, F., Li, J., Zhu, D.: Low-redundancy large linear arrays synthesis for aperture synthesis radiometers using particle swarm optimization. IEEE Trans. Antennas Propag. 64(6), 2179–2188 (2016)

14. Dorigo, M., Caro, G.D., Gambardella, L.M.: Ant algorithms for discrete optimization. Artif. Life **5**(5), 137–172 (1999)
15. Dorigo, M., Caro, G.D., Gambardella, L.M.: Ant algorithms for discrete optimization. AR Financ. Life **5**(5), 137–172 (1999)
16. Haupt, R.L.: Thinned arrays using genetic algorithms. IEEE Trans. Antennas Propag. **42**(7), 993–999 (1994)
17. Chen, K., He, Z., Han, C.: A modified real GA for the thinned linear array synthesis with multiple constraints. IEEE Trans. Antennas Propag. **54**(7), 2169–2173 (2006)
18. Peng, X.: Using genetic algorithm to optimize thinned planar arrays with arbitrary thinned factor. Telecommun. Eng. **47**(3), 153–158 (2007)
19. Zeng, W., Liang, Y., Huang, W.: An optimum method for thinned planar array based on iterative FFT algorithm. Telecommun. Eng. **2011**(11), 102–105 (2012)
20. Cen, L., Yu, Z.L., Ser, W., et al.: Linear aperiodic array synthesis using an improved genetic algorithm [J]. IEEE Trans. Antennas Propag. **60**(2), 895–902 (2012)
21. Heng L, Hongwei Z, Weimei L I, et al. Constraint optimization of planar thinned array antenna. Telecommun. Eng. (2016)
22. Jiang, Y., et al.: Synthesis of uniformly excited concentric ring arrays using the improved integer GA. IEEE Antennas Wirel. Propag. Lett. **15**(2016), 1124–1127 (2016)

A Novel Method to Classify Videos Based VBR Trace

Xiaojie Yu, Min Qiu, and Lizhi Peng[(✉)]

Shandong Provincial Key Laboratory of Network Based Intelligent Computing,
University of Jinan, Jinan 250022, People's Republic of China
yuxiaojie814@gmail.com, plz@ujn.edu.cn

Abstract. Video classification research has been studied for many years. Traditional video classification methods are based on text, sound, and visual content. However, all these approaches require that the video content can be inspected. If the video content can not be investigated. For example, the video frame is encrypted or transmitted on the network device, then we can only measure the size of the video frame bitrate. In this paper, we propose two novel feature extraction methods based on variable bit rate (VBR) trace. The first one is extracting features in sliding windows. The second one is based on change points techniques to obtain more reasonable windows. We carry out empirical studied on our data sets to discriminate the action videos from the other videos. The experiment shows that we can identify the action video with 87% g-mean.

Keywords: Video classification · VBR trace · Change points.

1 Introduction

In the past decade, Internet witnessed the burst of video, especially for the mobile Internet. All kinds of videos extremely enhanced user experiences. However, different video contents have posed a new challenge, that is how to identify the Internet video types. It is necessary for large video sites such as Netflix, YouTube, and Amazon to classify their videos to provide high quality video services. Schools need to ensure that students are exposed to health videos. From the view of Internet management, it is necessary to pick out illegal videos from other videos.

Traditional video classification is generally divided into four ways: text-based approaches, audio-based approaches, visual-based approaches, and those that used some combination of text, audio, and visual features [3,7,11,15,20,21,23]. Many of the standard classifiers such as Bayesian, support vector machines

This research was partially supported by the National Natural Science Foundation of China under grant No. 61972176, No. 61472164, No. 61672262, No. 61572230, and No. 61573166, the Shandong Provincial Key R&D Program under Grants No. 2018CXGC0706 and No. 2017CXZC1206.

(SVM) can be used for video classification. Gaussian mixture models (GMMs) and hidden Markov models (HMMs) are particularly popular on video classification in the past few years [3]. Much progress has been made in video classification in recent years. Convolutional Neural Networks (CNNs) has been proven to perform very well on video classification tasks [4,12,13]. However, all these techniques are based on condition that video contents can be inspected. If the video frame is encrypted or transmitted on a network device, then we can only measure the size of the video frame. In such cases, all these traditional techniques are invalid as the video contents cannot be inspected. Hence, in this work, we explore the method of time series classification based on video frame size.

Variable Bit Rate (VBR) Trace. Most popular streaming services use variable bitrate encoding. Therefore, the bitrate of an encoded video varies with its content. Variable bit rate encoding is also used on H.264 video. H.264 is the most widely used encoding standard for Internet video. In this standard, a video is encoded into a series of consecutive GOP (Group of pictures) groups. For each GOP, there is one I frame, several B frames and P frames. The I frame (intra coded picture) reference image is equivalent to a fixed image and is independent of other image types. Each image group starts with an I frame. A P frame (predictive coded picture) contains the difference information from the previous I or P frame. B frames (bidirectionally predictive coded pictures) contain difference information from previous and/or subsequent I or P-frames. VBR allows a higher bitrate to build more complex segment of media files while less space is allocated to less complex segments. Hence, the frame size changes with the bit rate. In this work, we choose B frame size traces as VBR traces.

The main contributions of this paper are summarized as follows:

- To the best of our knowledge, this paper is the first to use the change point method on the video frame size traces to explore the scene classification. We propose a new fusion function to obtain change points more accurately.
- We extract statistical features from variable bit rate (VBR) trace, resulting a larger and more effective feature set.
- We verified the effectiveness of the extracted features on our own data set, and further explored the impact of different parameters on classification.

The remainder of the paper is structured as follows. First, we introduce the background about VBR trace in Sect. 2. Then, we outline the related work in Sect. 3. Next, we present the framework in this work in Sect. 4. In Sect. 5, we describe in detail the method of extracting features. Implementation details and experimental results are described in Sect. 6. Discussion and future work are provided in Sect. 7.

2   Related Work

In general, the classification and matching of videos are mainly studied in two fields, one is the field of computer vision, and the other is the field of network security.

In the field of computer vision, there are many studies on video classification [4,12,13], mostly based on deep learning methods. They basically pay attention to the recognition of various actions. On the other hand, there are also research and explorations on video classification using Zero-shot learning [1,2,10,24].

In the field of cybersecurity, R Schuster et al. [22] showed that due to the segmentation prescribed by the MPEG-DASH standard, many video streams are uniquely characterized by their burst patterns. R Dubin et al. [6] and J Gu et al. [9] also explored the burst patterns to identify encrypted video streams. For the same reason, H Li et al. [16] and X Liu et al. [18] explored the action recognition on surveillance traffic.

Last but not least, FHP Fitzek et al. [8] present a publicly available library of frame szie traces of long MPEG-4 and H.263 encoded videos. They also present a thorough statistical analysis of the traces. Q Liang et al. [17] used fuzzy techniques to model and classify MPEG VBR videos.

Inspired by all these efforts, we explore a novel method to classify H.264 encoded videos. We extract features of VBR traces in following sections. And further present the effect of different parameters and feature combinations on the results.

3   The Framework

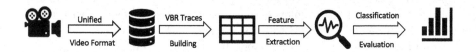

Fig. 1. Framework with four steps

3.1   A. Video Pre-processing

We first convert the videos with different formats to a single format using Axiom [19]. The target parameters are shown in Table 1.

Table 1. Format parameter

Video codec	Encode speed	HW accel	Quality	Pass	Pixel format	Frame rate
x264	Medium	off	High	2Pass	yuv420p	24

Then each movie is split into multi segments with fixed length of 120 s. And then, we pick out all the segments with actions to build the action movie set, and the left ones for the other movie set.

3.2   B. VBR Traces Building

The VBR data are extracted from the movie sets using FFmpeg, as VBR is the most effective method to get video information without inspecting the video contents. As we know, B frame is the dominant frame type in video data. Most differences between frames are contained in B frame. Therefore we only use the VBR trace of B frame. Each VBR trace is an array $D_i = (t_1, t_2, \ldots, t_n)$, thus all arrays with label form a vector sets $D = \{D_1, D_2, \ldots, D_m\}$. Obviously, the length of each row in vector sets is not same because the number of each segment is not equal.

3.3   C. Feature Extraction

Due to the high dimensional raw data and the varying length of the VBR traces, it is necessary to extract high-level semantic features to reduce the computing complexity and to achieve high classification performance. Inspired by [18], a basic idea is to calculate trace rate change C for each row data $D_i = (t_1, t_2, t_3, \ldots, t_n)$, where C is defined in Eq. 1.

As each VBR trace is essentially a time serial. We use a window sliding on each VBR trace to extract windowed-features. Then, some statistics are got from each window as the additional features. Detailed techniques will be introduced in the next section.

3.4   D. Classification

At the final step we utilize machine learning algorithms to discriminate the action movies from the other movies. To validate the effectiveness of the VBR trace and its features, we carry out our empirical studies using six well-known classic machine learning algorithms: Random Forests (RF), Logistic Regression (LR), Gaussian Naive Bayes (GNB), Decision Tree (DT), linear Suppor Vector Classification (LinearSVC), SVM with rbf kernel (SVM-rbf).

4   Extract Features

In this section, two novel feature extraction methods will be illustrated in detail. The first one is inspired by the method which is proposed in [18]. The second one is based on the change point detection techniques in statistics [14, 16]. Features we extracted are shown in Table 2.

In order to capture the information of VBR rate change, we first calculate the VBR trace rate change $C_i = (a_1, a_2, a_3, \ldots, a_{n-1})$ of the ith VBR trace $D_i = (t_1, t_2, \ldots, t_n)$. a_j represents the difference in frame size between the $(j+1)$-th and the j-th frame.

$$a_j = t_{j+1} - t_j, \qquad j \in [1, n-1] \tag{1}$$

Table 2. Features

Data type	Features
VBR trace	Mean, variance, skewness, kurtosis
Rate change	Mean, variance, skewness, kurtosis
DFT	Amplitude, phase

The mean values of the VBR trace and the frame size rate change: These features can show the intensity of scene changes in the videos. Given a VBR trace $D_i = (t_1, t_2, t_3, \ldots, t_n)$ and $C_i = (a_1, a_2, a_3, \ldots, a_{n-1})$, the mean values $\bar{t}$ and $\bar{a}$ are defined as:

$$\bar{t} = \frac{1}{n} \sum_{i=1}^{n} t_i, \qquad \bar{a} = \frac{1}{n-1} \sum_{i=1}^{n-1} a_i \qquad (2)$$

The variances of the VBR trace and the frame size rate change: These features can show the complexity of scene change. Given a frame size traces $D_i = (t_1, t_2, t_3, \ldots, t_n)$ and $C_i = (a_1, a_2, a_3, \ldots, a_{n-1})$, the variance t^{var} and a^{var} are defined as:

$$t^{var} = \frac{1}{n} \sum_{i=1}^{n} (t_i - \bar{t})^2$$

$$a^{var} = \frac{1}{n-1} \sum_{i=1}^{n-1} (a_i - \bar{a})^2 \qquad (3)$$

The skewness of the VBR trace and the frame size rate change: These features describe the symmetry of data distribution. Given a frame size traces $D_i = (t_1, t_2, t_3, \ldots, t_n)$ and $C_i = (a_1, a_2, a_3, \ldots, a_{n-1})$, the skewness t^{sk} and a^{sk} are defined as:

$$t^{sk} = \frac{\frac{1}{n} \sum_{i=1}^{n} (t_i - \bar{t})^3}{\left(\frac{1}{n-1} \sum_{i=1}^{n} (t_i - \bar{t})^2\right)^{\frac{3}{2}}}$$

$$a^{sk} = \frac{\frac{1}{n-1} \sum_{i=1}^{n-1} (a_i - \bar{a})^3}{\left(\frac{1}{n-2} \sum_{i=1}^{n-1} (a_i - \bar{a})^2\right)^{\frac{3}{2}}} \qquad (4)$$

The kurtosis of the VBR trace and the frame size rate change: These features describe the shapes of the distribution of the original data. Kurtosis is a measure of whether the distribution is peaked or flat relative to a normal distribution. Given a frame size traces $D_i = (t_1, t_2, t_3, \ldots, t_n)$ and $C_i = (a_1, a_2, a_3, \ldots, a_{n-1})$, the kurtosis t^{ku} and a^{ku} are defined as:

$$t^{ku} = \frac{\frac{1}{n}\sum_{i=1}^{n}(t_i - \bar{t})^4}{(\frac{1}{n}\sum_{i=1}^{n}(t_i - \bar{t})^2)^2} - 3$$

$$a^{ku} = \frac{\frac{1}{n-1}\sum_{i=1}^{n-1}(a_i - \bar{a})^4}{(\frac{1}{n-1}\sum_{i=1}^{n-1}(a_i - \bar{a})^2)^2} - 3 \tag{5}$$

Amplitude and Phase transformed from DFT: According to reference [18], we use DFT to obtain coefficients containing frequency information. We apply DFT in sliding window directly. Given a frame size traces $D_i = (t_1, t_2, t_3, \ldots, t_n)$, the coeffcients we get are complex numbers with the form of $z = a + bi$. Amplitude and phase were proven to be effective in practice [18]. Thus, we use these features. Amplitude and phase are defined as:

$$Amplitude = \sqrt{a^2 + b^2}, \qquad Phase = \arctan\frac{b}{a} \tag{6}$$

Sliding window: For each frame size traces $D_i = (t_1, t_2, t_3, \ldots, t_n)$, sliding window may get more detailed information. We do not fix the size of the windows, but the number of windows: m is fixed. A consequent issue is the impact of the parameter m, which will be explored in the empirical studies. Furthermore, we explored the effect of different m. For example, given a frame size traces $D_i = (t_1, t_2, t_3, \ldots, t_n)$, result is $D_i = (d_1, d_2, \ldots, d_j, \ldots, d_m)$, d_j is sub-sequence. The sub-sequece d_j is defined as:

$$d_j = \begin{cases} \{t_{[(j-1)\frac{n}{m}]}, \ldots, t_{j\frac{n}{m}}\}, & 1 \le j \le (m-1) \\ \{t_{[(j-1)\frac{n}{m}]}, \ldots, t_n\}, & j = m \end{cases} \tag{7}$$

Since the length of a scene in each video is not fixed, fixed length of sliding window is not reasonable. The perfect case is that a single window corresponds with a single scene. Therefore, we apply PELT algorithm [14] first to detect change points. Then, we get more reasonable length of window.

Change point detection for a time series data $y_{1:n}$, assume we get m change points with their positions $\tau = \{\tau_1, \tau_2, \ldots, \tau_m\}$ in $y_{1:n}$. Let $\tau_0 = 0$ and $\tau_{m+1} = n$. One commonly used method to identify multiple change points is to minimize

$$\sum_{i=1}^{m+1}[\mathcal{C}(y_{(\tau_{i-1}+1):\tau_i})] + \beta f(m) \tag{8}$$

Here $\mathcal{C}$ is a cost function for a segment and $\beta f(m)$ is a penalty guard against overfitting.

We present a weighted fusion cost function which combines cost function $\mathcal{C}_1$ for exponential distribution with changing mean and cost function $\mathcal{C}_2$ for normal distribution with variable variance. More formally, for a segmented subsequence

$y_{1:n}$ between $\tau_{i-1} + 1$ and τ_i, $n = \tau_i - (\tau_{i-1} + 1)$, we have

$$C_1 = -n(\log(\sum_{j=1}^{n} y_j)) \tag{9}$$

$$C_2 = n \log \sigma^2 + \frac{1}{\sigma^2} \sum_{j=1}^{n} (y_j - \mu)^2 \tag{10}$$

Here,

$$\sigma^2 = \frac{1}{n} \sum_{j=1}^{n} (y_j - \bar{y}) \tag{11}$$

$$\mu = \frac{1}{n} \sum_{j=1}^{n} y_j \tag{12}$$

Figure 2 shows a case study of comparing the methods using C_1, C_2 and the combined cost function. As shown in Fig. 2, the distribution of the change points obtained by the cost function C_2 is relatively dense. The distribution of the change points obtained by the cost function C_1 is relatively sparse. Hence, we use cost function $C = \theta_1 C_1 + \theta_2 C_2$. In our study, we set the parameters as $\theta_1 = 0.7, \theta_2 = 0.3$. We also carry out empirical studies to explore the impacts on these parameters.

Another problem is that some of the neighbour change points are too close to support reasonable segments. For the time of two change points T_{τ_i} and $T_{\tau_{i-1}}$, if $T_{\tau_i} - T_{\tau_{i-1}} > 0.5$ s, then we ignore τ_i.

5   Evaluation

5.1   A. Date Collection

Table 3. Collection of videos

Movies	Episodes
MIT 18.065	All
Avengers	2, 3
Transformers	1, 2, 3, 4, 5
Iron Man	1, 3
Pirates of the Caribbean	1, 2, 3, 4, 5

Collection of video is shown in Table 3. We first convert the videos with the parameters in Table 1 using [19]. Then each movie is split into multi segments

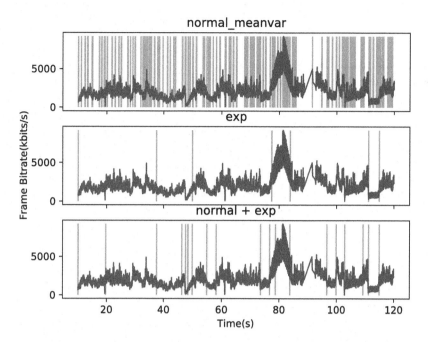

Fig. 2. The change points obtained by different functions. The first line and the second line are the results of normal distribution and exponential distribution, the last line is the result of the fusion of the two functions.

with fixed length of 120 s. And then we extract B frame traces on each segment. Finally, we got 2144 samples including 379 action scene samples and 1765 other scene samples. Obviously, the data sets is imbalanced, we over-sample minority classes by the Synthetic Minority Oversampling Technique (SMOTE) [5]. In this work, we use cross validation method to evaluate the performance of extracted features, so we split samples to 5 folds randomly.

5.2   B. Experimental Setup

We use six model to evaluate the effective of features. Firstly, we test on features which is extracted by fixed windows. As the Table 4 shown.

We can evaluate the effect of different number of windows. Secondly, for the features extracted by change points method, we choose a best model in last step to evaluate the performance of those features. We arrange the features between the change points τ_i and τ_{i+1} as (*time span, mean, variance, skewness, kurtosis*), and define them as features in an interval, called span features. Then different combinations of features are tested according to Table 5. We also use Wilcoxon's Sign Rank Test to test the difference between different features.

Table 4. Combinations of features

Features	1window	1window-DFT	9windows-DFT
(VBR trace) mean, variance, skewness, kurtosis	✓	✓	✓
(rate change) mean, variance, skewness, kurtosis	✓	✓	✓
(DFT) amplitude, phase	-	✓	✓

Table 5. Different combinations of features

Features	V1	V2	V3
span features	✓	✓	✓
(1 window) mean, variance, skewness, kurtosis	-	✓	✓
(rate change features of 1 window) mean, variance, skewness, kurtosis	-	-	✓

5.3   C. Performance Metrics

We use G-mean, Accuracy, F1-score to evaluate the performance of our features.
G-mean. We define g-mean as

$$G - mean = \sqrt{\frac{TP}{TP + FN} \times \frac{TN}{TN + FP}} \tag{13}$$

where TP and FP represent the true postives and the false positives of samples, respectively. Besides, TN and FN represent the true negative and false negative of samples, respectively.

Accuracy. we define accuracy as

$$accuracy = \frac{TP + TN}{TP + TN + FN + FP} \tag{14}$$

F1-score. we define f1-score as

$$f1 - score = \frac{2TP}{2TP + FP + FN} \tag{15}$$

5.4   D. Experimental Results

In this part, we carry out experiments to evaluate the effectiveness of features. As the Fig. 3(a) shown, when the number of windows m is 1, the performance of random forest is best. The performance of svm algorithm with rbf kernel is better than that with linear kernel. The results show that our data requires a nonlinear method to fit. And random forest with 600 trees have more powerful fitness.

As the Fig. 3(b) shown, we experiment on features obtained with different window numbers by using random forest model. As the number of windows m increases, the g-mean score and f1-score score decreases. The best g-mean score, g-mean score of feature $1windows\_DFT$, is higher 5.41% than feature

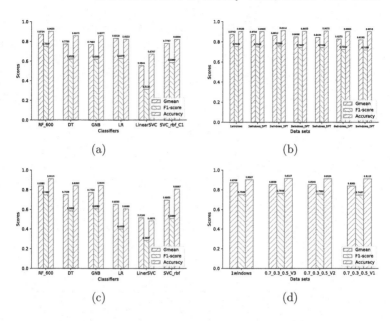

Fig. 3. The impact of different features on different models. (a) is the performance of features on six models when windows $m = 1$; (b) is the performance of the features obtained by the different numbers of windows on the random forest; (c) is the performance of Feature V1 on six models; (d) is the performance of the combination of several features of the two methods. Here, 0.7_0.3_0.5_V3 means $\theta_1 = 0.7$ and $\theta_2 = 0.3$, the span is 0.5 s, so we can ignore some change points as mentioned above.

$9windows\_DFT$'s. We guess that the fewer windows, the larger the window size, which can capture more macro fluctuation characteristics. Another phenomenon is that there is no significant difference between those with Fourier transform features and those without Fourier transform features. In theory, we believe that selecting the appropriate frequency domain characteristics can better reflect the fluctuation characteristics of the data. We guess the reason for this result may be that our method of selecting frequency domain features is not suitable.

As the Fig. 3(c) and (d) shown, for the features extracted by changepoints methods, The performance of random forest also is best. Decision trees and Gaussian Naive Bayes perform well. In the random forest experiment, there are no obvious differences between the three combinations of feature points based on change points method. And compared with the features extracted with only one window, the method of change points does not remind of obvious advantages. In theory, we think that the change points method is more reasonable, and the problem may lie in our treatment of features. Since the change point of each sample is different, the number of extracted features is different. In order to obtain training samples of equal length, we fill in the zeros behind the features, which causes a lot of information redundancy, so that the classifier does not get good results.

We conduct experiments on the change points data obtained by different combinations of θ_1 and θ_2. As the Fig. 4 and Fig. 5 shown, when $\theta_1 = 0.4$ and $\theta_2 = 0.6$, the result is the best one. And f1-score and accuracy, the result of feature 0.4_0.6_V2 is a little higher than the result of feature $1window$.

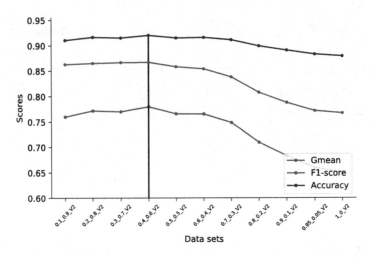

Fig. 4. Results on various selection of θ_1 and θ_2. For example, 0.1_0.9_V2 means $\theta_1 = 0.1$ and $\theta_2 = 0.9$. We obtain the Feature V2 to test.

In addition, through Wilcoxon's Sign Rank Test, we compared the differences between different feature combinations. Firstly, we do hypothesis testing on the best features of the two ideas. Secondly, we do hypothesis testing for different combinations of features in each idea. The result is shown in Table 6.

Table 6. The results of Wilcoxon's Sign Rank Test

Test Group	P-value	Result
(1window-DFT, v2)	0.0938	0
(1window-DFT, 1windows)	0.8438	0
(1window-DFT, 9windows-DFT)	0.4375	0
(V1, V3)	0.0313	1
(V1, V2)	0.0625	0
(V2, V3)	0.0625	0

The result of hypothesis testing show that there is no significant difference in performance between most of the features of our experiments. But for the best model in our experiments, such as random forest, the difference in different features is still obvious.

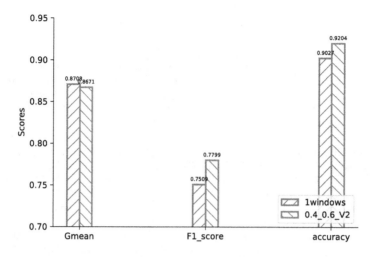

Fig. 5. Comparison between Feature 1window and Feature 0.4_0.6_*V*2

6   Conclusion and Future Research

In this paper, we explored a novel method to classifier videos. The VBR trace can show some semantic features which is useful to classification. Further, we explored the more effective features obtained by segmenting data using change points method. Basically, our features are effective in the binary classification of videos. But the result of the hypothesis test is not what we thought. We realize that there are still many unsolved things. We need to solve the problem of zero-filling of changing points. Maybe a faster and more effective change point algorithm can be used. The fusion of the objective function of the change point and the corresponding weight have a large adjustment space, etc. Finally, in the future, we can try the multi-classification task.

References

1. Bishay, M., Zoumpourlis, G., Patras, I.: Tarn: temporal attentive relation network for few-shot and zero-shot action recognition. arXiv preprint arXiv:1907.09021 (2019)
2. Brattoli, B., Tighe, J., Zhdanov, F., Perona, P., Chalupka, K.: Rethinking zero-shot video classification: end-to-end training for realistic applications. arXiv preprint arXiv:2003.01455 (2020)
3. Brezeale, D., Cook, D.J.: Automatic video classification: a survey of the literature. IEEE Trans. Syst. Man Cyber. Part C (Appl. Rev.) **38**(3), 416–430 (2008)
4. Caba Heilbron, F., Escorcia, V., Ghanem, B., Carlos Niebles, J.: ActivityNet: a large-scale video benchmark for human activity understanding. In: Proceedings of the IEEE Conference on Computer Vision and Pattern Recognition, pp. 961–970 (2015)
5. Chawla, N.V., Bowyer, K.W., Hall, L.O., Kegelmeyer, W.P.: SMOTE: synthetic minority over-sampling technique. J. Artif. Intell. Res. **16**, 321–357 (2002)

6. Dubin, R., Dvir, A., Pele, O., Hadar, O.: I know what you saw last minute-encrypted HTTP adaptive video streaming title classification. IEEE Trans. Inf. Forensics Secur. **12**(12), 3039–3049 (2017)
7. Fan, J., Luo, H., Xiao, J., Wu, L.: Semantic video classification and feature subset selection under context and concept uncertainty. In: Proceedings of the 2004 Joint ACM/IEEE Conference on Digital Libraries, pp. 192–201. IEEE (2004)
8. Fitzek, F.H., Reisslein, M.: MPEG-4 and H. 263 video traces for network performance evaluation. IEEE Netw. **15**(6), 40–54 (2001)
9. Gu, J., Wang, J., Yu, Z., Shen, K.: Walls have ears: traffic-based side-channel attack in video streaming. In: IEEE INFOCOM 2018-IEEE Conference on Computer Communications, pp. 1538–1546. IEEE (2018)
10. Hahn, M., Silva, A., Rehg, J.M.: Action2Vec: a crossmodal embedding approach to action learning. arXiv preprint arXiv:1901.00484 (2019)
11. Hauptmann, A., et al.: Video classification and retrieval with the informedia digital video library system (2002)
12. Karpathy, A., Toderici, G., Shetty, S., Leung, T., Sukthankar, R., Fei-Fei, L.: Large-scale video classification with convolutional neural networks. In: The IEEE Conference on Computer Vision and Pattern Recognition (CVPR), June 2014
13. Kay, W., et al.: The kinetics human action video dataset. arXiv preprint arXiv:1705.06950 (2017)
14. Killick, R., Fearnhead, P., Eckley, I.A.: Optimal detection of changepoints with a linear computational cost. J. Am. Stat. Assoc. **107**(500), 1590–1598 (2012)
15. Kobla, V., DeMenthon, D., Doermann, D.S.: Identifying sports videos using replay, text, and camera motion features. In: Storage and Retrieval for Media Databases 2000, vol. 3972, pp. 332–343. International Society for Optics and Photonics (1999)
16. Li, H., He, Y., Sun, L., Cheng, X., Yu, J.: Side-channel information leakage of encrypted video stream in video surveillance systems. In: IEEE INFOCOM 2016-The 35th Annual IEEE International Conference on Computer Communications, pp. 1–9. IEEE (2016)
17. Liang, Q., Mendel, J.M.: Mpeg VBR video traffic modeling and classification using fuzzy technique. IEEE Trans. Fuzzy Syst. **9**(1), 183–193 (2001)
18. Liu, X., Wang, J., Yang, Y., Cao, Z., Xiong, G., Xia, W.: Inferring behaviors via encrypted video surveillance traffic by machine learning. In: 2019 IEEE 21st International Conference on High Performance Computing and Communications; IEEE 17th International Conference on Smart City; IEEE 5th International Conference on Data Science and Systems (HPCC/SmartCity/DSS), pp. 273–280. IEEE (2019)
19. McManis, M.: Axiom: an FFmpeg interface for windows. https://axiomui.github.io
20. Roach, M., Mason, J., Xu, L.Q.: Video genre verification using both acoustic and visual modes. In: 2002 IEEE Workshop on Multimedia Signal Processing, pp. 157–160. IEEE (2002)
21. Roach, M., Mason, J.S.: Classification of video genre using audio. In: Seventh European Conference on Speech Communication and Technology (2001)
22. Schuster, R., Shmatikov, V., Tromer, E.: Beauty and the burst: remote identification of encrypted video streams. In: 26th {USENIX} Security Symposium ({USENIX} Security 17), pp. 1357–1374 (2017)
23. Xu, L.Q., Li, Y.: Video classification using spatial-temporal features and PCA. In: 2003 International Conference on Multimedia and Expo. ICME 2003, Proceedings (Cat. No. 03TH8698), vol. 3, pp. III-485. IEEE (2003)
24. Zhu, Y., Long, Y., Guan, Y., Newsam, S., Shao, L.: Towards universal representation for unseen action recognition. In: Proceedings of the IEEE Conference on Computer Vision and Pattern Recognition, pp. 9436–9445 (2018)

Research on Friendvertising-Counter Technology in Big Data

Pei Ren, Hui Liu, and Fengyin Li[✉]

School of Information Science and Engineering, Qufu Normal University,
Rizhao 276826, China
Lfyin318@126.com

Abstract. In today's society, the Internet is rapidly developing, Internet merchants can use the user information they have mastered to analyze consumer preferences. Then they conduct product recommendations to maximize profits. The accumulation of data on the behavior of consumers browsing, purchasing, and viewing advertisements on the Internet has become the basic source of information used by Internet companies to analyze users. The Internet merchant platform uses the behavioral preference data of the users that have been mastered before to analyze the different usage habits of users of different consumption levels and their usage requirements. However, combined with the characteristics of e-commerce, it can be found that this kind of killing phenomenon is not only reflected in the price differential pricing, but the quality difference and service difference on the same price basis may become the target of the merchant platform. The main contributions of this dissertation are as follows:(1) Research on big data killing against technology. (2) Design and implementation of big data killing system. The fuzzy Internet platform builds the consumer user portrait to achieve the goal of combating big data.

Keywords: Big data · User behavior preferences · User portraits · Django framework · Random browsing · Simulated orders

1 Introduction

In this society, every user has been marked with numerous labels. What kind of content do you like to see, what kind of products you buy, how much consumption power you have, who are your friends, which group do you prefer? In the eyes of the network platforms that grasping these basic data, there is an accurate "bias" towards consumers [3]. In many cases, this bias can be confusing, but it does affect daily decision-making: according to shopping records that determine purchasing power, e-commerce service platforms recommend what consumers may buy, and even rank also different reviews; many people search at the same hotel or airline ticket at the same time, and prices may rise; infrequently used accounts always receive coupons. Also, the higher the level of the account, the stronger

© Springer Nature Switzerland AG 2020
X. Chen et al. (Eds.): ML4CS 2020, LNCS 12487, pp. 283–289, 2020.
https://doi.org/10.1007/978-3-030-62460-6_25

the purchasing power of the account owner, the more likely it is to be recommended to buy more expensive items. In the era of big data, ordinary consumers have become the weak side. Although the Internet has been called "transparent" since its birth, in the current form, this transparency is not only asymmetric but also unfair. On the one hand, platform means centralization, platform has a large number of data bases [1], personal life trajectory and precise positioning of consumer preferences, so that individual behavior cant be hidden; on the other hand, as "big data" [2], as the "killing acquaintance" behavior exhibition, the platform can selectively hide from consumers and only show "limited truth" to consumers.

In recent years, with the rapid growth of mobile consumption and mobile payment in the world, the daily behavior preference data of ordinary consumers are mastered by Internet business companies. The behavior of user behavior preference data controlled by Internet business companies will lead to several problems. The first problem is user authorization and data ownership. The second one is the way in which the platform legitimately uses user data. The third one is how to protect users' privacy and right to know [12]. The deepest problem behind "Big Data Killing" is how to strengthen the protection of user data privacy, as well as how to ensure that user data is not used for unfavorable or impartial behavior to users. The research of "Big Data Killing" countermeasure technology is carried out by a trusted third party to protect users' behavior habits from being acquired by the platform, so that the platform cant get user portraits through algorithmic analysis, so that users' privacy can be protected [4].

2   Preliminary

(1) Web Services
HTTP is an application layer protocol designed within the framework of Internet protocol suite. Its definition assumes that an underlying reliable transport layer protocol and transmission control protocol (TCP) are commonly used. The uniform resource identifier (URI) scheme HTTP and HTTPS are used to identify and locate HTTP resources on the network through the uniform resource locator (URL). URIs and hyperlinks in HTML documents form interlinked hypertext documents [16]. Use HTTP and XML serialization and other web-related standards for delivery. Web service is a communication method that allows two software systems to exchange these data over the internet. Software systems that request data are called service requesters, while software systems that process requests and provide data are called service providers [13].

(2) Python Technology
Python is an explanatory, advanced and general purpose programming language. Python has dynamic type system and automatic memory management function [10]. Python currently has a variety of web application frameworks, such as zope, quixote, webware, skunkweb, PSO and twisted web. For new Python users,

this diversity of choices may be a problem, because generally, their choice of Web frameworks limits their choice of available web servers, and vice versa... In contrast, although Java has the same number of Web application frameworks, Java's "servlet" API enables applications written with any Java Web application framework to run in any Web server that supports the servlet API [9,15].

Django is a Python-based free open source Web framework that follows the model-view-template (MVT) architecture pattern [8]. Django's main goal is to simplify the creation of complex database-driven websites. The framework emphasizes reusability and "pluggability" of components, fewer code, low coupling, rapid development, and the principle of "don't repeat yourself". Django's configuration system allows third-party code to be inserted into regular projects, provided it follows reusable application conventions [14]. More than 2,500 packages can be used to extend the original behavior of the framework, providing solutions to problems that the original tools did not solve: registration, search, API provision and use, CMS, etc.

(3) Web Crawler Technology
Web crawler, sometimes referred to as spider or spider robot, usually referred to as crawler, is an Internet robot that browses the World Wide Web systematically and is usually used for Web spidering [6]. Web search engines and other websites use web crawlers or spider software to update their index of website content or other website content. Web crawlers copy pages, and search engines index downloaded pages so that users can search more effectively [5]. Crawlers consume resources on the system being accessed and often visit sites without permission. When accessing a large number of pages, scheduling, loading, and "courtesy" issues play a role. For public sites that do not want to be crawled, there are mechanisms to let the crawler know this. The crawler downloads the content and data of the web page to provide data support for the search engine system, this undoubtedly shows the importance of web crawlers in search engines. In addition to the text information that users want to read, the content of this page also contains hyperlink information. The hyperlink information crawler system in web pages has the ability to access other web pages on the network. Because the collection process of the crawler system looks like the behavior of the crawler or spider roaming on the network, it is called the network crawler system or the network spider system.

3   Big Data Friendvertising-Counter Scheme

3.1   Architecture

Firstly, the functions of the system are determined. Secondly, the functional modules of the system are designed. Then, the functions of the system are realized in turn. On the premise of the realization of the functional modules of the system, the details of the page are designed to make the system more complete. The overall framework of large data ripening countermeasure system is shown in Fig. 1:

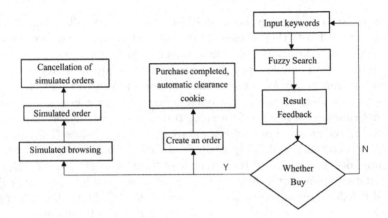

Fig. 1. Framework diagram of delivery system

3.2   Data Grabbing

The main function of the data grabbing module is to grab the commodity information of the existing group-buying website, store the commodity information in the document after simple processing, which is convenient for users to search and use in the system [7]. The basic idea of the data grabbing module is: first, we grab some parameters of the store ID through the list page, and construct a URL of the detail page locally, then we visit the detail page. Grabbing information, due to the limited number of pages, we can carry out classified grabbing, the specific flow chart as shown in Fig. 2:

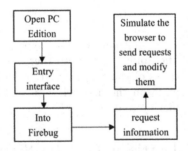

Fig. 2. Grab flow chart

3.3   Auto Clearing Cookies

In this section, we use the modules in Python to complete the automatic cleaning of Cookies. The specific process is shown in Fig. 3:

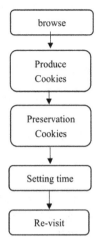

Fig. 3. Automatic clearance flow chart

3.4 Search Sorting

The purpose of sorting is to help users quickly find what they need through the search of fuzzy query, there are generally two viewpoints of fuzzy query. One is that the system allows certain differences between the searched information and the searched information. When entering product keyword information in the search box, similar product information will appear; the other is that the search will automatically synonym.

Technically speaking, in the products matched by user input keywords, the products most suitable for user needs rank first, while other products are placed in the corresponding position in order. Users use our big data ripening confrontation system to search, the big data ripening confrontation system presents the products searched on the page. When users click on the product trademark, they will enter the product details, and then find the order button to place the order. The general process of commodity search is shown in Fig. 4:

The main idea of the search algorithm is: we need to introduce price factors into the ranking to influence the final display price. If we take GMV as the goal, it can simply be expressed as cvr*price. At the same time, we want to control the role of price, so the goal is slightly modified: add a variable t to control the impact of price, the range of this t value is very limited. MAB or CMAB can be used to find the optimal solution.

We abstract this problem from the perspective of reinforcement learning, and take the commodity price grade (0–7, from low to high) of the first two clicks as the status. This state indicates the user's preference for the price of the goods he clicked on before. If he clicked on one item twice, it shows that the user prefers the low-price goods. It is likely that the user will only be interested in the low-price goods next. If the distribution of the state transition is stable, then a statistical model can describe this rule. In fact, the user's behavior is affected by

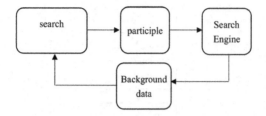

Fig. 4. Commodity search flow chart

our ranking model [11]. The reason why the user clicks on a product may be that the current ranking strategy only shows a product to the user, not necessarily the essential needs of the user. In the next user search process, we can choose one product to make the user's demand converge quickly. Choice two is to put some nearby products for the user to choose. If the user chooses other products and transfers the status, he may find a better path. The final revenue and all the strategies in our process are all the same. Relevantly, from each point of view, the strategy may not be optimal, but the overall situation may be optimal.

4   Conclusion

This paper studies in detail the use of existing technologies to combat the "ripening" phenomenon of big data. Internet commercial companies use different means to preference privacy of mobile phone users' behavior, use their own user behavior preference data to build user portraits for consumers, recommend goods or services through user portraits without the knowledge of consumers, and on this basis, summarizes the research goal and specific work of this article in detail. We combined with Python's advantages in system development and data processing, and eventually realized the big data ripening confrontation system.

References

1. Chen, J.: Big data: a survey. Mob. Netw. Appl. **19**(2), 171–209 (2014)
2. Gossett, E.: Big data: a revolution that will transform how we live, work, and think. Math. Comput. Educ. **47**(17), 181–183 (2014)
3. Gu, H.: Modeling of user portrait through social media. In: IEEE International Conference on Multimedia and Expo (ICME), pp. 13–15 (2018)
4. Gu, H.: Modeling of user portrait through social media. In: IEEE International Conference on Multimedia and Expo (ICME), pp. 17–19 (2018)
5. Moody, K.: SharpSpider: spidering the Web through web services. In: American Web Congress, pp. 154–160 (2003)
6. Mukhopadhyay, D.: A new approach to design domain specific ontology based web crawler. In: International Conference on Information Technology (2007)
7. Giorgini, P.: Goal-oriented requirement analysis for data warehouse design. In: ACM International Workshop on Data Warehousing & OLAP, pp. 189–231 (2005)

8. Aldanondo, M.: Mass customization and configuration: requirement analysis and constraint based modeling propositions. Integr. Comput. Aided Eng. **10**(2), 177–189 (2003)

9. Lesleyh, R.: Python phylogenetics: inference from morphology and mitochondrial DNA. Biol. J. Linn. Soc. **93**(3), 603–619 (2010)

10. Al-Rfou, R.: Theano: a Python framework for fast computation of mathematical expressions, pp. 129–201 (2016)

11. White, G.C.: Program MARK: survival estimation from populations of marked animals. Bird Stud. **46**(sup1), 125–140 (2013)

12. Feng, J.: Big data and privacy protection. Chin. J. Comput. **37**, 246–258 (2014)

13. Zeng, J.: Big data user portrait and precision marketing based on Weibo. Mod. Econ. Inf. (16), 306–308 (2016)

14. Wang, J.: Design and implementation of test work platform based on Django. Chin. New Technol. New Prod. (2015)

15. Fan, J.: A survey on web application servers. Technol. Cent. Softw. Eng. **14**, 1728–1739 (2003)

16. Rong, J.: Design and implementation of a deep web crawler. Comput. Modernization (3), 31–34 (2009)

A Survey of Researches on Personalized Bundle Recommendation Techniques

Miao Li, Xuguang Bao, Liang Chang$^{(\boxtimes)}$, Zhoubo Xu, and Long Li

Guangxi Key Laboratory of Trusted Software, School of Computer Science
and Information Security, Guilin University of Electronic Technology,
Guilin 541004, China
changl@guet.edu.cn

Abstract. The recommender system is widely used in various fields such as movies, music, and products. It has been an effective method to handle the preference matching problem by retrieving the most relevant information and services from a large amount of data. Most researches on recommender systems focus on improving the relevance of individual recommendation item. Nevertheless, in recommendation scenarios, users are often exposed to multiple items and may be interested in a collection of items. The platform can offer multiple items as a bundle to user in this case. That is called *Bundle Recommendation* problem, which refers to predict a user's preference on a bundle rather than an individual item. The larger scale data of the bundle compared to individual item results in information overload, thus, it is crucial to develop personalized bundle recommendation technology to help users quickly match a high-quality bundle which can improve the user experience and benefit both consumers and product providers. In this paper, we first review the main model methods of bundle recommender systems in recent years, including integer programming methods, association analysis methods, traditional recommendation methods, and recommendation methods based on deep learning. And then, we analyze the relationships of personalized bundle recommender systems compared with the traditional recommender systems. Finally, we discuss the difficulties and future development trend of personalized bundle recommender systems.

Keywords: Bundle recommendation · Recommender system · Data mining · Review

1 Introduction

The recent 10 years have witnessed the rapid development of Internet technology. The way people communicate, read the news, buy products, and watch movies has changed dramatically. The data of many applications present an explosive growth. Rich user data, on the one hand, makes it possible to mine user preferences and generate recommendation results, but on the other hand, it also poses great challenges to the extraction of available information. The recommender systems have been an effective tool to alleviate information overload [1], improve user experience, and increase the exposure of service providers for a long time, which are a process for users to match the items they are interested in [2]. Figure 1 is a schematic diagram of a recommendation

© Springer Nature Switzerland AG 2020
X. Chen et al. (Eds.): ML4CS 2020, LNCS 12487, pp. 290–304, 2020.
https://doi.org/10.1007/978-3-030-62460-6_26

process. It aims to speculate on user preferences and discover items that may be interesting to users, so as to help users save time and create a delightful user experience. As the Internet has developed into a platform for providing large-scale online services, the recommender systems meet the needs of users by reducing the efforts in proactive searches. They are widely utilized in industry including online shopping (Amazon, Tmall, etc.), consumer reviews (Meituan, etc.), music and movie service websites (163 music, etc.), mobile application stores (Andriod application store, etc.) and other areas.

Nevertheless, in various recommendation scenarios, especially e-commerce, users usually browse multiple items rather than a single item. In general, more than 1/3 of transactions contain two or more different products. In travel packages, users prefer a combination of a series of items. Meanwhile, service providers usually use discounts and other ways to encourage users to consume multiple products bundle [3]. Therefore, we should treat a set of items as an entirety to perform recommendation, rather than recommending them separately. This scenario where a collection of items needs to be recommended is called bundle recommendation.

Bundle sales [4] is a form of symbiotic marketing, which means that two or more brands or companies cooperate in the promotion process to expand their influence and achieve the effect of "1 + 1 > 2". Stremersch and Tellis [5] subdivided bundle sales into product bundle and price bundle. Price bundle means that some products which cannot be combined into a new product are given a discount when sold together; and the product bundle refers to that each product can be sold separately, or be combined into a new product for sale. As a new cross-industry and cross-brand sales method, product bundle increases product value, so more and more companies began to attach more attention to it. Traditional bundle recommendation [6, 7] is to mine a group of items that can be purchased together by mining effective information, without any restrictions on the relevance between recommended products. Although this method works well sometimes, it does not have personalization, nor can it solve the situation where users want to purchase a group of items with a common theme. Personalized bundle recommendation [8–11] refers to simultaneously recommending multiple items that have a specific relationship with each other [12], such as a complementary relationship, or an alternative relationship. The user selects the item he/she likes according to his/her preferences. The attractiveness of an item may depend on other items displayed to the user [13]. This requires predicting the user's preference for a set of items and matching, rather than a single item. Figure 2 shows a set of examples of personalized bundle recommendation lists, including clothing and accessories, and music in the same category. For users, a set of items that are related to each other can improve the shopping experience and get corresponding discounts; for sellers, bundle recommendations can increase the exposure of low-view items in the bundle and promote product sales.

In this paper, we mainly review the research and application of personalized bundle recommendation technology. The left of this paper is organized as follows. Section 2 focuses on how to generate the personalized bundle. In Sect. 3, we discuss the future work, and end this paper with a conclusion in Sect. 4.

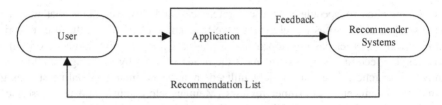

Fig. 1. Illustration of the recommendation process.

Fig. 2. Examples of bundle recommendations.

2 Research of Personalized Bundle Recommender System

The bundle recommender systems make use of user's historical data and background information to predict the user's preference for a bundle of items rather than a single item. Such as game recommendation [14], point of interest recommendation [15], music playlist recommendation [16], course recommendation [17], fashion recommendation [18, 19] and so on. Formalization of the bundle recommendation problem is given in [8]. Let N be the whole set of items, U be the whole set of users, K be the whole set of bundles. A bundle k is any combination of items, i.e., $k = \{n_1, n_2, ..., n_k\}$. U, N and K all have a large size in search space, and a utility function f is defined to calculate the recommendation score of bundle k to the user u. The research problem of bundle recommendation algorithm is to find the most interested bundle $k \in K$ for each user $u \in U$ by calculating the total recommendation score:

$$\forall_{u \in U}, k'_u = \arg \max_{k \in K} F(u, k) \tag{1}$$

On the one hand, only when a user is most satisfied with an item in the bundle will he chooses the bundle to consume. On the other hand, even if a user is interested in all the components of the bundle, he may not like the bundle because it is not a good match. So, the user-bundle interaction matrix is sparser [10] than the user-item interaction matrix in general. Both interactive information and side information need to be fully utilized to generate personalized recommendation results.

Bundle recommendations extend the traditional recommended research direction, which is an improvement of the relevance or profitability of individual items [20, 21]. From the current research of bundle recommender systems, it can be seen that the techniques are more and more widely utilized in real-life scenarios and have achieved ideal results. In the following, we introduce the bundle recommendation problem from different perspectives including integer programming techniques, association analysis techniques, traditional recommendation techniques, and recommendation techniques based on deep learning.

2.1 Integer Programming Techniques

In recommended domain, several efforts on bundle in recommender systems have been considered in vocation package recommendation [22], and they are modeled as a linear knapsack problem [23]. These works usually use approximation algorithms to discover the top-k products having better values and satisfying specific constraints. The modeling idea has also been applied to the recommendation of travel location list [24]. However, pairwise dependencies [25] among similar items aren't considered in their work, and cross-item dependencies are modeled as hard constraints, which brings complex computation and could not automatically recommend the optimal matching results to users according to their preferences.

In e-commerce, it is difficult to model a hard constraint between cross-items, and users are more likely to have different preferences for the item bundle. Considering above, Zhu et al. [8] presented a personalized method based on integer quadratic programming [26] for bundle recommendation in e-commerce. They first generate a candidate bundle set from the existing recommendation results, and then calculate the utility value of the candidate set to maximize the utility function based on user data. The utility function can be the conversion rate of the item and the total revenue, or profit of the bundled goods. The cross-dependencies between items are estimated from the historical data of users and combined with contextual information, product compatibility, and cost savings. Cross-item dependencies are strictly and explicitly considered. However, this method only considers the first and second terms of cross-item dependence in the approximate treatment, and ignores the higher-order terms of cross-item dependence, so as to give the sub-optimal result. Despite the fact that this method can be sufficient and feasible for a small or medium set of candidates, it fails on the much larger scale data set.

Similar work is presented in [7]. However, bundles are predefined by the retailer at different costs or prices which means that users must proactively select a set of items according to their preferences. This is contrary to what we expect. In general, these methods need to construct the bundle candidate set in advance to reduce the workload, and could not obtain an optimal result. In addition, these methods take more response time. However, the ideal recommender system should automatically and flexibly generate a high-quality bundle without manual involvements.

2.2   Association Analysis Techniques

In traditional marketing and economics domain, some researches [5] focus on solving the problem of product bundling or price bundling. The psychological impact and economic reasons for product bundling have been well explained, and the techniques of bundle design are well studied [27]. Scholars have also constructed mathematical models in different perspectives to innovate the way of bundle [28]. However, due to the variety of items and the high personalized needs of users, the traditional fixed combination can hardly meet the preferences of consumers. Thus, it is not applicable to our situation.

Data mining technology is widely used to analyze customers' preferences, so as to generate product portfolio to obtain more product exposure and profit [29]. Association analysis is an unsupervised learning algorithm that seeks interesting relationships in large data sets. These relationships can be presented in two forms: frequent item sets or association rules. Association rules are implied expressions with the form $X \rightarrow Y$, where X and Y are disjoint item sets, i.e., X and Y have no intersection set. The strength of association rules can be measured by its support and confidence. The support can be used for the frequency of a given data set, while the confidence determines the frequency of Y in a transaction containing X. The two measures of support and confidence are defined as follows, where N represents the total number of transactions:

$$\text{support}(X \rightarrow Y) = \frac{\sigma(X \cup Y)}{N} \tag{2}$$

$$\text{confidence}(X \rightarrow Y) = \frac{\sigma(X \cup Y)}{\sigma(X)} \tag{3}$$

A common strategy used by association rule mining algorithms is to decompose them into two sub tasks: frequent item set generation and rule generation. Apriori algorithm [30] and FP growth algorithm [31] are commonly widely used. Clustering analysis is a technique for finding the internal structures among data. It divides all data instances into similar groups which are called clusters. Based on the information and relationships of the objects in the data, cluster analysis first randomly selects an individual instance as the center of the initial cluster, and then merges the closest clusters one after another, until an acceptable group of data objects is obtained. The goal is to make objects in groups related to each other, while objects in different groups are unrelated. K-means algorithm [32] and DBSCAN algorithm [33] are some of the widely used methods. Besides, Naive Bayes algorithm [34–36], CART Tree [37], and Support Vector Machine [38, 39] are also widely used in the domain of data mining.

Existing data mining methods provide us with popular product portfolios and consumption patterns. Yang et al. [40] considered the product bundling method of online bookstores with different data sources. By integrating customer orders, browsing data and shopping cart data, they provided online users with more interesting product bundles. Miguéis et al. [41] proposed a clustering algorithm based on customer lifestyle. They divided each customer into different lifestyle groups according to the clustering similarity rules of customers' purchase history. Liao et al. [42] divided customers into low, medium and high groups according to their consumption frequency, and used Apriori algorithm to determine the product categories for each customer group. Kim et al. [43] used information about product categories to make multi-level rules. Chen et al. [44] combined customer behavior characteristics, demographic variables, and transaction database to develop a method of mining customer behavior changes. Jiao and Zhang [45] tried to improve the product portfolio by forming a clear decision support. However, due to the large scale of products in online e-commerce and the varied preferences of customers, these methods may generate several unnecessary frequent item sets or tedious low-quality bundles. Therefore, Fang et al. [46] proposed a customized product bundle method by integrating association rule mining, customer segmentation, and recommendation techniques (see Fig. 3). They used Apriori algorithm to extract the association rules of the product category. And in order to determine customer segmentation according to user's RFM indicators [47], the K-means algorithm was used. Sarwar et al. [48] also used the association rule mining algorithm to perform a similar analysis on the e-commerce recommendation.

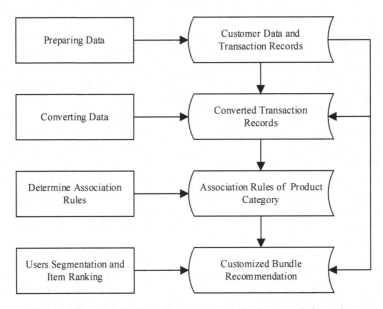

Fig. 3. The method of bundle recommendation by association rules.

Note that above methods are not personalized because they consider specific groups [49] rather than individual users. Although there are ways to make the rules "personalize" by making them conform to the user's historical transactions before they are used for recommendations, the model does not substantially learn the personalized associations between items. In most cases, when mining the correlation between different projects, only the frequency of the project is used, and the method of user segmentation is susceptible to subjective factors. In addition, bundle recommendation in the form of recommending a set of other products to users who have already purchased several products. Although the fact that such a recommendation may be useful, there is no guarantee that all of these products may actually be related to each other.

2.3 Traditional Recommender Techniques

The original purpose of association rule mining is not recommendation, but finding interesting association from the transaction data. The research was mainly focus on computational efficiency. The method based on association rules has two disadvantages. First, the items observed must all appear in the same transaction. Therefore, it may not be able to model associations that have not been seen before but may have been inferred. Second, the rules are universal and are applied to all users without personalization [54].

The traditional recommendation systems utilize the user's historical behavior record or similarity relationship to find the items that the user may be interested in. For example, Collaborative Filtering [50] uses a method of similar interest preferences among similar users to discover users' potential preferences for items [51]. Such as linear model matrix factorization [52], and nonlinear neural network model AutoRec [53]. However, most Collaborative Filtering algorithms are optimized using a dataset of isolated user-item tuples. The implicit assumption is that users are only interested in one item at a time. In fact, users can usually only buy multiple related products to fulfill specific needs. People on traveling may wish to visit several places in one travel. In these cases, the items that user seeks are not independent.

Le et al. [54] proposed an approach that factorizes basket-level associations to solve above problems. They gave a situation named *Basket-Sensitive* where the users already have a basket of items, and the task is to recommend several related items to the basket. The approach is to model the recommendation as a value function with several types of associations. This is different from the traditional market basket analysis [55] and does not independently recommend goods [56]. A similar work [57] considers association rules between different baskets. Liu et al. [58] estimated the possibility that consumers would purchase recommended items together with items that have already been purchased.

Zhang et al. [59] studied the problem of recommending list of multiple items to users. The list recommendation problem is related to the top-k [60] optimization problem, and learning-to-rank approaches have been widely used as an extension of MF model [61–63]. Xie et al. [64] generated a top-k bundle via sampling and preference elicitation for users in recommended list scenarios. Deng et al. [65] comprehensively discussed the complexity of top-k bundle recommendation algorithm. These methods usually modify the loss function of the matrix factorization model to fit the ranking task. However, they did not consider the recommendation list as an optimized entirety. As a result, they may ignore many relevant factors, such as the interactions between items or contextual information. A novel two-layer framework based on existing Collaborative Filtering algorithm was proposed by optimizing the click probability of the list for this deficiency in [66].

Nevertheless, there is no special restriction on the correlation among recommended items, and sometimes it cannot be applied to the situation where users want to purchase a bundle with a common theme.

2.4   Recommendation Techniques Based on Deep Learning

The recommended models based on deep learning can be divided into two categories in general: models based on representation learning, and models based on matching function learning. Representation learning methods learn the latent representation of users and items as an intermediate product, which makes it easier to calculate the matching score, thus it is not an end-to-end model [67–69]. While the models based on matching function learning is an end-to-end method, which directly fit the existing input [70, 71]. Their basic frameworks are shown in Fig. 4 and Fig. 5, respectively.

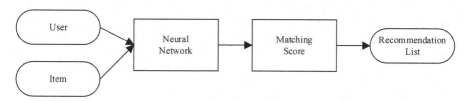

Fig. 4. Model based on match function learning.

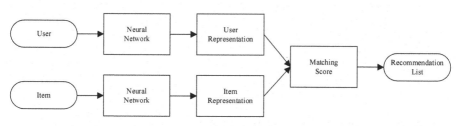

Fig. 5. Model based on representation learning.

To build a bundle recommender system, a common idea is to treat bundles as separate columns in user-bundle matrix to run CF methods like matrix factorization. Although technically feasible, this simple idea does not work well in predicting user-bundle interactions due to the following difficulties. First, a bundle consists of multiple items. Therefore, it is not appropriate to run CF methods. Second, the bundle-user interaction matrix is sparser than the user-item interaction matrix. Finally, the search space of bundle is more complicated. Chen et al. [10] proposed a new model named Deep Attentive Multi-Task, which takes special care of the above problems with a neural collaborative filtering framework [72]. There are two key designs in this method: 1) Using factorized attention network to obtain a bundle's representation [73]. 2) Jointing modeling (see Fig. 6) of user-bundle and user-item interactions [74]. Cao et al. [75] also proposed a joint model that only has shared layers.

In recent years, sequence generation methods have been successfully used in recommender systems [76, 77]. They use encoder-decoder architecture [78, 79] to generate sequences, and use beam search strategy [80] to predict sequences of indefinite length. It is crucial for bundle recommender systems to consider the potential bundle relationship between items displayed by the user's personalized sequence behavior. Yu et al. [81] proposed a new method based on Factorizing Personalized Markov Chain (FPMC) [82], which comprehensively explores potential bundle relationships from the user's perspective, and utilizes deep learning models to extract the semantic features involved. Thus, their work has succeeded in integrating the user-level sequence pattern and the potential bundle relationship extracted from the semantics associated with the product. However, duplicate or similar items are often seen in the generated bundles. In addition, the sequence generation method has the problem of insufficient representation of rich features. Bai et al. [9] first tried to use the sequence generation method to consider both quality and diversity. They used a determinant point process [83] to decompose the model and combined it with a neural network. At the same time, a feature-aware softmax is proposed to make up the problem of traditional seq2seq's insufficient representation of rich features. Thereby generating a high-quality and diverse bundle list.

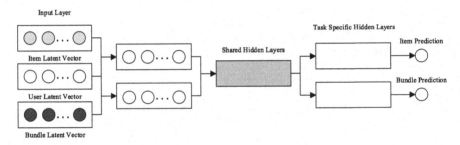

Fig. 6. Illustration of joint modeling.

The collection recommendations were presented by Kouki et al. [11]. They pointed out that given an anchor product pa, the goal of collecting recommendations is to generate a set of collected products $Pc = \{pc_1, ..., pc_k\}$, so that the product set $\{pa, pc_1, ...,\}$ is recommended to users. The product set Pc must satisfy a set of constraints, usually imposed by business logic. For example, all products belong to the same brand, or have related titles, and product descriptions. Their method first combines the product hierarchy with transaction data or domain knowledge to confirm the set of candidate products. Then, the siamese-biLSTM architecture [84, 85] is used to generate text embeddings for the products, which are used as input to the cosine similarity layer. Finally, the top similarity products can be selected to generate collection recommendations.

A graph is an abstract data structure that describes the relationship among entities through the definition of nodes and edges. Such as social network, commodity network, knowledge graph [86], etc. The graph Embedding is an important research direction, which has been successfully used in drug recommendation [87], music list recommendation [88], and other recommendation scenarios. Graph has the ability of propagation. It not only can effectively extract the direct association, but also can explore the relationship of the Second Degree and Third Degree through the walk strategy. Wang et al. [89] designed a two-stage recommendation framework based on graph embedding. The first stage is matching, and the second stage is ranking. In the matching stage, it is proposed to use side information to enhance the embedding procedure, which generates a set of candidate sets of similar products for users. In the ranking stage, this framework learns a deep neural network model and ranks the candidate products according to the preferences of each user.

3 Future Work

As an extensive research of the recommender systems, personalized bundle recommendation researches have made some progress. However, they still face several challenges and opportunities in the process of development. Including how to combine recommendation optimization with pricing, solve user-bundle interaction data sparsity and cold start issues, and improve the performance of the personalized bundle recommendation.

The growing trend of online shopping has triggered the development of increasingly complex product recommender systems. It leads to increased availability of data on consumer preferences, which companies in all industries can use to improve operations, revenue, and consumer satisfaction. Garfnkel et al. [7] optimized for the total purchase cost. Beladev et al. [90] produced bundle products by combining demand function and price modeling. But these methods do not take into account the discount of items in the bundle, nor are they dynamic pricing. Ettl et al. [91] built a dynamic model to recommend personalized discount product portfolios to online shoppers. The model considers the trade-offs between profit maximization and inventory management, and selects products related to consumer preferences.

Bundle sparsity and cold start issues should be carefully considered. Since the fact that users tend to interact with only a small number of items, it is difficult to train an accurate recommendation model, especially for users on a bundle.

Obviously, the new data and user's demand for recommendation accuracy are the main driving force. First, for the new data in bundle, how to quickly add it to the recommendation model in an appropriate way, and efficiently calculate the changes of users' preferences. Furthermore, how to quickly generate recommendation results based on the user's historical data. In this case, the efficiency and accuracy of the algorithm become the key point of researches.

4 Conclusion

Nowadays, with the rapid development of the Internet and the increasing demand for information from Internet users, personalized bundle recommendation services are to be in the ascendant. Compared with traditional recommender systems, personalized bundled recommendation can not only meet users' various needs in a better way, but also can capture intuitive reasons why different users may like the same bundle.

Therefore, many application services related to bundle recommendations have emerged including book bundle recommendation, travel route planning, etc. Although some achievements have been achieved, there are still several works to be furtherly explored, for example, how to effectively alleviate the sparsity and cold start problems, etc. Personalized bundle recommender systems are not only the central of our everyday lives but also highly indispensable in some industries. Therefore, they have important research significance and broad application scenarios.

Acknowledgements. This work was supported in part by grants (No. 61966009, No. U1811264, No. U1711263, No. 61762027) from the National Natural Science Foundation of China, in part by grants (No. 2019GXNSFBA245059, No. 2019GXNSFBA245049, No. 2018GXNSFDA281045, No. 2018GXNSFDA138090) from the Science Foundation of Guangxi Province, and in parts by grants (No. AD19245011, No. AA17202048, No. AA17202024) from the Key Research and Development Program of Guangxi Province.

References

1. Adomavicius, G., Tuzhilin, A.: Toward the next generation of recommender systems: a survey of the state-of-the-art and possible extensions. IEEE Trans. Knowl. Data Eng. **17**, 734–749 (2005)
2. Xu, J., He, X., Li, H.: Deep learning for matching in search and recommendation. In: The 41st International ACM SIGIR Conference on Research & Development in Information Retrieval, pp. 1365–1368 (2018)
3. Jasin, S., Sinha, A.: An LP-based correlated rounding scheme for multi-item ecommerce order fulfillment. Oper. Res. **63**, 1336–1351 (2015)
4. Drumwright, M.E.: A demonstration of anomalies in evaluations of bundling. Mark. Lett. **3**, 311–321 (1992)
5. Stremersch, S., Tellis, G.J.: Strategic bundling of products and prices: a new synthesis for marketing. J. Mark. **66**, 55–72 (2002)
6. Chen, Y.-L., Tang, K., Shen, R.-J., Hu, Y.-H.: Market basket analysis in a multiple store environment. Decis. Support Syst. **40**, 339–354 (2005)
7. Garfinkel, R., Gopal, R., Tripathi, A., Yin, F.: Design of a shopbot and recommender system for bundle purchases. Decis. Support Syst. **42**, 1974–1986 (2006)
8. Zhu, T., Harrington, P., Li, J., Tang, L.: Bundle recommendation in ecommerce. In: Proceedings of the 37th international ACM SIGIR Conference on Research & Development in Information Retrieval, pp. 657–666 (2014)
9. Bai, J., et al.: Personalized bundle list recommendation. In: The World Wide Web Conference, pp. 60–71 (2019)
10. Chen, L., Liu, Y., He, X., Gao, L., Zheng, Z.: Matching user with item set: collaborative bundle recommendation with deep attention network. In: Proceedings of the 28th International Joint Conference on Artificial Intelligence, pp. 2095–2101. AAAI Press (2019)
11. Kouki, P., et al.: Product collection recommendation in online retail. In: Proceedings of the 13th ACM Conference on Recommender Systems, pp. 486–490 (2019)
12. Wang, Z., Jiang, Z., Ren, Z., Tang, J., Yin, D.: A path-constrained framework for discriminating substitutable and complementary products in e-commerce. In: Proceedings of the Eleventh ACM International Conference on Web Search and Data Mining, pp. 619–627 (2018)

13. Yadav, M.S.: How buyers evaluate product bundles: a model of anchoring and adjustment. J. Consum. Res. **21**, 342–353 (1994)
14. Pathak, A., Gupta, K., McAuley, J.: Generating and personalizing bundle recommendations on steam. In: Proceedings of the 40th International ACM SIGIR Conference on Research and Development in Information Retrieval, pp. 1073–1076. ACM, Shinjuku (2017)
15. Pham, T.-A.N., Li, X., Cong, G.: A general model for out-of-town region recommendation. In: Proceedings of the 26th International Conference on World Wide Web, pp. 401–410 (2017)
16. Cao, D., Nie, L., He, X., Wei, X., Zhu, S., Chua, T.-S.: Embedding factorization models for jointly recommending items and user generated lists. In: Proceedings of the 40th International ACM SIGIR Conference on Research and Development in Information Retrieval, pp. 585–594 (2017)
17. Parameswaran, A., Venetis, P., Garcia-Molina, H.: Recommendation systems with complex constraints: a course recommendation perspective. ACM Trans. Inf. Syst. (TOIS) **29**, 1–33 (2011)
18. Jaradat, S.: Deep cross-domain fashion recommendation. In: Proceedings of the Eleventh ACM Conference on Recommender Systems, pp. 407–410 (2017)
19. Yin, R., Li, K., Lu, J., Zhang, G.: Enhancing fashion recommendation with visual compatibility relationship. In: The World Wide Web Conference, pp. 3434–3440 (2019)
20. Takács, G., Pilászy, I., Németh, B., Tikk, D.: Scalable collaborative filtering approaches for large recommender systems. J. Mach. Learn. Res. **10**, 623–656 (2009)
21. Herlocker, J.L., Konstan, J.A., Terveen, L.G., Riedl, J.T.: Evaluating collaborative filtering recommender systems. ACM Trans. Inf. Syst. (TOIS) **22**, 5–53 (2004)
22. Xie, M., Lakshmanan, L.V., Wood, P.T.: Breaking out of the box of recommendations: from items to packages. In: Proceedings of the Fourth ACM Conference on Recommender Systems, pp. 151–158 (2010)
23. Marchetti-Spaccamela, A., Vercellis, C.: Stochastic on-line knapsack problems. Math. Prog. **68**, 73–104 (1995)
24. Liu, Q., Ge, Y., Li, Z., Chen, E., Xiong, H.: Personalized travel package recommendation. In: 2011 IEEE 11th International Conference on Data Mining, pp. 407–416. IEEE (2011)
25. Rendle, S., Freudenthaler, C., Gantner, Z., Schmidt-Thieme, L.: BPR: Bayesian personalized ranking from implicit feedback. arXiv preprint arXiv:1205.2618 (2012)
26. Gallo, G., Hammer, P.L., Simeone, B.: Quadratic knapsack problems. In: Padberg, M.W. (ed.) Combinatorial Optimization. Mathematical Programming Studies, vol. 12, pp. 132–149. Springer, Berlin (1980). https://doi.org/10.1007/BFb0120892
27. Bakos, Y., Brynjolfsson, E.: Bundling information goods: pricing, profits, and efficiency. Manag. Sci. **45**, 1613–1630 (1999)
28. Prasad, A., Venkatesh, R., Mahajan, V.: Temporal product bundling with myopic and strategic consumers: manifestations and relative effectiveness. Q. Market. Econ. **15**(4), 341–368 (2017). https://doi.org/10.1007/s11129-017-9189-6
29. Karimi-Majd, A., Fathian, M.: Extracting new ideas from the behavior of social network users. Decis. Sci. Lett. **6**, 207–220 (2017)
30. Agrawal, R., Srikant, R.: Fast algorithms for mining association rules. In: Proceedings of 20th International Conference on Very Large Data Bases, VLDB, pp. 487–499 (1994)
31. Han, J., Pei, J., Yin, Y.: Mining frequent patterns without candidate generation. ACM SIGMOD Rec. **29**, 1–12 (2000)
32. Karypis, M.S.G., Kumar, V., Steinbach, M.: A comparison of document clustering techniques. In: Text Mining Workshop at KDD 2000, May 2000 (2000)
33. Ester, M., Kriegel, H.-P., Sander, J., Xu, X.: A density-based algorithm for discovering clusters in large spatial databases with noise. In: KDD, pp. 226–231 (1996)

34. Langley, P., Iba, W., Thompson, K.: An analysis of Bayesian classifiers. In: AAAI, pp. 223–228 (1992)
35. Lewis, D.D.: Naive (Bayes) at forty: the independence assumption in information retrieval. In: Nédellec, C., Rouveirol, C. (eds.) ECML 1998. LNCS, vol. 1398, pp. 4–15. Springer, Heidelberg (1998). https://doi.org/10.1007/BFb0026666
36. Ramoni, M., Sebastiani, P.: Robust bayes classifiers. Artif. Intell. **125**, 209–226 (2001)
37. Loh, W.-Y.: Classification and regression trees. Wiley Interdisc. Rev. Data Min. Knowl. Discov. **1**, 14–23 (2011)
38. Vapnik, V.: The Nature of Statistical Learning Theory. Springer, Heidelberg (2000). https://doi.org/10.1007/978-1-4757-3264-1
39. Vapnik, V.N.: An overview of statistical learning theory. IEEE Trans. Neural Networks **10**, 988–999 (1999)
40. Yang, T.-C., Lai, H.: Comparison of product bundling strategies on different online shopping behaviors. Electron. Commer. Res. Appl. **5**, 295–304 (2006)
41. Miguéis, V.L., Camanho, A.S., Cunha, J.F.: Customer data mining for lifestyle segmentation. Exp. Syst. Appl. **39**, 9359–9366 (2012)
42. Liao, S., Chen, Y., Lin, Y.: Mining customer knowledge to implement online shopping and home delivery for hypermarkets. Exp. Syst. Appl. **38**, 3982–3991 (2011)
43. Kim, C., Kim, J.: A recommendation algorithm using multi-level association rules. In: Proceedings IEEE/WIC International Conference on Web Intelligence (WI 2003), pp. 524–527. IEEE (2003)
44. Chen, M.-C., Chiu, A.-L., Chang, H.-H.: Mining changes in customer behavior in retail marketing. Exp. Syst. Appl. **28**, 773–781 (2005)
45. Jiao, J., Zhang, Y.: Product portfolio identification based on association rule mining. Comput. Aided Des. **37**, 149–172 (2005)
46. Fang, Y., Xiao, X., Wang, X., Lan, H.: Customized bundle recommendation by association rules of product categories for online supermarkets. In: 2018 IEEE Third International Conference on Data Science in Cyberspace (DSC), pp. 472–475. IEEE (2018)
47. Chen, D., Sain, S.L., Guo, K.: Data mining for the online retail industry: a case study of RFM model-based customer segmentation using data mining. J. Database Market. Customer Strategy Manag. **19**, 197–208 (2012)
48. Sarwar, B., Karypis, G., Konstan, J., Riedl, J.: Analysis of recommendation algorithms for e-commerce. In: Proceedings of the 2nd ACM Conference on Electronic Commerce, pp. 158–167 (2000)
49. Qi, S., Mamoulis, N., Pitoura, E., Tsaparas, P.: Recommending packages to groups. In: 2016 IEEE 16th International Conference on Data Mining (ICDM), pp. 449–458. IEEE (2016)
50. Breese, J.S., Heckerman, D., Kadie, C.: Empirical analysis of predictive algorithms for collaborative filtering. arXiv preprint arXiv:1301.7363 (2013)
51. Hu, Y., Koren, Y., Volinsky, C.: Collaborative filtering for implicit feedback datasets. In: 2008 Eighth IEEE International Conference on Data Mining, pp. 263–272. IEEE (2008)
52. Koren, Y., Bell, R., Volinsky, C.: Matrix factorization techniques for recommender systems. Computer **42**, 30–37 (2009)
53. Sedhain, S., Menon, A.K., Sanner, S., Xie, L.: AutoRec: autoencoders meet collaborative filtering. In: Proceedings of the 24th International Conference on World Wide Web, pp. 111–112 (2015)
54. Le, D.T., Lauw, H.W., Fang, Y.: Basket-sensitive personalized item recommendation. Presented at the (2017)
55. Russell, G.J., Petersen, A.: Analysis of cross category dependence in market basket selection. J. Retail. **76**, 367–392 (2000)

56. Pazzani, M.J., Billsus, D.: Content-based recommendation systems. In: Brusilovsky, P., Kobsa, A., Nejdl, W. (eds.) The Adaptive Web. LNCS, vol. 4321, pp. 325–341. Springer, Heidelberg (2007). https://doi.org/10.1007/978-3-540-72079-9_10
57. Wang, P., Guo, J., Lan, Y.: Modeling retail transaction data for personalized shopping recommendation. In: Proceedings of the 23rd ACM International Conference on Information and Knowledge Management, pp. 1979–1982 (2014)
58. Liu, G., Fu, Y., Chen, G., Xiong, H., Chen, C.: Modeling buying motives for personalized product bundle recommendation. ACM Trans. Knowl. Discov. Data (TKDD) **11**, 1–26 (2017)
59. Zhang, F.: Research on recommendation list diversity of recommender systems. In: International Conference on Management of e-Commerce and e-Government, pp. 72–76 (2008)
60. Cremonesi, P., Koren, Y., Turrin, R.: Performance of recommender algorithms on top-n recommendation tasks. In: Conference on Recommender Systems, pp. 39–46 (2010)
61. Rendle, S., Freudenthaler, C., Gantner, Z., Schmidtthieme, L.: BPR: Bayesian personalized ranking from implicit feedback. In: Uncertainty in Artificial Intelligence, pp. 452–461 (2009)
62. Shi, Y., Karatzoglou, A., Baltrunas, L., Larson, M., Oliver, N., Hanjalic, A.: CLiMF: learning to maximize reciprocal rank with collaborative less-is-more filtering. In: Conference on Recommender Systems, pp. 139–146 (2012)
63. Shi, Y., Larson, M., Hanjalic, A.: List-wise learning to rank with matrix factorization for collaborative filtering (2010)
64. Xie, M., Lakshmanan, L.V.S., Wood, P.T.: Generating top-k packages via preference elicitation. In: Very Large Data Bases, pp. 1941–1952 (2014)
65. Deng, T., Fan, W., Geerts, F.: On the complexity of package recommendation problems (2012)
66. Shalom, O.S., Koenigstein, N., Paquet, U., Vanchinathan, H.P.: Beyond collaborative filtering: the list recommendation problem. In: The Web Conference, pp. 63–72 (2016)
67. Zhuang, F., Zhang, Z., Qian, M., Shi, C., Xie, X., He, Q.: Representation learning via dual-autoencoder for recommendation. Neural Netw. **90**, 83–89 (2017)
68. Wu, L., Quan, C., Li, C., Wang, Q., Zheng, B., Luo, X.: A context-aware user-item representation learning for item recommendation. ACM Trans, Inf. Syst. **37**, 22 (2019)
69. Lian, J., Zhang, F., Xie, X., Sun, G.: Towards better representation learning for personalized news recommendation: a multi-channel deep fusion approach. In: International Joint Conference on Artificial Intelligence, pp. 3805–3811 (2018)
70. Cheng, H., et al.: Wide & deep learning for recommender systems. In: Conference on Recommender Systems, pp. 7–10 (2016)
71. Tay, Y., Luu, A.T., Hui, S.C.: Latent relational metric learning via memory-based attention for collaborative ranking. In: The Web Conference, pp. 729–739 (2018)
72. He, X., Liao, L., Zhang, H., Nie, L., Hu, X., Chua, T.: Neural collaborative filtering. In: The Web Conference, pp. 173–182 (2017)
73. Chen, J., Zhang, H., He, X., Nie, L., Liu, W., Chua, T.-S.: Attentive collaborative filtering: multimedia recommendation with item- and component-level attention (2017)
74. Yosinski, J., Clune, J., Bengio, Y., Lipson, H.: How transferable are features in deep neural networks. In: Neural Information Processing Systems, pp. 3320–3328 (2014)
75. Cao, D., He, X., Miao, L., An, Y., Yang, C., Hong, R.: Attentive group recommendation. In: International ACM SIGIR Conference on Research and Development in Information Retrieval, pp. 645–654 (2018)
76. Chen, X., et al.: Sequential recommendation with user memory networks. In: Web Search and Data Mining, pp. 108–116 (2018)

77. Liu, Q., Wu, S., Wang, D., Li, Z., Wang, L.: Context-aware sequential recommendation. In: 2016 IEEE 16th International Conference on Data Mining (ICDM), pp. 1053–1058 (2016)

78. Cho, K., et al.: Learning phrase representations using RNN encoder-decoder for statistical machine translation. arXiv: Computation and Language (2014)

79. Sutskever, I., Vinyals, O., Le, Q.V.: Sequence to sequence learning with neural networks. Computation and Language (2014)

80. Wiseman, S., Rush, A.M.: Sequence-to-sequence learning as beam-search optimization. In: Empirical Methods in Natural Language Processing, pp. 1296–1306 (2016)

81. Yu, W., Li, L., Xu, X., Wang, D., Wang, J., Chen, S.: ProductRec: product bundle recommendation based on user's sequential patterns in social networking service environment. In: International Conference on Web Services, pp. 301–308 (2017)

82. Rendle, S., Freudenthaler, C., Schmidtthieme, L.: Factorizing personalized Markov chains for next-basket recommendation. In: The Web Conference, pp. 811–820 (2010)

83. Chen, L., Zhang, G., Zhou, E.: Fast greedy MAP inference for determinantal point process to improve recommendation diversity. In: Neural Information Processing Systems, pp. 5622–5633 (2018)

84. Bromley, J., et al.: Signature verification using a "siamese" time delay neural network. Int. J. Pattern Recogn. Artif. Intell. 7, 25 (1993)

85. Koch, G.R.: Siamese neural networks for one-shot image recognition. Presented at the (2015)

86. Shou, W., Fan, W., Liu, B., Lai, Y.: Knowledge map mining of financial data. Tsinghua Sci. Technol. 18, 68–76 (2013)

87. Wang, M., Liu, M., Liu, J., Wang, S., Long, G., Qian, B.: Safe Medicine Recommendation via Medical Knowledge Graph Embedding. arXiv: Information Retrieval (2017)

88. Wang, D., Xu, G., Deng, S.: Music recommendation via heterogeneous information graph embedding. In: International Joint Conference on Neural Network, pp. 596–603 (2017)

89. Wang, J., Huang, P., Zhao, H., Zhang, Z., Zhao, B., Lee, D.L.: Billion-scale commodity embedding for e-commerce recommendation in Alibaba. In: Knowledge Discovery and Data Mining, pp. 839–848 (2018)

90. Beladev, M., Rokach, L., Shapira, B.: Recommender systems for product bundling. Knowl. Based Syst. 111, 193–206 (2016)

91. Ettl, M., Harsha, P., Papush, A., Perakis, G.: A data-driven approach to personalized bundle pricing and recommendation. Manuf. Serv. Oper. Manag. 22, 461–480 (2019)

Estimation of Motor Imagination Based on Consumer-Grade EEG Device

Zhenzhen Luo[1], Zhongyi Hu[1,2(✉)], and Zuoyong Li[3(✉)]

[1] College of Computer and Artificial Intelligence, Wenzhou University,
Wenzhou, People's Republic of China
lzzhen1314@163.com, hujunyi@163.com
[2] Intelligent Information Systems Institute, Wenzhou University,
Wenzhou, People's Republic of China
[3] Fujian Provincial Key Laboratory of Information Processing and Intelligent
Control, College of Computer and Control Engineering,
Minjiang University, Fuzhou, People's Republic of China
fzulzytdq@126.com

Abstract. Nowadays, classifying electroencephalogram (EEG) signals based motor imagery tasks is extensively used to control brain-computer interface applications, as a communication bridge between humans and computers. In this paper, we propose signal-to-image transformation and feature extraction methods for the classification of motor imagery. Specifically, a continuous wavelet transform is applied to decompose EEG signals into five rhythms and generate time-frequency images. Then, a gray-level co-occurrence matrix is used to extract global texture features on time-frequency images. Finally, the SVM classification model is optimized by using a grid search algorithm to select optimal parameter pairs (C, σ). To confirm the validity of the proposed methods, we experimented on self-collected data, which is obtained using a consumer-grade EEG device. The experimental result showed that this proposed method can achieve an acceptable classification accuracy of 90% for a two-class problem (left/right-hand motor imagery).

Keywords: Brain-computer interface (BCI) · Motor imagination · Electroencephalogram (EEG) · Continuous wavelet transform (CWT) · Gray-level co-occurrence matrix (GLCM)

1 Introduction

The brain-computer interface (BCI) is a system that realizes the communication between humans and machines. It can convert human brain electrical activity signals into corresponding control signals, and realize the purpose of brain electrical consciousness control machines [1,2]. For some special subjects (for example pilots, detoxifiers, paralyzed patients), it can reduce the burden on the staff and enable the paralyzed patients to achieve EEG-controlled mechanical arms or keyboard typing, which will have extraordinary significance.

© Springer Nature Switzerland AG 2020
X. Chen et al. (Eds.): ML4CS 2020, LNCS 12487, pp. 305–314, 2020.
https://doi.org/10.1007/978-3-030-62460-6_27

The key to realizing the brain-computer interface lies in the two links of feature extraction and classification [3–5]. There are two types of EEG feature extraction methods, one is to extract features based on EEG signals, such as autoregressive model (AR) [6], wavelet transform (WT) [7], neural network [8,9], and common spatial pattern (CSP) [10], etc. They are the most common methods. The other is descriptors to extract the feature of time-frequency images, such as the gray-level co-occurrence matrix (GLCM) [11] and local binary pattern (LBP) [12]. The AR model performs signal analysis in the frequency domain and cannot obtain time-domain information at the same time. Although the wavelet transform can obtain both time and frequency domain information, it is unable to obtain high-resolution time-frequency characteristics at the same time because it is constrained by the Heisenberg uncertainty principle. Both methods only extract features based on the channel signal energy, while ignoring the relevant information between the channels. Although neural networks have powerful functions, small sample data restricts its use. The common spatial pattern is the most common method for EEG signal classification. Its limitation is that the difference in data of different individuals will greatly affect the classification results. Now, more and more researchers are focusing on treating time-frequency images of EEG signals as natural images and using image processing methods for feature extraction, which not only visualizes feature extraction but also achieves good classification precision based on some descriptors.

For the classification of EEG signals for left and right-hand motor imagery, this paper firstly uses continuous wavelet transform to obtain EEG time-frequency images of motor imagination, and then uses a gray-level co-occurrence matrix descriptor to extract features based on time-frequency images, and finally uses SVM-RBF classifier to achieve classification. For a consumer-grade single-electrode EEG device, the experiment has achieved an acceptable classification result of 90%, which provides the possibility of implementing the portable brain-computer interface for consumer-grade EEG devices based on gray-level co-occurrence matrix algorithm.

The rest of this paper is organized as follows. Section 2 introduces the three aspects of experimental equipment, experimental data, and data preprocessing. Section 3 details the theory and implementation of the proposed method. The experiment result of motor imagination are reported in Sect. 4, and conclusions and future works are drawn in Sect. 5.

2   Experimental Data

2.1   Experimental Equipment

The experimental equipment is a consumer-grade brainwave sensor module device, and the brain sensor technology core of TGAM was developed by United states neurosky. The device size is $27.9 \times 15.2 \times 2.5$ (mm), and the brainwave output includes the original EEG signal, concentration, relaxation, blink, brain wave (delta, theta, low alpha, alpha, low beta, gamma). The sampling frequency is 512 Hz, and the hardware filter is 3 Hz–100 Hz, and the technical specifications of the UART serial port include a baud rate of 57600, 8 data bits, no parity bit and 1 stop bit.

2.2 Experimental Data

The experimental data is based on brainwave module biofeedback detection equipment for brainwave sensor TGAM and Bluetooth EEG. The experiment used a dry electrode with a sampling frequency of 512 Hz. A subject is in a quiet environment. After wearing the device, turn on the TGAM device switch and set the experimental device data (such as serial port, bit rate, etc.) on the serial assistant interface. The subject is seated in front of the computer in a comfortable and relaxed state, and then a motor imagination experiment is conducted. The schematic diagram of data collection is shown in Fig. 1.

Step 1: The screen presents a cross mark "⊕" to make the subject focus. If you are ready, go to step 2.

Step 2: Whether the picture of "Left Arrow" or "Right Arrow" appears on the screen, it is controlled by mouse click. When the subject clicks the button "LEFT", a picture of the left arrow appears, ready to start imagining EEG movement. If the subject is ready, click the "Left Start" button to add the start flag of the left hand motor imagination. After a period of time, click the "Left End" button and add the left end flag in real-time. Similarly, the right-hand motor imagination. If an experiment is completed, click the "Back" button to go to Step 3.

Step 3: Click the "Save" button to save the experimental data. If you continue the experiment, skip to Step 1, and repeat the experiment collection Steps.

The whole experiment process is controlled by the mouse clicks according to the subject's preparation. The experimental data comes from the EEG signals of some subjects, and the left and right movement imaginations are collected 20 times, respectively.

2.3 Data Preprocessing

The data collected by the experimental equipment is a hexadecimal non-numeric data packet, and about 512 raw data are sent per second. The purpose of running

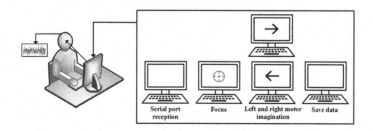

Fig. 1. The schematic diagram of data sampling

C code is to convert the raw data between adjacent start and end flags into decimal data, at the same time remove some illegal data (may be caused by the device not being worn well). Considering that the length of the collected EEG signal is not fixed, the subject controls the duration of the imagination. To facilitate subsequent time-frequency analysis and feature extraction, this paper fixes the data points of the EEG signal segment to 4097, and the sampling time is about 8 s.

3   The Proposed Method

To achieve the estimation of motor imagination based on consumer-grade EEG device, a time-frequency analysis, and feature extraction method based on motor imaging EEG data is proposed, the flow chart of which is shown in Fig. 2. The proposed method exploits time-frequency images from a unique perspective. It significantly extracts global texture features and has the nature of simplicity and efficiency. The following sub-sections will describe the theory and implementation of the proposed method.

3.1   Time-Frequency Analysis

Time-frequency analysis aims to high-resolution time-frequency images (i.e., TFIs). It is mostly used in the field of EEG signal processing and disease diagnosis. EEG signals usually have repetitive and non-stationary, and high-resolution TFIs are difficult to obtain. Based on this cue, many signal processing technologies have been developed to generate TFIs in recent years. For example, the short-time Fourier transform (STFT) method uses a fixed window size for phase shift so that it can be applied to non-stationary transformed EEG signals. However, due to the fixed window size, the problem of high-time resolution and high-frequency resolution cannot be achieved simultaneously. In this paper, the continuous wavelet transform (CWT) is used to solve this problem. It introduces a "time-frequency" window that changes with time, the purpose is to achieve a higher frequency resolution at low frequencies and a higher time resolution at high frequencies.

EEG signals of motor imagination can be analyzed by continuous wavelet transform for time-frequency analysis, and the overall time-frequency images of EEG signals and their segmentations are shown in Fig. 3. Specifically, the dbN method is used to decompose the EEG signal into five rhythms (i.e., delta rhythm (0-4 Hz), theta rhythm (4–8 Hz), alpha rhythm (8–12 Hz), beta rhythm (12–30 Hz), and gamma rhythm (30–40 Hz)). Then, the continuous wavelet transform is implemented to generate the overall time-frequency images and corresponding five ones, and its principle expression is:

$$CWT(s, \tau) = \frac{1}{\sqrt{s}} \int_{-\infty}^{+\infty} f(t)\psi^*(\frac{t - \tau}{s})dt \qquad (1)$$

where ψ^* is a complex conjugate function; s is scale, which can change the scaling transformation of the wavelet function; τ is as a translation variable, which corresponds to the time variable t and controls the wavelet function translation transformation.

3.2   Feature Extraction Based on Gray-Level Co-occurrence Matrix

The gray-level co-occurrence matrix (GLCM) is mostly used in image processing, pattern recognition, and other fields. It can effectively extract image texture features.

The GLCM algorithm has two variables, direction θ and distance d, which can be obtained by setting different parameter values to obtain the joint probability density between two pixel positions, which is defined as follows:

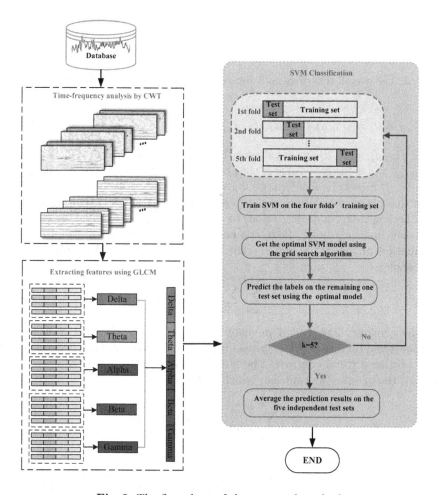

Fig. 2. The flow chart of the proposed method

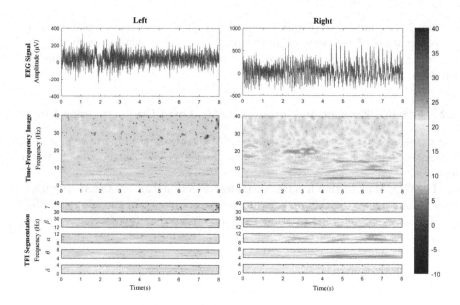

Fig. 3. The overall time-frequency images of EEG signals and their segmentations

$$P(i, j; d, \theta) = \{(x, y), (x + d_x, y + d_y) | f(x, y) = i, f(x + d_x, y + d_y) = j\} \quad (2)$$

where $f(x, y) = i$ is the gray value of the pixel at the position (x, y), and $f(x + d_x, y + d_y) = j$ is the gray value of the pixel at the adjacent position $(x + d_x, y + d_y)$ when (x, y) meets the fixed values θ and h.

In this paper, we will use four types of feature parameters (i.e., energy, contrast, homogeneity, and correlation) to characterize the texture features of time-frequency image. Among them, the energy reflects the uniformity of the gray distribution of the image and the thickness of the texture. The mathematical expression is:

$$C_1 = \sum_{i=0}^{L-1} \sum_{j=0}^{L-1} [P(i, j; d, \theta)]^2 \quad (3)$$

The contrast (also called moment of inertia) in GLCM can measure the sharpness and texture depth of grayscale images. The depth of the texture groove is proportional to its contrast. The larger the value away from the diagonal in GLCM, the greater the contrast, which is defined as:

$$C_2 = \sum_{i=0}^{L-1} \sum_{j=0}^{L-1} (i - j)^2 P(i, j; d, \theta) \quad (4)$$

The homogeneity's value is positively related to whether the diagonal elements of the GLCM have a larger value, and it is expressed as:

$$C_3 = \sum_{i=0}^{L-1} \sum_{j=0}^{L-1} \frac{1}{1 + |i - j|} P(i, j; d, \theta) \tag{5}$$

The correlation measures the similarity of spatial gray-level co-occurrence matrix elements in the row or column direction. The local gray-scale correlation in the image can be measured by the difference of the matrix element values.

$$C_4 = \sum_{i=0}^{L-1} \sum_{j=0}^{L-1} \frac{(ij)P(i, j; d, \theta) - \mu_x \mu_y}{\sigma_x \sigma_y} \tag{6}$$

where,

$$\mu_x = \sum_{i=0}^{L-1} \sum_{j=0}^{L-1} iP(i, j; d, \theta),$$

$$\mu_y = \sum_{i=0}^{L-1} \sum_{j=0}^{L-1} jP(i, j; d, \theta),$$

$$\sigma_x = \sum_{i=0}^{L-1} (i - \mu_x)^2 P(i, j; d, \theta),$$

$$\sigma_y = \sum_{i=0}^{L-1} (j - \mu_y)^2 P(i, j; d, \theta).$$

The experiment sets the distance $d = 1$ and $\theta = (0, \pi/4, \pi/2,$ and $\pi)$. GLCM extracts the EEG features of left and right-hand motor imagination, where each EEG data segment contains five frequency sub-bands. Therefore, the dimension of the feature vector is $5 \times (4 \times 4)$. Its visualization is shown in the step of using GLCM feature extraction in Fig. 2.

4   Experimental Results

The support vector machine (SVM-RBF) using radial basis functions as the kernel, and it acts on the left and right-hand motion imagery EEG signals' classification problem. For the performance of the SVM classifier, selecting the appropriate parameter values (C, σ) can obtain the optimal classification model, where C is the penalty parameter of the classifier and σ is the radius of RBF. As explained above, in our study, we have used a five-fold cross-validation approach with a grid search algorithm to optimize the two parameters and the best results were obtained with $C = 0.0313$ and $\sigma = 0.0313$.

The experimental data collected in this paper is based on consumer-grade single-electrode device. The gray-level co-occurrence matrix descriptor are used to extract time-frequency features from four aspects: energy, contrast, homogeneity, and correlation. The feature vector' dimension of each EEG signal segment is 80, and the amount of left and right-hand data is 40. Then, the extracted time-frequency features are used as input data to put into the SVM-RBF classifier by five-fold cross-validation. Finally, the average classification result is 90%.

Table 1. Comparison of two-class average accuracy (%) between studies on different motor imagery EEG datasets

Methods	Year	Dataset	Average accuracy
Lotte and Guan [13]	2011	(*2) Dataset IIa	89.07
		(*1) Dataset IIIa	
		(*1) Dataset IVa	
		(*2) Dataset IIa	
Yger et al. [14]	2015	(*1) Dataset IIIa	85.93
		(*1) Dataset IVa	
		(*2) Dataset IIa	
Mishuhina and Jiang [15]	2018	(*1) Dataset IIIa	91.91
		(*2) Dataset IIa	
Singh et al. [16]	2019	(*1) Dataset IIIa	92.22
		(*1) Dataset IVa	
Proposed method	–	Self-collected Dataset	**90**

Note: bold value indicates result obtained by the proposed method;
*1: represents the BCI Competition III, *2: represents the BCI Competition IV.

However, some researchers used BCI Competition III and BCI Competition IV as experimental datasets [13–16], which were provided by the Laboratory of Brain–Computer Interfaces (BCI-Lab), Graz University of Technology. In this dataset, the signals were recoreded from subjects using a 64-channel EEG amplifier. As shown in Table 1, Singh et al. [16] had achieved the higher classification result is 92.22%, it outperformed that of our proposed method by 2.22%.

It is worth noting that the data collected by most researchers are multi-channel EEG devices, which are not comparable to the classification results of our experimental device. For the two-class problem (left/right-hand motor imagery), the experiment achieved better classification accuracy of 90%.

5   Conclusions and Future Works

In this paper, we proposed a novel estimation of motor imagination method based on time-frequency images. The proposed method exploits time-frequency images from a unique perspective in comparison with conventional signal processing method. Specifically, the proposed method presents a useful feature extraction descriptor (i.e. gray-level co-occurrence matrix), and uses the descriptor to extract discriminative and effective features. The proposed method also perform the grid search algorithm and five-fold cross-validation to optimize the classification model. The experimental result on EEG signals of motor imagination demonstrates that the proposed method obtains an acceptable classification result of 90%.

However, the proposed method does not achieve high accuracy in motor imagination. In the future, we will collect more EEG data of motor imagination to perform multi-source data classification, which will further improve the classification effect.

Acknowledgment. This work was supported by the National Natural Science Foundation of China [U1809209, 61702376, 61972187, 61772254], the Major Project of Wenzhou Natural Science Foundation [ZY2019020], the Key Project of Zhejiang Provincial Natural Science Foundation [LSZ19F020001], Fujian Provincial Leading Project [2017H0030, 2019H0025], Government Guiding Regional Science and Technology Development [2019L3009], and Natural Science Foundation of Fujian Province [2017J01768, 2019J01756]. We acknowledge the efforts and constructive comments of respected editors and anonymous reviewers.

References

1. Daly, I., Scherer, R., Billinger, M., Müllerputz, G.: FORCe: fully online and automated artifact removal for brain-computer interfacing. IEEE Trans. Neural Syst. Rehabil. Eng. Publ. IEEE Eng. Med. Biol. Soc. **23**(5), 725 (2014)
2. Corsi, M.C., Chavez, M., Schwartz, D.: Integrating EEG and MEG signals to improve motor imagery classification in brain-computer interfaces. Int. J. Neural Syst. **29**(01), 1850014 (2019)
3. Lu, P., Yuan, D., Lou, Y., Liu, C., Huang, S.: Single-trial identification of motor imagery EEG based on HHT and SVM. In: Sun, Z., Deng, Z. (eds.) Proceedings of 2013 Chinese Intelligent Automation Conference. LNCS, vol. 256, pp. 681–689. Springer, Heidelberg (2013). https://doi.org/10.1007/978-3-642-38466-0_75
4. Sahu, M., Shukla, S.: Impact of feature selection on EEG based motor imagery. In: Fong, S., Akashe, S., Mahalle, P.N. (eds.) Information and Communication Technology for Competitive Strategies. LNNS, vol. 40, pp. 749–762. Springer, Singapore (2019). https://doi.org/10.1007/978-981-13-0586-3_73
5. Kumar, S., Sharma, A.: A new parameter tuning approach for enhanced motor imagery EEG signal classification. Med. Biol. Eng. Comput. **56**(10), 1861–1874 (2018)
6. Zhang, Y., Liu, B., Ji, X., Huang, D.: Classification of EEG signals based on autoregressive model and wavelet packet decomposition. Neural Process. Lett. **45**(2), 365–378 (2017)
7. Han, D., Li, P., An, S., Shi, P.: Multi-frequency weak signal detection based on wavelet transform and parameter compensation band-pass multi-stable stochastic resonance. Mech. Syst. Signal Process. **70–71**, 995–1010 (2016)
8. Shi, T., Ren, L., Cui, W.: Feature recognition of motor imaging EEG signals based on deep learning. Pers. Ubiquitous Compu. **23**(3–4), 499–510 (2019)
9. Hsu, W.Y.: Fuzzy Hopfield neural network clustering for single-trial motor imagery EEG classification. Expert Syst. Appl. **39**(1), 1055–1061 (2012)

10. Sid, A.B., Nawal, B., Mohamed, D.K.: CSP features extraction and FLDA classification of EEG-based motor imagery for brain-computer interaction. In: International Conference on Electrical Engineering (2016)
11. Li, Y., Cui, W., Luo, M., Li, K., Wang, L.: Epileptic seizure detection based on time-frequency images of EEG signals using gaussian mixture model and gray level co-occurrence matrix features. Int. J. Neural Syst. **28**(07), 1850003 (2018)
12. Boubchir, L., Al-Maadeed, S., Bouridane, A., Cherif, A.A.: Classification of EEG signals for detection of epileptic seizure activities based on LBP descriptor of time-frequency images. In: IEEE International Conference on Image Processing (2015)
13. Lotte, F., Guan, C.: Regularizing common spatial patterns to improve BCI designs: unified theory and new algorithms. IEEE Trans. Biomed. Eng. **58**(2), 355–362 (2011)
14. Yger, F., Lotte, F., Sugiyama, M.: Averaging covariance matrices for EEG signal classification based on the CSP: an empirical study. In: European Signal Processing Conference (EUSIPCO), pp. 2721–2725 (2015)
15. Mishuhina, V., Jiang, X.: Feature weighting and regularization of common spatial patterns in EEG-based motor imagery BCI. IEEE Signal Process. Lett. **25**(6), 783–787 (2018)
16. Singh, A., Lal, S., Guesgen, H.: Reduce calibration time in motor imagery using spatially regularized symmetric positives-definite matrices based classification. Sensors **19**(2), 379 (2019)

An Overview of Key Technologies and Challenges of 6G

Qingling Liu[1]([⊠]), Shahid Sarfraz[1], and Shubin Wang[2]

[1] Department of Information and Communication Engineering, Harbin Engineering University, Harbin 150001, China
{liuqingling, shahidsarfraz93}@hrbeu.edu.cn
[2] China Telecom Co. Ltd., Harbin Branch, Harbin, China
125338156@qq.com

Abstract. Significant increase has been witnessed in data usage and users over the years for communication. Development of technology is a necessity hence 5G (5th generation) system is about to launch commercially however over a few years even that won't be sufficient. 5G networks are being tested and released offering various noteworthy advanced technologies and are anticipated to move forward progressively in upcoming years. Keeping in light the ever-increasing demand, 6G will be the need of the hour. Researchers and scholars around the world instigated to turn their attention to what 6G might be in the next 10 years or more, and many initiatives are already taken in various countries to explore the possible 6G technologies. A major revolution has been attained in the design of communication networks through 5G networks for their capability of providing a single platform, allowing a diversity of different services, from enhanced mobile broadband communications to virtual reality and the internet of things (IoT). However, estimation of the increasing requirements for new facilities and envisaging the expansion of new technologies within a decade from now on, the fact is already imaginable to envision, that to gratify new needs of society. This article aims to extend the vision of 5G soon and contemplates about the ambitious technologies which will lead to the implementation of 6G networks.

Keywords: 6th generation technology (6G) · Artificial intelligence · Terahertz communication · Visible light communication · Intelligent reflecting surfaces · Radio stripes

1 Introduction

As the modern technological world becomes smarter, intelligent, and pervasive, the stream of data becomes more imperative. The last two decades have perceived never-ending progress in the global mobile data traffic [1, 2], and the changes in the field of telecommunication will remain happening for many years. The need for data traffic has increased significantly since the evolvement of communication technologies and assumed to exceed Petabytes by 2021. From 1G to 5G, each of these generations has many innovations as shown in Fig. 1.

© Springer Nature Switzerland AG 2020
X. Chen et al. (Eds.): ML4CS 2020, LNCS 12487, pp. 315–326, 2020.
https://doi.org/10.1007/978-3-030-62460-6_28

There are many limitations in 5th generation mobile communication technology although it is still in implementation process [3, 4], such as high data traffic, latency, security, energy efficiency, frequency bands for which researchers have already started to work on 6th generation (6G) system which will have various innovations and technologies which 5G and its preceding technologies lack. As networks will need to share more amount of data with high speed, machine type communication will get progress connecting not just people, but vehicles, devices, and sensors. There is no uncertainty that due to the concept of pervasive artificial intelligence (AI), 6G is becoming a hot topic in the scientific world. The rise of the massive usability of AI will be the main reason for the enfranchising of 6G.

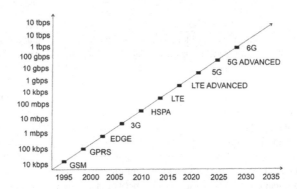

Fig. 1. Wireless roadmap to 2035

From data mining to network arrangement, AI will be present at all surfaces. To fulfill the requirements of users that are increasing rapidly each year along with their need for high data throughput with secure communication. 6G is expected to gain attention near 2030 and it will become the major requirement of users. Table 1 shows how the requirements and characteristics may become key performance indicators in 6G against 5G.

Table 1. Comparison of key characteristics of 5G and 6G

Characteristics	5G	6G
Data Rate UL	10 Gbps	1 Tbps
Data Rate DL	20 Gbps	1–10 Tbps
Latency Rate	1 ms	<0.1 ms
Spectral Efficiency (SE)	30 Bps	100 Bps
Visible Light Communication (VLC)	No	Yes
Pervasive AI	No	Yes
Real-Time Buffering	Not available	Available
THz Communication	No	Yes
Cell-Free Networks	Conceivable	Yes
Satellite Integration	No	Yes
Intelligent Reflecting Surfaces (IRS)	Conceivable	Yes
Uniform User Experience	50 Mbps	10 Gbps

In this paper, we will discuss various key technologies and challenges for 6G. We will try to determine the innovative aspects of the 6G technological development and explore the profound literature framework to get the answer about technological areas of 6G. The first section of this paper provides an overview of key technologies assumed to be used in 6th generation technology (6G). The second section provides the challenges and problems to deal with the limitations of 6G.

2 Key Technologies

There is no lack of conviction that 6G will look much better than 5G, but to achieve the goals for 6G some major leap forwards are required. There are various key technologies of 6G which we expect can fulfill the requirements for the improvement of the system. These key technologies include

2.1 Virtual Reality

Virtual reality or Artificial intelligence will be the main reason for the development of 6th generation communication technology. Since the advancement of IoT (Internet of Things), mobile communication technologies are becoming more and more important for better usage of technological devices. From self-driving cars to air traffic, every technology needs higher data throughput with low latency. Though 5G networks already offering downloading speed of up to 600 MB to 10 GB and have the potential to get significantly faster as compared to previous 4th generation technology which offers much less speed than 5G. But 6G will offer even much faster speed, the current estimate is that they could approach 1 TB per second. To achieve the goal of complete usage of artificial intelligence, researchers and scientists are already looking for 6G which will become a key enabling force behind an entirely new generation of applications for machine intelligence. Semantic communication and machine learning will have some major roles in AI for 6G [5, 6]. Based on Shannon's classical information theory, Semantic communication can tremendously improve the efficiency of communication by enabling semantic interference. Machine learning by enabling self-organization strategies can greatly enhance the communication system in 6G on the network level. Also in the process of deployment of AI, intelligent agents trained in the cloud using machine learning algorithms on Big Data will be deployed in the real world in the next decades which can unravel multiple optimization problems. Like 5G, 6G will not use the traditional algorithms of AI. To utilize the true power of AI, collaborative AI will be the key [7], which will revolutionize the world.

2.2 Terahertz (THz) Communication

Terahertz is a unit of frequency which is defined as one trillion (1012) cycles per second or 1012 Hz. Terahertz technology has the capability for employment in future wireless systems in a short-range. Terahertz communication is rising as the imminent technology to facilitate Terabits per second link (Tbps) with various spotlight features such as high throughput and trivial latency [8, 9]. Photonic technologies are being used for the generation of terahertz waves. Terahertz waves lie between the microwave band and infrared band in the electromagnetic spectrum as shown in Fig. 2. Terahertz (THz) frequency range (0.1 THz–3 THz) is the last span in the whole electromagnetic wave spectrum and is described as a THz GAP in the world of science.

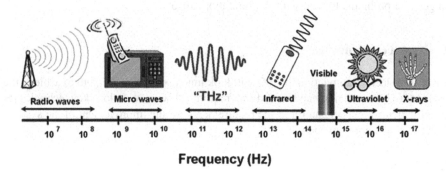

Frequency (Hz)

Fig. 2. Electromagnetic spectrum

Several issues limit the practicality of networks using lower frequency bands. To counter these limitations, terahertz communication technology can provide up to the Tbps link to fulfill the communication demand such as high throughput and low latency. THz is appropriate for developing a wireless telecommunication system that can provide a very high speed of 100 Gb/s. The efficacy of Terahertz technology is propitious for high-speed information transmission between electronic devices; creating wireless local area networks (WLANs) and wireless personal area networks (WPANs). Due to the limitation of transmission distance the THz wireless communications can be widely used for indoor application scenarios. The deployment of terahertz systems needs a strong understanding and precise modeling of channel conditions between the receiver (RX) and transmitter (TX). There are many key technologies for the realization of THz wireless systems including THz solid-state superheterodyne receiver, THz modulators, THz channel model, THz channel estimation, THz beamforming, and THz beam tracking. There are two different kinds of THz communication systems; Solid-state THz wireless communication system and spatial direct modulation THz communication system. The major difference in both of these systems is solid-state system is based on the frequency mixing mechanism, and the spatial direct modulation system is based on the baseband signals which are directly modulated into the radio frequency [10]. As we explore more about Terahertz (THz) communications, we find more technical challenges in the implementation of this communication system. Though THz provides huge bandwidth, the band deteriorates from high atmospheric losses. In THz band, antennas become smaller so to invoke communication we have to use high-gain directional antennas over distances surpassing a few meters. The concept of Ultra-Massive MIMO is formulated which depends on embracing ultra-dense frequency-tunable plasmonic nano-antenna arrays that are utilized which increases distance and also achieving higher data rates at THz frequencies [11].

2.3 Visible Light Communication

Visible light communication (VLC) can become a major technology for 6th generation wireless communication systems. VLC has great potential for progress over the next decade, bridging the existing efficiency gap between VLC and 5G technology that has already proved the experience of Gbps and will reach the Tbps with 6G technology. One potential alternative strategy for future 6G networks is to utilize the visible spectrum for visible light communication to have optical fiber-like output.

VLC is the type of communication in which data is sent wireless through the air with modulation of light waves from the visible spectrum with a range of 380 nm to 750 nm wavelengths [12]. This technology revolves around the principle of intensity modulation of solid-state infrastructure provided by light-emitting diodes (LEDs). One key advantage of VLC is providing an additional spectrum of approximately 300 THz of bandwidth which is much larger than traditional radio-frequency based access networks. VLC is one of the promising technology due to its features of non-licensed channels, high bandwidth, and low power consumption [13]. While the implementation of VLC technology, omnidirectional features can be achieved by using numerous transmitting elements [14].

2.4 Radio Stripes

Network densification was one of the major ideas for the deployment of massive MIMO 5G communication. Many large scale antennas were deployed on base stations distributed in many cells. Although there were many advantages of cellular massive MIMO networks like improved beamforming and facilitating more users in the large area through coordination between access points (APs) in small cells still it has some limitations in signal strength in beamforming and inter-cell interference which needs to be addressed. For this purpose, the new concept of cell-free massive MIMO is already in discussion in the world of wireless communication. Just like traditional MIMO networks, communication in cell-free massive MIMO will happen through coordinated multipoint. Deployment of this cell-free massive MIMO will happen with a congruous cost-effective framework Radio Stripes System (Fig. 3).

In February 2019, Ericsson proposed a radio stripes system. They presented that we can achieve great performance through distributed MIMO but it is inoperable to deploy it due to its high cost. To ease the deployment, we need to employ a radio stripe system. In the radio stripe system, the antennas and APUs are integrated inside a single cable [15]. Deployment of antenna elements with radio stripes system will not just make it easy to deploy large-scale antennas but it will also provide robust performance. At the Mobile World Congress (MWC) event in Barcelona, Ericsson suggested that radio stripes system will give pervasive effectuation and connectivity. From public transport to stations to shopping malls, deployment of radio stripes system is not just easy due to invisibility and cost-efficiency but also provides magnificent performance. This change

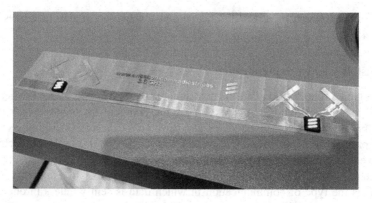

Fig. 3. Ericsson's radio stripe

of distributed antenna systems over a stripe is a great step towards future technologies and will play an important role in the deployment of 6G mobile systems.

2.5   Quantum Networks Communication

When the Quantum networks and quantum internet will be fully implemented on a wide scale the communication will be revolutionized, people will not only encounter the faster speed also the secure communication compared to the current system. The high data rate and security are the features that will play an important role in the usage of quantum communication in 6G technology [16]. Researchers employed the principle of entanglement, which tangled photons to transferal information among two nodes, where half of the photons are owned by the sender, while the receiver owns the other half. Photons are manipulated to communicate, causing an instant change in conforming photons. Entanglement, however, is the object of decoupling and the theorem of no cloning. Entangled particles become disentangled due to their strong interaction with the surrounding environment. No cloning theorem states that unknown quantum states cannot be copied.

Additionally, each node of a quantum network comprises of Quantum processors relying on qubits as a replacement of conventional bits. Qubits can also be defined as superposition and may occur in multi-state, which allows them to accomplish numerous calculations at one time whereas, the conventional bits are restrained to only 0 and 1 restricting them to one calculation at one time. While one quantum processor alters its photons state, the tangled photons in the equivalent quantum processor also alter, allowing them to transfer essential qubits. One of the advantages is, this is an unhackable communication system, any attempt of snoop or – the information will disengage the system. The information will be altered and notify that the hacking assault occurred. Though existing applications are inadequate but have been employed magnificently in quantum key distribution. Because the tangled photons instantly transmit information, this makes it faster than the conventional system.

To overcome the difficulty of long-distance communication academia has employed quantum repeaters. These repeaters are placed among the sender and receiver. The motive of these repeaters is to store the tangled photons by the sender and receiver. If accomplished entanglement swap with Bell state measurements, the photons of both receiver and sender can be tangled over a long distance. Although researchers have developed resourceful methods to suppress the problems still a handful of quantum repeaters are required even in primary quantum networks.

2.6   Large Intelligent Surface (IRS)

Large Intelligent Surface (LIS), also known as Intelligent Reflecting Surface (IRS) is considered as a prominent energy-efficient technology for the 6G communication system which can get unprecedented Massive MIMO output gains. 5G networks used Massive MIMO system for the communication system to get improved spectral and energy efficiency where base stations are equipped with a very large number of antenna arrays, thereby scaling up the conventional MIMO systems by many orders of magnitude. The difference which the IRS makes is that IRS contains low-cost passive reflecting elements [17], which are low-cost and consume less energy that can reconfigure the controlled propagation environment. The resulting IRS can be readily integrated into walls, ceilings, and facades of buildings. It has the potential to reduce energy consumption significantly.

Figure 4 shows communications using Intelligent Reflecting Surface (IRS) where the base station is out of the line of sight from the user equipment (UEs) due to tree. Each reflecting element induces a certain phase shift on the incident electromagnetic wave which will make the propagation channel more favorable for users. In 6G networks, IRS will play a fundamental role and will satisfy the various quality of services (QoS).

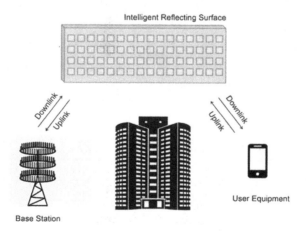

Fig. 4. IRS assisted communication system

3 Technological Challenges

There are many advantages of 6G over 5G and previous networks which will make way for its implementation but at the same time, there will be many hurdles that require special attention. Some of these hurdles are already being considered and addressed in 5G but no decisive answer was found.

3.1 Advanced Access Network

6G will provide very high data rates but an adequate growth of the backhaul capacity will be required [18, 19]. The deployment of VLC and THz communication systems will further increase the density of access points. These access points are geographically distributed and pervasive. For various types of applications and users, each of these access points will support very high data rate connections for communication. To avoid the creation of bottleneck, the backhaul networks in 6G have to manage the immense amount of data for communication between the access points and the centralized network to provide high data rate services to users. To cope with this challenge, there may be many solutions like quantum communications and exploring capacity of 6G access technologies for solutions of self-backhauling where radio stations provide both access and backhaul services. When the access and the backhaul share the same wireless channel with time, frequency, and space. The major benefit will be the easy deployment of dense network in a more integrated manner by counting on many control and data channels defined for providing access to the user equipment (UEs) as shown in Fig. 5.

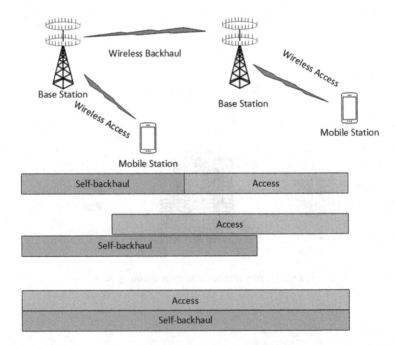

Fig. 5. Advanced backhaul architecture

3.2   Terahertz (THz) Frequencies

Recent development indicates that frequencies in the THz range and above will be considered for 6G. Many terahertz (THz) free bands will be available to satisfy the requirement of high data rates with increased bandwidth. 5G introduces mm-Wave with wider bandwidths for higher data rates but due to lack of propagation modeling and channel understanding, the 5G spectrum may not exceed 140 GHz. However, 6G will utilize spectrum beyond 140 GHz but still, there will be many challenges including the range of communication and size of antennas that needs to be addressed in the future. The propagation properties of mmWave and sub-mmWave (THz) are susceptible to environmental conditions; thus, the results are absorbent and dispersive [20]. The atmospheric situation is often complex, and therefore very unstable. Hence this band's channel modeling is relatively complex, and there is no ideal channel model in this band. In the recent development, Rohde and Schwarz presented the system at the EuMW2019 workshop held in Paris on mm-Wave and THz frequencies. The target of the workshop was on frequencies above 100 GHz, where the primary focus was on D-band (150 GHz) and H-band (300 GHz). The research resulted in a system that allows signal generation and signals analysis at 300 GHz and 2 GHz bandwidth. Fundamental research is on carrier frequencies above 300 GHz as it will be appropriate for THz communication.

3.3   Devices Capacity

As artificial intelligence will be the key factor of 6G communications. Like every other generation, 6G will also be defined by user equipment capability and requires very high computational power to run the algorithms of AI. UEs will need more power and to make them more efficient will be a major challenge for companies working on building UEs. Notables companies launched 5G enabled devices but the working of these devices is still under observation. Conventional devices are not energy efficient and they produce excessive heat that needs to be improved and devices will be designed with new materials and design to fulfill the requirements of emerging systems of the future.

3.4   Mobile Edge Computing

Edge computing is a technology which is proposed before 4G and remains as a challenge in its implementation. The concept of MEC enables cloud computing and IT services at the edge of the network for ease of users. Mobile edge computing MEC is used for the reduction of latency to the applications and services as well as much more bandwidth consumption saving [21], but there are some major challenges in implementing MEC from which some are addressed even in 5G but it further needs to be addressed in the research of 6G. Some of these challenges are mobile data and computation offloading, policy control, session management function (SMF), user plane function (UPF), edge cloud infrastructure, and convergence with network function virtualization (NFV). A layered architecture based on the NFV concept, WI Cloud can be used [22], for providing network function and compute resources which will change the conventional elements of network and cloud computing (Fig. 6).

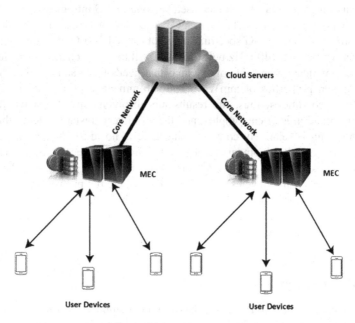

Fig. 6. Mobile edge computing architecture

3.5 Tactual Communication

Upcoming usage of holographic communication is to convert virtual views close to people's reality, behavior, environments, etc. Exchanging physical contact remotely via a real-time Internet connection is advantageous. The anticipated facilities involve telecommunications, the automated cooperative reader, and interpersonal communications that will enable random control to be applied across communication networks. To meet these strict requirements, the effective design of the communication framework between the rows must be carried out. For example, new physical layer diagrams (PHY) must be developed to enhance transfer and motivated protocol for the design of signaling systems, congestion of waveforms, etc. Wireless communication systems cannot meet that standard and it needs wireless fiber communication systems [23, 24].

3.6 Security

Security is a key issue for 6G wireless networks, especially when employing the Terrestrial Space Integrated Network (STIN) technology. In 6G other modes of security, such as advanced network security, should be considered collectively in addition to traditional physical layer security. Hence, new security solutions worth more extensive research, depending on low complexity and having high safety standards. To this extent, other physical layer security approaches proposed for 5G can be applied to 6G systems, like Low-Density Parity Check (LDPC)-based protected massive MIMO; protected mm-Wave techniques might also be sufficient for UM-MIMO and THz band applications. For integrated network security, diverse security domains need to have a suitable management objective for various functions. A centralized distribution control system is a good framework for STIN that takes diverse management into accounts and certificate less communication keys. These physical and network layer protection approaches will combine this comprehensive protection approach with efficient administration and operation, which effectively preserves sensitive information and anonymity on 6G networks [25].

4 Conclusion

In this paper, we surveyed key technologies that will help in the future to work more efficiently on 6G. 6G will provide a very high data rate and capacity, all around there will be no drop in quality of data throughput regardless of the number of user equipment (UEs) connected to the network during the same time. We have analyzed different technologies regarding the development of 6G standards and discussed how Terahertz (THz) communication can become a major difference between previous generations and the 6th generation communication system and how by using all of these technologies, the requirements of AI applications will be fulfilled. Due to innovation and an increase in demand for artificial intelligence, THz communication along with Radio Stripes and quantum networks will be able to fulfill the requirement of high data rates and security for applications. We also presented some major challenges for 6G, such as the range of communication and size of antennas in THz frequencies of THz communication system and the capability of devices to ascribe with new technologies.

Acknowledgment. This paper is funded by the International Exchange Program of Harbin Engineering University for Innovation-oriented Talents Cultivation.

References

1. Tariq, F., et al.: A Speculative Study on 6G (2019)
2. Zhao, Y., Yu, G., Xu, H.: 6G mobile communication network: vision. Challenges Key Technol. (2019). https://doi.org/10.1360/n112019-00033
3. Nawaz, F., et al.: A review of vision and challenges of 6G technology. Int. J. Adv. Comput. Sci. Appl. **11** (2020). https://doi.org/10.14569/ijacsa.2020.0110281
4. Saad, W., Bennis, M., Chen, M.: A vision of 6G wireless systems: applications, trends, technologies, and open research problems. IEEE Netw. 1–9 (2019)
5. Strinati, E.C., et al.: 6G: the next frontier: from holographic messaging to artificial intelligence using subterahertz and visible light communication. IEEE Veh. Technol. Mag. **14**(3), 42–50 (2019)

6. Nawaz, S.J., Sharma, S.K., Wyne, S., Patwary, M.N., Asaduzzaman, M.: Quantum machine learning for 6G communication networks: state-of-the-art and vision for the future. IEEE Access **7**, 46317–46350 (2019)
7. Stoica, R.-A., Abreu, G.: 6G: the wireless communications network for collaborative and AI applications (2019)
8. Yuan, Y., Zhao, Y., Zong, B., Parolari, S.: Potential key technologies for 6G mobile communications. Sci. China Inf. Sci. **63**(8), 1–19 (2020). https://doi.org/10.1007/s11432-019-2789-y
9. Ghafoor, S., et al.: MAC protocols for terahertz communication: a comprehensive survey (2019)
10. Chen, Z., et al.: A survey on terahertz communications. China Commun. **16**(2), 1–35 (2019)
11. Elayan, H., et al.: Terahertz band: the last piece of RF spectrum puzzle for communication systems (2019)
12. Matheus, L.E.M., et al.: Visible light communication: concepts, applications, and challenges. IEEE Commun. Surv. Tutor. **21**, 3204–3237 (2019)
13. Khan, L.U.: Visible light communication: applications, architecture, standardization, and research challenges. Digit. Commun. Netw. **3**(2), 78–88 (2017)
14. Chen, C., Bian, R., Haas, H.: Omnidirectional transmitter and receiver design for wireless infrared uplink transmission in LiFi, pp. 1–6 (2018)
15. Interdonato, G., et al.: Ubiquitous cell-free massive MIMO communications. EURASIP J. Wirel. Commun. Netw. (2019)
16. Hosseinidehaj, N., Malaney, R.: Quantum entanglement distribution in next-generation wireless communication systems (2016)
17. Wu, Q., Zhang, R.: Intelligent reflecting surface enhanced wireless network via joint active and passive beamforming. IEEE Trans. Wirel. Commun. **18**(11), 5394–5409 (2019)
18. Giordani, M., et al.: Towards 6G networks: use cases and technologies (2019)
19. Chowdhury, M.Z., Shahjalal, M., Hasan, M.K., Jang, Y.M.: The role of optical wireless communication technologies in 5G/6G and IoT solutions: prospects, directions, and challenges. Appl. Sci. **9**, 4367 (2019)
20. Golovachev, Y., Etinger, A., Pinhasi, G.A., Pinhasi, Y.: Propagation properties of sub-millimeter waves in foggy conditions. J. Appl. Phys. **125**, 151612 (2019)
21. Yu, Y.: Mobile edge computing towards 5G: vision, recent progress, and open challenges. China Commun. **13**(Suppl. 2), 89–99 (2016)
22. Li, H., et al.: Mobile edge computing: progress and challenges. In: 2016 4th IEEE International Conference on Mobile Cloud Computing, Services, and Engineering (MobileCloud) (2016)
23. Simsek, M., Aijaz, A., Dohler, M., Sachs, J., Fettweis, G.: 5G-enabled tactile internet. IEEE J. Sel. Areas Commun. **34**(3), 460–473 (2016)
24. Kim, K.S., et al.: Ultrareliable and low-latency communication techniques for tactile internet services. Proc. IEEE **107**(2), 376–393 (2019)
25. Yang, P., Xiao, Y., Xiao, M., Li, S.: 6G wireless communications: vision and potential techniques. IEEE Netw. **33**(4), 70–75 (2019)

Q-Learning-Based Adaptive Bacterial Foraging Optimization

Ben Niu[1,2] and Bowen Xue[1(✉)]

[1] College of Management, Shenzhen University, Shenzhen 518060, China
drniuben@gmail.com, isxuebowen@163.com
[2] Great Bay Area International Institute for Innovation, Shenzhen University,
Shenzhen 518060, China

Abstract. As a common biological heuristic algorithm, Bacterial Foraging Optimization (BFO) is often used to solve optimization problems. Aiming at increasing the solution accuracy and convergence performance while enhancing the capability of individual's self-learning and exploration, a Q-Learning-Based Adaptive Bacterial Foraging Optimization (QABFO) is proposed in this paper. The basic chemotaxis, reproduction and elimination/dispersal operations in standard BFO are redesigned in a Q-learning mechanism, and the Q-table will be updated on the basis of the changed fitness values in each iteration. In chemotaxis operation, modified search direction and secondary cruising mechanism are introduced into tumbling and swimming behaviors, with the purpose of improving the search efficiency and balancing local and global search. Additionally, a generation skipping adaptive reproduction is designed to control the accuracy and convergence of QABFO. Experimental results demonstrate that compared with BFO, PSO and GA, the proposed algorithm performs better in terms of accuracy and stability on most of the test functions and can effectively improve the premature convergence problem due to the original reproduction operation in BFO.

Keywords: Bacterial foraging optimization · Q-learning · Generation skipping adaptive reproduction

1 Introduction

Reinforcement learning (RL) is a trial and error way to consider the interaction between agents and the environment. Its purpose is to maximize the long-term future rewards. Nowadays, it has been a trend to improve biological heuristic algorithms with the mechanism of RL. As a typical algorithm of reinforcement learning, Q-learning has been applied to Genetic Algorithm (GA) [1, 2], Particle Swarm Optimization (PSO) [3, 4], Bacterial Foraging Optimization (BFO) [5, 6] and so on. Because of Q-learning algorithm, individuals in those algorithms can choose policies based on the rewards they get from interacting with the environment without external inputs.

Passino [7] first proposed BFO based on the foraging behavior, information exchange mechanism, growth and propagation of E. coli in the human intestine, in which chemotaxis, reproduction and elimination/dispersal operations are designed to

© Springer Nature Switzerland AG 2020
X. Chen et al. (Eds.): ML4CS 2020, LNCS 12487, pp. 327–337, 2020.
https://doi.org/10.1007/978-3-030-62460-6_29

solve optimization problems. Following Passino, a series of improvements on BFO have emerged during the recent years. On the one hand, some literature focused on the improvement and adjustment of the original three operations. Pang et al. [8] introduced an adaptive Lévy flight step-size mechanism into chemotaxis operation to regulate the search processes. Niu et al. [9] proposed CSRBFO with only chemotaxis and elimination/dispersal operations, which reduced computational complexity of BFO. On the other hand, some researches combined BFO with other classical algorithms. Nithya et al. [10] combined BFO with GA and studied the parameters in the dynamic nature of environment. Panwar et al. [11] investigated a novel combination of BFO and PSO, which was applied to a hydro dominating energy system. Han et al. [6] introduced reinforcement learning mechanism and cross operation into BFO, and tackled the problem of risk scheduling using a knowledge transfer matrix.

Based on the literatures above, we embed an improved BFO algorithm into the framework of Q-learning and propose the Q-learning-based adaptive bacterial foraging optimization (QABFO). In order to cater to the strengthening effect of Q-learning on local search and shortcomings like poor convergence performance and low solution accuracy in BFO, we make a series of improvements, including an enhanced chemotaxis to increase the search efficiency and avoid falling into local optimal solutions, and a generation skipping adaptive reproduction to improve premature convergence. In addition, the bacterial individuals pay more attention to the information interaction within the whole swarm while using its own Q-table, which contributes to the balance of exploration and exploitation.

This paper is organized as follows. In Sect. 2, we introduce BFO and Q-learning algorithms, explain how they combine with each other and show the structure and calculation of Q-table. In Sect. 3, we list the improvement of chemotaxis, reproduction and elimination/dispersal operations in BFO. Section 4 shows the experimental results and analyses and the conclusions are presented in Sect. 5.

2 Q-Learning-Based Adaptive Bacterial Foraging Optimization

2.1 Bacterial Foraging Optimization

Bacterial foraging optimization is a bionic random searching algorithm that simulates the foraging process of Escherichia coli. It includes three operations: chemotaxis, reproduction and elimination/dispersal. More detailed information is shown in [7].

2.2 Q-Learning

Q-learning is a value-based and iterative learning method in reinforcement learning. State, action and reward are three important terms in this algorithm. A Q-table records the cumulative rewards that can be obtained from the environment by selecting action in current state st. More details can be found in [12].

2.3 Combination of BFO and Q-Learning

In QABFO, we regard chemotaxis and elimination/dispersal operations as two alternative "actions/states" of a bacterium, the location of one bacterium represents a candidate solution. One bacterium delegates one agent and has its own sub Q-table. In a single iteration, a bacterium chooses an action with the highest accumulative Q-value in its sub Q-table. When the bacterium finishes this action, the global optimal solutions will be recorded and the Q-table will be updated based on the rewards generated by bacterial interaction with the environment.

When meeting the condition *iter* > *maxIter*/2, all the bacteria will be adaptively and generationally reproduced according to the rules in reproduction operation. It is worth noting that reproduction is not an action in Q-table, because compared with the chemotaxis and elimination/dispersal actions, the effect of reproduction operation on the improvement of fitness value is more obvious and there is no confrontation among them when making a choice.

Q-Table Structure. The whole Q-table of the bacterial swarm is constructed by sub Q-tables of Np individuals. All sub Q-tables are independent of each other and the choice of a feasible solution is parallel. In a sub Q-table, we regard the former action space as the next state space, the rows and columns represent the current state spaces (chemotaxis, elimination/dispersal) and the action spaces (chemotaxis, elimination/dispersal) of an individual, respectively.

$$Q = [Q1, Q2, \cdots, QNp] \tag{1}$$

For example, the sub Q-table of the 24th individual in 3746th iteration on Rosenbrock function is shown in Table 1.

Table 1. Sub Q-table of the 24th individual in 3746th iteration on Rosenbrock function.

Q-values		Action spaces	
		Chemotaxis	Elimination/Dispersal
State spaces	Chemotaxis	−5.0022e−01	1.7493e+00
	Elimination/Dispersal	9.9991e−01	1.3186e+00

Table 1 shows in the 3746th iteration, the accumulative rewards of choosing chemotaxis and elimination/dispersal actions in chemotaxis state for the 24th individual are −5.0022e−01 and 1.7493e+00. And in elimination/dispersal state, the accumulative rewards are 9.9991e−01 and 1.3186e+00.

Update of Q-Table. At the beginning, we set a Q-table as an empty table with zero values. In the first iteration, all bacteria perform chemotaxis actions. Then in the following iterations, we compare the current fitness value of each bacteria with its fitness value in last iteration and get a reward $r_{t+1}^i \in \{-1, 0, 1\}$.

$$r_{t+1}^i = \begin{cases} 1 \; if \; J_{t+1}^i < J_t^i \\ 0 \; if \; J_{t+1}^i = J_t^i \\ -1 \; otherwise \end{cases} \tag{2}$$

In Eq. (2), J_{t+1}^i is the new fitness value of ith individual. Then after chemotaxis and elimination/dispersal actions, the ith sub Q-table will be updated on the basis of the following recursive equations:

$$st + 1 = at \tag{3}$$

$$\alpha(t) = \alpha start - \frac{\alpha start - \alpha end}{tmax} t \tag{4}$$

$$Qi(st, at) = Qi(st, at) + \alpha(t)[r_{t+1}^i + \gamma \max_a Qi(st+1, a) - Qi(st, at)] \tag{5}$$

Equation (3) means the next state is equivalent to the current action. In Eqs. (4) and (5), t is the number of current iteration and $tmax$ is the number of total iterations, $\alpha(t) \in [0, 1]$ is a learning factor and $\gamma \in [0, 1]$ is a discount factor, $\alpha start$ and αend are the initial and final learning factors, respectively. Additionally, in the reproduction operation, a sub Q-table will be updated according to the position changes of bacterial individuals, thus causing the update of the whole Q-table.

3   Three Key Operations in QABFO

In view of the shortcomings of the original BFO and the influence of Q-learning mechanism on the proposed algorithm, we make some corresponding improvements on the traditional chemotaxis, elimination/dispersal and reproduction operations.

3.1   Enhanced Chemotaxis

Aiming to tackle with the common problems in traditional BFO algorithm, such as low search efficiency, easily falling into a local optimum and weakened global search ability due to self-learning mechanism in Q-learning, we mainly focus on the optimization of tumbling and swimming behaviors.

Modified Search Direction. In the tumbling process of classical BFO, each bacterium randomly chooses one direction containing D-dimensions. However, not every dimension can obtain a right direction, and there is mutual interference between those dimensions, which reduces the search efficiency. Therefore, inspired by Pang et al. [8], we use the following method to propose the direction vector $\Phi i'$ (shown in Fig. 1) to make bacteria tumble randomly on only one dimension.

The choosen dimension to tumble

$$\Phi_i{'}=(\underbrace{\ldots,0,0,\ldots,-1 \overset{\Updownarrow}{or} 1,\ldots,0,0,\ldots}_{D \ dimensions \ of \ \Phi_i{'}})$$

Fig. 1. Structure of the direction vector $\Phi_i{'}$.

- Step1: Randomly select a number from 1 and -1 as a direction of tumbling;
- Step2: Randomly select one dimension to tumble among the D-dimensions;
- Step3: Set the selected dimension value to 1, and other dimension values to 0 to build the direction vector $\Phi_i{'}$ of the ith bacterium.

Then, the location θ_d^i of ith bacterium at d^{th} dimension is calculated as follows:

$$C(t) = C_{start} - \frac{C_{start} - C_{end}}{t_{max}} t \tag{6}$$

$$\theta_d^i(t+1) = \theta_d^i(t) + C(t)\Phi_i \tag{7}$$

Where $C(t)$ is a self-adaptive swimming step unit determined by t and t_{max} [13], C_{start} is the initial swimming step and C_{end} is the final swimming step.

Secondary Cruising Mechanism. In the chemotaxis operation of classical BFO, a bacterium will stop its local search when encountering a worse fitness value. Aiming to enhance the search ability and avoid falling into a local optimal solution, we nest a secondary cruising mechanism into the process of bacterial swimming. When a bacterium reached a position with a worse fitness value, it can tumble and swim again until they meet the chemotaxis termination condition $m = N_s$, where m is the counter for swim length.

Due to the fact that a bacterium choose an action on the basis of a shared-nothing sub Q-table, the mechanism of Q-learning strengthens the capability of local search, making it easy to be trapped in local optimal solutions. In BFO, the original swarming mechanism based on attraction and repulsion signals can play a role in strengthening the global search ability. Therefore, in addition to considering the information exchange mechanism of bacterial swarming, we also take the global optimal fitness value J_{gbest} as the criterion $c_{Jgb}(c_{Jgb} = J_{gbest})$ for a bacterium to decide whether to continue the swimming behavior or to implement the secondary cruising mechanism:

$$\begin{cases} swim, \ c_{Jgb} = J_{t+1}^i & if \ J_{t+1}^i < c_{Jgb} \\ Secondary \ cruising & otherwise \end{cases} \tag{8}$$

3.2 Elimination/Dispersal

Because the environment in which bacteria live may have favorable or unfavorable changes, such as the rise and fall of temperature, the increase or decrease of food and so on, there are usually death and migration behaviors among bacterial population, which we call elimination/dispersal. It takes place with a certain probability, and we assume it to be P_{ed}. According to [5, 6], we update the position of ith bacterium as follows:

$$\theta^i(t+1) = \begin{cases} rand1(\theta_{\max} - \theta_{\min}) + rand2(\theta_{gbest} - \theta^i(t)) & rand3 > P_{ed} \\ \theta_{gbest} & otherwise \end{cases} \quad (9)$$

Where $rand1, rand2, rand3 \in (0, 1)$ are three random numbers and θ_{gbest} is the position of the global optimal bacterium. $\theta_{\min}, \theta_{\max}$ are the boundaries of the bacterial positions.

3.3   Generation Skipping Adaptive Reproduction

In our algorithm, reproduction is not an alternative action in the Q-table but it is still a necessary action for the bacteria swarm. In original BFO, the sorting operation is carried out first, and then only half of the individuals with higher fitness value will be kept. Then the swarm will reproduce to keep the amount of bacterial population unchanged. However, the search process will meet the termination of the algorithm quickly and the optimal fitness value will stay unchanged after meeting a sharp decline in a short time especially when combined with the Q-learning mechanism. The reason of the premature convergence is that the number of current optimal individuals and their offspring increases exponentially after each generation's reproduction operation, the speed of reserving the best is too fast and the range is too concentrated.

As a result, the way to reproduce is the key to control the convergence and accuracy of our algorithm. Thus we propose the generation skipping adaptive reproduction mechanism when meeting the condition $t > t_{max}/2$, this mechanism will be implemented several generations apart and the number of reserved optimal individuals N_{res} will increase with the number of iterations linearly.

Additionally, small intergenerational step size leads to premature convergence and local optimization while large step size weakens the ability to reserve the optimal individuals in reproduction operation. Thus, we set the intergenerational step size s_{re} to 5.

$$N_{res}(t) = \left\lfloor (t - \frac{t_{max}}{2}) \Big/ \frac{t_{max}}{2N_p} \right\rfloor + 1 \quad (10)$$

$$Swarm(1 : Np, t+1) = [Swarm_{sort}(1 : N_{res}(t), t); Swarm_{sort}(1 : N_p - N_{res}(t), t)] \quad (11)$$

In the equations above, $N_{res}(t)$ is the number of reserved optimal individuals in iteration t, N_p is the bacterial population size and $Swarm$ represents the location, fitness value and Q-value of the bacteria swarm. $Swarm_{sort}$ is the bacteria in descending order of health values.

Finally, the whole searching process in QABFO is clearly illustrated in Fig. 2.

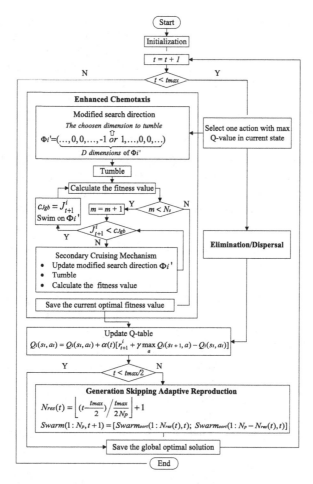

Fig. 2. The flow chart of QABFO.

4 Experiments and Analyses

4.1 Experimental Parameters Setting

We use six common benchmark functions to test the performance of QABFO, including three unimodel functions (Dixo_price, Schwefel and Rosenbrock) and three multimodel functions (Rastrigin, Ackley and Apline). In order to test the feasibility and effectiveness of Q-learning and the key improvements in QABFO algorithm, we select three biological heuristic algorithms BFO [13], PSO [5], and GA [15] for comparison. The parameter settings are consistent with the above literature.

Among the four algorithms, the dimension D of all benchmark functions is 30, the number of individuals N_p is 40, and the maximum iteration t_{max} in QABFO, BFO, PSO and GA is 10000. The elimination probabilities P_{ed} in QABFO and BFO are set to 0.25. More details of parameter settings are as follows.

- In QABFO, $N_s = 10$, $\gamma = 0.5$, $\alpha_{start} = 1$, $\alpha_{end} = 1$, $C_{start} = 0.01$, $C_{end} = 0.01$.
- In BFO, the number of chemotaxis, reproduction, elimination/dispersal and swimming are $N_c = 1000$, $N_r = 5$, $N_e = 2$, $N_s = 10$. The chemotaxis step $C = 0.1$.
- In PSO, the learning factors $c1, c2$ are set to 2 and the inertia weight $w = 0.9$.
- In GA, the crossover probability and mutation probability are $p_c = 0.65$ and $p_m = 0.1$, respectively.

4.2 Experimental Results and Analyses

We perform fifteen experiments on QABFO, BFO, PSO and GA for each benchmark function separately, and collate the mean, standard deviation, maximum, and minimum values of the optimal fitness values in Table 2. Then we obtain Fig. 3 based on the mean of optimal fitness values through fifteen trials for each algorithm.

Table 2. Comparison among QABFO, BFO, PSO and GA on six functions with thirty dimensions in fifteen experiments.

Functions	Metrics	QABFO	BFO	PSO	GA
Dixo_price	Mean	**5.16E−04**	5.33E+01	1.02E+00	2.37E+01
	Std	**5.57E−04**	2.81E+01	4.06E−01	5.18E+00
	Max	**1.71E−03**	1.33E+02	2.21E+00	3.36E+01
	Min	**1.06E−07**	1.93E+01	6.69E−01	1.58E+01
Schwefel	Mean	**3.84E−04**	7.04E+03	7.18E+03	1.11E+04
	Std	**7.36E−06**	1.97E+02	3.19E+02	5.66E+01
	Max	**4.10E−04**	7.34E+03	7.76E+03	1.12E+04
	Min	**3.82E−04**	6.79E+03	6.79E+03	1.10E+04
Rosenbrock	Mean	**1.69E−04**	2.55E+02	3.77E+01	1.96E+02
	Std	**1.38E−04**	7.94E+01	2.20E+01	3.73E+01
	Max	**4.77E−04**	4.09E+02	8.55E+01	2.80E+02
	Min	**4.70E−07**	1.51E+02	2.45E+01	1.40E+02
Rastrigin	Mean	**1.17E−03**	3.74E+02	8.24E+01	1.47E+02
	Std	**9.62E−04**	4.98E+01	2.39E+01	1.16E+01
	Max	**2.99E−03**	4.37E+02	1.35E+02	1.70E+02
	Min	**3.76E−05**	2.57E+02	4.58E+01	1.31E+02
Ackley	Mean	**2.91E−03**	2.12E+01	2.00E+01	1.15E+01
	Std	1.62E−03	1.16E−01	**3.40E−04**	6.30E−01
	Max	**7.90E−03**	2.14E+01	2.00E+01	1.31E+01
	Min	**8.86E−04**	2.10E+01	2.00E+01	1.05E+01
Apline	Mean	**8.81E−04**	9.57E+01	9.98E−01	1.52E+01
	Std	**6.03E−04**	1.04E+01	3.44E−01	1.47E+00
	Max	**2.35E−03**	1.12E+02	1.66E+00	1.74E+01
	Min	**3.02E−04**	8.11E+01	4.83E−01	1.28E+01

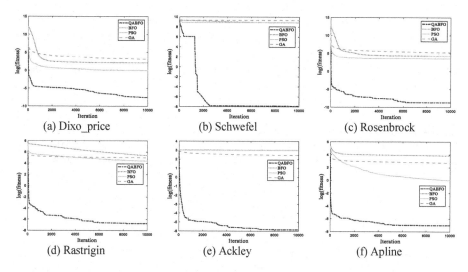

Fig. 3. Convergence curves of QABFO, BFO, PSO and GA on six benchmark functions.

From the experimental results in Table 2, we find that when using most of the benchmark functions, QABFO is superior to the other three algorithms in the four statistics, which shows that QABFO has high search accuracy and stability. For example, QABFO increases seven and eight orders of magnitude than BFO on Schwefel function when comparing the mean value and standard deviation value respectively. Nevertheless, in terms of multimodel like Ackley function, QABFO shows lower stability than PSO, but this gap is not obvious.

Figure 3 illustrates that QABFO can enhance the search ability and converges faster than BFO, PSO and GA algorithms on most of the benchmark functions. Besides, in comparison with BFO, the role of generation skipping adaptive reproduction operation in improving premature convergence is clearly reflected. However, in the later iteration part of the figures, QABFO does not converge on Dixo_price function.

5 Conclusions

This paper proposes a modified bacterial foraging algorithm (QABFO) with the consideration of Q-learning mechanism, which enables the bacterial individuals to determine their own actions based on the feedbacks they received from their interactions with the environment. In chemotaxis operation, we propose a single dimension direction selection and a secondary cruising mechanism. Then, we emphasize the global search capability by proposing an adaptive reproduction operation, through which the bacterial swarm has more opportunity to find better optimal fitness values. Finally, the proposed algorithm was compared with BFO, PSO and GA on six benchmark functions. The experimental results present that QABFO performs better on most of the functions with respect to search accuracy and convergence performance.

Our work has the following limitations that we can study in the future. First, this paper only considers single objective optimization problem, thus the multi-objective complex optimization based on the proposed QABFO will be one of our future research directions. Second, we only choose the chemotaxis and elimination/dispersal operations as two "actions/states" in Q-learning structure, and in the future, more alternative options could be explored, such as mutation and swarming.

Acknowledgement. This study is supported by Guangdong Province Soft Science Project (2019A101002075), Guangdong Province Educational Science Plan 2019 (2019JKCY010), Guangdong Province Bachelor and Postgraduate Education Innovation Research Project (2019SFKC46).

References

1. Teodoro, C.B., Viviana, C.M., Leandro, D.S.C.: Multi-objective optimization of the environmental-economic dispatch with reinforcement learning based on non-dominated sorting genetic algorithm. Appl. Therm. Eng. **146**, 688–700 (2019)
2. Young, D.K.: An efficient integration of the genetic algorithm and the reinforcement learning for optimal deployment of the wireless charging electric tram system. Comput. Ind. Eng. **128**, 851–860 (2019)
3. Almahdi, S., Yang, S.Y.: A constrained portfolio trading system using particle swarm algorithm and recurrent reinforcement learning. Expert Syst. Appl. **130**, 145–156 (2019)
4. Ding, S., Du, W., Zhao, X., Wang, L., Jia, W.: A new asynchronous reinforcement learning algorithm based on improved parallel PSO. Appl. Intell. **49**(12), 4211–4222 (2019). https://doi.org/10.1007/s10489-019-01487-4
5. Jiang, H., Dong, W., Ma, L., Wang, R.: Bacterial foraging algorithm based on reinforcement learning for continuous optimizations. In: Li, K., Li, W., Chen, Z., Liu, Y. (eds.) ISICA 2017. CCIS, vol. 873, pp. 41–52. Springer, Singapore (2018). https://doi.org/10.1007/978-981-13-1648-7_4
6. Han, C.J., Yang, B., Bao, T., Yu, T., Zhang, X.S.: Bacteria foraging reinforcement learning for risk-based economic dispatch via knowledge transfer. Energies **10**, 638 (2017)
7. Passino, K.M.: Biomimicry of bacterial foraging for distributed optimization and control. IEEE Control Syst. Mag. **22**(3), 52–67 (2002)
8. Pang, B., Song, Y., Zhang, C., Wang, H., Yang, R.: Bacterial foraging optimization based on improved chemotaxis process and novel swarming strategy. Appl. Intell. **49**(4), 1283–1305 (2018)
9. Niu, B., Liu, J., Wu, T., Chu, X.H., Wang, Z.X., Liu, Y.M.: Coevolutionary structure-redesigned-based bacterial foraging optimization. IEEE/ACM Trans. Comput. Biol. Bioinform. **15**(6), 1865–1876 (2018)
10. Nithya, S., Meena, K.: Genetic algorithm based bacterial foraging optimization with three-pass protocol concept for heterogeneous network security enhancement. J. Comput. Sci. **21**, 275–282 (2017)
11. Panwar, A., Sharma, G., Nasiruddin, I., Bansal, R.C.: Frequency stabilization of hydro–hydro power system using hybrid bacteria foraging PSO with UPFC and HAE. Electr. Power Syst. Res. **161**, 74–85 (2018)
12. Watkins, C.J.C.H., Dayan, P.: Q-learning. Mach. Learn. **8**(3), 279–292 (1992)
13. Niu, B., Wang, J.W., Wang, H.: Bacterial-inspired algorithms for solving constrained optimization problems. Neurocomputing **148**, 54–62 (2015)

14. Liu, Y., Passino, K.M.: Biomimicry of social foraging bacteria for distributed optimization: models, principles, and emergent behaviors. J. Optim. Theory Appl. **115**(3), 603–628 (2002)
15. Wang, H., Zuo, L., Liu, J., Yang, C., Li, Y., Baek, J.: A comparison of heuristic algorithms for bus dispatch. In: Tan, Y., Takagi, H., Shi, Y., Niu, B. (eds.) ICSI 2017. LNCS, vol. 10386, pp. 511–518. Springer, Cham (2017). https://doi.org/10.1007/978-3-319-61833-3_54

Counterfactual Retrieval
for Augmentation and Decisions

Nwaike Kelechi[1]([✉]) and Shuang Geng[2,3]

[1] School of Artificial Intelligence, Xidian University, Xi'an, China
kell21n@stu.xidian.edu.cn
[2] College of Management, Shenzhen University, Shenzhen, China
gs@szu.edu.cn
[3] Greater Bay Area International Institute for Innovation, Shenzhen University,
Shenzhen, China

Abstract. The optimal situation to make a decision is to have all variables in grasp. This however, almost never occurs. There has been research on counterfactuals as a way to provide more explainable systems and models. In furtherance of this research, this paper proposes CORFAD, Counterfactual Retrieval for Augmentation and Decisions. We explore user generated counterfactual tweets and by aggregating counterfactual statements that relate to pre-determined keywords, CORFAD simplifies data analysis by suggesting variables towards which future actions might have the greater or lesser effects towards a defined goal. This has the dual purpose of making synthetic counterfactual data generation more focused and less likely to generate non-useful explanations, while also able to stand alone to assist decision makers. This paper uses as test case, Counterfactual Statements connected with the Tesla Model 3 to explore insights that can guide decision-making in situations where multiple variables are possible and exist.

Keywords: Counterfactuals · Decision systems · Tweets

1 Introduction

The necessity of gaining insight into future effect given present cause, and investigating possible present effect given alternate past causes, has meant that causation and counterfactuals have been extensively studied. Even taking as reference a basic model whose states S and policy actions A over time T are recorded, generating counterfactuals to account for possible alternate states would soon become overwhelming, if there was no additional policy for the definition of which counterfactuals are useful or not. We go on to define the boundaries of a test case, as the experimental work in this paper is focused on counterfactual

This work was supported by the National Natural Science Foundation of China [71901150] and China Postdoctoral Science Foundation Grant [2019M663083], Guangdong Province Postgraduate Education Innovation Plan (2019SFKC46).

X. Chen et al. (Eds.): ML4CS 2020, LNCS 12487, pp. 338–346, 2020.
https://doi.org/10.1007/978-3-030-62460-6_30

tweets about the Tesla Model 3, a car available for purchase and in use by people around the world. Hypothetically, the decisions over which upgrade or combinations of upgrades will provide the most utility in the next manufacturing cycle will be taken with the consideration of variables across several domains [1], one of which will be customer feedback, and the exploration of decision making from real world Counterfactual tweets is the focus of this paper.

If the use case is framed as a question:

Would they be _____, if we did _____ ?

The spaces are left blank in part to show the many variations in which this question could be framed. This question now begins to look like a multi-armed bandit problem, such as described by [2]. But we can also express this using Pearl's do-calculus [3].

$$EU(x) = \sum_y Px(y)U(y) \tag{1}$$

Where the goal is to maximize the expected utility $EU(x)$, for upgrade (x), from a set of possible upgrades $do(X = x)$, $U(y)$ being the utility of outcome, and $P_x(y)$ the probability that an outcome $Y = y$ is realized had upgrade $do(X = x)$ been performed. We can quite simply insert Y and X respectively in the question. We might add that x can also be framed as a batch of actions, as the possible upgrades may be numerous and it could be difficult or needless to evaluate the utility of every single upgrade except those which contribute the highest utility.

Of particular note is that this question is futuristic, but unlike in many other applications of multi-armed bandits, Exploration and Exploitation strategies are not feasible for obvious reasons of time and expense, thus, given that we have past data, we resort to expressing it in counterfactual form, shifting the time of reference to the past [2].

Would they have _____ if we had _____?

Counterfactual statements come in various guises, and the example just given is an instance. The premise of a counterfactual statement is some event X that did not happen, and the possible action Y, if X had happened. X denotes the antecedent, which is the defining characteristic of the counterfactual, and Y denotes the consequent, which might only be implied or absent, as in the statement *I wish I had a Model 3*. We can thus express them in this way: if X, then Y or if X. Statements which qualify as counterfactual make up only a small fraction of the collective of user generated text that can be found on the internet, for example, only about 1 percent of tweets are counterfactual [4] and this mirrors the findings of our experiments where specific keyword searches on Twitter data, collated an occurrence of about 1.34%. The importance of Counterfactual Statements can be gauged from the reality that they have been studied across different domains for a long period of time, perhaps disproportionately to their occurrence. While there is a lot of extant research on counterfactuals, in various fields, we have not found any existing research on approaches to retrieve counterfactual feedback specific to keywords from tweets.

2   Related Work

There have been previous approaches to Synthetic counterfactual generation, and the technique adopted has usually been dependent on the use case. [6] demonstrated natural language counterfactual explanations to explain object recognition outputs, and another oft described application is in explaining loan rejections and housing prices, given available data from a built-up model. In the situations just described, the features of both models have boundaries, yet run into the difficulty of generating useful counterfactual explanations. However, there already exist tools able to generate counterfactuals, conditional on the availability of a pre-trained model and samples from a training data set. [7] By extracting real world counterfactual data, the search space for generating synthetic counterfactuals can be reduced, increasing the likelihood of generating useful counterfactuals. But again, with real world data such as tweets, there exists the inevitability of unreliability, the possibility that the author of the tweet may have been lying, [5], so that as with other social media data analysis models, we strive for safety in numbers. If instead, we had a significantly large number of semantically similar tweets from users largely saying *I wish that car had better acceleration*, we can consider such data actionable. There have not been publicly available implementations of retrieval of real-world counterfactuals similar to our purpose. There is the recognition that an accurate enough means of retrieval may have previously been unavailable, attributable perhaps to counterfactuals having implicit and explicit forms [8], and thus not reliably identified by the presence of specific words. Stochastic and linguistic rule methods have historically been very useful in Natural language tasks, and still are [9,10]. In Part-of-Speech tagging for instance, Probabilistic methods such as Conditional Random Fields (CRFs) and Hidden Markov Models (HMMs) are approaches to assign tags. Linguistic rules meanwhile, work very well for matching regular expressions and Context free grammars, but a draw back is that while they tend to work well in narrow and well-defined use cases, they do not seem to fare quite as well when adapted to a broad or generalized problem. The combination of a rule-based method and a supervised classifier was used by [4] to capture counterfactual tweets. They used words commonly found in counterfactuals (If, wish and other modals etc) to increase the likelihood of counterfactual tweets appearing in their searches and then manually built their train data set by annotating the tweets, also supplementing with tweets from each of the seven forms of counterfactuals they had identified as part of their work and then predicting on separate test data. Their work yielded an F1 score of 0.77.

3   Method

Newer language models have allowed the possibility of improved performance on many natural language tasks. But why should they be able to do this? A simple answer would be better architectures [11], more training data, and transfer learning [12]. Given that they are pre-trained on a large amount of data, 16 GB of uncompressed and text in the case of BERT [13], loosely related to the human way of reading books and getting an education,[1] Fine-tuning-tuning the models using domain specific data or feature extraction is important to achieve better results on tasks. The choice between fine-tuning and feature extraction depends on the system designer and specific task, as they can both be implemented across classification tasks with feature extraction faring slightly worse than fine-tuning, thus we opted for fine-tuning in building our model.We can think of this as a student revising his notes just before an examination. His revision notes might be a few pages he had jotted down in his study time,and thus we can understand that satisfactory fine-tuning can be achieved on a much smaller data set [14]. The data sets used for fine-tuning our models is derived from the SemEval2020 task; Modelling Causal Reasoning in Language: Detecting Counterfactuals [15].

The specific language models used in the experiment are the RoBERTa base model for the counterfactual retrieval and the BERT base model for the antecedent and consequent retrieval. The base models were chosen because of reduced computational requirements, enabling the experiments to be performed on a single GPU using Google Colab. While the larger models have marginally higher accuracy [13,19], on the downside they have higher computational requirements. [19] shows a comparative analysis of the performance differences of BERT and RoBERTa models in different language tasks.

Algorithm 1: Pipeline for Retrieving Counterfactuals

---

1 **Tweet Pre-processing** ;
2 Scrape Tweets;
3 Clean Tweets ;
4 **Prediction** ;
5 Load sequence language model ;
6 Predict over the data set;
7 Create a new data set with Counterfactual Tweets ;
8 Load token classification model ;
9 Predict over the data set ;
10 **Post processing**;
11 Extract antecedents and consequents;

3.1   Data Retrieval and Preparation

For this paper, we retrieved a small sample size of 10,000 tweets using the keywords *Tesla Model 3*, and *Model 3* and *The Model 3* from select days between October 2019 and Jan 2020. And while we experimented with other products with a worldwide reach such as DJI Mavic and Pepsi, It is intuitive that the

---

[1] A fair idea of 1 GB of text data is reading 1000 books, each of 600 pages, and containing 300 words per page.

frequency of tweets that refer to a particular product, event or place, will be dependent on the visibility of the said product or event or place among twitter users. Therefore, in generating tweets for a less visible product or event, a greater degree of creativity might be necessary, and other details like location, time of tweet, and inclusion of words frequently occurring in counterfactual statements can improve data generation. On the other hand, keywords which are language independent will return results across multiple languages, so that if the user wishes for a specific language, specifying tweet location or including common stop-words with the search keywords might be necessary [16]. We preserved original text as much as possible, getting rid only of hyperlinks, hashtags, white spaces and emojis. Ablation experiments showed that stop words were rightly preserved. The raw tweets, the cleaned tweets, and the code are available[2].

3.2   Prediction

We consider the entire text of a tweet or any other textual data being mined for counterfactual instances, as a sequence or a list of sequences, and the antecedent and consequent parts of each counterfactual statement as multi-word tokens. Thus we frame the detection of counterfactuals as a sequence-to-sequence classification task, and the extraction of the antecedent and consequent parts as a token classification task [17]. A counterfactual develops its meaning not from a single word but progressively along the length of its span. And while the length limitation of tweets helps to keep the sequences shorter, It should be added that in many instances, the antecedent and consequent might span only a part of the entire statement, so that the 512 sequence limit for BERT and RoBERTa is never reached. The Experiments are performed on Google Colab, using the Huggingface implementation of the models on Pytorch.[3, 4, 5]

4   Results

We show in Table 1, the number of counterfactuals retrieved from the data set, and in Table 2, a snapshot of the Counterfactuals. Table 3 shows the antecedents and consequents. 134 sentences identified as Counterfactual, reflects a frequency of occurrence of 1.34%.[6]

4.1   Further Results

Returning to the counterfactual question raised earlier, we have this:
Would they have _____ if we had _____?

---

[2] https://github.com/Kc2fresh/Counterfactuals.
[3] https://colab.research.google.com.
[4] https://huggingface.co.
[5] https://pytorch.org.
[6] This hinges on improvements made on the underlying model, which achieves an F1 score of 86.9% on the SemEval Post-Evaluation Leader-board.

Table 1. Data: Cf is Counterfactual

Dataset	Cf	Non-Cf	Total
Num	134	9866	10000

Table 2. A snapshot of retrieved Counterfactuals

Index	Counterfactual
63	Wish the model 3 had a nicer interior considering the price tag especially for the performance version
856	I do love the minimalist cabin of the tesla model 3 i just wish it was built out of nicer materials
1200	I will have had my model 3 for two years on June 6 i have 60 124 trouble free kms my daily commute is less 10 kms but i drive across the country to vacation spots instead of flying now
599	The tesla model 3 is amazing but it would be even better if the backup camera had horizontal guidelines
3282	My tesla model 3 warns me of a collision and it can even intervene i wish kobe s pilot had some similar tech in his helicopter

Assuming a large number of tweets were scraped giving rise to a large number of counterfactual statements, How might we fill in the blanks and bring about simplification. First, we might consider a method as described in Algorithm 9, as a means of simplification. In handling the consequents, we have to make a distinction between two types of counterfactuals, Upward counterfactuals, which express a negative consequent, and Downward Counterfactuals, which express a positive consequent. Thus, passing the consequents for example in Table 4 through a sentiment analysis filter, it can be seen that a positive instance represents dissatisfaction, while a negative instance would represent satisfaction. A neutral review may or may not be statistically valid. Also, handling the consequents in this way, compensates for the instances where no actual consequents exist, such as when the *wish* word is used. In such cases, the antecedent is passed as the consequent.

Algorithm 2: Grouping Antecedents

Result: Grouped list of Antecedent Entities
1 initialization: ;
2 **for** *antecedent in antecedents* **do**
3   extract entity e;
4   **if** *e is similar to item in list of Master words and Phrases* **then**
5 | append e to list of name: item in MW and P;
6   **else**
7 | add e to list of Master Words and Phrases;
8   **end**
9 **end**

Table 3. Antecedents and Consequents

Antecedent	Consequent
If the backup camera had horizontal guidelines	It would be even better
I just wish it was built out of nicer materials	
If i had money money	I ll go for the model x

Table 4. Sentiment Analysis of Consequents

Consequent	Sentiment
It would be even better	Positive
I just wish it was built out of nicer materials	Positive
I ll go for the model x	Neutral

5   Discussion

While the experiment took into account only a relatively small sample of tweets, it is expected that this should be able to scale to a much larger size [18]. For example, given a large enough data set, for an antecedent to be statistically significant, it might need to exceed a certain threshold, suggested as a product of relative frequency of occurrence and a pre-determined weight. We shall however, go on to explore the possibilities. What do the results tell about the Tesla Model 3? and how can we apply these results to generating useful synthetic counterfactuals for decision makers? or, can the user generated counterfactuals stand on their own as a decision making tool? For example, looking through the antecedents, we might for the purpose of our analysis, build up a list of possible upgrades:*upgrade interiors, horizontal lines in backup cameras, reduce car price.* Obviously, different costs and rewards are associated with these actions, and they can be represented accordingly when generating counterfactuals, so that only marginal variations in value should be accepted when generating counter-factuals for variables with large weights, for example *car price* and the consequents having a positive or negative value largely determines the direction for which counterfactual values are expected to be generated. Counterfactual explanations related to competitor products can also be observed as in Table 5, and this introduces another possibility of comparing attributes of cars manufactured by different automakers, and generating counterfactuals to explain why users might prefer a certain car over another.

Table 5. Counterfactuals comparing alternative car models

Index	Counterfactual
408	Bmw 3 series sales down threefold because of tesla model 3 betcha wish you had introduced something sportier than the i3 guys
794	Just hit 55 555 km on my 2018 leaf it s been a much better drive experience than any i c e vehicle but i wish i had waited for the model 3 instead at this point i ll wait until cybertruck to make the switch very poor temperature control on leaf battery

6 Conclusion

In this paper, we proposed CORFAD, Counterfactual Retrieval for Augmentation and Decisions. We applied CORFAD to real world tweets, and also explored the use cases for the retrieved counterfactuals, and how they can help create more explainable models and guide decision making. We showed alternate post-results processing of the antecedents and consequents for additional information extraction. Finally, we provide a pointer to future research, the exploration of counterfactual feed-back from other social media sources, and we expect in future, that the desire for more explainable models will continue to drive research towards more effective application of counterfactuals.

References

1. Nutt, P.C.: Models for decision making in organizations and some contextual variables which stipulate optimal use. Acad. Manag. Rev. **1**(2), 84–98 (1976). https://doi.org/10.5465/1976.4408670
2. Bottou, L., et al.: Counterfactual reasoning and learning systems: the example of computational advertising. J. Mach. Learn. Res. **14**(1), 3207–3260 (2013)
3. Pearl, J.: Causal and counterfactual inference. In: The Handbook of Rationality, pp. 1–41 (2018)
4. Son, Y., et al.: Recognizing counterfactual thinking in social media texts. In: ACL (2017). https://doi.org/10.18653/v1/P17-2103
5. Whitty, M.T.: Liar, liar! An examination of how open, supportive and honest people are in chat rooms. Comput. Hum. Behav. **18**(4), 343–352 (2002)
6. Hendricks, L. A., Hu, R., Darrell, T., Akata, Z.: Generating counterfactual explanations with natural language. arXiv preprint arXiv:1806.09809. (2018)
7. Ramaravind, K.M., Amit, S., Chenhao T.: Explaining machine learning classifiers through diverse counterfactual explanations. In Conference on Fairness, Accountability, and Transparency, 27–30 January (2020). https://doi.org/10.1145/3351095.3372850
8. Lewis, D.: Counterfactuals. John Wiley & Sons, Hoboken (2013)
9. Brill, E.: A simple rule-based part of speech tagger. In: Proceedings of the Third Conference on Applied Natural Language Processing, pp. 152–155. Association for Computational Linguistics (1992)
10. Manning, C.D., Manning, C.D., Schütze, H.: Foundations of Statistical Natural Language Processing. MIT Press, Cambridge (1999)

11. Vaswani, A., et al.: Attention is all you need. In: Advances in Neural Information Processing Systems, pp. 5998–6008 (2017)
12. Raffel, C., et al.: Exploring the limits of transfer learning with a unified text-to-text transformer. arXiv preprint arXiv:1910.10683 (2019)
13. Devlin, J., Chang, M.W., Lee, K., Toutanova, K.: BERT: pre-training of deep bidirectional transformers for language understanding arXiv preprint: 1810.04805. (2018). https://doi.org/10.18653/v1/N19-1423
14. Peters, M.E., Ruder, S., Smith, N.A.: To Tune or not to tune? Adapting pre-trained representations to diverse tasks. In: ACL (2019). https://doi.org/10.18653/v1/W19-4302
15. Yang, X., Obadinma, S., Zhao, H., Zhang, Q., Matwin, S., Zhu, X.: SemEval-2020 Task 5: counterfactual recognition. In: Proceedings of the 14th International Workshop on Semantic Evaluation (SemEval-2020) (2020)
16. Russell, M.A.: Mining the Social Web: Data Mining Facebook, Twitter, LinkedIn, Google+, GitHub, and More. O'Reilly Media, Inc. (2013). https://doi.org/10.1080/15536548.2015.1046287
17. Nwaike, K., Jiao, L. : Counterfactual detection meets transfer learning. In: Modelling Causal Reasoning in Language: Detecting Counterfactuals at SemEval-2020 Task [5] (2020, accepted)
18. Agerri, R., Artola, X., Beloki, Z., Rigau, G., Soroa, A.: Big data for natural language processing: a streaming approach. Knowl.-Based Syst. **79**, 36–42 (2015)
19. Liu, Y., et al.: RoBERTa: a robustly optimized BERT pretraining approach. arXiv preprint 1907.11692 (2019)

Firefly Algorithm Based on Dynamic Step Change Strategy

Jing Wang$^{(\boxtimes)}$, Fuqi Song, Aihua Yin, and Hui Chen

School of Software and Internet of Things Engineering, Jiangxi University
of Finance and Economics, Nanchang, China
wangjing@jxufe.edu.cn

Abstract. Firefly algorithm is a new heuristic intelligent optimization algorithm and has excellent performance in many optimization problems. However, like other intelligent algorithms, the firefly algorithm still has some shortcomings, such as the algorithm is easy to fall into the local optimal, and the convergence speed is slow in the later period. Therefore, this paper proposes a new firefly algorithm with dynamic step change strategy (DsFA) to balance the global and local search capabilities. Thirteen well-known benchmark functions are used to verify the performance of our proposed method, the computational results show that DsFA is more efficient than many other FA algorithms.

Keywords: Firefly algorithm · Heuristic intelligent optimization algorithm · Dynamic step change strategy

1 Introduction

Firefly algorithm was proposed by Xin-she Yang in 2008 [1] and it was a relatively novel optimization algorithm among swarm intelligence algorithms. The basic idea of the algorithm is to simulate the glowing characteristics of fireflies in nature, look for the brighter fireflies around, and gradually move to the position of the brightest fireflies to seeking the best solution. Its structure is simple, the process is clear, there are few parameters to be adjusted, and it has good searching ability, which quickly attracts the attention of a large number of researchers, and has been applied to many practical engineering optimization problems [2–5].

However, the theoretical basis of the firefly algorithm is not yet perfect, and it is difficult to avoid some of the defects of other swarm intelligent stochastic optimization algorithms, such as: the algorithm is easy to prematurely converge, the convergence rate is slow in the later period, and it is easy to fall into local optimization and other defects that need optimization. Therefore, in this paper, a step size that changes adaptively with the number of iterations was proposed. A larger step size was set in the early stage, as the number of iterations increases, the step size gradually decreases, which can effectively avoid the algorithm from falling into local optimum. And the initial attraction parameter was set to 0.4, so that the firefly population can be prevented from gathering to the local optimal value in a few iterations, thereby maintaining the diversity of the firefly population.

© Springer Nature Switzerland AG 2020
X. Chen et al. (Eds.): ML4CS 2020, LNCS 12487, pp. 347–355, 2020.
https://doi.org/10.1007/978-3-030-62460-6_31

The rest of this paper is organized as follows. In Sect. 2, firefly algorithm and its research status are briefly reviewed. Our approach DsFA is described in Sect. 3. Experimental results and analysis are presented in Sect. 4. Finally, the work is concluded in Sect. 5.

2 A Brief Review of Firefly Algorithm

There are several main concepts in the standard firefly algorithm: brightness, attractiveness, distance and movement.

Brightness: In FA, the light intensity I(r) is defined as:

$$I(r) = I_0 e^{-r^2 \gamma} \tag{1}$$

where I_0 is the initial brightness. The parameter r is the distance between two fireflies, γ is defined as the absorption coefficient of light intensity considering the loss of light in the propagation process.

Attractiveness: Firefly i attracts firefly j to move towards it when the brightness of firefly i is greater than firefly j. The attraction is written as:

$$\beta_{ij} = \beta_0 e^{-r^2 \gamma} \tag{2}$$

where β_0 is the maximum attraction, that is, the attraction when the distance is 0 between fireflies, γ is the light absorption coefficient, usually $\beta_0 = 1$, r_{ij} is the Euclidean distance between firefly i and firefly j.

Distance: The formula for calculating the distance between Firefly i and Firefly j is:

$$r_{ij} = \|x_i - x_j\| = \sqrt{\sum_{k=1}^{d} (x_{ik} - x_{jk})^2} \tag{3}$$

where d is the dimension of the variable, x_i and x_j are the spatial positions of firefly i and firefly j.

Movement: When the brightness of firefly i is greater than that of firefly j, firefly i attracts firefly j to move towards it. the moving formula is:

$$x_j(t + 1) = x_j(t) + \beta_{ij}(x_i(t) - x_j(t)) + \alpha \varepsilon_j \tag{4}$$

where t is the number of iterations; β_{ij} is the attractiveness of firefly i to j; α is the step size parameter, generally taking any number in [0, 1]; ε_j is a random number vector generated by a uniform distribution.

The algorithm framework of the standard firefly algorithm is as follows, FEs is the number of evaluations, MAXFEs is the maximum number of evaluations, and PS is the population size.

Algorithm1: Framework of FA	
1	Randomly initialize N fireflies (solutions) as an initial population $\{X_i \mid i = 1, 2, \ldots, N\}$;
2	Calculate the fitness v of each firefly X_i;
3	FEs = 0 and PS = N;
4	while this ≤ MAXFEs
5	for i= 1 to N
6	for j = 1 to N
7	if $f(X_j) < f(X_i)$
8	Move X_i towards X_j according to Eq. 4;
9	Calculate the fitness value of the new X_i;
10	FEs++;
11	end if
12	end for
13	end for
14	end while

3   Our Proposed Firefly Algorithm

3.1   Analysis of Attractive Parameters

The maximum attractive parameter β0 of the standard firefly algorithm is 1, and it can be seen from the analysis of the movement formula (4) that the attractive part plays the role of moving other individuals in the firefly group toward the current optimal individual during a certain iteration process. The attraction parameter is 1, which will cause the fireflies approach to the local optimal value quickly during a few iterations, thereby losing the population diversity as shown in Fig. 1.

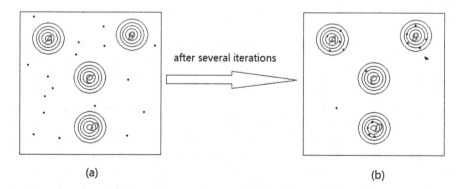

after several iterations

(a)   (b)

Fig. 1. Exploring state of firefly population with $\beta_0 = 1$

Figure 1 shows the movement process of the firefly population when the initial attraction parameter β0 is 1, and points A, B and D are local optimal solutions, C points are global optimal solutions, black dots represent firefly individuals with random distribution, and solid circles are two-dimensional equipotential lines of functions.

When the group evolves to not contain the global optimal solution, compared with the initial stage, the algorithm will lose the diversity of the population, and this process is irreversible, resulting in only a suboptimal solution in the later stage. In order to avoid this situation, the initial (maximum) attraction β0 of the algorithm was set to 0.4, so that as the algorithm iterates, the attraction part no longer tends to 1 quickly but to 0.4, in other words, the firefly population is proportional to a certain proportion Brighter fireflies approach, thereby maintaining the diversity of the population. as shown in Fig. 2.

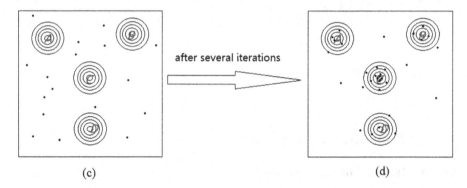

(c)   (d)

Fig. 2. Exploring state of firefly population while β_0=0.4

3.2 Analysis of Step Size

The design of the step size parameter has a great influence on the execution effect and efficiency of the algorithm. On the one hand, in the evolutionary iteration process of the algorithm, it is hoped that the step size is large and has strong global development ability, but at the same time, because the step size is too large, it may cause the firefly to span too large during the movement process, and skip the global optimal solution eventually leads to a reduction in the search accuracy of the algorithm; on the other hand, if a smaller step size is adopted, the local search capability of the algorithm will undoubtedly be improved, but at the same time it will also reduce the convergence speed of the algorithm, resulting in too slow convergence, Affect the execution efficiency of the algorithm. Therefore, how to grasp the size of the step size is extremely important for the performance of the algorithm.

According to the above, simply adopting the fixed step size in the original firefly algorithm is not feasible obviously, and does not adapt the needs of the actual problem. Therefore, we need to adjust the step size dynamically according to the needs of different evolution stages of firefly algorithm to balance and coordinate the relationship between global search ability and local search ability.

So, in the early stage of the algorithm evolution, we set a larger step size to ensure that the algorithm has a good global search ability. In the later stage of the evolution of the algorithm, we hope that the algorithm has a smaller step size and the group has a stronger convergence. Based on these changing characteristics of the step size, we design a step size decreased with the number of iterations model. And a control structure is added in the process of step change, in the control structure, the distance between the optimal individuals of the current generation and the previous generation is used to determine whether to reduce the step size to adapt the evolution needs of the next generation, the improved step size formula is as follows:

$$\begin{cases} \alpha(t+1) = (-0.3 * (t/T_{max}) + 0.9)\alpha(t) \\ \quad\quad \alpha(0) = 0.4(x_d^{max} - x_d^{min}) \end{cases} \tag{5}$$

Where t is the current number of iterations, x_d^{max} and x_d^{min} are the upper and lower limits of the objective function domain respectively.

3.3 The Framework of DsFA

According to the improvement of the attractiveness and step size in the adaptive firefly algorithm, we propose the algorithm framework of DsFA. The DsFA algorithm framework is shown below.

Algorithm2: Framework of DsFA

1	Randomly initialize N fireflies (solutions) as an initial population $\{X_i \mid i = 1, 2, ..., N\}$;
2	Calculate the fitness v of each firefly X_i;
3	FEs = 0 and PS = N;
4	while this ≤ MAXFEs
5	for i= 1 to N
6	for j = 1 to N
7	if $f(X_j) < f(X_i)$
8	Move X_i towards X_j according to Eq. 4;
9	Calculate the fitness value of the new X_i;
10	FEs++;
11	end if
12	end for
13	end for
14	Calculate the brightness difference between the best individual of the current generation and the previous generation
15	if the brightness between the two generations is 0
16	Update step size according to equation (5)
17	end if
18	end while

---

4   Experiments and Analysis

4.1   Benchmark Functions

In order to verify the performance of the algorithm, we adopted 13 internationally recognized benchmark functions for the algorithm minimum optimization test. The test function is shown in Table 1. Among them, D is the spatial dimension of the problem, function 1–6 is a unimodal function, function 6 is a discontinuous jump function and has only a minimum value, function 7 is a noisy quadratic function, function 8–13 is Multi-extreme multi-peak function

Table 1. Benchmark functions used in the experiments, where D is the problem dimension

Name	Function	Search Range	Global Optimum
Sphere	$f_1(x) = \sum_{i=1}^{D} x_i^2$	[−100, 100]	0
Schwefel 2.22	$f_2(x) = \sum_{i=1}^{D} \lvert x_i \rvert + \prod_{i=1}^{D} x_i$	[−10, 10]	0
Schwefel 1.2	$f_3(x) = \sum_{i=1}^{D} \left(\sum_{j=1}^{i} x_j \right)^2$	[−100, 100]	0
Schwefel 2.21	$f_4(x) = \max\{\lvert x_i \rvert, 1 \le i \le D\}$	[−100, 100]	0
Rosenbrock	$f_5(x) = \sum_{i=1}^{D}[100(x_{i+1} - x_i^2)^2 + (1 - x_i^2)^2]$	[−30, 30]	0
Step	$f_6(x) = \sum_{i=1}^{D} x_i + 0.5$	[−100, 100]	0
Quartic with noise	$f_7(x) = \sum_{i=1}^{D} i x_i^4 + random[0, 1)$	[−1.28, 1.28]	0
Schwefel 2.26	$f_8(x) = \sum_{i=1}^{D} - x_i \sin(\sqrt{\lvert x_i \rvert}) + 418.9829 D$	[−500, 500]	0
Rastrigin	$f_9(x) = \sum_{i=1}^{D}[x_i^2 - 10\cos 2\pi x_i + 10]$	[−5.12, 5.12]	0
Ackley	$f_{10}(x) = -20\exp\left(-0.2\sqrt{\frac{1}{D}\sum_{i=1}^{D} x_i^2}\right) - \exp\left(\frac{1}{D}\sum_{i=1}^{D}\cos(2\pi x_i)\right) + 20 + e$	[−32, 32]	0
Griewank	$f_{11}(x) = \frac{1}{4000}\sum_{i=1}^{D} x_i^2 - \prod_{i=1}^{D}\cos\left(\frac{x_i}{\sqrt{i}}\right) + 1$	[−600, 600]	0
Penalized 1	$f_{12}(x) = \frac{\pi}{D}\left\{\sum_{i=1}^{D-1}(y_i - 1)^2[1 + \sin(\pi y_{i+1})] + (y_D - 1)^2 + 10\sin^2(\pi y_1)\right\}$ $+ \sum_{i=1}^{D} u(x_i, 10, 100, 4), \; y_i = 1 + (x_i + 1)/4$ $u(x_i, a, k, m) = \begin{cases} u(x_i, a, k, m), \; x_i > a \\ 0, \; -a \le x_i \le a \\ k(-x_i - a)^m, \; x_i < -a \end{cases}$	[−50, 50]	0
Penalized 2	$f_{13}(x) = 0.1\left\{\sin^2(3\pi x_1) + \sum_{i=1}^{D-1}(x_i - 1)^2[1 + \sin^2(3\pi x_{i+1})]\right.$ $\left. + (x_D - 1)^2[1 + \sin^2(2\pi x_D)]\right\} + \sum_{i=1}^{D} u(x_i, 5, 100, 4)$	[−50, 50]	0

4.2   Experimental Setup

4.2.1   Experimental Environment Settings

The configuration of the experimental environment, the hardware information is as follows: the processor is Intel(R)Core(TM)i5-4258U, the CPU frequency is 2.4 GHz, and the running memory is 12 GB; the software information is: the programming software is IntelliJ IDEA 2019 version, and the operating system is 64-bit Windows 10.

4.2.2 Experimental Parameter Settings

We compare the data between DsFA and the standard firefly algorithm and the other three proposed algorithms. The relevant parameters are shown in Table 2. In order to ensure the reliability and comparability of the data, we unified the relevant parameters, as follows: The values of the parameters we designed: The number of firefly populations are 20; The maximum number of evaluations are 5.0E+05; The number of algorithm tests are 30; The dimension of the problem is 30.

Table 2. The parameter settings of different algorithms

	A	α_{min}	α_0	γ	β_0	β_{min}
FA	0.2	–	–	1.0 or $1/T^2$	1.0	–
MFA	–	–	0.5	$1/T^2$	1.0	0.2
WSSFA	–	0.04	–	1.0	1.0	–
VSSFA	–	–	–	1.0	1.0	–
DsFA	–	–	0.4	$1/T^2$	0.4	–

4.3 Comparison of Results

In Table 3, we recorded the experimental results of 13 classic objective functions of the DsFA test, where "Mean" is the average of the data of the algorithm running 30 times, and SD is the standard deviation. And "Best" and "Worst" correspond to the best and worst results of the 30 test results, respectively. Experimental results show that the algorithm has better performance on the 1, 2, 3, 4, 6, 8 and 10 functions.

Table 3. DsFA algorithm experimental result data

Function	Worst	Best	Mean	SD
f1	4.60E−45	1.50E−48	**2.55E−46**	8.49E−46
f2	3.01E−24	7.82E−26	**6.24E−25**	6.66E−25
f3	5.10E−18	3.20E−21	**3.81E−19**	1.03E−18
f4	7.67E−25	8.60E−27	**1.64E−25**	1.95E−25
f5	1.32E+02	1.56E+01	3.09E+01	3.24E+01
f6	0.0	0.0	**0.0**	0.0
f7	5.90E−02	1.20E−02	2.65E−02	1.16E−02
f8	4.31E−14	1.11E−14	**2.20E−14**	7.10E−15
f9	1.58E−02	0.0	3.45E−03	5.55E−02
f10	1.04E−01	1.57E−32	**1.57E−32**	8.35E−48
f11	1.10E−02	2.58E−32	3.66E−04	2.01E−03
f12	−+3.13E+03	−7.99E+03	−5.44E+03	1.58E+03
f13	5.77E+01	2.19E+01	3.55E+01	8.56E+01

Table 4. FA and DsFA algorithm experimental data comparison

Function	FA($\gamma = 0.1$)		FA($\gamma = 1/T^2$)		DsFA	
	Mean	SD	Mean	SD	Mean	SD
f1	6.67E+04	1.83E04	5.14E−02	1.36E−02	**2.55E−46**	**8.49E−46**
f2	5.19E+02	1.42E+02	1.07E+00	2.65E−01	**6.24E−25**	**6.66E−25**
f3	2.43E+05	4.85E+04	1.26E−01	1.86E−01	**3.81E−19**	**1.03E−18**
f4	8.35E+01	3.16E+01	9.98E−02	2.34E−02	**1.64E−25**	**1.95E−25**
f5	2.69E+08	6.21E+07	3.41E+01	6.23E+00	3.09E+01	3.24E+01
f6	7.69E+04	3.38E+03	5.24E+03	1.08E+03	0.0	0.0
f7	5.16E+01	2.46E+01	7.55E−02	1.42E−02	2.65E−02	1.16E−02
f8	1.10E+04	3.77E+03	9.16E+03	1.78E+03	**2.20E−14**	**7.10E−15**
f9	3.33E+02	6.28E+01	4.95E+01	2.39E+01	3.45E−03	5.55E−02
f10	2.03E+01	2.23E−01	1.21E+01	1.96E+00	**1.57E−32**	**8.35E−48**
f11	6.54E+02	1.69E+02	2.13E−02	1.47E−02	3.66E−04	2.01E−03
f12	7.16E+08	1.82E+08	6.24E+00	4.62E+00	−5.44E+03	1.58E+03
f13	1.31E+09	4.76E+08	5.11E+01	1.28E+01	3.55E+01	8.56E+01

Table 5. VSSFA, WSSFA, MFA and DsFA algorithm optimization results average comparison

Function	VSSFA Mean	WSSFA Mean	MFA Mean	DsFA Mean
f1	5.84E+04	6.34E+04	1.56E−05	**2.55E−46**
f2	1.13E+02	1.35E+02	1.85E−03	**6.24E−25**
f3	1.16E+05	1.10E+05	5.89E−05	**3.81E−19**
f4	8.18E+01	7.59E+01	1.73E−03	**1.64E−25**
f5	2.16E+08	2.29E+08	2.29E+01	3.09E+01
f6	5.48E+04	6.18E+04	**0.00E+00**	**0.0**
f7	4.43E+01	3.24E−01	1.30E−01	2.65E−02
f8	1.07E+04	1.06E+04	4.48E+03	**2.20E−14**
f9	3.12E+02	3.16E+02	6.47E+01	3.45E−03
f10	2.03E+01	2.05E+01	4.23E−04	**1.57E−32**
f11	5.47E+02	6.09E+02	9.86E−03	3.66E−04
f12	3.99E+08	6.18E+08	5.04E−08	−5.44E+03
f13	8.12E+08	9.13E+08	6.06E−07	3.55E+01

Table 4 records the experimental data comparison with two different versions of the FA algorithm proposed by scholar Yang, in which the middle algorithm is another version of FA that Yang proposed later, and suggests $\gamma = 1/T2$, where T is the definition of the objective function area. As can be seen from the table, compared with the previous two versions of FA, DsFA has a better performance in most objective function test results.

Table 5 shows the comparison results between our algorithm and other improved firefly algorithms. Among them, WSSFA [7] and VSSFA [8] were proposed by Yu et al. And MFA [6] was proposed by Fister et al. It can be seen from Table 5 that the DsFA algorithm has obvious advantages in optimizing functions 1–4, functions 6, 8, 10 and other functions. Compared with other proposed algorithms and standard firefly algorithms, the DsFA algorithm has better optimization results on some multi-peak functions. For the function f6, the DsFA always find the global optimal solution in these 30 test times.

5 Conclusion

This paper improves the attraction and step size parameter by analyzing the firefly's movement process and attraction method. First, by changing the initial attractiveness to 0.4 instead of 1, the fireflies fly to the brighter fireflies in a certain proportion, thereby avoiding the algorithm falling into the local optimal value and maintaining the diversity of the population. Then, we propose a step size improvement strategy that decreases with the number of iterations, and on this basis, a control structure is added to control the timing of step change. Experimental results show that DsFA has a better performance on most test function.

Although this article only improves the performance of the firefly algorithm in theoretical experiments, and has not been tested in actual problems, we will study this in future work and improve this algorithm.

Acknowledgments. The authors would like to thank anonymous reviewers for their detailed and constructive comments that help us to increase the quality of this work. This work was supported by the National Natural Science Foundation of China (No.: 61866014, 61862027 and 61962024), the National Natural Science Foundation of Jiangxi (No.: 20192BAB207032).

References

1. Yang, X.-S.: Nature-Inspired Metaheuristic Algorithms, Luniver Press (2008)
2. Jafari, O., Akbari, M.: Optimization and simulation of micrometre-scale ring resonator modulators based on p-i-n diodes using firefly algorithm. Optik **128**, 101–112 (2017)
3. Tuba, E., Mrkela, L., Tuba, M.: Support vector machine parameter tuning using firefly algorithm. In: 2016 26th International Conference Radioelektronika (RADIOELEKTRO-NIKA), pp. 413–418 (2016)
4. SundarRajan, R., Vasudevan, V., Mithya, S.: Workflow scheduling in cloud computing environment using firefly algorithm. In: 2016 International Conference on Electrical, Electronics, and Optimization Techniques (ICEEOT), pp. 955–960 (2016)
5. Shi, J.Y., et al.: Tracking the global maximum power point of a photovoltaic system under partial shading conditions using a modified firefly algorithm. J. Renew. Sustain. Energy **8**(3), 033501 (2016)
6. Fister Jr, I., Yang, X.-S., Fister, I., Brest, J.: Memetic firefly algorithm for combinatorial optimization arXiv preprint arXiv:1204.5165 (2012)
7. Yu, S., Su, S., Lu, Q., Huang, L.: A novel wise step strategy for firefly algorithm. Int. J. Comput. Math. **91**, 2507–2513 (2014)
8. Yu, G.: An improved firefly algorithm based on probabilistic attraction. Int. J. Comput. Sci. Math. **7**, 530 (2016)

Earthquakes Detection Scheme by Dynamic Time Warping on Smartphones

Yuqin Zhu$^{(\boxtimes)}$ ⓘ, Jiaxin Yang$^{(\boxtimes)}$, Bingjie Shao$^{(\boxtimes)}$ ⓘ, Liang Wang$^{(\boxtimes)}$ ⓘ, and Zhaohui Yuan$^{(\boxtimes)}$ ⓘ

School of Software, East China Jiaotong University, Nanchang, Jiangxi, China
yuanzh@whu.edu.cn, yangjiaxin_1994@163.com, shao632@163.com,
WL1998766WL@outlook.com, zyq13479473363@163.com

Abstract. With the rapid development of smart mobile devices and mobile communication networks, smart phones with built-in sensors can form a powerful sensing network to detect seismic events. However, the accuracy of the data collected by mobile phone sensors is not as good as the data obtained by professional seismograph, and the detection of seismic events by mobile phones also has artificial noises generated by the mobile phone itself and the environment, which leads to the need to improve the effectiveness of mobile phone systems for earthquake warning. In this paper, we propose a set of high-precision anomaly detection algorithms based on STA/LTA DTW. The effect of the algorithm is obtained through several sets of comparative experiments: the STA/LTA DTW high-precision anomaly event detection algorithm we proposed is more accurate than ordinary mobile phones for detecting earthquakes.

Keywords: Event detection · Sensing · Anomalous events

1 Introduction

The earthquake is extremely destructive and unavoidable. Effective earthquake warning can minimize injury and property damage. With the increasing usage of smart phones, earthquake warning through smart phones with built-in sensors has become the research focus of researchers [1–3]. However, the sensors built into ordinary smartphones are still not comparable to professional seismic instruments. Traditional seismic station instruments are precise and accurate, and are not disturbed by human factors. The sampling accuracy of the built-in sensor of the smart phone is low, and the sampling value of the sensor is easily affected by the activity of the mobile phone holder, resulting in frequent occurrence of false alarms for earthquake warning. When people are active, they suddenly change from one movement state to another. As shown in Fig. 1, a false alarm may be triggered by the state of the human body from rest to walking to running. The commonly used STA/LTA picking algorithm cannot distinguish between earthquakes and human actions, which makes false alarms appear in the earthquake warning system. This is a False warning.

© Springer Nature Switzerland AG 2020
X. Chen et al. (Eds.): ML4CS 2020, LNCS 12487, pp. 356–369, 2020.
https://doi.org/10.1007/978-3-030-62460-6_32

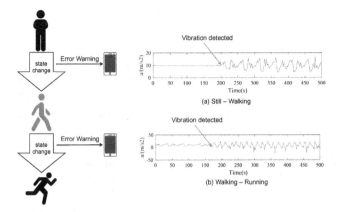

Fig. 1. Error warning of mobile phone system caused by the change of human motion state.

In this article, we propose a new scheme to reduce the negative impact of human activity on smartphone earthquake warning systems. First of all, the mobile phone sampled data will be affected by its own Gaussian noise and other shortcomings to carry out the corresponding data processing, the use of wavelet noise reduction to achieve Gaussian white noise removal, the use of feature functions for vibration event feature amplification processing to improve the system pick accuracy. Next, in order to reduce the impact of human activities on seismic anomaly detection, the dynamic time bending distance feature DTW of the time series signal of human daily behavior is analyzed, and on this basis, a double-layer threshold detection method is designed to reduce the false alarm rate. Finally, based on the abnormal event detection of smartphone multi-source motion sensor data fusion, the sensor detection quality is improved through the fusion of accelerometer and gyroscope data. The contributions of this research are summarized as follows:

- Using wavelet denoising to achieve Gaussian white noise removal, improving the system's picking accuracy.
- Proposed STA/LTA DTW high-precision anomaly detection algorithm, reducing the false alarm rate of the system.
- The data fusion technology of both acceleration sensor and gyroscope is used to improve the accuracy of the system.
- After a large number of experimental tests, the improvement effect of detection accuracy and false alarm rate was verified.

2   Related Work

2.1   Seismic Event Detection Method

All along, seismic event detection has been an important foundation for researching earthquake early warning. Commonly used seismic detection event detection methods are the time-to-length window mean value method in the time domain and the discrete Fourier in the frequency domain. Feature methods, etc. At present, the main seismic event detection methods are mainly through the identification of signal feature changes. Stevenson proposed a method of comparing the characteristics (amplitude or energy) of the long and short time window (STA/LTA) when detecting P waves of seismic signals [4]. Long time windows reflect the characteristic changes of background noise, and short time windows reflect the characteristic changes of seismic signals. The widely used STA/LTA method [5] refers to continuously calculating the ratio of the short-term average (STA) to the long-term average (LTA) on the signal characteristics and increasing the detection rate when the ratio exceeds a specified threshold. However, most of the existing related algorithms are suitable for accurate data collected by professional seismographs. When the seismic map shows a very low signal-to-noise ratio (SNR) or is affected by the human activities of the smartphone holder, it cannot be distinguished. An abnormal vibration caused by an earthquake or human activity may generate false alarms. In addition, because the STA/LTA method generally requires empirical adjustments to many parameters, making these methods difficult to adapt to the dramatic changes in different external environments and regions. Another important category of selection algorithms is based on autoregressive (AR) models [6] or wavelet processing methods [7]. They choose time instances to maximize the difference between the signals of the two AR models or wavelets before and after the selected time instance. Both are more accurate, but the AR model or wavelet will cause relatively high computational complexity and memory usage, so this method is not suitable for use in ordinary smartphones with limited resources.

2.2   Detection Methods Based on Mobile Phone Sensors

In the current existing research work, there are relatively few studies using smartphones to participate in seismic detection. Ishake [8] and QDS [9] detect the occurrence of an earthquake event by identifying whether the amplitude data collected from the mobile phone acceleration sensor exceeds a specified threshold. Due to the noise in the mobile phone itself and the daily activities of ordinary smartphone holders, this method Although the detection speed is fast, there are many error warnings, which are difficult to be the basis for decision-making in the processing center. The CSN [10] system also collects only the acceleration sensor data of the mobile phone, and then establishes a Gaussian mixture model to determine the distribution of the data. When data with a probability lower than a certain proximity is detected, an abnormal event is considered to occur. However, the acceleration data of the daily activities of smartphone holders vary, and there are problems in the establishment of the Gaussian mixture model. The MyShake system collects acceleration value data of human activities in daily life through mobile phone acceleration sensors, and then uses artificial neural networks to distinguish whether it is abnormal vibration or human activities. This method has accurate detection data, but the cost of training and calculation is high, and there is also the problem that training data is difficult to collect.

The seismic identification methods used by the above systems are summarized in Table 1.

Table 1. Seismic recognition method based on mobile phone sensor.

Systematic name	Data features	Recognition algorithm
Community Seismic Network	Time-frequency domain of sensor acceleration	GMM model anomaly detection
Ishake	Acceleration value of original sensor	Single threshold trigger
Quake Detection System	Sensor acceleration frequency domain	Average energy ratio method for long and short
MyShake	Time-frequency domain of sensor acceleration	Artificial neural nets

3 Motivation and Approach Overview

3.1 Motivation

In view of the actual research situation of using smartphones as sensing devices at home and abroad, there are still many deficiencies in using mobile phones for seismic detection. For example, most researches only use the acceleration sensor in the mobile phone to conduct research. However, as an ordinary sensor, the mobile phone sensor can only measure the abnormal value that occurs in a fixed time window to determine whether there is an abnormal vibration event. In addition, mobile phones, as our daily tools, are susceptible to human activities. Traditional seismographs can extract seismic P-wave signals from noise, and mobile phones need to be able to distinguish between human activity signals and seismic vibration signals for seismic detection Therefore, the traditional seismic event detection method cannot be directly applied to the mobile phone system to detect earthquakes, otherwise it may cause serious consequences due to false alarms. This article is based on a mobile sensing network system, using widely used high-density distribution smartphones as sensing nodes to achieve accurate seismic detection results.

3.2 Approach Overview

In this section, we will provide the working principle of STA/LTA DTW high-precision anomaly event detection method based on multi-sensor data fusion, as shown in Fig. 2.

First of all, it is the collection and processing of sensor data of ordinary smartphones. Our main consideration is that the data collected by the mobile phone

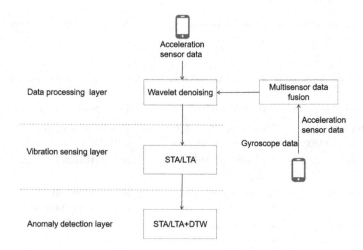

Fig. 2. Working principle diagram of high precision abnormal event detection method.

will be affected by the holders posture of holding the mobile phone and the Gaussian noise of the mobile phone itself, as well as the environmental noise. For these factors Adopt wavelet denoising and use feature function to amplify the signal to carry out corresponding data processing, and provide complete and effective data samples for the inspection of the next work-high-precision abnormal event detection method. Next, for the false alarm caused by human activities, we propose to add a layer of time series similarity measure to the traditional STA/LTA threshold algorithm to reduce the false alarm rate. The comparative experimental analysis shows the performance of the STA/LTA DTW algorithm. Because of the different brands of mobile phones, there is a certain difference in the data collected by the built-in sensor. The fusion of accelerometer and gyroscope data can improve the detection quality of the sensor. At the end of this article, the data fusion algorithm of the two is introduced in detail, and the analysis of The performance of the algorithm was tested.

4   Data Collection and Preprocessing

4.1   Data Acquisition

For the collection of daily human behavior event data, volunteers hold a smartphone or put the phone in their pockets, and then run or walk in daily life, up and down stairs, etc. The collection of abnormal vibration event data is that the volunteers stand on the laboratory shaking table to simulate the earthquake. In this article, we are using Samsung galaxys8, Huawei glory 10, and OPPOr10, three particularly common smartphones. The data collection is carried out from two aspects of daily human activities and abnormal vibration data. We divide the data to be collected into three types: Single act event, behavioral transformation events, anomalous event.

4.2   Data Preprocessing

Since the vibration of seismic P waves is vertical vibration, we choose to only process the Z-axis data when processing the data, and then observe the Z-axis data fluctuations. First, we use a nonlinear wavelet transform threshold method to denoise. The main principle is: the energy of noise is distributed in the entire wavelet area, and the energy of the effective signal is concentrated in a limited number of coefficients in the wavelet domain. Therefore, after wavelet decomposition, the wavelet transform coefficient of the signal is greater than the wavelet transform coefficient of noise Set thresholds for coefficients to achieve signal-to-noise separation. If $s(t)$ represents a valid signal and $w(t)$ is noise, then the original signal $f(t)$ is expressed as the sum of the two:

$$f(t) = s(t) + w(t) \tag{1}$$

In the first step, wavelet decomposition is performed according to the Mallet algorithm [11]. Let f_k be the discrete sampled data of the signal $f(t)$, $f_k = c_{0,k}$, then the orthogonal wavelet transform decomposition formula of the signal $f(t)$ is (2).

$$\begin{cases} c_{j,k} = \sum_n c_{j-1,n} h_{n-2k} \\ d_{j,k} = \sum_n d_{j-i,n} g_{n-2k} \end{cases} (k = 0, 1, 2, \ldots, N - 1) \tag{2}$$

where $c_{j,k}$ are scale coefficients, $d_{j,k}$ are wavelet coefficients, h and g are a pair of orthogonal mirror filter banks, j is the number of decomposition layers, and N is the number of discrete sampling points. In this step, the appropriate wavelet base number and decomposition layer number j will be selected, and the original signal wavelet will be decomposed into the j layer through the formula to obtain the corresponding wavelet decomposition coefficient. In the second step, threshold processing is performed, and the wavelet coefficients $d_{j,k}$ obtained in the previous step are thresholded. The commonly used threshold processing methods are the hard threshold method and the soft threshold method proposed by Dohono [12], Literature [13] proves that compared with the hard threshold method, the soft threshold method has stronger mathematical characteristics and better denoising effect. The obtained estimated signal is an approximate optimal estimate of the original signal, and the signal is smooth without additional oscillation. So this article uses the soft threshold processing method. The third step is signal reconstruction, inverse transformation of wavelet, the formula is shown in (3).

$$c_{j-1,n} = \sum_n c_{j,n} h_{k-2n} + \sum_n \hat{d}_{j,n} g_{k-2n} \tag{3}$$

Through experiments, we choose sym4 wavelet base, the decomposition level is 5 times, and the calculation formula of threshold is shown in (4).

$$\lambda = \sqrt{2 \log(N)} \tag{4}$$

Where N is the number of signal sampling points. The denoising results are shown in Fig. 3.

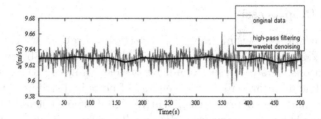

Fig. 3. Nonlinear wavelet denoising diagram.

The resulting signal is supposed to be a straight line that is stable near the acceleration value of gravity, but it is irregularly affected by Gaussian noise. After the original signal is filtered by a high-pass filter, the amplitude of the change is reduced but Gaussian noise still exists. The signal obtained after denoising using wavelet transform approximates a straight line. Wavelet transform denoising has achieved obvious results.

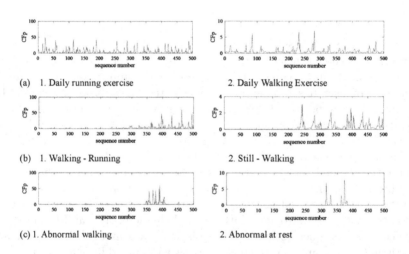

(a) 1. Daily running exercise   2. Daily Walking Exercise

(b) 1. Walking - Running   2. Still - Walking

(c) 1. Abnormal walking   2. Abnormal at rest

Fig. 4. Characterized sample data sequence diagram.

In order to highlight the vibration variation characteristics of the sampling sequence and improve the sensitivity of abnormal vibration data, we use the characteristic function to characterize the acceleration data instead of directly using the original data signal. In this paper, $|Y(i) - Y(i-1)|$ is selected as the feature function, and $CF(i) = |Y(i) - Y(i-1)|$. Characterize the collected data and the results are shown in Fig. 4.

5   Seismic Event Detection Scheme

High precision anomaly detection algorithm is divided into three layers. The first layer is mainly used to remove noise by wavelet transform, which has been introduced in detail in the data processing part. The second layer is "vibration sensing layer", Based on a wide range STA/LTA algorithms, which is mainly used to identify the vibration of mobile phone in the environment. As a result, the second layer can not exclude human interference; the third layer is the anomaly detection layer, by analyzing the DTW characteristics and simulation of the time series signals of daily behavior motion Different signal DTW characteristics of seismic motion time series to detect abnormal vibration. The anomaly detection based on the fusion of multi-motion sensor of smart phone is based on the above method, which combines the data of accelerometer and gyroscope.

5.1   Vibration Event Detection Based on STA/LTA Threshold Triggering Algorithm

This detection method is one of the most common detection methods at present. Its principle reflects the change trend of signal energy in a certain period of time through the ratio between STA and LTA. The long time window reflects the characteristic changes of the background noise, and the short time window reflects the characteristic changes of the target signal, that is, the seismic signal. When an earthquake occurs, the amplitude of the STA change of the signal characteristics in a short time is significantly larger than that reflecting the signal characteristics in a long time The change range of LTA makes the STA/LTA value abrupt. When the STA/LTA value is greater than the preset trigger threshold, it is determined that the mobile phone state has vibrated. The definitions of STA and LTA are shown in Eqs. (5) and (6).

$$STA = \sum_{i=1}^{N} \frac{X(i)}{N} \tag{5}$$

$$LTA = \sum_{j=1}^{M} \frac{Y(j)}{N} \tag{6}$$

In the formula, $X(i), (i = 1, 2, , N)$, represents the time series signal within a short time window, $Y(j), (j = 1, 2, , M)$, Represents the time series signal sampling value sequence within a long time window; M and N represent the number of sampling points in the LTA and STA windows, respectively. Then use the feature function as an input variable [14]. The feature function used in this article has been introduced in detail in the data processing part of the article. Introduce the characteristic function $CF(i) = |Y(i) - Y(i - 1)|$, and get the STA/LTA calculation formula as shown in (7).

$$R = \frac{STA}{LTA} \tag{7}$$

Determining the threshold of the STA/LTA threshold triggering algorithm is the key point of this method. If it is too high, it is easy to increase the missed alarm rate, while if it is too low, it will cause an increase in false alarms. This article analyzes and processes the STA/LTA threshold algorithm for the collected sample data, and takes the trigger threshold = 1.10, 1.15, 1.20, 1.25, 1.30, 1.50, 1.70 to determine whether the vibration detection effect is good or bad. Trigger threshold), false alarm rate (shock not triggered threshold), false alarm rate (shock not triggered threshold) three indicators to measure the effect, the calculation results are shown in Table 2 above.

Table 2. Accuracy, false alarm rate and false alarm rate under different thresholds

Threshold	Accuracy rate %	False alarm rate %	False alarm rate %
1.10	20.43	79.57	0
1.15	22.36	77.64	0
1.20	51.94	48.06	0
1.25	80.68	19.32	0
1.30	97.43	2.57	0
1.50	100	0	78.63
1.70	100	0	96.76

This paper analyzes the experimental results through the experimental method, and finally sets the threshold to 1.3. When threshold1 = 1.3, the accuracy rate is the highest, the false alarm rate is the lowest, and there is no false alarm rate.

5.2 Vibration Event Detection Based on STA/LTA Threshold Triggering Algorithm

The abnormal event signal is different from the regularity of human activities, and its signal is not very regular. There are large differences in the waveforms of abnormal events in different time periods. Through this difference, the time series similarity measure in adjacent time windows can be well used to distinguish whether the received signal is a human activity signal or an abnormal event signal. Here this article uses DTW (Dynamic Time Warping) to calculate the similarity between the two. We performed statistics on the DTW change rate of the time series signal fragments after the STA/LTA threshold was triggered in the behavior transformation events and abnormal events. As shown in Fig. 5, there is a clear dividing line between the behavior transformation events (C events) and abnormal events (E events) in the distribution of the eigenvalues of the data set, so we adopt a fixed threshold2 in this article to more accurately distinguish human Active events and abnormal events.

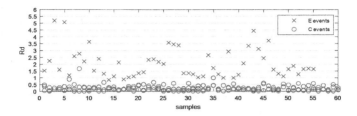

Fig. 5. Data set eigenvalue Rd value distribution.

Through the experiment threshold2 = 0.5,1.0,1.5,2.0 to judge the effect of its classification, the classification accuracy of the event is used as a measurement indicator, and the results are shown in Table 3.

Table 3. Correct rate of classification of behavior transformation events and abnormal events under different threshold2

Threshold2	Correct rate of behavior transformation events %	Correct rate of abnormal events %
0.5	100	71.43
1.0	97.81	96.22
1.5	89.05	97.06
2.0	85.31	100

It can be drawn from the table that when threshold2 = 1, the algorithm effect is optimized, so when $Rd < 1$, we determine that the event is an artificial event; when $Rd > 1$, the event is determined to be an abnormal event, that is an earthquake.

5.3   Seismic Event Detection Based on Multi-sensor Data Fusion

MEMS inertial sensors are only approximately calibrated by the manufacturer at the initial stage of use, the errors of the sensors will also change over time [15]. Therefore, the sensor calibration needs to be performed again to achieve more accurate results. In this paper, a multi-sensor fusion method is proposed, which uses extended Kalman filter to fuse triaxial accelerometer data and triaxial gyroscope data to realize the calibration of accelerometer. We selected several common smartphones on the market for experiments to verify the effectiveness of this calibration algorithm. The verification scheme consists of two groups of experiments, one set of experiments is to keep the mobile phone still on the horizontal desktop for 10 s, then rotate in the direction previously specified (90 degrees as a benchmark), first the mobile phone static for 10 s, then rotate. Another set of experiments is that the smartphone rotates continuously around all its axes. Finally, the accelerometer value and gyroscope data value are corrected using the calibration algorithm. The experimental results are shown in Fig. 6.

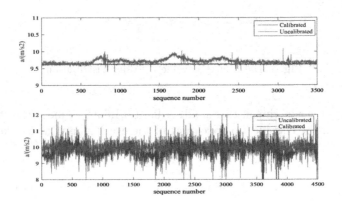

Fig. 6. Calibration algorithm experimental results.

We can see from the First picture that after rotation-stationary processing, there is a certain deviation in the data collected by the acceleration sensor. The second picture is a slow and continuous rotation effect diagram of the mobile phone around its own coordinate axis. The figure shows that the data collected by the acceleration sensor up and down fluctuation in a certain range. The experiment shows that the two groups of data after calibration have better effect presentation, the numerical amplitude is in the middle, and it is always in a stable range. Based on multi-sensor data fusion seismic event detection is more accurate data and then use the above section of the abnormal event detection method to detect. For details, see the anomaly detection method.

6   Seismic Event Detection Scheme

6.1   High-Precision Abnormal Event Detection Algorithm Framework Performance Evaluation

(1) This article uses traditional STA/LTA and the proposed algorithm to process the above 90 sets of data, we use the number of pickups (shock changes occur) and false alarms (action change events) And percentage to measure the improvement of the program performance. We compare the picking accuracy and false alarm rate of the traditional STA/LTA algorithm and the STA/LTA DTW dual threshold algorithm into Fig.7.

It can be concluded through experiments: Compared with the traditional STA/LTA single-layer threshold detection method, the STA/LTA DTW double-layer threshold detection method effectively reduces the early warning rate, and can perform more accurate early warning of abnormal events.

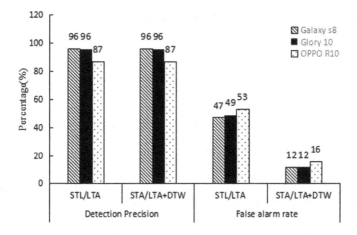

Fig. 7. Effectiveness of STA/LTA+DTW.

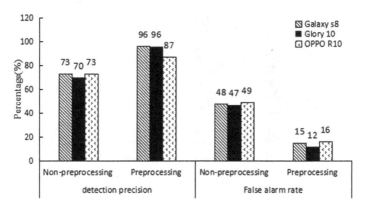

Fig. 8. Effectiveness of data preprocessing.

(2) Different from the traditional earthquake warning system, the signals collected in the mobile phone-based earthquake warning system are easily affected by noise, so we use wavelet denoising to achieve better results. We used the STA/LTA DTW algorithm to perform experiments on 90 sets of signals subjected to wavelet denoising and 90 sets of unprocessed signals. The results are shown in Fig. 8.

It can be seen from Fig. 8 that the picking accuracy and false alarm rate have changed positively before and after data preprocessing. From this we can conclude that by denoising the sensor data signal, the picking accuracy can be greatly improved, The false alarm rate is greatly reduced.

368   Y. Zhu et al.

6.2 Analysis of Abnormal Event Detection Results Based on the Calibration Algorithm

In order to improve the accuracy of the data collected during abnormal event detection, the calibration algorithm is applied to the data sampling process. In this experiment, we used Meizu V8, HTC826w and VivoY73. Ordinary smartphones, from which to collect acceleration values and gyroscope data in various states. The experiment consisted of 90 sets of data records, of which 30 sets were records of abnormal vibration events simulated by the shaking table; 30 sets were records of normal vibrations in daily life, and 30 sets were records of behavior-action transformations. The algorithm used for abnormal vibration detection is the new STA/LTA DTW double threshold picking algorithm proposed in this paper. The results are shown in Fig. 9.

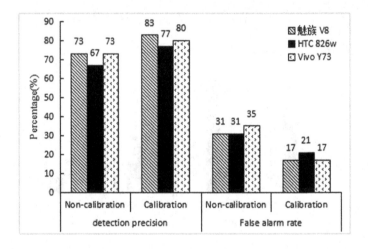

Fig. 9. The effectiveness of data fusion algorithms.

As can be seen from the figure, after multi-sensor data fusion, the anomaly detection accuracy of the three mobile phones has increased from 73%, 67%, and 73% to 83%, 77%, and 80%, respectively, and the accuracy has increased by an average of 9%. The false alarm rate has decreased from 31%, 31%, 35% to 17%, 21%, 17% respectively, and the false alarm rate has dropped by an average of 14%, which effectively improves the accuracy rate and reduces the false alarm rate, thereby significantly enhancing Mobile phone earthquake warning system.

7 Conclusion

This paper proposes a set of calibration-based STA/LTA DTW high-precision abnormal event detection methods. First of all, this method proposes the use of wavelet transform to achieve noise removal and the use of feature function for signal amplification to improve the pick-up rate. Then according to the shortcomings of mobile phones that are different from professional detection instruments and easily affected by external environment (that is, man-made actions), a high-precision abnormal event detection algorithm for STA/LTA DTW is proposed. Finally, through multi-sensor data fusion calibration, the effect of the detection scheme is optimized. Through experiments, compared with traditional methods, this detection method can reduce certain false alarm rate and missed alarm rate.

References

1. Kong, Q., Allen, R.M., Schreier, L., et al.: MyShake: A smartphone seismic network for earthquake early warning and beyond. Sci. Adv. **2**(2), e1501055–e1501055 (2016)
2. Cochran, E.S., Lawrence, J.F., Christensen, C., Jakka, R.S.: The quake-catcher network: Citizen science expanding seismic horizons. Seismol. Res. Lett. **80**, 26C–30 (2009)
3. Faulkner, M., Olson, M., Chandy, R., Krause, J., Chandy, K.M., Krause, A.: The next big one: Detecting earthquakes and other rare events from community-based sensors. In: International Conference on Information Processing in Sensor Networks, pp. 13C–24 (2011)
4. Stevenson, P.R.: Microearthquakes at Flathead Lake, Montana: A study using automatic earthquake processing. Bull. Seismol. Soc. Am. **66**(1), 61–80 (1976)
5. Allen, R.V.: Automatic earthquake recognition and timing from single traces. Bull. Seismol. Soc. Am. **68**(5), 1521C–1532 (1978)
6. Sleeman, R., Van Eck, T.: Robust automatic p-phase picking: An on-line implementation in the analysis of broadband seismogram recordings. Phy. Earth Planet. Inter. **113**(1–4), 265C–275 (1999)
7. Zhang, H., Thurber, C., Rowe, C.: Automatic p-wave arrival detection and picking with multiscale wavelet analysis for single-component recordings. Bull. Seismol. Soc. Am. **93**(5) 1904C–1912 (2003)
8. Reilly, J., Dashti, S., Ervasti, M., et al.: Mobile phones as seismologic sensors: Automating data extraction for the iShake system. IEEE Trans. Autom. Sci. Eng. **10**(2), 242–251 (2013)
9. Zambrano, A., Perez, I., Palau, C., et al.: Quake detection system using smartphone-based wireless sensor network for early warning. Rev. Iberoamericana De Automatica E Informatica Ind. **12**(3), 297–302 (2014)
10. Faulkner, M., Olson, M., Chandy, R., et al.: The next big one: Detecting earthquakes and other rare events from community-based sensors. In: International Conference on Information Processing in Sensor Networks, pp. 13–24. IEEE (2011)
11. Mallat, S.: A theory for multiresolution signal decomposition: The wavelet representation. IEEE Trans. Pattern Anal. Mach. Intell. **11**(7), 674–693 (1989)
12. Donoho, D.L., Johnstone, J.M.: Ideal spatial adaptation by wavelet shrinkage. Biometrika **81**(3), 425–455 (1994)
13. Donoho, D.L.: Denoising by soft-thresholding. IEEE Trans. Inf. **81**(3), 613–627 (1995)
14. Allen, R.: Automatic earthquake recognition and timing from single trace. Bull. Seismol. Soc. Am. **68**(5), 1521–1532 (1978)
15. Woodman, O.J., Woodman, C.O.J.: An introduction to inertial navigation. J. Navig. **9**(3), 696 (1956)

Towards Accurate Seismic Events Detection Using Motion Sensors on Smartphones

Qingping Cao$^{(\boxtimes)}$ ⓘ, Yuqin Zhu$^{(\boxtimes)}$ ⓘ, Mei He$^{(\boxtimes)}$ ⓘ, and Zhaohui Yuan$^{(\boxtimes)}$ ⓘ

School of Software, East China Jiaotong University, Nanchang, Jiangxi, China
{caoqingping23,HMruanjian}@outlook.com, zyq13479473363@163.com,
yuanzh@whu.edu.cn

Abstract. Smartphones equipped with motion sensors can be manipulated as a Community Seismic Network for earthquake detection. But, there still have many challenges such as the limited sensing capability of the off-the-shelf sensors and unpredictable diversity of daily operations by phone users in current smartphones, which yield poor monitoring quality. So we present a suite of algorithms towards detecting anomalous seismic events from sampling data contaminated by users operations, including a lightweight signal preprocessing method, a two-phase events picking and timing scheme on local smartphones, and a decision fusion scheme to maximize anomaly detection performance at the fusion center while meeting the requirements on system false alarm rate. We experimentally evaluate the proposed approach on networked smartphones and shake tables. The results verify the effectiveness of our approach in distinguishing anomalous seismic events from noises due to normal daily operation.

Keywords: Seismic processing · Events detection · Motion sensor

1 Introduction

Smartphones and tablets equipped with motion sensors have emerged as a powerful resource of sensor networks in earthquake early warning systems (EEWS)[1–3]. The built-in sensors on mobile devices such as accelerometers and gyroscopes can sample the vibrations of earthquakes similarly to the general seismostations that share the same basic principles. Moreover, the community sensing networks (CSN) composed by bestrewed intelligent devices can fill the blind spots in a monitored area of the highly accurate but expensive, sparsely placed seismostations in current seismic early warning systems. CSNs can leverage data fusion with a large number of nodes to compensate for the deficiency of their own perception accuracy, so using community-held sensors is a particularly promising opportunity in EEWS. But it also presents difficult challenges. The timely and accurate detection of seismic events by smartphones is the first prerequisite for

X. Chen et al. (Eds.): ML4CS 2020, LNCS 12487, pp. 370–383, 2020.
https://doi.org/10.1007/978-3-030-62460-6_33

action in seismic signal analysis. The rare events however, are often difficult or impossible to model and characterize as a priori. Moreover, the objective of equipping motion sensors on smartphones comes from casual games or man-phone interactions, so the off-the-shelf sensors are not qualified to meet the stringent performance required by mission-critical EEWS. More frustratingly, motion signals sampled by built-in sensors are often contaminated with noise caused by the phone holders daily operations, it is extraordinarily hard to draw correct conclusions from processing these signals with simple techniques.

Most of the existing works in seismic events detection focused on collecting measurements on shaking tables to estimate a suitable detection thresholds on smartphones to issue alarms, and then employing data fusion strategy to improve the detection precision [4,5]. The U.S. Geological Survey Did You Feel It is a polling based scheme for collecting reports of shaking and damage as experienced by individuals [6]. MyShake and iShake system are on-phone detection algorithms to separate earthquakes from other shakes, they issue earthquakes alarms by network detection [7]. Caltech presented an approach towards detecting rare events to maximize detection performance at fusion [3]. However, most of the current works are based on the measurements on shaking table, while take little account of the operations of phone users.

In this paper, we present schemes of distinguishing seismic events from routine activities of phone holders according to the signals sampled by built-in accelerometers. The contributions of this work are summarized as follows:

- A lightweight preprocessing algorithm which highlights the pattern of anomalous events from sampled data and reduce noise.
- A combined scheme for detecting and timing the real seismic events from daily operations of the phone holders.
- A decision fusion strategy is employed to eliminate the false alarms caused by human motions; and plenty of data are collected to verify the feasibility and accuracy of the proposed schemes.

2 Related Work

2.1 Seismic Events Detection

There have several algorithms for seismic events detection, P-phase picking have been proposed for decades. They are typically based on the identification of changes in the signal characteristics such as energy, frequency and features of the autoregressive models [8]. The widely adopted STA/LTA approaches [9] continuously compute the ratio of short-term average (STA) to long-term average (LTA) over a signal feature and raise a detection once the ratio exceeds a specified threshold. However, as most of the algorithms are based on accurate data sampled by dedicated seismostations, when the seismograms present a very low signal-to-noise ratio (SNR) or are contaminated with daily activities of the holders, they could produce false alarms. Moreover, the heuristic STA/LTA approaches often require empirical tuning of numerous parameters, that cause these methods difficult to adapt to different regions and various changes of the environments. Another important category of picking algorithms is based on autoregressive (AR) models [10] or wavelet processing methods [11]. They pick time instance to maximize the dissimilarity of two AR models or wavelets for signals before and after the picked time instance. Both of them are accurate and robust, however, the AR models or wavelets incur high computational complexity and memory usage, they would be inappropriate to be adopted in the resource-limited smartphones.

2.2   Community Seismic Networks

The Community Seismic Network and the Quake Catcher networks use low-cost MEMS accelerometers that plug into computers which are deployed in buildings to detect earthquakes [12]. These systems consisted of thousands of accelerometers but are hard to be expanded to be an ubiquitous sensing system, while the smartphones are very easy to be popularized. Caltech presents an anomaly events detection scheme which adopted data fusion on a processing center to determine whether an event is an earthquake or not [3]. Some crowd sensing projects use internet social media to detect earthquakes, they lease earthquakes words from tweets or posters in various languages to issue possible earthquakes [13], the short slab is that the message would be delayed due to the information posting and data collection. The similar work in Berkeley is MyShake and iShake system, which use smartphones as the node of crowd sensing networks to report earthquakes and the locations [1,7]. Unlike the above, we effort in distinguishing events from samples contaminated by daily operations on smartphones and utilizing data fusion to eliminate the false alarms.

3   Motivation and Approach Overview

3.1   Motivation

The fundamental problem of utilizing smartphones in earthquake detections is that the built-in sensors, accelerometers for example, are not made for the particular objective, most of them are unsuitable to issue accurate earthquakes. Meanwhile, the ambient noise in signals is unpredictable since owners pose their phones on diverse scenarios. And the differences of manufacturers lead to a large differences in smartphones hardware. Both of them cause serious false alarm rates, which results in challenges in designing the detection strategies. So we need to propose schemes to recognize the real events from the data contaminated by ambient noise, while reducing false alarms effectively.

3.2   Overview

The proposed system consists of plenty of cell phones and a decision center networked by cellular mobile internet. As depicted in Fig. 1. The application running on smartphones collects motion signals sensed by accelerometers at real-time, then applies a lightweight eigenfunction to amplify the features of anomalous tremors while dropping the influence of noise. Then, the refined signals are handed down to a lightweight P-phase picking algorithm. If a preliminary event is found, a high-accuracy events timing analyse algorithm will be triggered to figure the accurate time of tremors out or to deny that a true seismic event is occurring. Once a positive decision is made on local smartphones, the location and exact timing of the event will be transmitted to the fusion center, on which the number of positive decisions is compared to the number of registered devices located in the same areas. The decision center issues a global decision about earthquake if the ratio of positive number to whole exceeds a preset threshold which is analyzed in Sect. 5.3.

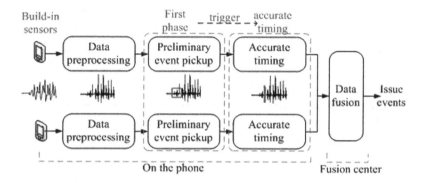

Fig. 1. Architecture of the system

The proposed approach has the following advantages. First, we employ a lightweight eigenfunction for noise reduction. The proposed technique is more practical for energy-constrained mobile phones. Secondly, a two-stage event detection algorithm is designed to lower the computational overhead. Since the decision of the first stage is made by a simple algorithm, STA/LTA for example, and only triggers the second stage where the accurate but resource expensive algorithm is executed. Moreover, by employing data fusion schemes, the method reduces false alarms as well as incurs low communication overheads as only transmitting a small amount of data to the fusion center.

4 Data Collection and Preprocessing

4.1 Data Collection

We collect the seismic data by simulating and recording on a computer-controlled shaking table which is for testing the stability of components of building structure. Smartphones are held by participants who standing or walking on the table, acting as usual as if they were on the ground. We use three different types of smartphones with built-in accelerometers to sample data in different scenes, and make the effort to keep matching with the real scenarios. Then, we summarize the actual data in daily activities and then classify them into nine types described in Table 1, which includes no event, regular vibrations, irregular vibrations, diminuendos shaking events, crescendos shaking events, low frequency vibration events, high frequency vibration events, persistent vibrations, and simulated seismic events which are controlled by shaking table.

Table 1. Classifications of recorded data

Event	Event types	Causes of shaking
E1	No vibrations	Stable or normal activities
E2	Regular vibrations	Built-in vibrating motor or other devices
E3	Irregular vibrations	Chaos activities
E4	Diminuendos shaking	From strenuous activities to calm
E5	Crescendos	From calm to strenuous activities
E6	Low frequency vibrations	Normal daily activities
E7	High frequency vibrations	High frequency of holders movements
E8	Persistent vibrations	Uninterrupted holders movement
E9	Simulated seismic events	Intermittently subjected to external shakes

4.2   Data Preprocessing

Due to the influence of people's daily operation and the low accuracy of the built-in sensors of mobile phones, the frequency of vibrations received by mobile phones can not directly reflect the spectrum changes, we employ transforming on signals to amplify the P-phase characteristics while reducing the influence of interferences. According to previous studies, threshold based methods such as STA/LTA and AIC methods are effective in the seismic phase identification in time domain, and the horizontal amplitude is notable [14]. The Allen eigenfunction, which was proposed by Allen in [9], can reflect and enhance the change of frequency and amplitude of signals sensitively. The calculation of Allen transform is simple, which is appropriate to be employed for preprocessing for real-time events picker in smartphones. We denote the original sampling record as $Y(i)(i = 1, 2...n)$ and the new time series $CF(i)$ which is transformed from $Y(i)$, can be defined as:

$$CF(i) = A^2 \sin^2 \omega \qquad (1)$$

where A is amplitude of signal, and ω is the circle frequency at time i. The specific calculation of $CF(i)$ can be derived as follows: Suppose the signal recorded at time i is $x(i), (i = 1, 2, ...n)$:

$$x(i) = A\cos(\omega i \Delta t + \phi) \tag{2}$$

After trigonometric transforming,

$$x(i-1)x(i+1) = A^2 \cos^2(\omega i \Delta t + \phi) - A^2 \sin^2 \omega \tag{3}$$

By substituting Eq. (2) into the above equation, we can get

$$A^2 \sin^2 \omega = x(i)^2 - x(i-1)x(i+1) \tag{4}$$

By replacing (1) with the above equation, the transforming CF(i) of original sampling record Y (i) can be calculated by:

$$CF(i) = Y(i)^2 - Y(i-1)Y(i+1) \tag{5}$$

5   Seismic Events Detection Scheme

Seismic events detection scheme in smartphones needs real-time and accurate picking and timing. However, the accurate but resource expensive strategies are inapplicable in battery powered mobile devices. In this section, we proposed a two phases scheme for smartphones for local detection and a decision fusion scheme for global detection. The first phase is a preliminary, its objective is to decide whether there is an event. Once a positive decision is made, it triggers a complex but accurate timing scheme as the second phase to report the exact events.

5.1   Preliminary Detection

The event picker in the first phase must be lightweight, so we use the STA/LTA algorithm [14,15]. The average energy ratio of long and short time windows is defined as [16]:

$$STA(i)/LTA(i) = \frac{\sum_{k_1}^{i} CF(i)/(i - k_1 + 1)}{\sum_{k_2}^{i} CF(i)/(i - k_2 + 1)} \tag{6}$$

where $CF(i)$ is time series after Allen transform, i is the current value at time i, k_1 and k_2 are start time before current time stamp i, and we set $k_2 \leq k_1 \leq i$ as to guarantee separating the long time window and the short one. If the STA/LTA value exceeds a pre-set threshold, the algorithm determines the occurrence of earthquake events, otherwise, no action is taken. The setting of the trigger threshold is the key parameter as it might launch the false alarms or miss the real anomalous events [16], we will analyze it later.

5.2   Accurate Timing

The STA/LTA method is the limited ability on false alarm elimination and, its picked event arrival time usually lags behind the real arrival time, in order to obtain accurate event pick up information, we introduce the AIC method, which is only triggered when the simple STA/LTA reports a positive decision to balance the resource consumption and system performance. The basic principle is that the minimum value on the AIC curve is the best boundary between the seismic signals and the environmental noise [17]. The AIC curve of seismic signal in a fixed time window is calculated. The minimum value in the curve is the location of the arrival time of P wave. Therefore, by constructing the maximum likelihood in a certain time window, we can obtain the arrival time of the P-wave.

However, AIC causes high computing complexity so is unsuitable for resource constraint smartphones, so we use a improved AR-AIC scheme proposed by Maeda [10], in which the AIC curve is solved out directly from the preprocessed time-series. Unlike the STA/LTA picker whose timing results often lags behind the real, the AR-AIC method determines the exact P-phase arrival time to a specific sampling point rather than the whole time window, which obtains accurate timing results even though its computation complexity is much high. Suppose the number of samples of the data window is $N, x(i)(i = 1, ..., N)$ is the i th value in the wave, then the AIC value can be calculated as:

$$AIC(k) = k \log\{var(x[1, k])\} + (N - k - 1) \log\{var(x[k + 1, N])\}$$

where var($\cdot$) is the variance. The exact time of P-phase of the event is chosen as the time with minimum value within all AIC values of the param time window on the wave.

5.3   Data Fusion and Threshold Setting

The local decisions made by a single smartphone are possible false alarms as the sampled data by built-in sensors are contaminated with phone holders daily operation. However, one of the most important advantages of leasing smartphones in earthquake detection is the mass of participants. So data fusion inevitably becomes the effective solution to reduce the false alarm rate while maintaining the detection probability. The fusion strategy adopted is decision fusion due to the low communication cost [18]. Specifically, the client phones send the positive local decisions 1 to the fusion center which compares the number of the received positive decisions (denoted by λ) to a threshold, if λ equals or is greater than the threshold, the global final positive decision will be issued and no action otherwise. Then the setting of threshold is the key to the system performance and we analyze how to set it as follows.

We use $\Lambda = \sum_{i=1}^{n} I_i$ to represent the summation of reports received by fusion center, where Ii represents the local decisions, $i = 1, ..., n$ is the number of smartphones. In decision fusion, $I_i = 1$ if smartphone i report positive local decision and 0 if no event found. Suppose a smartphone makes a decision under assumptions with or without evens (represented by H_1 and H_0, respectively). When no event occurs, the local decision of sensor $i : I_i|H_0$ follows Bernoulli distribution with success probability α_i [19]. Then the test statistic $\Lambda \mid H_0$ follows a generalize Binomial distribution, the probability mass function of $\Lambda \mid H_0$ is:

$$P(\Lambda = \lambda|H_0) = \sum_{|S|=\Lambda, \forall S} \prod_{i \in S} \alpha_i \prod_{j \in S^c} (1 - \alpha_j) \tag{7}$$

where S is the subset of smartphones with size λ and S^c is the complement of S. Similarly, the local decision of sensor $i : I_i|H_1$ follows Bernoulli distribution with success probability β_i, the probability mass function (PMF) of $\Lambda \mid H_1$ is:

$$P(\Lambda = \lambda|H_1) = \sum_{|S|=\Lambda, \forall S} \prod_{i \in S} \beta_i \prod_{j \in S^c} (1 - \beta_j) \tag{8}$$

Then we can get the cumulative distribution function (CDF):

$$F_{\Lambda|H_0}(x) = \sum_{\lambda=0}^{|x|} P(\Lambda = \lambda|H_0) \tag{9}$$

The system false alarm rate can be computed as $P_F = 1 - F_{\Lambda|H_0}(\eta)$. Similarly, the system detection probability can be calculated as $P_D = 1 - F_{\Lambda|H_1}(\eta)$. Note that α_i in Eq. (9) is replaced with β_i to produce the PMF of $\Lambda|H_1$.

However, the computational complexity of CDF is $O(2^n)$, so when the number of fusion nodes is large (which is suppose to be), it is infeasible to compute at runtime. Then we use an approximate equation as follows.

The local decision made by smartphones are independent, so the mean $\Lambda|H_0$ are given by:

$$E[\Lambda|H_0] = \sum_{i=1}^{n} E[I_i|H_0] = \sum_{i=1}^{n} \alpha_i \tag{10}$$

and the variance is:

$$Var[\Lambda|H_0] = \sum_{i=1}^{n} Var[I_i|H_0] = \sum_{i=1}^{n} \alpha_i - \alpha_i^2 \tag{11}$$

The Lyapunov condition for a sequence of Bernoulli random variables has been proved in [19]. Therefore, according to the Lyapunov Central Limit Theorem (CLT), when n is very large, $\Lambda|H_0$ follows Normal distribution:

$$\Lambda|H_0 \sim N(\sum_{i=1}^{n} \alpha_i - \sum_{i=1}^{n} \alpha_i - \alpha_i^2) \tag{12}$$

and similarly, we have:

$$\Lambda|H_1 \sim N(\sum_{i=1}^{n} \beta_i - \sum_{i=1}^{n} \beta_i - \beta_i^2) \tag{13}$$

Therefore, the false alarm rate and detection probability of the system are as follows:

$$P_F \cong Q(\frac{\lambda - \sum_{i=1}^{n} \alpha_i}{\sqrt{\sum_{i=1}^{n} \alpha_i - \alpha_i^2}}); P_D \cong Q(\frac{\lambda - \sum_{i=1}^{n} \beta_i}{\sqrt{\sum_{i=1}^{n} \beta_i - \beta_i^2}}) \tag{14}$$

where $Q(x) = \frac{1}{\sqrt{2\pi}} \int_x^\infty e^{-t^2/2} dt, Q(\cdot)$ is the Q-function of the standard normal distribution.

The system false alarm rate PF can be set as a prior, and the false alarm rates in local smartphones are obtained numerically as discussed at Sect. 5.1, both of them are sent to the fusion center at the initialization stage. So we can get the system threshold according to Eq. (14).

6   Performance Evaluation

6.1   Evaluation Implementation

The detection algorithm proposed above has been implemented on Android system through various types of smart phones. The shake table used in the experiment was originally for studying the earthquake resistant behaviors of building structures at The Structural Engineering and Vibration Laboratory in our university. We chose the perceptual quality S of detection as the performance reference by the detection probability p_d and the false alarm rate p_f. The phones recorded 20 sets of data for each types of motions in Table 1 while the shake table simulated the earthquakes. The reference time stamp of earthquakes is downloaded from shake table control computers as the ground truth. In other to determine the threshold on smartphones, we record plenty of samples and detect the events. As an example, the chosen threshold of one smartphone starts from

Table 2. Local decision thresholds of phone1

Thresholds	Accuracy (%)	False alarm rate (%)	Ratio S
0.1	100	68.02	1.47
0.15	100	64.07	1.56
0.2	100	49.23	2.03
0.25	98.21	45.32	2.17
0.3	79.64	47.57	1.67
0.35	41.79	44.36	0.94
0.4	29.17	25.69	1.14
0.45	26.04	19.44	1.34
0.5	19.79	18.75	1.06

0.1 to 0.5, increased by 0.05 in each round of detecting. According to analysis in reference [10], the length of short windows and long window are set to 0.5 and 10 s respectively. We record and load 90 records to calculate the thresholds which are shown in Table 2, then we can determine the threshold of this phone to be 0.25 according to the posted detection results. Although the calculation of thresholds for smartphones is labor extensive, but it is an one off job for each phone model, so it is viable.

6.2   Evaluation Implementation

In order to evaluate the effectiveness of the proposed event picker on local smartphones, we compared the results to the ground truth which is the exact starting time of shakes downloaded from the computer on the shaking table. We set the traditional P-phase picker as a baseline which is the widely adopted STA/LTA algorithm [16]. 9 different behavioral modes of the human activities discussed in Table 1 are simulated by several phone holders. Figure 2 depicts timing results of detecting an event, the arrival time obtained by traditional pickers lags behind the ground truth, while the proposed scheme can produce much more accurate results.

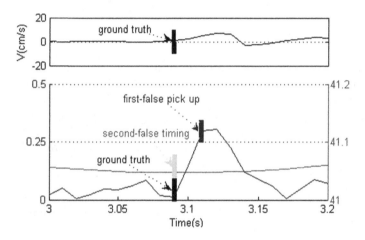

Fig. 2. An example of local detection.

Table 3 shows a typical timing results of anomalous events recorded by a phone while the phone holders post 9 activities. The results are similar to Fig. 2. However, decreasing the length of the short window can improve the precision, but it results in computing extensive and false alarms.

6.3   Effectiveness of Data Preprocessing

To verify the effectiveness of the proposed preprocessing scheme in eliminating sampling noise, we conduct plenty of experiments by 409 sets of samples on smartphones. Figure 3(a) depicts the relationship between the false alarm rate pf and the detection probability pd calculated from 90 set of data. The detection threshold is scaled from a small value which guarantees pd to be 100%, to a large value that the pd less than 50% or no false alarm issued. The blue curve represents the detection results with preprocessed data and the red curve represents no preprocessing employed. From the figure we can see that the curve

Table 3. The events timing of local detection.

Record	Ground truth(s)	STA/LTA(s)	STA/LTA+AIC(s)
E1	-	-	-
E2	0.98	0.99	0.98
E3	1.51	1.60	1.52
E4	2.38	2.43	2.37
E5	3.09	3.11	3.09
E6	1.57	1.59	1.57
E7	2.22	2.24	2.21
E8	2.16	2.17	2.16
E9	0.94	0.95	0.93

with preprocessing can achieve lower false alarm rate than the original one, the results verified that data preprocessing are benefit to the false alarm elimination.

The evaluation is also conducted on three different phones in the same scenario, the threshold is set as discussed in Sect. 6.4. Figure 3(b) is the results, in which we compare the false alarm rate with and without adopting the preprocessing, the average improvement of false alarm by data preprocessing in local decision is about 24%.

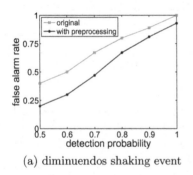

(a) diminuendos shaking event

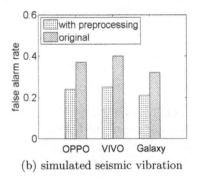

(b) simulated seismic vibration

Fig. 3. The Effectiveness of Preprocessing. (Color figure online)

6.4   Performance of Data Fusion

To validate the performance improvement of data fusion in the system, three smartphones participate in detecting earthquakes and sent the positive decisions to the fusion center for final issuing, specifically, three phones are held by three persons as usual on a shake table, while the shake table simulates an event.

Figure 4 depicts the received signals, where the first phone reports 3 false alarms and one event, and the other two report only one false alarm and both of them detect the events. As the threshold calculated by Eq. (14) is two, only one of three false alarms are issued, two of them have been eliminated.

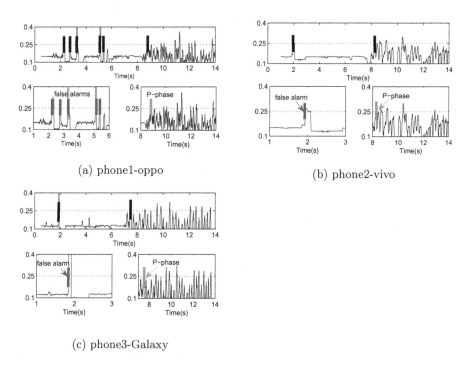

(a) phone1-oppo

(b) phone2-vivo

(c) phone3-Galaxy

Fig. 4. Simulated Seismic Vibration and False Alarms Reported by Three Phones. Upper is the Original Wave, Lower is the Local Zoom of Events.

At each phone we carry out 45 detections for different events described at Table 1. The fusion threshold is calculated by Eq. (14). First, we bound the system false alarm rate to PF = 0.1 as the requirement and calculate the threshold, compare the received detection probabilities with the results without fusion. Figure 5(a) shows that the PD doubles after fusion. Secondly, we set PD = 0.9 to determine the threshold as to guarantee the system missing rate, then compare the false alarm rate of after fusion with the results of single smartphones. The received results show that the false alarm drops dramatically compared with the detections only on single nodes, the improvement is effective.

As the area of shake table is too small to accommodate more participants at one time, we conduct numeric simulations on MATLAB as reproduce the effectiveness of fusion by large number of smartphones. We use a Guassan noise generater to simulate noise caused by environment and the fabrication difference of models of smartphones. Figure 5(b) is the comparison of the false alarm rate and the detection probability with different fusion numbers, while the guaranteed detection probability and false alarm rate are set to PD = 0.9 and PF = 0.1 respectively. The green curve shows the detection probability increases to 1, while the number of fusion members increases from 5 to 30. When the system detection probability is bound to 0.9, the system false alarm rate drops from 0.4 to 0 while the number of fusion members increases to 30. The results show in complete agreements with one analysed in Sect. 5.3.

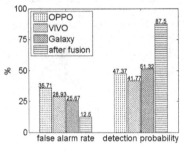

(a) diminuendos shaking event

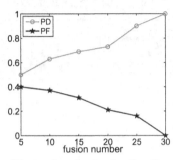

(b) simulated seismic vibration

Fig. 5. The effectiveness of data fusion. (Color figure online)

7   Conclusions

We develop a holistic scheme to accurate the anomalous events detection by smartphones, which pick the arrival times of events sampled by built-in motion sensors on smartphones. The purpose of this paper is to eliminate the false alarms caused by daily operations of phone holders. The proposed strategy is evaluated through extensive sampling and detection experiments by smartphones. The results show that our strategy can significantly reduce the false alarm rate caused by daily operations compared with traditional methods.

References

1. Kong, Q., Allen, R.M., Schreier, L., et al.: MyShake: a smartphone seismic network for earthquake early warning and beyond. Sci. Adv. **2**(2), e1501055 (2016)
2. Cochran, E.S., Lawrence, J.F., Christensen, C., Jakka, R.S.: The quake-catcher network: citizen science expanding seismic horizons. Seismol. Res. Lett. **80**, 26–30 (2009)
3. Faulkner, M., Olson, M., Chandy, R., Krause, J., Chandy, K.M., Krause, A.: The next big one: detecting earthquakes and other rare events from community-based sensors. In: International Conference on Information Processing in Sensor Networks, pp. 13–24 (2011)

4. Moumni, B., Frias-Martinez, V., Frias-Martinez, E.: Characterizing social response to urban earthquakes using cell-phone network data: the 2012 Oaxaca earthquake. In: 2013 ACM Conference on Pervasive and Ubiquitous Computing Adjunct Publication, pp. 1199–1208. ACM (2013)
5. Wilson, R., zu Erbach-Schoenberg, E., Albert, M., Power, D., et al.: Rapid and near real-time assessments of population displacement using mobile phone data following disasters, the 2015 Nepal earthquake. PLOS Curr. 1(8), 1 (2016)
6. Wald, D.J., Quitoriano, V., Worden, C.B., Hopper, M., Dewey, J.W.: USGS did you feel it? Internet-based macroseismic intensity maps. Ann. Geophys. 54(6), 688–709 (2012)
7. Dashti, S., et al.: iShake: using personal devices to deliver rapid semi-qualitative earthquake shaking information. GeoEng. Rep. 28, 1–51 (2011)
8. Withers, M., et al.: A comparison of select trigger algorithms for automated global seismic phase and event detection. Bull. Seismol. Soc. Am. 88(1), 95–106 (1998)
9. Allen, R.V.: Automatic earthquake recognition and timing from single traces. Bull. Seismol. Soc. Am. 68(5), 1521–1532 (1978)
10. Sleeman, R., Van Eck, T.: Robust automatic P-phase picking: an on-line implementation in the analysis of broadband seismogram recordings. Phys. Earth Planet. Inter. 113(1–4), 265–275 (1999)
11. Zhang, H., Thurber, C., Rowe, C.: Automatic P-wave arrival detection and picking with multiscale wavelet analysis for single-component recordings. Bull. Seismol. Soc. Am. 93(5), 1904–1912 (2003)
12. Clayton, R.W., Heaton, T., Chandy, M., et al.: Community seismic network. Ann. Geophys. 54(6), 738–747 (2012)
13. Earle, P.S., Bowden, D.C., Guy, M.: Twitter earthquake detection: earthquake monitoring in a social world. Ann. Geophys. 54(6), 708–715 (2012)
14. Qiang, M.: Study and application on earthquake early warning, pp. 305–318 (2008)
15. Earle, P.S., Shearer, P.M.: Characterization of global seismograms using an automatic-picking algorithm. Bull. Seismol. Soc. Am. 84(2), 366–376 (1994)
16. Shan, L.: Automatic P-arrival detection for earthquake early warning. Chin. J. Geophys. 56(7), 2313–2321 (2013)
17. Akaike, H.: Factor analysis and AIC. In: Parzen, E., Tanabe, K., Kitagawa, G. (eds.) Selected Papers of Hirotugu Akaike. Springer Series in Statistics (Perspectives in Statistics), pp. 371–386D. Springer, New York (1987). https://doi.org/10.1007/978-1-4612-1694-0_29
18. Varshney, P.K.: Distributed Detection and Data Fusion. Springer, New York (2012)
19. Tan, R., Xing, G., Wang, J., So, H.C.: Exploiting reactive mobility for collaborative target detection in wireless sensor networks. IEEE Trans. Mob. Comput. 9(3), 317–332 (2009)

A SEIR Model Optimization Using
the Differential Evolution

Dejiang Wang[1], Yafeng Sun[1], Ji Song[1], and Ying Huang[2](✉)

[1] School of Information Engineering, Jiangxi University of Science
and Technology, Ganzhou, China
[2] School of Mathematics and Computer Science, Gannan Normal University,
Ganzhou, China
nhwshy@whu.edu.cn

Abstract. The SEIR is a crucial mathematical model for solving infectious disease prediction and other problems in the field of artificial intelligence. It is used to effectively prevent and control infectious diseases by studying the infectious diseases' propagation speed, spatial range, transmission route, dynamic mechanism and other issues. In order to improve the prediction of infectious diseases in a certain area, a SEIR model optimization approach based on differential evolution (DE) algorithm is proposed in this paper. In this method, the differential evolution is used to optimization the related variables in the model. The overall prediction of the adjusted and optimized SEIR model algorithm is conformed to the regional development laws. The experimental results show that the SEIR infectious disease model optimized by DE algorithm is accurate and reliable in the analysis of COVID-19 propagation situation, and the model can be used to provide certain theoretical methods and technical support for future outbreak policy formulation.

Keywords: Differential evolution · SEIR model · Propagation dynamics · Epidemic analysis

1 Introduction

The SEIR is a significant mathematical model for solving infectious disease prediction and other problems in the field of artificial intelligence. It can be used to guide the effective prevention and control of infectious diseases by studying the propagation speed, spatial range, propagation path, dynamic mechanism and other issues of infectious diseases.

The infectious disease dynamic model is generated based on the infectious disease model promotion. The infectious disease dynamics [1] is an important method for carrying out theoretical quantitative research. According to the characteristics of population growth, the occurrence of disease and the laws of spread and development within the population, and the social factors related to it, a mathematical model that can reflect the dynamic characteristics of infectious diseases can be established. Through the quantitative analysis and numerical simulation of the dynamic behavior of the model, it analyzes the development process of the disease, reveals the epidemic law,

X. Chen et al. (Eds.): ML4CS 2020, LNCS 12487, pp. 384–392, 2020.
https://doi.org/10.1007/978-3-030-62460-6_34

predicts the change trend, and analyzes the causes of the disease epidemic. For the SARS epidemic in 2003, domestic and foreign scholars have established a large number of dynamic models to study its spreading laws and trends, and the effects of various isolation and prevention measures on epidemic control. By these models, lots of references are provided for decision-making departments. SIR or SEIR models are used to most of the studies on SARS propagation dynamics. The values of the two parameters of exposure rate and infection efficiency are commonly used to evaluate the effect of measures and fit actual popular data. Shi Yaolin [2] established a system dynamics model of SARS propagation, and carried out Monte Carlo experiments using data from Vietnam as a reference. Preliminary results indicate that the infection rate and its changes over time are the most important factors affecting the spread of SARS. Cai Quancai [3] established a propagation dynamics model that can quantitatively evaluate the effects of SARS interventions and fit the Beijing data well.

The improved SEIR infectious disease model used for infectious disease prediction in this paper can be found in [1]. In the model, based on the assumption that the law of population change is linear, for the epidemic situation of infectious diseases with incubation period (represented by the COVID-19), the classic SEIR model was improved. The four groups of classic SEIRs have been re-explained, and by setting parameter constraints to reveal the changes between the four groups.

For more researchers can understand and study the DE algorithm, Storn and Price established the official website of the differential evolution algorithm in 1997 [4]. The establishment of this website has received the attention and support of the researchers and carried out the differential evolution algorithm for related personnel. The DE algorithm has been applied by Store and Price, which plays an important role in promoting the research and application of differential evolution algorithm. This algorithm is based on the heuristic random search of population difference, using binary coding, which is divided into population initialization, mutation, crossover and selection [5]. Because binary coding is slower than real coding, DE algorithm is faster than classical genetic algorithm. Differential evolution (DE) algorithm is an optimization algorithm based on modern intelligence theory, the direction of optimization is guided by the search through the cooperation and competition between individuals [6]. The first of the algorithm is population initialization, and then the vector difference between any two individuals in the population is summed with the third individual to generate a new individual. The new individual is compared with the corresponding individual in the contemporary population. If the fitness of the new individual is better than that of the current individual, the new individual will be replaced in the next generation, otherwise the old individual will be preserved. Through continuous evolution, the excellent individuals are retained, the inferior ones are eliminated, and the search is guided to approach the optimal solution [7].

Based on mentioned the above, in order to make the prediction results obtained by the SEIR model more in line with the actual development, this paper adopts the DE algorithm to optimize the model parameters. On the basis of the original modified SEIR model, we introduce an adaptive strategy to dynamically optimize the parameters of the model and obtain the ideal optimization result.

The remainder of this paper is as follows. Section 2 introduces the back-ground of the SEIR model and DE algorithm. In Sect. 3, the SEIR optimization model using DE algorithm is explained in detail, and the experimental analysis and results are given in Sect. 4. Finally, Sect. 5 is a summary of this paper.

2   Related Work

2.1   The SEIR Model

The relationship between the SEIR infectious disease model in terms of population division and conversion is shown in Fig. 1.

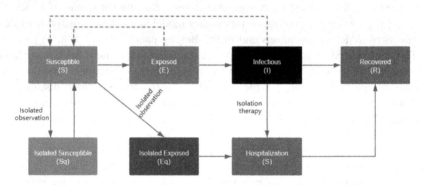

Fig. 1. The relationship of the SEIR model [8]

The control of the number of susceptible persons can be expressed as follows:

$$dS/dt = -[\rho c\beta + \rho cq(1 - \beta)]S(I + \theta E) + \lambda S_q \tag{1}$$

where q is the isolation ratio, β is the probability of infection, c is the contact rate, ρ is the effective contact coefficient, usually a fixed value of 1, ρc is the effective contact rate. The conversion rates of susceptible is S, isolated susceptible Sq, isolated latent Eq, and latent E are (1) $cq\ (1 - \beta)$, $\rho c\ q\beta(1 - q)$, and $\rho c\beta(1 - q)$, respectively. Considering the impact of non-isolated infected person I and latent person E on susceptible people, there are susceptible persons who have been released from isolation Sq re-transformed into S, and θ is the ratio of the latent person to the infected person's ability to transmit. Assume that the incubation period patients have the same infectious ability as those who have already shown symptoms, namely $\theta = 1$. λ is the isolation release rate, its value is $1/14$ and the isolation duration is $14\ d$ [9].

The modified SEIR kinetic equation for the COVID-19 epidemic is constructed as follows:

$$\begin{cases} dS/dt = -[\rho c\beta + \rho cq(1-\beta)]S(I+\theta E) + \lambda S_q \\ dE/dt = \rho c\beta(1-q)S(I+\theta E) - \sigma E \\ dI/dt = \sigma E - (\delta_I + \alpha + \gamma_I)I \\ dS_q/dt = \rho cq(1-\beta)S(I+\theta E) - \lambda S_q \\ dE_q/dt = \rho c\beta qS(I+\theta E) - \delta_q E_q \\ dH/dt = \delta_I I + \delta_q E_q - (\alpha + \gamma_H)H \\ dR/dt = \gamma_I I + \gamma_H H \end{cases} \qquad (2)$$

Among them, σ is the conversion rate of latent person to infected person, taking $1/7$ (the incubation period is 7d), α is the case fatality rate, δ_I is the isolation rate of infected persons, γ_I is the recovery rate of infected persons, δ_q is the conversion rate of quarantined latent persons to quarantined infected persons, and γ_H is the recovery rate of quarantined infected persons.

In the real cases, it can be found that since February 12 in 2019, Hubei Province and other regions changed the statistical method of newly diagnosed cases, the clinically diagnosed cases are included in the new cases, which caused a significant increase in officially announced new cases. The official published data is higher than the theoretical model prediction results in the original literature due to changes in statistical methods, so the model parameters are appropriately revised. The inclusion of some non-secondary confirmed cases will result in a lower average infection coefficient, and an increase in the total number of cases will lead to an increase in the contact coefficient. Considering a dynamic parameter adjustment method, the modified SEIR model after dynamic optimization is used to calculate the theoretical results of the number of infected people.

2.2 Differential Evolution

Differential evolution algorithm is an evolutionary algorithm for solving optimization problems. The evolutionary algorithm is regarded as a post-heuristic algorithm for its few requirements. Although the post-heuristic algorithm is applicable to a variety of optimization problems, the global optimal solution cannot be guaranteed to be found.

The differential evolution algorithm can be used to solve multi-dimensional real-coded optimization problems. Since it does not rely on the gradient information of the problem, it can solve non-differentiable optimization problems. Additionally, the differential evolution algorithm can also be used for discontinuous, noisy, and optimization problems that change over time.

Differential evolution is similar to genetic algorithm, including mutation operation, crossover operation, and elimination mechanism. The DE algorithm is also a greedy genetic algorithm with preserving ideas based on real coding [10]. The difference between the two solutions are randomly selected and added to the variable of the current solution member after scaling, so the probability distribution is not suited for DE to generate the next generation of solutions [11].

By perturbing the direction of the individual, the function value of the individual is reduced. Like other evolutionary algorithms, the gradient information of the function will not be used in the DE algorithm. Therefore, there is no requirement for the derivability or even continuity of the function and DE algorithm is highly applicable. There are some similarities between DE algorithm and particle swarm optimization algorithm, however, the correlation between multiple variables is considered in the differential evolution algorithm, considering the DE algorithm has a great advantage in variable coupling compared to particle swarm optimization. Therefore, the advantages of the differential evolution algorithm in the continuous domain optimization problem have been widely used, and triggered the upsurge in the field of evolutionary algorithm research.

The classic strategy operator of the DE algorithm is as follows:

$$v_i = x_i^1 + F \times \left(x_i^2 - x_i^3\right) \tag{3}$$

where *x1*, *x2*, and *x3* are three individuals selected from the current population, respectively, *i* denotes the *i-th* locus, and *F* is a quantifying factor that can be used to control the difference between the new individual and the parent individual *x1*. Because there are many parent individuals referenced in the DE operator, the newly generated offspring children and the original parent individuals are quite different, so DE algorithm performs well in global search capabilities and is often used to deal with complex optimization problems, meanwhile, it can avoid the algorithm falling into local optimum.

3   The Proposed Algorithm

For the dynamic optimization of model parameters, DE algorithm is used in this paper to dynamically optimize the parameters of the model based on real data, so that the prediction effect obtained by the model is more in line with the actual development.

Specific algorithm steps are as follows:

Step1: Initialize population control parameters: population size is *pop_size*, maximum evolution times denotes by *max_Iterate*, crossover probability is P_c, mutation probability is P_m.

$$\left\{X_i(0)|x_{i,j}^L \leq x_{i,j}(0) \leq x_{i,j}^U; i = 1, 2, \ldots\ldots, NP; j = 1, 2, \ldots\ldots, D\right\} \tag{4}$$

where X_i is the i-th individual and j is the j-th dimension.

$$x_{i,j}(0) = x_{i,j}^L + rand(0, 1)\left(x_{i,j}^U - x_{i,j}^L\right) \tag{5}$$

where $X_{i,j}^L$ and $X_{i,j}^U$ are the lower and upper bounds of the *j* dimension, respectively, and rand(0,1) represents random number in the interval [0,1].

Step2: Initialize *cn* cluster centers randomly and generate initial population *Chrom*, calculate the membership of each sample using Eq. (3) for each cluster center, and calculate the fitness value a of each individual using Eq. (3), where i = 1, 2,..., pop_size.

Step3: Set evolution iteration parameter *Iterate = 0*.

Step4: Perform genetic operations such as selection, crossover and mutation on the population *Chrom*, use the Eq. (4) and (5) to calculate the *cn* cluster centers and the membership of each sample, and use the Eq. (3) to calculate each individual's fitness value f_i. If $f_i > F_i$, the old one will be replaced by the new individual; otherwise, the probability $P = 1\ \exp((F_i - f_i)T)$.

Step5: Iterate = Iterate + 1. If Iterate < max_Iterate, turn back to **Step4**; otherwise, execute **Step6**.

Step6: $T_i = J * T_{i-1}$. If $T_i > T_{end}$, turn back to **Step3**; otherwise, execute to **Step7**.

Step7: Output the optimal solution.

Thus, *cn* evacuated clusters are obtained that in the different clusters are evacuated, and in the same clusters are dense.

4   Experiments and Analysis

4.1   Experimental Data

The model of this paper is solved by Euler numerical method with a time step of *0.01 (d)*. It should be stated that in the model of this article *I* is the current number of infected persons, defined as the confirmed cases announced on the day minus the cured cases and deaths.

Based on the original revised model, we crawled the time series of epidemic spread in various regions of China through crawlers, and used the data of the previous 30 days as training data to dynamically optimize the contact rate and effective contact coefficient based on DE algorithm.

For the feasibility assessment, this paper uses a comparison between the number of infected people obtained from the previous training and the actual infection data. Screen out populations that are more in line with real data development.

4.2   Experimental Analysis

In the case where the original model defines the static parameter values, the specific operation is shown in Fig. 2.

According to the running effect of the optimized and optimized dynamic parameters model, taking the Hubei Province infection prediction as an example, as shown in Fig. 3.

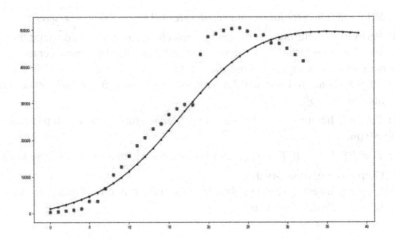

Fig. 2. The result of the original SEIR model algorithm

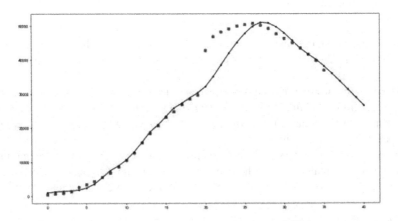

Fig. 3. The results of the SEIR model optimization for Hubei province

Through this experiment, the system found that for the epidemic situation of infectious diseases, the dynamic optimization method is used to predict the trend of the epidemic situation. It is more in line with the true epidemic trend than the prediction situation obtained under the previous fixed parameter situation. For different epidemics caused by different diseases, the system is also applicable by obtaining part of the time series or the epidemic sequence of similar epidemic. Figure 4 shows the effect of data testing in other regions.

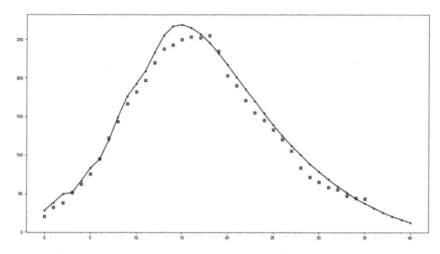

Fig. 4. The results of the SEIR model optimization for Shanghai city

5   Conclusion

From the perspective of epidemic prevention, although there are many factors that affect the spread of the epidemic, the main factors include the contact rate, the effective release coefficient, and the isolation ratio. The SEIR is a crucial mathematical model for solving infectious disease prediction and other problems in the field of artificial intelligence. It is used to effectively prevent and control infectious diseases by studying the infectious propagation speed, spatial range, transmission route, dynamic mechanism and other issues. In order to improve the prediction of infectious diseases in a certain area, a SEIR model optimization approach based on differential evolution (DE) algorithm is proposed in this paper. In this method, the differential evolution is used to optimization the related variables in the model. The overall prediction of the adjusted and optimized SEIR model algorithm is conformed to the regional development laws. The experimental results show that the SEIR infectious disease model optimized by DE algorithm is accurate and reliable in the analysis of COVID-19 propagation situation, and the model can be used to provide certain theoretical methods and technical support for future outbreak policy formulation.

Acknowledgement. This work was supported by the National Natural Science Foundation of China (Grant No. 61903089), the Jiangxi Provincial Natural Science Foundation (Grant No. 20202BAB202014).

References

1. Diekmann, O., Heesterbeek, H., Britton, T.: Mathematical Tools for Understanding Infectious Disease Dynamics, vol. 7. Princeton University Press (2012)
2. Ng, T.W., Turinici, G., Danchin, A.: A double epidemic model for the SARS propagation. BMC Infectious Diseases **3**(1), 19 (2003)

3. Michael, S., Shi, P., Tse, C.K.: Plausible models for propagation of the SARS virus. IEICE Trans. Fundam. Electron. Commun. Comput. Sci. **87**(9), 2379–2386 (2004)
4. Storn, R., Price, K.: Differential evolution–a simple and efficient heuristic for global optimization over continuous spaces. J. Global Optim. **11**(4), 341–359 (1997)
5. Ahuja, R.K., Orlin, J.B., Tiwari, A.: A greedy genetic algorithm for the quadratic assignment problem. Comput. Oper. Res. **27**(10), 917–934 (2000)
6. Fan, Q.Q., Yan, X.F.: Self-adaptive differential evolution algorithm with zoning evolution of control parameters and adaptive mutation strategies. IEEE Trans. Cybern. **46**, 219–232 (2015)
7. Awad, N.H., Ali, M.Z., Mallipeddi, R., Suganthan, P.N.: An improved differential evolution algorithm using efficient adapted surrogate model for numerical optimization. Inf. Sci. **451**, 326–347 (2018)
8. Li, M.Y., Muldowney, J.S.: Global stability for the SEIR model in epidemiology. Math. Biosci. **125**(2), 155–164 (1995)
9. Lekone, P.E., Finkenstädt, B.F.: Statistical inference in a stochastic epidemic SEIR model with control intervention: Ebola as a case study. Biometrics **62**(4), 1170–1177 (2006)
10. Tian, M., Gao, X.B.: Differential evolution with neighborhood-based adaptive evolution mechanism for numerical optimization. Inf. Sci. **478**, 422–448 (2019)
11. Zhang, J., Sanderson, A.C.: Jade: adaptive differential evolution with optional external archive. IEEE Trans. Evol. Comput. **13**, 945–958 (2009)

Multi-term Multi-task Allocation for Mobile Crowdsensing with Weighted Max-Min Fairness

Haibo Liu[1], Wenchao Jiang[2(✉)], Shasha Yang[3], Jianfeng Lu[1], and Dongjun Ning[4]

[1] Department of Computer Science and Engineering,
Zhejiang Normal University, Jinhua 321004, China
lhbzjnu@163.com, lujianfeng@zjnu.edu.cn
[2] School of Computer, Guangdong University of Technology,
Guangzhou 510006, China
jiangwenchao@gdut.edu.cn
[3] Xingzhi College, Zhejiang Normal University, Jinhua 321004, China
yssl3910109@126.com
[4] Taotall Technology Co., Ltd., Guangzhou 510635, China
donjonning@taotonggroup.com

Abstract. Mobile crowdsensing (MCS) has become a new paradigm of massive sensory data collection, analysis and exploration. Most studies in MCS tend to focus only on the goal of maximizing the social utility without considering the social fairness. The main challenge for considering social fairness in the multi-term multi-task allocation (MMA) problem lies in how to achieve a balance between social utility and social fairness in the multi-term. In order to maintain social fairness and stimulate mobile users to compete for sensing tasks, this is the first paper to introduce the weighted max-min fairness updated depending on the max-min fairness into the multi-term multi-task allocation problem. Using a deterministic local search (DLS) auction mechanism, we design a novel MMA algorithm which can work out the multi-task allocation problem and maintain the social fairness in the long term. Finally, extensive evaluation results show that our approach has a good performance which can balance utility and fairness with a relatively steady value of PoF.

Keywords: Mobile crowdsensing · Multi-term multi-task allocation · Auction mechanism · Weighted max-min fairness

This work was supported in part by the National Natural Science Foundation of China (No. 62072411, 61872323, 61751303), in part by the Social Development Project of Zhejiang Provincial Public Technology Research (No. 2017C33054), in part by the Natural Science Foundation of Guangdong Province (No. 2018A030313061), and in part by the Guangdong Science and Technology Plan (no. 2017B010124001, 201902020016, 2019B010139001).

X. Chen et al. (Eds.): ML4CS 2020, LNCS 12487, pp. 393–404, 2020.
https://doi.org/10.1007/978-3-030-62460-6_35

1 Introduction

With the popularity of Big Data and the massive increase of mobile devices, many investigations have focused on the development of mobile crowdsensing (MCS) which has become an efficient method to collect huge data and make decisions. So far, the idea of MCS has been extensively used in many aspects of scientific research such as network security [1], communication network [2], social network [3], etc. Although more and more applications have been stimulated to work out a variety of issues [4–7], there are also many fundamental problems such as the quality of data [8], tasks allocation [9], privacy preserving [10, 11] which need to be further researched in crowdsensing system.

More and more attention should be paid to the multi-task allocation which has direct and vital influence in MCS. There also exists a very extensive literature [12, 13] on the topic of the multi-task allocation problem of diverse applications scenarios considering different optimization objectives. Online multi-task allocation [7, 14–16] is one of the popular topics which mainly focus on the quality of data and the stability of crowdsensing system by predicting the mobility model of workers or using queue to control the arriving tasks [17]. It is unlike for all the online algorithm to compute the optimal result in the complicated and fickle online scenario. Comparing with online multi-task allocation problem, the offline one, which has more information about workers and requesters, can figure out a better solution with some other constraints by designing specific algorithm. Stackelberg game and Auction mechanism are the common ways to deal with the complex multi-task allocation problem in the most offline algorithm [18–20]. Although these methods can find an allocation scheme depending on its rules and tactics, most scenarios have ignored some crucial factors such as social fairness which may lead to a large number of workers unwilling to compete for tasks, especially in the long-term situation. In MCS, the typical process simply includes requesters' publishing tasks, tasks allocation, workers' performing tasks and receiving payment. We call this typical process one term. In most literature, the next more term will stiffly follow the first method to work out the multi-task problem which has ignored the fairness in the long term.

Fairness is an important social factor in resource allocation problem and there is also a large body of work in this area considering different definitions of fairness. Proportional fairness, Max-Min fairness and Kalai-Smorodinsky Fairness are the three common fairness form and each of them has its own character and applicational scenario. Proportional fairness which can look for a fair solution satisfying the proportional constraint, has been widely used in device-to-device communication networks [21], wireless sensor networks [22] and so on, but it is difficult to prove and compute the only one fair solution. Kalai-Smorodinsky fairness is similar with max-min fairness and has added some other constraint condition. The Max-Min fairness is the most flexible, adaptive and direct form which is satisfied with the common sense by making the participant obtaining the lowest utility, still receives highest possible utility.

Under the long-term situation, some participants would be unallocated in continuous terms and the Max-Min fairness can't be applied to this situation directly. In order to keep fairness in multi-term, we design the Weighted Max-Min Fairness based on the Max-Min Fairness to figure out the multi-term multi-task allocation (MMA) problem. Our main contributions are summarized as follows:

Table 1. Summary of parameters in this paper.

Variable	Description
$T = \{1, \ldots\ldots, \tau\}$	The set of term
$\mathcal{R} = \{r_1, \ldots\ldots, r_m\}$	The set of requesters
$\mathcal{W} = \{w_1, \ldots\ldots, w_n\}$	The set of workers
$\Gamma = \{\Gamma_1, \ldots\ldots, \Gamma_m\}$	The set of tasks
$K = \{\kappa_1, \ldots\ldots, \kappa_m\}$	The unit value set of tasks
$A = \{\alpha_1, \ldots\ldots, \alpha_n\}$	The bidding price set of workers
$\mathcal{C} = \{c_1, \ldots\ldots, c_n\}$	The cost set of workers
S_i	The interested tasks set of w_i
A_k	The kth allocation solution
u_j^r, u_i^w	The utility of requester j and worker i
σ_i	The weight of worker i
$\rho_{i,j}$	The payment of w_i from r_j

- The submodular function is taken advantage of to design a deterministic local search (DLS) auction mechanism to work out the multi-task allocation problem in one term by selecting a part of workers properly under the constraints of max-min fairness.
- We take the multi-term multi-task allocation problem into consideration with the weighted max-min fairness updated depending on the max-min fairness to stimulate workers and maintain social fairness in the long term.
- Extensive numerical evaluations show that our designed algorithm can have a good result which can balance utility and fairness with a relatively steady value of PoF, and attract more workers to compete for tasks.

In the rest of article, we first give a presentation on system model and problem formulation in Sect. 2, and design an auction mechanism to tackle out the multi-term multi-task problem in Sect. 3. Section 4 will do a simulation experiment and make a performance evaluation, and conclusions are drawn in the last section.

2 Model and Problem

2.1 System Model

A crowdsensing system usually includes three parts: a service platform, a set of requesters and a set of workers. As shown in Fig. 1, the typical transaction in MCS can be described as follows: First, each requester can publish a sensing task with its own description and send whole information to the service platform. Next, the platform spreads all the sensing tasks information to workers who are in the system at the same time. After reading and having a knowledge of tasks' detail, all workers will select some tasks based on their preference and give a feedback to the service platform. Consequently, depending on workers' tastes and tasks' value, the platform would adopt some strategy to select a part of workers to perform the sensing tasks. Then, each

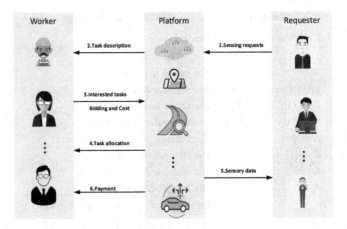

Fig. 1. The typical transaction in mobile crowdsensing.

worker uploads the sensing data to the MCS platform after completing the task. At last, requesters get their wanted sensory data and workers receive the payment from the platform. We call this whole process as one term. Table 1 has listed frequently used parameters in this paper.

In this paper, we focus on the multi-term scenario and divide time into discrete term $T = \{1, \ldots\ldots, \tau\}$. In one term t: $t \in T$, we use $\mathcal{R} = \{r_1, \ldots\ldots, r_m\}$ to denote a set of requesters and $\mathcal{W} = \{w_1, \ldots\ldots, w_n\}$ is a set of workers. Let each requester $r_j \in \mathcal{R}$ posts a sensing task $\tau_j \in \Gamma$ with unit value $\kappa_j \in K$, where the task set $\Gamma = \{\Gamma_1, \ldots\ldots, \Gamma_m\}$ and $K = \{\kappa_1, \ldots\ldots, \kappa_m\}$. At the same time, each worker competes for their interested tasks S_i with the bidding price $\alpha_i \in A$ and the cost $c_i \in C$ where the bidding price set $A = \{\alpha_1, \ldots\ldots, \alpha_n\}$ and the cost set $C = \{c_1, \ldots\ldots, c_n\}$. We assume that the platform can allocate no more than one task to each worker and all workers are honest who will try their best to finish work and the contribution increases with the bidding price.

Definition 1. (Requester's Utility) Then, the utility of requester j over the set of selected users S_j is defined as:

$$u_j^r = \left(\kappa_j \sum_{i \in S_j} \alpha_i\right)^\theta - \sum_{i \in S_j} \rho_{i,j} \tag{1}$$

Where $\rho_{i,j}$ is the payment which worker i gets from requester j.

Definition 2. (Worker's Utility) the utility of worker i can be described as followed:

$$u_i^w = \begin{cases} \rho_{i,j} - c_i, & i \in S_j \\ 0, & otherwise \end{cases} \tag{2}$$

Algorithm 1: Deterministic Local Search Auction

Input: $S = \{S_1, \ldots \ldots, S_m\}, \Phi = \{\sigma_1, \ldots \ldots, \sigma_n\}$

Output: U

1 find a worker i and the corresponding j where $\mu^r(\{i\})$ is the maximum
  among all $i \in N$

2 $U_j = U_j \cup \{i\}$, add U_j into U

3 **foreach** worker $i \in S \backslash U$ **do**

4   **if** $\mu^r(U \cup \{i\}) > (1 + \frac{\epsilon - \sigma_i}{n^2}) \mu^r(U)$ **then**

5       $U_j = U_j \cup \{i\} \leftarrow \arg\min \mu^r_{j \in S_i}$

6   **if** U_j not in U **then**

7   add U_j into U

8   **endif**

9   **endif**

10 **endfor**

11 **foreach** worker $i \in U$ **do**

12   **if** $\mu^r(U \backslash \{i\}) > (1 + \frac{\epsilon - \sigma_i}{n^2}) \mu^r(U)$ **then**

13       $U = U \backslash \{i\}$

14   go to line 3

15   **endif**

16 **endfor**

17 **return** U

2.2 Max-Min Fairness

It is obvious that there exist many feasible solutions in the multi-task allocation problem. Different allocated scheme may lead to the different utility of requesters and workers. What's worse, some solutions could give rise to unfairness. Therefore, a fair solution is essential for platform to attractive more workers to compete for tasks.

Definition 3. (Max-Min fairness) A solution is sought by making the participant obtaining the lowest utility, still receives highest possible utility. So, we are in search for a solution $x_{MM} \in X$ such that

$$x_{MM} = \arg max_{x \in X} \, min_{j=1,\ldots\ldots,k} \, \{\mu(x)\} \qquad (3)$$

Max-Min fairness has been widely used in resource allocation problem to maintain fairness. Based on the previous research, there must be at least as many as one solution existing. if having some same solutions, we can just choose one of solutions randomly. Although max-min fairness has a good performance, it can't adapt to the multi-term multi-task allocation scenario. Before we rewrite the form of max-min fairness, we divide workers into two parts based on the character of multi-term problem and the allocated result of workers: if workers had taken part in competing for tasks and hadn't been selected, we call these works PU (Participated and Unallocated). On the contrary, we call the other part of workers PA (Participated and Allocated).

Definition 4. (Workers' Weight) Different category of workers have different weight, the weight of workers is defined as:

$$\sigma_i = \begin{cases} \varepsilon, \ w_i = PU \\ 0, \ otherwise \end{cases} \tag{4}$$

Where ε is a very little number. Based on the weight of workers, we modify the form of max-min fairness and call it as weighted max-min fairness.

Definition 5. (Weighted Max-Min Fairness) Based on the definition of max-min fairness and the description of workers' weight, for every agent $i \in N$, the weighted max min fairness solution x is defined as:

$$x_{WMM} = \arg\max_{x \in M} \min_{k \in K} \mu(x) * w(x) \tag{5}$$

Where $w(x)$ is the weight of solution x.

2.3   Multi-term Multi-task Allocation Problem

Given the definition of workers' and requesters' utility in the previous section, we now study the multi-term multi-task allocation (MMA) problem under the constraint of weighted max-min fairness. We assume that there exist K allocation solutions and our goal is to find one to satisfy the definition of weight max-min fairness.

Definition 6. (MMA)   Under the constraint of weighted max-min fairness, the multi-term multi-task allocation problem can be defined as:

$$\begin{cases} \mu^r = max \sum_{j \in M} u_j^r \\ s.t. \ max_{i \in N} \min_{k \in K} u_i^w(A_k) * w(A_k) \\ w(A_k) = e^{\sum_{i \in S_k} \sigma_i} \end{cases} \tag{6}$$

Where A_k denotes the kth allocated scheme.

3   Auction Mechanism for MMA

In this section, we will specifically analyze the multi-term multi-task allocation problem. First, we propose the deterministic local search (DLS) auction mechanism to work out the workers selecting problem. Based on the DLS auction mechanism, we will give the detail of multi-term multi-task allocation algorithm.

3.1   Deterministic Local Search Auction Mechanism

Given the set S of workers, under the constraint of weighted max-min fairness, how to select a subset $\mho$ so that the μ^r is maximized over the all possible subsets? It is obvious that this allocation problem is the NP-hard problem and it is difficult to find the optimal solution. Therefore, we pay our attention to the alternative of the approximation algorithm. There exists a mount of studies assume that the utility function of requesters is monotone submodular, which is applied to many realistic scenarios. In order to find an approximate solution easily, we also use this submodular function as our utility function.

Algorithm 2: MMA Algorithm

Input: U_{t-1}

Output: U_t

1 check out all the workers and update their weight
2 update the task set $S \leftarrow S_t$
3 compute U using algorithm 1
4 **foreach** worker $i \in U$ do
5     $ñ_{i,j} \leftarrow á_i$
6   compute the worker i utility according to Eq.(2)
7 **endfor**
8 compute the utility of requesters according to Eq.(1)
9 **return** U_t,

Definition 7. (Submodular Function): Let ψ be a finite set, a function $f: 2^\psi \mapsto$ R is called the submodular function if and only if

$$f(X \cup \{x\}) - f(X) \geq f(Y \cup \{x\}) - f(Y) \tag{7}$$

for any $X \subseteq Y \subseteq \psi$ and $x \in \psi \setminus Y$.

Lemma 1: the utility u_j^r is a submodular function

Proof: Based on the Definition 7, For any $X \subseteq Y \subseteq \psi$ and $x \in \psi \setminus$, we need to prove that: $u_j^r(X \cup \{x\}) - u_j^r(X) \geq u_j^r(Y \cup \{x\}) - u_j^r(Y)$. The utility function is $u_j^r = \left(\kappa_j \sum_{i \in S_j} \alpha_i \right)^\theta - \sum_{i \in S_j} \rho_{i,j}$ and we use $v(S)$ to denote this function $\left(\kappa_j \sum_{i \in S_j} \alpha_i \right)^\theta$. So, we just need to prove $v(X \cup \{x\}) - v(X) \geq v(Y \cup \{x\}) - v(Y)$. From the derivation of this function $\left(\kappa_j \sum_{i \in S_j} \alpha_i \right)^\theta$, we know that it is a monotone increasing concave function. It obviously meets up the requirement.

As the previous description, we update the utility function with $V(S) = \sum_{j \in M} \left(\kappa_j \sum_{i \in S_j} \alpha_i \right)^\theta$. Therefore, we can rewrite the MMA problem with the submodularity function as follows:

$$\begin{cases} \mu^r = max(V(S) - \sum_{j \in M} \sum_{i \in S_j} \rho_{i,j}) \\ s.t. \max_{i \in N} \min_{k \in K} u_i^w(A_k) * w(A_k) \\ w(A_k) = e^{\sum_{i \in S_k} \sigma_i} \end{cases} \tag{8}$$

Where S is the set of selected workers. Therefore, we design a deterministic local search (DLS) auction based on the algorithm of [23]. The DLS auction can select workers step by step depending on the marginal utility. The detail of DLS auction can be described in the Algorithm 1. Based on the description of research [23], we know that the algorithm terminates, the set U is a $(1 + \frac{\epsilon}{n^2})$-approximate local optimum. The running time of DLS auction algorithm is $O(\frac{1}{\epsilon} n^3 m \log m)$.

3.2 MMA Algorithm

In the previous section, we make use of the submodularity function and design a local search auction mechanism to figure out the user selected problem. Next, we focus on the multi-term multi-task allocation problem. Different with the one-term multi-cycle multi-task problem, the MMA problem's previous allocation result has the influence on the next term allocation with the change of workers' weight. Based on the Algorithm 1, the following algorithm is designed to work out the MMA problem.

The key part of MMA algorithm is the step 3. The running time of this algorithm depends on the product of the number of terms and the time of Algorithm 1.

4   Simulation and Evaluation

4.1   Simulation Setup

In this part, we will provide some numerical experiments to check out the efficiency of our proposed solution for the MMA problem in crowdsensing system. We mainly analyze three aspects: the number of workers and requesters, the influence of some key parameters and the change of utility in multi-term. Next, we will give the value of some parameters. we assume that the value of $\kappa_j, \forall j \in [1, m]$, is subject to a Gaussian distribution $\kappa_1 \sim N(u_1, \sigma_1^2)$. The parameter α_i is same as before which is subject to a Gaussian distribution $\alpha_i \sim N(u_2, \sigma_2^2)$. The code of our algorithm is written in C++. All the experiments have been carried out on a standard desktop PC with an Intel Core i5 running at 2.3 GHz, and with LPDDR3 8 GB 2133 MHz, running MacOS Mojave 10.14.6 Editions.

4.2   Performance Evaluation

In Fig. 2(a), no matter with the fair solution or the greedy one, we observe that Requesters' Utility monotonically increases with the number of tasks m, where we set the number of workers n = 500 and $\sigma_1^2 = \sigma_2^2 = 5$. It is obvious that the more the number of tasks is, the more the profit will become. Comparing with Fig. 2(a), there isn't any monotonicity in Fig. 3(b) with both the fair one and the greedy one. We can

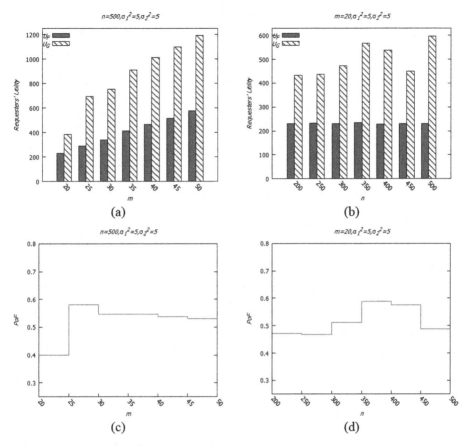

Fig. 2. Requesters' Utility verse intrinsic parameters: (a) m; (b) n. (c) and (d) are the corresponding PoF.

easily understand that when the number of tasks is fixed, the utility will fluctuate by selecting different set of workers. If we are patient enough, we will find that the utility of the fair algorithm has a slight oscillation comparing with the greedy one which is because the fair one doesn't consider the higher bidding price of worker firstly. While from Fig. 2(c) and Fig. 2(d), the value of PoF is in the range from 0.4 to 0.6 which is relatively stable as a whole.

Figure 3 illustrates the performance of our proposed DLS auction mechanism against intrinsic parameters σ_1^2 and σ_2^2. We assume that the value of σ_1^2 and σ_2^2 changes from 2 to 5 step by 0.5 where we set m = 20 and n = 500. Over all, we can draw that

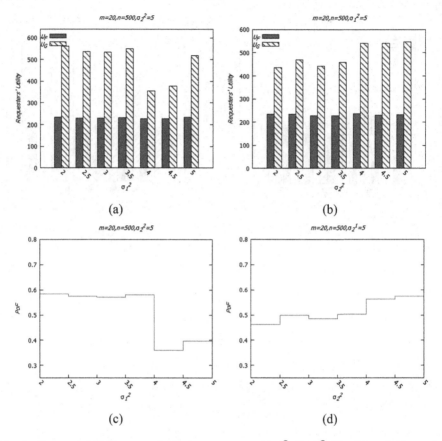

Fig. 3. Requesters' Utility verse intrinsic parameters: (a) σ_1^2; (b) σ_2^2. The (c) and (d) are the corresponding PoF.

these two parameters have a little influence on the Requesters' Utility from Fig. 3(a) and Fig. 3(b). Comparing Fig. 3(c) with Fig. 3(d), the parameter σ_1^2 which leads to the unit value of tasks has more effect on the result.

In Fig. 4, we evaluate the performance of MMA algorithm where we set m = 20, n = 500, $\sigma_1^2 = 5$ and $\sigma_2^2 = 5$. From Fig. 4(a), it is observed that the requesters' utility is stable in multi-term comparing with the greedy algorithm which the reason is same as the Fig. 2 (b). What's more, the value of PoF isn't too large which denotes that the MMA algorithm has a relatively good allocation result.

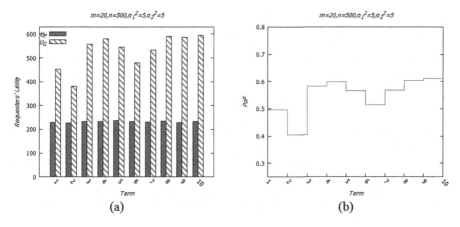

Fig. 4. (a): the requesters' utility in multi-term; (b): the corresponding PoF.

5 Conclusion

In this paper, we have proposed a deterministic local search (DLS) auction mechanism to work out the multi-term multi-task allocation problem under the weighted max-min fairness constraint. Firstly, we have modeled the multi-task allocation problem and introduced a more practical scenario: the multi-term allocation problem. Secondly, based on the definition of the max-min fairness, we propose the weighted max-min fairness to constrain the multi-term allocation. Thirdly, the property of submodularity function is taken advantage of to propose a deterministic local search (DLS) auction mechanism and a novel algorithm also designed to figure out the fair allocation scheme. Finally, evaluation results have demonstrated that our approach has a good performance which can balance utility and fairness with a relatively steady value of PoF.

References

1. Xiao, L., Li, Y., Han, G., Dai, H., Poor, H.V.: A secure mobile crowdsensing game with deep reinforcement learning. IEEE Trans. Inf. Forensics Secur. **13**(1), 35–47 (2018)
2. Sun, W., Liu, J.: Congestion-aware communication paradigm for sustainable dense mobile crowdsensing. IEEE Commun. Mag. **55**(3), 62–67 (2017)
3. Meng, Y., Jiang, C., Quek, T.Q.S., Han, Z., Ren, Y.: Social learning based inference for crowdsensing in mobile social networks. IEEE Trans. Mob. Comput. **17**(8), 1966–1979 (2018)
4. Jayaraman, P.P., Bártolo Gomes, J., Nguyen, H., Abdallah, Z.S., Krishnaswamy, S., Zaslavsky, A.: Scalable energy-efficient distributed data analytics for crowdsensing applications in mobile environments. IEEE Trans. Comput. Soc. Syst. **2**(3), 109–123 (2015)
5. Pryss, R., Schobel, J., Reichert, M.: Requirements for a flexible and generic API enabling mobile crowdsensing mHealth applications. In: 2018 4th International Workshop on Requirements Engineering for Self-Adaptive, Collaborative, and Cyber Physical Systems (RESACS), Banff, AB, pp. 24–31 (2018)

6. Zhang, J., Wang, D.: Duplicate report detection in urban crowdsensing applications for smart city. In: 2015 IEEE International Conference on Smart City/SocialCom/SustainCom (SmartCity), Chengdu, pp. 101–107 (2015)

7. Zhang, Y., Zhang, D., Li, Q., Wang, D.: Towards optimized online task allocation in cost-sensitive crowdsensing applications. In: 2018 IEEE 37th International Performance Computing and Communications Conference (IPCCC), Orlando, FL, USA, pp. 1–8 (2018)

8. Wang, J., Tang, J., Yang, D., Wang, E., Xue, G.: Quality-aware and fine-grained incentive mechanisms for mobile crowdsensing. In: 2016 IEEE 36th International Conference on Distributed Computing Systems (ICDCS), Nara, pp. 354–363 (2016)

9. Wang, L., Yu, Z., Zhang, D., Guo, B., Liu, C.H.: Heterogeneous multi-task assignment in mobile crowdsensing using spatiotemporal correlation. IEEE Trans. Mob. Comput. **18**(1), 84–97 (2019)

10. Zhou, P., Chen, W., Ji, S., Jiang, H., Yu, L., Wu, D.: Privacy-preserving online task allocation in edge-computing-enabled massive crowdsensing. IEEE Internet Things J. **6**(5), 7773–7787 (2019)

11. Wang, Z., et al.: Personalized privacy-preserving task allocation for mobile crowdsensing. IEEE Trans. Mob. Comput. **18**(6), 1330–1341 (2019)

12. Hu, A., Gu, Y.: Mobile crowdsensing tasks allocation for multi-parameter bids. In: 2017 IEEE 3rd Information Technology and Mechatronics Engineering Conference (ITOEC), Chongqing, pp. 489–493 (2017)

13. Tao, X., Song, W.: Location-dependent task allocation for mobile crowdsensing with clustering effect. IEEE Internet Things J. **6**(1), 1029–1045 (2019)

14. Zhang, Y., Zhang, D., Vance, N., Wang, D.: Optimizing online task allocation for multi-attribute social sensing. In: 2018 27th International Conference on Computer Communication and Networks (ICCCN), Hangzhou, pp. 1–9 (2018)

15. Meng, J., Tan, H., Li, X., Han, Z., Li, B.: Online deadline-aware task dispatching and scheduling in edge computing. IEEE Trans. Parallel Distrib. Syst. **31**(6), 1270–1286 (2020)

16. Xiao, M., Wu, J., Huang, L., Cheng, R., Wang, Y.: Online task assignment for crowdsensing in predictable mobile social networks. IEEE Trans. Mob. Comput. **16**(8), 2306–2320 (2017)

17. Wang, X., Jia, R., Tian, X., Gan, X.: Dynamic task assignment in crowdsensing with location awareness and location diversity. In: IEEE INFOCOM 2018 - IEEE Conference on Computer Communications, Honolulu, HI, pp. 2420–2428 (2018)

18. Nie, J., Luo, J., Xiong, Z., Niyato, D., Wang, P.: A Stackelberg game approach toward socially-aware incentive mechanisms for mobile crowdsensing. IEEE Trans. Wirel. Commun. **18**(1), 724–738 (2019)

19. Chen, X., Deng, B.: Task allocation schemes for crowdsourcing in opportunistic mobile social networks. In: 2018 International Conference on Computing, Networking and Communications (ICNC), Maui, HI, pp. 615–619 (2018)

20. Huang, H., Xin, Y., Sun, Y., Yang, W.: A truthful double auction mechanism for crowdsensing systems with max-min fairness. In: 2017 IEEE Wireless Communications and Networking Conference (WCNC), San Francisco, CA, pp. 1–6 (2017)

21. Li, X., Shankaran, R., Orgun, M.A., Fang, G., Xu, Y.: Resource allocation for underlay D2D communication with proportional fairness. IEEE Trans. Veh. Technol. **67**(7), 6244–6258 (2018)

22. Huang, J., Bi, J.: A proportional fairness scheduling for wireless sensor networks. In: 2015 International Conference on Identification, Information, and Knowledge in the Internet of Things (IIKI), Beijing, pp. 266–271 (2015)

23. Feige, U., Mirrokni, V.S., Vondrak, J.: Maximizing non-monotone submodular functions. In: 48th Annual IEEE Symposium on Foundations of Computer Science (FOCS 2007), Providence, RI, pp. 461–471 (2007)

An Improved Sensor Pattern Noise Estimation Method Based on Edge Guided Weighted Averaging

Wen-Na Zhang[1,2], Yun-Xia Liu[1,2(✉)], Jin Zhou[1,2], Yang Yang[3], and Ngai-Fong Law[4]

[1] School of Information Science and Engineering, University of Jinan, Jinan 250022, China
ujn_zhangwn@qq.com, {ise_liuyx,ise_zhouj}@ujn.edu.cn
[2] Shandong Provincial Key Laboratory of Network Based Intelligent Computing, University of Jinan, Jinan 250022, China
[3] School of Information Science and Engineering, Shandong University, Qingdao 266237, China
yyang@sdu.edu.cn
[4] Department of Electronic and Information Engineering, The Hong Kong Polytechnic University, Hong Kong, China
ngai.fong.law@polyu.edu.hk

Abstract. Sensor Pattern Noise (SPN) has proven to be an effective fingerprint for source camera identification. However, its estimation accuracy is still greatly affected by image contents. In this work, considering the confidence difference in varying image regions, an image edge guided weighted averaging scheme for robust SPN estimation is proposed. Firstly, the edge and non-edge regions are estimated by a Laplacian operator-based detector, based on which different weights are assigned to. Then, the improved SPN estimation is obtained by weighted averaging of image residuals. Finally, an edge guided weighted normalized cross-correlation measurement is proposed as similarity metric in source camera identification (SCI) applications. The effectiveness of the proposed method is verified by SCI experiments conducted on six models from the Dresden data set. Comparison results on different denoising algorithms and varying patch sizes reveal that performance improvement is more prominent for small image patches, which is demanding in real forensic applications.

Keywords: Sensor pattern noise · Edge detection · Weighted averaging · Source camera identification

1 Introduction

Digital images play an increasingly indispensable role in human life. It is also an important information carrier that can be used to testify incidents and provide legally acceptable evidence for courtroom purposes. However, the credibility of images is reduced when they are maliciously tampered, which is undoubtedly a loss. To this context, the development of digital image forensics technology [1–3], such as integrity

© Springer Nature Switzerland AG 2020
X. Chen et al. (Eds.): ML4CS 2020, LNCS 12487, pp. 405–415, 2020.
https://doi.org/10.1007/978-3-030-62460-6_36

verification, source device linking, authentication and source camera identification (SCI), has drawn more attention in the past decades.

Sensor pattern noise (SPN) has long been an effective method in SCI problems that it is a unique fingerprint to identify a specific device of the same brand and camera model [4]. After one have accumulated certain number of images (blue-sky images with large smooth areas are preferable [5]) from the image sensor, a set of residual images are calculated by subtracting the denoised version from the original images. Then, different strategies are adopted to estimate SPN by aggregating the residuals. Many research works [6–15] have been developed based on SPN method, which can be roughly divided into three categories.

Employing better image denoising algorithms contributes to more accurate SPN estimation. The wavelet domain adaptive denoising filter [16] first adopted by Lukas et al. [6] is a common choice for image denoiser in early years [6, 7]. As spatial domain image denoising methods are less influenced by artifacts, Kang et al. developed a series of SPN methods [8–10]. As a representative work, Zhang et al. proposed a block weighted averaging module [11], which based the block variance of all extracted residuals, further suppress the effects of scene content. In our previous attempt [12], the enhanced restoration capability of Multi-Scale Expected Patch Log Likelihood (MSEPLL) has been verified, especially for small patch sizes. Cortiana et al. [13] conducted comprehensive comparison of different denoising filters and found that the BM3D denoising algorithm [17] demonstrates the best performance in SCI applications. How to obtain better residual images less influenced by image contents is an important direction in SPN estimation.

The second group of works focus on **residual image or SPN enhancement.** The zero-mean(ZM) and Wiener filtering in Fourier domain(WF) techniques proposed by Chen et al. [5] are widely adopted in SCI fields [9–11]. Six models were proposed to suppress the influence of scene content in [7] while a spectrum equalization algorithm was proposed in [14] for SPN enhancement.

Residual aggregation strategy that works on how to fuse all information from multiple images also plays an important role in SPN estimation. Besides direct averaging in [4] and the maximum likelihood estimation method in [5], the reciprocal of the variance of the entire residual is adopted as weights in [15] by Lawgaly et al.

Considering the fact that different image contents contributes varyingly to SPN estimation, an improved SPN estimation method is proposed in this work. Firstly, a Laplacian operator-based detector is adopted to distinguish edge and non-edge regions. Then, by weighting edge and non-edge regions of the residual, effective sensor pattern noise estimation is performed. In this way, the estimated SPN is less influenced by image contents while the problem of effective residual aggregation is addressed simultaneously. The effectiveness of the proposed method has been verified by three comparative tests, and the experimental results show that identification accuracy of most camera devices has been improved.

The remainder of this paper is organized as follows. Section 2 introduces the relevant work of this paper and Laplacian operator-based edge detectors [18]. The proposed SPN estimation method and similarity measure is presented in Sect. 3 in detail. Section 4 discusses experimental results, while Sect. 5 concludes the paper.

2   Related Works

2.1   The Influence of Edge Region

Generally, multiple natural images containing different scene details are adopted in SPN estimation, while the acquisition of blue-sky images is impossible in real forensic applications. This will greatly degrade the accuracy of SPN estimation as shown in Fig. 1. Due to the imperfectness of current image denoising algorithms, there are plenty image content related structures in residual images (see Fig. 1(c)), as compared to the idea SPN shown in Fig. 1(a). It is easy to get the conclusion that the obtained residual image is highly correlated to the edge region (Shown in Fig. 1(d)) of the original image. This is in consistent with the fact that smooth region is beneficial to the extraction of SPN, while the texture/edge region interferes with the estimation of SPN [7].

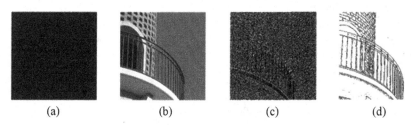

| (a) | (b) | (c) | (d) |

Fig. 1. The influence of edge region in SPN estimation. (a) The *SPN* estimated by blue-sky images. (b) An example of natural image. (c) Residual image extracted by GBWA [11]. (d) Edge image obtained by LOE [18].

There have been plenty works that tried to utilize this phenomenon to improve the SPN estimation accuracy. For example, the variance of image intensity is adopted as the texture complexity indicator [19], that only pixels in smooth region are utilized for further processing. In [20], Chan et al. studied the effect of image intensity as well as image texture features, based on which a nonlinear regression model is utilized for confidence map prediction, so that a pixel-wise weighting function could be obtained to penalize texture/edge pixels. In [21], a reliability map is obtained by inverted edge power, while a Gaussian filter is performed as well to make sure surrounding non-edge region are also assigned a lower weight.

In this work, we also adopt the same philosophy to unequaly weight edge, texture and smooth regions for SPN estimation. We will reply on a robust edge detector [18] for edge/non-edge region distinction. Meanwhile, we will show that the simple yet effective weighting strategy is a universal technique that benefits more accurate SPN estimation that it could be used in conjunction with several state-of-the-art image denoising algorithms.

2.2   The Laplacian Operator-Based Edge Detection Algorithm

In this section, we briefly introduce the Laplacian operator-based edge detectors [18], as we rely on this method for reliable edge/non-edge region distinguish.

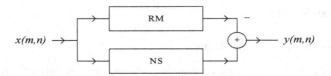

Fig. 2. The Laplacian operator-based edge detection model.

Based on the most popular Laplacian operator in edge detection, Xin Wang reformulated the Laplacian operator-based edge detection model (EDM) as shown in Fig. 2, where $x(m,n)$ and $y(m,n)$ represent the input and output images, respectively. The noise smoother (NS) is used to obtain edge information while smoothing noise and the round mean (RM) part is used to compute the local mean. Then, by a subtraction operation between the outputs of the two filters, the local high-frequency components of an image are obtained.

Considering the incorporation local non-linearity will benefit edge detection, the multistage median filter (MMF) is adopted as the noise smoother in this work. Imposing a Laplace distribution hypothesis of the output signal of the edge detection operator, the optimal MAP threshold T_0 is

$$T_0 = \frac{\sqrt{2}}{\sigma_{s1}} \sigma_{w1}^2.$$ (1)

where σ_{w1} and σ_{s1} are the standard deviation of noise and signal, respectively. The finally detected edge map E is obtained by

$$E(m,n) = \begin{cases} y(m,n) - \text{sgn}[y(m,n)]T_0, & |y(m,n)| > T_0 \\ 0, & |y(m,n)| \le T_0 \end{cases}$$ (2)

Readers may refer to [18] for more details in estimation of specific parameters.

3   The Proposed Edge Guided Weighted Averaging Method

In this section, we will first present the proposed edge guided weighted averaging method for SPN estimation. Then the framework of source camera identification and performance evaluation protocol is discussed.

3.1   SPN Estimation Based on Edge Guided Weighting

In order to reduce the influence of image contents as well as perform effective aggression from multiple residual images that corresponds to the same position in the same sensor, an image edge guided weighted averaging method is proposed.

As illustrated by the diagram in Fig. 3. that for each image, edge map E and residual images R are calculated simultaneously. Guided by the principle that non-edge region are more reliable thus higher weights should be assigned to, and edge region should be assigned with smaller weights. Considering the robustness of the LOE edge detector, a simple strategy is adopted that all pixels in edge region are equally weighted by a reduction parameter α without further distinguish in the edge intensity. Finally, the SPN is obtained by weighted average of residual images with respect to the weights. From the visual inspection of the obtained SPN, we see that it is less influenced by the image contents and looks more "white" as expected.

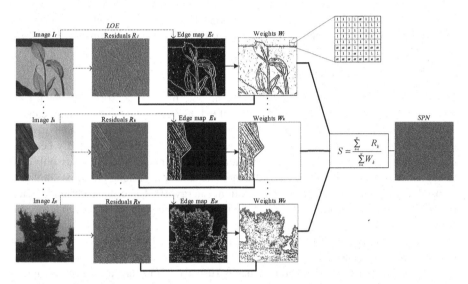

Fig. 3. The diagram of the proposed edge guided weighted averaging method for SPN Estimation.

To sum up, the proposed SPN estimation method is consisted of three steps as follows:

Step1. Obtain the residual image. Residuals image R is to subtract the denoised version from the original image I:

$$R = I - F(I), \tag{3}$$

where $F(\bullet)$ represents the denoising algorithm, We set the standard deviation of noise $\sigma_0 = 3$ when denoising following [5].

Step2. Obtain the weighting map. Utilizing LOE to obtain the edge region of image. In the weighting map W, the value of the edge region is set to α while non-edge is 1.

Step3. Obtain the camera SPN estimation and enhancement. Given a set of N images from the same camera instance, the estimated SPN is obtained by weighting average:

$$S = \frac{\sum\limits_{k=1}^{N} W_k R_k}{\sum\limits_{k=1}^{N} W_k}. \tag{4}$$

It is worth mentioning that the proposed edge guided weighted averaging method is a general SPN aggregation method that imposes no restriction on image denoising nor SPN enhancement algorithms. It could be adopted in conjunction with state-of-the-art SPN estimation or enhancement methods to further improve the estimation accuracy.

3.2   Source Camera Identification

In forensic applications, once the SPN of candidate imaging sensors have been estimated by the proposed edge guided weighted averaging method, source camera identification could be performed. To determine whether the image t under investigation was taken from a specific camera, one needs to calculate the similarity between the fingerprint of t (usually replaced by noise residue image when there is only one image at hand) and the SPN of the candidate camera. Among various similarity measurement, including Peak to Correlation Energy (PCE), cross-correlation, etc., normalized cross-correlation (NCC) is widely adopted due to its simplicity and stability.

As there is only one test image at hand in the testing phase, the influence of image content due to imperfection of denoising filters is more severe as compared with the case in SPN estimation where more images (usually 25/50) are available for aggregation. Based on previous discussion in assigning unequal weights to edge/non-edge regions, an edge guided weighted normalized cross-correlation (EWNCC), defined as

$$\rho_c = corr(W_t R_t, S_c) = \frac{(W_t R_t \bullet S_c)}{\|W_t R_t\| \bullet \|S_c\|}, \quad c = 1, 2, \ldots C \tag{5}$$

is proposed as the similarity measurement between noise residual R_t and the SPN of candidate camera S_c, W_t is the weighting map of the test image calculated according to the step2 in Sect. 3.1, and C is the total number of camera instances in consideration.

By assigning test image t to the camera that yields the largest NCC values among all C candidates, and then counting the number of correctly judgments (True) and wrong judgments (False) for each camera, the accuracy can be obtained as:

$$Accuracy_c = \frac{True}{True + False}. \tag{6}$$

4   Experiments and Discussion

4.1   Experimental Setup

To verify the effectiveness of the proposed algorithm, we conduct experiments on the public Dresden data set [22], following the experimental settings in [11]. All images from six cameras are selected for fairness in performance comparing, while details of the database are shown in Table 1. Depending on different settings, $N = 25$ or 50 randomly selected natural images are used for SPN estimation, while the remaining images are used for testing. Only central patches of sizes 64×64 and 128×128 are extracted for SPN estimation, as the source camera identification difficulty will greatly increase with the decline in patch size, which is demanding in real applications.

Table 1. Detail information of the experimental database.

Camera No.	Image resolution	Device information	No. of images in Dresden
No.1	3264×2448	Canon_Ixus55_0	224
No.2	3872×2592	Nikon_D200_1	380
No.3	3648×2736	Olympus_mju_1050SW_4	202
No.4	3648×2736	Panasonic_DMC-FZ50_1	415
No.5	3072×2304	Samsung_L74wide_0	232
No.6	3456×2592	Sony_DSC-H50_0	284

Several methods are selected for performance comparison, including the basis method [4] which is a pioneering yet effective method in this field, the Model 3 in [7] that is a representative of SPN enhancement methods, the GBWA method [11] and BM3D method [13] that provide the state-of-the-art performance. We strictly follow all parameter settings and implementation details. No post-processing is adopted by BM3D while Fourier domain 3×3 Wiener filtering is applied to GBWA estimated SPN that retained artifact due to same in-camera processing algorithm could be reduced in some extent as claimed by the authors [11].

4.2   Determination of Weighting Parameter

As previously discussed in Sect. 3.1, α is an important parameter that determines the relative contribution of non-edge pixels, thus would directly affect the SPN estimation accuracy. Take the extreme case that $\alpha = 0$ for example, where all edge pixels are excluded in SPN estimation that some useful information would be lost. This should be avoided as edge pixels contain certain information, whereas being less reliable. However, α should not be set too large. As in the other extreme case $\alpha = 1$, edge pixels are considered equally contributing to the SPN estimation, which is obviously against our motivation. Generally speaking, the detection accuracy will first increase and then drop with the increase of α.

To determine the optimal value of α, we take GBWA [11] and BM3D [13] as baseline, the average detection performance of the proposed edge guided weighting

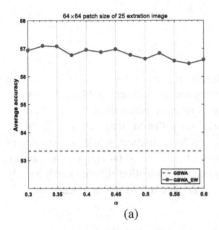
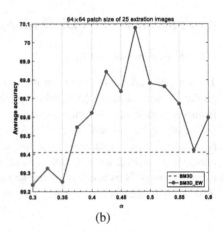

(a)   (b)

Fig. 4. Average detection accuracy of proposed edge guided weighting under various settings of α for (a) GBWA and (b) BM3D methods.

(denoted as "*_EW") method are depicted with respect to different setting of α in Fig. 4 (patch size is set to be 64×64, while 50 images are used for SPN estimation).

We see that the edge guided weighted algorithm outperforms the baseline for both GBWA and BM3D in most α settings, with average identification accuracy improvement of 3.47% and 0.16%, respectively. The performance improvement with respect to α also obeys the first rise and then decline tendency as expected. In comprehensive consideration of performance and parameter robustness, we set $\alpha = 0.475$ uniformly for both SPN and EWNCC computation.

4.3   Source Camera Identification Performance Comparison

To verify the effectiveness of the proposed algorithm, we conduct comprehensive experiments and show results in Table 2 and Table 3 with 25 images for SPN estimation, for patch sizes of 64×64 and 128×128, respectively. In each table, bold figures indicate the highest identification accuracy among all six methods. To study the effectiveness of edge guided weighting algorithm with respect to baseline, methods demonstrating better performance are highlighted with gray background for both GBWA and BM3D groups.

Table 2. Accuracy Comparison for 64×64 patch size of 25 extracted images.

Method	No.1	No.2	No.3	No.4	No.5	No.6	Average (%)
Basic	42.71	50.42	40.11	45.64	38.65	73.75	48.55
Model3	27.64	61.41	40.11	57.69	31.40	72.20	48.41
GBWA	37.19	62.25	47.46	59.23	36.71	77.22	53.34
GBWA_EW	41.71	65.35	45.76	68.72	41.06	77.99	56.77
BM3D	52.76	82.82	59.32	79.23	53.14	89.19	69.41
BM3D_EW	53.27	81.13	61.02	82.05	54.59	88.42	70.08

Table 3. Accuracy Comparison for 128×128 patch size of 25 extracted images.

Method	No.1	No.2	No.3	No.4	No.5	No.6	Average (%)
Basic	67.34	78.03	54.80	74.10	57.00	96.53	71.30
Model3	67.34	84.23	58.19	77.18	53.62	95.37	72.65
GBWA	71.36	87.04	75.71	81.03	63.29	95.75	79.03
GBWA_EW	74.37	91.27	67.80	87.44	72.46	94.21	81.26
BM3D	85.93	98.31	72.88	92.31	82.13	98.46	88.33
BM3D_EW	87.44	97.18	70.62	93.59	85.02	98.46	88.72

Generally speaking, BM3D based methods usually demonstrate best performance due to its powerful denoising ability. However, we find that the improvement of BM3D_EW over BM3D is very commendable. Furthermore, we can observe consistent performance improvement by the edge guided weighting for both GBWA and BM3D methods with average improvement of 2.83% and 0.53%, respectively.

We further investigate performance when increase the number of images to 50 for SPN estimation, while results are given in Table 4 and Table 5, while similar conclusions could be drawn. One may notice that GBWA algorithm achieved best performance in camera No.3 for patch size of 128×128. Further examination reveals that there are more flat and smooth regions in the images for Olympus in Dresden database. The block weighting mechanism in the GBWA [11] is an effective strategy that suits these types of images. This post-processing algorithm may be the reason for slightly better performance. However, averaged accuracy improvement over the GBWA method on the whole database is 3.43%, 2.23%, 3.87% and 1.53%, respectively. Meanwhile, we see that performance gain is more obvious for small patch size of 64×64, which is a very appealing property of the proposed method.

Table 4. Accuracy Comparison for 64×64 patch size of 50 extracted images.

Method	No.1	No.2	No.3	No.4	No.5	No.6	Average (%)
Basic	52.87	63.94	42.76	60.00	41.76	81.20	57.09
Model3	46.55	73.94	40.79	66.03	41.21	79.49	58.00
GBWA	55.75	72.12	47.37	70.41	45.60	87.18	63.07
GBWA_EW	62.07	75.15	50.66	75.89	51.10	86.75	66.94
BM3D	70.69	88.79	61.18	87.67	61.54	97.01	77.81
BM3D_EW	70.69	88.79	60.53	86.58	67.03	96.15	78.29

414   W.-N. Zhang et al.

Table 5. Accuracy Comparison for 128 × 128 patch size of 50 extracted images.

Method	No.1	No.2	No.3	No.4	No.5	No.6	Average (%)
Basic	81.03	86.97	57.24	83.84	63.74	98.72	78.59
Model3	74.71	89.09	65.13	84.93	62.64	98.29	79.13
GBWA	85.63	93.94	78.95	87.40	68.68	98.72	85.55
GBWA_EW	85.06	95.15	76.32	91.51	75.27	99.15	87.08
BM3D	94.25	99.09	78.29	95.62	89.56	100.00	92.80
BM3D_EW	92.53	98.18	75.00	95.34	92.86	100.00	92.32

5 Conclusions

In this paper, a sensor pattern noise estimation scheme based on edge guided weighted averaging is proposed. By assigning different weights to the edge and non-edge pixels in the process of SPN estimation, contributions of smooth regions are emphasized thus estimation accuracy gain is obtained. Furthermore, an edge guided weighted normalized cross-correlation is proposed as similarity measure to handle less reliable edge pixels in test image. Finally, the robustness of parameter setting and effectiveness of the proposed method is verified through a series of experiments where consistent accuracy improvement is observed.

Acknowledgments. This work was supported by National Key Research and Development Program (No. 2018YFC0831100), the National Nature Science Foundation of China (No. 61305015, No. 61203269), the National Natural Science Foundation of Shandong Province (No. ZR2017MF057), and Shandong Province Key Research and Development Program, China (No. 2016GGX101022).

References

1. Popescu, A.C., Farid, H.: Exposing digital forgeries by detecting traces of resampling. IEEE Trans. Sig. Process. **53**(2), 758–767 (2005)
2. Popescu, A.C., Farid, H.: Exposing digital forgeries in color filter array interpolated images. IEEE Trans. Sig. Process. **53**(10), 3948–3959 (2005)
3. Lin, Z., Wang, R., Tang, X., Shum, H.Y.: Detecting doctored images using camera response normality and consistency (2009)
4. Lukas, J., Fridrich, J., Goljan, M.: Digital camera identification from sensor pattern noise. IEEE Trans. Inf. Forensics Secur. **1**(2), 205–214 (2006)
5. Chen, M., Fridrich, J., Goljan, M., Lukas, J.: Determining image origin and integrity using sensor noise. IEEE Trans. Inf. Forensics Secur. **3**(1), 74–90 (2008)
6. Lukas, J., Fridrich, J., Goljan, M.: Detecting digital image forgeries using sensor pattern noise 6072 (2006)
7. Li, C.: Source camera identification using enhanced sensor pattern noise. IEEE Trans. Inf. Forensics Secur. **5**(2), 280–287 (2010)

8. Wu, G., Kang, X., Liu, K.J.R.: A context adaptive predictor of sensor pattern noise for camera source identification. In: 2012 19th IEEE International Conference on Image Processing (ICIP) (2012)
9. Kang, X., Chen, J., Lin, K., Anjie, P.: A context-adaptive spn predictor for trustworthy source camera identification. Eurasip J. Image Video Process. **2014**(1), 19 (2014)
10. Zeng, H., Kang, X.: Fast source camera identification using content adaptive guided image filter. J. Forensic Sci. **61**(2), 520–526 (2016)
11. Zhang, L., Peng, F., Long, M.: Identifying source camera using guided image estimation and block weighted average. J. Vis. Commun. Image Represent. **48**, 471–479 (2017)
12. Zhang, W., Liu, Y., Zou, Z., Zang, Y., Yang, Y., Law, B.N.: Effective source camera identification based on msepll denoising applied to small image patches (2019)
13. Cortiana, A., Conotter, V., Boato, G., De Natale, F.G.B.: Performance comparison of denoising filters for source camera identification. Proc. SPIE **7880**, 788007 (2011)
14. Lin, X., Li, C.: Preprocessing reference sensor pattern noise via spectrum equalization. IEEE Trans. Inf. Forensics Secur. **11**(1), 126–140 (2016)
15. Lawgaly, A., Khelifi, F., Bouridane, A.: Weighted averaging-based sensor pattern noise estimation for source camera identification, pp. 5357–5361 (2014)
16. Mihcak, M.K., Kozintsev, I.V., Ramchandran, K.: Spatially adaptive statistical modeling of wavelet image coefficients and its application to denoising **6**, 3253–3256 (1999)
17. Dabov, K., Foi, A., Katkovnik, V., Egiazarian, K.: Image denoising by sparse 3-d transform-domain collaborative filtering. IEEE Trans. Image Process. **16**(8), 2080–2095 (2007)
18. Wang, X.: Laplacian operator-based edge detectors. IEEE Trans. Pattern Anal. Mach. Intell. **29**(5), 886–890 (2007)
19. Matsushita, K., Kitazawa, H.: An improved camera identification method based on the texture complexity and the image restoration. In: International Conference on Hybrid Information Technology, pp. 171–175 (2009)
20. Chan, L., Law, N., Siu, W.: A confidence map and pixel-based weighted correlation for prnu-based camera identification. Digital Invest. **10**(3), 215–225 (2013)
21. Satta, R.: Sensor pattern noise matching based on reliability map for source camera identification, pp. 222–226 (2015)
22. Gloe, T., Bohme, R.: The 'dresden image database' for benchmarking digital image forensics, pp. 1584–1590 (2010)

Analysis of the Influence
of Stylized-CIFAR10 Dataset on ResNet

Dexin Wu, Jian Xu$^{(\boxtimes)}$, and Heng Liu

Software College, Northeastern University, Shenyang, China
xuj@mail.neu.edu.cn

Abstract. ResNet and other CNN networks have a very good performance in the field of image classification, and have developed rapidly in recent years.There are many explanations for the high performance of CNN, which are generally divided into two types: one is shape hypothesis, the other is texture hypothesis. It is found that the dependence of CNNs on texture or shape tends to come from datasets rather than model itself. In this paper, based on CIFAR10 dataset, the texture of the image is partially modified or completely removed, and the stylized image dataset with more shape information is generated. We carried out the experiments of different scale and various stylized-coefficient to study differences comprehensively and multilayered between the influence of stylized-cifar10 dataset with shape information and that of original one with both information and texture information.

Keywords: Stylize transfer · Machine learning · Residual network · Data augment

1 Introduction

With the development of science and technology and the improvement of GPU computing power, deep learning has been widely used in various fields such as computer vision [9], semantic segmentation [11], 3D behavior recognition and so on in recent years. Among all kinds of deep learning models, ResNet, proposed by He et al. [8], has impressive performance. Its main innovation lies in the residual network, which solves the problem of "gradient disappearance" when CNNs is in a deep layer. Now, some works have improved ResNet and obtained some variants of it. For example, Xie et al. [14] proposed ResNeXt, which can improve the accuracy and reduce the number of super parameters without increasing the complexity of parameters.

There are many explanations for CNNs' high-performance at present, which are generally divided into two types. One is *Shape Hypothesis* [6,10,15]. CNNs combines low-level features into complex shapes, and finally identifies objects. On the other hand, *Texture Hypothesis*. Some studies have found that CNNs trained with image texture information can also achieve high accuracy in ImageNet classification tasks [1,3].

© Springer Nature Switzerland AG 2020
X. Chen et al. (Eds.): ML4CS 2020, LNCS 12487, pp. 416–426, 2020.
https://doi.org/10.1007/978-3-030-62460-6_37

In order to study the relationship between the two hypotheses, Geirhos et al. [6] generated Stylized-ImageNet dataset through AdaIN style-transfer method [5] to force the model to learn shape information and reduce its texture bias. It is found in the experiment that ResNet-50 architecture can recognise object based on shape, and it is proved that it is the is the dataset affects the shape or texture inclination of the model, not the characteristics of the model itself, and the model trained by stylized-dataset has stronger performance on ordinary pictures.

In this paper, based on the CIFAR10 dataset made by Alex et al. and stylized transfer method [5], we generate the stylized-CIFAR10 dataset, and carry out experiments through ResNet model extending the conclusion under the ImageNet dataset to verify the texture or shape tendency of the deep learning model from pictures with different sizes and contents. It is helpful for the research of complex models based on texture shape data.

2 Related Work

2.1 Datasets

Imagenet dataset, proposed in 2009, [13] is currently an ongoing research effort aimed at providing researchers around the world easily. At present, the research on deep learning image applications, such as pattern recognition, object detection, classification, positioning and so on, is mostly based on this dataset. ImageNet dataset are easy to use with detailed documents. Now there are a total of 14, 197, 122 224×224 size images, which are divided into 21, 841 synsets. ILSVRC 2012 is often used in practical training, which can be regarded as a subset of the complete ImageNet.

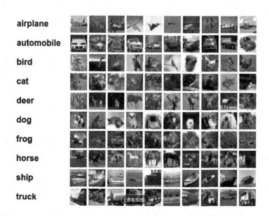

Fig. 1. The classes in the dataset and 10 random images from each class.

CIFAR10: the CIFAR10 dataset consists of 32×32 color images in 10 classes, with 6, 000 images in each class, as Fig. 1. There are totally 50, 000 training images and 10, 000 test images. Obviously, the image in CIFAR10 is smaller than that in ImageNet. The dataset is divided into five training batches and one test batch, each batch has 10000 images. The test batch contains exactly 1000 randomly selected images from each category. Training batches contain the remaining images in a random order, but some training batches may contain more images from one category than another. Overall, the sum of the five training sets contains exactly 5000 images from each class.

2.2   Shape and Texture

For CNNs' high performance, there are many explanations at present, which are generally divided into two kinds. One is shape hypothesis [6]. CNNs combine low-level features into complex shapes, and then identifies objects. For example, kriegeskorte et al. [6] think that the high-level unit of the model will learn representations of object shape in the picture. Ritter et al. [12] found that CNNs have so-called shape bias like children. Texture hypothesis, on the other hand, where some studies have found that although the overall shape structure is destroyed, CNNs can also classify texture images [4]. In addition, local information such as texture is also proved to be useful for ImageNet classification. Recently, some experiments show that the model can also achieve high accuracy in ImageNet tasks inputting texture information [1].

In order to study the relationship between the two hypotheses, Geirhos et al. [6] generate images with conflicting shape and texture information through the AdaIN style transfer method [5]. Experimental data shows that compared with the global shape of the object in the image, CNNs model has a higher judgment dependence on the local texture properties of it, as shown in Fig. 2. This conclusion, combined with the conclusion that the color [7] and size [2] of objects have little influence on CNNs performance, can prove local texture information plays an important role in object recognition CNN models.

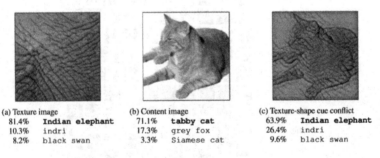

(a) Texture image	(b) Content image	(c) Texture-shape cue conflict
81.4% **Indian elephant**	71.1% **tabby cat**	63.9% **Indian elephant**
10.3% indri	17.3% grey fox	26.4% indri
8.2% black swan	3.3% Siamese cat	9.6% black swan

Fig. 2. Classification of a standard ResNet of Texture image, Content image, Stylize-image.

In addition, In [6], Stylized-ImageNet (SIN) dataset is generated to force the model to learn the shape information and reduce the texture bias of the models.

The experiment found that the model can also recognize objects in the shape data set, proving that the in which affects the shape or texture tendency of the model is the data set, But not the characteristics of the model itself, and the model trained by SIN data set has better performance in common pictures.

2.3   ResNet

ResNet is proposed to solve the degradation problem of deep neural network: when the number of network layers increases, the accuracy declines. It is not the performance degradation of test set caused by over fitting, nor the gradient disappearance problem solved by BN layer. In order to solve this problem, He [8] designed a better model structure. In the past few years, ResNet has been one of the most pioneering works in the field of deep learning. It enables deep learning training to show superior performance even after reaching hundreds of layers. In addition to image classification, the performance of many application models for target detection and face recognition has been improved.

In [8], the stacked layers are called a block. For a single block, the function that can be fitted is $F(x)$. If the expected potential mapping is $H(x)$, then using residual $H(x) - x$ instead of potential mapping becomes the learning goal. So it will be fitting $H(x)$ with $F(x) - x$. This is easier to optimize, because it is easier to let $F(x)$ learn to be 0 than to let $F(x)$ learn to be identity map. For redundant blocks, let $F(x) = 0$ to achieve identity mapping, which will not affect performance.

The block composed of $F(x) - x$ is called a Residual Block, as shown in Fig. 3.

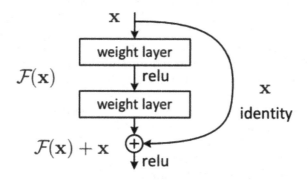

Fig. 3. A building block.

ResNet is very easy to modify and expand. By adjusting the number of channels in the block and the number of stacked blocks, the network can easily change the width and depth to get different expression capabilities, without worrying too much about the degradation of the network. As long as the training data is enough to gradually deepen the network, ResNet can get better performance.

3   Experiment Setup

3.1   Models and Datasets

The experimental model is based on a simple architectures of ResNet in Table 1 [8].

Table 1. The architecture of ResNet for CIFAR10 [8]

Output map size	32×32	16×16	8×8
Layers	$1 + 2n$	$2n$	$2n$
Filters	16	32	64

The configuration of this network is not the common ResNet, but the structure designed for CIFAR10.

The first layer is 3×3 convolution. Then we use a stack of 6n layers with 3×3 convolutions on the feature maps of sizes 32,16,8 respectively, with 2n layers for each feature map size. The numbers of filters are 16,32,64 respectively. The subsampling is performed by convolutions with a stride of 2. The network ends with a global average pooling, a 10-way fully-connected layer, and softmax. There are totally $6n + 2$ stacked weighted layers [8].

As the method of making stylized Imagenet data set in [6], we made a new dataset called stylized-CIFAR10 or SC, removed the texture of the image itself through AdaIN style transfer method [12], and randomly selected a painting style to replace it. It is worth noting that the size of CIFAR10 image is 32×32, which is so small that the shape of the object in the original image is not obvious. Therefore, after the stylized processing, some objects in the image are difficult to distinguish (even by human). The influence of this factor will be considered in later analysis.

In SC dataset, three stylized pictures are generated for each picture in original-CIFAR10 dataset (OC), that is, 15000 pictures are generated under each label, and then 5000 pictures and 50000 pictures are selected from 10 labels to form SC dataset. Mix OC dataset and SC dataset, and then randomly select 50000 pictures to get mixed-cifar10 dataset (MC).

3.2   Results on Both Datasets

We refer to ResNet model structure in [8], and make $Stack\_n = 3$, experiment on ResNet-18. Experimental results are shown in Table 2.

First, the network is trained on OC, and 87.9% accuracy is achieved in the original test set, but only 13.5% on the SC test set. In addition to the similarity of object shape information in the two datasets, the texture information is

Table 2. The accuracy of ResNet on OC, SC, MC

Train on	OC	SC	MC
OC	87.9%	41.3%	82.0%
SC	13.5%	31.3%	27.9%

extremely different, which also shows that the model will learn the texture information of the picture when it is trained on OC and consider the texture input when judging the picture on the test data, which is the same as the ImageNet experiment in [6].

It should be noted that after training on SC dataset, testing on OC is higher than that on SC, which may be because the shape information in SC images is different, and the shape characteristics in test SC may be less clear than that in the original test images. In addition, the model has a strong tendency to judge the shape of the object after training, and unclear shape information will greatly affect performance. This proves the conclusion of [6] to a certain extent that in object classification, CNNs relies more on local texture than global shape information, but it also leads to a guess: if we train the model based on texture and shape orientation respectively, which one is more robust when the input information (texture and shape) they tend to be damaged?

3.3 Mixed-CIFAR10

By mixing OC and SC datasets and selecting them randomly with equal probability, we generated Mixed-CIFAR10 (MC) dataset, including training set and test set. OC and SC account for 50% respectively. The experimental results are shown in Table 2.

Compared with OC-trained model, the performance of MC-training on OC test dataset is 6% lower than 87.9%, but the accuracy on SC test set is improved by 14%. This shows that the generalization performance of the MC-training model on the SC test data is enhanced by adding some SC to OC. This is an obvious result. The mixed dataset has the similar effect of data enhancement and adversarial training. Adding "adversarial samples" like stylized dataset to the training set can help the model improve the robustness against the aggressive input.

3.4 Different Proportion of SC in MC

After a simple experiment on MC generated by random sampling with equal probability, experiments are carried out on different MC datasets according to different proportions of SC datasets to study the performance changes of the model with different degrees of stylization. The experimental results are shown in Table 3.

The proportion of SC pictures is 0.1, 0.3 and 0.5 respectively. It can be seen that with the increase of the proportion, the accuracy of the model on OC test set

Table 3. The accuracy on different proportions of SC in MC

Prop of SC	0.1	0.3	0.5
OC	86.3%	84.3%	82.0%
SC	21.6%	25.9%	27.9%

and SC test set shows negative correlation and positive correlation respectively: from 0.1 to 0.3, accuracy on OC decreased by 2%, accuracy on SC increased by 4.3%; from 0.3 to 0.5, accuracy on OC decreased by 2.2%, accuracy on SC increased by 2%. It can be concluded that the negative effect of SC image on the accuracy of the original model may be greater than its positive effect on the model generalization robustness. This can also be concluded from the test results based on SC-training networks.

3.5 Different Coefficient of Stylization

In the above experiment, the transfer coefficient of stylized image is $\alpha = 1.0$, which is the default value of ImageNet experiment in [6], which means that the original image texture is completely removed and the image size of CIFAR10 dataset is only 32×32, resulting in serious distortion of the picture, some pictures even human eyes can not distinguish.

Table 4. The accuracy on different coefficient of SC

Coe of SC	0.05	0.5	1.0
OC	80.3%	81.4%	82.0%
SC with 1.0	14.6%	18.1%	27.9%

This may be due to the high stylization of the dataset, which completely removes the original image texture, and the image size of CIFAR10 dataset is only 32×32, resulting in serious distortion of the picture, some pictures even human eyes can not distinguish. Then we compare the performance of the model under different transfer coefficients. SC datasets with multiple coefficients can better verify the feasibility of stylized methods applied to data enhancement or other preprocessing methods. The stylization coefficient of SC dataset in the above experiments is the highest 1.0. In this part, we choose 0.05, 0.5 to compare with 1.0 as shown in Table 4. Note that the coefficients are different, but the mixing ratio is the same 0.5.

By observing the data in Table 4, an interesting phenomenon can be found by observing the data that the accuracy increases with the increase of the coefficient, in other words, these illegible pictures difficult to recognize with 1.0 coefficient can still help with training. This conclusion is a little counterintuitive. Besides, performance improvement is reflected not only in OC dataset but also in SC with 1.0.

3.6   Coefficients and Proportions

In the above, we explored the impact of different proportions of SC with 1.0 as in Table 4. Here Table 5 and Table 6 are results on SC with 0.5 and 0.05.The proportions are 10%, 30%, 50%, 70%, 90%.

Table 5. The accuracy on different proportions of SC with 0.5 in MC

Coe of SC	0.9	0.7	0.5	0.3	0.1
OC	70.6%	77.4%	81.4%	83.5%	86.1%
SC with 1.0	18.8%	18.3%	18.1%	17.8%	16.4%

Compared with 0.5 coefficient horizontally, the range of accuracy at 0.05 coefficient 71.3%–84.2% is more concentrated than 70.6%–86.1%, It shows that when the coefficient is 0.05, the performance of the model on SC is poor and there is no obvious change tendency of accuracy on SC, which may be because the low transfer coefficient makes the model unable to fit the stylized dataset well, which makes the change of accuracy on OC more susceptible to the influence of proportions rather than coefficients.

Table 6. The accuracy on different proportions of SC with 0.05 in MC

Coe of SC	0.9	0.7	0.5	0.3	0.1
OC	71.3%	76.9%	80.3%	83.4%	84.2%
SC with 1.0	15.2%	14.8%	14.6%	15.0%	14.8%

Under the two coefficients, the influence of SC pictures with different proportions on the model is shown in Fig. 4.

By fitting the trend line, it can be found that the performance of the model will decline with the increase of the ratio under the two coefficients, but the performance under 0.5 is better than that under 0.05, which is very interesting. With the coefficient of 0.05, the images is very close to the OC dataset, and the fitting degree of the original distribution is higher, but it is not as good as 0.5, which shows that the stylized dataset can help the model improve performance. This phenomenon is consistent with the conclusion shown in Table 4.

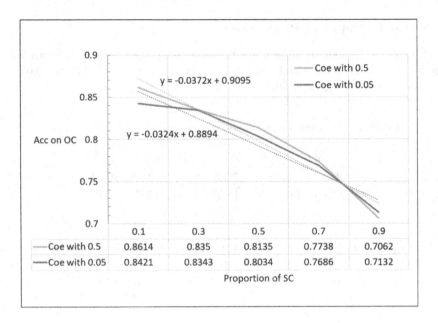

Fig. 4. Accuracy on OC with different proportions and coefficients of SC.

4 Conclusion

In Table 2, on one hand, the mixed dataset reduces the performance of the model on the original test set, but it also improves its performance on the stylized data, and the improvement is more significant. On the other hand, After training on SC dataset, testing on OC is higher than that on SC, which may be because the shape information in SC images is different, and the shape characteristics in test SC may be less clear than that in the original test images. This proves the conclusion that the model has a strong tendency to judge the shape of the object after training, and unclear shape information will greatly affect performance.

In Table 3, with the increase of the proportion, the accuracy of the model on OC test set and SC test set shows negative correlation and positive correlation respectively, further, the negative effect of SC is greater the positive.

In Table 4, we get an interesting conclusion: with the coefficient of 1.0, the texture is difficult to distinguish after being completely removed, but the negative effect on the model performance is lower than 0.5 and 0.05, and the performance of the model on the SC test set will be greatly improved.

Table 5 further validates the previous experiment. According to the conclusions, under the coefficient of 1.0, mixing with 10% stylized pictures can improve the performance of the model on the SC test set the most, and reduce the performance of the model slightly, which is different from the experimental conclusion under the ImageNet dataset in [6]: the model trained based on the SIN dataset improves the accuracy on the IN dataset. This may be due to image size and texture information characteristics of CIFAR10, which can not even retain shape information after texture removal.

It can be concluded that the stylized dataset can help the model to improve the processing ability of shape information with no or minor impact on the performance based original texture, while the effect of this method on small-scale images is not as good as that on large-scale images.

5 Remarks

In this paper, we verify the texture shape tendency of deep learning in CIFAR10 dataset. At present, there is a dependence of texture features in machine learning model recognition, but the degree of dependence is different in different size and different samples. This can help to improve the performance of the model in different tasks.

Interpretability of deep learning has always been an important research direction. Although the experiment can not describe its weight and bias parameters mathematically at present, from the perspective of bionics, the Texture-Shape method is more similar to the perspective of human recognition of objects. Texture-Shape datasets provide a new way of understanding complex models may appear in the future based on this kind of data.

Combined with the method of adversarial training, it can improve the robustness of the model by mixing the two kinds of data. It shows that the current model has the defect of texture bias in the robustness, and it is likely to make mistakes in the face of common samples with shape information or even adversarial inputs. On the other hand, this idea can be introduced into the methods of generating adversarial samples. For the model with texture (or shape) bias, the adversarial samples with opposite tendency (shape or texture) can be generated which may improve the effectiveness [3].

In the follow-up research, the above experiments with different proportion and coefficient can be further improved. In addition, different adversarial attack can be introduced. On the other hand, we can also explore better processing methods of shape bias and texture bias, such as feature fusion, integrated learning.

Acknowledgment. This work is supported by the National Natural Science Foundation of China (61872069), the Fundamental Research Funds for the Central Universities (N2017012).

References

1. Brendel, W., Bethge, M.: Approximating CNNs with bag-of-local-features models works surprisingly well on ImageNet. arXiv preprint arXiv:1904.00760 (2019)
2. Eckstein, M.P., Koehler, K., Welbourne, L.E., Akbas, E.: Humans, but not deep neural networks, often miss giant targets in scenes. Curr. Biol. **27**(18), 2827–2832 (2017)

3. Emin Orhan, A., Lake, B.M.: Improving the robustness of ImageNet classifiers using elements of human visual cognition. arXiv preprint arXiv:1906.08416 (2019)
4. Funke, C.M., Gatys, L.A., Ecker, A.S., Bethge, M.: Synthesising dynamic textures using convolutional neural networks. CoRR abs/1702.07006 (2017), http://arxiv.org/abs/1702.07006
5. Gatys, L.A., Ecker, A.S., Bethge, M.: Image style transfer using convolutional neural networks. In: Proceedings of the IEEE Conference on Computer Vision and Pattern Recognition, pp. 2414–2423 (2016)
6. Geirhos, R., Rubisch, P., Michaelis, C., Bethge, M., Wichmann, F.A., Brendel, W.: ImageNet-trained CNNs are biased towards texture; increasing shape bias improves accuracy and robustness. CoRR abs/1811.12231 (2018), http://arxiv.org/abs/1811.12231
7. Geirhos, R., Temme, C.R.M., Rauber, J., Schütt, H.H., Bethge, M., Wichmann, F.A.: Generalisation in humans and deep neural networks. CoRR abs/1808.08750 (2018), http://arxiv.org/abs/1808.08750
8. He, K., Zhang, X., Ren, S., Sun, J.: Deep residual learning for image recognition. CoRR abs/1512.03385 (2015), http://arxiv.org/abs/1512.03385
9. Krizhevsky, A., Sutskever, I., Hinton, G.E.: ImageNet classification with deep convolutional neural networks. In: Advances in Neural Information Processing Systems, pp. 1097–1105 (2012)
10. Kubilius, J., Bracci, S., de Beeck, H.P.O.: Deep neural networks as a computational model for human shape sensitivity. PLoS Comput. Biol. 12(4), e1004896 (2016)
11. Long, J., Shelhamer, E., Darrell, T.: Fully convolutional networks for semantic segmentation. CoRR abs/1411.4038 (2014), http://arxiv.org/abs/1411.4038
12. Ritter, S., Barrett, D.G., Santoro, A., Botvinick, M.M.: Cognitive psychology for deep neural networks: a shape bias case study. In: Proceedings of the 34th International Conference on Machine Learning-Volume 70, pp. 2940–2949. JMLR. org (2017)
13. Russakovsky, O., et al.: ImageNet large scale visual recognition challenge. Int. J. Comput. Vision 115(3), 211–252 (2015)
14. Xie, S., Girshick, R.B., Dollár, P., Tu, Z., He, K.: Aggregated residual transformations for deep neural networks. CoRR abs/1611.05431 (2016), http://arxiv.org/abs/1611.05431
15. Zeiler, M.D., Fergus, R.: Visualizing and understanding convolutional networks. In: Fleet, D., Pajdla, T., Schiele, B., Tuytelaars, T. (eds.) ECCV 2014. LNCS, vol. 8689, pp. 818–833. Springer, Cham (2014). https://doi.org/10.1007/978-3-319-10590-1_53

A Multi-objective Ant Colony Optimization Algorithm with Local Optimum Avoidance Strategy

Ying Wu[1], Zibo Qi[1], Ling Jiang[1], Changsheng Zhang[2]([⊠]), and Jian Xu[2]

[1] Shenyang Fire Science and Technology, Research Institute of MEM,
Shenyang, China
65126391@qq.com, {qizibo,jiangling}@syfri.cn
[2] Software College of Northeastern University, Shenyang, China
{zhangchangsheng,xuj}@mail.neu.edu.cn

Abstract. Ant colony optimization (ACO) algorithm has rapid convergence speed and competitive performance in multi-objective optimization. However, for complicated multi-objective problems (MOPs), it faces the issue of the local optimum trap, which hinders the global optimization of the multi-objective ACO. This paper proposes a multi-objective ACO algorithm with a local optimum avoidance (LOA) strategy, called MACO/D-LOA. The proposed strategy uses a matrix structure to record the paths that ants have visited. Then it controls the selected probability of the recorded paths. This mechanism enhances the exploration research capability of the multi-objective ACO while retaining the exploitation ability. Experimental results on typical test cases indicate that the proposed algorithm obtains competitive convergence results than state-of-the-art algorithms.

Keywords: Ant colony optimization · Multi-objective optimization · Discrete optimization · Decomposition strategy

1 Introduction

The Multi-objective problem (MOP) represents a kind of problem constrained by not only one optimization objective. In practice, the objectives are generally conflicted. In general, the goal of the MOP optimization is to get a group of nondominated solutions to approximate the shape and distribution of the MOP's Pareto front (PF), which shows different trade-offs of the contradictory objectives.

The decomposition-based strategy is efficient in MOP optimization. It decomposes the objective space into several sub-regions by a group of weight vectors, which construct a scalarized function for each sub-region, i.e., for decomposition-based strategy, there is one optimal solution in each sub-region. The algorithm collects optimums of sub-regions to approximate the PF.

© Springer Nature Switzerland AG 2020
X. Chen et al. (Eds.): ML4CS 2020, LNCS 12487, pp. 427–435, 2020.
https://doi.org/10.1007/978-3-030-62460-6_38

Ant colony optimization (ACO) algorithm is one of the most popular swarm intelligence algorithms. It constructs solutions using historical experiences heuristically, inspired by the foraging behavior of ant colonies. Specifically, the ACO utilizes a pheromone matrix to guide the searching process. The more promising paths accumulate more massive amounts of pheromone. Therefore, ants visit these paths with higher probability. In this way, the ACO can quickly converge to a high-quality solution.

Based on the characteristics of fast convergence of the ACO, combining the decomposition strategy with it has achieved ideal results in multi-objective optimization. Several sophisticated algorithms, such as the MOEA/D-ACO [6], MOACO/D-MMAS [12], and MOACO/D-ACS [2], have made satisfactory performance on benchmark test. Furthermore, in recent years, some decomposition-based ACO has been utilized in engineering areas like taxi-passenger matching [10] and community detection [5].

Although the decomposition-based ACO has rapid convergence speed, it faces the risk of being trapped in a local optimum. The main reason is the complicated MOP. There could be multiple promising sub-regions in the search space. Once the ants find one of these regions, the ACO leads them to pay more attention to this area; therefore, more pheromones accumulate on paths related to this region. This situation intensifies as the iteration progressed until the search scope of all ants focuses on one area. This phenomenon is called the local optimum trap (LOT).

Several approaches of adaptive pheromone evaporation rate [4] are proposed to avoid LOT for single-objective ACO by balancing the exploration and exploitation [8] of the ant colony. They failed in solving MOP because the search space of the MOP is more complicated.

This paper proposes a multi-objective ACO algorithm with a local optimum avoidance strategy, which utilizes a matrix to record to visited paths in the previous iteration. By comparing visited routes, the algorithm adjusts the pheromone matrices to balance the exploitation and exploration. In this way, the proposed approach forces the algorithm to perform the global search to get out of the LOT. This paper describes the algorithm framework of the decomposition-based ACO with the local optimum avoidance strategy. The proposed algorithm is named as MACO/D-LOA. A comparative experiment is implemented to test the optimization quality of MACO/D-LOA on multi-objective benchmark problems.

The remaining part of this paper is organized as follows: the second section introduces the details of the proposed MACO/D-LOA algorithm. Section 3 verifies the performance of MAOC/D-LOA through a comparative experiment. At last, the conclusion section summarizes the works of this paper and analyzes the potential research direction.

2   The Proposed MACO/D-LOA

This section describes the design and implementation of the proposed MACO/D-LOA and the LOA strategy.

2.1   The Local Optimum Avoidance Strategy

During the optimization procedure, when the algorithm is stuck in stagnation, it assumes that it might encounter the LOT. In this case, it executes the LOA strategy to shift the search behavior's focus on exploration, i.e., the LOA expands the search scope. Therefore, the algorithm could find a more promising region and escape from the LOT.

The LOA strategy is based on extra archives that record the visited solutions in different iterations. Since this paper transforms the search space of the discrete optimization problem into a directed acyclic graph (DAG), the LOA uses the matrix structure to represent the visited solutions as paths of the DAG. To be specific, in each iteration of an optimization process, the ant colony works out several solutions recorded in a matrix. And the algorithm reserves this matrix to the next iteration. For example, for the tth iteration, the ACO marks the solutions in a matrix P_c, which means the results of the current iteration. Meanwhile, the algorithm maintains the matrix that records the solutions of its former iteration, the $t - 1^{th}$ iteration, which is called P_f. By comparing the above two matrices, the MACO/D-LOA determines whether the LOT occurs. This judgment is based on the assumption that when falling into a locally optimal state, the solutions produced by the algorithm are highly similar.

Figure 1 illustrates the P_c and P_f. There are eight nodes numbered from A to H. Each element of the matrices represents an edge. For example, the element at the upper right matrix of the matrix represents the edge from node A to H. It is worth noting that since the search space is a DAG, the edge from node A to H is different from the one from H to A. If an edge is included in a solution, its state is recorded as 1 in the matrix. Otherwise, its state is 0.

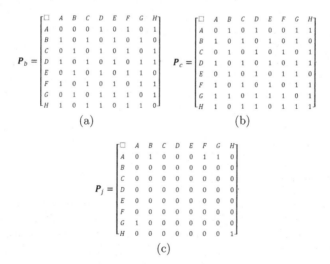

Fig. 1. An example of P_b, P_c, and P_j

The algorithm works out a matrix P_j to analyze the searching statement. Let $x_{i,j}$ be the elements of row i, column j of P_j, $y_{i,j}$ and $z_{i,j}$ are the elements at the same location in P_c and P_f, respectively. The MACO/D-LOA calculates the $x_{i,j}$ according to Eq. 1:

$$x_{i,j} = \begin{cases} 1, \text{if } y_{i,j} \neq z_{i,j} \\ 0, \text{otherwise} \end{cases} \tag{1}$$

When the percentage of the number of edges that is marked as 0 is greater than a threshold θ, the algorithm adjusts the pheromone information to guide the search behavior of ants for next iterations. For the decomposition-based strategy, each subproblem corresponds to an ant colony, i.e., each subproblem owns a pheromone matrix. For edge (k, l), its pheromone for subproblem j is updated according to Eq. 2:

$$\tau_{k,l}^{j} = \rho \cdot (\tau_{max} - \tau_{k,l}^{j}) \tag{2}$$

where $\tau_{k,l}^{j}$ is the pheromone of edge (k, l) in pheromone matrix of subproblem j, ρ is a zoom parameter, τ_{max} is the maximum value of pheromone on an edge.

After the above update, there is more pheromone content on the unvisited edges. In this case, the LOA strategy increases the selective probability of the unvisited edges and reduces the likelihood of the visited edges. Therefore, more ants will perform an exploration search for the following epochs.

2.2   Algorithm Framework

The Algorithm 1 shows the executing procedure of the proposed MACO/D-LOA algorithm. At first, the algorithm initializes the ant colony and the necessary variables and archives. When the algorithm begins, it firstly constructs a set of solutions, which are evaluated by the objective functions. Then the algorithm selects the optimal solution for each subproblem. The optimal solutions are utilized to update the nondominated solution set E. According to E, the MACO/D-LOA updates the pheromone matrices. After this, the LOA strategy updates the matrices P_c and P_f and uses them to calculate P_j. According to the percentage of the number of 0 in P_j, the LOA updates the pheromone matrices. MACO/D-LOA repeats the above processes until it meets the stop criterion. Finally, the algorithm outputs E to approximate the PF.

2.3   Performance Discussion

Assuming that MACO/D-LOA employs m ants to solve an n-dimensional search space optimization problem. The time complexity in the initialization phase is $T_1(n) = m + m * n + n^2 + 2$. The time complexity in the algorithm iteration process is $T_2(n) = m * n^2 + 2n^2 + 4$. Therefore, the time complexity of the algorithm is $T(n) = T_1(n) + MFE * T_2(n)/m$. Among them, MFE is the maximum number of iterations. Since $MFE \gg m$ and $MFE \gg n$, the worst-case time complexity of the algorithm is $O(n^2 * MFE)$.

Algorithm 1: Algorithm framework of MAOC/D-LOA

Input: The problem to be optimized; The stop criterion; The number of
  subproblems N; Threshold θ
Output: A non-dominated solution set $\boldsymbol{E}$;
1 initialize N weight vectors $\lambda^1, \lambda^2, ..., \lambda^N$;
2 initialize ants;
3 initialize heuristic information matrices and pheromone matrices;
4 initialize the $\boldsymbol{E}$ as NULL;
5 initialize $\boldsymbol{P}_c$ and $\boldsymbol{P}_f$ as NULL;
6 **while** *stop criterion == false* **do**
7 $\quad$ construct solutions;
8 $\quad$ evaluate solutions;
9 $\quad$ select optimal solution for each subproblem by Tchebycheff method;
10 $\quad$ update $\boldsymbol{E}$;
11 $\quad$ update pheromone matrices; **for** *each ant colony* **do**
12 $\quad\quad$ update $\boldsymbol{P}_c$;
13 $\quad\quad$ calculate $\boldsymbol{P}_j$;
14 $\quad\quad$ calculate number of 1 n_1 and number of 0 n_0;
15 $\quad\quad$ **if** $\frac{n_0}{n_0+n_1} > \theta$ **then**
16 $\quad\quad\quad$ | update pheromone matrices according to Eq. 2;
17 $\quad\quad$ **end**
18 $\quad\quad$ set $\boldsymbol{P}_f = \boldsymbol{P}_c$;
19 $\quad$ **end**
20 **end**
21 output $\boldsymbol{E}$;

---

3 Experimental Study

This section introduces a comparative study, which investigates the performance
of the proposed MACO/D-LOA.

3.1 Experimental Settings

This paper adopts nine two-objective Travelling Salesman Problems (TSPs)
as benchmark test cases to verify the algorithm performance. Each problem
is constructed by combining two single-objective problems form the TSPLIB.
For example, the test case kroAB100 is constructed by combining kroA100 and
kroB100.

This experiment compares the proposed algorithm with three typical
dominance-based ACOs [3], MACS [1], MOACO [7], and PACO [11], and a
state-of-the-art decomposition-based ACO, MOACO/D-ACS [2]. The iteration
number of all algorithms is uniformly set to 10,000. For every test case, each
algorithm runs 31 times independently. And the results of each independent
execution is evaluated by the IGD indicator.

The setting and updating of the heuristic matrix and pheromone matrix are as follows: Let $\eta_{k,l}^i$ be the heuristic information of the ith sub-problem cluster on link (k, l), it is calculated according to Eq. 3:

$$\eta_{k,l}^i = \frac{1}{\sum_{j=1}^q \lambda_j^i c_{k,l}^j} \tag{3}$$

Let $\tau_{k,l}^i$ be the pheromone of the ith sub-problem cluster on link (k, l), at the initialization stage, it is initialized as 1.

Before the construction of paths, for each ant i, the algorithm calculates the attractiveness of each edge. For edge (k, l), its attractiveness is computed according to Eq. 4:

$$\phi_{k,l} = \left[\tau_{k,l}^i + \Delta \times In(x^i, (k, l)) \right]^\alpha (\eta_{k,l}^i)^\beta \tag{4}$$

where Δ, α, and $\beta > 0$ are control parameters. The function $In(x^i, (k, l))$ is equal to 1 if edge (k, l) is in the current solution and otherwise $In(x^i, (k, l))$ is equal to 0.

For solution construction, the algorithm allocates a random start node for ant i at first. Next, the ant constructs a path node by node. Assuming a ant i is at node l, it generates a random number between 0 and 1. If the random number is smaller than a threshold r, ant i chooses the city k that the $\phi_{k,l}$ is the maximum. Otherwise, select a node randomly from feasible nodes by the roulette wheel selection approach. The ant repeats the node selection process until a complete path is constructed.

3.2   Performance Analysis Based on Hypervolume Indicator

Table 1 shows the mean value, minimum value, maximum value, and standard deviation of the repeated experiments. The bold number highlights the best results under the same test case. As shown in the table, the MAOC/D-LOA obtains the best on the average result, maximum result, and minimum result on all nine test cases. Furthermore, the results of the MACO/D-LOA are the best on standard deviation on five test cases (kroAD100, kroCE100, kroCE100, euclidAB100, kroAB200).

3.3   Performance Analysis Based on Hypothesis Test

This paper utilizes the Kruskal-Wallis hypothesis test [9] to investigate the significance of the difference between the experimental results of different algorithms. The significant level is set to 0.05 in this experiment. When the p-value, i.e., the results of this hypothesis test, is less than 0.05, there is a significant difference between the results of the MACO/D-LOA and the compared algorithm. The hypothesis results are shown in Table 2. According to the results, the MACO/D-LOA is significantly better than all its competitors on all test cases.

Table 1. Experimental results based on hypervolume indicator

Test case		MACO/D-LAO	MACS	MOACO	MOACO/D-ACS	PACO
kroAB100	Means	**1.840E−02**	2.221E−01	3.632E−01	3.608E−01	4.229E−01
	Max	**2.100E−02**	2.304E−01	3.810E−01	3.789E−01	4.392E−01
	Min	**1.340E−02**	2.088E−01	3.376E−01	3.434E−01	4.021E−01
	Standard	1.134E−03	9.251E−03	9.659E−03	**1.017E−03**	1.367E−03
kroAC100	Means	**1.770E−02**	2.150E−01	3.620E−01	3.623E−01	2.640E−01
	Max	**2.120E−02**	2.264E−01	3.737E−01	3.742E−01	2.822E−01
	Min	**1.190E−02**	2.000E−01	3.458E−01	3.471E−01	2.515E−01
	Standard	1.131E−03	1.807E−03	**4.110E−04**	3.568E−03	4.972E−03
kroAD100	Means	**2.390E−02**	2.247E−01	3.551E−01	3.531E−01	1.819E−01
	Max	**2.610E−02**	2.330E−01	3.656E−01	3.645E−01	2.005E−01
	Min	**2.010E−02**	2.120E−01	3.420E−01	3.349E−01	1.619E−01
	Standard	**1.409E−04**	1.590E−04	3.862E−03	4.628E−03	4.332E−03
kroCD100	Means	**2.540E−02**	2.299E−01	3.545E−01	3.533E−01	1.974E−01
	Max	**2.980E−02**	2.388E−01	3.785E−01	3.694E−01	2.106E−01
	Min	**2.120E−02**	2.184E−01	3.401E−01	3.256E−01	1.847E−01
	Standard	**9.409E−04**	1.111E−03	2.081E−03	2.729E−03	2.220E−03
kroCE100	Means	**2.440E−02**	1.915E−01	3.214E−01	3.203E−01	1.494E−01
	Max	**3.050E−02**	1.992E−01	3.432E−01	3.373E−01	1.599E−01
	Min	**1.990E−02**	1.817E−01	3.083E−01	2.920E−01	1.383E−01
	Standard	**7.226E−04**	9.192E−04	2.639E−03	3.491E−03	1.850E−03
euclidAB100	Means	**2.580E−02**	2.598E−01	3.661E−01	3.511E−01	2.052E−01
	Max	**3.010E−02**	2.712E−01	3.838E−01	3.629E−01	2.170E−01
	Min	**1.920E−02**	2.496E−01	3.504E−01	3.377E−01	1.937E−01
	Standard	**1.263E−03**	3.999E−03	2.087E−03	4.774E−03	7.286E−03
euclidCE100	Means	**8.200E−03**	4.127E−01	5.609E−01	3.852E−01	3.782E−01
	Max	**1.220E−02**	4.422E−01	5.693E−01	5.725E−01	3.827E−01
	Min	**5.600E−03**	9.630E−02	5.506E−01	2.006E−01	3.737E−01
	Standard	6.986E−04	9.836E−04	4.454E−03	1.671E−03	**2.782E−04**
kroAB150	Means	**2.080E−02**	2.284E−01	4.204E−01	2.978E−01	2.454E−01
	Max	**2.340E−02**	2.376E−01	4.299E−01	3.468E−01	2.622E−01
	Min	**1.860E−02**	2.222E−01	4.074E−01	2.468E−01	2.334E−01
	Standard	7.809E−04	1.705E−03	8.935E−04	1.790E−02	**8.200E−06**
kroAB200	Means	**2.520E−02**	2.444E−01	4.614E−01	2.552E−01	2.757E−01
	Max	**2.720E−02**	2.554E−01	4.710E−01	4.710E−01	2.889E−01
	Min	**2.200E−02**	2.381E−01	4.486E−01	4.020E−02	2.515E−01
	Standard	**7.427E−04**	3.732E−03	3.899E−03	2.082E−01	2.155E−03

3.4   Discussion

According to Table 1, the proposed algorithm has obtained superior mean, maximum and minimum results. Furthermore, the proposed algorithm obtains the best standard deviation on five of nine test cases, i.e., it can provide stable results. The above indicators verify the MACO/D-LOA has a competitive global search capability. In addition, the hypothesis test result shows that the proposed algorithm has significantly superior performance than peer algorithms. And as shown in Fig. 2, the MACO/D-LOA provides a PF with better convergence and distribution performance. Therefore, the proposed improvement is effective.

Table 2. Results of hypothesis test

Test case	MACS	MOACO	MOACO/D-ACS	PACO
kroAB100	1.10E−26	5.20E−58	8.60E−100	1.30E−94
kroAC100	7.40E−36	9.50E−100	3.50E−120	4.10E−30
kroAD100	1.30E−81	1.80E−134	1.30E−157	2.80E−52
kroCD100	3.60E−39	4.20E−92	5.90E−58	3.20E−21
kroCE100	1.40E−81	1.20E−134	1.30E−157	2.90E−52
euclidAB100	9.30E−51	3.90E−120	4.60E−72	1.40E−27
euclidCE100	2.10E−22	1.70E−119	1.00E−101	4.90E−42
kroAB150	3.50E−11	2.90E−46	9.80E−34	7.20E−18
kroAB200	3.50E−11	2.90E−06	5.10E−25	7.20E−18

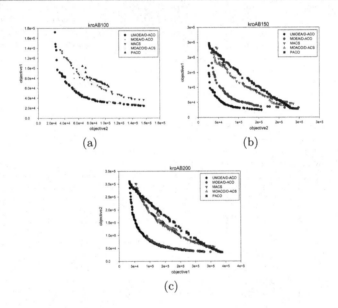

Fig. 2. Distribution of nondominated solutions

4   Conclusion

This paper proposes a modified multi-objective ACO algorithm, MACO/D-LOA, which has a local optimum avoidance strategy to help it in overcoming the LOT. The proposed approach utilizes extra matrix archives to store the historical experiences of the ant colonies. Based on this, the ant colonies adjust the selected probability of the visited paths to concentrate more on exploration searching. This strategy is simple and easy for implementation. It only introduces a limited memory footprint without increasing the complexity of the ACO framework. The experiments on multi-objective test cases show that the proposed algorithm has a competitive performance on complicated MOPs. For the future work, designing efficient searching strategies and improving the performance of ACO in high-dimensional objective space are promising research directions.

Acknowledgement. This paper is supported by the Key Project of National Natural Science Foundation of China (U1908212), the Fundamental Research Funds for the Central Universities (N2017013, N2017014).

References

1. Barán, B., Schaerer, M.: A multiobjective ant colony system for vehicle routing problem with time windows. In: Applied Informatics, pp. 97–102 (2003)
2. Cheng, J., Zhang, G., Li, Z., Li, Y.: Multi-objective ant colony optimization based on decomposition for bi-objective traveling salesman problems. Soft. Comput. **16**(4), 597–614 (2012)
3. Chengar, O., Savkova, E., Vladimirova, E., Sapozhnikov, N.: Pareto optimization using the method of ant colony. In: MATEC Web of Conferences, vol. 129, p. 03013. EDP Sciences (2017)
4. El Fachtali, I., Saadane, R., El Koutbi, M.: Improved vertical handover decision algorithm using ants' colonies with adaptive pheromone evaporation rate for 4th generation heterogeneous wireless networks. IJWMC **12**(2), 154–165 (2017)
5. Ji, P., Zhang, S., Zhou, Z.P.: A decomposition-based ant colony optimization algorithm for the multi-objective community detection. J. Ambient Intell. Humaniz. Comput. **11**(1), 173–188 (2020)
6. Ke, L., Zhang, Q., Battiti, R.: MOEA/D-ACO: a multiobjective evolutionary algorithm using decomposition and antcolony. IEEE Trans. Cybern. **43**(6), 1845–1859 (2013)
7. Lopez-Ibanez, M., Stutzle, T.: The automatic design of multiobjective ant colony optimization algorithms. IEEE Trans. Evol. Comput. **16**(6), 861–875 (2012)
8. Luger, J., Raisch, S., Schimmer, M.: Dynamic balancing of exploration and exploitation: the contingent benefits of ambidexterity. Organ. Sci. **29**(3), 449–470 (2018)
9. Ren, W.L., Wen, Y.J., Dunwell, J.M., Zhang, Y.M.: pKWmEB: integration of Kruskal-Wallis test with empirical Bayes under polygenic background control for multi-locus genome-wide association study. Heredity **120**(3), 208–218 (2018)
10. Situ, X., et al.: A parallel ant colony system based on region decomposition for taxi-passenger matching. In: 2017 IEEE Congress on Evolutionary Computation (CEC), pp. 960–967. IEEE (2017)
11. Skinderowicz, R.: Population-based ant colony optimization for sequential ordering problem. In: Núñez, M., Nguyen, N.T., Camacho, D., Trawiński, B. (eds.) ICCCI 2015. LNCS (LNAI), vol. 9330, pp. 99–109. Springer, Cham (2015). https://doi.org/10.1007/978-3-319-24306-1_10
12. Teixeira, C., Covas, J., Stützle, T., Gaspar-Cunha, A.: Multi-objective ant colony optimization for the twin-screw configuration problem. Eng. Optim. **44**(3), 351–371 (2012)

Education for Bilingual Children in the Age of Artificial Intelligence

Weiwei Zhou[✉] (iD)

School of Foreign Languages, Nanchang Institute of Technology,
Nanchang 330099, China
280925505@qq.com

Abstract. With the advancements of technology and the mobility of information and population, the number of bilingual children is greater nowadays than that in previous days. The education modes for them have also seen great changes in the age of Artificial Intelligence. AI technologies, emerging as one of the most significant impetus for the change of the world in the 21st century, have greatly altered the previous situation of education in all regions of the world. In this paper, the author firstly presents the current situations of both AI technologies and bilingual children. Then the ways AI can be integrated into the education for bilingual children have been discussed from the perspectives of bilingual children themselves, their families and schools. In spite of the benefits AI has brought to education, challenges are also noticeable at the same time. Therefore, external factors in technological and educational aspects and internal factors in psychological, physical and emotional areas should be carefully taken into consideration in the education for bilingual children.

Keywords: Artificial Intelligence · Education · Bilingual children

1 Introduction

Advancements in Artificial Intelligence (AI) are changing industries, economies and disciplines and casting effects on human activities all over the world. In July 2017, the Chinese State Council printed and distributed "The Development Plan of New Generation AI", in order to grab the huge strategic opportunities of AI, construct the first-mover advantage of AI and accelerate the construction of China into an innovative powerful country in technology and science. Later, in December 2017, Ministry of Industry and Information Technology of the People's Republic of China followed by printing and distributing "The 3-Year Action Plan of Promoting the Industrial Development of New Generation AI", aiming at pushing forward the deeper combination between AI and the real economy. The development and breakthrough in the AI field has significantly prompted the efficiency in production and the globalization while bilingualism, appearing as a common phenomenon, draws more and more attention from researchers and the public as a result.

At the same time, bilingual children, who need more assistance than other bilingual groups, are struggling for their new identities in the new countries with the linguistic barrier presenting as one of the biggest challenges. I decide to write about bilingual

© Springer Nature Switzerland AG 2020
X. Chen et al. (Eds.): ML4CS 2020, LNCS 12487, pp. 436–442, 2020.
https://doi.org/10.1007/978-3-030-62460-6_39

children and their education because of my experiences of meeting bilingual children in both China and the UK and I want to discover more about their development and how education is properly provided for them with the help of AI. In addition to this, what makes bilingual children different from other bilinguals are their potential of being balanced bilinguals and their particular learning abilities and processes that are distinct from adult learners.

Although bilingual children, their families and their teachers hold different opinions towards each other and different beliefs for the bilingual education, there is a close relationship between the three major subjects here and that is the reason why I want to emphasize it in this essay. I will focus on the potential assistance that AI can provide in building up a closer relationship between the three subjects so that better education can be offered to those bilingual children.

2 An Overview of Artificial Intelligence in Education and Bilingual Children

The new generation of AI has been influencing and changing the way human beings are living and it has been regarded as the important thruster for the 4th Industrial Revolution.

2.1 Artificial Intelligence in Education

The UNESCO has reported that "the systematic integration of Artificial Intelligence (AI) in education has the potential to address some of the biggest challenges in education today, innovate teaching and learning practices, and ultimately accelerate the progress towards Sustainable Development Goal 4" (2020). According to the "Artificial Intelligence Market in the US Education Sector Report" (2018), analysts forecast the Artificial Intelligence Market in the US Education Sector to grow at a Compound Annual Growth Rate of 47.77% during the period 2018–2022. Companies like iFLYTECH in China, Carnegie Learning and Fuel Education in the US, etc. have all applied AI to education from kindergarten through twelfth grade and more AI technologies have been applied to higher education in recent years. AI in education exerts an influence on learning style, learning opportunities, learning quality, teacher development, etc. and presents new challenges in equality, policies, privacy, ethics, etc. in education. One study found that 34 h on an AI education app are equivalent to a full university semester of language education.

Benefits have been brought by AI technologies to education both at school and at home. Firstly, it makes education universal to a greater extent. Learners can get access to education in any places and at any time due to the easy and convenient operation at their smartphones and tablets. Feedback can be given to them from their tutors in a real-time mode. Secondly, learners' personalized needs can be met while AI-based tools can adapt different levels of learning materials to learners based on their existing knowledge and abilities. In addition, AI technologies have also brought great benefits to teachers and parents. AI in education enables teachers to teach students in accordance with their aptitude when it provides possible ways for teachers to notice the precise gaps in students' knowledge. With the help of AI, parents spare no more time than before to follow the studies of their children and build up a closer relationship with their children's schools. All of those benefits also apply to the education of bilingual children.

2.2 Bilingual Children

Bilingual children constitute a larger proportion of younger learners than ever before because of a larger scale of international mobility of population.

Bilinguals. Since many worries have mounted on the education of bilingual children, it is difficult to explore anything related to bilingualism without a clear idea about "How bilingual is defined". According to the Webster Dictionary (1961), bilingual is defined as "having or using two languages especially as spoken with the fluency characteristic of a native speaker, a person using two languages especially habitually and with control like that of a native speaker". Compared to this definition, another one, put forward by Titone, defines bilingualism as "the individual's capacity to speak a second language while following the concepts and structures of that language rather than paraphrasing his or her mother tongue" (Titone 1972). Therefore, there is a gap between these two definitions that represent two kinds of views from scholars while Bloomfield's theory gives a definition bridging these two as follows:

In … case where … perfect foreign-language learning is not accompanied by loss of the native language, it results in bilingualism, native-like control of the two languages. After early childhood, few people have enough muscular and nervous freedom or enough opportunity and leisure to reach perfection in a foreign language; yet bilingualism of this kind is commoner than one might suppose, both in cases like those of our immigrants and as a result of travel, foreign study, or similar association. Of course one cannot define a degree of perfection at which a good foreign speaker becomes a bilingual: the distinction is relative (Bloomfield 1935).

Bloomfield addresses the possible factors that may result in the rise of bilinguals and the different categorized definitions of being bilingual. According to his definition, the bilingual children I will address here are those relatively perfect bilinguals, or in other words, dominant bilinguals.

The factors contributing to the development of bilingualism or even multilingualism are often linked to the international mobility of population and information. These gatherings of people and information contribute to the need for contact of language, making it possible for the rise of bilinguals. Li Wei made a list of possible elements leading to language contact: politics, natural disaster, religion, culture, economy, education and technology (Li 2000).

Situations Bilingual Children are in. The rise of bilingual children is mostly due to their families' and schools' decisions. For example, they resettle in a new country with their parents, their parents are from two different countries or speak two different languages, their parents want them to grow up as bilinguals to be more competent in job market in the future or their educational policies force them to be bilinguals. It is reported that they can become confused about the two languages and sometimes will mix the two languages up for use; they need longer time to develop their bilingual languages than those monolinguals. In addition, some bilingual children are found to suffer from mental stress such as anxiety, nervousness, and disappointment when they have to deal with situations in their second languages at the beginning stage. It is especially true for those immigrant children from minority language groups. However, despite that disadvantages may be found, advantages have been discovered for bilingual children in communicative, cultural cognitive (Li 2000) and linguistic aspects. Research has shown that bilingual children have better metalinguistic awareness and problem solving abilities than monolingual children (Fromkin, Rodman and Hyams 2003).

In recent years, more attention is drawn to research into the development of bilingual children among which I will focus my points on the education for bilingual children in their families and schools where most of their learning happens.

3   AI in Education for Bilingual Children

Policy makers, schools and parents of the bilingual children have realized the importance of adapting these children to their new language environment. For example, in the United States and Sweden, various kinds of bilingual programs such as transitional bilingual programs and enrichment bilingual programs have been carried out by involving the use of the minority children's mother tongues for teaching in order to help those bilingual children to fulfill the gaps between their mother tongues and the school languages (Bialystok and Cummins 1991). Many schools also begin to train teachers for the special need of the bilingual children so that teaching can be implemented in the right direction in a more effective way. As for some parents, even though they hold positive attitudes towards the maintenance of the mother tongues being spoken by their children, they feel the urgent need for their children to become engaged in the new language environment. With the integration of AI technologies into the education for bilingual children, all of those measures can be simplified, systematized and personalized.

3.1   AI for Bilingual Children

Bilingual children are struggling and mediating themselves to settle into the new language communities—this is the process that occurs in their inner minds. In the research conducted by Drury, she reports the voices and development of three 4-year-old bilingual children at home and school. It is discovered that these bilingual children tend to start as shy since they don't have the same experiences as the people around (Drury 2007) and they experience the "silent period" while they are getting accustomed to the new language environment and begin to acquire the knowledge of what is expected and "tune in to the sounds of setting" (Drury 2007), after which they gain improvement.

AI technologies can be integrated and applied during that "silent period" so as to strengthen the knowledge zone for each individual bilingual child. A level of differentiation in each individual child's needs can be recognized, recorded and told by AI technologies while human teachers are not able to do so if they have more than 20 students in class. Bilingual children in "silent period" do not need to talk much when intelligent platforms and smart products can evaluate their knowledge gaps by testing them and evaluate their mental state if children's faces can be scanned and read thus assessing the challenges they are ready for and adjusting response timely without interfering with them too much. By doing so, those bilingual children can get access to the most appropriate learning materials and discover the most suitable learning styles for themselves and timely and precise feedback can be provided as well. AI technologies provide children various choices on when and where they choose to study and the advancements in the technologies give considerable linguistic support to bilingual children to a great extent. Voice assistants such as Apple Siri enables children to communicate and search for variable learning materials without communicating with parents, teachers and peers.

3.2 AI for Family Education of Bilingual Children

The families of the bilingual children often fall into a dilemma of how their children can conform to the second language communities and how to maintain the mother tongues to keep their identities at the same time. Most of them expect high proficiency of their children's school performance. Yet, many minority parents feel that they can do nothing to help their children with the school curriculums and rely mostly on the school education. On the contrary, they can support their children at home through their own ways and find children's development of learning at home that is invisible to the teachers. Some children are reported that they rarely speak during the school time but as researches find, they actually practice their second languages and use their school knowledge while interacting with their families (Drury 2007). Parents, at this point, are supposed to notice these learning phenomena and provide appropriate assistance to the children.

In this case, the potential of AI to support children in study significantly encourages parents of bilingual children as tutoring is advancing greatly. Various learning platforms, programs and smart applications are available to family education thanks to the development in AI technologies with which parents are able to teach and communicate with their children at home and establish a more intimate relationship with their children's schools so that children's performance at school and family can be better synchronized and presented to each other.

3.3 AI for School Education of Bilingual Children

In addition to family education, school education plays an important part in the development of bilingual children since schools are one of the major communities where learning takes place. In the past, little attention was drawn to bilingual children's learning barriers in schools since people believed that to bilingual children's language learning and environment adaption would be natural processes. What's more, people argue that the unsuccessful academic performance in schools of bilingual children is owing to their failure to be bilingual. Real situations are unlike that and are far more complex. Until recent years, governments and schools realize how their policies have affected the academic performance of the bilingual children and are putting more energy and resources into the education for bilingual children. Take the principles for early years education set in the Curriculum Guidance for the Foundation Stage in England for example. It states as aiming to "foster personal, social and emotional well-being" by "promoting and inclusive ethos and providing opportunities for each child to become a valued member of that group and community so that a strong self-image and self-esteem are promoted" (QCA 2000). As what is indicated previously, governments and schools are supposed to make some improvements in providing special support for those bilingual children with the advancements in technologies, especially in AI technologies.

The key to promote bilingual children's learning at school is to construct AI-assisted intelligent campus. The first step is to improve and perfect hardware teaching facilities by making them "smart", such as introducing "smart classrooms", "smart libraries" and "smart management systems" so as to lay a firm foundation for children's learning. The second step is to equip the teachers with sufficient digital skills so that they are able to conduct efficient and effective teaching in this intelligent environment since bilingual children are in need of more assistance from teachers than other children both in language and cultural expressions. For example, the Third Space Learning system provided teachers with specific teaching techniques. Then children's intelligent learning profiles are expected to be built up because AI make immense and personalized databases possible and they can be built up based on the precise analysis of the children's personal information like age, sex, cognitive level, etc., their learning portfolio like learning experiences, testing scores, activities attended, etc. and other profiles like their personalities, hobbies, used applications, facial expressions, etc. Moreover, AI contributes greatly in the development of testing and evaluation systems. The quick calculation and analysis of the testing results and the automate tasks AI products can perform allow teachers to spare more time with each individual child. Besides, AI reinforces cooperative learning among bilingual children while language barriers and cultural differences can be overcome with the help of AI. For example, companies like Little Dragon have created educational games that can be co-played during school time by children whose emotions can be sensed and analyzed so that the most appropriate communicative modes can be established.

3.4   Challenges of AI in Education for Bilingual Children

The first challenge is to coordinate the work of different sectors such as education administration department, schools and families while integrating AI into the education of bilingual children since technologies are far more complicated than what we have imagined. Both technological and humanistic factors need to be taken into consideration during the process. The second challenge is to ensure the equity and completeness of the data collected. It is important to make the quality of data to the top of the list. The collection, systematization and analysis of the data should be attached great importance. The third challenge is related to ethical problems of AI. When children's personal information and private data are collected, it is important to keep regulations on the privacy and security of the children.

4   Conclusion

According to the facts analyzed above, the education for bilingual children is far more complicated than we have expected. There will be external factors in social and educational aspects and internal factors in psychological, physical and emotional areas influencing the development of bilingual children. As children's main learning context are families and schools, their parents and teachers should take up practical measures and think deeply about how they can scaffold these children. By collecting characteristic data and setting up database for each bilingual child, higher-quality learning environment, more advanced teaching and learning solutions and more novel learning materials have come into being. AI, a booming technological domain, broadens the possibility for education development whereas brings about known and unknown challenges at the same time.

References

Bialystok, E.: Language Processing in Bilingual Children. Cambridge University Press, Cambridge (1991)

Bloomfield, L.: Language. Allen and Unwin, London (1935)

Fromkin, V., Rodman, R., Hyams, N.: An Introduction to Language, 7th edn. Thomson Heinle, Boston (2003)

Lexalytics. https://www.lexalytics.com/lexablog/ai-in-education-present-future-ethics. Accessed 01 June 2020

Li, W.: The Bilingualism Reader. Routledge, London/New York (2000)

QCA (Qualifications and Curriculum Authority): Curriculum Guidance for the Foundation Stage. QCA, London (2000)

Research and Markets. https://www.researchandmarkets.com/reports/4613290/artificial-intelli gence-market-in-the-us. Accessed 01 June 2020

Titone, R.: Le Bilinguisme Precoce. Dessart, Brussels (1972)

UNESCO. https://en.unesco.org/themes/ict-education/action/ai-in-education. Accessed 02 June 2020

Webster, N.: Webster's Third New International Dictionary of the English Language. Bell & Sons, London (1961)

Application of Fuzzy Comprehensive Evaluation in Environmental Adaptability of Poultry House

Fenghang Zhang, Linze Li, Yuxuan Jiang, Zhunan Zhou, and Xiuli Wang[✉]

College of Information Science and Engineering, Shandong Agricultural University, Tai'an 271018, China
wxlmail@sdau.edu.cn

Abstract. Aiming at the problems of low accuracy and heavy workload in the evaluation of poultry house environment based on a single environmental factor, this paper selected five factors that have a great impact on the environment of the poultry house and established a multi-factor environmental evaluation model of poultry house based on the main body of temperature, humidity, ammonia (NH_3) concentration, carbon dioxide (CO_2) concentration, and hydrogen sulfide (H_2S) concentration. Through this system, the suitability of the poultry house environment can be judged more scientifically and accurately, and the evaluation process can be greatly simplified.

Keywords: Environmental Adaptability of Poultry House · Analytic hierarchy process · Judgment matrix · Consistency check · Fuzzy comprehensive evaluation method

1 Introduction

The domestic breeding industry is developing towards scale and standardization in recent years. The gap between China and the international advanced level in the fields of poultry disease control and poultry house feeding technology is gradually narrowing. However, there are still some gaps in the environmental control of poultry house compared with the world-class level [1–7]. The environment of poultry houses includes environmental factors such as temperature, humidity and feeding density [8], which play a crucial role in the growth and reproduction of poultry.

This paper combines the environmental factors of broiler growth and the actual situation of the poultry house, aiming at the problems of the existing method of environmental adaptation assessment by a single method. Using the fuzziness of the environment in the poultry house, a more scientific and accurate fuzzy evaluation model is established, the corresponding fuzzy judgment set, result set, etc. are

The paper is supported by the 2019 Science and Technology Development Plan (Guidance Plan) of Tai'an, China (Project No. 2019GX020).

determined, and the membership of the environment to the result set is obtained to determine the suitability of the environment.

2 Establishment of Poultry House Environmental Adaptability Evaluation System

2.1 Index Evaluation System

A variety of environmental factors in poultry houses interact with each other and restrict each other to form a complex, diverse, and non-linear system. At the same time, because the adaptability of broilers to the environment is not an exact value in the growth process, but a fuzzy concept in a certain range.

Combined with the work experience of relevant experts, five environmental factors which have a great influence on the health and growth of broilers were selected as the indicators of environmental adaptability evaluation based on the research of literature [9–11], including temperature, humidity, carbon dioxide (CO_2) concentration, ammonia (NH_3) concentration, and hydrogen sulfide (H_2S) concentration. According to the actual situation, the scope of environmental adaptability evaluation in poultry houses was given as shown in Table 1.

Table 1. Evaluation index system of poultry house environment

Evaluate	Temperature/ °C	Humidity/ %	CO_2 mass concentration/ (mg/m3)	NH_3 mass concentration/ (mg/m3)	H_2S mass concentration/ (mg/m3)
Suitable	21 ~ 23	60 ~ 65	0 ~ 1500	0 ~ 10	0 ~ 10
More suitable	16 ~ 21 or 23 ~ 26	50 ~ 60 or 65 ~ 70	0 ~ 1500	10 ~ 15	0 ~ 10
Unsuitable	>26 or <16	>70 or <50	>1500 or <0	>15	>10

2.2 Index Weight Parameter

To determine the influence relationship between the environmental factors of the poultry house more scientifically and accurately, the analytic hierarchy process (*AHP*) is used to determine the weight W of the environmental adaptability evaluation of the poultry house. The evaluation of environmental factors in the poultry house is carried out within a certain range. When all the impact factors are appropriate or inappropriate, but a certain impact factor is in the inappropriate range, a veto is adopted to evaluate it as inappropriate.

Hierarchical Analysis Model. In this paper, the environmental adaptability of the poultry house is taken as the standard layer O, the temperature, humidity, carbon dioxide (CO_2) concentration, ammonia (NH_3) concentration, and hydrogen sulfide (H_2S) concentration are taken as the standard layer C. The appropriate, relatively appropriate and inappropriate levels are taken as the measures layer to establish the hierarchical analysis model.

Construct Judgment Matrix. Based on establishing the AHP (*Aalytic Herarchy Pocess*) model, this paper constructs the judgment matrix based on the 1–9 scale method [15]. Temperature, humidity, carbon dioxide (CO_2) concentration, ammonia (NH_3) concentration and hydrogen sulfide (H_2S) concentration of the environmental factors to be compared are respectively expressed as T,H,C,N,S, i.e. Y = {T,H,C,N,S}. Any two elements y_i and y_j in Y are selected for comparison each time to construct the judgment matrix Q. The judgment matrix has the following properties: $\begin{cases} a_{ij} > 0 \\ a_{ij} = \frac{1}{a_{ji}} \\ a_{ii} = 1 \end{cases}$

According to the properties of the 1–9 scale method, we establish the judgment matrix A of the importance level of the poultry house, as shown in Table 2.

Table 2. Hierarchical matrix based on 1–9 scale method

A	T	H	N	C	S
T	1	4	5	5	4
H	1/4	1	2	3	2
N	1/5	1/2	1	2	2
C	1/5	1/3	1/2	1	1/2
S	1/4	1/2	1/2	2	1

Calculate the Weight of the Judgment Matrix. By normalizing each column element of the matrix and converting the contents of Table 2 into matrix A, we get the result of matrix *A* as shown in formula (1):

$$A = \begin{bmatrix} 1 & 4 & 5 & 5 & 4 \\ 1/4 & 1 & 2 & 3 & 2 \\ 1/5 & 1/3 & 1/2 & 1 & 1/2 \\ 1/5 & 1/2 & 1 & 2 & 2 \\ 1/4 & 1/2 & 1/2 & 2 & 1 \end{bmatrix} \tag{1}$$

Pass the matrix *A* through the formula: $\overline{b_{ij}} = b_{ij} / \sum_{k=1}^{n} b_{kj} (i,j = 1, 2, \cdots, n)$. And the normalization operation is performed to obtain the matrix *B*, as shown in formula (2).

$$B = \begin{bmatrix} 0.5263 & 0.6319 & 0.5556 & 0.3846 & 0.4211 \\ 0.1316 & 0.1580 & 0.2222 & 0.2308 & 0.2105 \\ 0.1053 & 0.0790 & 0.1111 & 0.1538 & 0.2105 \\ 0.1053 & 0.0526 & 0.0556 & 0.0769 & 0.0526 \\ 0.1316 & 0.0790 & 0.0556 & 0.1538 & 0.1053 \end{bmatrix} \tag{2}$$

Pass the matrix B through the formula: $\overline{w_i} = \sum\limits_{j=1}^{n} \overline{b_{ij}}(i = 1, 2, \cdots, n)$. And calculate the value of each row to the matrix, as shown in formula (3).

$$AW = [2.5191 \quad 0.9530 \quad 0.65970.3430 \quad 0.5251]^T \tag{3}$$

Normalize the matrix $\overline{w_i} = (\overline{w_1}, \overline{w_2}, \overline{w_3}, \cdots \overline{w_n})^T$, and normalize matrix $\overline{W}$ with formula $w_i = w_i / \sum\limits_{j=1}^{n} \overline{w_j}(i = 1, 2, \cdots, n)$ to get matrix W, as shown in formula (4).

$$W = [0.15 \quad 0.19 \quad 0.13 \quad 0.07 \quad 0.11]^T \tag{4}$$

After obtaining matrix AW and matrix W, $\lambda = 5.0000000000000002$ is obtained by formula: $\lambda = \frac{1}{n} \sum\limits_{i=1}^{n} \frac{(Aw)_i}{w_i}$

Then the maximum eigenvalue $\lambda = 5$ of matrix P' is calculated, and the corresponding eigenvector is WT = [0.15,0.19,0.13,0.07,0.11].

Therefore, the poultry house environment temperature, humidity, ammonia concentration, carbon dioxide concentration and hydrogen sulfide concentration correspond to the weight of 0.15, 0.19, 0.13, 0.07, 0.11 respectively.

Consistency Test. To judge the validity of the eigenvector W, a consistency test is carried out in this paper. Since the continuity of λ is related to aij, the larger the λ is than n, the more severe the inconsistency of A is. Therefore, the degree of inconsistency of A can be judged by the value of λ - n, and the inconsistent index can be defined, as shown in formula: $CI = \frac{\lambda - n}{n-1}$.

When CI = 0, there is complete consistency, CI is close to 0, there is satisfactory consistency, the larger the CI, the more serious the inconsistency. To measure the value of CI, we introduced random consistency index RI, as shown in Table 3.

Table 3. Average random consistency index

n	1	2	3	4	5	6	7	8	9	10	11
RI	0	0	0.58	0.90	1.12	1.24	1.32	1.41	1.45	1.49	1.51

Define the consistency ratio $CR = \frac{CI}{RI}$. Generally, when the consistency ratio $CR = \frac{CI}{RI} < 0.1$, it is considered that the inconsistency of A is within the allowable range and there is satisfactory consistency. After calculating $CI = \frac{0.0000000000000002}{4}$, $CR = \frac{CI}{1.12}$, it is clear that CR is much smaller than 0.1, that is, the hierarchical matrix passes the consistency test.

3 Fuzzy Comprehensive Evaluation of Poultry House Environment

3.1 Establish a Set of Evaluation Factors and Set up a Collection of Comments

The evaluation factor set is a set established by taking the factors in the criterion layer as elements, usually represented by $U = (u_1, u_2, ..., u_m)$, where the element u_i represents the ith factor in the criterion layer. Comment set is a set of possible results of the measure layer versus the criterion layer, usually expressed as $V = (v_1, v_2, ..., v_m)$, where the element v_i represents the ith evaluation result.

3.2 Membership Function

The membership function can be used to make a comprehensive evaluation of things that are affected by many factors. Its feature is that the evaluation results are expressed as a fuzzy set [12–14]. Although the membership function has certain subjectivity, it also should follow the corresponding rules.

Suppose an arbitrary mapping of the domain X to the closed interval [0,1].

$$\mu_A : X \rightarrow [0, 1]$$
$$x \rightarrow \mu_A(x)$$

They determine a fuzzy set A on X, μ_A is called the membership function of A, and $\mu_A(x)$ is called the membership degree of X to fuzzy set A, denoted as: $A = \{(x, \mu_A(x)) | x \in X\}$.

The fuzzy set A is completely characterized by the membership function μ_A. When $\mu_A(x) = \{0,1\}$, A degenerates into a normal set. The higher the degree to which μ belongs to A, the closer the membership degree $\mu_A(\mu)$ approaches 1 and vice versa, the closer it approaches 0.

Therefore, we need to establish the membership function of each element in the evaluation factor set $U = (u_1, u_2, u_3, u_4, u_5)$ to each element in the comment set $V = (v_1, v_2, v_3)$.

According to the formula in Table 3, the membership function corresponding to temperature and humidity can be expressed by the formula (5)–(7).

$$u(u_d) = \begin{cases} 0, u_d > b \\ \frac{b - u_d}{b - a}, a \leq u_d < b \\ 1, u_d < a \end{cases} \tag{5}$$

$$u(u_a) = \begin{cases} 0, u_a < a, u_a > d \\ \left(\frac{u_a - a}{b - a}\right)^k, a \leq u_a < b \\ 1, b \leq u_a \leq c \\ \left(\frac{d - u_a}{d - c}\right)^k, c < u_a \leq d \end{cases} \tag{6}$$

$$\mu(\mu_u) = \begin{cases} 0, u_u < c \\ \left(\frac{u_a-c}{d-c}\right)^k, c \leq u_u < d \\ 1, d < u_u \end{cases} \tag{7}$$

The membership function corresponding to carbon dioxide concentration, ammonia concentration, and hydrogen sulfide concentration can be expressed by formula (8)–(10).

$$u(u_d) = \begin{cases} 0, a > u_d, u_d > d \\ \frac{u_d-a}{b-a}, a \leq u_d < b \\ \frac{d-u_d}{d-c}, c < u_d \leq d \\ 1, b \leq u_d \leq c \end{cases} \tag{8}$$

$$u(u_a) = \begin{cases} 0 \quad, u_a > d \\ \left(\frac{u_a}{a}\right)^k, 0 \leq u_a < a \\ \left(\frac{u_a-b}{c-b}\right)^k, b < u_a \leq c \\ 1, a \leq u_a \leq b, c \leq u_a \leq d \end{cases} \tag{9}$$

$$u(u_u) = \begin{cases} 0, u_u < c \\ \left(\frac{u_u-c}{d-c}\right)^k, c \leq u_u < d \\ a, u^u > d \end{cases} \tag{10}$$

There are three elements in assessment set V, which are relatively appropriate, appropriate and inappropriate. Therefore, each factor in the evaluation factor set has three membership functions $u(u_d), u(u_a), u(u_u)$, which correspond to the comment set V, i.e. the elements of measure layer. a,b,c,d in the formula respectively represent the dividing points of the elements of the commentary set.

3.3   Establishment of Fuzzy Relation Evaluation Model

According to formula (5)–(10), the fuzzy relation matrix R can be obtained, as shown in formula (11).

$$R = (r_{ij}) = \begin{bmatrix} u_R(u_1,v_1) & u_R(u_1,v_2) & u_R(u_1,v_3) \\ u_R(u_2,v_1) & u_R(u_2,v_2) & u_R(u_2,v_3) \\ u_R(u_3,v_1) & u_R(u_3,v_2) & u_R(u_3,v_3) \\ u_R(u_4,v_1) & u_R(u_4,v_2) & u_R(u_4,v_3) \\ u_R(u_5,v_1) & u_R(u_5,v_2) & u_R(u_5,v_3) \end{bmatrix} \tag{11}$$

In the formula, $u_R(u_i,v_j)$ is the membership degree of u_i with respect to v_j.

According to the eigenvector W^T of matrix P' and membership matrix R, the poultry house environment evaluation matrix is established, as shown in formula (12).

$$B = W^T * R = (b_1, b_2, b_3) \tag{12}$$

Then, the maximum vector b_j of matrix B is obtained, that is, when $j = 1$, the evaluation result is appropriate. When $j = 2$, the evaluation result is more appropriate; When $j = 3$, the evaluation result is inappropriate.

4 Verification of Evaluation Results

Some data from selected test sites are shown in Table 4.

Table 4. Some experimental data

Time	Temperature °C	Humidity %	CO_2 mg/m3	NH_3 mg/m3	H_2S mg/m3
8:00	25.2	64.2	510.3	2.3	2.5
9:00	25.5	64.5	516.2	2.3	2.5
10:00	25.6	64.8	523.1	2.5	2.6
11:00	26.1	65	526.5	2.8	2.7
12:00	26.5	64.9	535.7	2.9	3.0
13:00	26.4	64.9	532.5	3.4	3.1
14:00	26.4	64.8	549.2	3.4	3.2
15:00	26.5	63	562.5	3.6	3.2
16:00	26.5	62.5	586.2	3.7	3.2
17:00	26.6	63	598.2	4	3.3

According to the actual situation of the poultry house, this paper makes further analysis. The humidity, carbon dioxide concentration, ammonia concentration, and hydrogen sulfide concentration in the data selected in this paper are all within the appropriate range of environmental evaluation indexes of the poultry house, and the temperature is within the appropriate range, which is very close to the appropriate range at the same time. Therefore, the appropriate and relatively appropriate respective membership values in the obtained results are 0.4876 and 0.4896, with very little difference. To avoid errors caused by inaccurate measurement of environmental data in poultry houses at a certain time point, this paper also selects a large number of data at different time points for testing to establish subordinate changes of environmental adaptability in poultry houses within one day, as shown in Fig. 1

In Fig. 1, the red curve indicates the membership degree relatively appropriate for the environment, and the yellow curve indicates the membership degree appropriate for the environment. Since the membership degree inappropriate for the environment is always 0, it is not shown in Fig. 1. From the line chart, it can be seen that the environment in the poultry house is at a relatively appropriate level from 8:00 to 17:00, and the environmental factors in the poultry house reach a suitable state at 16:00. With the substantial increase in carbon dioxide concentration, the environment once again reaches a more suitable state. This phenomenon also shows that the environmental

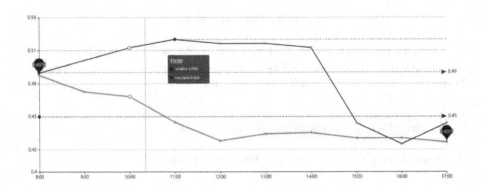

Fig. 1. Changes of environmental adaptability in poultry house in one day (Color figure online)

factors in poultry houses influence and restrict each other. This also proves that many factors need to be considered when analyzing the environmental adaptability of poultry houses.

5   Conclusion

The judgment matrix of five important factors affecting poultry houses is established by the 1–9 scale method 1–9, and the weights of the five factors are obtained by the analytic hierarchy process (*AHP*). The membership functions of temperature, humidity, ammonia concentration, carbon dioxide concentration, and hydrogen sulfide concentration on the result set are established by using the corresponding theories of fuzzy mathematics, and the evaluation matrix is finally obtained to get the adaptability evaluation of the current environment. Compared with the traditional method of evaluating the environmental adaptability through a single environmental variable, the method has higher accuracy and stronger stability greatly facilitating broiler breeders to control the environment and providing a theoretical basis for evaluating the environmental adaptability of poultry houses.

References

1. Lu, Z., He, X., Zhang, L., et al.: Effects of ambient temperature and humidity on nutrient metabolism of broilers and its regulation mechanisms. Chinese J. Animal Nutr. **29**(9), 3021–3026 (2017)
2. Chang, S., Liu, J., Ye, J., et al.: Study on prevention and control of animal infectious diseases in China from perspective of new development vision. Bull. Chin. Acad. Sci. **34**(2), 145–151 (2019)
3. Wang, K., Wu, J., Zhao, X.: Review of measurement technologies for air pollutants at livestock and poultry farms. Sci. Agric. Sinica **52**(8), 1458–1474 (2019)
4. Sun, Y., Wang, Y., Sa, R., et al.: Research progress on the effect of air quality in poultry houses on broiler health. Chin. J. Animal Nutr. **30**(4), 1230–1237 (2018)

5. Zou, H., Xing, J.: Research on prevention and control of pollution of livestock and poultry farming in Xingshan Town. Env. Sci. Manage. **44**(8), 73–77 (2019)
6. Pu, S., Li, T., Wang, H., et al.: Monitoring technology of air pollution generated by animal feeding operations: A review. J. Agro-Env. Sci. **38**(11), 2439–2448 (2019)
7. Zhu, C., Zhang, S., Tao, Z., et al.: The Production and Harzard of Ammonia in Poultry House and Its Effective Measures of Emission Reduction. Acta Ecologae Animalis Domastici **40**(6), 72–77 (2019)
8. Yuan, J., Zhang, K., Hu, X.: Study on the effect of environment factors on the growth of broiler chickens. Acta Ecologae Animalis Domastici **28**(6), 1182–1673 (2007)
9. Diao, H., Feng, J., Diao, X.: Effects of high ambient temperature on performance of laying hens and the mitigation results of nutritional measures. Chin. J. Animal Nutr. **29**(6), 1850–1855 (2017)
10. Zhang, H., Li, S., Zhan, X., et al.: The latest development of broiler production and environmental control. China Poult. **39**(13), 1–5 (2017)
11. Guo, T., Wang, J., Li, K., et al.: Effects of environmental temperature on growth performance, digestive function and indexes related with heat stress of yellow broilers in finishing period. Chin. J. Animal Sci. **54**(8), 107–111 (2018)
12. Tang, J., Li, X.: On the stability evaluation of the deep subway foundation pit based on the fuzzy mathematical theory. J. Saf. Env. **18**(6), 2135–2140 (2018)
13. Wei, K., Geng, J., Xu, S.: FMEA method based on fuzzy theory and D-S evidence theory. Syst. Eng. Electron. **41**(11), 2662–2668 (2019)
14. Wang, Z., Liang, X., Liu, X., et al.: comprehensive evaluation of groundwater quality based on fuzzy mathematical model and matter element extension model. Water Power **44**(9), 1–3 (2018)
15. Ge, S.: Determination of functional evaluation coefficient by 1–9 scale method. Value Eng. **01**, 33–34 (1989)

Performance Evaluation of Multirotor UAV by Considering the Balanced Pattern

Min Lv[1], Cong Lin[1(✉)], Tianran Ma[2], and Sheng Hong[3]

[1] China Academy of Information and Communications Technology,
Beijing 100191, China
Linc@cape.avic.com
[2] AVIC China Aero-Polytechnology Establishment, Beijing 100028, China
[3] Beihang University, Beijing 100191, China

Abstract. The multirotor UAV is a typical k-out-of-n pair: G model, which means that the two rotors distributed on the same axis must be synchronized operating. That is to say, if a rotor is failed, then the opposite one soluble shut down to keep the UAV in a balanced state. However, the above-mentioned model does not consider the effect of torque generated by rotating rotors. Thus, the neutralization of torque, which is ignored by k-out-of-n pair: G model, must be considered. In this situation, we employ the k-out-of-n pair: G balanced model to describe the balanced pattern of the multirotor UAV. We use the finite Markov chain imbedding approach to establish the system reliability calculating equations for the UAV and we also derive the performance evaluation indexes, the mean residual capacity and the expected time to failure, which can be used to determine the usage of the UAV. Then, we use some numerical examples to demonstrate it is worthy of involving the balance pattern in the system modeling process, otherwise, the we may obtain an over optimistic reliability evaluation result that misguides the operation of the UAV.

Keywords: System reliability · k-out-of-n pair: G balanced model · Performance evaluation · Finite Markov chain imbedding approach

1 Introduction

The two rotors distributed on the same axis of a multirotor UAV, e.g. Quadcopter, Hexacopter and Octocopter, must be synchronized operating, in order to keep the drone maintaining a balance pattern. It is roughly alike the cascading failure mode, which means the failure of a component may cause others failed, for more knowledge one can refer to [1–5].

In the UAV example, the failure of a rotor compels the shutdown of the opposite one. Therefore, the k-out-of-n pair: G model, which means there should be at least k pairs of rotors working so that the drone own the enough capacity for flying, may apply to describe the failure criterion for the multirotor UAV, see Fig. 1.

© Springer Nature Switzerland AG 2020
X. Chen et al. (Eds.): ML4CS 2020, LNCS 12487, pp. 452–462, 2020.
https://doi.org/10.1007/978-3-030-62460-6_41

However, the k-out-of-n pair: G model only considers the requirement from elevating force point of view, it ignores the influence of torque generated by the rotating rotors. Hence, Hua and Elsayed [6, 7], proposed the k-out-of-n pair: G balanced model, which not only requires the number of remaining rotors meets the minimal level of k pairs, but the remaining rotors must be distributed symmetrically so that the torque can be neutralized. In real world, if we know the performance degradation paths of the rotors, then we can obtain the reliability prediction of UAV, which further leads the determination on the usage of the drone.

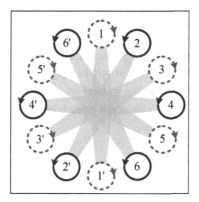

Fig. 1. The multirotor UAV with pair-wise distributer rotors.

In this paper, we employ the finite Markov chain imbedding approach (FMCIA) to derive the system reliability equation of the UAV. Then, we give out some performance indexes, e.g. the mean residual capacity and the expected time to failure or the drone. Next, we introduce some numerical examples to illustrate how the proposed methods are used to evaluate the performance of the UAV. Last, some conclusions are addressed.

2 System Reliability Modelling

The model we used to establish the system reliability of the UAV is k-out-of-n pair: G balanced model. But, for the convenience of readers, we first introduce how to use the FMCIA to obtain the system reliability of the k-out-of-n pair: G model, then we illustrate how to apply the method to the k-out-of-n pair: G balanced mode.

2.1   *k*-out-of-*n* Pair: G Model

To clarify the process of system reliability modeling with FMCIA, some assumptions are declared.

(a) The system is composed with n pairs of components and it is regarded as reliable only if the number of remaining pair of component, ω, is no less than k.

(b) The working probability of an arbitrary component at a certain time epoch is denoted as $p_i(t)$, where $i \in \{1, 2, \ldots, n, 1', 2', \ldots, n'\}$.

In terms of FMCIA, we define a Markov chain $\{Y(\theta), \theta = 1, 2, \ldots, n\}$ to describe the number of the working pairs of components when the θth pair is added into the system. Thus, the state space of the Markov chain should be $S(\theta) = \{0, 1, \ldots, k, k+1, \ldots n\}$, where state $s \in \{0, 1, \ldots, k-1\}$ represents the system is unreliable, otherwise it stands for reliable state.

Thus, the state transition probability matrix of Markov chain $\{Y(\theta), \theta = 1, 2, \ldots, n\}$ can be written as Eq. (1), where $p_\theta(t)p_{\theta'}(t)$ means the components on the θth axis are both working so that the number of working pairs is added by one, and $1 - p_\theta(t)p_{\theta'}(t)$ represents the θth pair is not contribute to the system so that the number of working pairs remains the same.

$$
\Lambda_\theta(t) =
\begin{bmatrix}
1 - p_\theta(t)p_{\theta'}(t) & p_\theta(t)p_{\theta'}(t) & & & \mathbf{0} \\
 & \ddots & & \ddots & \\
 & & & 1 - p_\theta(t)p_{\theta'}(t) & p_\theta(t)p_{\theta'}(t) \\
\mathbf{0} & & & & 1
\end{bmatrix}_{(n+1)\times(n+1)}
\tag{1}
$$

Based to assumption (a), the system reliability for the *k*-out-of-*n* pair: G model is defined as $R_{sys}(t) = P\{\omega \geq k\} = \sum_{s=k}^{n} P\{S(\theta) = s\}$. According to Fu and Koutras [8, 9], Cui *et al.* [10], Lin *et al.* [11, 12], the system reliability can be calculated by Eq. (2), where $\pi_0 = (1, 0, 0, \ldots, 0)_{1\times(n+1)}$ is the initial state, $\mathbf{U} = (0, 0, \ldots, 0, \underset{(k+1)^{th}}{1}, 1, \ldots 1)_{1\times(n+1)}$ is used to add up probability value of all working sates and T is an matrix transpose operator.

$$
R_{sys}(t) = \pi_0 \prod_{\theta=1}^{n} \Lambda_\theta(t) \mathbf{U}^T
\tag{2}
$$

2.2 *k*-out-of-*n* Pair: G Balanced Model

The challenge of the new model is how to define a system is in a balanced pattern. Hua and Elsayed [13] employ the concept of moment difference to determine whether or not the system is balanced given some pairs of components are failed. The trick of moment difference is to obtain tow imagine axis, $\{X(\mathrm{I}), X(\mathrm{II})\}$, perpendicular to each other so the remaining working components can uniformly distribute around them.

Let M_x represent the summation of the moment on axis x and E_x is the set of the components which locate within the range of $[-\frac{\pi}{2}, \frac{\pi}{2}]$ around axis x. Let γ_i stands for the state of component in E_x, i.e. $\gamma_i = 0$ if component i is failed, otherwise $\gamma_i = 1$. Let $\alpha_{i,x}$ represents the angle from the axis where component i locates to the axis x anticlockwise.

Thus, the summation of the moment on axis x can be calculated by Eq. (3). If and only if we can obtain the tow imagine axis, $\{X(\mathrm{I}), X(\mathrm{II})\}$ that satisfy the condition $M_{X(\mathrm{I})} = M_{X(\mathrm{II})} = 0$, the system is regarded as in a balanced pattern.

$$M_x = \sum_{i \in E_x} \gamma_i \cos \alpha_{i,x} \tag{3}$$

For the convenience of reader, we assume $n = 6$, see Fig. 1, to clarify how to obtain the system reliability for the k-out-of-n pair: G balanced model. It is obvious that if the components are all working, the system is definitely reliable; whereas, is all of them are failed, the system is in a failure state.

Table 1 lists all balanced pattern of the system given there are $o \in \{1, 2, \ldots 5\}$ pairs of components working. For example, when the system remains $o = 5$ pairs of working components, there is only one pattern that can make system in to balanced; when the system remains $o = 4$ pairs of working components, there are three patterns that can make system in to balanced.

Similarly, there are two patterns for $o = 3$, three patterns for $o = 2$ and one patterns for $o = 1$, respectively. The vector $\boldsymbol{\delta}_1^{(o)}$ represents the state of the pair-wised components on each axis.

Note: due to lacking of space in Table 1, we do not give the sequence number of each component in the schematic diagram. It is in accordance with that in Fig. 1.

Table 1. The balanced pattern, given o pairs of working components

o	Schematic for balanced pattern	$x(\mathrm{I})$	$x(\mathrm{II})$	$\delta_i^{(o)}$
5		$E_{x(\mathrm{I})}=\{4,3,2,1,6',5',4'\}$ $\gamma=(1,1,1,0,1,1,1)$ $\alpha=(\frac{3\pi}{12},\frac{2\pi}{12},\frac{\pi}{12},0,\frac{5\pi}{12},\frac{4\pi}{12},\frac{3\pi}{12})$	$E_{x(\mathrm{II})}=\{1,6',5',4',3',2',1'\}$ $\gamma=(0,1,1,1,1,1,0)$	$\delta_1^{(5)}=(\overset{1}{0},\overset{2}{1},\overset{3}{1},\overset{4}{1},\overset{5}{1},\overset{6}{1})$
4		$E_{x(\mathrm{I})}=\{4,3,2,1,6',5'\}$ $\gamma=(1,1,0,0,1,1)$ $\alpha=(\frac{5\pi}{24},\frac{3\pi}{24},\frac{\pi}{24},\frac{11\pi}{24},\frac{9\pi}{24},\frac{7\pi}{24})$	$E_{x(\mathrm{II})}=\{1,6',5',4',3',2'\}$ $\gamma=(0,1,1,1,1,0)$	$\delta_1^{(4)}=(\overset{1}{0},\overset{2}{0},\overset{3}{1},\overset{4}{1},\overset{5}{1},\overset{6}{1})$
4		$E_{x(\mathrm{I})}=\{5,4,3,2,1,6',5'\}$ $\gamma=(1,1,0,1,0,1,1)$ $\alpha=(\frac{3\pi}{12},\frac{2\pi}{12},\frac{\pi}{12},0,\frac{5\pi}{12},\frac{4\pi}{12},\frac{3\pi}{12})$	$E_{x(\mathrm{II})}=\{2,1,6',5',4',3',2'\}$ $\gamma=(0,1,0,0,0,1,0)$	$\delta_2^{(4)}=(\overset{1}{0},\overset{2}{1},\overset{3}{0},\overset{4}{1},\overset{5}{1},\overset{6}{1})$
4		$E_{x(\mathrm{I})}=\{4,3,2,1,6',5',4'\}$ $\gamma=(0,1,1,0,1,1,0)$ $\alpha=(\frac{3\pi}{12},\frac{2\pi}{12},\frac{\pi}{12},0,\frac{5\pi}{12},\frac{4\pi}{12},\frac{3\pi}{12})$	$E_{x(\mathrm{II})}=\{1,6',5',4',3',2',1'\}$ $\gamma=(0,1,1,0,1,1,0)$	$\delta_3^{(4)}=(\overset{1}{0},\overset{2}{1},\overset{3}{1},\overset{4}{0},\overset{5}{1},\overset{6}{1})$
3		$E_{x(\mathrm{I})}=\{4,3,2,1,6',5',4'\}$ $\gamma=(1,1,0,0,0,1,1)$ $\alpha=(\frac{3\pi}{12},\frac{2\pi}{12},\frac{\pi}{12},0,\frac{5\pi}{12},\frac{4\pi}{12},\frac{3\pi}{12})$	$E_{x(\mathrm{II})}=\{1,6',5',4',3',2',1'\}$ $\gamma=(0,0,1,1,1,0,0)$	$\delta_1^{(3)}=(\overset{1}{0},\overset{2}{0},\overset{3}{1},\overset{4}{1},\overset{5}{1},\overset{6}{0})$
3		$E_{x(\mathrm{I})}=\{4,3,2,1,6',5',4'\}$ $\gamma=(1,0,1,0,1,0,1)$ $\alpha=(\frac{3\pi}{12},\frac{2\pi}{12},\frac{\pi}{12},0,\frac{5\pi}{12},\frac{4\pi}{12},\frac{3\pi}{12})$	$E_{x(\mathrm{II})}=\{1,6',5',4',3',2',1'\}$ $\gamma=(1,0,1,0,1,0,1)$	$\delta_2^{(3)}=(\overset{1}{0},\overset{2}{1},\overset{3}{0},\overset{4}{1},\overset{5}{0},\overset{6}{1})$
2		$E_{x(\mathrm{I})}=\{4,3,2,1,6',5'\}$ $\gamma=(1,0,0,0,0,1)$ $\alpha=(\frac{5\pi}{24},\frac{3\pi}{24},\frac{\pi}{24},\frac{11\pi}{24},\frac{9\pi}{24},\frac{7\pi}{24})$	$E_{x(\mathrm{II})}=\{1,6',5',4',3',2'\}$ $\gamma=(0,0,1,1,0,0)$	$\delta_1^{(2)}=(\overset{1}{0},\overset{2}{0},\overset{3}{0},\overset{4}{1},\overset{5}{1},\overset{6}{0})$
2		$E_{x(\mathrm{I})}=\{4,3,2,1,6',5',4'\}$ $\gamma=(0,1,0,0,0,1,0)$ $\alpha=(\frac{3\pi}{12},\frac{2\pi}{12},\frac{\pi}{12},0,\frac{5\pi}{12},\frac{4\pi}{12},\frac{3\pi}{12})$	$E_{x(\mathrm{II})}=\{1,6',5',4',3',2',1'\}$ $\gamma=(0,0,1,0,1,0,0)$	$\delta_2^{(2)}=(\overset{1}{0},\overset{2}{0},\overset{3}{1},\overset{4}{0},\overset{5}{1},\overset{6}{0})$
2		$E_{x(\mathrm{I})}=\{5,4,3,2,1,6',5'\}$ $\gamma=(1,0,0,1,0,0,1)$ $\alpha=(\frac{3\pi}{12},\frac{2\pi}{12},\frac{\pi}{12},0,\frac{5\pi}{12},\frac{4\pi}{12},\frac{3\pi}{12})$	$E_{x(\mathrm{II})}=\{2,1,6',5',4',3',2'\}$ $\gamma=(1,0,0,1,0,0,1)$	$\delta_3^{(2)}=(\overset{1}{0},\overset{2}{1},\overset{3}{0},\overset{4}{0},\overset{5}{1},\overset{6}{0})$
1		$E_{x(\mathrm{I})}=\{5,4,3,2,1,6',5'\}$ $\gamma=(0,0,0,1,0,0,0)$ $\alpha=(\frac{3\pi}{12},\frac{2\pi}{12},\frac{\pi}{12},0,\frac{5\pi}{12},\frac{4\pi}{12},\frac{3\pi}{12})$	$E_{x(\mathrm{II})}=\{2,1,6',5',4',3',2'\}$ $\gamma=(1,0,0,0,0,0,1)$	$\delta_1^{(1)}=(\overset{1}{0},\overset{2}{1},\overset{3}{0},\overset{4}{0},\overset{5}{0},\overset{6}{0})$

Then, we should determine the possible ways that system may transit from a balanced pattern to another. So, we define $N_{i_1,i_2}^{(o)\to(o-1)}$ represent the ways a system can transfer from "the balanced pattern i_1, given o pair of working components" to "the balanced pattern i_2, given $(o-1)$ pair of working components". Figure 2 shows the number of possible ways that the system can transfer from a balanced pattern to another.

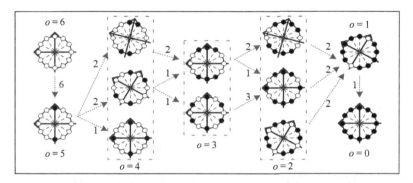

Fig. 2. The possible ways the system can transfer from a balanced pattern to another.

We define $\mathbf{Q}_{m_o \times m_{o-1}}^{(o)\to(o-1)} = \left[N_{i_1,i_2}^{(o)\to(o-1)} \right]$, where m_o stands for the number of balanced pattern give o pairs of components working. The meaning of m_{o-1} is similar, so we omit it. For example, we have

$$\mathbf{Q}^{(6)\to(5)} = 6, \ \mathbf{Q}^{(5)\to(4)} = \begin{bmatrix} 2 & 2 & 1 \end{bmatrix}, \ \mathbf{Q}^{(4)\to(3)} = \begin{bmatrix} 2 & 0 \\ 1 & 1 \\ 0 & 0 \end{bmatrix},$$

$$\mathbf{Q}^{(3)\to(2)} = \begin{bmatrix} 2 & 1 & 0 \\ 0 & 3 & 0 \end{bmatrix}, \ \mathbf{Q}^{(2)\to(1)} = \begin{bmatrix} 2 \\ 2 \\ 2 \end{bmatrix}, \ \mathbf{Q}^{(1)\to(0)} = 1.$$

Let η_o represents the number of possible ways that the system transfers from "all working components" to "a balanced pattern, given o pair of working components". It can be calculated by Eq. (4), where Σ means the summation for all elements in the matrix.

$$\eta_o = \begin{cases} \sum \prod_{o=n-1}^{o} \mathbf{Q}_{m_{o+1} \times m_o}^{(o+1)\to(o)}, & o = 0, 2, \ldots, n-1, \\ 1, & o = n. \end{cases} \tag{4}$$

Thus, we can obtain

$$\eta_6 = 1, \eta_5 = 6, \eta_4 = 30, \eta_3 = 48, \eta_2 = 144, \eta_1 = 288, \eta_0 = 288.$$

Finally, the system reliability of the k-out-of-n pair: G balanced model can be calculated by Eq. (5), where $\mathbf{V} = \left(\underbrace{0, 0, \ldots, 0}_{k}, \frac{\eta_k}{A_n^{n-k}}, \frac{\eta_{k+1}}{A_n^{n-k-1}}, \ldots, \frac{\eta_n}{A_n^0} \right)_{1 \times (n+1)}$. $\frac{\eta_o}{A_n^{n-o}}$ is the proportion that the system is in a balanced pattern, given o pairs of working components and $A_n^{n-o} = \frac{n!}{o!}$.

$$R_{sys}(t) = \pi_0 \prod_{\theta=1}^{n} \Lambda_\theta(t) \mathbf{V}^T \tag{5}$$

3   Performance Evaluation of Multirotor UAV

For the multirotor UAV, the performance should be evaluated from two aspects, i.e. if the remaining rotors can provide enough elevating lift so that the drone can carry its load and how long the drone can be used since some of the rotors may fail during flying, should be considered. Therefore, we use two indexes, the mean residual capacity and the expected time to failure, to answer those questions.

3.1   Mean Residual Capacity

In Eq. (5), we can obtain the system reliability by adding up all probability values that the UAV can be regarded as reliable. When evaluating the capacity, we define each pair of rotors contribute to the UAV with $\psi(t)=1$ capacity. Thus the mean residual capacity, $E[\psi(t)]$, can be calculated by Eq. (6), where the vector of $\mathbf{\Psi} = (0, 1, \ldots n)$ represents the capacity of the UAV at each state.

$$E[\psi(t)] = \pi_0 \prod_{\theta=1}^{n} \Lambda_\theta(t) \mathbf{\Psi}^T \tag{6}$$

3.2   Expected Time to Failure

Once a UAV is starting to operate a mission, there is no possibility that we can withdraw and repair it when failure happen. Thus, it is necessary to evaluate if the UAV, with current state of its components, can be used for a certain length of time. Thus, we apply the term of expected time to failure, $E[T_f] = \int_{t=0}^{\infty} R_{sys}(t)dt$, to measure the duration that the UAV can be operated without failure. Since the FMCIA only obtains the numerical result of the system reliability, we can use Eq. (7) to approximately calculate the expected time to failure, where $t_i = i\Delta t$.

$$E[T_f] \approx \lim_{u \to \infty} \sum_{i=0}^{u} R(t_i)\Delta t \qquad (7)$$

4 Numerical Examples

In this section, we use "2-out-of-n pair: G model" and "2-out-of-n pair: G balanced model" to show the difference of the performance evaluation results. We assume all rotors of the UAV are identical and their lifetime are all subjected to the same Weibull distribution with scale parameter $\lambda = 40$ and shape parameter $\beta = 2$, i.e. the working probability of a rotor is $p_i(t) = \int_t^\infty \frac{1}{20}\left(\frac{u}{40}\right)e^{-\left(\frac{u}{40}\right)^2} du$.

4.1 System Reliability Evaluation with 2-out-of-n Pair: G Model

Based on Eq. (2), the system reliability evaluation result is shown as Fig. 3. We can see the system reliability enhances as the number of n grows. However, we do not consider the balanced pattern, thus the result may not reflect the real reliability level of the UAV.

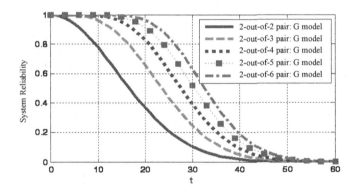

Fig. 3. The system reliability evaluation result with 2-out-of-n pair: G model.

4.2 System Reliability Evaluation with 2-out-of-n Pair: G Balanced Model

Based on Eq. (5), the system reliability evaluation result is shown as Fig. 4. We can see when the number of rotor reaches $n = 6$ pair, the system reliability will be dominated by the case when $n = 5$. It is because as the number of component failure, there are more unbalanced patterns that may occur. The result can be explained as "it is more optimal to design drone with five pairs of rotors than six pairs".

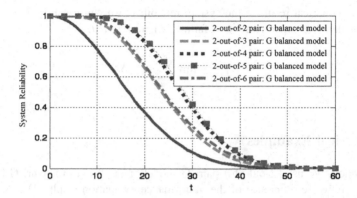

Fig. 4. The system reliability evaluation result with 2-out-of-n pair: G balanced model.

4.3 Comparison of the Mean Residual Capacity for the Two Models

Based on Eq. (6), the mean residual capacity evaluation result is shown as Fig. 5. We can see as the operating time goes by and the failure of rotors accumulates, the UAV with 5 pairs of rotors is more robust than that with 6pair. Besides, when considering the influence of balanced pattern, the performance evaluation result tends to be more conservative than using the k-out-of-n pair: G model.

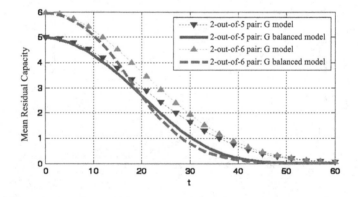

Fig. 5. The comparison of the mean residual capacity for the two models.

4.4 Comparison of the Expected Time to Failure for the Two Models

Based on Eq. (7), the expected time to failure evaluation result is shown as Fig. 6. We can see, when considering the balanced pattern, the average operating time of the UAV is discounted as the number of pairs reaches at $n = 5$ or $n = 6$. It is a more realistic performance evaluation so that we can use to determine whether or not to arrange the UAV conduct he mission with certain duration required.

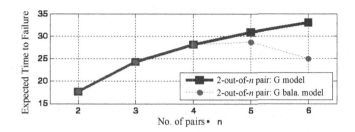

Fig. 6. The comparison of the expected time to failure for the two models.

5 Conclusions

In this paper, we use finite Markov chain imbedding approach to establish the system reliability calculating equations for the multirotor UAV according to the k-out-of-n pair: G balanced model. We also derive the performance evaluation indexes, the mean residual capacity and the expected time to failure. Then we use some numerical examples to explain the influence of balanced pattern, which is not considered in the k-out-of-n pair: G model. The findings we obtained in this paper, can be used to the design of an UAV to determine the control policy in case of rotors' failure and it can also be used in the operating phase if an UAV can be assign to a task for a certain duration according to its rotors degrading states.

Acknowledgements. This research is supported by National Natural Science Foundation of China with granted No. 71801198 and 61773001. The authors are appreciated to the National Key Research Program with granted No. 2019YFB1706001 and to the Industrial Internet Innovation Development Project with granted No. TC190H468.

References

1. Hong, S., Lv, C., Zhao, T., et al.: Cascading failure analysis and restoration strategy in an interdependent network. J. Phys. A Math. Theor. **19**(49), 195101 (2016)
2. Hong, S., Wang, B., Ma, X., et al.: Failure cascade in interdependent network with traffic loads. J. Phys. A Math. Theor. **48**(48), 485101 (2015)
3. Hong, S., Zhu, J., Braunstein, L., et al.: Cascading failure and recovery of spatially interdependent networks. J. Stat. Mech. Theor. Exp. **10**, 103208 (2017)
4. Hong, S., Yang, H., Zhao, T., et al.: Epidemic spreading model of complex dynamical network with the heterogeneity of nodes. Int. J. Syst. Sci. **11**(47), 2745–2752 (2016)
5. Hong, S., Zhang, X., Zhu, J., et al.: Suppressing failure cascades in interconnected networks: Considering capacity allocation pattern and load redistribution. Mod. Phys. Lett. B **5**(30), 1650049 (2016)
6. Hua, D., Elsayed, E.: Degradation analysis of k-out-of-n Pairs: G balanced system with spatially distributed units. IEEE Trans. Reliab. **65**(2), 941–956 (2016)
7. Hua, D., Elsayed, E.: Reliability approximation of k-out-of-n pairs: G balanced systems with spatially distributed units. IISE Trans. **50**(7), 616–626 (2018)

8. Fu, J., Koutras, M.: Poisson approximations for 2-dimensional patterns. Ann. Inst. Stat. **46** (1), 179–192 (1994)
9. Fu, J., Koutras, M.: Distribution theory of runs: a Markov chain approach. J. Am. Stat. Assoc. **89**, 1050–1058 (1994)
10. Cui, L., Xu, Y., Zhao, X.: Developments and applications of the finite Markov chain imbedding approach in reliability. IEEE Trans. Reliab. **59**(4), 685–690 (2010)
11. Lin, C., Cui, L., Coit, D., Lv, M.: Reliability modeling on consecutive-kr-out-of-nr: F linear zigzag structure and circular polygon structure. IEEE Trans. Reliab. **65**(3), 1509–1521 (2016)
12. Lin, C., Cui, L., Coit, D., Lv, M.: Performance analysis for a wireless sensor network of star topology with random nodes deployment. Wireless Pers. Commun. **97**(3), 3993–4013 (2017)
13. Hua, D., Elsayed, E.: Reliability estimation of k-out-of-n Pairs: G balanced systems with spatially distributed units. IEEE Trans. Reliab. **65**(2), 886–900 (2016)

AdvJND: Generating Adversarial Examples with Just Noticeable Difference

Zifei Zhang[(⊠)], Kai Qiao, Lingyun Jiang, Linyuan Wang, Jian Chen,
and Bin Yan

Academy of Information Systems Engineering, PLA Strategy Support Force
Information Engineering University, Zhengzhou 450001, China
zhangzf2014@qq.com, qiaokai1992@gmail.com,
yunlord@outlook.com

Abstract. Compared with traditional machine learning models, deep neural networks perform better, especially in image classification tasks. However, they are vulnerable to adversarial examples. Adding small perturbations on examples causes a good-performance model to misclassify the crafted examples, without category differences in the human eyes, and fools deep models successfully. There are two requirements for generating adversarial examples: the attack success rate and image fidelity metrics. Generally, the magnitudes of perturbation are increased to ensure the adversarial examples' high attack success rate; however, the adversarial examples obtained have poor concealment. To alleviate the tradeoff between the attack success rate and image fidelity, we propose a method named AdvJND, adding visual model coefficients, just noticeable difference, in the constraint of a distortion function when generating adversarial examples. In fact, the visual subjective feeling of the human eyes is added as a priori information, which decides the distribution of perturbations, to improve the image quality of adversarial examples. We tested our method on the FashionMNIST, CIFAR10, and MiniImageNet datasets. Our adversarial examples keep high image quality under slightly decreasing attack success rate. Since our AdvJND algorithm yield gradient distributions that are similar to those of the original inputs, the crafted noise can be hidden in the original inputs, improving the attack concealment significantly.

Keywords: Adversarial attack · Just noticeable difference · Attack concealment

1 Introduction

Deep neural networks (DNNs) are effective for completing many important but difficult tasks like computer vision [1–4], nature language processing [5–8], etc., and can achieve state-of-the-art performances in these tasks. Furthermore, they have approached human levels of performance in some specific tasks. Thus, we can assume that artificial intelligence is moving toward human intelligence step by step. However, Szegedy made an intriguing discovery that DNNs are vulnerable to adversarial examples [9], and he first proposed the concept of adversarial examples in image classification. A good-performance DNN model misclassifies inputs modified by

© Springer Nature Switzerland AG 2020
X. Chen et al. (Eds.): ML4CS 2020, LNCS 12487, pp. 463–478, 2020.
https://doi.org/10.1007/978-3-030-62460-6_42

adding small, imperceptible perturbations, which is hard to distinguish for humans. And adversarial examples are used to attack such applications like face recognition [10, 11], autonomous driving car [12, 13] and malware detection [14]. Obviously, adversarial examples are blind spots of deep models. The problem of generating adversarial examples can be regarded as an optimization problem, in which the target perturbations are minimized when the predicted label is not equal to the true label. The mathematical formula is decribed as follows:

$$
\begin{aligned}
&\min \ D(x, x + r) \\
&\text{s.t.} \ f(x+r) \neq f(x).
\end{aligned}
\tag{1}
$$

Let x be the input to the model, r the perturbation, $D(x, x + r)$ the distortion function between adversarial examples and their original inputs, and $f(x)$ the predicted label of the model. As shown in formula (1), there are two requirements for generating adversarial examples. One is to generate a misclassified example to attack successfully, and the other is to generate the smallest possible distortion value. These requirements ensure that the adversarial examples are similar to the original inputs and that high image fidelity is guaranteed. Because of the security threat of DNNs, adversarial examples have garnered significant attention among researchers, especially in the security critical applications. Classic methods for generating adversarial examples on deep learning have been established. Based on the adversarial setting criteria to sort, white-box attack represents to directly acquire all information, like training datasets, model architecture and so on. However, black-box attack means to get information by querying model indirectly. And the proposed methods usually use the L_p norm (L_0, L_2, L_∞), to classify the adversarial examples, which is used for constraining the perturbations. That is, in the definition of the distortion function $D(x, x + r)$, the L_p norm is used as a distance metric to measure the similarity between the adversarial examples and the original inputs. Typically, Jiawei Su et al. [15] proposed the one pixel attack method with the L_0 norm constraint, which changes by only one or several pixels [16, 17] in a picture but results in a significant changes compared with the original image of the poor attack concealment with obvious altered traces. Additionally, a lower attack success rate is resulted. Szegedy et al. proposed a method to generate adversarial examples with box-constrained L-BFGS [9] via back-propagation to obtain gradient information. Moosavi-Dezfooli et al. proposed a method to search the minimum perturbations to a classified boundary, named DeepFool [18], with the high images fidelity and attack success rates. Both of them take the L_2 norm constraint, which interferes the entire picture. Adversarial examples which satisfy the L_2 norm constraint are similar to the original inputs [18, 19]. However, it is time consuming to generate adversarial examples, which is inefficient. Goodfellow et al. proposed the fast gradient sign method (FGSM) [20] with the L_∞ norm constraint, which fastly generates adversarial examples by maximizing the loss function, with low image fidelity and attack success rate. Furthermore, Kurakin Alexey et al. proposed an iterative fast gradient sign method (I-FGSM) [21] to improve FGSM. We herein mainly discuss the L_∞ norm constraint, restraining the maximum distance difference between the adversarial example and the original input. Generally, perturbations are increased to ensure the adversarial examples' high attack success rate; however, the adversarial examples obtained in this manner exhibit poor concealment. To alleviate the tradeoff between the attack success rate and image fidelity, we propose a method that adds visual model coefficients in the L_∞ norm constraint. Because the L_∞ norm constraint is an objective metric, the distribution of perturbation is disordered and some noisy pixels are sensitive to the human eyes. Sid Ahmed Fezza et al. [22] thought the L_p norm did not correlate with human judgement and were not suitable as a distance metric. Adil Kaan Akan et al. [23] defined the machine's just noticeable difference with regularization terms, other than just noticeable difference of human visual perception. And they generated just noticeable difference adversarial examples, which attacked successfully just right. Different from that, we take the visual model coefficients into consideration, and think it can be added in the constraint to improve the images quality and guarantee high image fidelity. In fact, the visual subjective feeling of the human eyes is added as a priori information in the constraint to control the distribution of perturbations. In our study, we integrate the just noticeable difference (JND) coefficients into the L_∞ norm constraint of the distortion function to complete above mentioned task.

JND coefficients are critical values at which a difference can be detected. Additionally, they reflect that the human eyes can recognize the threshold of an image change. In general, the JND model is applied in image encoding. There exists redundancy in images, which without de-redundancy would be transported with lower efficiency. And JND could determine the amount of tolerated distortions to guarantee the quality of the images. Image encoding with JND coefficients can improve coding efficiency significantly [24–26], called perceptual coding. In this study, we used the JND model of the image domain to hide noise. As shown in Fig. 1, after adding Gaussian noise with a variance of 0.01 in the original input, the image is significantly interfered. When we constrain the noise with JND coefficients to control the distribution of noise, a human visual system (HVS) cannot distinguish the difference between the original input and the JND image, which proves the noise concealment ability of JND coefficients.

Original Image   Gaussian Noise Image   JND Image

Fig. 1. JND coefficients hide Gaussian noise. Left column: the original image. Middle column: the Gaussian noise image. Right column: the JND image.

JND coefficients can hide Gaussian noise because a region with large JND coefficients is a region with complex image textures. Additionally, it is difficult for our

HVS to notice these changes in these regions, which are also called visual blind spots of the human eyes. The larger the JND coefficients, the higher are the thresholds, the greater is the redundancy, the smaller is the sensitivity of the human eyes, and the more noise can be embedded. Therefore, perturbations in regions with large JND coefficients are less likely to be detected. We integrate JND coefficients into the existing adversarial attack methods. Namely, we add JND coefficients to the norm constraint and define this method as AdvJND. The primarily contributions of this study are as follows:

- We suggest a method to integrate JND coefficients for generating adversarial examples. We add the visual subjective feeling of the human eyes as a priori information in the constraint to decide the distribution of perturbations and generate adversarial examples with gradients distribution similar to that of the original inputs. Hence, the crafted noise can be hidden in the original inputs, thus improving the attack concealment significantly.
- We demonstrate that generating adversarial examples with our algorithm costs less time than algorithms with the L_2 norm constraint like DeepFool, when the image quality and the attack success rate of their methods are approximate. Such fact proves that our AdvJND algorithm is more efficient.

In Sect. 2, we provide the implementation algorithm of AdvJND. The effects of AdvJND are shown in Sect. 3. In Sect. 4, we draw the conclusions.

2 Methodology

In our AdvJND algorithm, we should get some information in advance, like the original image's JND coefficients and the original perturbations from the target model's gradients. Hence, we compute the JND coefficients in Sect. 2.1, and adopt FGSM and I-FGSM methods to yield the original perturbations in Sect. 2.2. In Sect. 2.3, we introduce the complete AdvJND algorithm.

2.1 JND Coefficients

The JND coefficients are based on the representation of visual redundancy in psychology and physiology. The receiver of image information is the HVS. A JND spatial model in the image domain primarily includes two factors: luminance masking and texture masking. On one hand, according to the Weber's law, the luminance contrast of perception in HVS increases with the practical's luminance. On the other hand, since the complex texture area and excess noises are both high-frequency information, so that excess noises could be hided in the texture area easily. To better match the HVS characteristics, X. K. Yang [27] designed a nonlinear additive model for masking to give consideration to both luminance adaption and texture. And texture masking is determined by the average background luminance and the average luminance difference around a pixel [28, 29]. The JND coefficient of each pixel is obtained experimentally [27]. The formula is

$$jnd(i, j) = \max(f_1(bg(i, j), mg(i, j)), f_2(i, j)), \tag{2}$$

where $f_1(i, j)$ is the texture masking function, $f_2(i, j)$ is the luminance adaption function, $bg(i, j)$ and $mg(i, j)$ represent gradient changes of the average background luminance and neighboring points at point (i, j), respectively.

Due to the visual redundancy in the image, there is a chance to embed noises in it. Furthermore, it is necessary for us to determine the magnitude of embedding noises to guarantee imperceptibility. Luckily, JND coefficients is related with HVS's sensitivity and helpful to embedding noises without perceptibility, which improves the attack concealment.

2.2 Adversarial Attack Methods

The paper is based on the white-box adversarial attack setting, instead of Curls & Whey [30], which concerntrates on improving adversarial image quality under the same query times in black-box setting.

In this section, we review the related studies of adversarial attack. We primarily introduce the FGSM and its extended algorithm I-FGSM and obtain the original perturbations from them. And our method performs improvements based on the FGSM and I-FGSM. The reason why we choose I-FGSM as a baseline is that I-FGSM is the state-of-the-art white-box attack based on L_∞ norm constraint.

FGSM. The basic concept of the FGSM [20] is to optimize in the direction of increasing loss function, i.e., generating adversarial examples in the positive direction of the gradient. It exhibits two characteristics. One is that it generates adversarial examples fast, as it only performs one back-propagation without iteration. Another is that it measures the distance between the adversarial example and the original input using the L_∞. These are the two main reasons for the obvious perturbations.

$$p = \varepsilon \cdot sign(\nabla_x J(\theta, x, y)) \tag{3}$$

$$x^{\mathrm{adv}} = x + p, \tag{4}$$

where ε represents the upper limit of perturbation, $\nabla_x J(\cdot)$ represents the gradient value of the loss function to the original input via back-propagation, p represents the perturbation, x represents the original input, and x^{adv} represents the generated adversarial example.

I-FGSM. The I-FGSM [21] is the expansion of the FGSM, which computes perturbations iteratively instead of in a one-shot manner. Specifically, a ε single value that changes in the direction of the gradient sign is replaced by a smaller α value; subsequently, the upper limit of the perturbation ε is used as limiting the constraint.

$$x_0^{adv} = x \tag{5}$$

$$\text{Clip}_{x,\varepsilon}\{x\} = \min(1, x + \varepsilon, \max(x - \varepsilon, x)) \tag{6}$$

$$x_{t+1}^{adv} = \text{Clip}_{x,\varepsilon}\{x_t^{adv} + \alpha \cdot sign(\nabla_x J(\theta, x, y))\}. \tag{7}$$

The I-FGSM achieves adversarial examples of better image quality than the one-shot FGSM. Meanwhile it implies more time costs.

2.3   AdvJND Methods

First, we are to calculate the JND coefficients of the original input and then normalize the processed JND coefficients to the L_∞. Specifically, we normalize the original input pixels to [0,1], and calculate the JND coefficients on each channel independently to simplify the calculation. Although the JND coefficients can reflect the edge information to some extent, for a more obvious edge area and a better discrimination, we calculate the power values of the JND coefficients, which allow large values to become larger, and small values to become smaller, that is, values representing edge areas are dramatically larger than smooth areas. In this paper, we square the image's JND coefficients.

$$jnd_2 = jnd \times jnd. \tag{8}$$

On the other hand, after squaring, the obtained JND coefficients are close to the order of 1e–3. If perturbations added are directly controlled at 1e–3 or similar, it would be difficult to attack the image successfully although the perturbations obey the image's gradient distribution. Thus, we discard the absolute values of the JND coefficients instead of their relative values, that is, we take JND coefficients to control the distribution of perturbations indirectly.

$$\lambda = \frac{p_{ori}}{\max(jnd_2)} \tag{9}$$

$$k = \lambda \times jnd_2. \tag{10}$$

p_{ori} represents the original perturbations from the FGSM or I-FGSM method, represents the scaled value, and k is the JND coefficients' relative values, which provide the critical information of the image texture location. Although the obtained adversarial examples are similar to the original inputs, their attack success rates are still lower than original adversarial examples'. In most cases, the large values of k primarily locate in the regions with complex textures, in which noise can be hided efficiently, and the small values of k locate in the smooth areas, in which our HVS are sensitive and easy to notice. Therefore, we decide the final values of k based on the location information. And our strategy is to reduce the small values of k in multiplies and calculate the final perturbations as follows.

$$\begin{cases} t = 1, & if \ k \geq \rho \\ t = \gamma, & if \ k < \rho \end{cases} \tag{11}$$

$$p_{out} = k \times t. \tag{12}$$

We obtained the experience value experimentally. The threshold value $\rho = \varepsilon/2$, the reduced multiple $\gamma = 1/4$, and p_{out} represents the final adversarial perturbations. The AdvJND method is summarized in **Algorithm 1**.

Algorithm 1 takes the FGSM method as an example to show the complete process of our AdvJND algorithm to generate adversarial examples. If we implement our AdvJND algorithm based on the I-FGSM method, take the output x^{adv} as the input x, and repeat the procedures from step 3 to step 9 until satisfying the minimum condition or the maximum iterations.

3 Experiments

In this section, experiments on the FashionMNIST [31], CIFAR10 [32], and MiniI-mageNet datasets (using 1000 images from ILSVR2012 [33] test dataset, 1925 pictures in total, and the reason why we take the MiniImageNet dataset is that it can not guarantee the high recognition accuracy in classification tasks with the whole ImageNet dataset, and in order to show the effectiveness of our attack algorithm, we validate the MiniImageNet with high accuarcy.) are used to validate our AdvJND method, and these datasets correspond to network architectures LeNet-5 [34], VGG16 [35], and Inception_v3 [36], respectively. We demonstrate the advantages of the FGSM-JND and I-FGSM-JND algorithms over the original attack methods in Sect. 3.1. And the proposed AdvJND algorithm adopts a general approach of the constraint to generate adversarial examples. In Sect. 3.2, we compare the efficiency between the I-FGSM-JND and DeepFool algorithms.

Algorithm 1 AdvJND: restrain JND coefficients to L_∞ norm

1 input: an image x, superior limit ε.

2 output: an adversarial example x^{adv}.

3 Computer JND coefficients of the image x

$$jnd(i,j) \leftarrow \max\left(f_1\left(bg(i,j), mg(i,j)\right), f_2(i,j)\right).$$

4 Calculate the original perturbations p_{ori} $p \leftarrow \varepsilon \cdot sign\left(\nabla_x J(\theta, x, y)\right)$.

5 Square JND coefficients $jnd_2 \leftarrow jnd \times jnd$.

6 Normalize JND coefficients to L_∞ norm $k \leftarrow \dfrac{p_{ori}}{\max(jnd_2)} \times jnd_2$.

7 Set thresholds $\begin{cases} t \leftarrow 1, & if\ k \geq \rho \\ t \leftarrow \gamma, & if\ k < \rho \end{cases}$.

8 Obtain Perturbations p_{out} $p_{out} \leftarrow k \times t$.

9 Get the final adversarial example $x^{adv} \leftarrow x + p_{out}$.

10 return x^{adv}.

3.1   AdvJND

The core of AdvJND is integrating JND coefficients into the L_∞ constraint. More similar adversarial examples are generated though the attack success rate, slightly decreasing within an acceptable scope.

FGSM vs. FGSM-JND. The FGSM-JND is obtained by integrating JND coefficients into the FGSM. As shown in Fig. 2, the perturbations generated by the FGSM are distributed over the entire image, but the perturbations generated by the FGSM-JND are distributed over the edge region of the "pants". The adversarial examples generated by FGSM are rough and modified obviously, but the adversarial examples generated by our algorithm are smooth and more similar to the original inputs, since our FGSM-JND algorithm can effectively control perturbations in such smooth regions with the location of small JND coefficients and mainly hide noise in regions with the location of large JND coefficients to ensure its adversarial capacity.

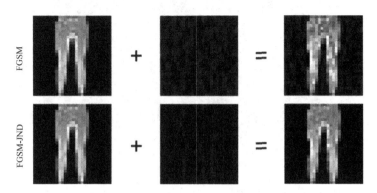

Fig. 2. FGSM vs. FGSM-JND on the FashionMNIST dataset.

I-FGSM vs. I-FGSM-JND. The I-FGSM-JND is obtained by integrating JND coefficients into the I-FGSM. In Fig. 3, the I-FGSM generates more obvious perturbations, especially in the smooth background region. However, the perturbations generated by the I-FGSM-JND primarily focus on regions of complex texture in the images (e.g., the "bird" in row 1), which is not sensitive to the HVS, and perturbations in it cannot be detected easily. And even in smooth regions like the body of the "bird", our I-FGSM-JND generates smaller and fewer perturbations in such regions.

From a different perspective, we can explain this phenomenon with the histograms of oriented gradients (HOG) [37], which is a feature descriptor of an image and reflects outline and texture information of an image. We herein config the HOG basic settings with 8 orientations, pixels per cell and cell per block. In Fig. 4, even though the HOG of the adversarial examples (e.g., still the "bird" in row 1) generated by the I-FGSM-JND can mainly be perturbed by a small noise texture in the background, the outline of "bird" can be recognized. By contrast, FGSM-JND's adversarial examples are covered with noise but cannot be recognized, that is, all the magnitudes and directions of textures are messy and even we can't distinguish the target and background. On the other hand, the HOG descriptors of the "bird" in row 2 and the "dog" in row 3 are clearer than that of the "bird" in row 1, especially in the background regions. It is most likely that the background in row 1 is more complex, where JND coefficients is larger and we can add more noise. The texture complexity reflects the information of the edge, which is related with gradient. Thus, the gradients distribution of adversarial examples generated by the I-FGSM-JND is more similar to those of the image inputs.

Original Methods vs. Improvement Methods. In Fig. 5, we select 10 adversarial examples randomly and enlarge their local regions (marked by a red box in the same place) to see more information in detail. For example, in row 8, we enlarge the sky to observe. The FGSM method generates distinct perturbations and the I-FGSM can produce more refined perturbations by iterating the FGSM method, which also proves that it is useful to iterate. To our surprise, integrating JND coefficients into the

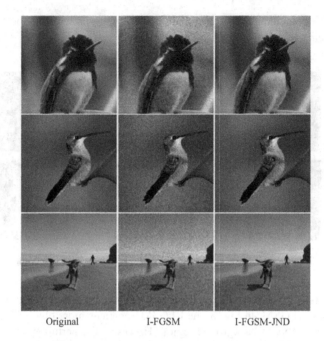

Original   I-FGSM   I-FGSM-JND

Fig. 3. I-FGSM vs. I-FGSM-JND on the MiniImageNet dataset.

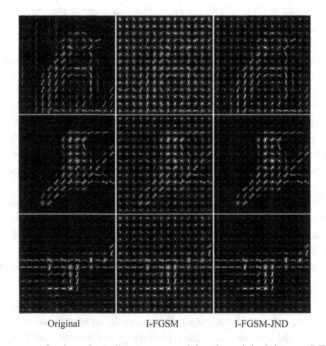

Original   I-FGSM   I-FGSM-JND

Fig. 4. Histograms of oriented gradients generated by the original inputs, I-FGSM, and I-FGSM-JND in Fig. 3.

constraint, we can get smaller perturbations than the I-FGSM method. For all images, we can conclude that our AdvJND algorithm improves the image quality obviously, especially in smooth regions with simple texture. And I-FGSM-JND algorithm performs best. There is no doubt that it works when we take the JND coefficients as a priori information to control the distribution of gradients.

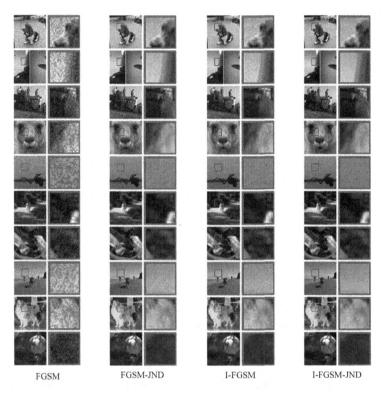

FGSM   FGSM-JND   I-FGSM   I-FGSM-JND

Fig. 5. Ten adversarial examples were generated by the FGSM, FGSM-JND, I-FGSM, and I-FGSM-JND with epsilon 0.1; their local enlarged images on the MiniImageNet dataset are shown on the right orderly. (Color figure online)

As shown in Table 1, the non-attack method means taking the original images as inputs without epsilon, and the attack success rate, namely (1-recognition accuracy), of the AdvJND algorithm is lower than or equivalent to that of the original attack method, which sacrifices a little attack success rates to improve the images fidelity. This is especially obvious in the FGSM and FGSM-JND. Because the FGSM is a one-step attack method, its effect on the attack success rate is larger than that on the image fidelity, which leads the gap of the attack success rate between the FGSM and FGSM-JND a little large. And by iterating, the attack success rate is higher and the image fidelity becomes better, meanwhile, the gap of the attack success rate between the I-FGSM and I-FGSM-JND decreases.

Table 1. Comparison of recognition accuracy between the original attack and AdvJND attack on the FashionMNIST, CIFAR 10, and MiniImageNet datasets.

Attack methods	Epsilon	FashionMNIST/LeNet5	CIFAR10/Vgg16	MiniImageNet/Inception_v3
Non-attack	0.0	92.33	83.4	97.82
FGSM	0.2	12.94	9.02	43.64
FGSM-JND		29.48	9.22	58.49
I-FGSM		5.69	7.51	1.3
I-FGSM-JND		16.57	7.52	2.44

On the other hand, the performance of the FashionMNIST dataset, whether the attack success rate or the gap of the attack success rate between the original attack algorithm and our AdvJND algorithm, is worse than other datasets. It can be considered that the improvement effect of our AdvJND algorithm is a little critical about images because the JND coefficients are related to the the texture complexity of the image. However, such FashionMNIST dataset prefers simple textures and smooth backgrounds, and the MiniImageNet dataset includes more practical images in our real life with more complex textures. We know that the function of the JND coefficients are small in smooth images and the effects of the JND coefficients are not obvious, which explains why our AdvJND algorithm performs better on the MiniImageNet and CIFAR10 datasets than the FashionMNIST dataset.

3.2   I-FGSM-JND vs. DeepFool

The attack success rate of the I-FGSM-JND algorithm is slightly higher than that of DeepFool, but the average of time consuming for the I-FGSM-JND algorithm to generate an adversarial example is approximately only half of the DeepFool (in Table 2). The times are computed using a NVDIA GTX 1080Ti GPU. This is because DeepFool takes the smallest distance to the nearest classification boundary as the minimum perturbations. So, it must traverse the classification boundary and obtain the smallest distance. In case of the situation of 1000 classes, the disadvantage of time-consuming will be more obvious. Thus, the efficiency of the I-FGSM-JND algorithm is significantly higher than that of DeepFool, and the I-FGSM-JND is more suitable as a universal attack method (Fig. 6).

Similar to integrating the JND coefficients in the L_∞ norm, the subjective visual information of the human eyes is used as a priori information to improve the image quality of the adversarial examples. Furthermore, we can consider to embed the appropriate visual model coefficients into the L_2 norm constraint as a priori information which can provide a better search strategy or reduce the search space to decrease the iteration or traversal times to improve the efficiency.

Table 2. The efficiency of generating adversarial examples with the I-FGSM and DeepFool.

Method	Attack success rate (%)	Average time of generating an adversarial example (s)
I-FGSM-JND	97.45	0.7
DeepFool	96.36	1.41

Fig. 6. I-FGSM-JND vs. DeepFool on the MiniImageNet dataset.

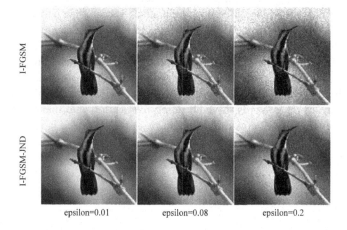

Fig. 7. Adversarial examples generated by the I-FGSM and I-FGSM-JND with epsilon 0.01, 0.08, and 0.2

4 Conclusions

Large perturbations lead the adversarial examples' high attack success rate and bad image fidelity with poor concealment. To alleviate the tradeoff between the attack success rate and image fidelity, we herein proposed an adversarial attack method using AdvJND and used JND coefficients to relate the subjective feeling of human eyes and the image quality evaluation metric. The human eyes are not sensitive to changes in complex texture regions, which provides a chance for us to embed more noise in these regions. Our experimental results demonstrated that the HOG descriptors of adversarial examples generated by the AdvJND algorithm were similar to those of the original inputs; thus, noise could be hidden effectively in the original inputs. Our approach can be incorporated into the new proposed L_∞ norm-based attack method to build adversarial examples that are similar to the original inputs. In future work, other metrics of human visual evaluation can be integrated into the L_2 norm constraint to improve the efficiency of generating adversarial examples.

Appendices

Explore the Influence of Epsilon on Image Quality. The epsilon is crucial for improving the attack success rate. In this section, we present the attack success rate and image fidelity of AdvJND attacks by changing the epsilon value.

When the epsilon increases from 0.01 to 0.2, the attack success rate improves, too. Simultaneously, the gap between the I-FGSM and I-FGSM-JND decreases gradually. When the epsilon is 0.2, the difference in the attack success rate between the I-FGSM and I-FGSM-JND is less than 0.009. However, in terms of image quality (in Fig. 7), the adversarial examples generated by the I-FGSM with epsilon 0.01 and those by the I-FGSM-JND with epsilon 0.2 with higher attack success rate are similar.

Therefore, adversarial examples generated by AdvJND are more similar to the original inputs when the attack success rates of the original attack and AdvJND attack are equivalent. In other words, by embedding the a priori information of the human eyes' subjective feeling, the algorithm based on AdvJND attack is more effective for alleviating the tradeoff between the attack success rate and image fidelity and achieves to generate adversarial examples with more higher image quality.

References

1. Lecun, Y., Boser, B., Denker, J., et al.: Backpropagation applied to handwritten zip code recognition. Neural Comput. **1**(4), 541–551 (1989)
2. Krizhevsky, A., Sutskever, I., Hinton, G.E.: ImageNet classification with deep convolutional neural networks. In: NIPS 2012, pp. 1097–1105, MIT Press (2012)
3. He, K., Zhang, X., Ren, S., et al.: Deep residual learning for image recognition. In: CVPR 2016, pp. 770–778. IEEE (2016)

4. Huang, G., Liu, Z., Van Der Maaten, L., et al.: Densely connected convolutional networks. In: CVPR 2017, pp. 4700–4708. IEEE (2017)
5. Hinton, G., Deng, L., Yu, D., et al.: Deep neural networks for acoustic modeling in speech recognition: the shared views of four research groups. IEEE Signal Process. Mag. **29**(6), 82–97 (2012)
6. Bahdanau, D., Cho, K., Bengio, Y.: Neural machine translation by jointly learning to align and translate. In: ICLR 2015, OpenReview (2015)
7. Sutskever, I., Vinyals, O., Le, Q.V.: Sequence to sequence learning with neural networks. In: NIPS 2014, pp. 3104–3112, MIT Press (2014)
8. Andor, D., Alberti, C., Weiss, D., et al.: Globally normalized transition-based neural networks. arXiv Preprint arXiv:1603.060426 (2016)
9. Szegedy, C., Zaremba, W., Sutskever, I., et al.: Intriguing properties of neural networks. In: ICLR 2014, OpenReview (2014)
10. Sharif, M., Bhagavatula, S., Bauer, L., et al.: A general framework for adversarial examples with objectives. ACM Trans. Priv. Secur. **22**(3), 1–30 (2019)
11. Bose, A.J., Aarabi, P.: Adversarial attacks on face detectors using neural net based constrained optimization. In: MMSP 2018, pp. 1–6, IEEE (2018)
12. Eykholt, K., Evtimov, I., Fernandes, E., et al.: Robust physical-world attacks on deep learning visual classification. In: CVPR 2018, pp. 1625–1634, IEEE (2018)
13. Papernot, N., McDaniel, P., Goodfellow, I., et al.: Practical black-box attacks against machine learning. In: ACCC 2017, pp. 506–519, ACM (2017)
14. Hu, W., Tan, Y.: Black-box attacks against RNN based malware detection algorithms. In: AAAI 2018, pp. 245–251, AAAI (2018)
15. Su, J., Vargas, D.V., Sakurai, K.: One pixel attack for fooling deep neural networks. IEEE Trans. Evol. Comput. **23**(5), 828–841 (2019)
16. Carlini, N., Wagner, D.: Towards evaluating the robustness of neural networks. In: SP 2017, pp. 39–57, IEEE (2017)
17. Papernot, N., McDaniel, P., Jha, S., et al.: The limitations of deep learning in adversarial settings. In: EuroS&P 2016, pp. 372–387, IEEE (2016)
18. Moosavi-Dezfooli, S. M., Fawzi, A., Frossard, P.: DeepFool: a simple and accurate method to fool deep neural networks. In: CVPR 2016, pp. 2574–2582, IEEE (2016)
19. Moosavi-Dezfooli, S.M., Fawzi, A., Fawzi, O., et al.: Universal adversarial perturbations. In: CVPR 2017, pp. 1765–1773. IEEE (2017)
20. Goodfellow, I.J., Shlens, J., Szegedy, C.: Explaining and harnessing adversarial examples. In: ICLR 2015, OpenReview (2015)
21. Kurakin, A., Goodfellow, I., Bengio, S.: Adversarial examples in the physical world. arXiv Preprint arXiv:1607.02533 (2016)
22. Fezza, S.A., Bakhti, Y., Hamidouche, W., et al.: Perceptual evaluation of adversarial attacks for CNN-based image classification. In: QoMEX 2019, pp. 1–6. IEEE (2019)
23. Akan, A.K., Genc, M.A. Vural, F.T.: Just noticeable difference for machines to generate adversarial images. arXiv Preprint arXiv:2001.1106 (2020)
24. Shen, D.F., Wang, S.C.: Measurements of JND property of HVS and its applications to image segmentation, coding, and requantization. In: Digital Compression Technologies and Systems for Video Communications, pp. 113–121 (1996)
25. Xiao, W.: An H. 264 encode mode decision algorithm based on JND. J. Univ. Electron. Sci. Technol. China **42**(1), 121–124 (2013)
26. Li, Y., Liu, H., Chen, Z.: Perceptually lossless image coding based on foveated JND. In: IRI 2015, pp. 72–75, IEEE (2015)
27. Yang, X., Ling, W., Lu, Z., et al.: Just noticeable distortion model and its applications in video coding. Signal Process.: Image Commun. **20**(7), 662–680 (2005)

28. Chou, C.H., Chen, C.W.J.: A perceptually optimized 3-D subband codec for video communication over wireless channels. IEEE Trans. Circ. Syst. Video Technol. **6**(2), 143–156 (1996)
29. Chou, C.H., Li, Y.C.: A perceptually tuned subband image coder based on the measure of just-noticeable-distortion profile. IEEE Trans. Circ. Syst. Video Technol. **5**(6), 467–476 (1995)
30. Shi, Y., Wang, S., Han, Y.: Curls & whey: boosting black-box adversarial attacks. In: CVPR 2019, pp. 6519–6527, IEEE (2019)
31. Xiao, H., Rasul, K., Vollgraf, R.: Fashion-MNIST: a novel image dataset for benchmarking machine learning algorithms. arXiv Preprint arXiv:1708.07747 (2017)
32. Cifar10. http://www.cs.toronto.edu/~kriz/cifar.html
33. Russakovsky, O., Deng, J., Su, H., et al.: Imagenet large scale visual recognition challenge. Int. J. Comput. Vis. **115**(3), 211–252 (2015)
34. LeCun, Y., Bottou, L., Bengio, Y., et al.: Gradient-based learning applied to document recognition. Proc. IEEE **86**(11), 2278–2324 (1998)
35. Simonyan, K., Zisserman, A.: Very deep convolutional networks for large-scale image recognition. In: ICLR 2015, OpenReview (2015)
36. Szegedy, C., Vanhoucke, V., Ioffe, S., et al.: Rethinking the inception architecture for computer vision. In: CVPR 2016, pp. 2818–2826, IEEE (2016)
37. Dalal, N., Triggs, B.: Histograms of oriented gradients for human detection. In: CVPR 2005, pp. 886–893, IEEE (2005)

Squeeze Criterion GANs: Double Adversarial Learning Method

Yan Gan[1,2]([✉]), Tao Xiang[1], and Mao Ye[2]

[1] College of Computer Science, Chongqing University, Chongqing 400044, China
shiyangancq@gmail.com, txiang@cqu.edu.cn
[2] School of Computer Science and Engineering,
University of Electronic Science and Technology of China, Chengdu 611731, China
cvlab.uestc@gmail.com

Abstract. Generative adversarial networks (GANs) have attracted much attention since it is able to effective learn from an unknown real distribution. However, the instability of the training process greatly affects the quality of the generated images. To address this problem, the network structure-based, loss-based variant model and some training techniques are proposed. Unfortunately, there are some problems with the above methods, such as the limited effect of stabilizing the training process, the complex mathematical derivation, and the lack of universality of training techniques for different tasks. To this end, we propose a novel squeeze criterion GANs. In this method, we design a pseudo real module to synthesize adversarial sample and the double identity discriminator is designed. Then, the generated image and adversarial sample, as well as the generated image and real image form double adversarial learning. Through double adversarial learning, it forms a squeeze criterion to stabilize the training process of generator and discriminator. Finally, experimental results show that the proposed method has well portability and stabilizes the training process of existing GANs, and improves the quality of generated images.

Keywords: GANs · Adversarial sample · Double adversarial learning · Instability

1 Introduction

In recent years, GANs [1] have attracted much attention due to the fact that it is able to implicitly learn an unknown real distribution. It has achieved amazing results in many applications, including image synthesis [2–5], video synthesis [6], text generation [7] and other applications [8]. However, the unstable training process of GANs is a notoriously challenging.

Supported by the National Key R & D Program of China (2018YFE0203900), National Natural Science Foundation of China (61773093).

© Springer Nature Switzerland AG 2020
X. Chen et al. (Eds.): ML4CS 2020, LNCS 12487, pp. 479–493, 2020.
https://doi.org/10.1007/978-3-030-62460-6_43

To solve this challenging, many variant models have been proposed. In this paper, we divide them into the network structure-based, loss-based variant model and some training techniques. First of all, the network structure-based variant model involves designing novel network structure. For example, in the feature extraction layers of generator and discriminator, Radford et al. [9] use the convolutional neural network to replace the multi-layer perceptron in the original GAN, and then they design the DCGAN model. Mirza et al. [10] design a conditional GANs model. They add a conditional information (label or semantic information) to a generator and discriminator. Zhang et al. [11] employ the non-local model and introduce self-attention to the GAN framework, then they design the SAGANs model. It enables both the generator and the discriminator to efficiently model relationships between widely separated spatial regions. Although these variant models based on network structure can improve the performance of model training and improve the quality of image synthesis, their effect on stable training process is not enough. Moreover, few researchers have added an auxiliary module to stabilize the training process.

Secondly, to overcome the training instability caused by JS divergence, the researchers propose the loss-based variant model. For instance, Arjovsky et al. [12] use Wasserstein distance instead of JS divergence to build the model, and then the WGAN model is proposed. Mao et al. [13] build the LSGANs model through Person χ^2. EBGANs model [14] is modeled by the total variance. However, the mathematical derivation behind these variants is too complex to be understood.

Moreover, in order to stabilize the training process, some training techniques are proposed. For example, Pan et al. [15] skillfully integrate Instance Normalization (IN) and Batch Normalization (BN) as building blocks, and design the IBN-Net which remarkably enhances a CNN's modeling ability on one domain, as well as its generalization capacity on another domain without finetuning. Miyato et al. [16] point out that Spectral Normalization (SN) is added into a generator and discriminator to stabilize the training process. Odena et al. [17] propose a "regularization" technique (called Jacobian Clamping) to stabilize the training process, which softly penalizes the condition number of the generator Jacobian. Zhang et al. [18] propose a simple, effective training stabilizer based on the notion of consistency regularization. Other training techniques include different learning rate [19], orthogonal regularization [20], feature matching [21] and so on. However, these training techniques are also limited to different applications and they are not universal. Therefore, their portability is poor.

To sum up, in order to improve the stability of GANs training process and consider the portability of the model, we introduce the concept of adversarial sample. Then, we propose a novel squeeze criterion GANs applied to image synthesis. It is a double adversarial learning method. Specifically, on the one hand, the generated image and the adaptive synthesized adversarial sample form an adversarial sample constraint to achieve the purpose of learning from the adversarial sample. On the other hand, in order to further learn from the real image, the generated image and the real image form another real image constraint. With the double adversarial constraints mentioned above, the training instability of the generator and discriminator is effectively suppressed.

Our contributions are as follows:

(1) To improve the training stability of generator and discriminator, a novel squeeze criterion GANs is proposed. In this method, the generated image and adversarial sample, as well as the generated image and real image form double adversarial learning.
(2) We tactfully design a pseudo real module to adaptively synthesize adversarial sample and double identity discriminator is designed. Furthermore, this pseudo real module is trained with existing GANs.
(3) Experimental results show that the proposed method can stabilize the training process of generator and discriminator respectively, and improve the quality of the generated images.

2 Double Adversarial Learning Method

2.1 Problem Analysis

GANs defines an implicit learning process of the unknown real distribution through the two-player game rule. Its min-max objective function [1] is given by:

$$\min_{G_\theta} \max_{D_\omega} L = E_{x \sim p_{data}}[log D_\omega(x)] + E_{z \sim p_z}[log(1 - D_\omega(G_\theta(z)))], \qquad (1)$$

where G_θ and D_ω represent the generator with parameter θ and the discriminator with parameter ω, respectively. x is a real sample. z is an input noise.

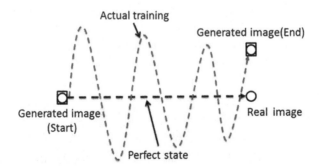

Fig. 1. The explaining of original GANs. The ideal situation is that the generated image is infinitely close to the real image. As shown by the black dotted arrow. However, the actual training process is oscillating, resulting in a large difference between the generated image and the real image. As shown by the dotted red arrow. (Color figure online)

In theory, if GANs is sufficiently trained, it can generate images that are very close to real images. That is, under the role of adversarial training, we want the generated image to be close to the real image. The dotted black arrow is shown in Fig. 1. However, in practice, due to the unstable training process, the generated image distribution is quite different from the real image distribution. The dotted red arrow is shown in Fig. 1. The instability is most likely the result of simple adversarial training.

Therefore, we propose double adversarial learning method. This method constructs a squeeze criterion to constrain the generation process. We will describe our method in detail below.

2.2   Model Framework

In the training process of GANs, it is difficult to be trained effectively, resulting in the difference between the generated image distribution and the real image distribution. In addition, considering the portability and ease of understanding of the model, we introduce the concept of adversarial sample. Then a novel squeeze criterion GANs is proposed, namely double adversarial learning method. In the propsed method, the adversarial sample and real images are able to guide the generator to generate better images gradually. The proposed model framework is shown in Fig. 2.

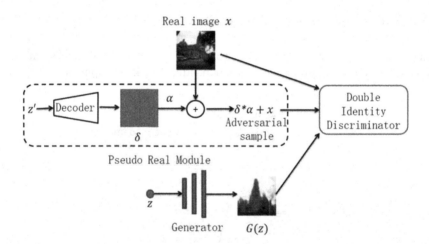

Fig. 2. Double adversarial learning method. Compared with the original GANs model, our method deliberately adds a pseudo real module (It is shown in the dotted box) and designs a double identity discriminator.

For the sake of the presentation, we assume that z and z' are random noises. They have the same dimension $(1 \times m)$. First of all, a randomly sampled noise z generates an image $G(z)$ by the generator G. Similarly, the random noise z'

generates a noise image δ by the decoder De. Secondly, the generated image δ multiplies by the adjustment parameter α and then adds the real image x to form the adversarial sample $x + \alpha * \delta$. In this paper, we assume that the generated images $G(z)$, δ, and adversarial sample have the same dimensions as the real image $x(n \times n)$, so that they can participate in the training of discriminator. In particularly, at the first few training steps, we assume that the discriminator recognizes the generated adversarial sample as a real sample. And in the subsequent training steps, it identifies the generated adversarial sample as a fake sample. Through this pseudo-real hypothesis and the mode of adversarial learning, the image generated by the generator is gradually closer to the adversarial sample, and then further closer to the real image. Therefore, the discriminator is called a double identity discriminator. Finally, the adversarial sample is trained with the GANs model.

2.3   Pseudo Real Module

In order to reduce the instability of generator and discriminator during training, a simple and portable pseudo real module is designed. It outputs an adversarial sample. As shown in the dotted box of Fig. 2.

Specifically, the adversarial sample (AS) is formed as follows in this paper. Firstly, we input a random noise z' into the decoder to generate a noise image, which is given by:

$$\delta = De(z'). \tag{2}$$

Then, the adversarial sample is obtained by adjusting real image x and noise image $\alpha * \delta$ during training:

$$AS = x + \alpha * \delta, \tag{3}$$

Finally, we further normalize δ, as follows:

$$\delta = \delta/||\delta||_F, \tag{4}$$

where the subscript F is the F-norm and we set $F = 2$.

On the one hand, the adversarial sample participates in the training of generator. On the other hand, it also participates in the training of discriminator. Through adversarial training, the pseudo real module has learned to adaptively adjust the instability of generator and discriminator. Finally, it not only stabilizes the GANs training process, but also forces the generated image to align firstly the adversarial sample and then towards the real sample.

2.4   Double Identity Discriminator

The original discriminator is only trained with real images and generated images, which makes the training process of the discriminator unstable and leads to its failure to learn a well classification decision hyperplane. Finally, it affects the

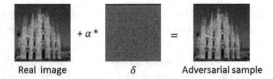

Real image δ Adversarial sample

Fig. 3. The example of adversarial sample formation processes.

quality of the generated image. In addtion, inspired by adversarial sample [22] which is very close to the real image (See Fig. 3), we introduce it to train the discriminator. For this reason, we tactfully design a double identity discriminator. As shown in Fig. 4.

Since the real image is very close to the adversarial sample, at the first few training steps, we believe that the discriminator should treat the synthesized adversarial sample as the real image (See the if branch in Fig. 4). Then, at subsequent training steps, it treats the adversarial sample as a fake image (See the else branch in Fig. 4). In other words, the generated image is firstly aligned to the adverarial sample. Then the generated image is closer to the real image. Using the adversarial sample, generated image and real image to train the discriminator, on the one hand, the pseudo real module can adaptively handle the instability of generator and discriminator. On the other hand, the adversarial sample expands the training data, which enables the discriminator to learn a better classification decision hyperplane.

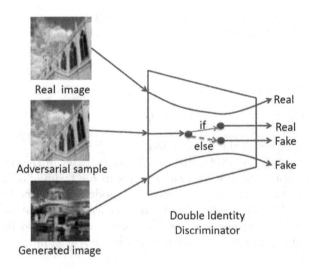

Fig. 4. The example of double identity discriminator. Compared with the general discriminator, the discriminator we designed increases the recognition of adversarial sample.

According to the previous analysis, the loss function of GANs discriminator after modification is given by:

$$L_{DAL}^{D} = E_{x \sim p_{data}}[log D_\omega(x)] + E_{z \sim p_z}[log(1 - D_\omega(G_\theta(z)))] + R(AS), \quad (5)$$

where AS is an adversarial sample. $R(AS)$ represents the recognition result of an adversarial sample. Its specific form is:

$$R(AS) = \begin{cases} E_{AS \sim p_{AS}}[log D_\omega(AS)], if\, step < threshold; \\ E_{AS \sim p_{AS}}[log(1 - D_\omega(AS))], if\, step \geq threshold. \end{cases} \quad (6)$$

In a follow-up experiment, we set $threshold = 1000$ and maximize L_{DAL}^{D} in the optimization process.

2.5   Objective Function of Generator

According to the previous analysis, in order to train the pseudo real module with the GANs model, and to achieve double adversarial learning, we tactfully add the adversarial sample part to the generator's loss function. Its specific form is given by:

$$L_{DAL}^{G} = E_{z \sim p_z}[log(1 - D_\omega(G_\theta(z)))] + E_{AS \sim p_{AS}}[log(1 - D_\omega(AS))], \quad (7)$$

where the $E_{AS \sim p_{AS}}[log(1 - D_\omega(AS))]$ means that we want the adversarial sample to be as consistent as possible with the real image. The goal is to make the generated image as close to the adversarial sample as possible, and then align it with the real image. Finally, we minimize L_{DAL}^{G} in the optimization process.

2.6   Theoretical Analysis

In this section, we mainly analyze how the squeeze criterion GANs stabilizes the training process through double adversarial learning.

First of all, through the pseudo real module, we can synthesize an adversarial sample. In the generator's loss function, we want the adversarial sample to be as real as possible, which forces it to be very close to the real image.

Then, on the one hand, we construct an adversarial learning by the adversarial sample and generated image. It forms a kind of adversarial sample constraint. The blue arrow is shown in Fig. 5. Concretely, the adversarial sample constraint is determined by the following formula:

$$\min_{G_\theta} \max_{D_\omega} L_{ASC} = E_{AS \sim p_{AS}}[log D_\omega(AS)] + E_{z \sim p_z}[log(1 - D_\omega(G_\theta(z)))]. \quad (8)$$

On the other hand, we use the generated image and the real image to construct another adversarial learning, so that the generated image is able to learn from the real image. This forms a real image constraint. The red arrow is shown in Fig. 5. The specific form of real image constraint is:

$$\min_{G_\theta} \max_{D_\omega} L_{RIC} = E_{x \sim p_{data}}[log D_\omega(x)] + E_{z \sim p_z}[log(1 - D_\omega(G_\theta(z)))]$$
$$+ E_{AS \sim p_{AS}}[log(1 - D_\omega(AS))]. \quad (9)$$

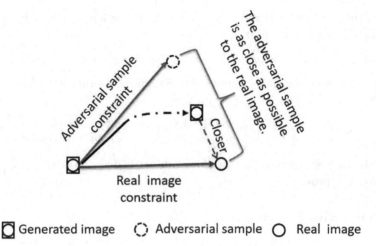

Fig. 5. The explaining of squeeze criterion in double adversarial learning method. We construct double adversarial learning by the adversarial sample and generated image, as well as the generated image and real image. (Colr figure online)

To sum up, a kind of constraint space of squeeze criterion (The triangular region is shown in Fig. 5) is formed tactfully by double adversarial learning. Under the double adversarial learning, the mapping space of the generator and discriminator is relatively small. Further, it reinforces the constraints of the generator and discriminator. Finally, the stability of generator and discriminator training is effectively controlled.

In this constraint space of squeeze criterion, at the first several training steps, the discriminator treats the adversarial sample as a real image, which forces the generated image to learn from the adversarial sample (The black solid line is shown in Fig. 5). At the following training steps, the discriminator regards the adversarial sample as a fake sample. It forces the generated image to come closer to the real image (The dotted black arrow is shown in Fig. 5).

2.7 Method of Transportability

In order to further verify the portability of squeeze criterion in the stable training process, we apply it to the Hinge loss [11] and LSGANs loss [13]. In the extended different loss functions, we directly add the adversarial sample to the generator's loss function and the corresponding discriminator is replaced with the double identity discriminator.

At the beginning, we apply our method to the Hinge loss [11]. The loss function of corresponding discriminator is given by the following equation:

$$
\begin{aligned}
L_{DAL}^{D-Hinge} = \ & -E_{x \sim p_{data}}[\min(0, -1 + D_\omega(x))] \\
& - E_{z \sim p_z}[\min(0, -1 - D_\omega(G_\theta(z)))] + R^{Hinge}(AS),
\end{aligned} \quad (10)
$$

and $R^{Hinge}(AS)$ is the recognition of adversarial sample. It is given by:

$$R^{Hinge}(AS) = \begin{cases} -E_{AS\sim p_{AS}}[\min(0, -1 + D_\omega(AS))], if\, step < threshold; \\ -E_{AS\sim p_{AS}}[\min(0, -1 - D_\omega(AS))], if\, step \geq threshold. \end{cases} \quad (11)$$

The loss function of the corresponding generator is given by:

$$L_{DAL}^{G-Hinge} = -E_{z\sim p_z}[D_\omega(G_\theta(z))] - E_{AS\sim p_{AS}}[D_\omega(AS)]. \quad (12)$$

In the process of optimization, we minimize $L_{DAL}^{D-Hinge}$ and $L_{DAL}^{G-Hinge}$.

Then, the proposed method is applied to the LSGANs loss [13] and the loss function of the corresponding discriminator is given by:

$$L_{DAL}^{D-LSGANs} = \frac{1}{2} * E_{x\sim p_{data}}[(D_\omega(x) - b)^2] + \frac{1}{2} * E_{z\sim p_z}[(D_\omega(G_\theta(z)) - a)^2]$$
$$+ \frac{1}{2} * R^{LSGANs}(AS). \quad (13)$$

In a similar way, the expression of $R^{LSGANs}(AS)$ is:

$$R^{LSGANs}(AS) = \begin{cases} E_{AS\sim p_{AS}}[(D_\omega(AS) - b)^2], if\, step < threshold; \\ E_{AS\sim p_{AS}}[(D_\omega(AS) - a)^2], if\, step \geq threshold. \end{cases} \quad (14)$$

In the LSGANs loss case, the corresponding generator is given by:

$$L_{DAL}^{G-LSGANs} = \frac{1}{2}*E_{z\sim p_z}[(D_\omega(G_\theta(z))-c)^2]+\frac{1}{2}*E_{AS\sim p_{AS}}[(D_\omega(AS)-c)^2]. \quad (15)$$

In the experiment, we set $a = 0$, $b = c = 1$ respectively and we minimize $L_{DAL}^{D-LSGANs}$ and $L_{DAL}^{G-LSGANs}$.

3   Experiments

3.1   Experimental Settings

Datasets. To verify the effectiveness of the proposed double adversarial learning method, we conduct experiments on the LSUN [23] and CelebA [24] datasets. Then, the specific settings of experimental datasets are shown in Table 1.

Baseline Models. To evaluate the performance of the double adversarial learning method, we compare the proposed method with the GANs [1], Hinge [11] and LSGANs [13] loss functions. Then, we select six models as baseline models. Thereinto, Jacobian Clamping [17] is a class of constraining generator method. We add Jacobian Clamping into the GANs loss, denote as GANs-JC model. Similarly, consistency regularization [18] is a kind of constraining discriminator method. We add it into GANs loss, denote as GANs-CR model. In particular, according to the description in reference [18], we construct $T(x)$ with a linear manner. That is $T(x) = 0.99 * x + 0.01 * G(z)$ and x is a real image. Moreover,

Table 1. The settings of experimental datasets.

Name	Number of training image	Image size
LSUN	126,227	64 * 64
CelebA	202,599	64 * 64

Table 2. Baseline models.

Baseline model	Loss function
GANs [1]	BCE loss
GANs-JC [17]	BCE loss
GANs-CR [18]	BCE loss
WGAN-SN	Hinge loss
SAGANs [11]	Hinge loss
LSGANs [13]	LSGANs loss

WGAN-SN model adopts the framework of WGAN [12]. We add the SN constraint [16] to its generator and discriminator. Specifically, the baseline models are shown in Table 2.

Implementation. When we implement the GANs, GANs-JC, GANs-CR, WGAN-SN and LSGANs models, we employ basic network structure [3]. For the SAGANs model, we use the public code to train model [11]. Since the proposed method adds a decoder in the pseudo real module, we design a five-layer decoder, as shown in Table 3. In particular, to fairly compare the performance of all models, we train them all half a million times.

Evaluation Metrics. Firstly, in order to evaluate the stability of the proposed method in the GANs training process, we use the coefficient of variation (CV) [25] to measure the model. If the value of coefficient of variation is smaller, the GANs model is more stable. Secondly, in order to evaluate the quality of the generated images, we choose Frechet Inception Distance (FID) [19] to quantitatively analyze the performance of the model. If the value of FID is smaller, the generated image is closer to the real image at the feature level.

Specifically, to compute the coefficient of variation, we need to record the loss values of the discriminator and generator in the training process. In this paper, we record the loss value every 10 training steps. Then, we are able to calculate the mean (m) and standard deviation (S) of discriminator and generator loss values, respectively. Finally, we compute the CV [25] according to the following formula:

$$CV = \frac{S}{m} * 100\%. \tag{16}$$

Table 3. Basic network structure of decoder. In which, the "BN" and "SN" represent Batch Normalization and Spectral Normalization.

Decoder
ConvTranspose2d, BN(SN), ReLu
ConvTranspose2d, BN(SN), ReLu
ConvTranspose2d, BN(SN), ReLu
ConvTranspose2d, BN(SN), ReLu
ConvTranspose2d, Tanh

Furthermore, to compute the FID, we assume that the activations of real images and generated images are respectively $N(\mu_{real}, C_{real})$ and $N(\mu_{fake}, C_{fake})$. Then the FID [19] is given by:

$$FID = ||\mu_{real} - \mu_{fake}||^2 + Tr(C_{real} + C_{fake} - 2(C_{real} * C_{fake})^{1/2}), \quad (17)$$

where $[\mu_{real}, C_{real}]$ and $[\mu_{fake}, C_{fake}]$ are the mean and covariance of real images and generated images.

3.2   Parameter Selection

Since the proposed method adds an additional manual adjustment parameter α when synthesizing adversarial sample, we mainly discuss its selection here. The flow of parameter selection is as follows. We first set different values based on experience. Then, we judge whether the parameter is appropriate according to the coefficient of variation mentioned in the evaluation metrics. If the value of coefficient of variation is small, this setting is appropriate. Otherwise, we continue to repeat the experiment.

In particular, we select the GANs-CR model as testing model and choose the LSUN dataset as testing dataset. On the basis of the GANs-CR model, we add the pseudo real module to the GANs-CR model, and adopt double adversarial learning, which is recorded as GANs-CR-DAL. The experimental results of parameter selection are shown in Table 4. According to the experimental results, when $\alpha = 0.05$, the corresponding CV values of discriminator and generator are the smallest in the LSUN dataset, so we set $\alpha = 0.05$ for the LSUN dataset. Similarly, in the CelebA dataset, we set the same α value.

3.3   Experimental Results

Comparison Model Stability. In order to verify that double adversarial learning can stabilize the training process of exiting GANs models, we measure the performance of each model by the coefficient of variation.

The testing results of coefficient of variation are shown in Table 5. Compared with the GANs, GANs-CR, WGAN-SN, SAGANs and LSGANs models, our

Table 4. Results of parameter selection.

α	CV/Discriminator	CV/Generator
0.5	11.8489%	5.6601%
0.05	**0.8568%**	**5.6459%**
0.005	1.5060%	5.6620%

Table 5. The statistical results of coefficient of variation on LSUN and CelebA datasets.

Model	CV of D/LSUN	CV of G/LSUN	CV of D/CelebA	CV of G/CelebA
GANs	163.3980%	46.7639%	261.0661%	115.0887%
GANs-DAL	3.2490%	18.1081%	10.4636%	27.0361%
GANs-CR	149.7030%	7.5872%	27.3170%	7.7460%
GANs-CR-DAL	0.8568%	5.6459%	9.8402%	6.1650%
WGAN-SN	111.1594%	36.8428%	79.3350%	35.3127%
WGAN-SN-DAL	2.0769%	12.3719%	1.6919%	8.8965%
SAGANs	97.5319%	30.5657%	79.2351%	36.2593%
SAGANs-DAL	1.6939%	10.2432%	1.7781%	12.8960%
LSGANs	98.0059%	11.3318%	328.6026%	11.1030%
LSGANs-DAL	24.0592%	18.0994%	9.4394%	23.4612%

method obtains much smaller coefficient of variation. In particular, our method is very effective for the training of stability discriminator. In addition, our method can stabilize the training process of generator in different degrees. Except for the testing result of the LSGANs-DAL model in the LSUN dataset. Finally, the experimental results of the coefficient of variation demonstrate that the proposed method can stabilize the training process of discriminator and generator respectively. Therefore, our method can improve the stability of existing GANs models.

Comparison Generated Image. In order to compare the quality of images generated by each model, we use FID evaluation metric. Specially, to be fair, we select 64 generated images as testing images for every model.

Then, the results of FID testing are shown in Table 6. Compared with the GANs, GANs-JC, GANs-CR, WGAN-SN, SAGANs and LSGANs models, our method can obtain much smaller FID value. Except for GANs-JC model's experiment in the CelebA dataset. The results of FID testing show that our double adversarial learning method improves the performance of baseline models in different degrees. By comparing the FID of generated image, it can be seen that the image generated by our method is closer to the real image at the feature level.

Table 6. Results of FID testing. Among them, "T" stands for 10,000 training times.

Model	FID/LSUN	FID/CelebA
GANs	188.408	181.853
GANs-JC	189.372(6T)	163.922(6.5T)
GANs-DAL	179.649	166.917(2T)
GANs-CR	200.394	191.304
GANs-CR-DAL	199.025(1T)	161.336(5T)
WGAN-SN	192.454	175.214
WGAN-SN-DAL	186.973(2T)	158.472
SAGANs	181.196	175.362
SAGANs-DAL	178.556	160.391(26T)
LSGANs	185.529	174.504(2.5T)
LSGANs-DAL	185.143(2T)	157.822(2T)

4 Conclusion

In order to improve the training stability of existing GANs models' generators and discriminators, we propose a squeeze criterion GANs. It is a double adversarial learning method. In this method, we introduce the concept of adversarial sample. Then, a pseudo real module and double identity discriminator are designed. On the one hand, through an adversarial learning, the adversarial sample which is synthesized adaptively by the pseudo real module and the generated image form a kind of adversarial sample constraint. On the other hand, through another adversarial learning, the generated image and the real image form a real image constraint. The above double adversarial learning constraints constitute a squeeze criterion. It is used to stabilize the training process. Furthermore, it forces the generated image to learn from the adversarial sample in the first few training steps. The resulting images are then forced to learn from real samples. Finally, the experimental results show that the proposed method has well portability. It is able to stabilize the training process of generator and discriminator respectively, and improves the quality of the generated images.

References

1. Goodfellow, I., Pouget-Abadie, J., Mirza, M., et al.: Generative adversarial nets. In: Advances in Neural Information Processing Systems, pp. 2672–2680. MIT Press, Cambridge (2014)
2. Zhu, J.Y., Park, T., Isola, P., et al.: Unpaired image-to-image translation using cycle-consistent adversarial networks. In: Proceedings of the IEEE International Conference on Computer Vision, pp. 2223–2232. IEEE, Piscataway (2017)
3. Gan, Y., Liu, K., Ye, M., Zhang, Y., Qian, Y.: Generative adversarial networks with denoising penalty and sample augmentation. Neural Comput. Appl. **32**(14), 9995–10005 (2019). https://doi.org/10.1007/s00521-019-04526-w

4. Zhang, H., Xu, T., Li, H., et al.: StackGAN++: realistic image synthesis with stacked generative adversarial networks. IEEE Trans. Pattern Anal. Mach. Intell. **41**(8), 1947–1962 (2018)

5. Gan, Y., Liu, K., Ye, M., et al.: Sentence guided object color change by adversarial learning. Neurocomputing **377**, 113–121 (2020)

6. Wang, T.C., Liu, M.Y., Zhu, J.Y., et al.: Video-to-video synthesis. In: Advances in Neural Information Processing Systems, pp. 1144–1156. MIT Press, Cambridge (2018)

7. Li, Y., Pan, Q., Wang, S., et al.: A generative model for category text generation. Inf. Sci. **450**, 301–315 (2018)

8. Hong, Y., Hwang, U., Yoo, J., et al.: How generative adversarial networks and their variants work: an overview. ACM Comput. Surv. **52**(1), 1–43 (2019)

9. Radford, A., Metz, L., Chintala, S.: Unsupervised representation learning with deep convolutional generative adversarial networks. arXiv preprint arXiv:1511.06434 (2015)

10. Mirza, M., Osindero, S.: Conditional generative adversarial nets. arXiv preprint arXiv:1411.1784 (2014)

11. Zhang, H., Goodfellow, I., Metaxas, D., et al.: Self-attention generative adversarial networks. In: International Conference on Machine Learning, pp. 7354–7363. ACM, New York (2019)

12. Arjovsky, M., Chintala, S., Bottou, L.: Wasserstein generative adversarial networks. In: International Conference on Machine Learning, pp. 214–223. ACM, New York (2017)

13. Mao, X., Li, Q., Xie, H., et al.: On the effectiveness of least squares generative adversarial networks. IEEE Trans. Pattern Anal. Mach. Intell. **41**(12), 2947–2960 (2018)

14. Zhao, J., Mathieu, M., LeCun, Y.: Energy-based generative adversarial network. arXiv preprint arXiv:1609.03126 (2016)

15. Pan, X., Luo, P., Shi, J., Tang, X.: Two at once: enhancing learning and generalization capacities via IBN-net. In: Ferrari, V., Hebert, M., Sminchisescu, C., Weiss, Y. (eds.) ECCV 2018. LNCS, vol. 11208, pp. 484–500. Springer, Cham (2018). https://doi.org/10.1007/978-3-030-01225-0_29

16. Miyato, T., Kataoka, T., Koyama, M., et al.: Spectral normalization for generative adversarial networks. arXiv preprint arXiv:1802.05957 (2018)

17. Odena, A., Buckman, J., Olsson, C., et al.: Is generator conditioning causally related to GAN performance? In: International Conference on Machine Learning, pp. 3849–3858. ACM, New York (2018)

18. Zhang, H., Zhang, Z., Odena, A., et al.: Consistency regularization for generative adversarial networks. arXiv preprint arXiv:1910.12027 (2019)

19. Heusel, M., Ramsauer, H., Unterthiner, T., et al.: GANs trained by a two time-scale update rule converge to a local nash equilibrium. In: Advances in Neural Information Processing Systems, pp. 6626–6637. MIT Press, Cambridge (2017)

20. Brock, A., Donahue, J., Simonyan, K.: Large scale GAN training for high fidelity natural image synthesis. arXiv preprint arXiv:1809.11096 (2018)

21. Salimans, T., Goodfellow, I., Zaremba, W., et al.: Improved techniques for training GANs. In: Advances in Neural Information Processing Systems, pp. 2234–2242. MIT Press, Cambridge (2016)

22. Goodfellow, I.J., Shlens, J., Szegedy, C., et al.: Explaining and harnessing adversarial examples. arXiv preprint arXiv:1412.6572 (2014)

23. Yu, F., Seff, A., Zhang, Y., et al.: LSUN: construction of a large-scale image dataset using deep learning with humans in the loop. arXiv preprint arXiv:1506.03365 (2015)
24. Liu, Z., Luo, P., Wang, X., et al.: Deep learning face attributes in the wild. In: Proceedings of the IEEE International Conference on Computer Vision, pp. 3730–3738. IEEE, Piscataway (2015)
25. Abdi, H.: Coefficient of variation. Encycl. Res. Des. **1**, 169–171 (2010)

A Feature-Based Detection System of Adversarial Sample Attack

Fangwei Wang[1,2], Yuanyuan Lu[2], Qingru Li[1,2],
and Changguang Wang[1,2(✉)]

[1] Lab of Network and Information Security of Hebei Province,
Hebei Normal University, Shijiazhuang 050024, China
{fw_wang,wangcg}@hebtu.edu.cn, liqingru2006@163.com
[2] College of Computer and Cyber Security, Hebei Normal University,
Shijiazhuang 050024, China
1656326360@qq.com

Abstract. With the increase of malware, traditional malicious detection methods are not suitable to high-intensity detection work. In response to this question, many malware detection methods based on Machine Learning (ML-based) are proposed to address this problem. However, the ML-based detection method is vulnerable to the attack from adversarial samples. To overcome the limitation, we present our model. We protect the classification model from adversarial example attack by quantifying the similarity between the extracted image features and the expected features of the prediction class. Experimental results demonstrate that our model can detect the misclassification caused by adversarial samples with a higher accuracy than that of the Resnet-50.

Keywords: Malware detection · Adversarial samples · Feature extraction · Data visualization

1 Introduction

Malware is a program that deliberately implements an attacker's harmful intent, such as gaining unauthorized access, stealing useful information, disrupting normal operations and affecting computers adversely [1,2]. Data from Tencent mobile security lab showed that the number of new viruses added in the first quarter of 2017 increased by 21.42% year-on-year. The total number of viruses reached 4.65 million, a 33-fold increase than in 2014. Therefore, how to accurately detect different kinds of malwares, especially their variants, is a challenge nowadays.

In the field of malicious code classification and detection, there are currently two directions: static method and dynamic method. The static detection technology is simple to realize, but the detection technology with the static characteristics of the program is often disturbed by shell, deformation, variation and other technologies. It will increase the difficulty of reverse analysis and poor detection

© Springer Nature Switzerland AG 2020
X. Chen et al. (Eds.): ML4CS 2020, LNCS 12487, pp. 494–500, 2020.
https://doi.org/10.1007/978-3-030-62460-6_44

effect. Dynamic detection technology detects the behavior of malicious code by running it in the virtual machine environment and detects it by the behaviour characteristics of the runtime. The dynamic method has high accuracy, but the analysis process is complex. In recent years, machine learning methods have been used to detect malware, especially visualization techniques has been utilized in ML-based detection methods. The application of machine learning to the malware detection has greatly improved the detection efficiency.

Unfortunately, researches show that machine learning models are vulnerable to adversarial samples. An adversarial sample is a malicious input sample which is typically created by applying a small but intentional perturbation, such that the attacked model misclassifies it with high confidence [3]. The adversarial sample is designed to affect the classification results of the classifier. At present, the most effective method for solving adversarial attacks is adversarial training. However, there are still some problems need to be solved, such as single detection target and low detection accuracy. In this paper, owing to the shortcomings of existing methods, we propose a method to detect adversarial attacks by quantifying the similarity between the extracted image features and the expected features of the prediction class. The advantage of this approach is that it can be implemented on any visual malware detection method based on machine learning. Our model can effectively detect adversarial attacks.

The rest of this paper is organized as follows. Section 2 compares the proposal against related work. Section 3 presents the architectural design of our proposed model. Section 4 analyzes the experiment results. Section 5 concludes this paper.

2   Related Work

At present, the application of machine learning methods to the malware detection has received an increasing attention to more and more foreign and domestic scholars. Recurrent neural networks (RNNs) were the first choice for most deep learning based malware detection systems. RNN-based malware detection systems are practicable that machine instructions extracted from malware and sequential information contained in API calls are useful for detecting malware [4,5]. Convolutional neural networks (CNNs) are often used to classify images because they extract local hierarchical features from data samples, regardless of location [6,7]. However, we speculate that CNN may be a better candidate for malware detection compared to RNN. Adding duplicate API calls or computer instructions in the image space is a translation or distortion of the features that can be trained to recognize malware by the use of the CNNs. The gray-scal image is one of the most popular and effective methods of identifying malware. Nataraj et al. firstly proposed this method [8], in which the k-nearest neighbor (K-NN) method is used to classify malware images by computing Euclidean distance. Nataraj et al. used binary texture analysis based on images and dynamic analysis to compare and analyze the classification of malware [9]. The results show that this method is more accurate than dynamic analysis in malware classification. Recently, Kalash et al. [10] explored a deep learning approach, which converts malware binary files to gray-scale images and subsequently trains a CNN framework for further classification. In general, these ML-based visualization methods can achieve a higher accuracy. In addition, the ratio of true positive to false positive also indicates better robustness. The appearance of the adversarial sample brings a serious security threat to traditional ML-based detection.

Adversarial techniques have developed rapidly in recent years. Researchers have proposed several methods to detect adversarial sample attack. Training adversarial samples is one of the countermeasures to make neural networks more robust. Zhang et al. [11] and Huang et al. [12] injected adversarial samples into the model in the training stage, and the results showed that adversarial training improved the robustness of DNNs. However, when the attacker uses different attack strategies, the effect of adversarial training is not effective. Meng et al. introduced MagNet as an effective defense strategy. It was proved to be an effective defense against gray box attack, and was provided that the attacker knew all about the network and defense strategy [13]. Pouya et al. proposed Defense-GAN which is trained to simulate the distribution of unperturbed images [14]. The results showed that the system can defend against most attack, because it does not assume knowledge of generating adversarial samples. However, at present, there are still some problems such as low accuracy and unsatisfactory effect. Adversarial techniques in malware detectionis still worth researchers' further studying.

In this paper, the proposed method performs adversarial detection on the existing ML-based malware detection model. The existing ML-based malware detection model can guarantee the high precision, and our method can improve the precision of the adversarial detection on this basis.

3   Architectural Design of the Proposed Model

In this section, the proposed method is described in detail. Figure 1 shows the flow chart of our model. First, the model converts the dataset into a gray-scale image through data visualization. Next, the feature of the data sample is extracted. Meanwhile, the image samples are used for ML-based malware classification. We perform feature extraction on the classification results. Finally, we judge whether it is an adversarial sample or not by the similarity between the extracted image features and the expected features of the prediction class.

3.1   Data Visualization

Visualization technique collects binary files of malware which can be read as 8-bit unsigned integers and be visualized as gray-scale images [14,15]. The value is between 0 (black) and 255 (white). The specific steps are as follows:

Step 1: reading any hexadecimal malicious code file in the samples in binary form, every 8 bits as a basic unit.

Step 2: converting the binary sequence in the basic unit into an unsigned integer variable, and the range of the variable is in [0, 255], then the value is mapped to the gray-scale value of any pixel in the image.

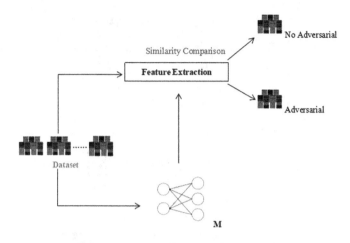

Fig. 1. Flow chart of the proposed model

Step 3: storing the gray-scale value corresponding to each pixel read into the new matrix according to a fixed width (128 bits in this paper). Repeating the above steps until all files are read. In order not to affect the final analysis result, if the content which the last read is less than 8 bits it is filled with 0.

Step 4: saving the matrix corresponding to the malicious file as an uncompressed PNG picture.

The entire process of dataset generation is showed in our experiment. In the following experiment part of Sect. 4, we will describe the process of generating adversarial samples. The dataset generation is shown in Fig. 2.

3.2 Feature Extraction

After the malware samples are converted into gray-scale image, it can be classified by image recognition technology. Image texture is the key component of image feature to extract the gray-scale image feature of malware. There are many kinds of texture feature extraction algorithms for a gray-scale image. The model adopts the GIST texture feature extraction algorithm.

GIST algorithm [8] was first used in the scene recognition field. Considering the characteristic of large amount of image data and distinct feature vectors of image texture in this experiment, the GIST algorithm is introduced to the feature extraction process of malicious code gray image. In order to reduce the complexity of analysis model, feature extraction and transformation, we use six characteristics to describe the subjective feelings of human beings towards images. They are coarseness, contrast, directionality, linelikeness, regularity and roughness.

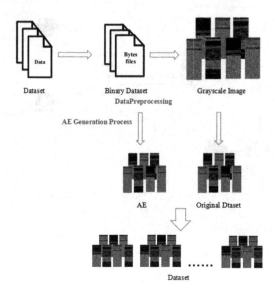

Fig. 2. Process of data generationl

3.3 Adversarial Sample Detection

The adversarial sample is designed to affect the classification results of the classifier. X represents the input sample and Y represents the classification result corresponding to the classification model of X. In this paper, the model extracts the original features and the post-classification features. The similarity distance between the features is calculated to determine whether the sample is an adversarial sample or not. In the following, we introduce the technical operations and algorithm for detecting malware in great detail, shown in Algorithm 1.

Algorithm 1. Pseudocode for the proposed algorithm

Input: Data X, ML-based model M, Feature extraction F
Output: Class Y, α

1: Result: $t \in \{-1,1\}$;
2: $F = GIST()$;
3: $f_1 = F(x)$;   // Extracted features;
4: $f_2 = F(y)$;   // Extracted features;
5: Detection: $d = cossim(f_1, f_2)$;
6: If $d < \alpha$: $t = 1$;
7:      else: $t = -1$;
8: If $t = -1$: $y = x$;
9: Store the feature vectors of adversarial images (y) into a feature set and input it
   to the classifier.

---

4   Experiment Results and Analysis

4.1   Datasets

The proposed model is evaluated with 1000 samples. It includes malicious samples, adversarial samples and benign samples. Malicious samples are randomly selected from Kaggle Microsoft Malware Classification Challenge (BIG 2015) [16]. The adversarial samples are generated by the FGSM [11] algorithm, which is described in the following.

Given an image x and its corresponding true label y, the FGSM attack sets the perturbation δ to:

$$\delta = \varepsilon \times sign(\nabla x J(x,y)),$$

where ε represents the distortion between adversarial samples and original samples. $sign(\Delta)$ denotes the sign function, $\nabla x J(x,y)$ calculate the gradient of the cost function J around the current value x of the model parameters θ.

In our model, we choose Resnet-50 as the ML-based model. The experimental environment is set up on Windows operating system. The performance of the classification models is evaluated using accuracy. Table 1 shows the classification results of different models.

Table 1. Classification results of the different models

Setup	No adversarial sample		Adversarial sample (FSGM)	
Model	Resnet-50	Our model	Resnet-50	Our model
Accuracy	85.5%	80.2%	34.2%	70.5%

5   Conclusion

In this paper, based on the existing machine learning model, we proposed a method to detect and defend adversarial sample attacks by quantifying the similarity between the extracted image features and the expected features of the prediction class. We trained our model in different scenarios and compared it with other models. Extensive evaluation shows that our model can protect the host with our detection model from adversarial sample attacks. However, the accuracy of our experimental results is not very high.

In the future, we will try to train our model with more datasets. The advantage of our method is that it can be implemented on any visual malware detection method based on machine learning. Next, we will try to experiment our method on more classification models.

Acknowledgments. This work was supported by the National Natural Science Foundation of China under Grants No. 61572170 and 61672206, Program for Hundreds of Outstanding Innovative Talents in Higher Education Institutions of Hebei Province (III) under Grant No. SLRC2017042, and Natural Science Foundation of Hebei Province of China under Grant No. F2019205163, and department of Human Resoueces and Social Security of Hebei Province under Grant No. 201901028.

References

1. Bayer, U., Moser, A., Kruegel, C., Kirda, E.: Dynamic analysis of malicious code. J. Comput. Virol. **2**(1), 67–77 (2006)
2. Gandotra, E., Bansal, D., Sofat, S.: Malware analysis and classiffication: a survey. J. Inf. Secur. **5**(2), 56–64 (2014)
3. IGoodfellow, I., Shlens, J., Szegedy, C.: Explaining and harnessing adversarial samples. arXiv preprint arXiv:1412.6572 (2015)
4. Rhode, M., Burnap, P., Jones, K.: Early stage malware prediction using recurrent neural networks. Comput. Secur. **77**(8), 578–594 (2018)
5. HaddadPajouh, H., Dehghantanha, A., Khayami, R., Choo, K.K.R.: A deep recurrent neural network based approach for Internet of things malware threat hunting. Future Genera. Comput. Syst. **5**(1), 88–96 (2018). https://doi.org/10.1016/j.future.2018.03.007
6. Wang, W., Zhao, M., Wang, J.: Effective android malware detection with a hybrid model based on deep autoencoder and convolutional neural network. J. Ambient Intell. Humanized Comput. **10**(8), 3035–3043 (2018). https://doi.org/10.1007/s12652-018-0803-6
7. Vasan, D., Alazab, M., Wassan, S., Naeem, H., Safaei, B., Zheng, Q.: IMCFN: image-based malware classification using fine-tuned convolutional neural network architecture. Comput. Netw. **171**(4), 107138 (2020). https://doi.org/10.1016/j.comnet.2020.107138
8. Nataraj, L., Karthikeyan, S., Jacob, G., Manjunath, B.S.: Malware images: visualization and automatic classiffication. In: Proceedings of the 8th International Symposium on Visualization for Cyber Security, New York, NY, USA, pp. 1–7. ACM (2011)
9. Nataraj, L., Yegneswaran, V., Porras, P., Zhang, J.: A comparative assessment of malware classiffication using binary texture analysis and dynamic analysis. In: Proceedings of the 4th ACM Workshop on Security and Artificial Intelligence, New York, NY, USA, pp. 21–30. ACM (2011)
10. Kalash, M., Rochan, M., Mohammed, N., Bruce, N.D.B., Wang, Y., Iqbal, F.: Malware classification with deep convolutional neural networks. In: 2018 9th IFIP International Conference on New Technologies, Mobility and Security (NTMS), pp. 1–5 IEEE (2018)
11. Zhang, C., Yang, X., Tang, Y., Zhang, W.: Learning to generate radar image sequences using two-stage generative adversarial networks. IEEE Geoence Remote Sens. Lett. **17**(3), 401–405 (2020)
12. Huang, R., Xu, B., Schuurmans, D., Szepesvári, C.: Learning with a strong adversary. arXiv preprint arXiv:1511.03034 (2015)
13. Meng, D., Chen, H.: MagNet: a two-pronged defense against adversarial samples. [Online]. Available: https://arxiv.org/abs/1705.09064. (2017)
14. Parmuval, P., Hasan, M., Patel, S.: Malware family detection approach using image processing techniques: Visualization technique. Int. J. Comput. Appl. Technol. Res. **7**(20), 129–132 (2018). https://doi.org/10.7753/IJCATR0703.1004
15. Liu, X., Zhang, J., Lin, Y., Li, H.: ATMPA: attacking machine learningbased malware visualization detection methods via adversarial examples. In: Proceedings of the International Symposium on Quality of Service (IWQoS 2019), Phoenix, AZ, USA, pp. 1–38. IEEE (2019)
16. Wang, L., Liu, J., Chen, X.: Microsoft malware classification challenge. [Online]. Available: https://arxiv.org/abs/1802.10135v1 (2018)

GF-Attack: A Strategy to Improve the Performance of Adversarial Example

Jintao Zhang[1,2], Zhenghao Liu[1,2], Liren Wu[1,2], Liwen Wu[1,2], Qing Duan[1,2,3(✉)], and Junhui Liu[1,2,3(✉)]

[1] Engineering Research Center of Cross-border Network Security, Ministry of Education, Kunming, China
{qduan,hanks}@ynu.edu.cn
[2] National Pilot school of software, Yunnan University, Kunming, China
[3] Key Laboratory in Software Engineering of Yunnan Province, Kunming, China

Abstract. As CNN's powerful visual processing function is widely recognized, its security has attracted people's attention. A large number of experiments prove that CNN is extremely vulnerable to adversarial attack. Existing attack methods have better performance in white-box attack, but in actual situations, attackers can usually only perform black-box attack. The success rate of black-box attack methods is relatively low. At the same time, the most attack methods will attack all pixels of the image, which will cause too much interference in the adversarial example. To this end, we propose an enhanced attack strategy GF-Attack. We recommend distinguishing between the attack area and the non-attack area and combining the information of the flipped image during the attack. This strategy can improve the transferability of the generated adversarial examples and reduce the amount of interference. We conducted single model and ensemble models attack on eight models, including normal training and adversarial training. We compared the success rate and distance of the adversarial examples generated by the enhanced method using the GF-Attack strategy and the original method. Experiments show that the improved method by GF-Attack is superior to the original method in the black-box setting and white-box setting. Increased maximum success rate **9.13%**, reduced pixel interference **404K**.

Keywords: Adversarial attack · Adversarial example · Flip image · Grad-Cam · Transferability

1 Introduction

Recently, deep learning has made a significant contribution to autonomous vehicles [1,4], surveillance [22], malicious code detection [2], as well as drones [25] et al. While an common challenge naturally risen, that is how to reduce the potential security risk of deep learning models. To illustrate the risks and threats

X. Chen et al. (Eds.): ML4CS 2020, LNCS 12487, pp. 501–513, 2020.
https://doi.org/10.1007/978-3-030-62460-6_45

related to deep learning models, we first review a practical scenario: if the learning mode is unable to correctly identify obstacles or other vehicles after being adversarial attack, the autonomous vehicle may have an accident; If someone attacks the model of the facial payment system, which will make the model make a wrong judgment, the user may suffer losses. A large mount of senarios illustrated that it is great importance of enhancing security of deep learning model. Therefore, there has been a host of works on the security of deep learning models. Among the variety of research threads, adversarial attack [24] is one of the main methods to affect the safety of learned models. Adversarial attack aims at making the model makes the wrong decision by the use of small noise disturbances. By modeling the attacking and defencing process, more robust deep learning models are obtained. Adversarial attack can be divided into black-box attack and white-box attack. The difference lies in whether the attacker knows a priority knowledge about deep learning models, such as deep neural network structure, parameters, and hyperparameters, training samples, learning results of a given sample, etc.

After knowing the structure and parameters of a given learned model, the white-box attack can always generate adversarial examples to abuse the learned model. For instance, FGSM (Fast Gradient Sign Method) [6] generates example by once gradient ascent; Iterative fast gradient sign method I-FGSM (Iterative FGSM) [8] fools the learning model by using multiple gradient ascents. However, the knowledge of structure and parameters of a learned model is a strong pre-condition that limited the application scenario of white-box attack. Hence, to settle the limitation, the black-box attack comes into sight. Different from white-box attack, black-box attack emphasizes the transferability of adversarial examples between different learning model [10,13]. For instance, an adversarial example misclassified by $VGG16$ must also be misclassified on $Inception-v1$. The current attack algorithm has a problem of poor transferability, and all pixels of the sample must be modified to achieve the attack. The latter leads to the enormous difference between the original samples and adversarial examples. For this problem, PS-MIFGSM [23] only attacks the areas that the model considers necessary, adopting this method can indeed reduce the amount of modification to adversarial examples, but this also leads to the problem of low transferability of adversarial examples.

To put an end to poor transferability of attack algorithms, in this paper, we visualized the attention areas of different models and found that the attention areas of different models are different. Therefore, applying the PS-MIFGSM method to limit the attack area, although the amount of modification in the adversarial examples reduce, this also results in a significant decline in transferability. To solve this problem, we fuse the gradient information of the flipped image on the attack area. Compared with PS-MIFGSM, our propose GF-Attack can combine with different attack methods. The initial results of these methods are shown in Fig. 1.

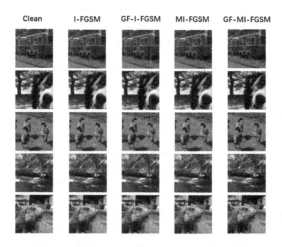

Fig. 1. Adversarial examples generated by different attack methods. In contrast, we found that I-FGSM and GF-I-FGSM have few image changes, but the success rate of white-box attack is low. A lot of changes have been made to MI-FGSM and GF-MI-FGSM. Observation shows that, due to the limitation of the attack area, GF-I-FGSM and GF-MI-FGSM are mainly committed to attacking the area that identifies the main body of the target object.

The original contributions of this paper as follows:

– We propose a novel attack enhancement strategy called GF-Attack. It enhances the conventional method by attacking a specific area by combining the gradient of the flipped image. Applying this strategy can improve the transferability of the generated adversarial examples and reduce the amount of modification.
– We experimentally evaluated the success rate of the attack under the ImageNet dataset and the amount of modification in the adversarial examples generated compared to the original image. The results show that the adversarial examples generated by the enhanced method of GF-Attack strategy are superior to the original method in terms of transferability and amount of modification.

The remainder of this paper organized as follows: In Sect. 2 reviews the work related to adversarial attacks. In Sect. 3, we explore the reasons for the low transferability of adversarial examples and propose corresponding enhancement algorithms based on two existing algorithms. In Sect. 4, we show the experimental effect. Section 5 discussed how to employ the GF-Attack strategy in different situations.

2 Related Work

Despite the performance of deep neural networks in many research and application fields is well, Szegedy et al. [21] first pointed out that there are security holes in neural networks in 2014. By making a small disturbance on a picture, the picture can be the high confidence is misclassified by the learning model, and even the image can be classified into a specified label. Since then, the research about adversarial attacks has flourished. GoodFellow et al. [6] argued in 2015 that the root cause of adversarial attacks is the linear nature of deep neural networks in high-dimensional space, rather than the complexity of neural networks previously suspected. At the same time, on the premise of this hypothesis, an efficient algorithm for generating adversarial example fast gradient descent method FGSM was proposed. Its experimental results show that a classifier with good test results cannot learn the true meaning of the classified samples, but can only construct a model. When it encounters some unlikely points in the space, it will expose the limitations of the model function. So, when deep neural networks are used in applications that require extremely high in the field of security, adversarial examples will definitely bring huge security risks. Since then, Madry et al. [11] proposed an improved I-FGSM algorithm in 2017 and added multiple iterative attacks on the basis of the FGSM algorithm, and the effect is more significant. Dong et al. [3] proposed the MI-FGSM attack in 2018, the momentum factor is added on the basis of the iterative attack to strengthen the attack effect. Although the above attack methods have achieved excellent results, however, the disturbances cover the whole image, which will increase the difference between the adversarial example and the real sample. Su et al. [18] proposed an extreme counter-attack method in 2017, using a differential evolution algorithm to iteratively modify each pixel to generate an adversarial sample, and compare it with the real example, according to specific criteria, choose to retain the best attack effect of the adversarial samples to achieve adversarial attacks. This kind of adversarial attack does not need to know any information on network parameters or gradients, and it can be made by changing the only one-pixel value in the image.

On the other hand, CNN was first proposed by Lecun et al. [9] and made breakthrough progress in the application of handwritten digit recognition. Later it was widely used in image recognition [5], speech detection [19], bioinformatics [14,17] and many other fields. Since CNN will directly affect the pixel value of the image in the processing process, it can extract broader, deeper, and more characteristic feature information. R. Selvaraju et al. [15] proposed a method that Grad-Cam directly finds the areas in the image that contribute most to the classification. Because the convolutional layer contains rich semantic information, and this semantic information will be incomprehensible to humans after being pooled. Therefore, Grad-cam uses the feature map of the last convolutional layer for visualization before merging to explain which region of the image the CNN made the corresponding prediction. The above researches show that the deep neural network model does not mean that the amount of information obtained for the entire image is equal during the processing of image information, and it pays more attention to certain specific areas.

Inspired by I-FGSM, MI-FGSM, Grad-Cam, and PS-MIFGSM, this paper proposes an adversarial attack enhancement strategy named GF-Attack that can works with the gradient-based attack algorithm to eectively reduce the amount of modication of adversarial examples as well as enhance the transferability. Our work in this paper is as follows: **1)** We propose the GF-Attack strategy to distinguish the attack and non-attack areas through Grad-Cam and combine the gradient of the flipped image during the attack. **2)** The GF-Attack strategy is combined with I-FGSM and MI-FGSM, respectively, to enhance the attack effect. **3)** In the experimental part, the improved algorithms GF-I-FGSM and GF-MI-FGSM based on GF-Attack were used to attack the images in the subset of ImageNet dataset. We compare the results with the adversarial examples generated by the original algorithm to get the success rate and the amount of modification of the adversarial examples. **4)** Give recommendations for employing the GF-Attack strategy in different situations.

3 Method

This section will introduce the GF-Attack strategy mentioned above in detail. As an attack enhancement strategy, GF-attack can combine with other attack methods. First, the Grad-Cam to obtain the attack area and the non-attack area. Next, the attack method applies to acquire interference information. It is worth noting that the gradient of the flipped image needs to be fused. Finally, the interference information is used to the image and then restore the non-attack area.

We give the targets of adversarial attacks, let the output of the DNN before the softmax layer as $z(x)$, then the output of the network can be expressed as:

$$y(x) = Softmax(z(x)) \tag{1}$$

y^{real} denote the label of input x, then the purpose of the adversarial attack is to find a Δx such that:

$$\underset{||\Delta x||_p}{arg\min}(x + \Delta x) \neq y^{real} \tag{2}$$

Where $||\cdot||_p$ presents the L_p norm of the vector. It is usually computationally impossible to solve this formula accurately, so the author of FGSM proposed a fast gradient sign method [6], which can convert into the following optimization problem:

$$\underset{x^{adv}}{arg\max} L\left(x^{adv}, y^{real}\right)$$
$$s.t. ||x - x_{adv}||_p \leq \varepsilon \tag{3}$$

x_{adv} represents the generated adversarial examples, ϵ limits the perturbation size, i.e.:

$$x_{adv} = x + \Delta x \tag{4}$$

y^{real} signify as one-hot encoding in the network, and $L(\cdot)$ represents the loss of the network, usually using logits layer $z(x)$ cross-entropy loss to generate adversarial examples.

Next, we will introduce several different adversarial attacks, analyze their shortcomings, and apply the GF-Attack strategy to enhance.

3.1 Fast Gradient Sign Methods and Its Derivatives

Fast Gradient Sign Method (FGSM): FGSM [6] is a One-step attack method, which uses the gradient of the loss function $\nabla_x L\left(x, y^{real}\right)$ in the input image for gradient ascent. The update equation is:

$$x^{adv} = x + \varepsilon \cdot sign(\nabla_x L\left(x, y^{real}\right)) \tag{5}$$

Iterative Fast Gradient Sign Method (I-FGSM): I-FGSM [8] expands based on FGSM, converts it from One-step to Iter-step attack, the process can be expressed as follow:

$$x_t^{adv} = x_{t-1}^{adv} + \alpha \cdot sign(\nabla_x L(x_{t-1}^{adv}, y^{real})) \tag{6}$$

In Iter-step, to satisfy the constraints in Eq. 3, using the clip method to limit the amount of disturbance in adversarial examples, or setting α as ε/T, where T represents the number of iterations.

Comparing the above two attack methods, the adversarial example produced by the One-step attack has a higher transferability, but the success rate of the white-box attack is shallow. In contrast, Iter-step performs better in white-box attacks, but the generated adversarial examples have lower transitivity and are not suitable for black-box attacks. Furthermore, this problem is caused by over-fitting occurred during the iteration process.

Momentum Iterative Fast Gradient Sign Method (MI-FGSM) [3]: It recommends to increase the momentum factor based on I-FGSM, not fall into the optimal local state, and stabilize the attack direction. Compared with the above attacks, MI-FGSM has better performance in black-box attack and white-box attack. The MI-FGSM process is as follow:

$$g_t = \mu \cdot g_{t-1} + \frac{\nabla_x L(x_{t-1}^{adv}, y^{real})}{||\nabla_x L(x_{t-1}^{adv}, y^{real})||_1} \tag{7}$$

$$x_t^{adv} = x_{t-1}^{adv} + \alpha \cdot sign(g_{t-1})$$

When the number of iterations $T = 1$, MI-FGSM is converted to FGSM, it is worth mentioning that the above methods are an attack on all pixels of the pictures. It will lead to a more substantial L_2 norm between the adversarial example and the original image, and make the visual change of the adversarial examples more obvious.

3.2 Grad-Cam

Grad-Cam is a method proposed by Ramprasaath R. Selvaraju [15] to solve the interpretability problem of CNN in 2017. It uses the last convolutional layer in the CNN to obtain the feature activation map because the last convolutional layer contains the richest classification information and is also the easiest to visualize on CNN. First, using the category output to distinguish the last convolutional layer to obtain $\partial y^{real}/\partial A_{ij}^{k}$ where y^{real} is the classification result A_{ij}^{k} is the value of the I, j position of the k-th feature map. Then calculating the weight a_k^{real} by Eq. 8.

$$a_k^{real} = \frac{1}{Z}\sum_i \sum_j \frac{\partial y^{real}}{\partial A_{ij}^k} \tag{8}$$

Where Z is the size of the feature map, it is then obtaining the visualization result of Grad-Cam through formula Eq. 9 and the calculated weight information is the critical area in the feature map that determines the classification result. The Relu function is used to remove the influence of negative values, and we only focus on the weight of positive values in the feature map on the classification results.

$$W_{Grad-Cam}^{real} = Relu(\sum_k a_k^{real} A^k) \tag{9}$$

3.3 Transferability of Adversarial Examples

Although Iter-step attacks can achieve better performance in white-box, in terms of transportability, which is needed to improve for the generated adversarial examples. Figure 2 shows the results of Grad-Cam visualization of the same picture using different models. It can found that different models have different attention areas for images, and the transferability of adversarial examples is highly related to the gradient of the white-box model. Therefore, different models have different areas of concern, which is one of the reasons for the lack of transferability of adversarial examples.

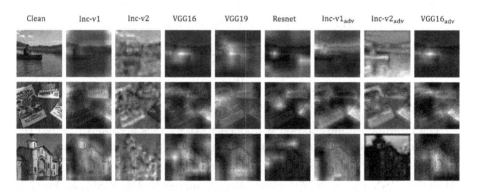

Fig. 2. Using Grad-Cam to visualize the results of different models. The model with adv in the subscript indicates adversarial training. From the figure, we can see that the attention areas of different models are very different, especially the model after adversarial training is quite different from the usual training model.

3.4 GF-Attack Strategy

To solve the problems of significant sample variation and poor transferability mentioned in Sects. 3.2 and 3.3, we proposed the GF-Attack strategy. This strategy can be used in combination with any process that uses gradients to attack. It not only effectively reduces the L_2 norm between the adversarial example and the original input but also improves the transferability of the generated adversarial examples by combining the gradient information of the flipped image to attack the critical areas of the model.

The basic process of GF-Attack is as flow: **1.** With the result generated by Grad-Cam, the sample can be divided into attack area and non-attack area; **2.** Finding the original image $\nabla_x L(x, y^{real})$ and flip image $\nabla_{x^{flip}} L(x^{flip}, y^{real})$ loss gradient perform weighted fusion to obtain interference information; **3.** According to the attack area and non-attack area, applying the interference information to the attack area, the non-attack area remains unchanged, and finally obtaining the adversarial samples. The following will introduce the enhanced attack method generated by combining the GF-Attack strategy with the two currently commonly used methods.

First, employing Eq. 10 to distinguish the attack area of the sample:

$$A_{ij}^* = W_{Grad-Cam}^{real}[q] \tag{10}$$

$W_{Grad-cam}^{real}$ is the weight value of the trajectory output by Grad-Cam. The first q sites are selected as the attack area, after sorting in descending order, and the remaining regions are non-attack areas.

GF-I-FGSM: This method is an improvement to I-FGSM. Based on Eq. 6, the gradient information of the flipped image is added, and Eq. 10 is used to calculate the attack area to attack the specific area.

$$g = \beta \cdot \nabla_x L(x_{t-1}^{adv}, y^{real}) + (1 - \beta) \cdot \nabla_{x^{flip}} L(x_{t-1}^{adv-flip}, y^{real}) \tag{11}$$

$$x_t^{adv} = x_{t-1}^{adv} + \alpha \cdot sign(g) \tag{12}$$

$$A_{ij}^{ori} = 0, ij \in A_{ij}^* \tag{13}$$

$$x_t^{adv} = A_{ij}^{ori} + x_t^{adv} \tag{14}$$

The interference information is applied to the attack area and restored the non-attack area to the corresponding region in the original image by using Eq. 13 and Eq. 14.

GF-MI-FGSM: The GF-Attack strategy is added to MI-FGSM, so Eq. 7 is converted to:

$$g = \beta \cdot \frac{\nabla x L(x_{t-1}^{adv}, y^{real})}{||\nabla x L(x_{t-1}^{adv}, y^{real})||_1} + (1 - \beta) \cdot \frac{\nabla x L(x_{t-1}^{adv-flip}, y^{real})}{||\nabla x L(x_{t-1}^{adv-flip}, y^{real})||_1} \tag{15}$$

$$g_t = g + g_{t-1} \tag{16}$$

$$x_t^{adv} = x_{t-1}^{adv} + \alpha \cdot sign(g_t) \tag{17}$$

When an adversarial example combined with flip gradient information obtain, the same processing as Eq. 13 and Eq. 14 in GF-I-FGSM is performed to distinguish the attack area from the non-attack area.

4   Experiment and Discussion

4.1   Experimental Preparation

Dataset: We selected 1216 images from ImageNet as the dataset, and the size of all pictures is preset to $3 \times 224 \times 224$.

Network: Eight models including the normal training model and the adversarial training model are used to the next experiment. The normal training model is as follow: $VGG16$ [16], $VGG19$ [16], $Inception-v1$ [20], $Inception-v2$ [20], $Resnet-v1-50$ [7]; The adversarial training model is as follow: $Inception-v1_{adv}$, $Incpetion-v2_{adv}$, $VGG16_{adv}$. Adversarial training uses a training method that incorporates adversarial examples [12].

Assessment Criteria: In adversarial attacks, success rate and the paradigm distance between the adversarial example and the original sample are used to evaluate the performance of the attack method. In this article, we use Eq. 18 to calculate the amount of change. This means that if the attack is successful, the single adversarial sample will calculate the L_2 average distance from the single pixel of the original sample; otherwise, it will be set to 64. The entire final distance is regarded as the average distance of 1,216 adversarial examples.

$$Distance(x^{adv}) = \begin{cases} 64, & y^{adv} = y^{real} \\ ||x^{adv} - x||_2, & y^{adv} \neq y^{real} \end{cases} \tag{18}$$

4.2   Single Model Attack

First, the proposed GF-Attack strategy is employed in a single-model attack, applying one of the models as a white model, and calculating the success rate and the distance mentioned in the previous section on the eight models. The results are shown in Table 1. The first column is the attacked white-box model, and the first row is the model used to test the adversarial examples. When the row and column models are the same, it is expressed as a white-box attack. Otherwise, it is a black-box attack.

As can be seen from Table 1 (the first column represents the model used for the white-box attack, the first row represents the different test models), adding GF-Attack to different methods compared to the original method significantly improves the success rate and the transferability of adversarial examples. GF-MI-FGSM is the most powerful of all arrangements. Taking the normal trained $Resnet-v1-50$ as a white-box model, $inc-v2$ as the black-box model to test the

Table 1. Success rate of black-box and white-box using different methods (single model)

Model	Function	inc_{v1}	inc_{v2}	res_{v1}	vgg_{16}	vgg_{19}	$inc_{v1_{adv}}$	$inc_{v2_{adv}}$	$vgg_{16_{adv}}$
inc_{v1}	I-FGSM	99.92%	25.58%	19.24%	12.09%	14.23%	0.00%	0.00%	5.43%
	GF-I-FGSM	99.92%	**27.80%**	19.24%	**15.79%**	**15.05%**	0.00%	0.00%	**6.41%**
	MI-FGSM	99.92%	65.38%	64.64%	51.32%	50.82%	1.23%	0.33%	26.89%
	GF-MI-FGSM	99.92%	**70.64%**	63.08%	**55.76%**	**53.04%**	**1.40%**	0.33%	**28.78%**
inc_{v2}	I-FGSM	17.60%	**99.75%**	6.00%	3.13%	6.33%	0.00%	0.00%	3.13%
	GF-I-FGSM	**20.07%**	99.42%	**7.15%**	**3.45%**	**7.40%**	0.00%	0.00%	**3.45%**
	MI-FGSM	53.54%	**99.84%**	34.87%	21.05%	37.17%	0.66%	0.58%	21.05%
	GF-MI-FGSM	**56.09%**	99.75%	**39.80%**	**22.20%**	**41.28%**	**1.07%**	**0.90%**	**22.20%**
res_{v1}	I-FGSM	29.77%	20.07%	100.00%	20.81%	19.57%	0.08%	0.00%	9.70%
	GF-I-FGSM	**34.54%**	**22.70%**	100.00%	**23.36%**	**20.89%**	0.08%	0.00%	**10.28%**
	MI-FGSM	73.19%	61.92%	100.00%	64.80%	62.09%	1.23%	**0.82%**	38.16%
	GF-MI-FGSM	**75.90%**	**67.76%**	100.00%	**67.85%**	**65.46%**	**1.32%**	0.74%	**40.13%**
$inc_{v2_{adv}}$	I-FGSM	2.22%	1.56%	0.58%	0.74%	0.99%	3.54%	99.59%	1.07%
	GF-I-FGSM	**2.80%**	**1.81%**	**0.66%**	**0.82%**	**1.15%**	**4.77%**	99.59%	**1.56%**
	MI-FGSM	5.51%	6.09%	3.78%	4.28%	3.37%	22.37%	100.00%	4.61%
	GF-MI-FGSM	**6.17%**	**7.73%**	**4.61%**	**5.10%**	**3.54%**	**31.50%**	100.00%	**6.25%**

success rate, the adversarial examples generated by GF-MI-FGSM have a 67.76% success rate, 61.92% for MI-FGSM, and only 20.07% using I-FGSM. When the adversarial training model $inc\text{-}v1_{adv}$ is used as a black-box model, the success rate of attacks using GF-MI-FGSM is 31.50%, while the values of MI-FGSM and I-FGSM are respectively 22.37% and 3.54%. Those results strongly suggest that the GF-Attack strategy can significantly improve the transferability of adversarial examples. We also found that the adversarial examples generated using the adversarial training model as a white-box attack have a higher success rate on the model, but the transferability is usually lower, such as $Inc\text{-}v2_{adv}$ is selected as the white-box model in the adversarial examples generated, all methods on the model reached more than 99%. Still, for other models, especially the ordinary training model, the attack success rate is often less than 8%. The reason for this phenomenon may be that although the structure of the model for adversarial training has not changed, the focus area of the model has changed (see Fig. 2).

Next, we adopt the formula mentioned in 4.1 to calculate the distance of the adversarial example generated under the experimental settings in Table 1. The results are shown in Table 2. The normal training model is used as a white-box model to attack the maximum reduction value of 2.69, which indicate that the sum of the reduced L_2 norm in the $3 \times 224 \times 224$ image by the GF-Attack strategy is 404920.32, which proves that our approach can effectively reduce the amount of modification in the sample. The adversarial training model is used as a white-box model for attacking, by attacking $Inc\text{-}v2_{adv}$ and using $Inc\text{-}v1_{adv}$ as a test model, the disturbance quantity can be reduced by 4.3. It can be seen that when the attack success rate is the same but not 0, the improved GF-Attack algorithm is superior to the original attack algorithm in the amount of modification and most aspects by combining Table 1 and Table 2. These data illustrate that the success rate of adversarial examples produced by the improved algorithm increases, and the amount of modification decreases. In the attack with $Inc-v2$ as the white-box, we can also observe that although the attack success rate is slightly lower than the original algorithm, the adversarial example changes little compared to the original image, which further shows that GF-Attack has a significant effect.

Table 2. Distance of black-box and white-box using different methods (single model)

Model	Function	inc_{v1}	inc_{v2}	res_{v1}	vgg_{16}	vgg_{19}	$inc_{v1_{adv}}$	$inc_{v2_{adv}}$	$vgg_{16_{adv}}$
inc_{v1}	I-FGSM	12.34	50.62	53.82	57.62	56.50	64	64	61.13
	GF-I-FGSM	12.08	49.37	53.77	55.64	56.02	64	64	60.61
	MI-FGSM	16.46	32.72	32.96	39.37	39.61	63.42	63.84	51.10
	GF-MI-FGSM	16.53	30.28	33.76	37.29	38.62	63.35	63.84	50.19
inc_{v2}	I-FGSM	54.85	12.61	60.32	60.86	60.68	64	64	62.36
	GF-I-FGSM	53.55	12.51	60.43	60.23	60.10	64	64	62.19
	MI-FGSM	38.69	17.04	46.90	47.44	46.38	63.7	63.72	54.02
	GF-MI-FGSM	37.53	17.13	45.22	45.18	44.47	63.5	63.57	53.51
res_{v1}	I-FGSM	48.43	53.49	12.34	53.08	53.7	63.95	64	58.9
	GF-I-FGSM	45.91	52.09	12.10	51.69	52.97	63.95	64	58.59
	MI-FGSM	29.03	34.35	16.44	32.96	34.29	63.41	63.60	45.74
	GF-MI-FGSM	27.74	31.57	16.43	31.58	32.72	63.38	63.64	44.84
$inc_{v2_{adv}}$	I-FGSM	62.86	63.2	63.71	63.62	63.49	62.20	12.54	63.44
	GF-I-FGSM	62.55	63.06	63.66	63.57	63.40	61.52	12.44	63.18
	MI-FGSM	61.31	61.03	62.13	61.91	62.35	53.15	15.69	61.75
	GF-MI-FGSM	61.01	60.25	61.76	61.53	62.28	48.85	16.01	60.97

4.3 Ensemble Models Attack

The experimental results of a single model attack show that GF-Attack can effectively improve the transferability of adversarial examples and optimize the amount of modification, but the attack success rate is relatively low in the black-box attack. To further verify the reliability of GF-Attack, we use the ensemble attack strategy to test. The ensemble attack is caused by Y. Liu [10], a proposed method that can simultaneously attack multiple networks, achieves the effect of improving the transferability of adversarial examples by fusing the gradient information of numerous different networks. We use the hold-out method to select one model at a time as the retention model, and the other models are employed for ensemble attacks with a weight of 1/7. Comparing the success rate and distance of the original method with the GF-Attack strategy improved process, and the result can be found in Table 3.

In Table 3, the first line indicates that each hold-out model is defined as a black-box model. We can see that the success rate of black-box attacks has been dramatically improved after using the ensemble strategy, especially in the standard training model. At the same time, in terms of success rate and change between adversarial example and the original sample, the adversarial examples generated using GF-MI-FGSM are usually better than other methods. Still, if the model of retained is an adversarial training model, the effect of adding GF-Attack will slightly decrease. It is because the attack area is limited with the addition of the Grad-cam area, and the adversarial training model is significantly different from the standard training model. This problem can be improved by adjusting the parameter q in Eq. 10.

Table 3. Comparison of success rate and distance of ensemble attacks

Model	Function	inc_{v1}	inc_{v2}	res_{v1}	vgg_{16}	vgg_{19}	$inc_{v1_{adv}}$	$inc_{v2_{adv}}$	$vgg_{16_{adv}}$
Hold-out	I-FGSM	77.06%	70.64%	72.37%	97.53%	93.59%	0.33%	0.00%	**86.76%**
	GF-I-FGSM	**82.15%**	**77.63%**	**75.08%**	**97.70%**	**94.74%**	0.33%	0.00%	85.69%
(success rates)	MI-FGSM	90.63%	90.05%	87.66%	98.44%	**98.11%**	5.35%	**2.38%**	**88.32%**
	GF-MI-FGSM	**91.86%**	**90.46%**	**88.57%**	**98.60%**	98.11%	5.35%	1.89%	88.08%
Hold-out	I-FGSM	24.53	27.80	26.91	14.15	16.14	63.84	64	**19.7**
	GF-I-FGSM	**21.79**	**24.12**	**25.40**	**13.89**	**15.34**	**63.83**	64	20.09
(distance)	MI-FGSM	21.89	22.18	23.27	**18.07**	**18.26**	61.61	**62.99**	**22.78**
	GF-MI-FGSM	**21.28**	**21.92**	**22.84**	18.12	18.36	**61.60**	63.23	22.95

5   Conclusion

The GF-Attack strategy proposed in this paper effectively reduces the amount of change of the adversarial example by distinguishing the attack area and the non-attack area and mixes the gradient of the flipped image to improve the transferability of the adversarial example. The experimental results show that the adversarial examples generated by adding the GF-Attack strategy can maintain a high success rate in the white-box attack, and the amount of image change is much smaller than the original formula, so it is unlikely to be discovered. In the black-box attack, GF-Attack can significantly improve the transitivity of adversarial example, and the paradigm distance is also lower than the original method. We suggest that the size of the target area can be appropriately reduced when a small amount of interference is pursued. On the contrary, the size of the target area should be increased in the black-box attack, which can solve the problem of poor transferability of adversarial example due to the different attention areas of different models, especially the adversarial training model.

Acknowledgment. This work was supported in part by the National Natural Science Foundation of China under Grant 61762089, Grant 61663047, Grant 61863036, and Grant 61762092, and in part by the Science and Technology Innovation Team Project of Yunnan Province under Grant 2017HC012.

References

1. Bojarski, M., et al.: End to end learning for self-driving cars. arXiv, Computer Vision and Pattern Recognition (2016)

2. Cogswell, M., Ahmed, F., Girshick, R., Zitnick, L., Batra, D.: Reducing overfitting in deep networks by decorrelating representations. arXiv, Learning (2015)
3. Dong, Y., et al.: Boosting adversarial attacks with momentum, pp. 9185–9193 (2018)
4. Flepp, B.: Off-road obstacle avoidance through end-to-end learning. In: Advances in Neural Information Processing Systems (2005)
5. Girshick, R., Donahue, J., Darrell, T., Malik, J.: Rich feature hierarchies for accurate object detection and semantic segmentation, pp. 580–587 (2014)
6. Goodfellow, I., Shlens, J., Szegedy, C.: Explaining and harnessing adversarial examples. arXiv, Machine Learning (2014)
7. He, K., Zhang, X., Ren, S., Sun, J.: Deep residual learning for image recognition, pp. 770–778 (2016)
8. Kurakin, A., Goodfellow, I., Bengio, S.: Adversarial examples in the physical world. arXiv, Computer Vision and Pattern Recognition (2016)
9. Lecun, Y., Bottou, L.: Gradient-based learning applied to document recognition. In: Proceedings of the IEEE, pp. 2278–2324 (1998)
10. Liu, Y., Chen, X., Liu, C., Song, D.: Delving into transferable adversarial examples and black-box attacks. arXiv, Learning (2016)
11. Madry, A., Makelov, A., Schmidt, L., Tsipras, D., Vladu, A.: Towards deep learning models resistant to adversarial attacks. arXiv, Machine Learning (2017)
12. Madry, A., Makelov, A., Schmidt, L., Tsipras, D., Vladu, A.: Towards deep learning models resistant to adversarial attacks (2017)
13. Moosavidezfooli, S., Fawzi, A., Fawzi, O., Frossard, P.: Universal adversarial perturbations, pp. 86–94 (2017)
14. Prasoon, A., Petersen, K., Igel, C., Lauze, F., Dam, E.B., Nielsen, M.: Deep feature learning for knee cartilage segmentation using a triplanar convolutional neural network, vol. 16, pp. 246–253 (2013)
15. Selvaraju, R.R., Das, A., Vedantam, R., Cogswell, M., Parikh, D., Batra, D.: Grad-cam: why did you say that? Visual explanations from deep networks via gradient-based localization (2016)
16. Simonyan, K., Zisserman, A.: Very deep convolutional networks for large-scale image recognition (2014)
17. Singh, R., Lanchantin, J., Robins, G., Qi, Y.: Deepchrome: deep-learning for predicting gene expression from histone modifications. Bioinformatics 32(17), 639–648 (2016)
18. Su, J., Vargas, D.V., Sakurai, K.: One pixel attack for fooling deep neural networks. IEEE Trans. Evol. Comput. 23(5), 828–841 (2019)
19. Swietojanski, P., Ghoshal, A., Renals, S.: Convolutional neural networks for distant speech recognition. IEEE Signal Process. Lett. 21(9), 1120–1124 (2014)
20. Szegedy, C., et al.: Going deeper with convolutions, pp. 1–9 (2015)
21. Szegedy, C., et al.: Intriguing properties of neural networks. arXiv, Computer Vision and Pattern Recognition (2013)
22. Van Etten, A.: You only look twice: Rapid multi-scale object detection in satellite imagery. arXiv, Computer Vision and Pattern Recognition (2018)
23. Wu, L., Liu, Z., Zhang, H., Cen, Y., Zhou, W.: Ps-mifgsm: focused image anti-attack algorithm. J. Comput. Appl. 1–8 (2019)
24. Yuan, X., He, P., Zhu, Q., Li, X.: Adversarial examples: attacks and defenses for deep learning. IEEE Trans. Neural Netw. 30(9), 2805–2824 (2019)
25. Zeggada, A., Melgani, F., Bazi, Y.: A deep learning approach to uav image multi-labeling. IEEE Geosci. Remote Sensing Lett. 14(5), 694–698 (2017)

War: An Efficient Pre-processing Method for Defending Adversarial Attacks

Zhaoxia Yin$^{(\boxtimes)}$ (iD), Hua Wang (iD), and Jie Wang (iD)

Anhui Province Key Laboratory of Multimodal Cognitive Computation,
School of Computer Science and Technology, Anhui University,
Hefei 230601, China
yinzhaoxia@ahu.edu.cn

Abstract. Deep neural networks (DNNs) have achieved extraordinary successes in many fields such as image classification. However, they are vulnerable to adversarial examples generated by adding slight perturbations to the input images, leading incorrect classification results. Due to the serious threats of adversarial examples, it is necessary to find a simple and practical way to defend against adversarial attacks. In this paper, we present an efficient preprocessing method called War (WebP compression and resizing operation) for defending adversarial examples. WebP compression is first performed on the input sample to remove the imperceptible perturbations from the adversarial example. Then, the compressed image is appropriately resized to further destroy the specific structure of the adversarial perturbations. Finally, we can get a clean sample that can be correctly classified by the model. Extensive experiments show that our method outperforms the state-of-the-art defense methods. It can effectively defend adversarial attacks while ensure the classification accuracy on the normal samples drops slightly. Moreover, it only requires a particularly short pre-processing time.

Keywords: Deep neural network · Image classification · Adversarial examples · Webp compression · Resizing operation

1 Introduction

In recent years, deep learning [13,18] has made breakthroughs in many fields, especially in computer vision [24,27]. The emerging technologies break some limitations of traditional machine learning [6,17]. However, Szegedy et al. [21] made the first attempt to discover the blind spot of deep neural network (DNNs) in the field of image classification. As reported, one can fool DNNs by deliberately adding imperceptible perturbations to the images, thus the concept of adversarial examples is raised. As shown in Fig. 1, on the left is a clean sample, which can be correctly classified by the model, whereas the image on the right is added

This research work is partly supported by National Natural Science Foundation of China (61872003, U1636206).

© Springer Nature Switzerland AG 2020
X. Chen et al. (Eds.): ML4CS 2020, LNCS 12487, pp. 514–524, 2020.
https://doi.org/10.1007/978-3-030-62460-6_46

with some deliberately designed perturbations, which can make the model mis-classified. The existence of adversarial examples attracted people's attention, which may bring serious threats to researches in some security-sensitive fields, such as automatic driving [2] and identity recognition [7].

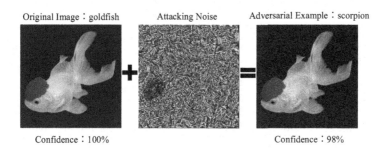

Original Image : goldfish   Attacking Noise   Adversarial Example : scorpion

Confidence : 100%   Confidence : 98%

Fig. 1. The generation processes of an adversarial example.

In order to better comprehend the deep neural networks and overcome the influence of adversarial examples, a series of attack methods and defense methods are proposed. However, the current defense researches have lagged behind attack researches. Moreover, many defense methods pay little attention to the real-word applications, and often ignore the high calculation cost. Therefore, it is necessary to develop more effective and practical methods to defend against adversarial attacks.

In this paper, we propose a simple but efficient preprocessing module to defend against adversarial examples, called War. The defense framework is shown in Fig. 2. First, both the clean samples and the adversarial examples are prepro-cessed by the War module, then we fed the processed samples into DNNs for classification, finally both can be correctly classified.

Our scheme mainly relies on the WebP [11] lossy compression. WebP lossy compression is specially designed to reduce the image details that are difficult to be perceived by human beings and to compress the image volume, which can effectively remove the imperceptible perturbations in adversarial examples. As we all know, JPEG compression [16] is a good method to defend the adversarial examples, but when the perturbations are strong, it needs to enhance the com-pression level to remove the these noises, at the same time, the image may appear block effect, and the image distortion will be serious. Since the loop filtering is introduced into WebP compression, blocking artifacts can be eliminated. Fur-thermore, with a same compression quality factor, the image volume obtained by WebP compression is 40% smaller than that of JPEG compression, which can save a lot of server broadband resources and data space.

Numerous experiments are carried out on the ImageNet dataset [9] to show the performance of the proposed method. Experimental results demonstrate that the overall defense effect of WebP compression is better than JPEG compression,

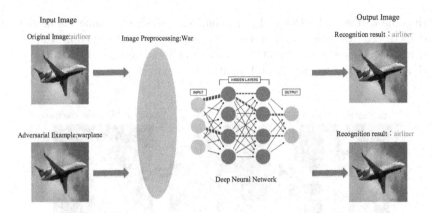

Fig. 2. The overall framework of the proposed defense method.

especially in the case of low and medium bit rates. Combining WebP compression and resizing operation, namely War, can achieve better defense effects. The proposed scheme can effectively resist three kinds of adversarial attacks include IFGSM [10], DeepFool [14] and C&W [1], and achieve a higher classification accuracy than HGD [12] and Comdefend [8]. Moreover, due to the low computational complexity of the proposed method, the preprocessing time on a single image is shorter.

2   Related Work

In this part, we first introduce several state-of-the-art attack methods, and then present the most advanced defense methods.

2.1   Attack Methods

Fast Gradient Sign Method (FGSM). [5] FGSM is an algorithm that quickly generates adversarial examples, it adds perturbations to the image by calculating the loss of the image classifier. Given an input image, it requires to find the maximum direction of the gradient change, and add adversarial perturbations in this direction, resulting in incorrect classification results. The generated adversarial example is formulated as follows:

$$x^{adv} = x + \epsilon \cdot sign(\nabla_x J(x,y)) \tag{1}$$

where $J(x,y)$ denotes the cross entropy cost function, x is the input image, y is the true label of the input image, and ϵ is the hyper parameter that determines the magnitude of the perturbation.

IFGSM. [10] IFGSM is an iterative version of FGSM, it applied FGSM multiple times with small perturbation instead of a large perturbation. After each iteration, the pixels are properly cropped while ensuring that the result remains near the input image x:

$$x^{(i)} = clip_{x,\epsilon}(x^{(i-1)} + \epsilon \cdot sign(\nabla_{x^{(i-1)}} J(x^{(i-1)}, y))) \tag{2}$$

DeepFool. [14] DeepFool algorithm is a non-target attack method, it generates adversarial examples by calculating the minimum adversarial perturbations. It first explores the nearest decision boundary, and then slightly modifies the image in each iteration to reach the boundary, so that the model classification results in error. Compared with FGSM, when the attack success rates are consistent, the perturbation generated by this method is smaller, making it more difficult to be detected.

Carlini and Wagner (C&W). [1] The distortion of C&W algorithm is calculated through three methods $(L_0, L_2, L\infty)$. In terms of the attack success rate achieved with minimal perturbations, it is more effective than previous methods. CW_L2 has the best performance, which is an optimization-based attack method that can generate adversarial examples by solving the following optimization problems:

$$\|x - x^{'}\|_2 + \lambda max(-\kappa, Z(x^{'})_\kappa - max\{Z(x^{'})_{\kappa'} : \kappa^{'} \neq \kappa\}) \tag{3}$$

Where κ controls the confidence that the image is misunderstood by the model, i.e. the confidence gap between the sample category and the real category. $Z(x^{'})_{\kappa'}$ is the logical output of category $\kappa^{'}$.

2.2   Defense Methods

The purpose of defense is to improve the robustness of the model to adversarial examples, so that it can correctly classify adversarial examples while ensuring that the loss of classification performance to normal samples is small.

Modifying the Neural Network. Adversarial training [23] is one of the most effective defense methods. It takes adversarial examples as part of the training set to train the model, and forces decision boundaries to become smoother, making model more robust. Gradient Masking [15] improves model robustness by modifying model gradients. However, both methods require a large amount of training data, which is time-consuming and complicated.

Modifying Input Data. Before inputting the sample to the classifier, the PixelDefend [19] can convert the disturbed image into a clean image. PixelDefend eliminates perturbations by simulating the spatial distribution of images, but when the space is too large, the simulation results will be poor. Xie et al. perform arbitrary transformations [25] to destroy the specific structure against perturbation, making the adversarial examples attack fail. Liao et al. regard these imperceptible adversarial perturbations as noises [12], and developed a high-level representation guided by denoiser to destroy these noises, but it requires a large number of adversarial examples to train it. Thang et al. cut down the fooling rates of the DNNs by rotating the adversarial images [22]. Jia et al. developed the Comdefend preprocessing module [8], they design two convolutional neural networks to compress and reconstruct the image to remove perturbation while ensuring low image distortion. Das et al. take JPEG compression [3] to remove the perturbations in the adversarial pictures.

3   Our Proposed Defense Method: War

3.1   WebP Compression

The WebP lossy compression is based on the predictive encoding method in VP8 video encoding to compress image data, whose the basic steps are similar to the steps of JPEG compression. It is specially designed to reduce the image details that are difficult to be perceived by human beings to compress the image volume, which can remove imperceptible perturbations in adversarial examples. As we know, JPEG compression has an excellent effect on defending adversarial attacks, but in the case of low and medium bit rates, it is prone to block effects, resulting in poor image quality and loss of classification accuracy. However, the loop filtering [4] is introduced in WebP lossy compression, which can be used to eliminate the blocking effect caused by quantization of DCT coefficients from block transformation. WebP compression not only can effectively remove adversarial perturbations, but also ensure that the compressed image quality still high. In addition, the predictive coding technique used in WebP compression reduces the special color. With a similar compression quality, the image volume obtained by WebP compression is 40% smaller than that of JPEG compression, which can save a lot of server broadband resources and data space. The degree of image compression is represented by Quality Factor, which varies from [0,100]. A high quality factor indicates a small degree of compression. Conversely, a low quality factor indicates a great degree of compression.

3.2   Resizing Operation

Resizing operation changes the size of the image, it consists of two steps: first, it is necessary to adjust the image to a specific size, and then reset the image pixel value. Resizing image will change the number of pixels, and the pixel values will also be reset, which plays an important role in destroying the specific structure of adversarial perturbation without affecting human eyes to normally extract image features. It is best to control the increase or decrease of the number of pixels caused by resizing image to be about 10% of the total number of pixels in the original image. In this case, the classification accuracy for normal samples is basically not affected, and it can also play a good performance on defending adversarial attacks.

3.3 War: WebP Compression + Resizing Operation

This paper proposes a simple and effective preprocessing method to defend adversarial attacks, called War, which combines image compression and resizing operation. As described in Fig. 3, before the image is fed into the DNNs, we first perform WebP compression, and then resize the compressed image. After preprocessing by the War module, both adversarial examples and normal samples can be correctly classified by DNNs.

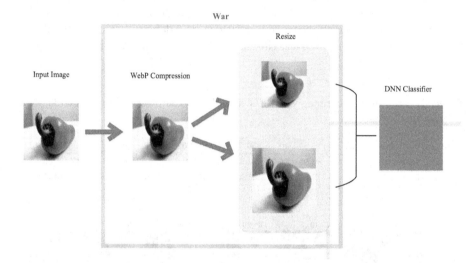

Fig. 3. The specific processing of the War scheme.

4 Experiments

4.1 Experimental Setup

– **Dataset:** In the experiments, we randomly 5,000 images selected from the ILSVRC 2012 verification set [9], which consists of 50,000 images and contains 1000 classes.
– **Neural Networks:** We test with three trained networks, inception_v3 [20], ResNet 34 and ResNet 101 [26], the recognition accuracies were 83%, 73% and 76%, respectively.
– **Attack Methods:** Three advanced attack methods, IFGSM, DeepFool and CW_L2, are used to generate adversarial examples.

4.2   Evaluation and Analysis

Algorithm Comparison. First, we compare the defense effects of JPEG compression and WebP compression on ResNet34. We choose a set of adversarial examples that can attack successfully, and they are generated by various attack algorithms under different perturbation amplitudes. The two compression methods are used for defense, and experimental results are shown in Table 1. The average Top1 accuracy of the model in WebP compression is 3.1% higher than JPEG compression, especially in the case of medium and low bit rates. Since WebP compression does not have the square effect as JPEG compression, the image distortion is smaller, so the classification accuracy of the model is significantly improved. In Fig. 4, we show some example images under different compression quality factors. We can clearly see that when the degree of compression is relatively large, JPEG compression will appear obvious square, while WebP compression with the loop filtering, the image distortion is smaller. Especially when destroying relatively large perturbations, the defense capability of WebP compression is better, moreover, the visual quality of the compressed image is higher.

Table 1. The Top1 accuracies of JPEG and WebP compression on ResNet34 with different quality factors.

QF	0	10	20	30	40	50	60	70	80	90	100	average
JPEG	16.1%	67.8%	78.0%	83.9%	84.7%	81.4%	80.5%	78.8%	73.0%	62.7%	14.3%	65.6%
WebP	55.1%	74.6%	77.0%	77.0%	78.8%	81.4%	79.6%	81.4%	77.0%	66.0%	8.0%	**68.7%**

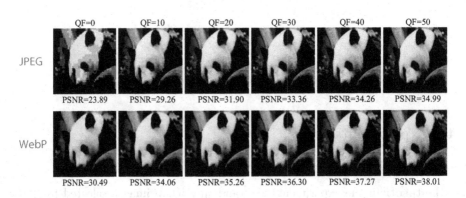

Fig. 4. Comparison of the sample quality between JPEG and WebP under different quality factors. PSNR(dB)

Next, we combine WebP compression and resizing operation, which is our proposed War, and compare it to using WebP compression alone for adversarial defending on Inception_v3. As illustrated in Fig. 5(a) and Fig. 5(b), the effect of combining the two methods will be significantly improved. We only need to take a small degree of compression then to resize the image, which can effectively destroy the adversarial perturbations while ensuring that the visual quality of the processed image is still high.

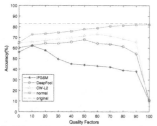 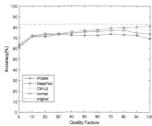

(a) The Top1 accuracies of input pictures under different quality factors.

(b) The Top1 accuracies of input pictures processed by War.

Fig. 5. The Top1 accuracies of WebP compression and War method on Inception_v3.

Performance Evaluation. To quantitatively evaluate the performance of the War method, we compare the method with two advanced defense methods, HGD [16] and Comdefend [17] on the ResNet101 and Inception_v3 respectively. Details are shown in Table 2, we can see that the proposed method can effectively resist IFGSM, DeepFool and CW_L2 attacks. The Top 1 accuracy on the same model is increased by more than 10% compared with the HGD, and is increased by more than 7% compared with the Comdefend.

Table 2. The performance of War method is compared with the HGD and Comdefend methods.

Model	Defense	Normal	IFGSM	DeepFool	CW_L2
*ResNet*101	No	76%	12%	1%	0%
	HGD [12]	54%	52%	52%	50%
	Comdefend [8]	67%	56%	53%	53%
	War	71%	64%	66%	69%
Inception_v3	No	83%	49%	11%	0%
	HGD [12]	70%	61%	60%	60%
	Comdefend [8]	74%	64%	60%	60%
	War	77%	71%	76%	78%

Next, we compare the processing time taken by the three preprocessing methods on single image. The HGD method needs to train denoiser with the generated adversarial images, which takes much time than others. The Comdefend method first compresses the image using a compressed convolutional neural network, and then reconstructs the original image using a reconstructed convolutional neural network. As shown in Fig. 6, the processing time used in HGD and Comdefend methods are 2.7 s and 1.2 s, respectively. Since our method does not need to train the networks and the calculation complexity is relatively low, so the time consumption is less, the processing time is only 0.5 s, which is more suitable for real-time defense.

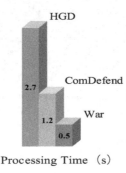

Processing Time (s)

Fig. 6. The processing time of three different preprocessing methods.

5   Conclusion

To find a simple and efficient method to resist the attack of adversarial examples, in this paper, we propose the War module to preprocess the model inputs to defend against adversarial examples. This method does not need to change the structure of the model. It only needs to perform WebP lossy compression on the input image, and then resize the image appropriately. WebP lossy compression can effectively remove adversarial noises, and the resizing image operation can further destroy the specific structure of adversarial perturbations. Finally, the processed adversarial images can be correctly classified by the model like normal samples. The experimental results show that the WebP compression method used in the proposed War has better defense effect than JPEG compression. The proposed method does not need to train the model or reconstruct the image, thus saving the processing time. More importantly, our scheme can effectively defend against adversarial examples while ensuring the loss of classification accuracy on normal samples is tiny.

References

1. Carlini, N., Wagner, D.: Towards evaluating the robustness of neural networks. In: 2017 IEEE Symposium on Security and Privacy (SP), pp. 39–57. IEEE (2017). https://doi.org/10.1109/SP.2017.49

2. Chen, C., Seff, A., Kornhauser, A.L., Xiao, J.: Deepdriving: learning affordance for direct perception in autonomous driving. In: International Conference on Computer Vision, pp. 2722–2730 (2015)
3. Das, N., et al.: Keeping the bad guys out: protecting and vaccinating deep learning with jpeg compression. arXiv preprint arXiv:1705.02900 (2017)
4. Ginesu, G., Pintus, M., Giusto, D.D.: Objective assessment of the webP image coding algorithm. Signal Process. Image Commun. **27**(8), 867–874 (2012). https://doi.org/10.1016/j.image.2012.01.011
5. Goodfellow, I.J., Shlens, J., Szegedy, C.: Explaining and harnessing adversarial examples. In: International Conference on Learning Representations (2014)
6. Huang, L., Joseph, A.D., Nelson, B., Rubinstein, B.I., Tygar, J.D.: Adversarial machine learning. In: Proceedings of the 4th ACM Workshop on Security and Artificial Intelligence, pp. 43–58 (2011)
7. Irons, J.L., et al.: Face identity recognition in simulated prosthetic vision is poorer than previously reported and can be improved by caricaturing. Vis. Res. **137**, 61–79 (2017). https://doi.org/10.1016/j.visres.2017.06.002
8. Jia, X., Wei, X., Cao, X., Foroosh, H.: Comdefend: an efficient image compression model to defend adversarial examples. In: Proceedings of the IEEE Conference on Computer Vision and Pattern Recognition, pp. 6084–6092 (2019)
9. Krizhevsky, A., Sutskever, I., Hinton, G.E.: Imagenet classification with deep convolutional neural networks. In: Advances in Neural Information Processing Systems, pp. 1097–1105 (2012). https://doi.org/10.1145/3065386
10. Kurakin, A., Goodfellow, I., Bengio, S.: Adversarial examples in the physical world. arXiv preprint arXiv:1607.02533 (2016)
11. Lian, L., Shilei, W.: Webp: a new image compression format based on vp8 encoding. Microcontrollers Embed. Syst. **3**, 47–50 (2012)
12. Liao, F., Liang, M., Dong, Y., Pang, T., Hu, X., Zhu, J.: Defense against adversarial attacks using high-level representation guided denoiser. In: Proceedings of the IEEE Conference on Computer Vision and Pattern Recognition, pp. 1778–1787 (2018)
13. Markatopoulou, F., Mezaris, V., Patras, I.: Implicit and explicit concept relations in deep neural networks for multi-label video/image annotation. IEEE Trans. Circuits Syst. Video Technol. **29**(6), 1631–1644 (2019)
14. Moosavi-Dezfooli, S.M., Fawzi, A., Frossard, P.: Deepfool: a simple and accurate method to fool deep neural networks. In: Proceedings of the IEEE Conference on Computer Vision and Pattern Recognition, pp. 2574–2582 (2016). https://doi.org/10.1109/CVPR.2016.282
15. Papernot, N., McDaniel, P., Goodfellow, I., Jha, S., Celik, Z.B., Swami, A.: Practical black-box attacks against machine learning. In: Proceedings of the 2017 ACM on Asia Conference on Computer and Communications Security, pp. 506–519. ACM (2017). https://doi.org/10.1145/3052973.3053009
16. Raid, A.M., Khedr, W.M., El-Dosuky, M.A., Ahmed, W.: Jpeg image compression using discrete cosine transform - a survey. Int. J. Comput. Sci. Eng. Surv. **5**(2), 39–47 (2014)
17. Sabharwal, A., Selman, B.: S. russell, p. norvig, artificial intelligence: a modern approach, Third edition. Artificial Intelligence, 175(5–6), 935–937 (2011)
18. Schmidhuber, J.: Deep learning in neural networks. Neural Netw. **61**, 85–117 (2015)
19. Song, Y., Kim, T., Nowozin, S., Ermon, S., Kushman, N.: Pixeldefend: leveraging generative models to understand and defend against adversarial examples. arXiv preprint arXiv:1710.10766 (2017)

20. Szegedy, C., Vanhoucke, V., Ioffe, S., Shlens, J., Wojna, Z.: Rethinking the inception architecture for computer vision. In: Proceedings of the IEEE Conference on Computer Vision and Pattern Recognition, pp. 2818–2826 (2016). https://doi.org/10.1109/CVPR.2016.308
21. Szegedy, C., et al.: Intriguing properties of neural networks. In: International Conference on Machine Learning (2014)
22. Thang, D.D., Matsui, T.: Image transformation can make neural networks more robust against adversarial examples. arXiv preprint arXiv:1901.03037 (2019)
23. Tramèr, F., Kurakin, A., Papernot, N., Goodfellow, I., Boneh, D., McDaniel, P.: Ensemble adversarial training: attacks and defenses. arXiv preprint arXiv:1705.07204 (2017)
24. Wang, X., et al.: Reinforced cross-modal matching and self-supervised imitation learning for vision-language navigation. In: Proceedings of the IEEE Conference on Computer Vision and Pattern Recognition, pp. 6629–6638 (2019)
25. Xie, C., Wang, J., Zhang, Z., Ren, Z., Yuille, A.: Mitigating adversarial effects through randomization. arXiv preprint arXiv:1711.01991 (2017)
26. Zagoruyko, S., Komodakis, N.: Paying more attention to attention: improving the performance of convolutional neural networks via attention transfer. arXiv preprint arXiv:1612.03928 (2016)
27. Zamir, A.R., Sax, A., Shen, W., Guibas, L.J., Malik, J., Savarese, S.: Taskonomy: disentangling task transfer learning. In: Proceedings of the IEEE Conference on Computer Vision and Pattern Recognition, pp. 3712–3722 (2018)

A High-Recall Membership Inference Attack Based on Confidence-Thresholding Method with Relaxed Assumption

Lulu Wang[1], Xiaoyu Zhang[1(✉)], Yi Xie[1], Xu Ma[2], and Meixia Miao[3]

[1] State Key Laboratory of Integrated Service Networks (ISN), Xidian University,
Xi'an, China
tris.wanglu@gmail.com, xiaoyuzhang@xidian.edu.cn, yixie1997@gmail.com
[2] School of Software, Qufu Normal University, Qufu, China
xumasysu@gmail.com
[3] School of Cyberspace Security, Xi'an University of Posts and Telecommunications,
Xi'an, China
miaofeng415@163.com

Abstract. Membership inference attack (MIA) aims to infer whether a given data sample is in the target training dataset or not, which poses a severe privacy risk in particular data-sensitive fields like the military, national security department, as well as enterprise. Observing that a model generated from adversarial training is more vulnerable against MIA, a novel attack method based on confidence-thresholding was proposed by Song et al. recently. However, it is not a straightforward work to deploy such an attack into real-world application scenarios, since shadow training and redundant assumptions are prerequisites. To address the above issues, in this paper, we propose an improved confidence-thresholding method with relaxed assumption, evaluating the prediction accuracy as the threshold. Our attack can be released without using shadow training and an additional dataset. Instead of collecting an additional dataset, attackers use their target data records, which are needed to be inferred about membership, to achieve MIA. As a result, our proposed attack against robust model has an overwhelming advantage on model recall with fewer accuracy and precision loss. Extensive experiments are conducted on real-world data, *i.e.*, Yale Face, and the results show that our proposed MIA attack is effective and feasible.

Keywords: Membership inference attack · Confidence-thresholding method · Relaxed assumption attack

1 Introduction

Machine learning (ML) has been widely used as an important tool to solve problems in various fields, such as health analytic [17], advertising [8,22,28], industry [9], and education [4]. Recently, the rapid development of cloud computing

© Springer Nature Switzerland AG 2020
X. Chen et al. (Eds.): ML4CS 2020, LNCS 12487, pp. 525–539, 2020.
https://doi.org/10.1007/978-3-030-62460-6_47

[2, 3, 30] further contributes to the wide deployment and exploiting of machine learning. Then, the cloud-based machine learning has been drawn more attentions from both academia and industry. However, there are still some problems needed to be focused on, especially on the security [1, 5, 7, 23, 25, 27] and privacy [6, 10–16, 18–21, 24, 26, 29] related issues against machine learning models. One significant threat is the privacy leakage from the training sets of machine learning models. Since the training data of machine learning models contains some private information about data providers, the attack aiming at the training set of models should be paid attention to. This kind of attack is called membership inference attack (MIA) [15, 18, 19], an attack to determine whether a given data record is used to train the target model.

MIA aimed at machine learning models is firstly presented in [19] by using the shadow training method. Shadow training is then used to perform MIA in different scenarios, some of which are feasible under weaker assumptions compared to the MIA presented in [19]. However, when using shadow training, there are some assumptions too strong to be satisfied. Besides, shadow training method is a little bit sophisticated since it needs to construct shadow models to simulate target model in order to collect and obtain data with label "member" and "non-member" and then train a classifier to separate "member" from "non-member". Even though there is an improvement of shadow training with only one shadow model proposed in [18], it is still complicated, especially compared to confidence-thresholding method.

Confidence-thresholding method is proposed by Yeom et al. [26], with less computation and assumptions. The key idea of this method is to compare the confidence of target data record with a threshold. When the confidence is larger than the threshold, we predict the data record as "member" of training set of target model; otherwise, predict it as "non-member". Song et al. [20] preformed MIA on robust models using this confidence-thresholding method. Comparing to shadow training method, this method is less complicated but with similar performance. However, the used threshold needs to be chosen using shadow training and thus needs an additional dataset for training. To avoid leveraging shadow training and redundant assumptions for getting a proper threshold, there is another confidence-thresholding method presented by Salem et al. [18]. Instead of using an additional dataset to obtain threshold, the authors suggested generating random data points in the feature space of the target data point utilized to choose threshold. This method is quite simple for an attacker to achieve because the only assumption is knowing the feature space of target data point, which is already know when having the target data point. However, based on substantial and extensive experiments, we found that the threshold-choosing method using randomly generated data points to achieve MIA on a robust model did not work well. The first reason may be that the randomly generated data records are far different from real data points, which are meaningless, just some noise pictures. Besides, the generated data points nearly have the same label by the prediction of the target model. For example, they are very likely to be classified into the same class, which for Yale Face dataset is class 3. Therefore, it is not surprise that the result is unsatisfied when using this confidence-thresholding method directly on the scenario of [20] since the generated data have poor performance.

Aiming at improving attack performance proposed in [20] against robust model, we design a novel confidence-thresholding method based on MIA presented in [18], called accuracy-based confidence-thresholding attack. Through experiments, we find out that when we use model accuracy as threshold to achieve attack, there is a good performance of MIA. Therefore, we try to evaluate the model accuracy through computing the probability that the predicted label equals to the true label. Instead of collecting an additional dataset, attackers use the target data records they already have to evaluate the prediction accuracy. The whole attack algorithm is based on a relaxed assumption compared to the existed MIA and subtly avoids the disadvantage of randomly generated data used for choosing threshold. To further measure our proposed attack model, we apply our attack on the real-world dataset Yale Face. The results of experiments show that our proposed attack has higher recall than the original confidence-thresholding method and with less accuracy and precision loss. Table 1 compares three different confidence-thresholding method. Our method outperforms other methods in overall since it is less complicated than the method in [20] and has a better performance compared to the method in [18].

Table 1. Comparison among three different confidence-thresholding MIA against robust model. Confidence-choosing indicates which kind of confidence from confidence vector attacker choose as the threshold.

Attack scheme	Shadow training	Additional dataset	Confidence-choosing
Attack in [20]	Yes	Yes	True label confidence
Attack in [18]	No	No	Maximum confidence
Our attack	No	No	True label confidence

1.1 Our Contributions

Our contributions are summarized as follows:

- We propose a novel accuracy-based membership inference attack, which has an overwhelming advantage over model recall and with almost no accuracy loss and less precision loss in contrast with the original confidence-thresholding method.
- Our proposed attack method has relaxed assumptions comparing to the existing MIA method under the condition that the target model is a robust model, without using shadow training to simulate the target model for getting labeled dataset to train an attack model or choose a threshold.
- We experimentally evaluate our attack method on the real-world dataset Yale Face, and the results show that our proposed attack is efficient and effective.

1.2   Organization

The rest of this paper is organized as follows. Section 2 gives a brief description of the background and problem statement. Our proposed high-recall MIA attack method is presented in detail in Sect. 3. Experimental setup and the corresponding experiment results are demonstrated in Sect. 4 and Sect. 5, respectively. Finally, Sect. 6 concludes this work and discusses future work.

2   Problem Statement

In this section, we first formalize the threat model, which gives an overall description of the problem we focus on, MIA. Then, we briefly introduce adversarial examples that play an important role in our attack method.

2.1   Threat Model

In this paper, we consider MIA in an black-box setting. The attack scenario contains two participants, i.e., model provider and attacker. The detail is described below.

– **Model Provider:** Model provider trains a classification model to provide service to the Internet users. Thus, the trained model is available to attacker, receiving output by querying data record. We suppose that the output of the target model is a confidence vector, indicating the probability that data belongs to each class. Formally, when inputting x to classifier, it outputs y_{pred}. The classification algorithm can be formulated as

$$M_{target} : x \rightarrow y_{pred},$$

where M_{target}, x and y_{pred} denote the target model, the input data record, and the confidence vector that the target model outputs, respectively.

– **Attacker:** The goal of attacker is to find out whether if the target data belongs to the training set of the target model provided by model provider. Attacker can only black-box access to the target model. The attack model takes (x_{target}, y_{target}) as input and outputs the label about "member" or "non-member". It can be formalized by

$$M_{attack} : (x_{target}, y_{target}) \rightarrow \{\text{"member"}, \text{"non} - \text{member"}\},$$

where M_{attack}, x_{target} and y_{target} represent the attack model, the target data record and the class label of this data record, respectively.

2.2   Adversarial Examples

Adversarial examples (AE) are examples with noise added on original examples (also called clean examples or benign examples). The purpose of adversarial example is to mislead machine learning models to output wrong prediction. For example, if the output of a machine learning model on a benign example is label a, the adversarial example with unnoticed change on this benign example makes the machine learning model output a label other than a. There are two different kinds of adversarial examples, targeted AE and untargeted AE. Targeted AEs represent the adversarial examples that can make ML model predict it as a specific class, while untargeted AEs mislead ML models to any wrong labels. In this paper, the AEs mentioned are untargeted AEs. In our proposed attack, the target model is a robust model, trained with adversarial examples. Besides, we queries untargeted AE to the target model in order to achieve our attack.

3   Our Proposed Attack

In this section, we first give a high description of our proposed attack, called accuracy-based confidence-thresholding attack. This attack is based on confidence-thresholding method. Then, we separate the attack model into two parts and describe them in detail. The two parts are threshold-choosing process and inference process.

3.1   High Description

Accuracy-based attack is used to achieve membership inference attack, determining if a data record is used to train the target model. The main idea of it is to choose a threshold that is similar to the accuracy of the target model when querying adversarial examples. To be clear, the adversarial examples used in this paper are untargeted AE. Since attacker has a set of data record that needs to be inferred, this set of data can be used to launch an attack. Therefore, the assumption of the proposed attack is that attacker has a target dataset containing data records needed to be inferred, which is satisfied in any situation, obviously. This dataset should stick with class labels, the class they belong to. Figure 1 illustrates the detailed attack process.

3.2   An Improved Threshold-Choosing Method

Threshold-choosing method takes labels and predictions of data in the target dataset as input and outputs a proper threshold for attacking. First of all, attacker has a target dataset, containing data records with their class labels. Then, attacker generates the adversarial examples of them by adding perturbation and queries the adversarial examples to the target model M_{target}, getting predictions $y_{pred}^1, ..., y_{pred}^m$. Next, attacker uses threshold-choosing method to get $threshold$. The threshold-choosing method first estimates the accuracy of target

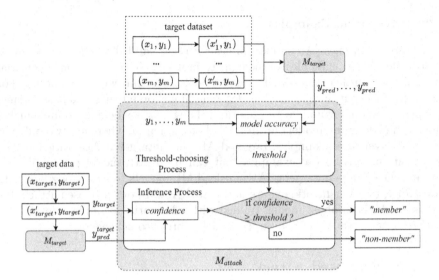

Fig. 1. The attack process of our proposed attack, including threshold-choosing process and inference process. Threshold-choosing method is used to obtain a proper threshold for attacking. After receiving threshold, inference part compares it with the confidence of target data in order to distinguish "member" from "non-member".

model by comparing the true label y and prediction y_{pred} of each data record in the target dataset. Then, it collects the true-label confidence of each data record in the target dataset that represent the probability of predicting correctly. After that, choose confidence that is the smallest value which is equal to or larger than model accuracy as the threshold used to attack. Besides, if the choosing threshold is equal to 1, we change it to a value smaller than 1. The reason for it is that threshold 1 results in a bad recall. The algorithm of threshold-choosing method is shown in Algorithm 1.

3.3   Inference Process Using Chosen Threshold

Since the threshold is set using Algorithm 1, we can implement inference process, which is based on the confidence-thresholding method. Taking a target data (x_{target}, y_{target}) that attacker wants to infer as an example, we will describe the inference process thoroughly. Attacker first queries target model M_{target} with the target data to receive the confidence vector y_{pred}^{target}. Then, select the confidence corresponding to the true label of target data in the confidence vector as *confidence*. The key step of inference process is to compare *confidence* with *threshold* chose in threshold-choosing process. If *confidence* is equal to or larger than *threshold*, then it is predicted as "*member*" of training set; otherwise, it is labeled as "*non-member*".

Algorithm 1. An improved method to choosing threshold

Input: target dataset $X_{target} : \{x_1, x_2, ..., x_m\}$ with labels $\{y_1, y_2, ..., y_m\}$
Output: threshold
1: $count = 0$ ▷ The number of correct predictions
2: $con\_vec = [\,]$ ▷ An empty list to store confidence of each data
3: **for each** $i \in x_{target}$ **do**
4:     $x_i' = x_i + r_i$ ▷ Generate adversarial example
5:     $y_{pred}^i = M_{target}(x_i')$ ▷ Query the target model to get its confidence vector
6:     $con\_vec.append(y_{pred}^i[y_i])$ ▷ Remember the confidence of adversarial example
    belonging to the class of true label in list con_vec
7:     **if** $argmax(y_{pred}^i) == y_i$ **then** ▷ Compare prediction with the true label
8:         $count+ = 1$
9:     **end if**
10: **end for each**
11: $acc = count/m$
12: $threshold = [i$ for i in con_vec if $i \geq acc$ and i-acc is the minimum$]$
13: **if** $threshold = 1$ **then** ▷ If threshold is chose to 1, adjust it.
14:     $con\_vec\_no\_1 = [i$ for i in con_vec if $i \neq 1]$ ▷ con_vec without 1
15:     $threshold = con\_vec\_no_1[size(con\_vec\_no\_1)/5]$
16: **end if**
17: **return** $threshold$

3.4 Brief Analysis on the Advantages of Accuracy-Based Attack

Accuracy-based attack requires less computational budget and has easy-satisfied assumption. There are two reasons we concluded below.

- Comparing with existing MIAs, our attack is performed without using shadow training. Shadow training method needs to train shadow models to simulate target model in order to get data with label "member" and "non-member". The removal of shadow training saves computation and storage overhead.
- Attackers have a target dataset with true class labels, which easy to achieve since the size of this target dataset needed is 100, which is not huge. Even though the number of data records attackers want to infer is less than 100, it is not hard for attackers to get more. Due to the fact that the reason for our attack needing this dataset is to estimate the accuracy of the target model on adversarial examples, attackers can just generate different AEs of existing data records. The attack result when dataset size is less than 100 is illustrated in Sect. 5. Similarly, the class labels of data records are not tough to obtain for attackers even if through artificially label them.

4 Experimental Setup

We implement our experiments on a Laptop equipped with one GTX 1660Ti GPU with 6 GB of memory.

4.1 Dataset

Yale Face. The dataset and the target model are similar to those used in [20]. The Yale Face database contains total 2,432 images of 38 people, with each person of 64 images under various lighting. But 18 of them are lost, remaining 2,414 images. The remaining dataset is divided into training set (with 50 images of each person) and testing set (514 images). Each image has a dimension of 168 × 192.

4.2 Target Model

The target model is a convolutional neural network (CNN) with the convolution kernel size 3 × 3. The CNN model consists of 4 blocks, and the number of output channels of each block is (8, 16, 32, 64). Each block contains two convolutional layers with strides of 1 and 2, respectively. After the convolution layer, there are two fully connected layers, each containing 200 and 38 neurons. The robust model uses the PGD-based adversarial training defense. The l_∞ perturbation budget (ϵ) is set to 8/255 when training a robust model.

Figure 2 illustrates the accuracy of the training set and testing set under different iterations. Based on this figure, we can say that the model performs well after 5,000 iterations. To prove that accuracy-based attack works well when the target model has high accuracy on the adversarial examples of the testing set, our experiments mainly focus on the model of 5,000 iterations.

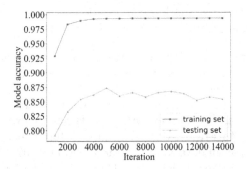

Fig. 2. Target model accuracy on training/testing dataset with different iterations.

4.3 Attack Criteria

- **Attack Accuracy:** This criteria is the fraction that attacker correctly predict "member" or "non-member" of training set for unknown data records. The number of "member" and "non-member" data may not equal, but they should have the same impact on attack accuracy. Therefore, we calculate it as

$$accuracy = \frac{1}{2} \times \frac{TP}{P} + \frac{1}{2} \times \frac{TN}{N},$$

where TF refers to true positive (namely predicting "member" when it is member), TN denotes true negative (namely predicting "non-member" when it is non-member), P is for positive (total number of positive data) and N is for negative (total number of negative data).

- **Attack Precision:** This criteria represents the proportion of true "member" in the predicted "member". The calculation is

$$precision = \frac{\frac{TP}{P}}{\frac{TP}{P} + \frac{FP}{N}},$$

where FP denotes False Positive (predicting "member" when its true label is "non-member").

- **Attack Recall:** This criteria shows how well can attacker recognize member in the training set. It can be calculated by

$$recall = \frac{TP}{P}.$$

4.4 Attack Model

We separate the training set and the testing set into two equal datasets with equal training data and testing data. One of them is used to get threshold and the other can be used as the testing set for attack in order to compute attack performance. Denote them as $data\_1$ and $data\_2$.

- **Our attack:** Randomly choose 100 data records from $data\_1$ as the dataset used by the attacker to infer. Through the 100 data records with their true labels, attacker can calculate a threshold used to perform accuracy-based attack by Algorithm 1. The whole procedure of attack is shown in Sect. 3.
- **Attack in [18]:** Randomly generate 100 data records and use them to get threshold by the confidence-thresholding method in [18].
- **Attack in [20]:** The original attack in [20] skips the procedure of choosing threshold. Therefore, the whole experiment results are the best results when implementing attack because it chooses the default threshold that can achieve the largest attack accuracy. To compare with our attack, we adjust the attack to a more realistic way. The attack changes as below:

Reconstruction of attack in [20]

1. Randomly choose 50 training data records and 50 testing data records from $data\_1$. This subset is then used as dataset that attacker hold.
2. Find out the best threshold that can make the subset achieve the largest attack accuracy. The specific method is to loop all confidence of true label of 100 data records to compute attack accuracy and look for the confidence with the largest accuracy.
3. Implement MIA using the obtained threshold.

---

5   Experiments

In this section, we evaluate the performance of our proposed attack through three criteria: accuracy, precision, and recall.

5.1   Overview of Results

The performance of our proposed attack as well as attack in [20] is shown in Fig. 3. The target model is trained through 5,000 iterations. We implement both attacks 100 times. We can tell that the accuracy of our attack is higher comparing with attack in [20], with little precision loss but a high recall gain. As shown in Fig. 2, this model has a well performance on testing set, which indicates **our attack can achieve a better attack performance in contrast to attack in [20]**. Besides, the performance of the confidence-thresholding method in [18] aimed at a robust model is also shown in Fig. 3, which shows that directly applied method in [18] does work well.

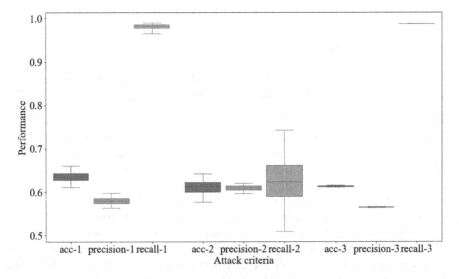

Fig. 3. The comparison of the performance of our attack, attack in [20], and attack in [18] against model trained with 5,000 iterations. The boxplots show the distribution of attack accuracy, precision, and recall. *acc*-1(2)(3), *precision*-1(2)(3) and *recall*-1(2)(3) represent attack accuracy, precision and recall of our attack (attack in [20]) (attack in [18]).

5.2   Attack Performance on Different Target Model

In Fig. 4, we can see that for models trained less than 7,000 iterations, our attack has higher accuracy, whether it is average, minimum, or maximum of accuracy.

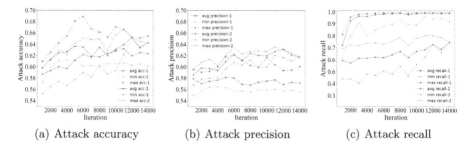

(a) Attack accuracy   (b) Attack precision   (c) Attack recall

Fig. 4. The comparison between our attack and attack in [20] through their (a) Attack accuracy, (b) Attack precision, and (c) Attack recall on models with different iterations. Each subfigure contains one attack criteria and the criteria is divided into three sub-criteria. Take *accuracy* as an example, we calculate the average accuracy, minimum accuracy, maximum accuracy among 100 attacks. In (a), *avg_acc*-1(2), *min_acc*-1(2) and *max_acc*-1(2) represent average accuracy, minimum accuracy and maximum accuracy of our attack (attack in [20]).

For models training with iterations varying from 7,000 to 10,000, the maximum and minimum accuracy of our attack are still much high than the accuracy of attack in [20], except for the minimum accuracy of model with iteration 8,000, where the minimum accuracy of attack in [20] is slightly higher than our attack's. The average accuracies of attacks on models of 7,000 to 10,000 iterations are kind of similar, apart from the average accuracy on model with 8,000 iterations. For model with more than 10,000 iterations training, the accuracy of our attack is almost not higher than the accuracy of attack in [20]. However, we can observe the reducing trend of test dataset classification accuracy of model after trained 10,000 iterations from Fig. 2. Therefore, **our attack performs a better MIA on well-performance model compared to the attack in** [20].

The recall of our attack is much higher than the recall of attack in [20], even the minimum recall of our attack is always larger than the maximum recall of attack in [20]. Recall reveals how well can attacker recognize data in training set, which is consistent with the purpose of membership inference attack. Therefore, recall is a significant standard to assess attack performance. Even though the precision of our attack is slightly lower than the precision of attack in [20], it can be ignored under the huge gap between the recall of two attacks. **Our attack has an extremely high attack recall, with almost higher than 90%.**

5.3   Attack Performance of Skewing Dataset

In Fig. 5, when the number of training set in target dataset gradually ascends and the number of testing set descends, the accuracy of both attacks has an increase. The difference is that the minimum and average accuracy of attack in [20] grow faster than of our attack. The result is that the minimum and average accuracy of attack in [20] are higher than the minimum and average accuracy of our attack when the proportion of data size of training set and testing set is

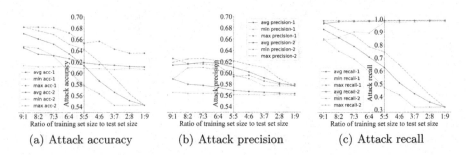

(a) Attack accuracy   (b) Attack precision   (c) Attack recall

Fig. 5. The performance change when data in target dataset is skewing to training set or testing set. The comparison between our attack and attack in [20] is achieved from three categories, i.e., (a) Attack accuracy, (b) Attack precision, (c) Attack recall. Each subfigure contains one attack criteria and the criteria is divided into three sub-criteria. Take *accuracy* as an example, we calculate the average accuracy, minimum accuracy, maximum accuracy among 100 attacks. In (a), *avg_acc*-1(2), *min_acc*-1(2) and *max_acc*-1(2) represent average accuracy, minimum accuracy and maximum accuracy of our attack (attack in [20]).

9:1. At the same time, there is a slight fluctuation for attack precision of both attacks. The attack recall of attack in [20] has witnessed a dramatic growth since the threshold of attack be chosen is lower during the change. When the ratio is 9:1, it is similar to the recall of our attack.

When the size of testing set in target dataset tends to be higher than the size of training set, the performance of attack in [20] has an obvious decrease, including *accuracy*, *precision* and *recall*. By contrast, the performance of our attack remains stable. It can tell that **our attack has a stable performance compared to the attack in [20]**.

5.4   Attack Performance Without Enough Target Data Records

The above attacks are based on that the size of the target dataset is 100, namely the number of data that the attacker wants to infer is larger than 100. However, when the dataset size is less than 100, attacker can still implement the attack. Since the target dataset is used to estimate the model accuracy, attacker can just generate more adversarial examples of the same benign example to achieve the goal. The performance of the attack with different dataset size is demonstrated in Fig. 6. When model iteration is 5,000, the attack accuracy and precision of our attack have witnessed a slight increase when the data size attacker has for inference drops. The recall of our attack decreases faster when dataset size is less than 50. We also test different models to get the overall results. The results show that the trend of performance change over dataset size variance is similar for different target models. When dataset size is larger than 50, the attack works well, just like when dataset size is 100. Even if the size of the target dataset is less than 50, the attack performance is not decreasing sharply. Therefore, **our**

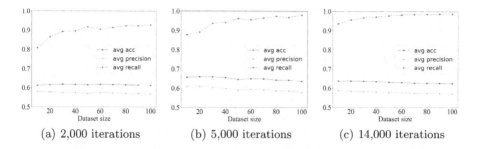

Fig. 6. The performance when changing the size of the target dataset that attacker has. This experiment is done on models trained with different iterations, i.e., (a) 2,000 iterations, (b) 5,000 iterations, and (c) 14,000 iterations. Each subfigure demonstrates the average value over the three criterias of attack performance when performing our proposed attack 100 times.

proposed attack works well even if the size of the target dataset that the attacker has is small.

6 Conclusion and Future Work

In this paper, we design a novel confidence-thresholding selection method, and then we further propose a membership inference attack based on this method. Compared to the original method, the proposed MIA attack has an overwhelming advantage over model recall and without almost no accuracy and precision loss. Besides, it relaxes the original complicated assumptions, neither needing to have an additional dataset labeled with "member" or "non-member" of target model nor using shadow training to simulate target model for collecting labeled dataset. Finally, the extensive experiments operated on the real-world dataset Yale Face demonstrate that our proposed attack is feasible and effective.

This work focuses on using untargeted adversarial examples to perform MIA and does not take the targeted adversarial examples into consideration, which would remain as a significant topic of future research. In addition, there is still an assumption that needs a dataset with true classification labels, which should be removed in the future work to achieve no assumption attack in its true sense.

Acknowledgment. The authors would like to acknowledge the support of the National Natural Science Foundation of China (No. 61902315).

References

1. Biggio, B., Nelson, B., Laskov, P.: Poisoning attacks against support vector machines. In: International Conference on Machine Learning (ICML), pp. 1467–1474 (2012)

2. Chen, X., Li, J., Ma, J., Tang, Q., Lou, W.: New algorithms for secure outsourcing of modular exponentiations. In: Foresti, S., Yung, M., Martinelli, F. (eds.) ESORICS 2012. LNCS, vol. 7459, pp. 541–556. Springer, Heidelberg (2012). https://doi.org/10.1007/978-3-642-33167-1_31

3. Chen, X., Huang, X., Li, J., Ma, J., Lou, W., Wong, D.S.: New algorithms for secure outsourcing of large-scale systems of linear equations. IEEE Trans. Inf. Forensics Secur. 10(1), 69–78 (2015)

4. Ciolacu, M., Tehrani, A. F., Beer, R., Popp, H.: Education 4.0–fostering student's performance with machine learning methods. In: Proceedings of the 2017 IEEE 23rd International Symposium for Design and Technology in Electronic Packaging (SIITME), pp. 438–443 (2017)

5. Elsayed, G., et al.: Adversarial examples that fool both computer vision and time-limited humans. In: Proceedings of the Advances in Neural Information Processing Systems, pp. 3910–3920 (2018)

6. Fredrikson, M., Jha, S., Ristenpart, T.: Model inversion attacks that exploit confidence information and basic countermeasures. In: Proceedings of the 22nd ACM SIGSAC Conference on Computer and Communications Security, pp. 1322–1333 (2015)

7. Goodfellow, I. J., Shlens, J., Szegedy, C.: Explaining and harnessing adversarial examples. In: International Conference on Machine Learning (2015)

8. Guo, H., Tang, R., Ye, Y., Li, Z., He, X.: DeepFM: a factorization-machine based neural network for CTR prediction. In: Proceedings of the Twenty-Sixth International Joint Conference on Artificial Intelligence (IJCAI), pp. 1725–1731 (2017)

9. Isele, D., Cosgun, A., Subramanian, K., Fujimura, K.: Navigating intersections with autonomous vehicles using deep reinforcement learning. In: 2018 IEEE International Conference on Robotics and Automation (ICRA), pp. 2034–2039 (2017)

10. Leino, K., Fredrikson, M.: Stolen memories: leveraging model memorization for calibrated white-box membership inference. arXiv preprint arXiv:1906.11798 (2019)

11. Long, Y., Bindschaedler, V., Gunter, C.A.: Towards measuring membership privacy. arXiv preprint arXiv:1712.09136 (2017)

12. Long, Y., et al.: Understanding membership inferences on well-generalized learning models. arXiv preprint arXiv:1802.04889 (2018)

13. Mao, Y., Zhu, X., Zheng, W., Yuan, D., Ma, J.: A novel user membership leakage attack in collaborative deep learning. In: Proceedings of the 2019 11th International Conference on Wireless Communications and Signal Processing (WCSP), pp. 1–6 (2019)

14. Melis, L., Song, C., De Cristofaro, E., Shmatikov, V.: Exploiting unintended feature leakage in collaborative learning. In: Proceedings of the 2019 IEEE Symposium on Security and Privacy (SP), pp. 691–706 (2019)

15. Nasr, M., Shokri, R., Houmansadr, A.: Comprehensive privacy analysis of deep learning: passive and active white-box inference attacks against centralized and federated learning. In: Proceedings of the 2019 IEEE Symposium on Security and Privacy (SP), pp. 739–753 (2019)

16. Rahman, M.A., Rahman, T., Laganiére, R., Mohammed, N., Wang, Y.: Membership inference attack against differentially private deep learning model. Trans. Data Priv. 11(1), 61–79 (2018)

17. Raví, D., et al.: Deep learning for health informatics. IEEE J. Biomed. Health Inform. 21(1), 4–21 (2016)

18. Salem, A., Zhang, Y., Humbert, M., Berrang, P., Fritz, M., Backes, M.: ML-Leaks: model and data independent membership inference attacks and defenses on machine learning models. In: 26th Annual Network and Distributed System Security Symposium (2019)
19. Shokri, R., Stronati, M., Song, C., Shmatikov, V.: Membership inference attacks against machine learning models. In: Proceedings of the 2017 IEEE Symposium on Security and Privacy (SP), pp. 3–18 (2017)
20. Song, L., Shokri, R., Mittal, P.: Privacy risks of securing machine learning models against adversarial examples. In: Proceedings of the 2019 ACM SIGSAC Conference on Computer and Communications Security (CCS), pp. 241–257 (2019)
21. Song, C., Ristenpart, T., Shmatikov, V.: Machine learning models that remember too much. In: Proceedings of the 2017 ACM SIGSAC Conference on Computer and Communications Security (CCS), pp. 587–601 (2017)
22. Shan, Y., Hoens, T.R., Jiao, J., Wang, H., Yu, D., Mao, J.C.: Deep crossing: web-scale modeling without manually crafted combinatorial features. In: Proceedings of the 22nd ACM SIGKDD International Conference on Knowledge Discovery and Data Mining, pp. 255–262 (2016)
23. Shafahi, A., et al.: Poison frogs! targeted clean-label poisoning attacks on neural networks. In: Proceedings of the Advances in Neural Information Processing Systems, pp. 6103–6113 (2018)
24. Wang, Z., Song, M., Zhang, Z., Song, Y., Wang, Q., Qi, H.: Beyond inferring class representatives: user-level privacy leakage from federated learning. In: Proceedings of the IEEE INFOCOM 2019-IEEE Conference on Computer Communications, pp. 2512–2520 (2019)
25. Yang, C., Wu, Q., Li, H., Chen, Y.: Generative poisoning attack method against neural networks. arXiv preprint arXiv:1703.01340 (2017)
26. Yeom, S., Giacomelli, I., Fredrikson, M., Jha, S.: Privacy risk in machine learning: analyzing the connection to overfitting. In: Proceedings of the 2018 IEEE 31st Computer Security Foundations Symposium (CSF), pp. 268–282 (2018)
27. Yuan, X., He, P., Zhu, Q., Li, X.: Adversarial examples: attacks and defenses for deep learning. IEEE Trans. Neural Netw. Learn. Syst. 30(9), 2805–2824 (2019)
28. Zhang, W., Du, T., Wang, J.: Deep learning over multi-field categorical data. In: Ferro, N., et al. (eds.) ECIR 2016. LNCS, vol. 9626, pp. 45–57. Springer, Cham (2016). https://doi.org/10.1007/978-3-319-30671-1_4
29. Zhang, X., Chen, X., Liu, J., Xiang, Y.: DeepPAR and DeepDPA: privacy-preserving and asynchronous deep learning for industrial IoT. IEEE Trans. Ind. Inf. 16(3), 2081–2090 (2019)
30. Zhang, X., Jiang, T., Li, K.C., Castiglione, A., Chen, X.: New publicly verifiable computation for batch matrix multiplication. Inf. Sci. 479, 664–678 (2019)

Smart Watchdog: A Lightweight Defending Mechanism Against Adversarial Transfer Learning

Yong Ding[1,2], Wenyao Liu[1(✉)] ⓘ, Yi Qin[3], and Yujue Wang[1]

[1] Guangxi Key Laboratory of Cryptography and Information Security,
School of Computer Science and Information Security, Guilin University
of Electronic Technology, Guilin 541004, China
1466002758@qq.com
[2] Cyberspace Security Research Center, Peng Cheng Laboratory,
Shenzhen 518055, China
[3] School of Mathematics and Computational Sciences, Guilin University of Electronic
Technology, Guilin 541004, China

Abstract. Most traffic sign recognition tasks rely on artificial neural network. As a kind of transfer learning method, knowledge distillation has improved the robustness of neural network models to a certain extent and saved time for model training. However, the weights of the original model (teacher model) and the new model (student model) are similar. The adversarial examples of the teacher model are easy to transfer and can successfully attack the student model. In order to solve this problem, this paper proposes a lightweight defense mechanism to reduce the similarity between the weight of the student model and the weight of the teacher model, and the dropout-randomization method is applied in the input layer of the student model to reduce the input probability of the adversarial examples. Moreover, we evaluate the precision and the recall of the improved model, the results show that the robustness of the model is significantly improved under the Carlini-Wagner (CW) attack and Project Gradient Descent (PGD) attack.

Keywords: Transfer learning · Knowledge distillation · Weight · Dropout

1 Introduction

With the development of society and the improvement of people's living standard, cars have been popularized and intelligent transportation system [15] has emerged. As a part of the intelligent transportation system, traffic sign recognition will help to improve the road safety of vehicles. At present, most traffic identification is completed by neural network models. The accuracy, real-time performance and robustness of the model are very important factors in the study

X. Chen et al. (Eds.): ML4CS 2020, LNCS 12487, pp. 540–549, 2020.
https://doi.org/10.1007/978-3-030-62460-6_48

of traffic sign identification [1,8]. Wrong identification results can lead to serious safety accidents. Therefore, in-depth research on the traffic sign recognition model is very necessary. Although the recognition technology of neural network model is becoming more and more perfect, there are remain some difficult problems to be addressed. For example, the training of the neural network models requires a lot of labeled data, which leads to high training costs. In addition, ordinary model training still has the problems of low training efficiency and poor robustness.

With the rise of artificial intelligence, the idea of transfer learning is applied to machine learning [20]. The parameters of the large model and the example "knowledge" learned are directly transferred to the similar new task model, then the data set for the new task is used to conduct "secondary training", so as to quickly build the model with high accuracy and simple structure. In 2014, Bengio et al. [21] studied the transferability of each layer feature in deep learning, and proposed that initializing the network with the parameters of a large model can improve the generalization performance. In the era of intelligent big data, in the face of increasing data volume and data types, transfer learning solves the problem of how to effectively learn from externally discrete data in the case of insufficient examples and incomplete tags in machine learning tasks [16,17].

While opening up a shortcut to model construction, transfer learning also brings new problems. Because the model parameters of the original model and the new model are similar, the student model is vulnerable to the adversarial examples of the teacher model [22]. So far, there is no good solution to this problem.

1.1 Related Work

With the rapid development of machine learning in recent years, transfer learning has been widely used in the field of machine learning [14]. Especially in the engineering field, transfer learning has made considerable progress, whether in speech recognition to deal with regional accents or in training self-driving cars in advance through video game simulations.

At present, many traffic sign recognition models are acquired by some classical deep convolutional neural network transfer learning. For example, AlexNet, proposed by Alex in 2012, takes Relu function as an activation function and uses dropout mechanism to prevent overfitting [11]. ResNet, proposed by He et al. in 2015, avoids the situation of continuously deepening the neural network and saturating the precision of the model, making it possible to train super deep neural networks [4]. As well as the features of multi-gpu implementation, CNN has become the core algorithm model in image recognition and classification, which has brought about the explosion of deep learning. However, there are problems with low efficiency, low recognition accuracy, and poor robustness in the student model.

Among them, one example of transfer learning is the distilled neural network model [18]. Although knowledge distillation can save time in labeling data sets, it also gradually exposes its disadvantages. Even if the attacker knows nothing about the model structure, parameters and training set of the student model, when the teacher's parameters and training set model are public, the student model is vulnerable to attack. In 2017, Carlini et al. [2] proved that CW attack algorithm can reliably find the adversarial examples of teacher model, while it can be transferred to student model.

1.2 Our Contributions

To address the above mentioned issues, the dropout mechanism was used in the input layer of the distilled student model to inactivate the input pixels in a certain proportion. This prevents some adversarial examples from being input into the student model and reduces the attack rate. Then, we choose the CW_2 attack algorithm and PGD attack algorithm to generate an adversarial example and load it into the improved distillation student model to observe the performance of it. The results show that our improved model can resist both attacks.

2   Preliminaries

This section briefly introduces the distillation student model and its related concepts.

2.1   Distillation Neural Network

Model distillation is a process of distilling the feature information and important parameters learned by the large-scale neural network model, and using the distilled small-grained "knowledge" to guide the training of the simplified network model [6]. The specific process is as follows:

Step 1. Pre-training a teacher model with complex structure, and the last layer of the teacher model is softmax layer:

$$Softmax\ (x_i, T) = \frac{e^{x_i/T}}{\sum_{j=1}^{j} e^{x_i/T}} \tag{1}$$

where x_i represents neurons in the last layer of the examples, and the value of T in the softmax layer is gradually changed from 1 to 100. The larger the value of T is, the softer the probability distribution is. In this step, the soft label is obtained.

Step 2. Assess the success rate of the attack against the teacher model. Different values of T were set to observe the recognition accuracy of the teacher model. When the attack success rate is the lowest, the value of T is T_z. The value of T is set to T_z for the soft label training of the student network.

Step 3. The test set is used to test the student model, where the value of T is 1. Our experiment will prove that the trained model has the characteristics of high precision, strong generalization ability and strong robustness.

2.2 Soft Targets

The label data of image examples are generally discrete and a example only has one category target. These labels are called hard targets, which correspond to the input data, for example: [0, 0, 1, 0]. But in practice, there are great similarities among many categories [9]. For example, cats in some images are so similar to dogs in color, size and other characteristics. However, the model has a similar probability of classifying them as cats or dogs. Discrete tags do not exhibit such similarities. When the model trained with hard labeled examples is put into application, it is easy to classify the image into other categories with similar characteristics.

To solve this problem, we train the distillation neural network to obtain the output of softmax layer, and convert the discrete calibration of examples into the target with "the possibility of each category" , which is the soft target, such as [0.001, 0.002, 0.98, 0.017]. Soft targets can retain the generalization ability of complex models while converting them into small ones.

2.3 Softmax Function

Softmax function is used in the multi-classification process to map the output of multiple neurons to the interval (0, 1) for multi-classification. It is defined as:

$$S_i = \frac{e^i}{\sum_j e^j} \tag{2}$$

In the neural network model, the softmax value of the i-th category is the ratio of the index of this category to the sum of the indices of all categories.

2.4 Generating Adversarial Examples

In general, given an input example x of a model, its target is $t = C(x)$, we can find another example x' that is close to x in the distance metric, so that $C(x') = t$, then we call x' for adversarial example.

In this paper, the CW attack and PGD attack algorithms are used to generate adversarial examples.

CW Attack. CW attack is a type of optimization-based attack. The L_P norms are used to measure the similarity between clean examples x and adversarial examples x' [13], which are defined as $||x - x'||_p$, and the p-norm is:

$$||v||_p = \left(\sum_{i=1}^{n} |v_i|^p \right)^{\frac{1}{p}} \tag{3}$$

when $p = 0$, the L_0 distance represents the number of changes of the example pixels. When p takes 2, the L_2 distance is the standard Euclidean distance between the pixels of the clean example x and the pixels of the adversarial example x'. When p is $+$, the L_∞ distance limits the maximum change of each pixel.

In this paper, we can find adversarial examples with distortion below the L_2 metric to achieve the target attack on the student model, where the objective function defined as follows:

$$minimize||\frac{1}{2}(tanh(w) + 1) - x||_2^2 + c \cdot f(\frac{1}{2}(tanh(w) + 1)) \tag{4}$$

The adversarial examples can be mapped into the $tanh$ space, x can be transformed in $(-\infty, +\infty)$. Since $C(x') = t$ is highly non-linear and difficult to solve, we optimize it into the following form [2]:

$$f(x') = max(max\{Z(x')_i : i \neq t\} - Z(x')_t, -\kappa) \tag{5}$$

where $z(x')_t$ represents the output vector of the adversarial example x' of the model without softmax function, and its maximum value corresponds to the category of the adversarial example finally classified. The value of $z(x')$ different from that of class t is $z(x')_i$, κ is the confidence level, and c is a superparameter used to balance the relationship between two losses.

PGD Attack. Project Gradient Descent attack is an iterative attack based on Gradient. In each iteration, the disturbance is clipped to the specified range. If the model can withstand PGD attacks, that means it may be able to withstand other attacks. Therefore, we adopt PGD algorithm to attack the student model before and after the improvement. The main idea is to make the change direction of the example characteristics and the increase direction of the gradient value of the loss function exactly the same. Multiple iterations are carried out, the value of the loss function will increase, and the neural network model will classify the example incorrectly. The objective function of the PGD attack is:

$$max_{||\delta||_\infty \leq \gamma} l(f(x_0 + \delta; w), y_0) \tag{6}$$

where x_0 is the source example, δ is the parameter of preturbing, γ constrains the permissible transformations, w is the weight of student model, y_0 is the ground-truth label, and $l()$ is used as the metric loss value. The adversarial examples are updated through gradient projection descent iteration:

$$x_{t+1} = \prod_\gamma x^t + \alpha sign(\nabla_x l(f(x_0 + \delta; w), y_0)) \tag{7}$$

where $\prod_\gamma = x||x - x_0||_\infty \leq \gamma$.

3   The Design of Smart Watchdog

3.1   Overview

In order to prevent the transfer of adversarial examples, make the distillation student model have better robustness and ensure the high classification accuracy of the student model, the distillation student model is improved.

Here, we intend to use dropout on the input layer of the student model to make the input neurons randomly inactivated in a certain proportion, so as to filter out some adversarial examples and resist the attack of adversarial examples of teacher model to some extent.

In the training process, Keras framework [10, 19] was selected to assemble and initialize our model, and the teacher model and student model were constructed based on the convolutional neural network . In order to get the soft targets, the softmax function which can change the T value is applied in the last layer of the teacher model. The soft targets and weights trained by the teacher model are used to train the student model. In addition, we select the pulse based SGD optimizer to perform random gradient descent, and select a example randomly for learning each time, namely: SGD updates each example in a gradient manner. However, SGD only updates once at a time. The gradient is calculated at a faster rate, and new examples can be added during the gradient descent. Finally, the CW-attack algorithm and PGD attack algorithm are used to attack the student model before and after the improvement, and the precision of the improved model are evaluated.

3.2 Dropout Layer

Although knowledge distillation saves time for training the model with simple structure and improves the model classification accuracy, the robustness of the model is also sacrificed to some extent.

Specifically, we add a dropout layer before the input layer of the distilled student model. When the examples are propagated forward, the input neuron is inactivated with a certain probability of p, and only $1 - p$ neurons transmit the example to the next layer. The example sets participate in each round of training in a certain proportion, which can avoid overfitting of the student model due to simplified structure and large data set to some extent. On the other hand, it can filter out some of the adversarial examples to improve the robustness of the distilled student model. The compromise between improving the accuracy of classification and improving the robustness of the neural network model is realized.

4 Evaluation

4.1 Parameter Settings

We construct the model architecture to evaluate the robustness of the improved distillation student model. The structure of our distillation neural network model is shown in Table 1 and the hyper parameters of the model are shown in Table 2.

Table 1. Model architecture

Layer type	Teacher model	Student model
Convolution+ReLU	$3 \times 3 \times 32$	$3 \times 3 \times 64$
Convolution+ReLU	$3 \times 3 \times 32$	$3 \times 3 \times 64$
Max Pooling	2×2	2×2
Convolution+ReLU	$3 \times 3 \times 64$	$3 \times 3 \times 128$
Convolution+ReLU	$3 \times 3 \times 64$	$3 \times 3 \times 128$
Max Pooling	2×2	2×2
Fully Connected+ReLU	200	256
Fully Connected+ReLU	200	256
Softmax	10	10

Table 2. Training parameters of the model

Parameter	Teacher model	Student model
Learning Rate	0.1	0.01(decay 0.5)
Delay Rate	1×10^{-6}	1×10^{-6}
Dropout	0.0	0.5
Batch Size	128	128
Epochs	50	50

4.2 Datasets

The MNIST data set and the CIFAR-10 data set were used in our experiments.

MNIST dataset contains training examples (60,000 handwritten digits) and corresponding training set labels, 10,000 test sets and corresponding test set labels. The images in it are all 28 * 28 grayscale images, with each pixel being an 8-bit byte.

The CIFAR-10 dataset consists of 60,000 32 * 32 pixel color images divided into 10 categories, each containing 6,000 images, 50,000 images were used for training the model and 10,000 were used for testing.

4.3 Performance Measure

Precision. Precision is the proportion of the number of examples correctly classified in the test example set to the total number of examples [3]. Generally,

$$Precision = \frac{TP}{TP + FP} \qquad (8)$$

where TP is the number of true positive examples, that is, the number of examples correctly classified as positive examples. FP is the number of false positive examples that the number of examples misclassified as positive examples.

Precision is a measure of the generalization ability of a model. The higher the precision of the model is, the stronger the generalization ability of the model is. We evaluate the precision of the distillation student model before and after the improvement respectively, which is shown in Table 3.

Table 3. Precision for student distillation models

Model	Dataset	Dropout	CW_2	PGD
Before improvement	MNIST	0.0	46.9%	37.3%
	CIFAR	0.0	43%	38.6%
After improvement	MNIST	0.5	64.6%	61.4%
	CIFAR	0.5	65.4%	67.7%

As can be seen from Table 3, under the CW attack, the precision of the unimproved model is only about 45%. When the dropout value is only 0.5, the precision of the improved model reaches about 65%. Moreover, as the dropout value increases, the precision of the model increases accordingly. Compared with the CW attack, the PGD attack seems to be more effective on the model. Before improving the model, the precision of the model is less than 40%; on the basis of our improved scheme, the precision of the model trained on the MNIST dataset reaches more than 60%, and the precision of the model trained on the CIFAR dataset reaches 65% the above.

Recall. The recall represents the proportion of examples that are predicted to be correct. There are two possibilities. One is to predict the original positive class as a positive class (TP), and the other is to predict the original positive class as a negative class (FN). The representation of recall is as follows:

$$Recall = \frac{TP}{TP + FN} \tag{9}$$

Table 4. Recall for student distillation models

Model	Dataset	Dropout	CW_2	PGD
Before improvement	MNIST	0.0	57.7%	68.1%
	CIFAR	0.0	58.3%	67.2%
After improvement	MNIST	0.5	53.9%	58.7%
	CIFAR	0.5	56.5%	52.1%

It is easy to see that if the training efficiency and robustness of the model are improved, the recall of the model drops slightly (Table 4).

5   Conclusion

Transfer learning provides a shortcut for saving the time of marking data, improving the efficiency of training model and improving the classification accuracy of small model. However, it also brings a new problem, that is, adversarial examples will attack the student model in a "transfer" way. In order to solve this problem, we put forward the "Watchdog" scheme and combine it with distillation neural network. It can realize the compromise between improving the accuracy of ordinary convolutional neural network and ensuring the robustness of the model.

In this paper, we also launched CW_2 attack and PGD attack against the students models before and after improvement. The experiment results showed that our improved scheme can indeed resist the "transfer" attack of adversarial examples on the student model to a certain extent. In addition, "Watchdog" can be used in combination with any existing defense methods, such as feature squeezing [5] and network pruning [7,12]. As for the defense effect, it needs to be further verified.

Acknowledgements. This article is supported in part by the National Natural Science Foundation of China under projects 61772150, 61862012, and 61962012, the Guangxi Key R&D Program under project AB17195025, the Guangxi Natural Science Foundation under grants 2018GXNSFDA281054, 2018GXNSFAA281232, 2019GXNSFFA245015, 2019GXNSFGA245004 and AD19245048, and the Peng Cheng Laboratory Project of Guangdong Province PCL2018KP004.

References

1. Berger, M., Forechi, A., De Souza, A.F., de Oliveira Neto, J., Veronese, L., Badue, C.: Traffic sign recognition with VG-RAM weightless neural networks. In: 2012 12th International Conference on Intelligent Systems Design and Applications (ISDA), pp. 315–319. IEEE (2012)
2. Carlini, N., Wagner, D.: Towards evaluating the robustness of neural networks. In: 2017 IEEE Symposium on Security and Privacy (SP), pp. 39–57, May 2017
3. Goutte, C., Gaussier, E.: A probabilistic interpretation of precision, recall and F-Score, with implication for evaluation. In: Losada, D.E., Fernández-Luna, J.M. (eds.) ECIR 2005. LNCS, vol. 3408, pp. 345–359. Springer, Heidelberg (2005). https://doi.org/10.1007/978-3-540-31865-1_25
4. He, K., Zhang, X., Ren, S., Sun, J.: Deep residual learning for image recognition. In: Proceedings of the IEEE Conference on Computer Vision and Pattern Recognition, pp. 770–778 (2016)
5. He, W., Wei, J., Chen, X., Carlini, N., Song, D.: Adversarial example defenses: ensembles of weak defenses are not strong. In: Proceedings of the 11th USENIX Conference on Offensive Technologies, pp. 15–15 (2017)
6. Hua, Y., Ge, S., Li, C., Luo, Z., Jin, X.: Distilling deep neural networks for robust classification with soft decision trees. In: 2018 14th IEEE International Conference on Signal Processing (ICSP), pp. 1128–1132. IEEE (2018)

7. Huang, G.-B., Saratchandran, P., Sundararajan, N.: A generalized growing and pruning RBF (GGAP-RBF) neural network for function approximation. IEEE Trans. Neural Netw. **16**(1), 57–67 (2005)
8. Huang, Z., Yuanlong, Y., Jason, G., Liu, H.: An efficient method for traffic sign recognition based on extreme learning machine. IEEE Trans. Cybern. **47**(4), 920–933 (2016)
9. El Jelali, S., Lyhyaoui, A., Figueirasvidal, A.R.: Designing model based classifiers by emphasizing soft targets. Fundamenta Informaticae **96**(4), 419–433 (2009)
10. Ketkar, N.: Introduction to keras. Deep Learning with Python, pp. 97–111. Springer, Berlin (2017)
11. Krizhevsky, A., Sutskever, I., Hinton, G.E.: Imagenet classification with deep convolutional neural networks. In: Advances in Neural Information Processing Systems, pp. 1097–1105 (2012)
12. Luo, J., Wu, J., Lin, W.: Thinet: a filter level pruning method for deep neural network compression. In: Proceedings of the IEEE International Conference on Computer Vision, pp. 5068–5076 (2017)
13. Luo, X., Chang, X., Ban, X.: Regression and classification using extreme learning machine based on $l1 - norm$ and $l2 - norm$. Neurocomputing **174**, 179–186 (2016)
14. Pan, W., Zhong, E., Yang, Q.: Transfer learning for text mining. Mining Text Data, pp. 223–257. Springer, Berlin (2012)
15. Kashif Naseer Qureshi and Abdul Hanan Abdullah: A survey on intelligent transportation systems. Middle-East J. Sci. Res. **15**(5), 629–642 (2013)
16. Raina, R., Battle, A., Lee, H., Packer, B., Ng, A.Y.: Self-taught learning: transfer learning from unlabeled data. In: Proceedings of the 24th International Conference on Machine Learning, pp. 759–766 (2007)
17. Tan, Q., Yu, G., Domeniconi, C., Wang, J., Zhang, Z.: Incomplete multi-view weak-label learning. In: IJCAI, pp. 2703–2709 (2018)
18. Tang, Z., Wang, D., Zhang, Z.: Recurrent neural network training with dark knowledge transfer. In: 2016 IEEE International Conference on Acoustics, Speech and Signal Processing (ICASSP), pp. 5900–5904. IEEE (2016)
19. Tokui, S., Oono, K., Hido, S., Clayton, J.: Chainer: a next-generation open source framework for deep learning. In: Proceedings of Workshop on Machine Learning Systems (LearningSys) in the Twenty-Ninth Annual Conference on Neural Information Processing Systems (NIPS), vol. 5, pp. 1–6 (2015)
20. Weiss, K., Khoshgoftaar, T.M., Wang, D.D.: A survey of transfer learning. J. Big Data **3**(1), 1–40 (2016). https://doi.org/10.1186/s40537-016-0043-6
21. Yosinski, J., Clune, J., Bengio, Y., Lipson, H.: How transferable are features in deep neural networks? In: Advances in Neural Information Processing Systems, pp. 3320–3328 (2014)
22. Zhou, W., et al.: Transferable adversarial perturbations. In: Proceedings of the European Conference on Computer Vision (ECCV), pp. 452–467 (2018)

A Poisoning Attack Against the Recognition Model Trained by the Data Augmentation Method

Yunhao Yang, Long Li[✉], Liang Chang, and Tianlong Gu

Guangxi Key Laboratory of Trusted Software, Guilin University of Electronic
Technology, Guilin 541004, China
lilong@guet.edu.cn

Abstract. The training model often preprocesses the training set with the data augmentation method. Aiming at this kind of training mode, a poisoning attack scheme is proposed in this paper, which can effectively complete the attack. For the traffic sign recognition system, its decision boundary is changed by the way of data poisoning, so that it would incorrectly recognize the target sample. In this scheme, a "backdoor" belonging to the attacker is added to the toxic sample so that the attacker can manipulate recognition model (i.e., the target sample is classified into expected categories). The attack is difficult to detect, because the victim will take a poison sample as a healthy one. The experimental results show that the scheme can successfully attack the model trained by the data augmentation method, realize the attack function against the selected target, and complete the attack with a high success rate. It is hoped that this work will raise awareness of the important issues of data reliability and data sources.

Keywords: Data augmentation · Poisoning attack · Traffic sign · Recognition system

1 Introduction

With the development of technologies such as big data and artificial intelligence, driverless technology is accelerating from research and development to application. However, since the introduction of driverless vehicles into the public eye, its security issues are also attracting the attention of the whole society. Applications for driverless vehicles rely on systems based on the Convolutional Neural Network (CNN) model to make decisions automatically, as a result, attention has been focused on potential vulnerabilities introduced by the CNN algorithm. In the driverless system, the recognition system model that classifies traffic signs is the most vulnerable place to attack. The attackers can manipulate the driverless system only by making minor changes to the traffic signs. When a driverless system and a human driver are driving at the same time, the automatic recognition system misjudges traffic signs, which can be catastrophic.

In order to achieve effective test results, CNN usually contains millions of weights. Therefore, powerful computing power and abundant training data are needed to train

© Springer Nature Switzerland AG 2020
X. Chen et al. (Eds.): ML4CS 2020, LNCS 12487, pp. 550–561, 2020.
https://doi.org/10.1007/978-3-030-62460-6_49

the model. Individuals and some enterprises often do not have such powerful resources, so they use cloud computing or other external computing tools for model training, but the data may be transferred to less protected systems, which is a good opportunity to create attacks. Transferring the knowledge learned in one scenario to another can effectively reduce the training cost. Such a pattern is often referred to as transfer learning. The biggest advantage of transfer learning is that it can use limited data to train a robust classifier. The principle of transfer learning is a pre-trained feature extraction network (pre-model), and only the final network layer (softmax layer) will be trained for a specific task.

At present, the driverless system mainly faces the big data security risk such as poisoning attack [1], evasion attack [2] and so on. Poisoning attack is a common attack method in the training phase. The attacker changes the learning algorithm logically and threatens the machine learning model by modifying and deleting the training data or injecting the elaborate poisoned data into the training set. The most common type of poisoning attack is model skew, in which the attacker contaminates the training data in such a way that the classifier tilts towards its own preferences in categorizing health data and poisoned data. This kind of poisoning attack has misled the discriminative model in application scenarios such as DoS attack detection [3], PDF malware classification [4] and sentiment analysis [5].

In the evasion attack, the attacker adjusts or manipulates the sample, causing the machine learning model to make a wrong judgment on the sample in the test phase. At present, this attack method has been widely used in various scenarios, such as malicious documents specially used to evade antivirus programs, e-mails trying to evade spam filters, etc. For example, someone has added graffiti to traffic signs to make the recognition system recognize "STOP" traffic sign as "Speed Limit 45" traffic sign [6].

The purpose of poisoning attack and evasion attack is to destroy the integrity of the model by generating adversarial samples. Once the attacker destroys the integrity of the model, the prediction results of the model will be disturbed or even manipulated. The theoretical basis of the above two kinds of attacks on CNN is based on two important aspects: first, the relationship between high-dimensional neurons and features is not one-to-one, but many-to-many; Second, adding some targeted and imperceptible perturbations to the original sample will change the features of the sample, which will lead to the misclassification of the target by CNN. The difference is that the poisoning attack mainly changes the decision boundary of the model by injecting the poisoned data into the training set in the training phase, while the evasion attack is to confuse the predicted results of the model through the adversarial datas in the test phase.

2 Related Work

Traditional poisoning attacks often indiscriminately reduce the accuracy of the test, rather than targeting a specific sample, which makes the attack easy to detect. The early attacks were mainly to damage the spam filtering system by poisoning Bayes Classifier [7] and attack Support Vector Machine (SVM) by using the poison sample of the gradient rise strategy training [8]. In recent years, many scholars have found that the poisoning attack has a disastrous impact on CNN. Steinhardt et al. [9] proved through experiments that even if there are sufficient preventive measures in advance, when the attacker is allowed to modify 3% of the training set, the test accuracy will be reduced by 11%. Muñoz et al. [10] proposed a scheme to generate poison samples, and trained the poison samples with the back-gradient optimization method, which increased the damage to the model. Inspired by the generative adversarial network (GAN) [11], the auto-encoder is selected as the generator, which greatly speeds up the generation of poison samples [12].

In order to make the attack more difficult to detect, the attacker designs targeted poisoning attack, this attack mode poses a great threat to the learning model. Targeted backdoor attack [13] cause the selected test data to be misclassified by adding a "backdoor" to the poison sample and injecting a small number of poison samples into the training set. Trojaning attack [14] generates a Trojan trigger for the discrimination model. Once the model is triggered, it will misclassify the targeted samples, but it will not have any impact on the unmarked samples.

However, in the above studies, a variety of hypotheses are proposed that are limited to the experimental environment. For example, attackers usually have a certain degree of control over the marking process of training set samples. This is an unintended departure from real-world scenarios, where training sets will be reviewed by specialists and qualified samples marked by examiners. Suciu et al. [15] proposed a poisoning attack scheme that did not control the marking process of the training set. However, in order to achieve the ideal attack effect, each batch of training set required at least 12.5% (up to 100%) of the poison samples, which was impossible in practice.

In an attack scheme, Ali Shafahi et al. [16] craft a poison sample called "clean-label", which would completely trick the examiner into labeling the sample and poison it with a high success rate. However, this scheme does not take into account that the training set will be preprocessed before the actual training model, which will change the features of the poison samples, resulting in the attack cannot achieve the desired effect. The target of the attack is a transfer learning model, but the data set used in the attack is the original data set to train the model, which lacks some objectivity. In order to enable the traffic sign recognition model to identify objects with different perspectives, brightness and sizes (i.e., the adaptability of the recognition process to new samples) in a robust manner, the model trainers usually perform data augmentation operations such as random noise addition, image flipping, random cutting, etc., on the training set before training. When training the traffic sign recognition model, the trainer often considers to improve the adaptability of the recognition model to new samples. The better way to solve this problem is to do some data augmentation operations on the training set before training, such as changing the brightness, image flipping and image cutting. Therefore, this paper can still achieve the purpose of poisoning attack after data augmentation. The main contributions of this paper are as follows:

1) The proposed scheme is able to complete the poisoning attack even after the traffic sign data is augmented. When utilizing the traffic sign training model, it is one of the most common methods for model trainers to do data augmentation on the training set, because this operation can increase the generalization ability of the model. However, in the process of making poison samples in this paper, the poison

samples were processed by the method of data augmentation in advance, which enhanced the adaptability of poison samples to data augmentation.

2) The scheme proposed in this paper will produce poisoning attack with "hidden backdoor", victim will correctly mark the label of the poisonous sample of traffic signs (the label seen by human eyes). The trainer and the recognition system will make different decisions on the sample, and the poisoning attack can be completed by making use of the decision difference. In short, it's hard for victims to suspect, the poison samples injected into the training set will be treated as healthy samples by the auditor, but it will change the decision boundary of the recognition system during the training.

3) This scheme realizes the poisoning attack on the designated target of the traffic sign recognition system. When the driverless recognition system can be manipulated to classify the target into the categories the attacker wants, it undoubtedly poses a great threat to driverless vehicles. For example, after the completion of the poisoning attack, the recognition system will be "No Enter" sign mistakenly identified as "No Parking" sign is easy to cause traffic accidents.

3   Recognition System and Adversary Model

3.1   Recognition System

This paper systematically studies the poisoning attacks against the Inception-V3 recognition system model, which is essentially an improved CNN model. The traditional CNN to improve the utilization of network computing resources is simply to stack the convolution layer in large quantities, which is easier to overfit and difficult to calculate. And Inception-V3 is a network with excellent local topology structure, can make the CNN layer to get better image features. A normally working system model consists of the testing phase in the middle part of Fig. 1 and the training phase shown on the left side of Fig. 1 (Ideal world). The training process includes such preprocessing methods as data augmentation and standardization. The preprocessing will increase the generalization ability of the model without loss of generality. In the test phase, the preprocessed new samples are put into the model after training, and the model will automatically make decisions on the samples. The poisoning attack process against this model is shown in the training stage (Adversarial world) on the right of Fig. 1. Firstly, poisoned data is injected into the training set and preprocessed the training set. Then, the training set is used to train the recognition system model. The training to complete the model by studying the features of poisoned data changed the decision boundary.

3.2   Adversary Model

Building an adversary model [17] usually requires four aspects: adversary strategy, adversary target [18], adversary knowledge [19] and adversary capability [20]. The adversary strategy of this scheme is to change the decision boundary of the model by injecting poison samples into the training set and further manipulate the model to

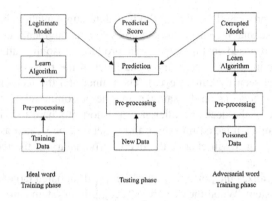

Fig. 1. System architecture

output error labels. Adversary target is to create a targeted attack that destroys the integrity of the model. The attacker can induce the model to predict the target sample to the designated category of the attacker. Except for the wrong prediction of the target, the overall performance of the model after poisoning is not obvious. In this paper, the adversary knowledge is set as that the attacker does not know the training data, but knows the model and its parameters. This also makes sense to attack a migration learning model that is pre-trained on a standard dataset. The adversary capability is set to be slightly weaker, requiring no control over the training process of the model at all (e.g., marking samples, collecting and screening samples).

4   Attack Scheme

4.1   The Theory of Crafting Poison Samples

The paper defines the category into which the attacker wants the target to be classified as the backdoor category, and selects a backdoor sample b in the backdoor category. Define t as the target sample, and when the attack succeeds, t will be misclassified into the backdoor category. Define p as an elaborated poison sample, x is defined as the feature representation of the poison sample in the input layer (i.e., the low-level feature), while $f(x)$ represents the feature of the sample in the bottleneck layer (also known as high-level feature). It should be noted that if the low-level features of the two samples are similar, it means that the human eye sees the two samples as the same, while the high-level features of the two samples will be identified as the same by the recognition system. Because of the high complexity and nonlinearity of $f(x)$, the loss of high-level feature of p and t can be continuously reduced in the training process, and the low-level feature of p and b can be ensured to be similar at the same time. In this paper, by minimizing the loss of high-level features of poison samples and target samples, the model will always classify poison samples and target samples into the same category; it is ensured that the low-level features of the poison sample are similar to the low-level features of the backdoor sample, so that the human eye will see no difference between the two samples. Therefore, the poison samples that are injected into the training set will be marked as backdoor category's label, and in the test phase, the model will classify the poison samples and the target samples into the backdoor category at the same time, so that the target samples will get "backdoor" from the backdoor category. At this point, the equation is used to represent the poison sample as:

$$p = \underset{x}{\mathrm{argmin}}\|f(t) - f(x)\|_2^2 + \alpha\|b - x\|_2^2 \tag{1}$$

The first term in Eq. (1) represents the loss of the high-level features of the target sample and the high-level features of the poison sample, in the process of minimizing the loss, the poison samples will keep approaching the target samples in the feature space. The second term represents the loss of the lower level features of the poison sample and the backdoor sample, minimizing this loss means that the appearance of the two samples is infinitely close, and the parameter α controls the degree of optimization.

Data augmentation can not only prevent training overfitting by expanding the sample size, but also enhance the generalization ability and stability of the model. Common methods of data augmentation include image clipping, image inversion, brightness adjustment, etc. If the training set is preprocessed by means of data augmentation before the training model, the above attacks will not achieve the desired effect.

Since the data augmentation will only preprocess the training set, and no measures will be taken for the test set, this means that only need to consider the influence of the poison samples on the feature space after transformation, and do not need to consider the influence of the target samples after processing. Therefore, in the case that the target preprocesses the training set with the data augmentation method, only the data augmentation operation $\phi(x)$ is used to replace x in the first item of Eq. (1), and the x in this objective function is optimized, the target equation is as follows:

$$p = \underset{x}{\mathrm{argmin}}\|f(t) - f(\phi(x))\|_2^2 + \alpha\|b - x\|_2^2 \tag{2}$$

4.2   Optimizing Poison Samples

The process of obtaining p by optimizing Eq. (2) is shown in Algorithm 1. Firstly, the backdoor sample is taken as the initial value of the poison sample, and the objective function is optimized based on it. In Eq. (2), the first term represents the Euclidean distance, while the second term represents the Frobenius norm. Therefore, in this paper, the first and second terms are optimized in different ways, but the consistency of the two terms should be ensured. For the first term, gradient descent is used to minimize the Euclidean distance between $f(\phi(x))$ and $f(t)$. For the second term, an approximate algorithm can be used to solve it, using Eq. (3) to continuously minimize the Frobenius norm of x and b.

$$x_i = (x_{i-1} + \lambda\alpha b)/(1 + \alpha\lambda) \tag{3}$$

$$\alpha = \alpha_0 \cdot 2048^2 / d_b \tag{4}$$

During the experiment, setting the number of the most optimized maxIters in Algorithm 1 to 1500, the initial learning rate λ is 255×100, decay coefficient φ is 0.5, constant M to 50. Since the dimensions of each traffic sign sample are different, in order to control the optimization degree of Frobenius norm of each sample, the coefficient α is calculated by Eq. (4), set α_0 to 0.25, d_b to represent the dimension of the backdoor sample, and 2048 is the number of neurons in the bottleneck layer in the Inception-V3 model.

Algorithm 1 Poison Sample Generation

Input: target sample t, base sample b, learning rate λ, decay coefficient φ, constant M

Output: poison sample p

Initialize x: $x_0 \leftarrow b$

Define: $L_p(x) = \left\| f(\phi(x)) - f(t) \right\|^2$

for $i = 1$ to *maxIters* do

$\hat{x}_i = x_{i-1} - \lambda \nabla_x L_p(x_{i-1})$

$x_i = (\hat{x}_i + \lambda \alpha b)/(1 + \alpha\lambda)$

if $(i < M)$

if $(x_i > \frac{\sum_1^i x_i}{i})$

$\lambda = \varphi \cdot \lambda$

else

if $(x_i > \frac{\sum_{i-M+1}^i x_i}{M})$

$\lambda = \varphi \cdot \lambda$

end for

4.3 Dataset

Our experiment is based on the standard data set of traffic signs in three countries (see Table 1). The data set has been organized by previous work, which evaluated the model through hold-out validation. All data sets have been split into training sets and test sets in proportion. In order to make the results objective, the paper followed this segmentation and carried out our experiments on it.

Table 1. Dataset characteristics

Dataset	Classes	Samples	Split
Chinese traffic signs [21]	58	6164	75:25
German traffic signs [22]	43	50000	80:20
Belgian traffic signs [23]	62	6454	75:25

It can be seen from Table 1 that the distribution of traffic sign categories is unbalanced in different countries, and the number and sample size of categories contained in each country are different. Therefore, this paper selects different target samples and backdoor samples for different countries. In this paper, the traffic signs that lead to serious traffic accidents are first considered as the experimental subjects; and secondly, in order to obtain better experimental results, the traffic signs with large numbers of samples will be used as experimental subjects. The traffic signs selected in this paper are shown in Table 2. For traffic signs in China, the total number of samples is 1098. Select "No Entry" as the target category, the number of samples is 598;"No Parking" is a backdoor category with 500 samples. There were 823 training samples and 275 test samples. For traffic signs in Germany, there are a total of 2911 samples; "Speed Limit 30" was selected as the target category, and the number of samples was 1500;"Speed Limit 100" is a backdoor category with 1411 samples; There were 2037 training samples and 874 test samples. For traffic signs in Belgium, there are a total of 726 samples; Select " No Parking " as the target category, the number of samples is 290;" No Entry " is a backdoor category with 436 samples; There were 545 training samples and 181 test samples.

Table 2. Experimental sample

Dataset	Backdoor class	Target class	Samples	Train samples	Test samples
Chinese	No Parking	No Entry	1098	823	275
Belgian	No Entry	No Parking	726	545	181
German	Speed Limit 100	Speed Limit 30	2911	2329	582

5   Experimental Result

Clipping is not only a method to increase the number of samples, but also a method to weaken the sample noise (i.e., reduce the background unrelated to the recognition target) and increase the stability of the model, so image clipping is often used to preprocess the training set. Therefore, the paper first considers how to poison the model when the trainer preprocesses the training set with image clipping. A clipping operation was selected as shown in Fig. 2(a). The clipping will retain 80% of the original sample. Since the light on traffic signs will change with time, to enhance the adaptability of the model to the samples with different brightness, the trainer will augment the training set by adjusting the sample brightness (such as Fig. 2(b)), and then train the model with the augmented training set. Therefore, the paper also considers the poisoning attack about training set adjusting brightness. When the car is driving on the horizontal ground, the system must recognize traffic signs from different angles, and the trainer will flip the sample horizontally (such as Fig. 2(c)) to preprocess the training set. Therefore, this paper also considers the poisoning attack of the model through the training of horizontal flip preprocessing.

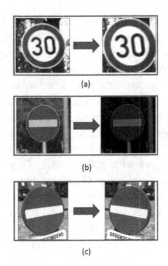

Fig. 2. Data augmentation

If the same sample appears in the training set and the test set, it will be selected as both a poison sample and a backdoor sample, and the resulting attack effect will be reduced. During the experiment, in order to avoid data redundancy, duplicate samples in the data set are removed before crafting poison samples. Figure 3 illustrates the production process of poison samples. By optimizing Eq. (2), poison samples with "hidden backdoors" can be obtained. During the experiment, only one poison sample was injected into the training set at a time, and then performed data augmentation on the training set. After the training set is augmented, the Adam optimizer (the learning rate is set to 0.001) is used to train recognition model for 100 epochs, and tested the performance of the model. The eventually poisoned model judged the target samples as the backdoor category with an especially high degree of confidence.

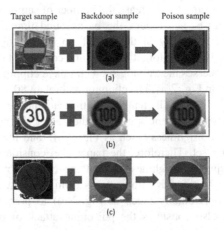

Fig. 3. Craft poison sample

During the test phase, for each target sample, the success of the attack on it (i.e., the target sample was classified into the backdoor category) will be recorded, the success rate of the attack for every 10 samples at that time will be calculated. Figure 4 records the attack success rate in the test phase of the training sets in three countries. Each time a poison sample was injected into the training set, a total of 150 experiments were conducted on the Chinese dataset, a total of 150 experiments were conducted on the Belgian dataset, and a total of 300 experiments were conducted on the German dataset. In the face of different data augmentation methods, the test performance of the model at the beginning is slightly different, but they all tend to be similar in the end. Table 3 illustrates the success rate of the final poisoning of data sets in three countries under different data augmentation methods. It was found that the reason why the attack did not achieve a 100% success rate was that the model training did not achieve complete overfitting (i.e., the classification accuracy of the model to the training set was up to 100%). After the model is attacked, the target sample and the poison sample are always classified into the same category. Therefore, in the training phase, whether the recognition model can fully learn the features of poison samples is the key factor for the success of poisoning attack.

Table 3. Final attack success rate

	Image Cropping	Flip Horizontal	Adjust Brightness
Chinese	98.00%	98.00%	98.67%
Belgian	98.67%	99.33%	98.67%
German	97.67%	98.33%	97.33%

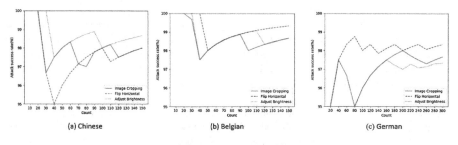

(a) Chinese   (b) Belgian   (c) German

Fig. 4. Attack success rate

6 Conclusion and Future Work

CNN is often regarded as a black box model, because its decision-making algorithm is not interpretable, which brings some difficulties to the security defense of CNN. This paper studies the poisoning attack of driverless traffic sign recognition system. Aiming at the training method of data augmentation, this paper proposes a poisoning attack scheme for the selected target. The proposed scheme attacks the model in the training phase and aims to manipulate the model in the test phase. The method makes it difficult for the model to distinguish two samples by training the poison samples which are similar to the high-level features of the target samples. This attack is highly covert because it poisons non-suspect (i.e., correctly labeled) samples and does not degrade the performance of non-target samples. In order to attack the model of training after data augmentation, this paper selects three methods of image clipping, brightness adjustment and horizontal flip to expand the training set, and attacks this model with a high success rate. The "correctly labeled" poison sample itself can inhibit the defensive effect of adversarial training. If the victim utilizes the poison sample to complete the adversarial training, the trained model will automatically misclassify the healthy samples.

The data sources of most models are easy to be controlled by the attacker. The paper hope to further understand the novel attacks against the traffic sign recognition system through this study, and provide a research foundation for the next research on the corresponding defense mechanism. In the course of the experiment, the training model with poison samples was slightly overfitting, and it was hoped that the following work could achieve the normal training model and the ideal attack effect. This experiment only attacked the known recognition system model, and it is expected that the future work can produce a migration of poison samples, which can complete the attack on the unknown model (i.e., black box attack).

Acknowledgement. This work is supported by the Natural Science Foundation of China (Nos. U1811264, U1711263, 61966009), and the Natural Science Foundation of Guangxi Province (Nos. 2019GXNSFBA245049, 2019GXNSFBA245059, 2018GXNSFDA281045).

References

1. Barreno, M., Nelson, B., Sears, R., Joseph, A.D., Tygar, J.D.: Can machine learning be secure? In: Proceedings of the 2006 ACM Symposium on Information, Computer and Communications Security (AsiaCCS), pp. 16–25. ACM, Taipei, Taiwan, China (2006)
2. Laskov, P.: Practical evasion of a learning-based classifier: a case study. In: 2014 IEEE Symposium on Security and Privacy(S&P), pp. 197–211. IEEE, San Jose, California, USA (2014)
3. Rubinstein, B.I., et al.: Antidote: understanding and defending against poisoning of anomaly detectors. In: Proceedings of the 9th ACM SIGCOMM Internet Measurement Conference (CIM), pp. 1–14. ACM, Chicago, Illinois, USA (2009)
4. Xiao, H., Biggio, B., Brown, G., Fumera, G., Eckert, C., Roli, F.: Is feature selection secure against training data poisoning? In: Proceedings of the 32nd International Conference on Machine Learning(ICML), pp. 1689–1698. ACM, Lille, France (2015)
5. Newell, A., Potharaju, R., Xiang, L., Nita-Rotaru, C.: On the practicality of integrity attacks on document-level sentiment analysis. In: Proceedings of the 2014 Workshop on Artificial Intelligent and Security Workshop (AISec), pp. 83–93. ACM, Scottsdale, Arizona, USA (2014)

6. Eykholt, K., et al.: Robust physical-world attacks on deep learning visual classification. In: Proceedings of the IEEE Conference on Computer Vision and Pattern Recognition(CVPR), pp. 1625–1634. IEEE, Salt Lake City, Utah, USA (2018)
7. Nelson, B., et al.: Exploiting machine learning to subvert your spam filter. In: Proceedings of the 1st Usenix Workshop on Large-Scale Exploits and Emergent Threats (LEET), pp. 1–9. USENIX Association, San Francisco, California, USA (2008)
8. Biggio, B., Nelson, B., Laskov, P.: Poisoning attacks against support vector machines. In: Proceedings of the 29th International Conference on Machine Learning(ICML), pp. 1467–1474. ACM, Edinburgh, Scotland, UK (2012)
9. Steinhardt, J., Koh, P.W.W., Liang, P.S.: Certified defenses for data poisoning attacks. In: Advances in Neural Information Processing Systems (NeurIPS), pp. 3517–3529. MIT Press, Long Beach, California, USA (2017)
10. Muñoz-González, L., et al.: Towards poisoning of deep learning algorithms with back-gradient optimization. In: Proceedings of the 10th ACM Workshop on Artificial Intelligence and Security (AISec), pp. 27–38. ACM, Dallas, Texas, USA (2017)
11. Goodfellow, I., et al.: Generative adversarial nets. In: Advances in Neural Information Processing Systems (NeurIPS), pp. 2672–2680. MIT Press, Montreal, Quebec, Canada (2014)
12. Feng, J., Cai, Q.-Z., Zhou, Z.-H.: Learning to confuse: generating training time adversarial data with auto-encoder. In: Advances in Neural Information Processing Systems (NeurIPS), pp. 11971–11981. MIT Press, Vancouver, British Columba, Canada (2019)
13. Chen, X., Liu, C., Li, B., Lu, K., Song, D.: Targeted backdoor attacks on deep learning systems using data poisoning. arXiv preprint arXiv:1712.05526 (2017)
14. Liu, Y., et al.: Trojaning attack on neural networks (2017)
15. Suciu, O., Marginean, R., Kaya, Y., Daume III, H., Dumitras, T.: When does machine learning FAIL? generalized transferability for evasion and poisoning attacks. In: 27th USENIX Security Symposium (USENIX Security), pp. 1299–1316. Usenix Association, Baltimore, Maryland, USA (2018)
16. Shafahi, A., et al.: Poison frogs! Targeted clean-label poisoning attacks on neural networks. In: Advances in Neural Information Processing Systems (NeurIPS), pp. 6103–6113. MIT Press, Montreal, Quebec, Canada (2018)
17. Biggio, B., Fumera, G., Roli, F.: Security evaluation of pattern classifiers under attack. IEEE Trans. Knowl. Data Eng. 26(2), 984–996 (2013)
18. Huang, L., Joseph, A.D., Nelson, B., Rubinstein, B.I., Tygar, J.D.: Adversarial machine learning. In: Proceedings of the 4th ACM Workshop on Security and Artificial Intelligence (AISec), pp. 43–58. ACM, Chicago, Illinois, USA (2011)
19. Lowd, D., Meek, C.: Adversarial learning. In: Proceedings of the eleventh ACM SIGKDD International Conference on Knowledge Discovery in Data Mining (SIGKDD), pp. 641–647. ACM, Chicago, Illinois, USA (2005)
20. Barreno, M., Nelson, B., Joseph, A.D., Tygar, J.D.: The security of machine learning. Mach. Learn. 81(2), 121–148 (2010). https://doi.org/10.1007/s10994-010-5188-5
21. TSRD. http://www.nlpr.ia.ac.cn/PAL/TRAFFICDATA/RECOGNITION.HTML. Accessed 17 May 2020
22. Šegvic, S., et al.: A computer vision assisted geoinformation inventory for traffic infrastructure. In: 13th International IEEE Conference on Intelligent Transportation Systems (ITSC), pp. 66–73. IEEE, Funchal, Portugal (2010)
23. Mathias, M., Timofte, R., Benenson, R., Van Gool, L.: Traffic sign recognition—how far are we from the solution? In: The 2013 International Joint Conference on Neural networks (IJCNN), pp. 1–8. IEEE, Dallas, Texas, USA (2013)

Adversarial Text Generation via Probability Determined Word Saliency

Gang Ma, Lingyun Shi, and Zhitao Guan[✉]

School of Control and Computer Engineering, North China Electric Power
University, 102206 Beijing, China
guan@ncepu.edu.cn

Abstract. Deep learning (DL) technology has been widely deployed in many
fields and achieved great success, but it is not absolutely safe and reliable. It has
been proved that research on adversarial attacks can reveal the vulnerability of
deep neural networks (DNN). Although many methods of adversarial attack and
defense have been proposed in the field of images, the research on textual
adversarial samples is still few. It is challenging because text samples are sparse
and discrete and the added perturbation might lead to grammatical errors and
semantic changes. Thus, there are some special restrictions on textual adversarial samples. We propose a synonyms substitution-based adversarial text
generation via Probability Determined Word Saliency (PDWS). In our method
PDWS, the word saliency and the optimal substitution word are determined by
the optimal replace-ment effect. The replacement effect is the probability change
caused by replacing one word with its substitution word. We evaluate our attack
method on two popular text classification tasks using CNN and LSTM. The
experimental results show that our method gets higher misleading rate and less
perturbation rate than the baseline methods.

Keywords: Adversarial attacks · Adversarial text · Nature language
processing · Deep neural networks · Deep learning

1 Introduction

Deep Learning technology has made great progress in many domains such as audio
recognition, computer vision and nature language processing (NLP). Although widely
used, DL Models have been proved are easily misled by adversarial samples [1, 2],
which is crafted from clean samples by adding some elaborated perturbation.

DL technology is widely applied in the NLP tasks [3], such as machine translation,
sentiment analysis, malicious text classification. In daily life, people increasingly rely
on the comments of previous users when shopping online, watching movies, and
searching for information. The more positive the user's comments, the higher the
product score, and the more it will stimulate the user's trust. Most of the various
scoring mechanisms utilize text sentiment classification technology based on deep
learning. Therefore, an attacker can change the score by disturbing normal user
comments, making the system no longer reliable or even useless.

Deep learning-based text classification technology has also been deployed in online
content detection, to filter out impolite, rude, and illegal speech. The existence of

© Springer Nature Switzerland AG 2020
X. Chen et al. (Eds.): ML4CS 2020, LNCS 12487, pp. 562–571, 2020.
https://doi.org/10.1007/978-3-030-62460-6_50

adversarial attack makes the model's ability to filter out declines, causing the original green and healthy network environment being polluted, and bringing a lot of misleading information to network users.

Thus, NLP tasks are also greatly threatened by adversarial samples and the research on the textual adversarial sample attack and defense is urgent and important, which can help us better understand the misbehavior of DL models and further help to improve their performance.

Although there are numerous existing methods for either attack [1, 4–6] or de-fense [5, 7, 8] in image domain, the researches in textual adversarial sample are still very few. It is mainly because textual adversarial attacks should satisfy not only misclassification but also imperceptibility [9] and the imperceptibility is difficult to satisfy. Imperceptibility requires the adversarial samples so close to the original that humans cannot percept. In the text domain, imperceptibility indicates high semantic similarity, appropriate words usage, and little spelling and grammar errors. Misclassification rate refers to the magnitude that the adversarial samples attack misleads the model to make wrong classification prediction.

Focusing on misclassification rate and imperceptibility, we propose a Probability Determined Word Saliency (PDWS) method to generate textual adversarial sample. In our method PDWS, we build synonyms candidate pool and determine the optimal substitute word according to the optimal replacement effect of the synonyms. The word saliency and replacement order are determined by the best replacement effect of each word in the text samples.

We evaluate our attack method on two popular text classification tasks using CNN and LSTM. Experiment results show that PDWS can greatly mislead the DNN model and get high misclassification rate. At the same time, PDWS can keep the number of replaced words at a low level, which means it is difficult for humans to perceive.

2 Related Work

Previous researchers tried to transfer the image adversarial sample generation method to the text field. Many of them refer to Ian Goodfellow's FGSM [1] method. Some researchers performed the gradient-based method to determine the saliency of words [10, 11] and used nearest neighbor search in embedding space to determine the replacement words [10, 12]. In terms of modifications, Samanta et al. [11] performed different perturbation operations according to different parts of speech. Alzantot et al. [12] used genetic algorithms to generate adversarial samples iteratively.

Some scholars preferred the saliency-based modification method. Gao et al. [13] proposed a novel word saliency scoring function, then performed character level replacement, deletion, and insertion to map the modified words to UNKNOWN in the embedding space. Li et al. [14] used Jacobian matrices to determine word saliency and applied the method to real-world applications. Ren et al. [15] comprehensively considered the scoring function and replacement effect to determine the words saliency. Liang et al. [16] used the word frequency information to determine the words saliency and select candidate words.

Although they can successfully fool the DL models, it can continue to improve in terms of semantic maintenance and grammatical accuracy.

3   Adversarial Attack in Text Domain

3.1   Adversarial Samples

The goal of a pre-trained text classification model is to correctly map all the samples from the input dataset to the label set. It can correctly classify a clean sample x to a true label y. Which is,

$$\arg\max_{y_i \in Y} P(y_i|x) = y_{true} \tag{1}$$

where $y \in Y = \{y_1, y_2, ..., y_k\}$ is label set containing k classes. $P(y_i \mid x)$ indicates the prediction confidence of model towards sample x on label y_i.

The adversarial attack method aims to generate the adversarial samples x' to change the prediction results, which is generated by adding some slightly elaborated perturbations Δx to the original sample x.

$$\arg\max_{y_i \in Y} P(y_i|x') \neq y_{true}, x' = x + \Delta x \tag{2}$$

The perturbations Δx should be small enough that it is difficult for humans to perceive. It means little grammar errors and semantic changes.

3.2   Our Method

Our method has two key issues: finding candidate words and establishing replacement order. First, for each word, build a candidate pool and calculate the best substitute word. Then establish the replacement order and perturb the original samples to obtain the adversarial samples. The process is shown as Fig. 1.

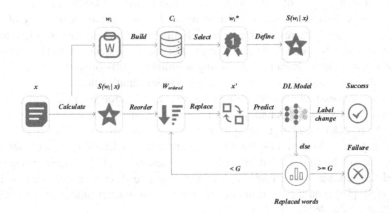

Fig. 1. Flow chart of our method

Optimal Substitute Word w_i*. We built our synonyms candidate pool C_i by using Hownet [17], a sememe-based lexical database. Sememe means the minimum indivisible semantic units of meaning.

Named Entities (NEs) are abbreviations or words or phrases with special meanings in the corpus, such as person names, place names, locations and organizational names. And for them, we will set up their candidate pool by using NEs that occur frequently in the corpus but rarely in the current class.

To decide an optimal candidate word for replacement, we calculate the replacement effect of all the candidate words of w_i. The Replacement Effect is defined as follows,

$$R(w_{ij}|x) = P(y_{true}|x) - P(y_{true}|x'_{ij}) \qquad (3)$$

Where $x = w_1 w_2 \ldots w_i \ldots w_n$, $x_{ij}' = w_1 w_2 \ldots w_{ij} ' \ldots w_n$, w_{ij} means the j-th candidate word in Ci. $P(y_{true} \mid x)$ indicates the prediction confidence of model towards sample x on label y_{true}. $R(w_{ij} \mid x)$ is the replacement effect of w_{ij}, which indicates the decreased confidence between x and x_{ij}' under the classier towards the true label.

The optimal substitute word w_i* is exactly the one that achieves the best replacement effect,

$$w_i^* = \arg\max_{w_{ij} \in C_i} R(w_{ij}|x) \qquad (4)$$

$R(w_i$* $\mid x)$ indicates the best attack effect that we can get when we modify w_i in x, and the corresponding perturbed sample is x_i* $= w_1 w_2 \ldots w_i$* $\ldots w_n$. In this way, we can decide the optimal substitute words and optimal replacement effects for all words (Table 1).

Table 1. An instance of candidate pool.

Original word	Interesting
Synonymy Candidate pool	funny, colorful, vivid, amusing, worthy, great, realistically, humorous

The Order of Replacement. Our word replacement order is mainly determined based on the optimal replacement effects of each word. In general, if the word that has significant saliency is modified, the prediction result will change obviously.

The word saliency is defined by optimal replacement effect, just as follows,

$$S(w_i|x) = R(w_i^*|x) \qquad (5)$$

It indicates the saliency of w_i is the greatest replacement effect we can get when modifying w_i. Then we sorted the words in sample x by word saliency to get the replacement order.

To get the adversarial sample, we greedily craft the original sample x under this order. We iteratively replace the words with its corresponding optimal substitute word until the text label changes or the number of changed words gets to G.

When performing **PDWS** attacks, we iteratively replace each word with its w_i* in this order until the predicted label changes or the number of replaced words reaches the upper limit G (Table 2).

Table 2. An instance of substitute-based adversarial sample.

Original sample positive	This movie is interesting, it tells some stories about Christian.
Adversarial sample negative	This movie is great, it tells some stories about Christian

PDWS Algorithm. The Algorithms are shown as follows.

Algorithm 1 Build C_i and calculate $wi*$

Input: clean sample $x = w_1, w_2, \cdots, w_n$, word w_i
      classifier model, ground truth label y_{true}
Output: Optimal substitute word w_i*
  1: Initialize: $x' \leftarrow x$.
  2: **for** word w_i in x **do:**
  3:      build candidate pool C_i for w_i;
  4: **end for**

  5: **for** word w_i in x **do:**
  6:   **for** candidate word w_{ij} in C_i **do:**
  7:      Compute $R(w_{ij}|x)$ according to Eq.3;
  8:   **end for**
  9:   $w_i* = \text{argmax}_{wij} R(w_{ij}|x)$;
10: **end for**

In Algorithm 1, lines 2-4 build candidate pool C_i for every word in clean sample x and lines 5-10 calculate optimal substitute word $wi*$.

In Algorithm 2, lines 11-13 calculate word saliency $S(w_i \mid x)$ for all words in clean sample x, line 14 reorder the words by $S(w_i \mid x)$. Line 15-22 aims to generate adversarial samples, i.e. replace the words in $W_{ordered}$ until the predicted label changes or the number of replaced words reaches G, then Correspondingly return "success" or "failure".

Algorithm 2 Perturb x and get adversarial sample x'

Input: clean sample $x = w_1, w_2, \cdots, w_n$, ground truth label y_{true},
    classifier model, threshold G

Output: adversarial sample x'

11: **for** word w_i in x **do:**

12:     $S(w_i|x) = R(w_i^*|x)$;

13: **end for**

14: $W_{ordered} \leftarrow$ **Sort**$(w_1, w_2, \cdots, w_n)$ according to $S(w_i|x)$
                 in descending order;

15: **for** word w_i in $W_{ordered}$ **do:**

16:     $x_i' \leftarrow$ replace w_i in x' with w_i^*;

17:     $x' = x_i'$;

18:     **if** argmax$_{yk}$ $P(y|x') \neq y_{ture}$:

19:         **return** x'.

20:     **else if** number of replaced words $> G$:

21:         **return** none.

22: **end for**

---

4 Experiment

In this section, we evaluate our method on two popular text classification tasks using CNN and LSTM. Then use some metrics to discuss the performance.

4.1 Dataset

We use AG's News dataset and IMDB dataset to evaluate our method. AG's News dataset contains over one million news articles, and those samples are classified into four classes: Sports, World, Sci/Tech and Business. Each class has a collection of 30,000 training samples and 1,900 testing samples. IMDB dataset contains 50000 positive and negative reviews and each review contains an average of 200 words.

4.2 Target Model and Baseline Method

We use LSTM, Bi-directional LSTM (BDLSTM) and the word-based CNN [18] as our target model to evaluate our proposed method.

    Our baseline methods are as follows. All of them use Hownet to build candidate pools except PWWS.

PWWS. PWWS [15] is also a replacement-based attacking method. In the original literate it uses Wordnet to build candidate pool and we retain its original settings.

WS. The word replacement order in WS [11] is based on the change in confidence before and after deleting the word.

Random. There is no pre-built word replacement order in Random. We will randomly choose a word every time we replace the sample.

4.3   Experimental Settings

We test the PDWS and other baseline methods on two different datasets. In each set of experiments, we randomly selected 3,000 clean samples from the dataset to attack. We set the maximum number of replacement words to 30.

4.4   Evaluation Metrics

We mainly use two metrics to evaluate the performance of the attacking method, Misled Rate (MR) and Perturbed Rate (PR). Misled rate refers to the decrease in the classification accuracy rate before and after the attack, reflecting the ability of the attack method to fool the model. Perturbed Rate refers to the average percentage of words replaced after the attack in each sample. The lower the value is, the higher the similarity between the produced adversarial sample and the corresponding clean sample.

4.5   Attacking Results

The attacking results are shown as follows.

Table 3. The misleading rate of different attack methods on various models and datasets.

Dataset	Model	Accuracy	PWWS	WS	Random	PDWS
Agnews	Word_CNN	0.9010	0.7870	0.7790	0.7510	**0.8050**
	Word_LSTM	0.9150	0.7230	0.7080	0.7140	**0.7520**
IMDB	Word_CNN	0.8285	0.6940	0.4715	0.4800	**0.7895**
	Word_BDLSTM	0.5395	0.5295	0.5110	0.4935	**0.5340**

Experimental results show that our method PDWS performs better than all the baseline attacking methods. Table 3 shows the Misleading rate of different attacking methods on various models and datasets, where the third column shows the prediction accuracy of the model on clean samples. We know that the greater the misleading rate, the stronger the attack capability of the method. In each set of experiments, PDWS can achieve the maximum misleading rate, which means that PDWS can fool the model to the greatest extent and make it misclassified.

Table 4 shows the Perturbed Rate of different attack methods on two datasets and corresponding models. PDWS obtained the lowest replacement rate in all sets of experiments, which means that the number of modified words is the smallest. Therefore, it can maintain the similarity with the original sample as much as possible.

Table 4. The perturbed rate of different attack methods on various models and datasets.

Dataset	Model	PWWS	WS	Random	PDWS
Agnews	Word_CNN	0.1151	0.1994	0.2194	0.1086
	Word_LSTM	0.1614	0.2495	0.2588	0.1404
IMDB	Word_CNN	0.0417	0.1068	0.106	0.0230
	Word_BDLSTM	0.0264	0.0548	0.0621	0.0195

Table 5 shows some adversarial sample instances of Agnews dataset on Word-CNN model, where the original words are in brackets and the substitutes word of the adversarial samples are colored red. The first and second columns respectively represent the model's predicted labels and confidence on the original clean sample and the corresponding adversarial sample. We can find that in the instances only one word's replacement can change the prediction result of the model. Although it is difficult for humans to recognize the perturbations between the samples, it has successfully misled the DNN model to make different predictions (Color figure online).

Table 5. Adversarial sample instances of Agnews dataset on word-CNN model.

Original	Adversarial	Adversarial samples
Sports 90.76%	World 67.91%	Italian Stefano Baldini has won the men's marathon in a time of 2:10:54. Naturalized Iraqi (American) Keflezighi was a surprise runner-up with Brazil's Vanderlei Lima finishing third.
Sci/Tech 60.18%	Business 43.54%	Dogs are Training to Sniff Out Cancer. Experts have trained unwanted dogs into super sniffers that can hear of (detect) drugs or bombs. Now they're focusing on a new threat: prostate cancer.

Through the above evaluation, we can find that there are still some defects in the current DNN model, which makes it easy to be attacked. This limits the applications of deep learning-based text classification technology. The study on adversarial samples helps us to find the vulnerabilities, and to improve the DNN model's performance.

5 Conclusion

In this paper, we propose a Probability Determined Word Saliency method (PDWS) to generate textual adversarial samples. We determine the optimal replacement word and word saliency by the optimal replacement effect. We evaluate our attack method on two popular text classification tasks using CNN and LSTM. The experimental results show that our method gets higher misleading rate and less perturbation rate than the baseline methods, indicating that the generated adversarial samples are very similar to the original samples. In the future we will further study the transferability of PDWS and corresponding defense methods.

Acknowledgements. The work is partially supported by the National Natural Science Foundation of China under Grant 61972148, Beijing Natural Science Foundation under grant 4182060.

References

1. Goodfellow, I.J., Shlens, J., Szegedy, C.: Explaining and harnessing adversarial examples. In: 3rd International Conference on Learning Representations 2015, ICLR, San Diego, USA (2015)
2. Nguyen, A., Yosinski, J., Clune, J.: Deep neural networks are easily fooled: High confidence predictions for unrecognizable images. In: Proceedings of the IEEE conference on computer vision and pattern recognition 2015, CVPR, pp. 427–436 (2015)
3. Wang, W., Wang, L., Tang, B., Wang, R., Ye, A.: Towards a robust deep neural network in text domain a survey. arXiv preprint arXiv:1902.07285 (2019)
4. Kurakin, A., Goodfellow, I., Bengio, S.: Adversarial examples in the physical world. arXiv preprint arXiv:1607.02533 (2016)
5. Tramèr, F., Kurakin, A., Papernot, N., Goodfellow, I., Boneh, D., McDaniel, P.: Ensemble adversarial training: attacks and defenses. arXiv preprint arXiv:1705.07204 (2017)
6. Dong, Y., et al.: Boosting adversarial attacks with momentum. In: Proceedings of the IEEE conference on computer vision and pattern recognition, CVPR, pp. 9185–9193 (2018)
7. Wong, E., Kolter, Z.: Provable defenses against adversarial examples via the convex outer adversarial polytope. In: International Conference on Machine Learning, ICML, pp. 5286–5295 (2018)
8. Song C., He K., Wang L.: Improving the generalization of adversarial training with domain adaptation. arXiv preprint arXiv:1810.00740 (2019)
9. Ling, X., Ji, S., Zou, J., Wang, J., Wang, T.: DEEPSEC: a uniform platform for security analysis of deep learning model. In: 2019 IEEE Symposium on Security and Privacy (SP), pp. 529–546 (2019)
10. Papernot, N., McDaniel, P., Swami, A., Harang, R.: Crafting adversarial input sequences for recurrent neural networks. In: 2016 IEEE Military Communications Conference, MILCOM, pp. 49–54 (2016)
11. Samanta, S., Mehta, S.: Towards crafting text adversarial samples. arXiv preprint arXiv: 1707.02812 (2017)
12. Alzantot, M., Sharma, Y., Elgohary, A., Ho, B.J., Chang, K.W.: Generating natural language adversarial examples. In: Proceedings of the 2018 Conference on Empirical Methods in Natural Language Processing, EMNLP, pp. 2890–2896 (2018)
13. Gao, J., Lanchantin, J., Soffa, M.L., Qi, Y.: Black-box generation of adversarial text sequences to evade deep learning classifiers. In: 2018 IEEE Security and Privacy Workshops, SPW, pp. 50–56 (2018)
14. Li, J., Ji, S., Du, T., Li, B., Wang, T.: Textbugger: generating adversarial text against real-world applications. arXiv preprint arXiv:1812.05271 (2019)
15. Ren, S., Deng, Y., He, K., Che, W.: Generating natural language adversarial examples through probability weighted word saliency. In: Proceedings of the 57th Annual Meeting of the Association for Computational Linguistics, ACL, pp. 1085–1097 (2019)

16. Liang, B., Li, H., Su, M., Bian, P., Li, X., Shi, W.: Deep text classification can be fooled. In: Proceedings of the 27th International Joint Conference on Artificial Intelligence, IJCAI, pp. 4208–4215 (2017)
17. Qi, F., Yang, C., Liu, Z., Dong, Q., Sun, M., Dong, Z.: Openhownet: an open sememe-based lexical knowledge base. arXiv preprint arXiv:1901.09957 (2019)
18. Kim, Y.: Convolutional neural networks for sentence classification. In: Proceedings of the 2014 Conference on Empirical Methods in Natural Language Processing, EMNLP, pp. 1746–1751 (2014)

Adversarial Example Attacks in the Physical World

Huali Ren[1,2] and Teng Huang[1,2(✉)]

[1] Institute of Artificial Intelligence and Blockchain, Guangzhou University,
Guangzhou, China
[2] College of Cyber Science, Nankai University, Tianjin, China
renhualione@163.com, huangteng1220@buaa.edu.cn

Abstract. Deep learning has made major breakthroughs in many problems that are difficult to solve by traditional algorithms, and has become a cutting-edge technology in the field of artificial intelligence. Deep neural network is the most widely used model in deep learning. However, recent research has shown that deep neural networks are vulnerable to adversarial examples, resulting from small-magnitude and carefully crafted perturbations added to the input that mislead the model. It will bring serious security risks to systems which based on deep learning. Therefore, adversarial example has attracted much attention in the field of artificial intelligence. Adversarial examples are generated in the digital world and extended to the physical world. This paper comprehensively investigates the attack work of adversarial examples in the physical world. Firstly, the related concepts of adversarial examples and typical generation algorithms are introduced, with the purpose of discussing the challenges of adversarial attacks in the physical world. Then, we enumerate the practical applications of adversarial examples in classification tasks and target detection tasks. Finally, we give the future research direction of adversarial example attack in the physical world. By reviewing the existing literature, it is helpful to improve the shortcomings of the existing works and propose more effective attack methods.

Keywords: Deep learning · Adversarial example · Physical world

1 Introduction

Deep learning [28] allow a computational model constructed by multiple processing layers to learn abstract data representations. During the training process of the model, the back propagation algorithm is used to indicate how to adjust its internal parameters, so that it achieves good performance. Deep learning has made breakthrough progress on issues that the machine learning and artificial intelligence community have been attempting to understand, such as natural language processing [19], computer vision [18], speech recognition [20], and other fields. Therefore, deep learning has become a cutting-edge technology in the field of artificial intelligence.

© Springer Nature Switzerland AG 2020
X. Chen et al. (Eds.): ML4CS 2020, LNCS 12487, pp. 572–582, 2020.
https://doi.org/10.1007/978-3-030-62460-6_51

Deep neural networks (DNN), a deep learning model, is an extension of the traditional machine learning model perceptron. The expressive ability of the model is enhanced by adding multiple fully connected hidden layers and different activation functions. In the field of computer vision, DNN can even reach human recognition accuracy [23,27]. Based on the success of DNN, it has been applied to various systems in the physical world (for example, self-driving cars and robots).

Recent studies have shown that the state-of-the-art deep neural network is vulnerable to adversarial examples in the form of subtle and imperceptible perturbations to inputs that mislead the output of the model [1–4,14,15,25]. The attacker can even specify the prediction result of the model. In particular, the adversarial examples generated for one model may successfully attack another model, which shows that adversarial example has transferable characteristics [1]. The emergence of adversarial examples brings serious security risks to the system that based on deep learning model, such as automatic driving, face recognition system. Therefore, it has become the focus of attention in the field of artificial intelligence and cross fields.

The adversarial examples are generated in the digital world and applied in the physical world. In daily life, a series of systems operate in a noisy and changing environment. The level of these noises is often greater than the perturbations, and it can destroy the perturbations generated only by the digital algorithm. In addition, in the digital world, attackers can directly modify the input data of the model. But in the physical world, the system captures signal data through various sensors. The attacker cannot access the input data of the model. Therefore, whether the adversarial examples generated in the digital world can be applied to the changing physical environment, and make the system with the deep model as the core error become an important research direction.

Recent work [6–8,10,12] has also shown that adversarial examples can be successfully applied in the real-world, bringing potential security threats to people's lives. Kurakin et al. [3] printed the adversarial example pictures on paper, and successfully cheated the Inception v3 model after being photographed by the camera. Evtimov et al. [5] placed black and white stickers on road signs to deceive the classifier. Athalye et al. [27] manufactured a 3D printed tortoise, which was mistaken for rifle or jigsaw puzzle.

In order to illustrate the future research direction of adversarial examples in the physical world, this article conducts a comprehensive investigation of the existing physical world adversarial examples attack works. The second part introduces the related concepts, the generation algorithm, and the challenges of adversarial examples in the physical world. From the perspective of the attack task, we review the related work of the attack image classifier and target detector. Finally, the future research direction of the physical world against attack is discussed.

2 Background

2.1 Related Concepts

Adversarial examples. Szegedy et al. [1] first proposed the concept of adversarial examples. The study found two "unconventional" phenomena of neural networks. Among them, one is the vulnerability of neural networks in image classification. The attacker generates samples with offensive characteristics by adding carefully crafted, small-magnitude, and imperceptible perturbations to the clean samples. Since the added perturbation is very small, it will not significantly affect the data distribution [4]. Such samples can make the neural network with high classification confidence and accuracy output wrong results. The research calls this kind of samples added with attack disturbances as adversarial examples. Its mathematical model is shown in formula (1).

$$minimize||\delta||_2, \ s.t. f(x + \delta) = l, x + \delta \in [0,1]^m \qquad (1)$$

Where $x + \delta$ is an adversarial example composed of clean samples x and perturbations δ, and l is the true label of x. f Represents the classification model, f(.,.) which is a mapping function that maps the input image to a label output.
Non-target attacks. The model output is any category other than the real category, so the attack is successful. In (1), $f(x + \delta) \neq l$.
Targeted attacks. The model not only outputs an error, but the output is a category specified by the attacker, and the attack is successful. Targeted attacks are harder to achieve than non-targeted attacks. In (1), $f(x + \delta) = y$ and $y \neq l$, where y is the prediction category that the attacker wants the model output.
White-box attacks. The attacker knows the internal structure, weight parameters, and training algorithm of the attack model.
Black-box attacks. In contrast to white-box attacks, the attacker knows nothing about the attack model.

2.2 Adversarial Example Generation Algorithm

In the white-box setting, researchers have proposed a series of adversarial example generation algorithms. The Fast gradient sign method(FGSM) was proposed by Goodfloow et al. [2]. In the paper, the researchers add perturbations to the direction of the gradient change in the loss function. Therefore, the attacker can quickly modify the distance between the real label and the predicted label. However, FGSM has a low attack success rate because it only performs one calculation when generating a perturbation. Basic iterative method (BIM) [3] and Iterative least-likely class method (ICML) [3] are improvements to FGSM. They change the single step calculation of FGSM into multiple small step iterative attacks, and adjust the perturbation direction to be consistent with or opposite to the change direction of loss function gradient. The Deepfool [14] attack is proposed based on the existence of a classification hyperplane that can separate different data sets in the depth model. Jacobian-Based Saliency Map(JSMA) [24] algorithm finds salient points by calculating the forward guide number (Jacobian matrix) and adds disturbance to the salient points with high sensitivity. Perturbations generated by universal adversarial perturbations(UAP) [4] algorithm can be added to multiple images, all of which are misclassified. C&W [15] is currently the strongest attack algorithm.

In the black-box setting, adversarial example generation algorithms include One-pixel, MI-FGSM, etc. One-pixel [16] algorithm is based on the idea of differential evolution(DE) and is a single-pixel attack. It only considers the number of pixels to be modified without considering the intensity of the Perturbations. The MI-FGSM [25] algorithm is another extension of the FGSM. It adds a momentum term to BIM to accelerate convergence and avoid falling into the local extremum of optimization.

2.3   Practical Adversarial Examples Attack

The adversarial examples are generated in the digital world and are actually exploited in the physical world. Kurakin et al. [3] proved that adversarial examples can be applied to the real-world. Researchers generates adversarial images using FGSM, BIM and ILCM algorithms. These images are printed on paper, and then physically transformed into the classification model by taking photos and cropping with mobile phone cameras. The experimental results show that most of the adversarial images after "photo transformation" make the image classifier recognize errors. But their work attack effects are very limited in changing physical states, including distance, angle, lighting, etc.

Although a series of changes in the physical environment have affected the adversarial example to attack the real system, if the attacker eliminates these effects, a robust sample is generated. So, it is obvious that this will bring a serious security threat to people's lives. For example, when the police track criminals through surveillance, if the criminal understands how the adversarial example attacks the face recognition system, he will successfully escape the hunt [17]. A self-driving car driving on a highway that completely relies on the output of the model, when it recognizes a road sign incorrectly [5,8], or makes a steering decision when it should go straight [6], then it is very likely Lead to danger. The detailed work will be mentioned in the third part.

2.4   Challenges in Physical World

In the digital world, the attacker has "digital level" access to the input. For example, the attacker can make arbitrary pixel-level modifications to the input image of the classifier. However, in real applications, attackers cannot control the sensors and data pipes of the system. At the same time, the perturbation must survive in various environmental transformations. This part mainly introduces the challenge of adversarial attack in the physical world and the mitigation methods proposed by some work.

Environmental Conditions. Under different environmental conditions such as light, distance, and sensor viewing angle, the image sent by the sensor into the model will be different from the original image. Specifically:

a. Sensor viewing angle: The real physical world is in a three-dimensional space. The adversarial example may be captured by the sensor under various viewing angles. To make the attack successful, the perturbations should remain aggressive in all perspectives.

b. Light: The intensity of natural light and the color of ambient light can affect the imaging of the adversarial example in the sensor.

c. Distance: The size of the captured sample is affected by the distance between the target and the sensor.

Spatial Constraints. In the digital space, adversarial perturbations can be added to any part of the image, including background imagery. However, for physical targets, the image of the object often does not have a fixed background due to changes in the distance and angle from the camera, Therefore, if a perturbation is added to the background, it is not necessarily in the captured target image. In order to better realize the adversarial example attack in the physical world, perturbations should be added to objects, such as road sign attacks [5].

Printability. In order to fabricate perturbation for theoretical calculations, every pixel of it should be able to be printed by existing equipment, such as adversarial patches. Due to the limitation of the color gamut of modern printing equipment, some theoretically calculated colors may not be completely and accurately restored. In particular, there may be errors during the printing process. Therefore, the attacker should consider the errors caused by printing when optimizing the generation of adversarial examples. Sharif et al. [17] first proposed the use of non-printable score (NPS) to measure this error, and added NPS to the optimized objective function. The NPS definition for a pixel p is described as (2). Where P is a printable RGB triplet. The NPS value describes the maximum distance between the perturbation pixel and any pixel in P. According to its definition, the value will be low when the pixel p' is close to a printable color p chosen from the printable color set P. In the poster sticker attack of Road sign [5], pedestrian detection [7], and steering decision attack [6], NPS has become a part of its optimization function.

$$NPS(p') = \prod_{p \in P} (p' - p) \tag{2}$$

Imperceptibility. If the generated perturbation is semantically irrelevant, or the adversarial image is different from other people's knowledge of the object, this will arouse other people's suspicion and destroy the concealment of the perturbation. At the same time, for physical systems that use sensors to capture data, perturbation data needs to be perceived by the sensors, such as camera. Because these systems are only mechanical output prediction labels, and do not pay attention to the real label of the object. Therefore, the generated attack pattern should be perceivable by the sensor and have good smoothness to the human eye. For this reason, Sharif et al. [17] introduced a smooth limiting function TV in the optimization objective, which is defined as (3). Where $\delta_{i,j}$ is the pixel value at the (i,j) coordinates in the perturbation. The value will be low when the smoother the perturbation pixels and the stronger the concealment.

$$TV(\delta) = \sum_{i,j}(\sqrt{(\delta_{i,j} - \delta_{i+1,j})^2 + (\delta_{i,j} - \delta_{i,j+1})^2}) \tag{3}$$

In order to successfully implement an attack in the physical world, the attacker should consider the challenges in the physical world mentioned above.

2.5   Image Classification Tasks

Traditional image classification tasks are based on people's cognition of things and find out some different characteristics between things to distinguish, for example, the classification of common cat and dog pictures. The advent of the era of big data has promoted the rapid development of deep learning. Researchers began to extract features from a large amount of image data, and use the extracted feature data to train a classifier. The model is constantly adjusted through the back propagation of the neural network.The main image classification models include: LeNet-5 [21], AlexNet [23], VGG [22], and ResNet [26].

2.6   Target Detection Task

Different from the image classification task, the target detection task must not only identify the category of each object in the picture, but also mark the position of the object in the picture through the bounding box. At present, object detectors are mainly divided into two categories: One type is a two-step framework that first marks the bounding box of the object, and then classifies and recognizes it, such as the series of R-CNN algorithms (Fast RCNN [29], Faster RCNN [30], Mask RCNN [31]); one is a one-step framework that uses a convolutional neural network (CNN) to predict the categories and positions of targets in the picture at the same time, including YOLOv2 [32], SSD [33] etc.

3   Adversarial Attack in the Physical World

3.1   Adversarial Attacks for Classifier in the Physical World

The classifier mainly extracts the features of the image and classifies the feature vector. Currently, attacks on classifiers in the physical world include: road signs, confrontation camera stickers, and steering decisions.

Road Sign. Evtimov et al. [5] attacked a road sign recognition system which plays an important role in automatic driving safety. They proposed an algorithm for generating attacks in a white-box setting, Robust Physical Perturbations (RP2), which generates robust adversarial perturbations in a series of dynamic physical environments (distance, angle, and resolution). The samples with this perturbation successfully mislead the two road sign classifiers that they built: LISA-CNN and GTSRB-CNN. In addition, two methods are used to attack classifiers, including object constrained post and stick attacks. These black and white stickers imitate common graffiti in life, so it won't arouse people's suspicion. Non printable score (NPS) [17] is added to the optimization objective function, in order to deal with the non printability challenge of color. Mask calculates the projection of the perturbations on the target surface, which can limit the spatial position of the perturbations. At the same time, samples are extracted from the dynamic physical world and the target image distribution of synthetic transformation, so as to enhance the robustness of perturbation to environmental changes. In fifield settings, the object constrained poster printing attacks makes the classifier stop sign recognizing 100% as the sign of speed limit 45.

Aishan Liu et al. [8] puts the adversarial patch generated by generator G on the sensitive area found by attention model M, they also realizes the attack on road signs. In automatic driving, these attacks may lead to property damage and even user casualties.

Adversarial Camera Stickers. Different from the work of manipulating the target object itself [5,7], Juncheng B. Li et al. considered an alternative method to fool the classifier by physically manipulating the camera itself. In the paper [10] proposed an adversarial camera sticker attack with "universal" perturbations(universal perturbations in digital space were considered by Moosavi-Dezfooli et al. [4]), which can make most pictures of a certain type of target be misclassified. They place a mainly-translucent sticker on the camera lens with a carefully crafted dot pattern. In the target image captured by the camera, these dot patterns are like some fuzzy points produced by the camera itself, which are not obvious to the viewer of the photo and are often ignored, but can cause the target to be classified as different by the ResNet model. This method is to inject perturbations in the light path between the camera and the object, which is highly concealed.

3.2   Adversarial Attacks for Object Detection in the Physical World

Different from the image classifier, the Object detector not only needs to identify the classification of each object in the picture, but also marks the position of the Object in the picture through the candidate bounding boxes. The current attacks on Object detectors include pedestrian detection, lidar and infrared attacks.

Pedestrian Detection. In [7], Simen Thys et al. successfully applied the adversarial example attack from the classifier to the Object detector. In the white box setting, the researchers used the adversarial patch to attack the object detector deployed with the YOLOv2 model. The person is successfully prevented from being detected under the camera, by placing a 40 * 40 size patch on the person. During the experiment, the bounding box of multiple attackers was obtained through the target detector, and patches were randomly initialized and placed in the relative part of the bounding box. The image of the attacker captured by the camera is input to person detectors, and the target and category score are output. Their optimization goal is to minimize the total loss, which is composed of the non-printability score (NPS) [17], the total variation (TV) [17], and the maximum objectness score. Under the condition of a fixed model, the pixels of the patch are continuously modified through the backpropagation algorithm, so that the person detectors cannot detect the presence of an attacker. In [4,9], it was proposed to wear a T-shirt printed with a perturbationed picture to attack the human body detector. Even if the movement causes the person's posture to change, the detection can be successfully avoided.

Lidar. The perception system composed of camera, lidar and radar is an important system to ensure the safety of autonomous driving. In the past, most of the research on adversarial attacks focused on camera-based perception, and there were few explorations to ensure security based on lidar perception.

Yulong Cao et al. [12] the first to show a Lidar attack against fake point spoofing in a white box setting. They place an attacking device near the self-driving car, and when the synchronized photodiode captures the laser pulses fired by the victim's lidar, the delay component is triggered. Then the delay component triggers the attack laser after a period of time to attack the pulse period of the subsequent victim's lidar, thereby generating a point cloud of objects that do not exist in the actual scene. But blindly generating fake points to attack often fails, because the lidar perception module includes three stages: pre processing, DNN-based object detection, and post processing, which will be detected in the machine learning-based object detection process. In [12], the researchers used the Adv-LiDAR algorithm to add perturbations to the fake point cloud, so that it successfully avoided the target detector, and entered the obstacle list after post-processing.

In particular, they also demonstrated two attack scenarios, including emergency brake attack and AV freezing attack (traffic jam). In addition, in paper [11], the researchers used LiDAR-Adv to generate a 3D printable physical adversarial object, which was placed on the road without being detected by LiDAR. James Tu et al. [13] placed the generated 3D adversarial object in the keyword area on the rooftop of any target vehicle to evaded the lidar detector with an 80% success rate.

4 Future Work Directions

At present, the adversarial example on the physical world are basically concentrated on a certain type of sensor attack. In different fields, the final decision may be obtained through comprehensive consideration of multiple or multiple type sensors. In order to successfully attack, researchers can be considered in the future.

5 Conclusion

In recent years, adversarial example attacks in the physical world have received widespread attention. And we believe that this will be a long-term task, which is not only interesting but also crucial. At the same time, understanding its attack principles in the physical world will help us design better defense programs. Further ensure the safety of deep learning models hidden behind various systems, especially for areas with high safety requirements such as intelligent driving and face recognition.

References

1. Szegedy, C., Zaremba, W., Sutskever, I, et al.: Intriguing properties of neural networks. arXiv: Computer Vision and Pattern Recognition (2013)
2. Goodfellow, I., Shlens, J., Szegedy C., et al.: Explaining and harnessing adversarial examples. arXiv: Machine Learning (2014)
3. Kurakin, A., Goodfellow, I., Bengio, S., et al.: Adversarial examples in the physical world. arXiv: Computer Vision and Pattern Recognition (2016)
4. Moosavidezfooli, S., Fawzi, A., Fawzi, O., et al.: Universal Adversarial Perturbations. In: Computer Vision and Pattern Recognition, pp. 86–94 (2017)
5. Eykholt, K., Evtimov, I., Fernandes, E., et al.: Robust Physical-world attacks on deep learning visual classification. In: Computer Vision and Pattern Recognition, pp. 1625–1634 (2018)
6. Zhou, H., Li, W., Zhu, Y., et al.: DeepBillboard: systematic physical-world testing of autonomous driving systems. arXiv: Computer Vision and Pattern Recognition (2018)
7. Thys, S., Van Ranst, W., Goedeme, T., et al.: Fooling automated surveillance cameras: adversarial patches to attack person detection. arXiv: Computer Vision and Pattern Recognition (2019)
8. Liu, A., Fan, J., Ma, Y., et al.: Perceptual-sensitive GAN for generating adversarial patches. In: National Conference on Artificial Intelligence, vol. 33(01), pp. 1028–1035 (2019)
9. Wu, Z., Lim, S., Davis, L.S, et al.: Making an invisibility cloak: real world adversarial attacks on object detectors. arXiv: Computer Vision and Pattern Recognition (2019)
10. Li, J., Schmidt, F.R., Kolter, Z., et al.: Adversarial camera stickers: a physical camera-based attack on deep learning systems. arXiv: Computer Vision and Pattern Recognition (2019)

11. Cao, Y., Xiao, C., Yang, D., et al.: Adversarial objects against LiDAR-based autonomous driving systems. arXiv: Cryptography and Security (2019)
12. Cao, Y., Xiao, C., Cyr, B., et al.: Adversarial sensor attack on LiDAR-based perception in autonomous driving. In: Computer And Communications Security, pp. 2267–2281 (2019)
13. Tu, J., et al.: Physically realizable adversarial examples for lidarobject detection. CoRR, abs/2004.0054 (2020)
14. Moosavidezfooli, S., Fawzi, A., Frossard, P., et al.: DeepFool: a simple and accurate method to fool deep neural networks. In: Computer Vision and Pattern Recognition, pp. 2574–2582 (2016)
15. Carlini, N., Wagner, D.: Towards evaluating the robustness of neural networks. In: IEEE Symposium on Security And Privacy, pp. 39–57 (2017)
16. Su, J., Vargas, D.V., Sakurai, K., et al.: One pixel attack for fooling deep neural networks. IEEE Trans. Evol. Comput. **23**(5), 828–841 (2019)
17. Sharif, M., Bhagavatula, S., Bauer, L., et al.: Accessorize to a crime: real and stealthy attacks on state-of-the-art face recognition. In: Computer and Communications Security, pp. 1528–1540 (2016)
18. He, K., Zhang, X., Ren, S., Sun, J.: Deep residual learning for image recognition. In: 2016 IEEE Conference on Computer Vision and Pattern Recognition (CVPR), pp. 770–778 (2016)
19. Sutskever, I., Vinyals, O. Le, Q.V.: Sequence to sequence learning with neural networks. In: NIPS (2014)
20. Hinton, G., Deng, L., Yu, D., et al.: Deep neural networks for acoustic modeling in speech recognition: the shared views of four research groups. IEEE Signal Process. Mag. **29**(6), 82–97 (2012)
21. Lecun, Y., Bottou, L.: Gradient-based learning applied to document recognition. IEEE **86**(11), 2278–2324 (1998)
22. Simonyan, K., Zisserman, A.: Very deep convolutional networks for large-scale image recognition (2014). arXiv:1409.1556
23. Krizhevsky, A., Sutskever, I., Hinton, G.: Imagenet classification with deep convolutional neural networks. Commun. ACM, **60**(6), 84–90 (2017)
24. Papernot, N., McDaniel, P., Jha, S., et al.: The limitations of deep learning in adversarial settings. In: 2016 IEEE European symposium on security and privacy (EuroS&P), pp. 372–387(2016)
25. Xie, C., Zhang, Z., Zhou, Y., et al.: Improving transferability of adversarial examples with input diversity. In: Computer Vision and Pattern Recognition, pp. 2730–2739 (2019)
26. He, K., Zhang, X., Ren, S., et al.: Deep residual learning for image recognition. In: IEEE conference on computer vision and pattern recognition. IEEE Computer Society, pp. 770–778 (2016)
27. Athalye, A., Engstrom, L., Ilyas, A., et al.: Synthesizing robust adversarial examples. In: International conference on machine learning. pp. 284–293 (2018)
28. LeCun, Y., Bengio, Y., Hinton, G.: Deep learning. Nature **521**(7553), 436–444 (2015)
29. Girshick, R.: Fast R-CNN. In: IEEE international conference on computer vision. pp.1440–1448 (2015)
30. Ren, S., He, K., Girshick, R., et al.: Faster R-CNN: towards real-time object detection with region proposal networks. IEEE Trans. Pattern Anal. Mach. Intell. **39**(6), 1137–1149 (2017)
31. He, K., Gkioxari, G., Dollár, P., et al.: Mask R-CNN. In: 2017 IEEE International Conference on Computer Vision (ICCV). IEEE (2017)

32. Redmon, J., Farhadi, A.: YOLO9000: better, faster, stronger, pp. 6517–6525 (2017)
33. Liu, W., et al.: SSD: single shot multibox detector. In: Leibe, B., Matas, J., Sebe, N., Welling, M. (eds.) ECCV 2016. LNCS, vol. 9905, pp. 21–37. Springer, Cham (2016). https://doi.org/10.1007/978-3-319-46448-0_2

Querying Little Is Enough: Model Inversion Attack via Latent Information

Kanghua Mo[1,2(✉)], Teng Huang[1,2], and Xiaoyu Xiang[1]

[1] Institute of Artificial Intelligence and Blockchain, Guangzhou University,
Guangzhou, China
mokanghua@gmail.com,
huangteng1220@buaa.edu.cn
[2] College of Cyber Science, Nankai University, Tianjin, China

Abstract. With the development of machine learning (ML) technology, various online intelligent services use ML models to provide predictions. However, attacker may obtain privacy information of the model through interaction with online services. Model inversion attacks (MIA) is a privacy stealing method that utilizes ML models output values to reconstruct input values. In particular, an indispensable step of implementing proposed MIA approaches is that the attacker query the auxiliary datasets entirely. However, in reality, it will be inefficient to transfer huge datasets to online services to get prediction values of inference models. More seriously, the huge transmission may cause the administrator's active defense. In this paper, we propose a novel MIA scheme which reduce queries on auxiliary datasets, by utilizing latent information of primitive models as high dimension features. We systematically evaluate our inversion approach in convolutional neural networks (CNN) classifier on LFW, pubFig, MNIST datasets. The experimental results show that even with a few queries of the inference model, our inversion approach still work accurately and outperforms than previous approaches. As conclusion, our method proves that implementing MIA does not require querying all auxiliary data on the classifier model, making it more difficult for the administrator to defend against the attack and elicit more investigations for privacy-preserving.

1 Introduction

Machine learning, especially deep learning models, have shown that multi-layer neural networks can achieve state-of-the-art performance on a wide range of traditional tasks. In order to make better use of the advantages brought by ML, various online service systems that based on ML model are applied. For example, developers can get face attributes, facial features positioning, and eye-openness levels by using the API provided by Apple's face-tracking APIs in the ARKit [2], Which technology is based on ML. What's more, developers can not only use other people's ML models but also share and trade their own ML models on Amazon [1,19] on-line markets for profit and collaboration with others.

© Springer Nature Switzerland AG 2020
X. Chen et al. (Eds.): ML4CS 2020, LNCS 12487, pp. 583–591, 2020.
https://doi.org/10.1007/978-3-030-62460-6_52

Although these ML models bring conveniences to many users, they also provide convenience for attackers to obtain models owners privacy information. In particular, the prediction results provided by these models could be sensitive, which gives rise to an important question: how much information about owner/user privacy do the prediction results reveal?

There are a lot of work about model inversion attacks that try to reconstruct user's private data with prediction results, which are mainly divided into two class of approaches. First class approach inverts a model by making use of gradient-based optimization in the data space [5,13,20] to find the most representative sample of a certain class. For example, model inversion attack [5] was proposed to infer training classes against neural networks by generating a representative sample for the target class. It casts the inversion task as an optimization problem to find the "optimal" data for a given class. The other class approach [4,14] are training second inverted model that acts as the inverse of the original classifier. To maximally reconstruct the images, they train the second model using full prediction vectors on the same training data of the classifier and the input of the second model is the prediction results while the output is the user's data; Ziqi et al. [22] apply MIA focus on adversarial scenario where an adversary is given the classifier and incomplete prediction result by background knowledge alignment.

But so far, most of the model inversion attacks require the same (similar) distribution training dataset and the entire queries to the inference model. As an attack method, querying the entire dataset will reveal the attacker's intentions, and it is easier for the administrator to detect. In this paper, we propose a novel MIA to reduce the queries times of auxiliary dataset, by using another model's hidden layer published on the market as an auxiliary information. Compared with state-of-the-art approaches, under the same settings, it's required queries times are significantly reduced, and the recovered data is almost the same as the conventional method.

Contributions. In summary, we make the following contributions in this paper.

1) We propose a novel scheme that requires only a few queries for model inversion attack.
2) In contrast to conventional methods, our method not only reduces the number of queries, but also has a more aggressive nature.
3) The user's private data can be reconstructed to provide an idea for other attack methods through our scheme.

2   Background

2.1   Model Inversion Attacks

The curious but honest attacker hopes to reconstruct original data based on the prediction value leaked by the users. Besides, he knew nothing about the details

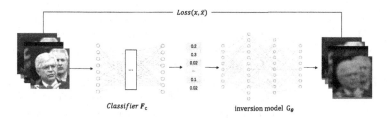

Fig. 1. General model inversion attack workflow. The attacker query x in an on-line black-box classifier F_c to get the prediction result, and then feed it into a shadow model G_θ locally to reconstruct the $\bar{x}$. So, attacker needs to upload all the datasets to get prediction values.

of the origin model F_c such as structure, training datasets, hyper-parameters, etc. After the model was released, attacker is able to query the model in the form of black-box and get the full prediction values. At this stage, in addition to being clear about the input format, output dimensions, and labels, the attacker will also have the following background knowledge about F_c:

Although there is no actual datasets of F_c, attacker can obtain some generalized data D_{aux} from the distribution P_a from other ways. For example, in a MIA attack against face recognition, although it is not known which individuals are specifically composed of training datasets, the attacker can download image resources containing human faces from public sources. Although these resources are not completely aligned with the F_c training datasets, they can reflect certain high-dimensional features to a certain extent.

The general MIA attack framework is shown in Fig. 1. The attacker trains G_θ to minimize the following objective:

$$R(G_\theta) = \frac{1}{|D_{aux}|} \sum_{x \in D_{aux}} L(G_\theta(F_c(x)), x) \tag{1}$$

where Function $L()$ is to measure the quality of reconstructed images such as L_2 distance. It means that we have to get the prediction value of all the datasets of D_{aux}, which has the following defects:

1) Efficiency and API's consumption issues. In practice, it is not easy to obtain the prediction values of all auxiliary datasets. It takes time to transfer data and to obtain the prediction results.
2) A large number of queries will attract the attention of model publishers. They realize that someone may carry out MIA attacks and may take active defense measures, such as deliberately returning false results.

2.2 Feature Extraction Models

Feature extraction models refer to those models that can reflect the contents of the image in high-dimensional features. Most of the existing image classification methods employ traditional global feature extraction techniques (e.g., color,

GIST [15]) or local features (e.g., SIFT [12] and HoG [3]) to generate feature representation for images. Compared with traditional methods, convolutional neural networks (CNN) model is a novel end-to-end feature proposal model and has demonstrated a strong capability for image classification. Some recent work [16,17,21] showed that the CNN models pretrained on large datasets are with data diversity, e.g., ImageNet, can be directly transferred to extract CNN visual features for various visual recognition tasks, such as image classification and object detection. Further more, recent related studies have shown that middle layers feature in CNN model can complement high-level semantic features [8]. Inspired by the above work, We can use the middle layer information provided by a pretrained CNN to improve MIA. We can download the pretrained models from the models market such as AlexNet [9], VGG [18], ResNet [6], etc. In this paper, we remove the fully connected layer behind the models and only reuse the previous convolutional layer and fixed the weight.

3   MIA Schemes

Due to the reality and the inevitable attack defects of the previous MIA approaches, we intend to simplify procedure, i.e. reduce queries times of inference model. We propose a novel MIA attack scheme that pre-trains G_θ to learn the high-dimensional features of the dataset on another model $\hat{F}$, which handles similar tasks. And then we train G_θ to learn the mapping between prediction values and $\hat{F}$ high-dimensional features rather than prediction values and original inputs. In regard to models detail, we remove the fully connected layer of $\hat{F}$, leaving the first layer to the last layer of the convolutional layer, whose input structure (w, h, c) and output structure is n, which corresponds to the number of neurons at s-th layer of G_θ. What's more, G_θ shares the input format of k with prediction values, and shares the same output format with $\hat{F}$.

Our scheme is shown in Fig. 2. First, we locally obtain high-dimensional features of all auxiliary dataset (D_{aux}) in the primitive model which act as feature extraction model. Secondly, We sample part of the data from D_{aux} and feed them into the classifier model to obtain the prediction results. Based on these two sets , we can train the inversion model to minimize the following empirical loss over the training sets D_{aux} and D_{query}:

$$R(G_\theta) = \frac{1}{|D_{aux}|} \sum_{x \in D_{aux}} L(G_\theta^{s \to m}(\hat{F}(x)), x) \tag{2}$$

$$+ \frac{1}{|D_{query}|} \sum_{x \in D_{query}} \left\| G_\theta^{1 \to s}(F_c(x)) - \hat{F}(x) \right\|_2 \tag{3}$$

where $L(\hat{x}, x)$ is a distance metric to measure reconstructed images quality. D_{query} is random sampling from D_{aux}. $G_\theta^{i \to j}$ represents the layers i to j of neural network G_θ. $\hat{F}$ trains on D_{aux} except full connect layer. $\hat{F}$ shares the input format of images size, and shares the same output format with $G_\theta^{1 \to s}$.

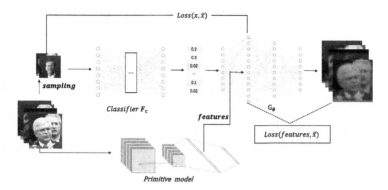

Fig. 2. Our scheme workflow. Firstly, the images which need to really query F_c were drawn from the auxiliary set's distribution. Secondly, by utilizing all the auxiliary images' high-dimensional features on other models (primitive models) that handle similar tasks. Finally, we optimize loss function to obtain the inversion model G_θ of F_c.

The implementation process of our plan is mainly divided into two steps. Firstly, we obtain all the high-dimensional features of D_{aux} on $\hat{F}$, and utilize them as the inputs of $G_\theta^{s \to m}$, iteratively training on D_{aux} as the reconstruction outputs until $G_\theta^{s \to m}$ convergence. This phase is agnostic for administrator. Secondly, We sample a certain amount of data from D_{aux} as D_{query} to obtain its prediction values provided by F_c and its m-dimensional features on $\hat{F}$, and use them as training datasets to train the $1 \to s$ inter-layers of G_θ until $1 \to s$ inter-layers convergence. Concerning the model inversion attack, G_θ is essentially the inverse of the classifier model F_c, mapping from the low-dimensional prediction values to the distribution $\mathbb{E}_{x \sim p_x}$. Since this process learns directly from $Y \longmapsto X$, the process of training G_θ needs to learn a large number of parameters, so a large number of queries are required. As the solution, by referring to the information of the sample in the latent layer of the model that handles similar tasks, additional information to be learned as $Y \longmapsto features \longmapsto X$, so the dependence on the number of queries is greatly reduced.

4 Experimentation

In this section, we evaluate the effect of our approach on different datasets. As comparison, we also use the conventional method under the same settings. For reproduction, the code is available on github[1].

MNIST [11] A handwritten digital dataset is composed of 60000 training datasets and 10000 test datasets in 10 class. In order to unify the setting, we resize its into $224 * 224 * 3$. The same action is taken for the following datasets.

PubFig [10] A large, real-world face dataset consisting of 5,8797 images of 200 people collected from the Internet. These images are taken in completely

---

[1] https://github.com/mostprise77/querying_little_MIA.

uncontrolled situations with non-cooperative subjects. Thus, there is large variation in pose, lighting, expression, scene, camera, imaging conditions and parameters, etc.

LFW [7] A face datasets consists of about 13,000 images of human faces crawled from the web. It is collected from 1,680 participants with each participant having at least two distinct images in the dataset. In our evaluation, we only consider people with more than 40 images, which leaves us with 19 classes. The face dataset is challenging for facial recognition, as the images are taken from the web and not under a controlled environment, such as a lab. It is also worth noting that this dataset is not similar with PubFig.

4.1   MNIST

Firstly,training a CNN Classifier model F_c with training datasets D_{train}, its accuracy on test dataset D_{test} is 98%. Secondly, we download the Vgg-16 [18] model pre-trained in Imagenet from the model market, and remove the last two layers of full connection layer, called $\hat{F}$. Its input size are $(224 * 224 * 3)$ and output size are 4096 dimensional vectors. Finally, G_θ is an input format of 10-dimensional vector (number of class). The number of neurons in the second layer is the same as output size in the $\hat{f}$, i.e. 4096 layers, followed by the conventional upper sampling layer. we use $tanh()$ as activation function.

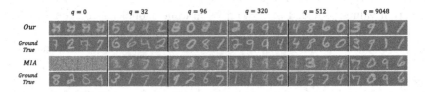

Fig. 3. Effect of variable query times for the inversion model G_θ on the inversion quality. We perform the inversion against MNIST classifier and present attack results on randomly chosen train data. The $|D_{aux}| = q$ we use is drawn from the test data distribution. For the previous MIA [22] in the third row, we use the same settings.

Training G_θ Phase. Before querying F_c in the form of black-box, we use $\{(\hat{F}(x), x)|x \in D_{test}\}$ to optimize empirical error 2 locally. When training, fix the first layer of the model, inject the $\hat{F}(x)$ directly into the second layer of G_θ,optimizing the loss function with SGD [23] training until convergence. Secondly, we use the budget n-times query model F_c,i.e. $|D_{query}| = n$. We assume that we can get all the prediction values(if not, use the cropping method mentioned in [22] to be fully feasible here) to form the dataset $\{(F_c(x), \hat{F}(x))|x \in D_{query}\}$. In the same way, we fix the sampling layer on the G_θ and train the weight w between the first layer and the second layer.

As a comparative experiment, we train a $\hat{G}$ with the same dataset according to the method of conventional MIA.

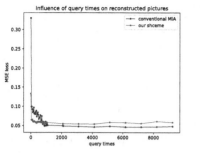
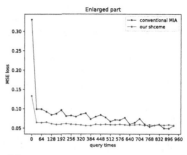

(a) Experimental results from 0 to 100% queries times

(b) Zoom in on the front part of (a)

Fig. 4. MNIST images' reconstruction quality comparison

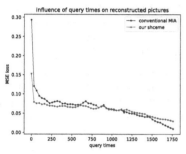
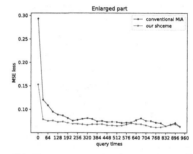

(a) Experimental results from 0 to 100% queries times

(b) Zoom in on the front part of (a)

Fig. 5. LFW images' reconstruction quality comparison

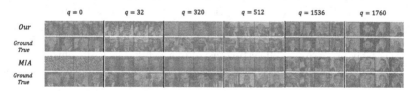

Fig. 6. Effect of variable query times for the inversion model G_θ on the inversion quality. We perform the inversion against PubFig classifier and present attack results on images randomly chosen from LFW.

Evaluate Phase. We use the data of training F_c as test dataset to evaluate the reconstruction effect between G_θ and $\hat{G}_\theta$. The results are shown in the Fig. 4 and 3.

Summary. We can see clearly that when budget $n < 700$, our scheme reconstruct images efficiently and achieve good results even with $n = 32$. When $n > 800$, the loss of conventional methods is smaller, but in practice, it is difficult to query all the datasets without being detected by the administrator. So, in queries budget limit settings, our scheme outperform than conventional methods.

4.2 LFW and PubFig

In this section, we use PubFig as the training dataset for F_c and LFW as the training dataset for G_θ. They differ greatly in environment, light, and structure etc., and the biggest common denominator is the inclusion of human faces. We used the same settings as the previous section, and the experimental results are shown in the Fig. 5 and 6.

Summary. The same experimental phenomenon also appeared on the face dataset. In particular, because there are more details in the face than hand-written digits, we and the traditional method need a larger part of D_{aux} to generate recognizable samples. We can clearly see that the sample generated when $q = 0$ is a meaningless face, and the attack has a preliminary effect when $q = 512$. But there is no doubt that when the number of queries is close to the entire dataset, the quality generated by the traditional method is better. Compared with handwritten digits, the reconstruction gap between the traditional method and our method is greater. We leave the optimization work under this setting in the future.

References

1. Amazon: Machine learning at aws. https://aws.amazon.com/machine-learning/
2. apple: Arfaceanchor.blendshapelocation. https://developer.apple.com/
3. Dalal, N., Triggs, B.: Histograms of oriented gradients for human detection. In: 2005 IEEE Computer Society Conference on Computer Vision and Pattern Recognition (CVPR 2005), vol. 1, pp. 886–893. IEEE (2005)
4. Dosovitskiy, A., Brox, T.: Inverting visual representations with convolutional networks. In: 2016 IEEE Conference on Computer Vision and Pattern Recognition (CVPR), pp. 4829–4837 (2016)
5. Fredrikson, M., Jha, S., Ristenpart, T.: Model inversion attacks that exploit confidence information and basic countermeasures. In: Proceedings of the 22nd ACM SIGSAC Conference on Computer and Communications Security, pp. 1322–1333 (2015)
6. He, K., Zhang, X., Ren, S., Sun, J.: Deep residual learning for image recognition. In: 2016 IEEE Conference on Computer Vision and Pattern Recognition (CVPR), pp. 770–778 (2016)
7. Huang, G.B., Mattar, M., Berg, T., Learned-Miller, E.: Labeled faces in the wild: a database forstudying face recognition in unconstrained environments (2008)
8. Kataoka, H., Iwata, K., Satoh, Y.: Feature evaluation of deep convolutional neural networks for object recognition and detection. arXiv preprint arXiv:1509.07627 (2015)
9. Krizhevsky, A., Sutskever, I., Hinton, G.E.: Imagenet classification with deep convolutional neural networks. Commun. ACM **60**(6), 84–90 (2017)

10. Kumar, N., Berg, A.C., Belhumeur, P.N., Nayar, S.K.: Attribute and simile classifiers for face verification. In: 2009 IEEE 12th International Conference on Computer Vision, pp. 365–372. IEEE (2009)
11. LeCun, Y.: The mnist database of handwritten digits (1998). http://yann.lecun.com/exdb/mnist/
12. Lowe, D.G.: Distinctive image features from scale-invariant keypoints. Int. J. Comput. Vis. **60**(2), 91–110 (2004)
13. Mahendran, A., Vedaldi, A.: Understanding deep image representations by inverting them. In: 2015 IEEE Conference on Computer Vision and Pattern Recognition (CVPR), pp. 5188–5196 (2015)
14. Nash, C., Kushman, N., Williams, C.K.I.: Inverting supervised representations with autoregressive neural density models. In: The 22nd International Conference on Artificial Intelligence and Statistics, pp. 1620–1629 (2018)
15. Oliva, A., Torralba, A.: Modeling the shape of the scene: a holistic representation of the spatial envelope. Int. J. Comput. Vis. **42**(3), 145–175 (2001)
16. Oquab, M., Bottou, L., Laptev, I., Sivic, J.: Learning and transferring mid-level image representations using convolutional neural networks. In: Proceedings of the IEEE Conference on Computer Vision and Pattern Recognition, pp. 1717–1724 (2014)
17. Sharif Razavian, A., Azizpour, H., Sullivan, J., Carlsson, S.: CNN features off-the-shelf: an astounding baseline for recognition. In: Proceedings of the IEEE Conference on Computer Vision and Pattern Recognition Workshops, pp. 806–813 (2014)
18. Simonyan, K., Zisserman, A.: Very deep convolutional networks for large-scale image recognition. In: International Conference on Learning Representations (ICLR 2015) (2015)
19. tencent: facerecognition. https://cloud.tencent.com/product/
20. Várkonyi-Kóczy, A.R.: Observer-based iterative fuzzy and neural network model inversion for measurement and control applications. In: Rudas, I.J., Fodor, J., Kacprzyk, J. (eds.) Towards Intelligent Engineering and Information Technology. SCI 2009, vol. 243, pp. 681–702. Springer, Berlin (2009). https://doi.org/10.1007/978-3-642-03737-5_49
21. Wei, Y., et al.: Cnn: Single-label to multi-label. arXiv preprint arXiv:1406.5726 (2014)
22. Yang, Z., Zhang, J., Chang, E.C., Liang, Z.: Neural network inversion in adversarial setting via background knowledge alignment. In: Proceedings of the 2019 ACM SIGSAC Conference on Computer and Communications Security (CCS 2019), pp. 225–240 (2019)
23. Zhang, T.: Solving large scale linear prediction problems using stochastic gradient descent algorithms. In: Proceedings of the Twenty-First International Conference on Machine Learning, p. 116 (2004)

Efficient Defense Against Adversarial Attacks and Security Evaluation of Deep Learning System

Na Pang[1(✉)], Sheng Hong[2], Yang Pan[1], and Yuqi Ji[3]

[1] Xingtang Telecommunications Technology Co., Ltd., Beijing 100083, China
sunnypxn@163.com, pyl21123@gmail.com
[2] School of Cyber Science and Technology, Beihang University, No. 37,
Xue Yuan Road, Beijing 100191, China
shenghong@buaa.edu.cn
[3] School of Optics and Photonics, Beijing Institute of Technology,
No.5, Zhong Guan Cun South Street, Beijing 100081, China
Jiyuqi2018@126.com

Abstract. Deep neural networks (DNNs) have achieved performance on classical artificial intelligence problems including visual recognition, natural language processing. Unfortunately, recent studies show that machine learning models are suffering from adversarial attacks, resulting in incorrect outputs in the form of purposeful distortions to inputs. For images, such subtle distortions are usually hard to be perceptible, yet they successfully fool machine learning models. In this paper, we propose a strategy, *FeaturePro*, for defending machine learning models against adversarial examples and evaluating the security of deep learning system. We tackle this challenge by reducing the visible feature space for adversary. By performing white-box attacks, black-box attacks, targeted attacks and non-targeted attacks, the security of deep learning algorithms which is an important indicator for evaluating artificial intelligence systems can be evaluated. We analyzed the generalization and robustness when it is composed with adversarial training. *FeaturePro* has efficient defense against adversarial attacks with a high accuracy and low false positive rates.

Keywords: Neural networks · Adversarial examples · Deep learning · Defense

1 Introduction

Recent breakthroughs in pattern recognition, automatic control and decision-making assistance are bringing deep neural networks (DNNs) into the center of artificial intelligence system. The lack of interpretability results in a black-box for users and makes counter-intuitive classification [1]. Szegedy et al. [2] showed the neural networks models are vulnerable to maliciously generated inputs which remain imperceptible. A neural network classifier can completely output any wrong prediction with high confidence through designed subtle disturbances to the input. Such maliciously generated inputs are called adversarial examples. The existence of adversarial examples magnifies the security hazards of deep learning and severely limits its application in

© Springer Nature Switzerland AG 2020
X. Chen et al. (Eds.): ML4CS 2020, LNCS 12487, pp. 592–602, 2020.
https://doi.org/10.1007/978-3-030-62460-6_53

realistic tasks, especially for scenarios that require high accuracy [3]. The attack is shown in Fig. 1. A picture of a strawberry, a neural network could have 99.58% confidence level is classified as strawberry, but the new formed after adding adversarial noise picture, neural network will misclassify it as a lion with 97.66% confidence.

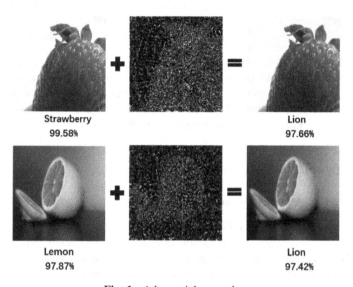

Fig. 1. Adversarial examples.

Adversarial samples fool neural network by different generation strategies, indicating that the deep neural network has hidden features and blind areas through the process of back propagation. The root cause of adversarial samples is the linearity of high-dimensional spaces [4]. The initial perturbation passes through the deep stacking of high dimensions in the process of backward transmission, and finally the accumulated value will be large enough to change the classification result. It is necessary to further study the defense methods of the adversarial samples and security evaluating methods of deep learning system.

Traditional works to defend against adversarial samples focused on adversarial training, which requiring to generate all known adversarial samples. Specifically, each training is computationally expensive. Gradient regularization is another effective defense method [5]. By adding regular terms to the cost function, the generalization ability can be improved. Defense distillation extracts knowledge from a complex structure to a simple structure, thereby reducing the computational complexity [6]. Most of them modify the deep neural networks (DNNs) models.

We propose a new strategy called *FeaturePro* to reduce success rate of adversarial attacks and evaluate the security of deep learning system. It is not necessary to change the deep neural networks (DNNs) models. The key idea of *FeaturePro* is to reduce feature spaces which is available to be used by adversary. The DNN models are smoothed during training. If different prediction generates after reducing feature spaces, the sample is to be considered as an adversarial sample. In particular, our contributions are:

- We propose a feature protecting based method to defend against adversarial attacks, while not impacting the DNN models.
- We evaluate the security of deep learning system and could provide security defense solutions.
- We show empirically that *FeaturePro* is robust to reduce the success rate of adversarial attacks.

The rest of the paper is structured as follows: In Sect. 2 we review different methods to generate adversarial attacks. Section 3 describes details of our proposed strategy, including protecting and evaluating methods. The experiments and results are shown in Sect. 4. Finally, we draw conclusion in Sect. 5.

2 Background and Related Works

2.1 White-Box Adversarial Attacks

White-box adversarial attacks obtain all the knowledge inside the deep neural networks (DNNs) model, including network architecture, network parameters, and training data as well. The objective function and constraints are modified so that we can make use of the similar method as the neural network training to generate the adversarial samples [7].

The fast gradient sign method (FGSM) is proposed to efficiently search for adversarial examples [8]. Given a normal image x, FGSM calculates a similar image x' to fool the classifier. The adversarial example x' is calculated by optimizing the loss function $Loss(x, l_x)$ which is the cost of classifying image x' as its label l_x while remaining the perturbation imperceptible.

$$x' = x + \varepsilon \cdot sign(\nabla_x Loss(x, l_x))$$

Jacobian saliency map approach (JSMA) looks for adversarial examples by changing only a few pixels instead of modifying the whole image [9]. The pixel is modified one at a time, and the adversarial saliency map is calculated to reflect how this pixel increases.

DeepFool uses a L_2 minimization-based formulation to search for minimal perturbation [10].

$$\Delta(x, x') := argmin_z \|z_2\|, subject\ to : g(x + z) \neq g(x)$$

The image is perturbed by a small vector at each iteration, and the perturbations are accumulated when the image modifies its label.

2.2 Black-Box Adversarial Attacks

Black-box adversarial attacks only rely on the input and output of the neural network model, and do not need to understand the structure and weight information of the network [11]. Such attacks can be effective on a variety of neural networks, but the success rate is lower than that of white-box attacks. The principle of the black-box attack is that the adversarial sample is migratable, and there is a continuous subspace in the adversarial sample space. This subspace will be shared by different neural network models, so it can achieve the migration against the sample. When the dimension of the model is higher, the subspace of the model is more likely to intersect with other models, and the more vulnerable it is to black-box attacks.

One pixel attack only change one pixel to fool a network classifier [12]. The differential evolution algorithm iteratively modifies each pixel to generate a sub-image. In contrast to the parent image, we retrain the sub-image which have the most hidden attack effect according to the selection criteria to realize adversarial attacks.

Universal perturbations for steering to exact targets (UPSET) in [13] is proposed to produce a perturbation to fool a classifier. The key idea of UPSET is the residual gradient network, generating anti-disturbance for targeted categories. The image could be classified into the targeted category no matter when the disturbance is added to any image.

2.3 Defenses Against Adversarial Attacks

Adversarial training is the first line of defense against adversarial attacks. By continuously adding adversarial samples into the training model, the accuracy of classification model is continuously improved. To ensure the effectiveness, this method requires the use of all known adversarial samples which is not available.

Simply stacking the denoising autoencoder onto the original network will make it even more vulnerable. The deep compression network method introduces the smooth penalty term of the compressed autoencoder during the training process, which makes the output less sensitive, so as to hide the gradient information [14].

Extra 'pre-input' layer trains them to modify the adversarial samples so that the classifier predicts the clean image as adversarial sample [15, 16]. By extracting the characteristics of the difference between the input and target, the separated detectors are trained.

3 Proposed Method

FeaturePro is for evaluating the security of deep learning system and defending against adversarial examples. It contains two main phases as illustrated in Fig. 2: the security evaluation phase and the defense phase against adversarial examples.

- **Security evaluation of deep learning system**
  The security of deep learning system has been in a non-standard state, which has affected the wide application of deep learning. We perform white-box s and black-box

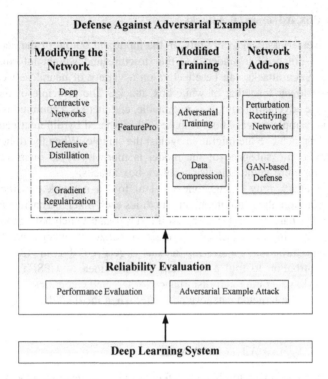

Fig. 2. Security evaluation and of defense of *FeaturePro*.

attacks for adversarial samples. White-box attacks are based on known classifier parameters and training data, while black-box attacks are to attack the model under the condition that the classifier model parameters and training data set are unknown.

- **Defense against adversarial examples**

    Changing or switching inputs can defend against adversarial attacks. Reducing feature spaces which is available to be used by adversary is necessary. If different prediction generates after reducing feature spaces, the sample is to be considered as an adversarial sample. Other defense methods contain three main phases: modifying the network, modified training and network add-ons. The modifying the network phase includes deep contractive networks [17], defensive distillation [6], and gradient regularization [5]. The modified training phase includes adversarial training [18, 19] and data compression [20, 21]. The network add-ons phase includes perturbation rectifying network [15] and GAN-based defense [22, 23]. Feature protecting can be combined with, such as adversarial training to improve the defense performance without changing the deep neural networks model.

3.1   Security Evaluation of Deep Learning System

Security is the ability of the deep learning algorithm to correctly complete the expected function under the specified conditions and within the specified time, without causing system failure or abnormality. Performance evaluation contains accuracy, precision and recall. The security evaluation process is shown in Fig. 3.

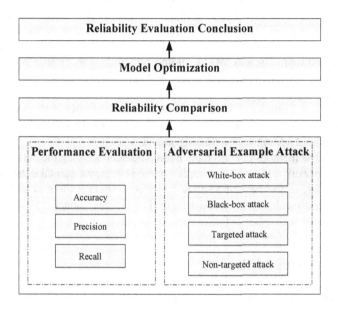

Fig. 3. Security evaluation process.

Attacks on intelligent algorithms includes black-box attacks, white-box attacks, targeted attacks and non-targeted attacks Black-box attacks contain one pixel attack and universal perturbations [24], while the white-box attacks contain the fast gradient sign method, Jacobian saliency map approach and Deepfool [25, 26]. The evaluation system analyzes whether the algorithm has the ability of adversarial attacks detection and whether it has a model parameter adaptive inspection modulse.

The system evaluates the defense strength of the deep learning algorithms and discovers the security defects of deep learning algorithms based on the misclassification rate and robustness of various attacks. By adding adversarial examples to retrain the model, the robustness and the security of the deep learning algorithm can be greatly improved.

For each targeted attack algorithm, it can apply defense algorithm one by one to defend and then record the scores of security of each adversarial defense algorithm separately. According to the results of security protection, we recommend the corresponding efficient defense against adversarial attacks to the user, that is, security hardening suggestions.

3.2 Defense Against Adversarial Examples

FeaturePro is to reduce success rate of adversarial examples, without changing the deep neural networks (DNNs) models. The deep neural networks models are smoothed during training. It is not necessary to expose too many features easily used by the adversary.

The sliding window mechanism is adopted to search for the mean pixel. *FeaturePro* makes use of the average of adjacent pixels of the image in the window to replace the center pixel. The pixels of the window at the edge of the image are also replaced by mean pixel. The nearby pixels are similar so that the image noise can be successfully reduced. The size of the sliding window varies from nine to the whole image. In order to obtain the best defense effect, this parameter can be adaptively changed.

The adversarial attacks will be detected when it generates different classification results after reducing the noise. The samples which is likely to be adversarial will be discarded, without adding to the training model.

Other defense methods contain three main phases: modifying the network, modified training and network add-ons. For simple typical attacks, we can take targeted defense methods. So far, in the face of various adversarial attacks, there is still not enough effective defense mechanisms to resist them. For complex attacks, Feature protecting can be combined with other defenses.

4 Experiments and Results

The architecture of *FeaturePro* is shown in Fig. 4. It is divided into platform layer, data layer, function layer and presentation layer. The platform layer contains the underlying operating system, programming language, and deep learning framework used. The data layer contains the image data storage module and the generated adversarial samples. The function layer includes the defense function of adversarial samples, the performance evaluation of the deep learning algorithm, and the adversarial samples generation module oriented to the operation interface. The presentation interface provides the function of user interaction with the background.

We use data from the ILSVRC2012 to attack the ResNet50 model. The ResNet50 model adopts a residual network design. It can effectively solve the problem of gradient disappearance during training.

Four attack algorithms, FGSM, DeepFool, JSMA and CW2, were performed in the experiment. The security evaluation result is shown in Fig. 5. The success rate of FGSM attack can reach 96.7%, and each image takes 0.212 s. The success rate of DeepFool is 94.6%, and each image takes 1.425 s. The success rate of JSMA is 94.2%, and each image takes 29.511 s, while the success rate of CW2 is 73.1%, and each image takes 0.653 s.

Figure 6 shows the defense effects of GanBased, Auto Encoder, Feature Squeezing, and *FeaturePro* against the four attacks. The percentage represents the classification

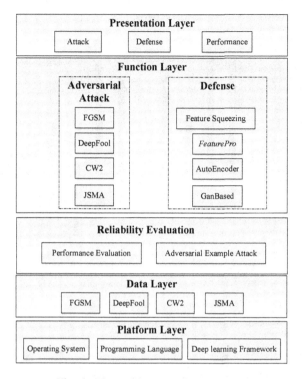

Fig. 4. The architecture of *FeaturePro*.

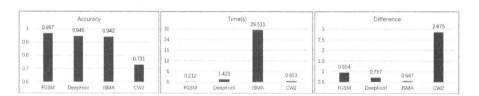

Fig. 5. Security evaluation.

accuracy of the model on the corresponding adversarial sample set or normal sample set after adding the defense algorithm. The accuracy of normal samples and the time-consuming of a single picture are shown in Fig. 7.

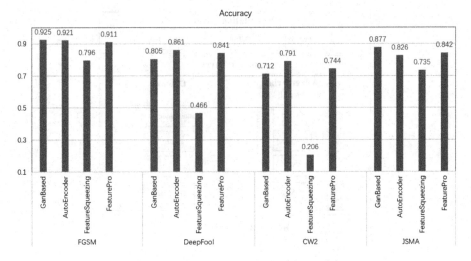

Fig. 6. Defense against adversarial samples.

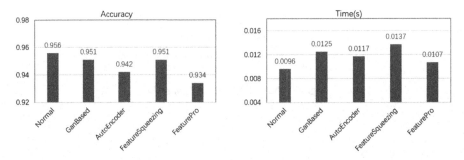

Fig. 7. The accuracy of normal samples and the time-consuming of a single picture.

5 Conclusion and Future Work

The existence of adversarial samples poses a huge challenge to the safety of intelligent driving and intelligent video. We proposed *FeaturePro*, a strategy for evaluating the security of deep learning system and defending against adversarial examples for deep neural networks. It reduces the success rate of adversarial examples without changing change the deep neural networks (DNNs) models.

Multitasking, strong migration, high concealment, and strong attack against adversarial samples are the inevitable trend of current attack algorithms. Research on adversarial attacks and defense will be a long-term task, which is not only interesting but also crucial. On the one hand, the study of adversarial samples allows people to analyze the operating mechanism of deep neural networks from a new perspective. On the other hand, efficiently resisting adversarial samples must also be the ultimate goal of artificial intelligence in the future.

Acknowledgments. The authors are highly thankful for National Key Research Program (2019YFB1706001), National Natural Science Foundation of China (61773001), Industrial Internet Innovation Development Project (TC190H468).

References

1. Montavon, G., Samek, W., Müller, K.: Methods for interpreting and understanding deep neural networks. Digital Signal Process. **73**, 1–15 (2017)
2. Szegedy, C., et al.: Intriguing properties of neural networks. arXiv preprint arXiv:1312.6199 (2013)
3. Papernot, N., et al.: Distillation as a Defense to Adversarial Perturbations against Deep Neural Networks. In: 2016 IEEE Symposium on Security and Privacy (SP), pp. 582–597. IEEE (2015)
4. Kurakin, A., Goodfellow, I., Bengio, S.: Adversarial examples in the physical world. arXiv preprint arXiv:1607.02533 (2016)
5. Gu, S., Rigazio, L.: Towards deep neural network architectures robust to adversarial examples. arXiv preprint arXiv:1412.5068 (2014)
6. Papernot, N., Mcdaniel, P.: On the effectiveness of defensive distillation. arXiv preprint arXiv:1607.05113 (2016)
7. Moosavi-Dezfooli, S.M., et al.: Universal adversarial perturbations. In: Proceedings of the IEEE conference on computer vision and pattern recognition, pp. 1765–1773. IEEE (2017)
8. Goodfellow, I.J., Shlens, J., Szegedy, C.: Explaining and harnessing adversarial examples. arXiv preprint arXiv:1412.6572 (2015)
9. Papernot, N., et al.: The limitations of deep learning in adversarial settings. In: 2016 IEEE European Symposium on Security and Privacy (EuroS&P), pp. 372–387. IEEE (2016)
10. Moosavi-Dezfooli, S.M., Fawzi, A., Frossard, P.: DeepFool: a simple and accurate method to fool deep neural networks. In: Proceedings of the IEEE conference on computer vision and pattern recognition, pp. 2574–2582 (2016)
11. Liu, Y., et al.: Delving into transferable adversarial examples and black-box attacks. arXiv preprint arXiv:1611.02770 (2016)
12. Su, J., Vargas, D.V., Kouichi, S.: One pixel attack for fooling deep neural networks. IEEE Trans. Evol. Comput. **23**(5), 828–841 (2017)
13. Sarkar, S., et al.: UPSET and ANGRI: Breaking high performance image classifiers. arXiv preprint arXiv:1707.01159 (2017)
14. Mardani, M., et al.: Deep generative adversarial networks for compressed sensing automates MRI. arXiv preprint arXiv:1706.0005 (2017)
15. Akhtar, N., Liu, J., Mian, A.: Defense against universal adversarial perturbations. In: Proceedings of the IEEE Conference on Computer Vision and Pattern Recognition, pp. 3389–3398 (2017)
16. Lee, H., Han, S., Lee, J.: Generative adversarial trainer: defense to adversarial perturbations with GAN. arXiv preprint arXiv:1705.03387 (2017)
17. Silver, D., et al.: Mastering the game of go without human knowledge. Nature **550**(7676), 354–359 (2017)
18. Sankaranarayanan, S., et al.: Regularizing deep networks using efficient layerwise adversarial training. arXiv preprint arXiv:1705.07819 (2017)
19. Li, B., Sim, K.C.: Improving robustness of deep neural networks via spectral masking for automatic speech recognition. In: 2013 IEEE Workshop on Automatic Speech Recognition and Understanding, pp. 279–284. IEEE (2013)

20. Bhagoji, A.N., et al.: Enhancing robustness of machine learning systems via data transformations. In: 2018 52nd Annual Conference on Information Sciences and Systems (CISS), pp. 1–5. IEEE (2017)
21. Das, N., et al.: Keeping the bad guys out: protecting and vaccinating deep learning with jpeg compression. arXiv preprint arXiv:1705.02900 (2017)
22. Shen, S., et al.: APE-GAN: Adversarial perturbation elimination with gan. arXiv preprint arXiv:1707.05474 (2017)
23. Zantedeschi, V., Nicolae, M.I., Rawat, A.: Efficient defenses against adversarial attacks. In: Proceedings of the 10th ACM Workshop on Artificial Intelligence and Security, pp. 39–49 (2017)
24. Akhtar, N., Mian, A.: Threat of adversarial attacks on deep learning in computer vision: a survey. IEEE Access 6, 14410–14430 (2018)
25. Smith, L., Gal, Y.: Understanding measures of uncertainty for adversarial example detection. arXiv preprint arXiv:1803.08533 (2018)
26. Dumont, B., Maggio, S., Montalvo, P.: Robustness of Rotation-Equivariant Networks to Adversarial Perturbations. arXiv preprint arXiv:1802.06627 (2018)

Author Index

Printed in the United States
By Bookmasters